Prior to *The Mitford Girls*, Mary S. Lovell has written five major biographies, including the international bestseller *Straight on till Morning: The Biography of Beryl Markham*. She lives in Gloucestershire.

For further information on books by Mary S. Lovell, please visit her website at www.marylovell.com

Praise for *The Mitford Girls*

'This is an excellent book – calm, dispassionate and respectful of its subjects' *Daily Telegraph*

'By drawing on new sources, Lovell presents a fresh version of the Mitford story . . . Lovell's book proves that there was something extraordinary about those six well-bred girls from Gloucestershire' *Independent*

'Lovell's never-a-dull-moment biography animates usually under-rated players such as the girls' mother, Lady Redesdale, who once lectured Hitler on the importance of wholemeal bread, and Pam, the second eldest and "most rural" Mitford Girl, who had a sky-blue Aga to match her eyes' *Daily Mail*

THE MITFORD GIRLS

The Biography of an Extraordinary Family

Mary S. Lovell

An *Abacus* Book

First published in Great Britain by
Little, Brown and Company in 2001
Reprinted 2001 (four times), 2002
This edition published by Abacus in 2002
Reprinted 2002 (four times)

A CIP catalogue record for this book
is available from the British Library

ISBN 0 349 11505 2

Typeset in Garamond by M Rules
Printed and bound in Great Britain
by Clays Ltd, St Ives plc

Abacus
An imprint of
Time Warner Books UK
Brettenham House
Lancaster Place
London WC2E 7EN

www.TimeWarnerBooks.co.uk

This book is for
Graeme, Shari, Robyn and Imogen
With all the love in the world

CONTENTS

Family Tree

SELECT FAMILY TREE, SHOWING MEMBERS OF THE FAMILY WHO APPEAR IN THIS BOOK

MITFORD LINE:

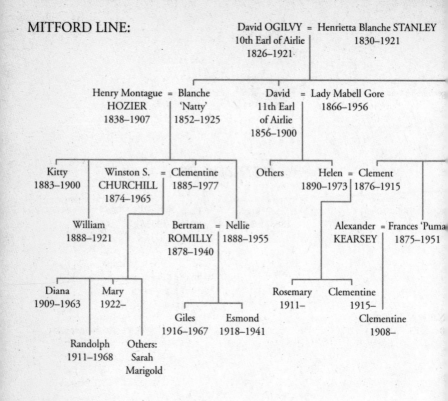

David OGILVY = Henrietta Blanche STANLEY
10th Earl of Airlie   1830–1921
1826–1921

Henry Montague = Blanche
HOZIER   'Natty'
1838–1907   1852–1925

David = Lady Mabell Gore
11th Earl   1866–1956
of Airlie
1856–1900

Kitty   Winston S. = Clementine
1883–1900   CHURCHILL   1885–1977
1874–1965

Others   Helen = Clement
1890–1973 | 1876–1915

William
1888–1921

Bertram = Nellie
ROMILLY   1888–1955
1878–1940

Alexander = Frances 'Puma'
KEARSEY   1875–1951

Diana   Mary
1909–1963   1922–

Rosemary   Clementine
1911–   1915–

Giles   Esmond
1916–1967   1918–1941

Clementine
1908–

Randolph   Others:
1911–1968   Sarah
Marigold

DISTAFF:

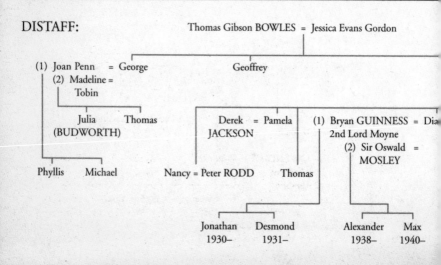

Thomas Gibson BOWLES = Jessica Evans Gordon

(1) Joan Penn = George
(2) Madeline =
Tobin

Geoffrey

Julia   Thomas
(BUDWORTH)

Derek = Pamela
JACKSON

(1) Bryan GUINNESS = Dia
2nd Lord Moyne
(2) Sir Oswald =
MOSLEY

Phyllis   Michael

Nancy = Peter RODD   Thomas

Jonathan   Desmond
1930–   1931–

Alexander   Max
1938–   1940–

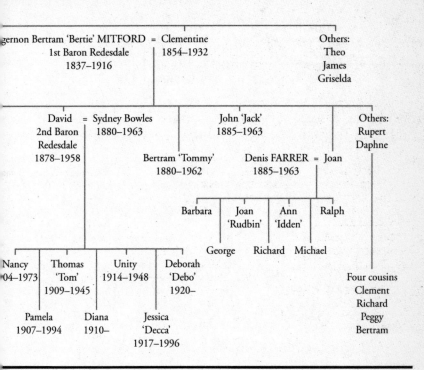

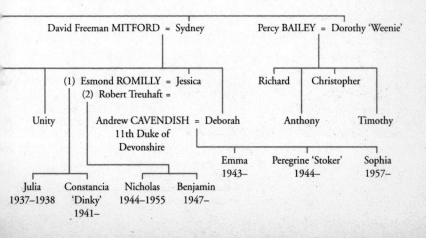

INTRODUCTION

During the course of researching and writing this book I have often been asked the question that people ask endlessly of a biographer: 'Who are you writing about at the moment?' In answering, 'The Mitford family,' I have noticed that recognition begins at about the age of fifty. In other words, if the questioner is over the age of fifty I generally receive a sage nod, below that the polite enquiry, 'And who are they?'

'They' were six beautiful and able sisters, Nancy, Pam, Diana, Unity, Jessica ('Decca'), and Deborah ('Debo'). Nancy wrote a series of sparkling bestselling novels, the best known of which are *The Pursuit of Love* and *Love in a Cold Climate*, and for which she drew largely upon her family for characters. Decca launched her writing career when she wrote a bestselling memoir of her early life called *Hons and Rebels*. These three books spawned a genre, which is called by the family the Mitford Industry. Later, both Diana and Debo also produced bestselling books. Yet the Mitford sisters are not known merely for producing literature: they also led extraordinarily full lives, quite independent of each other.

The bones of the sisters' childhood with their private languages, family jokes and endless nicknames are well known to people of my generation (over fifty), so I have tried to make the story intelligible to readers new to it without dwelling over-much on material about the girls' childhood that has been told and retold, except when necessary for continuity or when it added measurably to the narrative. What I set out to do was explore the relationships between the sisters, drawing on per-sonal interviews, family papers and correspondence not previously seen outside the family, as well as extensive published sources.

When I began researching, I suppose I had in mind – because of the above books – a frothy biography of life in Society between the wars. Of course I knew of the polarized ideologies of Diana, Unity and Decca but I had not realized how quickly or how completely the mirth of the sisters' childhood disintegrated into conflict, unexpected private passions, and tragedies.

The girls' parents, Lord and Lady Redesdale – David Freeman Mitford and his wife Sydney – are perhaps better known to pos-terity (thanks again to the above-mentioned books) as 'Farve' and 'Muv'. They were honest, well-meaning, salt-of-the-earth, admit-tedly slightly eccentric, socially retiring minor aristocrats; thoroughly nice people who, because of their extraordinary daughters, were propelled unwillingly, blinking and unprepared, into an international spotlight. Yet if there is a heroine in this book it is surely Sydney. Her loyalty to, degree of concern for and tactful support of all her daughters were unflagging, even when pre-Second World War polemics caused the disintegration of her formerly happy marriage. This strength may come as a surprise to those who recall the 'Muv' of her daughters' writings as a slightly batty, absent-minded and vague personality almost disassociated from the reality of her children's lives.

Although politics plays a major part in the story of the sisters, this is not a political book, so anyone expecting a stand against Unity or Diana and the far right, or Decca and the far left, must look elsewhere. I accept each of these protagonists as she was, and, in Diana's case, as she still is. This book seeks to explore the richness of the personalities, not to judge them. The reader is as capable as I am of forming his or her own opinions based on the evidence, and an individual social ideology. Rather, I hope to illustrate the complex loyalties and love, disloyalties and even hate, and above all the laughter that ran through this family's relationships – they could always find humour even in their own misfortunes. Lord Longford, who has known the family for seventy years, told me, 'You have to look at that family as *fun*. They were enormous fun.'[1]

Two of the sisters are triumphantly alive as I write this book. Diana, at ninety, is still chic and articulate; Debo, serene and utterly charming, celebrated her eightieth birthday in March 2000, yet apparently possesses the energy levels of someone half her age. She is a busy CEO directing a large, successful and constantly expanding organization that employs hundreds of people.

The mere fact that this book deals with nine personalities, three of whom have already been the subject of independent biographies,[2] means that for reasons of space much fascinating detail has had to be pruned. For those interested in delving further a bibliography is included. I have had to resist the temptation to explore a multiplicity of players on the twentieth-century world stage with whom various members of the Mitford family came into contact: from Winston Churchill, Anthony Eden, Adolf Hitler, Paul Joseph Goebbels, Benito Mussolini, Hermann Goering, and General de Gaulle, to the Duke and Duchess of Windsor, Max Beaverbrook, John and Bobby Kennedy, and Aly Khan; from George Bernard Shaw, Lytton Strachey, Evelyn Waugh, Diana Cooper, Emerald Cunard, John Betjeman and Cecil Beaton, to Katherine Graham, Maya Angelou, Salman Rushdie and Jon Snow. A complete list of the celebrities, heroes and anti-heroes who moved in and out of the lives of the sisters would take pages. Suffice it to say that it is simply not possible to tell the story of the relationships between the members of the family and also indulge the luxury of exploring these fascinating side issues. For the same reason many less well-known personalities who were close to the sisters have had to slip through these pages as mere shadows: their first cousins, for example, who were an important part of their growing-up years, dear family friends, such as Mrs Violet Hammersley, who was like a character from a Victorian novel with her furious pessimism, love of gossip and great affection for the family, and Lord Berners, talented, generous, and eccentric in the grand manner. Then there was a literal host of Decca's friends in California, among many others.

I hoped to discover some explanation for the diverse range of opinion between the Mitford sisters. They had sprung from a privileged background, but it was no more privileged than that of their childhood friends' and their cousins', who had a similar upbringing and education without becoming celebrities. Had Nancy's colourful portraits of 'Uncle Matthew' and 'Aunt Sadie' been true reflections of her parents, much might be explained. But Nancy's portraits *were* only colourful exaggerations. And these six girls, brought up in exactly the same way yet developing in such an individual manner, seem to have taken the twentieth century by the throat. It is not so much that they were historically important – except perhaps in the case of Diana, who as the second wife of Sir Oswald Mosley became arguably the most hated woman in England for a while, and was imprisoned without trial for most of the Second World War on the insistence of Labour ministers in the wartime coalition government – but that they are so much larger than life – easily as interesting as the characters in Nancy's novels.

As political alternatives both Communism and Fascism are probably equally unpalatable to the majority, so it is natural to be curious that Decca seems wholeheartedly accepted by the media, while Diana has always been regarded as a *bête noire*. The difference may lie in that Decca looked back at the historical picture, and on learning that Stalin had massacred 10 million people in the early thirties, publicly admitted that she had been wrong about parts of the Communist ideology she had so passionately espoused.[3] On the other hand Diana, although deploring the unspeakable atrocities perpetrated by the Nazis, and Hitler's subsequent activities, has always rejected hindsight to rewrite the contemporary opinions of Hitler that she formed prior to 1939. She liked and admired him as a man when she met him, and she still believes that 'It is not a question of right or wrong, but the impressions of a young woman in the thirties. Of course it would be easy just to deny these, but it would not be very interesting, or true.'[4] She has, still, only to put pen to paper, or appear on the radio, for the word 'unrepentant' to be hurled about by her critics.

I have been fortunate enough to meet four of the sisters. I contacted Debo and Diana first to research this book. I met Pam at a dinner party in Gloucestershire, in the eighties, where I was introduced to a pleasant woman by the name of Pamela Jackson, who was interested in my hunter, Flashman, and his breeding.[5] During dinner a remark made about a television programme in which the Mitfords had featured made me suspect who she might be, and when the ladies retired I asked my hostess if Mrs Jackson was one of the Mitford sisters. 'Oh, yes, she's the second eldest,' she replied. 'Wonderful eyes, hasn't she? She ordered her Aga to match them, you know.' I didn't quite believe this, but some years later I watched a television programme in which Pam was interviewed in her kitchen, and there was the amazing blue Aga. Recently I was told a story about her, which is probably true. Apparently at a dinner party she was placed next to Lord Louis Mountbatten, who said to her, 'I know who you are, you're one of the Mitford girls, aren't you?' 'Yes, that's right,' Pam replied kindly. 'And you are . . .?'

'Meet' is perhaps the wrong word to describe my contact with

Decca. I was packing in a hotel room in California one morning in 1986 when the phone rang and the caller identified herself as Decca Treuhaft which meant little to me. 'Jessica Mitford then?' she continued, in a delightfully deep and fruity English voice. I was there to see a publisher in Berkeley, about a book of short stories by Beryl Markham which I had compiled. Decca, who lived near Berkeley, had learned from a mutual friend that I was in town and telephoned to see if we could meet. She had been given a pre-publication review copy of my biography of Beryl Markham, and was kind enough to say that she had enjoyed it. So much so, she told me, that she was going to pass on her copy to a well-known Hollywood lawyer[6] with the suggestion that it would make a good movie.[7]

I was due to leave the area within the hour for an appointment in Santa Barbara with an old friend of Markham's who had eluded me for months. At the time, meeting him seemed more important so I never saw Decca in person, though we spoke several times afterwards by telephone. Perhaps it was just as well I did not know then of Decca's devastating reputation as a book critic – I simply thought of her as the author of the highly entertaining *Hons and Rebels*, the only book of hers that I had read – for the Markham book was my first biography and I was nervous about the reviews. In a later telephone conversation I told her I was coming to San Francisco on a book-signing tour. We could not meet then because she was going out of town, but she told me a favourite story. A famous writer was in Australia on a book-signing tour. As one woman handed him a book he asked her name and duly wrote, '*To Emma Chisit with best wishes . . .*' 'It turned out,' Decca chuckled, 'that the woman had only been asking the price.'

It was a typical Decca conversation. I experienced only the warm and generous facets of her clever, complex nature, and was surprised to find, during research, that she could also be implacable and vindictive. I bitterly regret, now, that I did not *make* time to take up her several kind invitations to visit her in Oakland. Life, and research for other books, got in the way and she died before this book was ever thought of.

With the assistance of Decca's family, however, I was able to access her private papers, and as the first biographer to see them was privileged to a behind-the-scenes view of the Mitford sisters through family letters covering more than sixty years. As well as letters she received, Decca kept copies of almost every letter she wrote and was so naturally funny that it was all I could do not to laugh out loud in the hushed sanctity of the Rare Books and Manuscripts Department of the University Library where I was researching.[8] The letters to Decca, especially from Debo, for the two kept up a regular correspondence from the 1960s until Decca's death in 1996, are equally amusing, not in terms of repeatable jokes but in their reactions to everyday events; what several of their contemporaries describe as a 'Mitford way of talking'. Their irreverent and hilarious comments on daily life, and every subject under the sun from the Royal Family to growing old, are not really part of a biographical study, but thankfully will not be lost to a dusty archive, for Decca's letters are presently being compiled for publication.[9]

Debo was initially concerned that my lengthy research into Decca's papers would give me a biased view of the family relationships. But I also had access to the unpublished papers of diarist James Lees-Milne and the objective correspondence between him and the other sisters covering a period of more than seventy years, particularly from Diana who wrote to him from the age of fourteen in 1924 until his death in December 1997. Furthermore, both Debo and Diana and other members of the family have been unfailingly helpful in submitting to interviews, patiently answering my letters of enquiry, and suggesting people to whom I should talk. Debo was also kind enough to allow me access to some Mitford family papers in the remarkable Chatsworth archives, and to help me in any number of ways since then. She is the youngest Mitford sister, and she possesses an endearing characteristic of treating everyone with whom she comes into contact in exactly the same way, always showing the same intelligent interest in what people have to say to her.

Diana invited me to visit her in her flat in the heart of Paris. Warned before our first meeting by a mutual friend that Diana was extremely deaf ('she's ninety this year') I was not sure what to expect, or even that it would be possible to conduct a formal interview. I found a beautiful woman, in a lovely setting. Willowy, smiling, warm and self-assured, she might have been a youthful seventy-odd. As she had recently been fitted with two hearing-aids she was able (to my relief) to hear speech perfectly, though not (to her regret) music. Her physical beauty took me by surprise. Everyone I had met spoke of Diana's remarkable beauty as a young woman, but somehow one does not expect a woman of ninety to be beautiful *per se* and, indeed, recent photographs of her are not flattering. I suspect that her beauty lies as much in her attitude and sharp intelligence as her skin texture, bone-structure, delicate colouring, thick soft white hair and those blue Mitford eyes. She speaks clearly and evenly, going over old ground without hesitation, displaying mild passion when the name of her late husband, Sir Oswald Mosley, crops up. Her memory is phenomenal and she is known to be utterly truthful (which has frequently rebounded on her when she might have done better to prevaricate, as others have done). Although she would rather I had not written this book she could not have been more helpful to me in its preparation

Mary S. Lovell
Stroat, Gloucestershire
February 2001

1

VICTORIAN ROOTS

(1894–1904)

Sydney Bowles was fourteen years old when she first set eyes on David Freeman Mitford. He was seventeen, classically handsome, as were all members of his family, and with luminous blue eyes. Dressed comfortably in an old brown velveteen keeper's jacket, he stood with his back to the fire, one foot casually resting on the fender. As Sydney entered the brightly lit library of his father's country house at Batsford in Gloucestershire, she was dazzled by light and warmth after a drive through dark winter lanes in the waggonette from the station. Her first impression as she walked through the hall had been of the sweet smell of beeswax, woodsmoke and oriental spices, but as soon as she saw David all this was forgotten. At that moment, Sydney wrote in an unpublished memoir, she lost her heart.

It was 1894. Sydney's father Thomas Bowles, a 'consistently eccentric, back-bench MP'[1] had taken his children to visit his good friend Lord Redesdale, Algernon Bertram 'Bertie', universally pronounced 'Barty', Mitford.[2] Both men were high achievers, and hugely successful personalities in their own fields.

Tall, angular, and dressed in the shapeless sailor suit that was the prescribed all-purpose day-wear for Victorian children,

Sydney felt all the natural frustration of a teenager wanting to look older to impress this handsome and apparently confident young man with her newly blossoming womanhood. Yet she was miserably aware that her outfit labelled her a child, along with her siblings. At fourteen she was scarcely more, but Sydney's had been an unusual childhood for the time.

Thomas Bowles was a widower and for some months, ever since he had purchased a substantial London house in Lowndes Square, Sydney had been its young chatelaine, in sole charge of the running of the household and the not inconsiderable finances of the establishment. Her father was Member of Parliament for King's Lynn. A man of character, he had a vast network of friends and entertained a good deal. Sydney apparently managed her responsibilities with distinction, failing only in the area of being able to control the male servants. Quarrelling footmen and drunken butlers were amused by her rather than respectful of her, and caused her a good deal of heartache. From that time, until the end of her life, she only ever employed women as indoor servants.

Prior to his buying the London house, the children of 'Tap' Bowles had spent much of the previous six years at sea, on their father's boats. Shortly after the death of his wife, when Sydney was eight, Bowles took them aboard his 150-ton sailing schooner *Nereid* and set off on a year-long voyage to the Middle East.[3] His published log of the voyage[4] gives details of horrendous storms, weathered with aplomb by his four motherless children while their governess and nurse were prostrated with seasickness. After their return to England, during election campaigns, he made his second yacht, the *Hoyden*, his temporary home and campaign headquarters; his children often accompanied him on those electioneering trips, and each year during the parliamentary summer recess the family lived on the yacht, usually sailing to France. So, though she had been as protected as any upper-class girl in the Victorian era, Sydney's exceptional experiences had given her a seriousness beyond her years.

We do not know what David Mitford thought of Sydney at that first meeting. His insouciant pose, which so impressed Sydney, disguised his status as the undervalued second son of the extraordinarily energetic Bertie Mitford. David lived in the shadow of his elder brother Clement, who was adored by everyone – if asked, David would probably have said he lived in Clement's sunlight. It was Clement who would one day inherit the title and family fortune, and he was as outgoing and confident as his father, a notable traveller, linguist, writer and MP. Like his father, Clement had attended Eton, an experience he found wholly enriching. Three further sons followed David and at least one, Jack (known as Jicksy, who was 'brave as a lion and clever as a monkey' and his parents' favourite child), attended Eton. David, however, was sent to Radley, which was considered second rate.

No secret was made of the fact that this choice of school was deliberate. Lord and Lady Redesdale did not wish Clement's career at Eton to be affected by David's behaviour. All his life David was liable to erupt in sudden violent rages if upset or frustrated. Unlike his gifted father, he was a poor reader and slow to learn, and his only real interest was in country sports. It seems probable that he suffered from undiagnosed dyslexia for he was not unintelligent, as his adult speeches in the House of Lords and his surviving letters reveal, and he spoke and wrote fluent French. Described by a grandson as 'impulsive, naïve and rather humble, with a touching idealism',[5] David was sensitive and disliked team games, so he was never popular at Radley, and he loathed his time there. And there is no doubting his fearsome temper: on one occasion having been locked in his room as a punishment for some misdemeanour he heated a poker in the fire until it became red hot, then threatened to attack his father and kill him with it. He was eventually released and calmed by 'Monsieur', the French tutor who taught them so well that all of the Redesdale children were bilingual and all lessons were conducted in French.

Monsieur, who became known as 'Douze-Temps' because of his demonstrations of rifle drill, '*Un! Deux! Trois!*...', had served in the Franco-Prussian War and kept the boys – especially David – spellbound with stories of his experiences.

When Sydney first met him, David must have been experiencing a huge sense of relief that his years at the hated boarding-school had come to an end. He had hoped to make a career in the Army (perhaps because of Monsieur's influence), but having failed the written examination for Sandhurst it was decided that he would emulate many younger sons of good family by going east, to Ceylon, to make his fortune as a tea-planter.

Sydney's teenage crush on him did not last. While David was in Ceylon she grew up and was launched into Society. She had been educated at home, latterly by a very able governess (who subsequently became Thomas Bowles' mistress).[6] There was talk of Sydney going to Girton, the women's college at Cambridge, and she went to view the college, but for some unknown reason the idea was dropped.[7] Only a handful of women attended university at the end of the nineteenth century; perhaps Sydney did not wish to be regarded as a 'blue-stocking'. With her tall, slender figure, a cloud of light brown hair, generous sulky mouth, and large blue eyes she was pronounced beautiful, and she thoroughly enjoyed the experience of being a débutante: the dances and balls and parties, riding in the crowded Row with her father, which was 'like an amusing party taking place every day',[8] and, especially, meeting new people.

But above everything, Sydney – in common with her father – loved the sea. Those weeks every summer when Tap's family lived aboard his yacht and sailed to Trouville or Deauville were the highlight of her young life. At Trouville Tap gravitated naturally towards the artistic community which gathered there, and among his acquaintances were Boldini and Tissot. More important to Sydney was Paul-César Helleu, a fashionable portrait painter who liked to spend his summers with his family, aboard his yacht the *Étoile*. The Bowles and Helleu families met when the *Hoyden* and *Étoile* were moored up alongside each other, and from this small incident would spring a lifelong family friendship. After that they met every year and Helleu painted several portraits of Sydney at the height of her beauty.[9]

It was inevitable that Sydney would receive the attentions of young men and she fell in and out of love with several, some more suitable than others. In London ice-skating was a favourite pastime, and her instructor, a Swede named Grenander, was one of the men she particularly favoured. 'I love being with him,' she wrote in her diary, 'I would do almost anything he asked me. I would let him call me Sydney, I would even let him kiss me . . .'[10] It was Grenander who came to her aid when she fell and hurt herself badly. Because of her attachment to him, Sydney managed stoically not to cry, or even wince, at the shattering pain as he manipulated what was later diagnosed as a broken ankle. But she realized that there was no future for her in a relationship with a skating professional, and eventually the infatuation faded.

One relationship ended sadly when the young man was killed in the Boer War. But the suitor who made the greatest impression on her was Edward 'Jimmy' Meade. Her love for Jimmy, in 1903, was apparently both deep and passionate, and was moving towards an engagement when Sydney discovered that he was a womanizer. She wisely broke off the relationship, and it was generally believed in London Society that she took up with David Mitford on the rebound.

David spent less than four years in Ceylon where evidently he did not take to the life of a planter. While he was on his first home leave in 1898, events unfolding in South Africa intervened in his future. Paul Kruger's ultimatum concerning the independence of the Dutch republics of Transvaal and the Orange Free State provoked war between the British and the Boers. This gave David the opportunity to be both a patriot and to engage in the career he had always longed for. With all thoughts of a return to Ceylon forgotten, he enlisted in the ranks of the Royal Northumberland Fusiliers. His elder brother Clement also fought in the Boer War, serving in the crack regiment of the 10th Hussars.

David's letters to his parents confirm his early intuition that the Army was the career he would enjoy above all others. His commanding officer, Lord Brabazon, took a liking to the earnest and gallant young man and appointed him as his orderly, which David modestly considered 'lucky'. Shortly afterwards, in March 1900, he received a flesh wound in the leg (his second wound of the war). Writing from the hospital at Bloemfontein, he asked his father to try to get him a commission, '. . . after this it would not be very difficult, and then I would have the career I always wanted'.[11] It was not to be. In the following year, while in the thick of fighting, David was badly injured in the chest and lost a lung. He was nursed in the field hospital for four days, and when it was suspected that he might live he was carried back to camp in a bullock cart, his wound swarming with maggots. He recovered, and was invalided home in early 1902.

Clearly, while David had been planting tea and soldiering, and Sydney was running her father's home and making her début in Society, there had been some further contact between the two, for while David was in hospital he dictated a love letter to Sydney, to be given to her in the event of his death. Since their fathers were the closest of friends they would have met quite naturally at each other's homes, and probably also at Prince's ice-skating rink, for both David and Sydney were excellent skaters and regular patrons there. After his homecoming Sydney – with her experience of losing a boyfriend in the war – would undoubtedly have been especially sympathetic to a man shipped home wounded.

In fact, little is known of the courtship of David and Sydney.

Photographs confirm what witnesses recall: they made a handsome couple. He was tall with handsome patrician features, tanned skin and strikingly blue eyes. She was almost his height, elegant and self-composed. It is not difficult to see why she was reckoned a beauty as a young woman. What is not apparent from old photographs is the humour they shared. According to several contributors, David had 'a terrific sense of fun – better than any professional comedian', while several people commented on Sydney's understated, dry wit. When David went to see Tap, to request the hand of his daughter, Tap replied dauntingly, 'Which daughter?' Having established that it was Sydney they were discussing (surely Tap was teasing?), Sydney's father naturally wished to know how David intended to support her. 'Well,' said David, 'I've got £400 a year, and these.' And he held up his large competent-looking hands.[12]

When they married on 6 February 1904, some ten years after that first meeting, Sydney was twenty-four years old. A couple of stories survive; the first was apparently widely circulated in London Society at the time. It was whispered that when she walked up the aisle of St Margaret's Church, Westminster, towards her bridegroom, she was in tears, weeping – they said – for Jimmy Meade. The other story was that a few days before her wedding day a married friend told Sydney what to expect on her wedding night. Sydney was dumbfounded, 'A gentleman would *never* do anything like that,' she said.[13]

The couple honeymooned aboard the *Hoyden*, and later visited Paris, after which they settled down in a modest house in Graham Street, a few steps from Sloane Square. By the standards of their class they were relatively poor. Apart from the allowance of £400 a year from David's father, Sydney had a small income from Tap. However, even combined, this income was not enough to live on in comfort, and here Tap was able to assist the young couple in a practical manner. It was not to be expected that, as a self-made man, he would hand over large sums of money to the newly-weds, but he was happy to give David a job. Among Tap's most successful business ventures had been the founding of several magazines. The first of these, *Vanity Fair*, had since been sold on, but he still owned the *Lady* (founded in 1885 and named at the suggestion of the Reverend Charles Dodgson), and he offered David the position of office manager.

It must be said that it might have been a better business move had he made Sydney office manager, for she had a natural ability in accounting and enjoyed bookkeeping. David, however, hated being indoors, hated office work and office hours, and hardly ever bothered to read a book. There is a family legend that he had once read Jack London's *White Fang* and found it so good he thought it unnecessary ever to read another book. Since there are references in some of his letters to books that he was reading it is safe to say that this was a joke and not fact. But he was not bookish and can have had little interest in a women's magazine in which half the space was (and still is) given over to small advertisements for domestic staff and holiday accommodation.

Indeed, the act for which he is best remembered during his days at the offices of the *Lady* is unconnected with the administration of the magazine itself. When the twenty-seven-year-old David arrived for work he found that the cellars of the building, and no doubt those adjoining it, were infested with rats. In Ceylon householders encouraged a mongoose to take up residence in their gardens to control rats and snakes, and by a piece of good fortune David had brought one home with him. He set it to work with significant success. The image of David spending his days hunting rats, to simulate country pursuits in order to avoid the office work he loathed, was fostered by Nancy through her character Uncle Matthew, and is not based on fact. He remained at the *Lady*, working in friendly harmony with Sydney's eldest brother George (who was general manager and co-owner with his father) until the outbreak of war in 1914, and from all accounts tried hard to live up to his father-in-law's trust in him. George Bowles had been president of the Union at Cambridge, and editor of *Granta*. Would such a man have tolerated David as a passenger for ten years? It seems unlikely, and it is even less likely that Tap would have continued to employ David if he had not made *some* positive contribution. As for David, he described the first year of his marriage in correspondence as 'a year of the greatest happiness to me', so it is unlikely that he found the work too irksome.

There is another, lesser-known, anecdote dating from David's time at the *Lady*. His salary was paid weekly, in cash in an envelope, as all employees were paid in those days, and it was his custom to hand over his entire wages to Sydney but for a very small sum. For many years, every Friday afternoon, after he was paid, he would wander over to Covent Garden Market and buy the most perfect peach he could find. This he presented to Sydney. She always received it with every sign of enthusiasm and would eat it after supper, sometimes offering him a piece or two. Twenty years passed before he learned by accident that Sydney loathed peaches. She had never told him, knowing that it would spoil his pleasure at having cleverly discovered a gift that he considered both economical and acceptable.[14]

With David's salary the couple had a joint income of around a thousand pounds a year, and on this Sydney's meticulous household accounts reveal that they employed five female servants. However, they lived quietly, seemingly content in each other's company, and their limited social life revolved mostly around the Bowles or the Mitford families. The fact that the couple's first child, a daughter, was born on 28 November a little more than nine months after their marriage was probably partially responsible for this. Sydney was initially disappointed for she had wanted, and absolutely expected, a boy, but David was ecstatic. They thought of calling the child Ruby but later decided upon Nancy. Though worried about 'my Sydney', as he affectionately referred to his wife (for the baby weighed nine and a half pounds at birth and the mother was uncomfortable for some days afterwards), David thought the baby 'the prettiest child . . . our happiness is very great,' he wrote to his mother. Unusually for the time he had insisted on being present at her birth, and he reported that Sydney had been 'sweet and brave'.

It seems such an ordinary story, this handsome but otherwise unremarkable young couple settling down to a quietly happy marriage, looking forward to further children. Though they had no great prospects they were content with their lot in life. There was absolutely no indication that their children – there would be seven in all – would be so extraordinary that they would make the family a household name.

2

EDWARDIAN AFTERNOON
(1904–15)

In the first decade of their marriage, life was simple and happy. David did not care to go into Society much, and although Sydney would probably have liked to[1] she deferred to David's wishes. David worked at the *Lady* during the week, and often at weekends they visited their parents in the country. Perhaps the attribute of David's that Sydney found so attractive was his sense of humour. 'She should really have married a more social man,' one of her children said, 'but she never complained . . . and she laughed tremendously at my father's jokes; he could be brilliantly funny.'[2]

That David was deeply in love with Sydney is obvious from letters he wrote to his parents.[3] It is more difficult to quantify Sydney's feeling for David. Her teenage diary and more especially her responses to her children as adults prove that she was sensitive and loving, though she always found it difficult to show affection. This was not necessarily unusual for a woman of her class at that time, but in Sydney's case it was probably due to the example set by her parents.

Sydney remembered her mother as 'delicate', kind and rather remote, though her letters apparently reveal her as an 'affectionate and solicitous' personality.[4] Tap Bowles, left to bring up a family of four small children, the youngest of whom was only two, was a good father according to his lights, and his children worshipped him, but there is no doubt that he had some odd ideas about child-rearing. Clever, successful, opinionated Tap provided an adventurous life for his children, but although he doted on his youngest child Dorothy, always known as Weenie, there was a lack of warmth in the rearing of his other children.[5] He did not believe, for example, in celebrating birthdays, and even though Sydney was running his home by the age of fourteen, she did not own a single party frock. Indeed, Tap did not think to provide her with any clothes other than her sailor suits until she was seventeen and needed to be 'brought out'. Clearly, then, the lack of a mother affected Sydney in ways that would have been important to most children. Four of Sydney's children commented that she seemed 'remote and unaffectionate' as they were growing up, and stated that they never became close to her, in the sense that they liked and appreciated her, until they were adults. It is probable that she did not know *how* to behave with her children.

So why did Sydney – a pretty girl, whose greatest enjoyments in life were sailing, visiting France and ice-skating, and who loved the parties and dancing she attended as a débutante – marry David, who was a countryman at heart, actively disliked meeting new people and regarded 'abroad' with suspicion and horror? There can be no other reason but that she fell in love with him. He was a kind man and he was very funny. He made her laugh and unquestionably loved her. Many successful marriages have been founded on less.

For Sydney, life changed only minimally after her marriage. Even motherhood scarcely ruffled her cool serenity, for her babies, as they appeared, were cared for by a series of nurses and nannies. Being in charge of an establishment was no novelty to her, having run her father's house for ten years, and her own home was cared for by staffing levels that seem extravagant today but – bearing in mind Sydney's lifelong financial prudence – were probably merely adequate in a world where there were no electrical appliances, detergents or easy-care fabrics. Advertisements in the *National Press* (cost, a halfpenny) for domestic servants reveal that a cook might command thirty pounds a year, a housemaid eighteen and a general servant twelve.

In a house that Nancy described as 'minute',[6] there was a cook, a parlourmaid, a housemaid, a kitchen maid, a nanny and a nursemaid. Nancy once asked her mother, 'What did you do all day?' and received a reply to the effect, 'I lived for you all.' Apart from overseeing the staff Sydney's daily life would have consisted of letter-writing, reading, shopping – principally at the Army and Navy Stores and Harrods – visiting her sister Weenie, who had taken over the running of their father's house after Sydney's marriage, and keeping her household accounts, which are almost a work of art in their dark blue leather bindings, tooled in gold.

Sydney was a good manager, and was of the school of thought that 'a lazy master makes a lazy servant'. A note among her papers states that one of the reasons she so loved being aboard a sailing ship was 'the beautiful cleanness . . . there is no luxury where there is dirt; and where everything is shining clean there is luxury'.[7] A close family friend has described Sydney as 'acutely perceptive, well read and fastidious; surprised by nothing and amused by everything . . . she encouraged her children's interest in music, the arts and reading, and the mental independence that would distinguish them . . . one of her peculiar charms was her patrician reserve . . .'.[8] Judging from photographs of her various homes, she might easily, in another age, have made a name for herself as an interior designer. What is more she accomplished her furnishing and decorating schemes at minimal cost, for they were simple, relying more on her own natural style and good taste than on colours or artifice. One odd event jars this neat pattern of Edwardian days. The adult Nancy claimed that Sydney once confided to her that early in her marriage she nearly ran away with another man. She only stayed, she said, because of Nancy, who was two years old at the time.[9] But Nancy's stories have always to be taken with a grain of salt, for she invented freely, always teasing, always seeking to entertain or shock.

Three years after Nancy's birth another girl, Pamela, was born. Two years later, in 1909, Sydney gave birth to the long-awaited son, Tom, and quickly became pregnant again. Diana arrived only a year after Tom, so that she always felt they were 'almost twins'. Although Sydney is said to have cried when she learned that her fourth baby was another girl, her disappointment was quickly dispelled, for Diana was beautiful from the first. Like all the Mitford children, except Nancy, Diana was blond-haired with clear fair skin and remarkable blue eyes. Nancy was dark, and her green eyes were later described by Evelyn Waugh, John Betjeman and sister Decca as triangular in shape.

When Nancy was born Sydney had engaged Lily 'Ninny' Kersey, daughter of the captain of Tap's yacht, as her nanny. This worked beautifully until the arrival of Pam when the thoroughly spoiled little Nancy engaged in a series of jealous rages, alternating with plaintive cries of, 'Oh, Ninny, I do wish you would still love me.' Sydney overheard her daughter's sad request and thought it best to engage a new nanny. Norah Evans came to look after the two little girls and remained until after Tom's birth. She was replaced by a woman who has gone down in Mitford history as 'the unkind nanny'. She is remembered for several things, first for her bad-fairy prediction on Diana's birth, 'She's too beautiful; she can't live long,' and for banging Nancy's head against the wooden bedpost, presumably as an effective form of punishment since she had been prohibited from uttering 'a single angry word' to the Mitford children. The head-banging came to the notice of David and Sydney, and Nancy wrote, 'My mother retired to bed, as she often did when things became dramatic, leaving my father to perform the execution. There was a confrontation in the nursery as of two mastodons; oddly enough, throughout the terrifying battle which ensued, I felt entirely on the side of the nanny.'[10]

The marvellous outcome of this traumatic episode was the recruitment of Laura Dicks. White-faced and red-haired, everything seemed against her at her interview. She was thirty-nine and Sydney feared at first that she would be too old to care for the lively young family. Furthermore, although Miss Dicks was very religious she was Nonconformist, and she supported the Liberal Party. In a conventional household, to whom the Church of England was the personification of the Conservative Party at prayer, such things mattered. But Miss Dicks' face when she first beheld baby Diana, and her genuine cry of delight, 'Oh, what a lovely baby,' must have convinced Sydney that this nanny could probably be trusted not to bang little heads against bedposts. She became known as 'Nanny Blor' and remained with the family for almost thirty years. She was a kind but firm surrogate mother to them, and in return they loved her. That she was also tactful and understanding was revealed by her manner on her first day in the Mitford household. As she went into the nursery Nancy was sitting reading, her 'furious little round face . . . concealed behind the book'.[11] The book (unusual perhaps for a six-year-old) was *Ivanhoe* but Blor made no comment, merely taking off her shiny black straw bonnet, and cape, and hanging them carefully behind the door before settling down to work without disturbing the child.

In common with their contemporaries, the Mitford children saw little of their parents. They would be dressed and taken down to the dining room after breakfast to say 'good morning'. Nancy recalled such an occasion when she was six, about the time that Blor joined the household. She entered the room, which she recalled was painted white with a green wreath papered around the cornice, to find her parents sitting at the table reading black-edged newspapers. To her surprise they appeared upset and they told her that the King, Edward VII, had died. Some days later she watched as the funeral cortège passed along the road under the balcony of her grandfather Redesdale's house.

Usually the Mitford children spent much of their time in the nursery with daily walks in the park, and occasional treats such as visits to the zoo, Harrods' pet shop, or one of the Kensington museums. Sometimes an aunt, uncle or grandparent would take them out to tea or to a pantomime. After nursery tea each day they would be dressed in their best clothes and taken down to spend an hour with their parents, after which they were bathed and put to bed. They were sometimes allowed to play with the children of the Norman family, who lived across the street, Hugh, Richard, Mark and Sibell. Ronald Norman was the brother of the banker Montagu Norman.[12] Another frequent visitor to the Mitfords', throughout their childhood and long after, was an enigmatic figure, Violet Hammersley, always referred to as Mrs Ham, or the wid (widow), by the children. She had known Sydney as a teenager and was present at every family celebration, crisis or drama, expressing her opinion (always pessimistic) with the confidence of a member of the family. But as well as friends such as the Normans and Mrs Hammersley, there were the cousins.

David was one of nine children, and Sydney was one of four. Their respective siblings produced, between 1910 and 1927, twenty-one children with the surnames Mitford, Farrer, Kearsey, Bowyer, Bowles and Bailey, and many of these first cousins were to play major parts in the lives of the Mitford children as they grew up and visited each other's homes. But the network of kinsmen who were to people the lives of the Mitford children were rooted further back in the family tree.

Both of David's parents – 'Bertie' Mitford (Bertram, 1st Lord Redesdale) and Lady Clementine Ogilvy – came from large families, and he remained close to many of them and to their numerous offspring.* Clementine's sister, Lady Blanche ('Aunt Natty'), married Henry Hozier and was mother to another Clementine (who married Winston Churchill) and Nellie (who married Colonel Bertram Romilly). David's children became close friends of the Churchill children, but friendship with the Romilly boys, Giles and Esmond, was not encouraged because Sydney disapproved of the feckless Nellie.

However, there are more complicated relationships involved than those shown in the official family tree. Although Nellie Romilly was regarded as permissive, her mother was even more so. 'Aunt Natty' Hozier's marriage was desperately unhappy and she was credited with at least nine lovers. She was more discreet than Nellie, perhaps, but it was widely believed – and this is well known in both the Churchill and Mitford families – that she had a love affair with her brother-in-law, Bertie Mitford (David's father), and that he was the natural father of Clementine. A few biographers have hinted at the facial similarity between David Mitford and his first cousin Clementine Hozier Churchill.[13] If the gossip is true this would be hardly surprising for David Mitford and Clementine would then be half-brother and sister, rather than first cousins.

In addressing this question, one of Clementine Churchill's daughters stated that her mother never learned the identity of her natural father though she knew he was not Henry Hozier.[14] Bertie Mitford is the most likely suspect, even though the poet and writer Wilfred Scawen Blunt claimed that Natty confessed to him that her two elder daughters were fathered by Captain George 'Bay' Middleton, known by his foxhunting contemporaries as 'the bravest of the brave', and to history as the dashing lover of the sporting Empress, Elizabeth of Austria.[15] This, however, must be set against the fact that Natty told a close friend,

*See family tree, page x.

just before the birth of Clementine, that the child she was carrying was 'Lord Redesdale's'.[16]

As for Natty's daughter, naughty Nellie Romilly, it was whispered that her brother-in-law, Winston Churchill, fathered one of *her* two sons, Esmond. There is a remarkable physical resemblance between the young Winston Churchill and Esmond Romilly, and as an adult Esmond certainly hinted at times that he was Winston's natural son, but this is jumping ahead of the story.[17] None of these dark family secrets touched David and Sydney's family and Aunt Natty was a great favourite of the children, which suggests she possessed considerable charm.

By the time Nanny Blor joined the family, Nancy was partially exempted from the dull nursery timetable. She had begun to attend the Frances Holland day school conveniently situated in the same street as the Mitfords' home.

Nancy makes no mention of the school in her scraps of autobiography, but admits to being 'vile' to her sisters and brother in those early years. It seems that while she loved her siblings in one sense, she never recovered from the halcyon period when, as an only child, she had the undiluted attention of her parents and nanny. Pam became the main target for Nancy's retribution and temper tantrums (an echo of her father's), and barbed teasing became second nature to Nancy and the ethos of the Mitford nursery. Recalling Nancy's childhood Sydney wrote, 'You were terribly spoiled as a little child, and by all. It was [Aunt] Puma's[18] idea. She said you must never hear an angry word and you never did, but you used to get into tremendous rages, often shaming us in the street . . . Puma adored you and in fact until Pam was born you reigned supreme . . .'[19] But throughout all Nancy's tempers and teases and general naughtiness Nanny Blor was scrupulously fair and even-handed with all her charges. 'I would have been much worse but for Blor,' Nancy admitted, '[she] at least made me feel ashamed of myself.'[20]

At about this time Sydney rented the Old Mill Cottage, in

High Wycombe,[21] as a retreat for her family from the heat of the summer in London. High Wycombe is on the southern side of the Chiltern Hills and the cottage, part of what was then a working mill, was on the outskirts of the town and gave the impression of being in the country. In subsequent years moving out to High Wycombe enabled the Mitfords to let their London house during the Season, which brought in some much-needed extra income, and eventually Sydney purchased the cottage with some help from her father.

The entire household went with Sydney and David to the Old Mill Cottage – Nancy, Pam, Tom and baby Diana, accompanied by Nanny Blor, Ada the nurserymaid, and all the staff, which had been increased to include Willie Dawkins, 'the hound boy'. The latter's job was to look after the family's menagerie of David and Sydney's three dogs, innumerable small creatures such as mice, hamsters and grass snakes purchased by the children from Harrods' pet shop, and Brownie, a miniature pony David had spotted on the eve of their trip while he was on his way to work at the *Lady*. He bought it on a whim and brought it home in a hansom cab to spend the night in an unused box room.[22] On the following day they took the pony with them to High Wycombe but hit a snag when the guard refused to allow it into the goods van. Refusing to be outdone, David exchanged the family's first-class tickets for third-class ones, and they all – family, animals and servants – clambered into an empty compartment (in those days trains had no corridors). Today the point of this story would be the novelty of taking a pony into a passenger compartment. At the time, however, the impact was quite different. It was unheard of for a family of the Mitfords' status to travel other than first class.

The act of buying the pony, with its attendant inconveniences, done with the sole intention of pleasing his children, is far more characteristic of David than the vivid larger-than-life caricature of him as the terrifying, bellowing 'Uncle Matthew' brandishing his 'entrenching tool',[23] in Nancy's novels. Much has been made by Mitford biographers of his violent temper, but although he undoubtedly suffered lifelong from spectacular outbursts, most of these could be better described as strong irritation coupled with periods of muttering under his breath (which were, more often than not, justifiable; Debo said, 'the fact that we couldn't always judge his mood made things exciting and we used to practise . . . to see how far we dared go before he turned and bellowed at us').[24] His reputation has suffered greatly from the spectre of Uncle Matthew.

The caricature overshadows the immense charm of the real David. There are stories of him playing noisy games with his children and their cousins, of his chasing them as they ran around the house screaming with delight and pretended terror. He was always ready to play games, it seems, and there was an endearing childlike element in his make-up. Debo recalled that 'he was wonderfully funny and the source of all the jokes in the family'. Several nieces have recounted how he was 'so funny that our sides ached with laughing'.[25] On the other hand, one said, 'He was very tall and rather frightening when he used to stand in the garden cracking his stock-whip . . .'[26] His relationship with Nancy was close; he was immensely fond of his eldest child and she was devoted to him. Their repartee at the dining table was outstanding: 'When they were on form together,' Debo recalls, 'they were funnier than anything I have seen on the stage. I still remember the *pain* of laughing at them.'[27] Nancy teased him with her quick wit and he replied in his uniquely funny turn of phrase, half serious, half aware of how droll were his remarks.[28]

One of David's dogs was a bloodhound and the major participant in a favourite game they called 'child hunt' in which the hound would hunt 'the cold boot'. The quarry, or the 'hares' – as the participating children were called – were given a head start and would set off running across fields, laying as difficult a trail as possible by running in circles, through 'fouled' land such as fields containing sheep or cattle, and crossing and recrossing streams. When they could run no more they would stop and sit down while they waited for the hound to find them. Invariably the hound would then jump all over them while licking their faces before 'poor old Farv', red-faced from pursuit, caught up to reward the animal with pieces of raw meat.

In a televised version of one of Nancy's books, these child hunts were given a more sinister connotation with the children running terrified through woods while their father, on horseback, thundered after them with a pack of hounds baying. In fact the children loved it – they thought the hound was '*so* clever'.[29] In her novel Nancy had referred to 'four great hounds in full cry after two little girls' and 'Uncle Matthew and the rest would follow on horseback'.[30] As a result, fiction overlaid fact, and during research for this book I met people who believed, and read articles that stated, that the Mitfords led the lives of the fictional Radletts, and at least one American journalist was convinced that David had 'hunted' his poor abused children with dogs.

There was never any pressure to conform and the children grew as they wanted. There were no half-measures in their behaviour. 'We either laughed so uproariously that it drove the grown-ups mad, or else it was a frightful row which ended in one of us bouncing out of the room in floods of tears, banging the door as loud as possible.'[31]

Sydney's role at this stage in the children's lives appears less involved than David's, at least as far as the children's memories go, but it was she who drove them around in a cart called 'the float'. It had enormous thin wheels and Diana recalls that when they came to a hill the children were made to get out and walk, to spare the horse.[32] Sydney enjoyed living in the country, though she took no direct part in field sports. After her marriage, there is no record of her shooting or hunting, though as a girl she rode well and often, and when she accompanied her father to

Scotland in 1898 she was regarded as 'a brilliant shot'.[33] As they grew up she encouraged her children to follow the hounds of the Heythrop Hunt and join their father when he fished and shot, but if they were not interested she was unconcerned. Many of her friends would have said she was a countrywoman, but she enjoyed London too.

In the same year that Sydney rented Old Mill Cottage for the first time, 1911, Pamela, who was not quite four years old, caught poliomyelitis, or infantile paralysis. There was no known successful treatment then for this frightening disease and it was as much feared by parents then as meningitis is today. It was often a killer, and those children who survived were usually crippled for life. Pam's illness must have severely tested Sydney's unconventional theories on doctors and nursing. She had inherited her strongly held opinions from her father, who believed that doctors and medications usually did more harm than good, and that, left to its own devices, the body would heal itself. Possibly Tap's lack of confidence in doctors stemmed from a bitter experience: he arrived home from work one day to find his wife, Jessica, dying, following an abortion performed by her doctor in the belief that for her to continue with her four-month pregnancy (her fifth child) would prove fatal.[34]

As part of the regime for keeping the 'good body' in good order Tap Bowles had decreed a number of unfashionable rules for his motherless children. The system had worked admirably, and Sydney saw no reason to adopt an alternative one for her own children. Most of the rules concerned regular exercise and personal hygiene, and were merely common sense, but others perplexed the children's carers by defying received childcare practices. The children were to have no medication of any kind – not even a weekly dose of 'something to keep them regular'; no vaccination ('pumping disgusting dead germs into the Good Body!'); their bedroom windows were always to be open six inches, winter and summer. Other dictates seemed positively eccentric: they were never to eat pork products, rabbit, hare or shellfish (the laws given in the Pentateuch, 'as dictated by Moses in the Old Testament'),[35] nor be allowed to eat between meals; nor were they ever to be forced to eat anything they did not want to eat – one child ate nothing but mashed potatoes for two years.[36] Sydney was not alone in adopting unusual health ethics. She and her brother Geoffrey, 'Uncle Geoff', composed letters to the newspapers on 'murdered food' (refined white sugar and flour with the wheatgerm removed). Uncle Geoff was convinced that England's decline was connected to a reduction in the use of natural fertilizers on the soil and was violently opposed to pasteurized milk. The children found his writings on the subject and his letters to *The Times* causes for hilarity (really, it was *too* embarrassing to have an uncle who wrote to the newspapers about manure, and expounded further in his book *Writings of a Rebel*).

During Pam's illness, however, Sydney overrode her theories and called in one doctor after another, six in all. It was only after being told there was little that could be done for the desperately sick child that she reverted to the one medical practitioner both Tap and she trusted. He was a Swede called Dr Kellgren, and an osteopath rather than a qualified doctor.[37] His treatments consisted of massage and exercise, an early form of intense physiotherapy (which pre-dated Elizabeth Kenny's groundbreaking treatments for polio). The treatment he gave Pamela worked: other than a slight weakness in one leg during her childhood she made a complete recovery.

At about this time David hit on a scheme to end their financial problems. With his growing family, their limited income must have been the cause of constant worry to him. Stories of the rich strikes in the Klondike a decade earlier, perhaps bolstered by his spell of active service in South Africa, seem to have persuaded him that gold-mining might be the answer. On hearing that a new goldfield had been discovered in Ontario, he staked several

claims to forty acres near the small township of Swastika, in the
Great Lakes area. Only small quantities of gold had been found
there so far, but a big seam was believed to exist.

Over the next twenty years or so, David would travel to
Ontario many times to work the claim. He had already been
there alone when, in the spring of 1912, he and Sydney decided
to go together and – the biggest treat — they were to sail on the
maiden voyage of the *Titanic*. Fortunately, something happened
to make this impossible, and their departure was delayed until
autumn of the following year. There, Sydney and David lived in
a sturdy, well-built wooden cabin, which they called 'the shack'.
It was basic but it had everything they needed. There were no
staff and Sydney did everything herself, including cooking and
pumping the water by hand. She even made her own bread, and
continued to do this for the remainder of her life.[38] David, photographed in corduroy knickerbockers, canvas gaiters, warm
workmanlike shirt and a leather waistcoat, enjoyed the time he
spent there. It was a tough, masculine environment and he felt at
home with the miners, who treated him with respect and taught
him how to crack a stock-whip that he had been given by an
Australian miner. He worked hard and found tiny traces of gold;
just enough to keep him enthusiastic. Meanwhile, there was a
massive strike on a neighbouring property owned by Harry
Oakes, a prospector who had been mining unsuccessfully for
some years. The Tough-Oakes mine proved the biggest gold mine
in Canada, and was a mile or so to the east of David's land, at
Kirkland Lake. Oakes purchased a lakeshore claim and burrowed
under the lake after his landlady told him about tiny nuggets and
flakes of gold she had seen in the streams as a child. He struck
gold almost immediately and issued half a million shares at
thirty-five cents each. Within two years each share was worth
seventy dollars and Oakes had kept the majority for himself.[39]

It is not difficult to see why David remained keen, although
the mining project eventually came to nothing. Furthermore,

he and Sydney were at their closest in the shack at Swastika through the winter in that inhospitable climate, and it was one of the happiest times of David's life. It was there that Sydney conceived their fifth child.

When the couple returned to London it was to a slightly larger house at 49 Victoria Road, off Kensington High Street. The new baby was born there, in August 1914, four days after Herbert Asquith declared war to cheering crowds gathered at Downing Street. Prior to the outbreak of hostilities, David had been on the point of leaving for his gold mine in Canada, but as he watched the situation deteriorate he became anxious to 'do his bit'. Although he had been classified as permanently unfit because he had only one lung, and knowing it was unlikely he would be allowed to see action, he nevertheless rejoined his old regiment. On 8 August he got a twelve-hour leave, and the latest addition to his family obliged by being born while he was at home.[40] It was a girl. The parents, still hoping for a second boy, were disappointed, but soon came round. There was time for another boy. In David's absence Sydney called her Unity after an actress (Unity Moore) she admired,[41] and then Grandfather Redesdale said that she *must* have a topically apposite second name so they added Valkyrie, after Wagner's Norse war-maidens. Almost from the time of her birth she was known in family circles as 'Bobo', but with hindsight, Unity Valkyrie's unusual name, combined with the place of her conception, Swastika, seems almost like an eerie prophecy which the fifth Mitford child had no alternative but to fulfil.

At the time, though, all that the family thought of was the onset of the Great War. While Sydney was lying-in at Victoria Road, the children were sitting on the balcony of Grandfather Redesdale's town house looking down on troops of men marching along Kensington High Street on their way to the slaughterhouse that lay in France. Nancy recalled that she was a miniature *tricoteuse*, knitting an 'endless scarf' in wool of a disagreeable shade of purple, 'for a soldier'. All the children did this knitting, even Tom – and the entire nation felt personally involved in the war.

Within a short time David had managed to persuade the doctors that he was fit enough to be sent to the front as one of a group of sorely needed officer reinforcements for the regiment's 1st Battalion. Before he left, and with his previous experience of war in mind, he set up an elaborate code so that Sydney could learn the most up-to-date news in a seemingly casual letter, merely from the manner and punctuation of the way he addressed her, or mentioned various fictional family members. For example, 'Tell this to Nelly', meant 'We are marching north.'

He returned home unexpectedly on embarkation leave to find his house strangely quiet. As usual during August Sydney had taken the children to spend the month with their grandfather Bowles in a rented cottage on the south coast, overlooking the Solent and the Isle of Wight.[42] However, the cook had received disturbing news by that morning's post. The cottage had been burned to the ground during the previous night and though she was expecting Mrs Mitford back later that day she was unable to tell David whether anyone had been hurt. Fortunately, they had escaped unscathed with only the loss of Diana's teddy bear (a great sadness to her), but it must have been a traumatic few hours for David while he waited for the family's return to London by train.

In subsequent years Nanny Blor usually took the children to her family home at the seaside resort of Bexhill in Sussex, to spend part of the summer months. Sometimes they stayed at the neighbouring town of Hastings with St Leonards where Nanny's twin sister[43] lived. During these holidays the children enjoyed climbing 'the perilous cliffs', and 'the scrumptious teas of brandy snaps, *shop-butter*, biscuits and marmalade'.[44] More than seventy years later Debo still recalls the delight of the sea, waves and sand to children brought up in the country. They bathed daily in the icy waters of the English Channel, with Nanny sitting waiting for them, wearing her beige cotton gloves. 'The comforting feel of holding her hand in its fabric glove is with me now, a refuge in time of trouble,' Debo wrote. 'She waited with striped bathing towels stretched out, wrapping [us], rubbing the sand into our mauve arms and legs, which was part of the sensation of well-being after bathing. We were rewarded with a Huntley and Palmer's ginger biscuit and a hot drink out of the ever-present Thermos.'[45]

David's first spell at the front ended in January 1915 when he suffered a complete breakdown of health, no doubt due to the effect of the cold and rain of that first winter of the war on his one remaining lung. He was invalided home and it was there, while he was recovering, in the early spring that he received terrible news. His elder brother, the family's golden child, Clement, had been killed in the fighting within a month of being awarded the DSO. Everyone was distraught with grief and Pam, who was about seven at the time, always recalled her father weeping openly at the news. She had not realized until then that grown-ups could cry. Clement left a three-year-old daughter Rosemary, and a young widow, Helen, just three months pregnant with her second child. If it was a boy, he would be heir to the Redesdale title. If it was a girl, David would inherit, but he, like the rest of his family, was so devastated by loss that it is almost certain he gave little thought to what this would mean to him in pecuniary terms. In any case his father was very much alive and expected to remain so for many years.

Once he recovered from his infection David was determined to return to the front. He knew that the Army was desperate for officers because the life expectancy of a junior officer at the front was so short. With his experience and service record he managed again to get himself passed fit. He was appointed transport officer to the 2nd Battalion and shortly after he rejoined his regiment in France the second battle of Ypres began. Every night,

and often twice a night, he had to get supplies through to his battalion on the other side of the town of Ypres, which was under
constant heavy bombardment. David's method was to quicken
the pace of the horses as they approached the town and lead the
wagons through Ypres at full gallop until they were clear of the
Menin Gate. His men worked in two shifts but David refused
any relief and personally accompanied every convoy, for which he
was mentioned in dispatches. Not only was his battalion never
without its supplies, but remarkably David never lost a man.
Although his children do not recall him mentioning the war in
later years, he did say modestly to a fellow officer that although
no one could call his work 'a picnic . . . it was of course a very soft
job compared with the trenches'.[46]

In October 1915 David and Sydney learned that Clement's
posthumous child was a girl, named Clementine.[47] David
became his father's heir but it made little obvious difference to
him, absorbed in the fight, and in contact with normal family life
only by letters and occasional periods of leave.

Several letters, written by Nancy to her father in France, survive. She had been learning French after David's mother told
Sydney, 'There is nothing so inferior as a gentlewoman who has
no French.' In her first attempt at writing to him in French, in
April 1916, Nancy tells him of a robin's nest in their garden, that
she had heard a cuckoo, and about her pet goat: '*Ma chèvre est
très bonne, elle aime beaucoup le soleil, et elle mange les chous que je
lui donne*'. David's delightful response is in verse:

> *Unusual things have come to pass*
> *A goat gets praised for eating grass!*
> *A robin in a tree has built!*
> *The coo coo has not changed its lilt!*
> *And I have no desire to quench*
> *My child's desire for learning French —*
> *Might I ask without being rude,*

Who pays the bill for Bon Chèvre's food?
Are cabbages for goats war diet?
Or are they given to keep her quiet.

His letters to his children, written in a tidy script, were always laced with fun, and he obviously took with good humour the numerous nicknames they bestowed on him such as 'jolly old Farve of Victoria Road' and 'Toad' or 'Toad-catcher'. In turn he had pet names for his children: he called Nancy 'my little Blob-nose', or more often 'Koko' after the character from *Mikado*, because he considered that her high cheekbones, dark curly hair and green eyes gave her a slightly oriental look.

Sydney was able to meet David on at least one occasion while he was on leave in Paris. Her news was worrying: with the loss of his salary from the *Lady*, she found it difficult to manage on her allowance and his Army pay. Then her father wrote to say that, due to increased taxation, he had no alternative but to reduce her allowance. Fortunately, Lord Redesdale came to the rescue with the offer of a house on his land at Batsford. It was called Malcolm House and was next to the church. Sydney was not enthusiastic about moving to the deeply rural part of Gloucestershire, but she could not bear the thought of debt. The London house was let and the children were delighted to be living in 'the real country' at last.

It was while the children were visiting their grandfather that six-year-old Diana developed appendicitis. Sydney had no option but to call in a doctor for what was a potentially fatal condition. Appendectomy was still regarded as highly dangerous and the surgery had to be performed 'on the kitchen table'. Put to bed in one of the guest bedrooms, the patient made a rapid recovery, thanks – she suggests – to the comfort and luxury of her surroundings.

Shortly after this the children saw seventy-nine-year-old Grandfather Redesdale for the last time. He was very ill and yellow with jaundice. He died in August 1916, his death undoubtedly hastened by the loss of Clement on whom he had pinned all his hopes for the future.

David now became the 2nd Lord Redesdale. Eight months later he was invalided home again, this time suffering from extreme exhaustion. As he convalesced the Army, recognizing his service record and his new responsibilities, gave him a home posting. He was made assistant provost marshal, based in Oxford from where he could travel to Batsford by motorcycle in an hour, a journey he made once a week.

3

NURSERY DAYS
(1915–22)

After a decent interval Sydney, the new Lady Redesdale, moved into Batsford with her lively brood. David's mother, Clementine, the dowager Lady Redesdale, tactfully moved to Redesdale Cottage in Northumberland.

In 1917, when Sydney moved in, Batsford was rather different from how it had been on her first visit in 1894 when she had met David and been overwhelmed by light, warmth and exotic scents. With only the ailing elderly Redesdales in residence for some time, many of the huge rooms had been closed off and the furniture shrouded in dust covers. Wartime restrictions and lack of money meant things did not change when Sydney took over. She opened only those rooms essential to house her family in comfort.

David's father left an estate valued at £33,000 gross.[1] After tax and other bequests David was left with just under £17,000. According to the Bank of England, this equates to a present-day monetary value of more than £600,000, although it must be said that the properties and chattels could not be purchased today for seven or eight times that amount. It was a useful inheritance, but most of it was not in cash but land and property in

Gloucestershire, Oxfordshire and Redesdale in Northumberland, and the income was insufficient to run Batsford House and its estate.

Bertie, the 1st Lord Redesdale, was said to have inherited a fortune from an uncle. In addition to this he had enjoyed a successful career heading the Board of Works under Disraeli for twelve years, and he had had royalties from several books, especially his runaway bestseller *Memories*, which detailed his life as a diplomat in Russia, China and latterly Japan. In fact, he had been successful at anything to which he turned his hand – eminent Victorian traveller, writer, linguist, yachtsman, senior civil servant, MP, garden designer, and horse breeder. Although he moved in the rather fast (and costly) circles of the Prince of Wales' set there is no evidence that he was a notable spendthrift or gambler. It appears that, apart from a wife who had little concept of living within her allowance, he spent most of his fortune on demolishing a perfectly good Georgian house at Batsford in 1880, and building the Victorian Gothic mansion with its elaborate gardens, arboretum and huge stables that still occupies the site. From the start it was obvious to David and Sydney that Batsford would have to be sold, but they could not even consider doing so until after the war.

Few women of her class were as financially prudent as Sydney but running the vast house with its five staircases on a limited budget must have taxed even her ingenuity. Although the family was technically better off because of David's inheritance, they had merely swapped one form of relative poverty for another. Some of Sydney's economies have gone down in family history, and one caused much merriment for it somehow made its way into the *Daily Sketch* under the headline, 'Peeress Saves Ha'pence' when she decided to save on the cost of washing, starching and ironing several dozen table napkins each day. Yet it was not ha'pence she was saving, but a considerable amount over a year, for the household would have used close to two hundred napkins a week.

Napkin rings were unacceptable, and paper napkins unthinkable and expensive, so the family did without. She also provided hard, shiny Bromo lavatory paper, which discouraged any extravagance in that department. Further aid to the exchequer came when the four Norman children were boarded out at Batsford for the duration of the war because their parents, Ronald and Lady Florence, were anxious to get them out of London with the threat of Zeppelins. So the Mitford children had built-in companions, as well as the children in the village as playmates.

At this point Unity was still a toddler in the sole charge of Nanny, but the others, Nancy (thirteen), Pam (ten), Tom (seven) and Diana (six), and the Norman children were all taught by a governess, Miss Mirams, in the schoolroom. David and Sydney were not alone in believing that it was unnecessary to educate girls beyond reading, writing and basic arithmetic to enable them to keep household books, French (essential for a well-bred girl), and enough geography and history to prevent them appearing ignorant in polite society. Music, needlework and deportment were also included. Only Tom was to go away for formal education and David made no financial allowance to educate the girls, assuming that Sydney would be responsible for this. Later, Sydney would herself teach her three younger children to read (they all had to be able to read aloud *The Times* leader by the age of six), and the basics of arithmetic, history and geography, before they joined the schoolroom at about eight. In those early days at Batsford, though, she was too busy to teach them, with the demands of a large, though well-staffed, house and a growing family as well as another pregnancy.

On 11 September 1917, Sydney gave birth to her sixth child, another girl whom they called Jessica after Sydney's mother, but the baby was known from the start as Decca. If there was ever any doubt about the relationship between David and Sydney, and the basis of their marriage, it is dispelled by a letter from

Aunt Natty written a few weeks before the birth of Decca. Sydney, she writes, 'is good – unselfish – beautiful – and she and her husband [are] the greatest lovers . . .'[2]

Miss Mirams, the second governess Sydney recruited, seems to have been something of a paragon. She taught the children in two groups, and in the early days Nancy, quick, bright and a voracious reader, was way ahead on her own. Pam, Tom and Diana formed a younger group with Sibell and Mark Norman. Pam, like David, was a slow learner and had difficulty even in keeping up with her two younger siblings. In later life dyslexia was diagnosed,[3] but throughout her childhood Nancy and her younger sisters teased her about her slowness. However, the standard of Miss Mirams' teaching became obvious when Tom applied for a place at Lockers Park Preparatory School. Many of the applicants would have had a conventional pre-prep education but Tom's entrance exam marks resulted in his being placed in the highest new-boy form. Certainly, then, the education the girls received in the schoolroom was not sub-standard and Miss Mirams' teaching was supplemented with exploration of the Batsford library, the repository of the remarkable book collection made by Bertie Redesdale throughout his adult life.

To pay the governess's salary of about £150 a year, and to fund the necessary books and teaching aids, Sydney set out to make money from eggs and honey, which she sold locally at first, but which later went up to London by train to smart clubs. She employed a full-time man to look after the five hundred hens, but she washed the eggs herself: 'I never sell an unwashed egg,' she told a visitor, and advised him that keeping chickens was no good as a project unless you knew what you were doing.[4] Soft-shelled or cracked eggs were eaten by the family, the hens ate all kitchen waste, and when they became too old to lay they became 'boiling fowl'. She managed the beehives herself, with the help of the redoubtable Miss Mirams. Other than to ensure the garden was well kept by the outside staff and produced sufficient fruit and vegetables for the kitchen, she was never much interested in it, and her hen-and-hive activities were merely a way of earning extra income. She always cleared a hundred pounds a year from her chickens, after expenses, and she tried to pass the ethic of prudent management on to her children. As soon as they were old enough they were all encouraged to keep chickens, pigs and even calves. They paid 'rent' to David for the land and stables, bought the feed from, and sold the produce to, the estate and were allowed to keep as pocket money any profits from their enterprise. Pam once fought her father over the matter of rent when she discovered at a tenants' supper that she was paying more, *pro rata*, for her small piece of land than the local farmers on their commercial acreage. Pam shone at stock-rearing, Nancy was not interested, and Diana recalls that she did it as well as she could because it was her only source of pocket money.

In 1918 Miss Mirams left and a succession of governesses followed her. Each summer a mademoiselle came to teach them French. During these visits only French was allowed to be spoken at the table, and Diana remembered that meals were often very quiet.[5] Even when French was not the order of the day, mealtimes could be fraught. It was one of David's foibles that he could not bear sloppiness and crumbs: spills irritated him beyond reasonable complaint, and since there were no napkins to disguise the results of a moment of clumsiness the children learned to be extra careful. Woe betide the child or unwary guest who dropped a spot of soup on 'the good tablecloth' or inadvertently scraped a knife across 'the good plate'.[6] The child would be yelled at, the guest (depending on status) glared at or David would explode to himself, not quite *sotto voce*, '*Filthy* beast!'

In 1918 Tom went off to boarding school aged eight. He was never homesick or bullied, and thoroughly enjoyed it. Perhaps in comparison with the teasing and bullying by his sisters at home prep school seemed tame. He particularly appreciated being allowed to eat sausages every day for breakfast. In the Mitford home the only person allowed this pork product was David, and naturally the children 'longed' for anything forbidden them. Tom's letters home lingered on this treat, a good tease on his sisters. Sometimes, though, Mabel the parlourmaid would take a chance and retrieve a leftover sausage as a treat for the girls who 'danced around the pantry with a delicious end of a congealing sausage', Debo recalled.[7]

When the war ended there was general rejoicing but there was a sting in the tail for the Mitford children. They had hoped the war would go on for ever for they had been told repeatedly that when it was over Batsford would have to be sold because they were too poor to live there. Almost their last memory of life at Batsford was a fête held by Sydney to raise funds for wounded soldiers. Just before it was due to be opened Sydney looked at her white elephant stall and thought it was understocked. She rushed into the house and began to gather 'odds and ends' to fill up the gaps. Most of these were priceless Oriental antiques brought back from the Far East by Bertie. David and the children managed to buy a few back, but the rest were snapped up by villagers and antiques dealers for coppers. The children learned from this: in subsequent years when it came near the time for summer fêtes they hid their toys.

In 1919 Batsford was sold, and David bought Asthall Manor near the Cotswold village of Swinbrook in Oxfordshire. He never intended the house to be their permanent home for he owned some hillside land on the other side of, and overlooking, Swinbrook, where he planned eventually to build a house for his family close to his pheasant coverts. But far from pining for Batsford, Sydney and the children fell in love with Asthall, a generous Jacobean gabled manor house, in a gentle green valley amid rolling hills. Only David, Pam and Diana were made uneasy by the ghosts of Asthall, for no one else appeared to see or sense them, or if they did they ignored them like the family in *The Canterville Ghost*. The haunting took several manifestations:

footsteps could be heard at night on the paving stones around the house, and sometimes the trickle and drip-drip of non-existent water. The nursery windows overlooked the churchyard, and although they were forbidden to watch funerals, they did. It was fertile soil in which Nancy could plant her own brand of scary ghost stories. Once, Decca and Debo fell into a newly dug grave and Nancy told them it meant 'bad luck, *forever*'.[8]

The elder children agreed that the best thing of all was the library. It was housed in a converted barn linked to the main house by a covered way, which they called 'the cloisters', and contained a good collection of books from Grandfather Redesdale's library at Batsford. The volumes had been chosen mainly by ten-year-old Tom, at his father's request, for David did not feel competent to make the selection himself. Furnished with comfortable armchairs and a grand piano, it was a desirable place to the children for they were hardly ever bothered by grown-ups there, and provided they behaved reasonably, replaced any books where they found them, and did not make too much mess, they were left alone. On the other hand, if they tried to read a book in the house, Nancy once said, it was almost guaranteed to attract a remark from David such as, 'If you've got nothing to do run down to the village and tell Hooper . . .' Hooper, called by the children 'Hoops' or 'Choops', was the groom, much loved by Pam and Debo despite a fearsome temper which, Sydney later told them, was due to shell-shock and bad experiences during the First World War. 'When Bobo once did something to annoy him, something with one of the ponies,' Debo wrote, 'he yelled at her, "I'll take yer in that wood and do for yer!"'[9]

The old Lords of the Manor of Swinbrook were the Fettiplaces. They had bought the estate in 1504 and their manor house was said to be 'one of the glories of Elizabethan England'. The family died out at the end of the eighteenth century, and the manor was purchased by a Mr Freeman of London. He lived quietly enough according to locals but he was, in fact, an infamous masked highwayman who even stooped to robbing his own guests as they rode home. Apprehended by Bow Street Runners, he was hanged at Tyburn in 1806; his estate became Crown property and the glorious manor house was demolished. Earl (the uncle from whom 'Bertie' inherited his fortune, but not the title of earl) Redesdale bought the Swinbrook estate, *sans* manor house, in 1810 for its sporting interests, and did little beyond collecting rents on the farms, building a few cottages and using the property for shooting parties.

When David inherited it, the village of Swinbrook was no more than a hamlet of 150 souls. Apart from a scattering of cottages built of honey-coloured stone and a few farmhouses, mostly owned by the estate, it consisted of the twelfth-century church, a village school, the Swan Inn on the very edge of the village, and the shop, which doubled as a post office and 'sold four kinds of sweets – toffee, acid drops, Edinburgh rock and butterscotch'.[10] Acid drops cost a penny-ha'penny a quarter, were weighed on the same brass scale as letters, and were sold in squares of paper deftly twisted into a cone by the postmistress.

Apart from the closure of the village shop, little has changed, and Swinbrook today still has a timeless, left-over-from-yesteryear ambience. Its narrow lanes, leading to the tiny village green, are still bordered with willows, beeches and silver birch, and in the spring its verges are full of primroses and blue cranesbill. The rolling hills are dotted with sheep and, apart from the occasional car passing through – there are faster routes to the comparative metropolis of Shipton-under-Wychwood than via Swinbrook – the prevailing sounds are birdsong, sheep, the trickle and splash of water from myriad streams, the shrieks of swallows and house-martins wheeling furiously overhead, and the far-off echoing ring of a horse's hoofs on a paved road. As a child Decca always thought that when William Blake penned, '. . . up in the sky the little birds fly, and the hills are all covered with sheep . . .' he was writing about Swinbrook.[11]

When they moved to Asthall the family was almost complete, but Sydney had one final attempt at producing another son, and in 1920, when she was forty, her seventh and last child was born. As usual David was present at the birth, and as he came out of the room Mabel the parlourmaid was waiting anxiously for news. 'One look at His Lordship's face,' she said in later years, 'told me everything.' It was another girl. They called the baby Deborah, quickly shortened to Debo. Many years later Mabel would gloat that 'His Lordship's face was like thunder. I don't think anyone looked at Miss Debo for three months . . . but she came up trumps in the end, didn't she?'[12] In the meantime, Nancy saw a tease in the situation. For years she tormented Debo with the line, 'Everyone cried when you were born.' She was sixteen, and Sydney asked her to be godmother to the new baby, fearing that she herself might not live to see Debo grow up. Pam was now thirteen, Tom eleven, Diana ten. Unity was six, and Jessica three.

As well as attending lessons, the older children rode out every day except Sunday with Captain Collinson, the agent, or Hooper. Although most of the children regarded Hooper as a grumpy old devil, Pam always referred to him as 'Hoops. *Sweet* Hoops . . .'[13] David could no longer ride: in the early days at Asthall his horse had reared up and fell on him, breaking his pelvis and afterwards riding became too uncomfortable. Sydney, who as a débutante had been a keen rider, had long ago given it up, but Nancy, Diana and, later, Debo were good horsewomen, and hunted side-saddle with the local pack of foxhounds, the Heythrop. They were joined by any visiting cousins on the daily rides, Rosemary and Clementine Mitford (daughters of the late Uncle Clement), for example, who often stayed at Asthall while their mother spent the winter in the Sudan, where her second husband was a government game warden. 'I remember riding a huge horse as a small child,' Clementine wrote, recalling a less than happy incident sixty-five years earlier when she was eight and Nancy was eighteen, 'and Nancy and Pam cantering ahead; Nancy looking like a Constantin Guys drawing, and Pam – not so glamorous but kinder to poor me. And Hooper, so disapproving (almost like a male Blor) I suppose because my riding clothes were all wrong. I remember the torture and embarrassment of the stirrup leathers biting into one's legs because I was wearing socks and thin knickers . . .'[14]

Neither Tom, Unity nor Decca ever took to hunting, though Diana tried patiently to teach Decca to trot round a field on her little pony Joey. On Sundays they all went out coursing with David and one of his brothers, 'Uncle Tommy', who came to luncheon and brought his whippet. They enjoyed these physically active days, beating through fields of winter crops to put up hares. When one jumped up, the whippet and David's lurcher would be unleashed, while David and Uncle Tommy leaned on their thumb-sticks and watched with countrymen's interest in venery. Since Sydney would never allow hares to be eaten, the children could never think what happened to those killed by the hounds after David popped them into the hare pockets he had designed into all his country clothes. Probably they were presented to his workers or tenants.

The children's enjoyment of field sports, which bred in most of them a oneness with the annual rhythms of their environment, did not stretch to condoning the traps set in the pheasant coverts by David's gamekeeper, Steele, who regarded anything that was not a pheasant as 'vermin'. As well as stoats, weasels and foxes, the bloody victims of these monstrous contraptions sometimes included hedgehogs, badgers and even the occasional feral cat. All the children made it a point of honour to visit the traps regularly and spring the captives, to the fury of the gamekeeper whom they all hated.

Although Nancy has traduced life in the country and portrayed it in novels as boring, and even Diana was less than complimentary of it when she was a teenager, waiting endlessly for escape into the glittering world of grown-ups, all the children had a happy childhood – even Decca who, though she never took to riding like the others, only became truly unhappy when she reached adolescence. There were always cousins and family visiting, always 'something going on', their cousin Rosemary recalled, far more so than in other houses that she and her sister visited.[15] Apart from endless games that the children themselves thought up and organized, in the summer there were tennis parties and trips to Stratford about once a month. There was the annual 'Bailey Week' at the Stow-on-the-Wold home of their four Bailey cousins, Richard, Anthony, Christopher and Timothy, the sons of Aunt Weenie and Colonel Percy Bailey. Bailey Week included cricket, tennis, walks and riding, picnics and dancing. It was like a mini Season, and the girls enjoyed it immensely. Even years later when Pam was a débutante and in the full throes of a London Season she wrote to Sydney of how much she was looking forward to Bailey Week. During the winter there was hunting and coursing, weekends when the house was full of guests for one of David's shoots, weekly trips to Oxford, where they skated at the rink behind the Regal cinema and browsed the latest books at Blackwell's, and the ever-popular rainy-day occupation of dressing up and putting on plays.

Church attendance on Sunday was compulsory for the Mitford children. Although the church at Asthall adjoined their home, the living of that parish was not in David's gift,[16] so he preferred to attend the church at Swinbrook where he could keep the clergyman in check. Here, with his family ranged beside him in a pew he had donated after a significant win on the Grand National in 1918, David watched hawk-like to see that the vicar did not stray from the wonderful liturgy of *the* prayer book with an extempore petition, or try to slip in a modern composition among the favourite traditional hymns he chose himself ('We don't want any of those damn complicated foreign tunes'), and that the sermon was kept to ten minutes, timed to the second by his stop-watch. Invariably, David also read the lesson and took the collection.

Despite the short sermons and the fascinating tombs of the long-dead Fettiplaces, the girls were bored in church and spent their time trying to make Tom 'blither' – giggle. Later, after Tom got his own flat in London and returned for weekends this mainly consisted of emphasizing certain words in prayers or psalms to try to make him react. From what they overheard of their brother's bachelor life it was considered especially important by his sisters that he be reminded often of the seventh commandment, 'Thou shalt not commit adultery.' Often it worked, and Tom giggled helplessly to the delight of the girls. Occasionally, he got his own back. When she was nine Decca had discovered a good wheeze where she would apply to manufacturers for free samples of products. One she particularly enjoyed was Benger's baby food. 'It was lovely,' she recalled. 'It tasted like Horlicks.' After a gap of about six months she sent off for another sample, which duly arrived, and then one day there came a loud knock at the door, and 'that awful Tuddemy [Tom] caused Mabel to call me, saying that the Benger's man was at the door wanting to see the baby. Total terror! [I had] visions of life imprisonment for fraud . . .'[17]

At Asthall Christmas was kept in the old-fashioned way with a party for the children of the tenants (still recalled by some who attended), and a fancy-dress party for the family and guests. There was a huge dressing-up box, from whose contents everyone had to concoct a character. For many years Pam was the fair Lady Rowena (Ivanhoe's betrothed), while Nancy, who began as the tragic bride in the mistletoe-bough legend (an incident said to have taken place at nearby Minster Lovell),[18] progressed as she grew older to a tramp who used to chase 'Lady Rowena' around the house lifting up the skirt of her red dress 'to see her knickers'.[19] The various characters of those long-ago parties are preserved in photographs in the

Chatsworth archives: headless men, cavaliers, nurses, pierrots, gypsies and French aristocrats.[20]

Secret societies were much in vogue among the younger children, and Unity and Decca, who called each other Boud (pronounced 'Bowd' not Bood), developed their own secret language called Boudledidge in which they became so fluent that they could tell rude stories to each other in front of unsuspecting grown-ups. Another of the societies was the Society of Hons formed by Decca and Debo, later made famous by Nancy in her novels. The two youngest children were keen on chickens – it was how they earned their pocket money – so they originally called their club the Society of Hens and began to call each other 'Hen' (and did so until Decca's death in 1996). The change from Hens to Hons came about, Decca explained, from a poem culled from two sources: one was a Burns poem, in which the line 'John Anderson, my Jo John' became 'My Hon Henderson my Ho Hon' and the second, 'Lars Porsena of Clusium', which spawned the 'Honnish lines': 'Hon Henderson my Ho Hon/By the nine gods she swore/That the great house of Henderson/Should suffer wrong no more'. So the Society of Hens became the Society of Hons, with its carefully written-down set of rules – to break one made one a Counter Hon – and initiation tasks that included frog-hopping across the tennis court, turning two somersaults while running forward and answering a series of general-knowledge questions.[21] The H was always pronounced in Hon, as it is in hen. It was never, as later came to be believed, a society for girls entitled to the prefix 'Honourable'.

The initial *raison d'être* of the society was to wreak vengeance on 'the Horrible Counter Hons', chief of whom, at the time of founding, was Tom, for some now-forgotten misdemeanour during his school holidays. Decca recalled that Nancy was elected Head of the League against Tom and badges were made, emblazoned with 'League against Tom. Head: Nancy'.[22] But empires crumble, and among Sydney's effects was also found a small homemade badge in Debo's childish hand, 'Leag against Nancy; Head Tom'.[23] The Society of Hons even had its own Honnish language; this was not so comprehensive as Boudledidge and borrowed freely from it.

In her memoir Decca recalled the inevitable squabbles that occur between a group of lively siblings with significant age disparities. The anti-Tom, or anti-Tuddemy (his name in Boudledidge)[24] campaign was merely 'the curious Honnish mirror-world expression of our devotion to him', she explained. 'For years he was the only member of the family to be "on Speakers" with all the others.' In spite of temporary alliances, which were generally formed for the purpose of defeating a governess, Decca wrote that her real childhood enmities were not with her older sisters but with her near contemporaries, Unity, who was three years older, and Debo, who was three years younger. 'Relations between Unity, Debo and me were uneasy, tinged with mutual resentment,' she recalled. 'We were like ill-assorted animals tied to a common tethering post.'[25] Elsewhere she would write of the boredom of the endless years of the schoolroom where she felt she had learned nothing. 'The one advantage was unlimited time to read. The library with Grandfather Redesdale's collection was for me a heavenly escape . . . it never occurred to me to be happy with my lot.'[26]

The only survivor of these three youngest children, Debo, cannot recall any of this smouldering resentment during their childhood, and believes it was something that occurred much later, after Decca grew up and became a rebel. But there is no doubting that Unity, Decca and Debo were all worlds apart in opinion, even at a young age. The squabbles and teasing that went on almost continuously were dealt with summarily by Nanny Blor or Sydney, with the quelling put-down, 'You are *very* silly children!'

Nancy 'ached' to learn more than was available to her at home. But though she could wheedle David in most things, he always turned sticky when she brought the subject round to education.

He feared that if they went to school his daughters would meet the wrong sort of girls and would be made to play hockey and develop thick calf muscles. Any such outburst as 'It's not fair, Tom has been allowed . . .' usually received the unanswerable reply, 'Tom's a boy.' She never stopped pleading, though, and at last, in 1921, when she was sixteen, Sydney sent her as a boarder to nearby Hatherop Castle School to be 'finished'. Although it subsequently became a formal educational establishment, Hatherop Castle then took about twenty of 'the right sort' of pupils, the nucleus of whom were the children of the family who lived in the Elizabethan manor house that housed the school. Lady Bazely, a widow who later married Commander Cadogan, had one Cadogan daughter and two Bazely daughters. Like the Redesdales she would not have dreamed of sending her daughters to public school, so she set up a small PNEU (Parents' National Education Union) school and invited the daughters of suitable neighbouring families to attend.

Nancy thoroughly enjoyed her time at Hatherop. The main curriculum, as well as sport (tennis, netball and swimming), was taken by the formidably able Miss Essex Cholmondeley, whom the girls adored. Mademoiselle Pierrat taught French, and there was an unnamed music teacher who gave them piano lessons. Once a week, on Wednesdays, there was dancing. It was important to young women with a London Season to face that they danced well. They all looked forward to this class and it was especially pleasurable for Nancy because Nanny brought Pam – now sufficiently recovered from polio to dance, although she never shone at the classes – and Diana from Asthall in the outside dickey seat of a Morris Cowley to join in the lessons. In the winter months, in their dancing dresses, the two younger girls arrived blue with cold, despite being wrapped up in David's old trench coats. Afterwards they travelled home in the same way through the bitter darkness. 'Strangely enough, we looked forward to these outings,' Diana recalled.[27] But while she enjoyed the dancing classes Diana shuddered at the idea of being sent away from Asthall to school like Nancy.

During her time at Hatherop, Nancy was introduced to the Girl Guide movement, and when she returned home suggested to her mother that she form a Swinbrook troop with herself as captain, Pam and Diana as her lieutenants, the members to be recruited from the village girls. Sydney thought it an excellent idea and the good-natured Pam fell in willingly with the scheme. Diana was horrified, which made the project even more attractive to Nancy as a long-running tease on her sister.

Nancy inspired teasing in her younger siblings to a greater or lesser degree, but she was the Queen of Teasers – 'a cosmic teaser', Decca would write. She seemed to know exactly what would irritate her victims most, fastening on any insecurities with devastatingly accurate effect. 'She once upset us,' Debo recalled, 'by saying to Unity, Decca and me, "Do you realize that the middle of your names are nit, sick and bore?"'[28] One friend likened her humour to the barbed hook hidden beneath a riot of colourful feathers in a fishing fly. And barbed is an apt word, for there was often a cruel element to her teasing, which caused real distress. For example, while Nancy longed to go to school Diana could not stand the thought of it: she became physically ill at the idea, and was therefore an easy victim of Nancy's tease that she had overheard their parents discussing to which school they might send Diana. That this might cause her younger sister to lie awake at nights worrying did not concern Nancy. It was 'a good tease' and that made it all right. Pam recalled that when they were debs Nancy would find out the name of the young man Pam most fancied and tell her that she had seen him out with another girl.

Nancy called Debo 'Nine' until she married, saying it was her mental age, and she took advantage of Debo's sentimental nature by writing poems and stories to make her cry. One was about a match: 'A little houseless match/It has no roof, no thatch/It lies alone it makes no moan/That little houseless match . . .' So effective was this that eventually Nancy had only to hold up a box of matches for tears to well in Debo's eyes. Unity caught on to this form of entertainment and invented a story about a Pekinese puppy. Decca retold it in her autobiography: 'The telephone bell rang. Grandpa got up from his seat and went to answer it. "Lill ill!" he cried . . . Lill was on her deathbed, a victim of consumption. Her dying request was that Grandpa should care for her poor little Pekinese. However, in all the excitement of the funeral the Peke was forgotten, and was found several days later beside his mistress's grave, dead of starvation and a broken heart.'[29] Soon, like Nancy with the box of matches, all the sisters had to do to reduce Debo to floods of tears was to whisper ominously, 'The telephone bell rang . . .'

But despite her cruel streak, Nancy's sheer funniness endeared her to everyone, even when they were the butt of a painful tease, for she went to great lengths to make them laugh. Here, her skill in acting and disguise – learned in countless home-produced plays – came in useful. During the general strike of 1926 Pam helped to run a temporary canteen on the main road to Oxford for strike-breaking truck drivers. According to Decca, Pam was the only one who knew how to make tea and sandwiches, and how to wash up, and she was given the early shift each day because she was an early riser. One morning at 5 a.m., while Pam was alone in the shack waiting for a customer, a filthy tramp lurched in from the half-light and asked for 'a cup o' tea, miss'. When Pam started nervously to pour it he nipped round the counter, slipped a grimy arm around her waist and thrust his hideously scarred face into hers, slurring, 'Can I 'ave a kiss, miss?' Pam screamed, tried to run, fell over and broke an ankle. The tramp was Nancy. On another occasion, when the Redesdales were selling a house, a potential buyer, a fearsomely plump matron with a pouter chest, whiskers and garlicky breath, came to inspect the house. She was shown round courteously by members of the family until she burst into peals of laughter. Nancy again. During both these incidents the sisters were entirely taken in.

Sydney was so impressed with the standard of teaching at Hatherop School that she recruited a Miss Hussey, who had been trained in the PNEU programme at Ambleside, as governess. All the younger girls were taught by this system. Far from being a sub-standard education, as some Mitford biographers have suggested, PNEU was and is a highly regarded, reliable and time-tested system of teaching.[30] It concentrates on a good basic education but one of its important precepts is to encourage a child to learn through the senses and independent exploration, rather than being spoon-fed with information. Regular, independently marked examinations check the pupil's progress. If there was a drawback it was that reading was then taught phonetically so that spelling remained a problem for the girls into their teens. And, although this is jumping ahead in the story, the end result of the Asthall schoolroom education speaks for itself. Four of the girls, Nancy, Decca, Diana and Debo, would become bestselling writers and were what would now be regarded as A and B grade pupils, therefore potential university material. Furthermore, educated in such a small isolated group, the children's personalities were allowed to develop and flower individually, even though they were always inevitably lumped together as 'the Mitford sisters'. It is clear, with hindsight, that they were gifted children, but one wonders how they might have turned out if they had been educated in the arena of a formal school and taught to a pattern.

Nevertheless, the standard of teachers in the Asthall schoolroom varied, for not all were PNEU trained, and to one 'geography' meant a study of the Holy Land, and tracing the journeys of St Paul in coloured inks.[31] Decca claimed to have been bored with the schoolroom from an early age and jealous of the children of literature who had such adventurous lives. Once, it is said, she burst out, 'Oliver Twist was *so lucky* to live in a fascinating orphanage.'[32]

David had no involvement in his daughters' schooling. Apart from serving on the local bench and the local county council, David took his seat in the House of Lords regularly and was chairman of the House of Lords' Drains Committee, which attempted to improve the building's antiquarian plumbing system. In his spare time he did the things he liked best. He rose at dawn, or before daybreak in winter. The housemaids, scurrying round trying to do their dusting and get the grates cleared and fires lit before the family woke up, would encounter him, in his Paisley dressing-gown, wandering amiably about the house, humming a favourite tune, with his vacuum flask of tea under his arm.[33] After breakfast, served promptly at eight-thirty for he could not abide latecomers to the table, he dealt with the running of the farms and the estate. Then, in his habitual corduroy breeches, canvas gaiters and comfortable jacket, thumb-stick in hand, he walked his coverts discussing maintenance with Steele, organized shoots, and went hare coursing or fishing. He no longer hunted, but he usually went to the meets to see his daughters off. There was also the annual rite of 'chubb fuddling'*, hilariously described by Nancy in *Love in a Cold Climate*.

The Windrush is a notable trout river that flows gin-clear through the valley past Swinbrook and below Asthall Manor. David owned fishing rights there, just as the fictional 'Uncle Matthew Radlett' owned the rights to a similar trout stream, which flowed beneath his fictional Cotswold home, Alconleigh;

It was one of his favourite possessions. He was an excellent dry-fly fisherman and was never happier, in and out of the fishing season, than when messing about in the river in waders and planning glorious improvements for it . . . He built dams, he dug lashers, he cut the weeds and trimmed

---

*Nancy's spelling, but in the OED it is given as 'chub'.

the banks, he shot the herons, he hunted the otters, and he restocked with young trout every year. But he had trouble with the coarse fish, especially the chubb, which not only gobble up baby trout but also their food . . . One day he came upon an advertisement . . . 'Send for the Chubb Fuddler'. The Radletts always said that their father had never learnt to read, but in fact he could read quite well, if really fascinated by his subject, and the proof is that he found the Chubb Fuddler like this all by himself.[34]

The chub fuddler came by appointment, and scattered the river with treated groundbait. The fish came surging to the surface in a feeding frenzy, whereupon every able-bodied man in the village, equipped with rakes, landing-nets and wheelbarrows hauled them out to be used in chub pies or as garden manure. The annual visit of the chub fuddler was a real-life event, and surely there is a heartfelt memory behind the incident when Uncle Matthew yells at Fanny, the narrator of *Love in a Cold Climate*, 'Put it back at once, you blasted idiot – can't you see it's a grayling? Oh my God, *women* – incompetent.'[35]

It is precisely because Nancy Mitford was so adept at recycling her own experiences, weaving the often improbable eccentricities of the real-life Mitfords with the slightly mad fictional Radletts, that the lines between fact and fiction became so indistinct, and helps to explain why the Mitfords were destined to become almost a national institution. In reality the Mitford family did not lead a truly exceptional life. They lived in what they regarded as a sort of upper-class poverty, with parents who were apparently unable to show overt affection to their children. 'Muv', with her strong sense of the work ethic, her dutiful local charity work and keen interest in the Women's Institute, appeared preoccupied to her children, but this was probably because she was always busy. 'Farve' was an eccentric country squire with loudly expressed jingoistic opinions. Like the fictional Uncle Matthew he ranted about 'the Hun' and 'bloody foreigners', believed that 'wogs begin at Calais', and that it was not necessary for women to be highly educated. All these traits were shared by many others of their class, described by one friend, Frank Pakenham,* as 'minor provincial aristocracy – the same as us'.[36]

What lifted the Mitfords from the ranks of the ordinary among their peers were not their lifestyles but their exceptional personalities: David's utterances make him appear eccentric by today's standards but he was essentially a kind man. Sydney's 'vagueness and preoccupation' veiled a deep love and sense of responsibility to her children. Far from drifting about in a haze she was a hard-working chatelaine, in every way involved with village life and always sympathetic to the problems of those less fortunate than her own family. As a result she was highly valued locally. 'She used to say,' Debo recalled, 'that the people who deserved praise, medals or whatever successful people got were the women who brought up families on the tiny amounts of money their husbands earned.'[37] But what chiefly made the Mitford family 'different' were the girls.

Nancy's brilliance as a novelist is arguably the primary reason why the Mitford family is still remembered, and is constantly being rediscovered by new readers. But the Mitford girls were first noticed publicly before Nancy's most famous books were written, when three of them, Diana, Unity and Decca, independently made newspaper headlines. In itself this was shaming for David and Sydney, who believed that the name of a decent woman should appear in the newspapers only twice: first on her marriage, and second in her obituary.

Nancy's private correspondence, and memoirs and letters written by Diana and Decca, show that despite their constant gales of laughter there was an incipient unhappiness among the Mitford

*Later Lord Longford.

girls as they grew up. This seems to be centred in a discontent with Sydney as a mother: they wanted more from her than she could give, or knew how to provide. Probably they wanted more physical contact, to be praised and told that they were loved, and the lack of this bred in them a basic insecurity, which lurked beneath their exuberant display of self-confidence and high spirits. But, again, Sydney was not unusual in her class and in that era.

Years later Nancy would say, 'I had the greatest possible respect for her; I liked her company; but I never loved her, for the evident reason that she never loved me. I was never hugged or kissed by her as a small child – indeed, I saw little of her . . . when we first grew up she was very cold and sarky with me. I don't reproach her for it, people have a perfect right to dislike their children.'[38] Decca agreed, claiming that it was her mother's implacable disapproval of her as a child that hurt most. 'I actively loathed her as a teenager (especially an older child, after the age of fifteen), and did not respect her. On the contrary I thought she was extremely schoopid [*sic*: a family spelling] and narrow minded – that is sort of limited minded with hard and fast bounds on her mind. But then, after re-getting to know her [as an adult] I became immensely fond of her and really rather adored her.'[39] Decca was fair minded enough to add, 'She probably didn't change, as people don't, especially after middle age. Most likely we did.' This sounds rather like Mark Twain's comment that when he was fourteen his father was so ignorant that he could hardly bear to be near him. 'But when I got to twenty-one I was astonished at how much he had learned in only seven years.' Diana, too, felt this childhood estrangement from her mother, though Debo never did, perhaps because as the last child left at home she received the full share of attention from both parents.

Sydney's actions and reactions, as her daughters made their own adult lives, show that far from being uninvolved she was deeply loving. Children sometimes appear to believe that parents have an inbuilt guide to perfect parenting and that an inability to deliver what they want or need is a deliberate act of neglect. But parenting is a hit-and-miss affair, depending on many ingredients: the age of the parents, the relationship between them, the behaviour of their own parents towards them and their reaction to it, and also the demeanour of the child. Parents, too, apparently, often have an inbuilt confidence that their children, given the same upbringing they themselves received, will grow up with the same values and beliefs. But there is no magic formula to good parenting and parents get only one crack at it with each child. They cannot rehearse and go back, learning from past mistakes if they get it wrong. Invariably, too, children grow up with a ragbag of selective memories.

In 1921 Sydney took the children to Dieppe for the summer, renting Aunt Natty's house there. The children adored it and were so busy with seaside activities that they hardly noticed two major family tragedies that traumatized the grown-ups. One day Sydney received a telegram advising that Natty's only son, Bill, had shot himself because of his debts. He had been an addicted gambler and had been bailed out several times by his brother-in-law, Winston Churchill. This time he felt he could no longer carry on and it fell to Sydney to break the dreadful news of his suicide to his mother, who was staying near by. A pall of sadness hung over the holiday but the children, it seems, were not aware of it. Decades later Sydney told Decca how Natty's daughter Nellie, then in her early twenties and unmarried, had once come to her in Dieppe in deep despair and begged for the loan of eight pounds. It was a gambling debt, she said, a debt of honour and must be paid. 'Muv went straight to Aunty Natty,' Decca recalled disapprovingly. The debt was honoured, 'and Nellie was bitterly punished. Muv told me this, but simply couldn't see what a vile thing it was to have done. I guess it's that awful disapproving quality that I always hated about her.'[40] Decca was four at the time of Bill's death, and probably seven when Nellie begged Sydney for help. In writing as she did many years later, Decca made no connection between the two incidents.

The other bad news received on that holiday concerned Sydney's father, Tap. He was in Spanish Morocco at Algeciras on holiday when he died suddenly. He had been a former member of the parliamentary committee on Gibraltar, so it was deemed appropriate that he should be buried there with full naval honours. His estate was just under £60,000, almost twice what Bertie Redesdale had left, and Sydney inherited just under a quarter of it, including a 19 per cent share in the *Lady*.[41]

4

ROARING TWENTIES
(1922–9)

In a sense, Nancy's seventeenth birthday in November 1921 was a watershed in the life of the family. She was the first to leave the nest, and her flight heralded the beginning of the end of an era of comfortable and inconspicuous family life. Although it would take another fifteen years to reach a nadir, change took place inexorably as, one by one, the girls reached adulthood and went out into the world.

But this was still in the future when Nancy set out on a school trip with immense excitement. A friend of hers, Marjorie Murray, attended a school in Queen's Gate, whose headmistress had arranged to take a group of four girls on a cultural tour to France and Italy. Europe had only recently returned to some semblance of normality after the 1914–18 war, and somehow Nancy contrived to be in the party. It was her first experience of being free of the family and she found it intoxicating.

Her letters home are full of enthusiastic superlatives: Paris was 'heavenly . . . we don't want to leave . . . Why doesn't one always live in hotels? It is so lovely . . .' Pisa was also '*too* heavenly . . . the buildings . . . so white in the middle of such green grass', and Florence '*too* lovely, *too* romantic . . . quite beyond description . . .

last night we went for a walk on the river and a man with a guitar and a girl with a heavenly voice serenaded us. I gave them two lire . . . and they went on for hours. It was *too* delicious . . .' The art galleries were beyond words: 'How I love the pictures. I had no idea I was so fond of pictures . . . if only I had a room of my own I would make it a regular picture gallery . . . how shall I tear myself away? Thank you *so* much for sending me. I have never been so happy in my life before, in spite of minor incidents such as fleas . . .' The colours in Florence were 'marvellous' and 'the blue sky is heavenly. I can't like Venice as much as this.'[1] But she loved Venice too, 'quite heavenly . . . in a quite different way to Florence. Here it is more the place that one likes, there it is the things, statues, pictures and buildings . . .'

To be sure, everything was not entirely perfect. Her home-made clothes made her feel conspicuous beside her more smartly dressed companions; she had less spending money than they did, and while she was allowed to wear her hair up, David's decree that she might not wear make-up rankled: 'both [Jean] and Marjorie powder their noses the whole time. I wish I could. I'm sure for travelling one ought.'[2] But it was the sort of trip Nancy had longed for, and although she did her best to appear a *femme du monde* in her letters to her parents, tales of juvenile pranks nudge the accounts of visits to art galleries, boat excursions and firework displays. In one she describes how a girl jumped on another's bed and burst the hot-water bottle, making 'such a mess! We "ragged in the dorm" violently after that and an old lady came along and . . . that rather shut us up!' On another she tells of how she met and discussed Ruskin with a nice 'old man' she met in the hotel restaurant and to whom she had 'talked for ages . . . The others say he isn't old, but he is really, quite 45.'[3]

When Nancy returned from the trip, her head filled with images of terracotta-roofed towns baking in hot sunshine, of flowers and colour, and blue waters, life for her would never be the same again. She could not see how she would ever afford to realize her dream of European travel, and Asthall seemed excruciatingly parochial: Pam was wrapped up in her love of the country, Diana – her quick intelligence already disappointed by an inadequate curriculum – was bored by the three younger sisters' eternal squabbling and giggling in their private languages, playing with their animals, or re-enacting their fantasy of being kidnapped by white slavers. That game went on for years: all respectable young women were warned constantly until the beginning of the Second World War never to speak to strangers, 'unless they are in uniform', for fear of ending up in a South American house of ill-repute. The younger Mitford girls rather fancied the idea, especially Unity who went out of her way to attract and appeal to any lurking white slavers.

The younger children were quick to realize when they were being patronized by Nancy, and although they loved the elder sisters – especially the jokes they told, which made them all *roar* with laughter – their hero-worship was patchy. 'Nancy was too sharp-tongued and sarcastic to be anyone's Favourite Sister for long,' Decca noted. 'She might suddenly turn her penetrating emerald eyes in one's direction and say, "Run along up to the school-room; we've had quite enough of you." Or, if one had taken particular trouble to do one's hair in ringlets, she was apt to remark, "You look like the eldest and ugliest of the Brontë sisters today."'[4] Pam, with what they regarded as her own brand of bucolic bliss – she loved gardening, animal husbandry and cooking – although innately kind and with no trace of cruelty in her humour (she had been the butt of Nancy's all her life), was almost as vague as Sydney, and not really suitable as a role model. But Diana, who resembled 'a *Vogue* cover artist's conception of the goddess of the chase', although bored and rebellious, was unfailingly kind to them, laughing at their jokes, pushing them forward to perform in Boudledidge to visitors, helping them with French, piano practice and riding. She was definitely Favourite Sister material. It was she who patiently encouraged

Decca, who never took to horses, as she bumped inexpertly round a paddock on her little pony Joey. 'Do try to hang on this time, darling,' Diana would tell her, as she picked her sister off the muddy ground for the umpteenth time. 'You know how cross Muv will be if you break your arm again.' It was Decca's proud boast to have had two broken arms before the age of ten, and – even better – an unusual bone-setting job had made her double-jointed in one elbow, which she delighted in demonstrating. Diana was also a Favourite Cousin, for that year – 1921 – Randolph Churchill visited Asthall and fell in love with her: she so resembled his mother, with her blonde elegance, beautiful features and huge sapphire-blue eyes, and no matter which way she turned her head it was a joy.[5]

Nancy always had a willing audience in her envious younger siblings for her stories about her trip, and she had her coming out dance to organize and look forward to. This did not quite live up to her imaginings for her dance programme of waltzes, polkas, foxtrots, one-steps and cotillions was filled with the names of family friends and kinsmen, rather than handsome dark-haired prospective lovers. Later she parodied the occasion mercilessly in *The Pursuit of Love*, describing the run-up to the ball where every man they knew was pressed into service as a dancing partner, 'elderly cousins and uncles who had been for many years forgotten' were 'recalled from oblivion and urged to materialize'. The longed-for magical evening came at last. Tall, with a fashionably slim, boyish figure, her dark curly hair worn up, for her request to have it 'shingled' had been vetoed by both parents, Nancy wore a straight dress with silver bugle beads, very *à la mode*:

This then is a ball. This is life, what we have been waiting for all these years, here we are and here it is, a ball, actually going on now, actually in progress round us. How extraordinary it feels, such unreality, like a dream. But, alas, so utterly different from what one had imagined and expected . . . the women so frowsty . . . but above all the men, either so old or so ugly. And when they ask one to dance . . . it is not at all like floating away into a delicious cloud, pressed by a manly arm to a manly bosom, but stumble, stumble, kick, kick . . .[6]

However, at the time Nancy loved it, just as she enjoyed being a débutante yet denigrated it in the same manner in her novels. This early-twenties era was excitingly different, and not just to Nancy. The post-war generation of young people (dubbed Bright Young Things or BYTs) erupted into Society determined to change the world for the better now that the war to end all wars was over. Their background was upper class, of course, but talented gatecrashers, working-class *émigrés* like Noël Coward, were not unwelcome. The aim was pleasure, set against a background of 'larks' and jazz music played on wind-up gramophones with trumpet amplifiers, and shameless new dances like the 'Black Bottom', and songs like 'I Love my Chili Bom Bom' or 'Squeeze up Lady Lettey'. Girls shingled their hair, wore slave bangles and cloche hats, and dressed in shapeless, waistless dresses designed to 'move' across an uncorseted body and display the lower legs, clad in silk stockings and high-heeled shoes. They smoked cigarettes in long holders and drank cocktails with names like 'Horse's Neck'. Their elders, the Edwardian generation who had fought a world war, and whose mores were still Victorian, were satisfyingly shocked.

Nancy's letters sparkle with accounts of dances and parties, shoots and hunt balls which entailed 'staying over'; and her hosts would provide mounts so that she could hunt, which she loved.[7] Although she was not, in her first Season of 1923, in the thick of Society, she was instantly popular, which was a triumph for her, though the edge was often taken off her enjoyment by her wardrobe. At home her new clothes had seemed so grown-up and glamorous, but compared with those of her fellow-débutantes she felt they looked what they were: homemade. Her allowance was £125 a year,[8] out of which she had to clothe herself and pay all incidentals such as laundry, hairdressing, books, family presents for birthdays and Christmas, tips to the staff when she visited country houses, trains and taxi fares. Although £125 would have been a significant sum to a working-class man or woman – it was almost what Sydney paid the governesses' for a year's work, for example, and seven pounds more than she paid the Stobies, her cook and handyman[9] – it would not have gone far in the life Nancy led.

Her introduction to different circles from the county set of her childhood began with her first dance: a distant cousin, Kathleen Thynne,[10] had written to Sydney to suggest she invite her brother, Lord Henry Weymouth. Nancy went on seeing him afterwards as a casual friend. He was 'on the fringe' of a clever Bohemian group at Oxford and he introduced her to some of these men. Another important source of introductions was Nina Seafield, with whom Nancy spent some months in Scotland.[11] Nina introduced Nancy to her cousin, Mark Ogilvie-Grant, who introduced her to his friends John Sutro, Robert Byron, Harold Acton and Brian Howard, who regarded Nancy's wit as 'pyrotechnical'. They comprised a group of Oxford aesthetes who were star players in what is now known as the Brideshead generation; Brian Howard was, of course, the model for Anthony Blanche, the leading character in Evelyn Waugh's *Brideshead Revisited*. It has often been stated, incorrectly, that Nancy's initiation into this group 'whose talent and intelligence were often veiled by flippancy',[12] was effected through Tom at Oxford, but he was only fourteen and still at Eton when Nancy made her début in Society and gathered her own circle of friends. She impressed these young men, many of whom were homosexual, with her unusual manner of speaking, her brilliantly irreverent and exuberant witticisms and her sense of the absurd. She had three hectic Seasons, but as she became increasingly involved with the Brideshead set, the attraction of hunt balls and dances palled. She began to see such events through their eyes, and found them increasingly 'boring'.

Nancy faced considerable difficulty in spending time with her new friends. Society, and the behaviour of upper-class women, was still governed by a complicated set of unwritten rules, which had remained unaltered since the days of the Regency, and would be difficult now to envisage. No young girl was ever seen out in town without a chaperone, and there were still parts of London – clubland in St James's, for example – where no respectable lady would be seen at all, even in a carriage. In the country, near one's own home, different rules applied: girls could walk and ride out alone, without any impropriety, though they were usually cautioned to ride in pairs for reasons of safety. But in London Nancy needed a companion – her mother, a younger sister, a member of staff, or Nanny – to accompany her if she wanted to walk round the corner to Harrods.

In addition there was David's hatred of anyone outside the family circle and mistrust of young men in general. 'According to my father,' Decca wrote, 'outsiders included not only Huns, Frogs, Americans, blacks and all other foreigners but also other people's children . . . almost all young men – in fact the whole teeming population of the earth's surface, except for some, though not all, of our relations and a very few tweeded, red-faced country neighbours to whom my father had for some reason taken a liking.'[13] Realizing that David's bark was worse than his bite ('we were never punished,' Diana wrote), Nancy braved her father's outbursts and his downright rudeness to her friends, and invited them home for tea or dinner, and sometimes even to stay for the weekend. There was only one telephone in the house: it looked like a black daffodil and was installed in David's study. Debo recalls how on one occasion Nancy's friend Peter Watson[14] 'was bold enough to ring up and ask to speak to her. Without moving his mouth from the instrument my father shouted into

the hall, "Nancy, it's that hog Watson wants to speak to you."[15]
Nancy's male guests had to stand firm in the face of being called
'damned puppy' if they were unfortunate enough to venture an
opinion that disagreed with David's own (not difficult), and
what sounded like 'sewer!' for merely daring to exist.[16]

In fact the word was not 'sewer'. Years later Sydney told Decca,
'I daresay you don't know that Sewer is really SOOR, or PIG in
Tamil. It was all you children who turned it into Sewer and I
think Farve was delighted at the idea. But which is worst, Pig or
Sewer, is hard to say.'[17] The word (more usually spelled *sua*),
was one of the few things learned by David long ago in Ceylon,
but before Sydney's explanation, young male visitors were warned
that they might well be described to their faces by Farve as
'sewers'.[18] And terrifying as it was to face David in a temper,
before too long men were *boasting* of being a 'Swinbrook Sewer',
although this often meant having to outface David who, as
dinner ended, was liable to call down the table to Sydney, 'Have
these people no homes of their own?'[19]

Sydney enjoyed having visitors to stay, and although of
Nancy's Oxford aesthetes she was often heard to exclaim disapprovingly, '*What* a set!' she sometimes threw her weight behind
Nancy's requests to entertain her friends, so that David found
himself vanquished, and subsided, muttering under his breath.
While the aesthetes regarded themselves as sensitive, thinking
and amusing, the athletes, their college opponents, considered
themselves clean-living and sporty. These opposing legions
inevitably contained hooligans on one side and hedonists on the
other, so it was not unknown for the streets of Oxford to rever-
berate with pitched battles between the 'Hearties' and the 'Arties'.
The hearty athletes were Conservative, patriotic nationalists, supporting the old order of things, King, country and fox hunting.
The arty aesthetes espoused romanticism, Oscar Wilde, pacifism
and were often anti-field sports and even ('heavens!') socialists.

Had Nancy's friends been Hearties, David might have been

better able to accept them, but it was an anathema to him to have groups of effeminate young men wearing violet-scented hair cream arriving at his home in noisy open sports cars. They lounged about the house dressed in Oxford bags with 28-inch bottoms, loud Fair Isle sweaters and silk ties, making silly jokes and roaring with laughter at everything that David and his generation regarded as sacred, and speaking at the table in the affected phraseology that appeared to pass for good conversation: 'how *too* utterly divine', 'not much cop', 'good show!' To them the Boer War, in which David and his brothers had fought and been wounded, was 'the Bore War', while Blake's 'Green and Pleasant Land' became 'Green Unpleasant Land – ha, ha, ha!' Sometimes, David could stand it no longer and let fly at the unfortunate youths with a barrage of oaths. One male guest was turned out of the house for wearing a comb in his breast pocket ('a man carrying a *comb*!'), and on another for venturing an opinion that he thought it was time, more than a decade after the end of the war, that Britain stopped producing anti-German propaganda. 'Be quiet!' David roared. 'And don't talk about what you don't understand!' This was followed by a furious aside: 'Young swine!'

The offender on this occasion, James Lees-Milne, was a meek, sensitive young man, who had been a friend of Tom from their first months at Eton, and whose parents lived at Broadway, a nearby Cotswold town. Although quelled and terrified by David's tirade, he held no grudge and remained a friend of the family for the rest of his life. David was not a grudge-bearer either and soon welcomed him back. Later Lees-Milne fell secretly in love with Diana, but he always had a particular affection for Sydney:

> She presided over her wilful, and be it said, deeply
> devoted family, with imperturbable serenity, pride and
> sweetness. It was often my privilege to stay at Asthall and

later Swinbrook . . . To their callow and unsophisticated guests their home seemed a perfect Elysium of culture, wit and fun. The source of those cloudless days was . . . that enigmatical, generous, great-minded, matriarchal figure, with her clear china blue eyes and divinely formed, slightly drooping mouth, which expressed worlds of humour and tragedy.[20]

Of David he wrote that, although he had a dual personality, 'I cannot see that the children had in him much to complain about. He was to them Dr Jekyll, indulgent and even docile. He submitted placidly to their ceaseless teasing, particularly Nancy's with its sharp little barb, barely concealed like the hook of an angler's fly beneath a riot of gay feathers.'[21]

Nancy was not so forgiving and viewed David's outbursts with dismay, sometimes trembling with despair and rage at the indignities heaped upon her guests. As an elderly woman she recalled that one young man had been picked up and shaken like a rat by her father, who growled through clenched teeth, 'I'd rather take a housemaid shooting than you, *Lord Clive*.'[22] 'Really,' she complained to Tom, over the Lees-Milne incident, 'parties here are *impossible* . . .'[23] Unity, Decca and Debo could be relied upon to make any discomforted guest feel even more uneasy: if applied to for advice ('What do you think I should do?') they would invariably break into a well-rehearsed chorus of one of the popular songs of the First World War – 'Oh we don't want to lose you, but we think you ought to go . . .' When David took an occasional liking to one of Nancy's visitors it was almost as bad as being disliked, for the hapless guest was then expected to be at the breakfast table, bright and shining, at eight-thirty sharp – not regarded as a 'reasonable' time by Nancy's contemporaries. And, worse, one was likely to be greeted by a cheery David rubbing his hands and sharing the information that one of his favourite dishes was on the menu: 'Brains for breakfast, old chap . . .' This information had such a particular effect on one young man that Unity, Decca and Debo made it the subject of yet another refrain, the words of which rang merrily: 'Brains for breakfast, Mark, Brains for breakfast, Mark, Oh the damned sewer, Oh the damned sewer . . .'

Nancy was being paid back handsomely for her years of teasing the others, for all this terrorizing, offence and ridicule made it difficult for her to pursue her Oxford friendships. Outside débutante dances – which were not an all-year-round activity, and which were not top of the list as entertainment for aesthetes – and home, she had few ways of meeting them. At one point she found a way of circumventing the system. On the pretext of spending a day with a girlfriend visiting Tom at school the two girls would take the train to Eton, drop off some small treat for him, then take the next train to Oxford where they would spend the rest of the day with Nancy's friends. It was all quite innocent, and the young people met in tea-rooms for amusing conversation, but on one occasion a neighbour of the Redesdales spotted Nancy and Brian Howard walking in Oxford without a chaperone. There followed, Nancy wrote to Tom, 'a hell of a row'. David was furious and roared at her that her reputation was ruined and that no respectable man would marry her. He told her that had she been a married woman her action would have been grounds for divorce. She was condemned to house detention and missed several balls.

By now, though, Nancy was virtually inured to rows at home about her friends and continued to invite them, despite her father's snarls, teeth grinding and insults. In fact, she was not above engaging David, head on, in rows that caused furious silences at meals. In 1924, aged twenty, she went so far as to have her long hair bobbed without permission ('Well, anyhow,' commented Sydney briefly, 'no one will look at you twice now'), and to wear trousers at home, which made David apoplectic with rage. When he was cross with Nancy, he would be out on the lawn as soon as it was light, cracking his stock-whip in impotent fury. Visiting cousins found this frightening. But the rows were only the tip, as it were, of the real relationship between Nancy and her father, who sparked each other off, provoking the hilarious repartee that listeners found so amusing.

When Tom began to invite his Oxford friends – 'the Fat Fairs', as Nancy called them – David found them more acceptable, but Nancy had broken the ice, just as she made things easier for Pam, who came out in 1924. Pam, however, was never a rebel and her year in France in 1923, where she was sent to improve her French, was incident-free. Unlike all of her sisters (except Debo, much later), Pam loved the country and for her it was not just 'a nice place to live', she felt a positive affinity with farming and animals and eventually made a semi-career of it. It was her undisguised enjoyment of domesticated pursuits such as cooking, which the others regarded as boring and 'womanly', that led to her lifelong nickname in the family, Woman, sometimes shorted to Woo. But though she lacked Nancy's vivacity, Pam's sense of humour was as well developed as that of any of the Mitford girls and she had her own court of admirers. She was always known as 'the quiet sister', but her letters to Sydney from France are full of her excitement about the invitations she had received to balls and dances and with pages of detailed discussion about the clothes she would need: '. . . a blue-mauve is very fashionable now and it is such a lovely colour . . . I ought to have that colour or a white but I think white rather dull, don't you? Besides my coming out dress will have to be white . . .' She describes a ride in a tank with gusto: '. . . I should love to do the whole thing over again. I hardly think I have ever enjoyed anything so much,' and she made a lot of a fancy-dress party to be held later in the week when all her group had decided to dress as Arab women. 'What fun,' she wrote, 'the wretched young men won't be able to know which is which of us.'[24]

Each débutante had to have her own social function so during the London Season there would be a dinner-dance or ball every night from Monday to Thursday. The whole point of the Season was, of course, to find a husband. It was a way of introducing well-bred girls to eligible and suitable young men. Newspapers gave amounts of space to Society activities that today would be considered disproportionate, and journalists were quick to nominate a girl as 'Deb of the Year', and an event as 'the Ball of the Season' or 'the Wedding of the Year'. It was regarded as a triumph for a girl to find a husband in her first Season, or at least receive a few marriage proposals, and it goes without saying that beautiful heiresses were the first to be snapped up.

Nancy was attractive, and her sharp wit was a great asset for those intelligent enough to appreciate it. She took up the ukelele, on which she would sing popular new songs such as 'Conchita', '. . . she was the child of a hidalgo/and he called her Conchita . . . Sitting by the open casement/There was Conchita the fair/And Count Don Fernando seeing/Ventured to approach her there . . .'; and 'Ukelele Lady', 'If you like-a ukelele lady, ukelele lady like-a you . . . If you like-a linger where it's shady, ukelele lady linger too . . .' in her light plummy voice. Her gaiety made her popular, although not necessarily marriageable, but unlike other girls she never took offence at being 'looked over as though in a horse market', or rebelled against the system; she enjoyed herself, noted everything from the good to the absurd and filed it away in her memory for later. Nothing was wasted.

With Nancy's first Season Sydney had embarked on what was to be her role for many years, as each of her girls came out. She was the chaperone. By 10 p.m. she would have eaten a light supper, and – in evening dress – she would turn down her bed, collect the girls, check them over and take them to whatever function they were attending. While her daughters enjoyed the dinner, and the dancing that followed, Sydney would sit on one of the ubiquitous hired gold chairs that lined the walls of the ballroom, along with the other chaperones. At first she probably enjoyed this, and sometimes David accompanied her to the more important functions or even, rarely, went in her place. She would have met many mothers or aunts she knew, all doing the same thing, and unlike David she had always enjoyed meeting new people and 'chatting'. Often a ball would go on until the early hours before the girls reappeared, glowing with enjoyment, and though Sydney hated late nights, this was reward enough for her. She never discovered, apparently, that sometimes her daughters slipped out of the back of a house through french windows and a garden exit, to visit nightclubs before returning to a party that had become dull.

On the morning after a party the débutantes were allowed to sleep in, to recover for the following evening. Sydney, however, was always up and dressed and at the breakfast table by eight-thirty carrying out her daily routine of menu planning and making up the daily shopping list, for even in town she always insisted on good, plain, fresh food. The younger children clamoured for attention, too, and although Unity had now graduated to the schoolroom, Sydney still gave a full quota of daily PNEU lessons to Decca and Debo. It was she, too, who arranged the considerable wardrobe needed by a débutante, and planned the dinners or dances for her daughters, which would have taken considerable organization although the girls thought it was simply a matter of opening up the ballroom, arranging a few flowers and cooking lots of kedgeree. Then, too, as spring ran into summer, when she longed to be at Swinbrook for the loveliest part of the year, she was stuck in London. By the time Debo came out in 1938 Sydney must have been heartily tired of this punishing routine, yet she never complained. It was a refined and rather unusual kind of martyrdom and, it goes without saying, was taken for granted by the girls.

Pam's coming-out dance was a fancy dress and Pam was

attired as Madame de Pompadour: '. . . I felt very self-conscious because I was rather fat,' she told a niece. 'In fact I did not enjoy any of the dances I went to when I came out, though I used to write in my diary what a good time I had had. I suppose I wrote it with an eye to be read in the future, and I did not want to be considered a failure at parties.'[25] Diana blamed Nancy for this: 'She was very unkind to Pam and undermined her self-confidence.'[26] The greatest preoccupation for both Diana and Pam in 1925 was to get permission to have their hair bobbed like Nancy. Even the younger sisters were recruited to bombard the parents: 'Darling Muv,' the eight-year-old Decca wrote, when their parents went off to Ontario, 'I hope you had a good crossing? Diana and poor Pam want more than ever to have their hair off and Pam did not enjoy her visit at all because everyone says, "Oh yes I like short hair best" and "Why don't you have your hair off?" Please do let them have it. Please. Love from Eight.'[27]

Decca's best friend at that time was not a sister, or even a brother, but a pet lamb called Miranda. All the children had dogs and Miranda was treated like one of these: she went everywhere with Decca, to church, for walks, to bed sometimes, if she could be smuggled in without Nanny noticing. She was terrified for her pet when sheep-dipping time came round: 'I used to go in with Miranda because I feared her eyes would be damaged by the virulent poisons in the dip, so I'd hold a hanky over her eyes.' Nanny used to get cross because her bathing suits got full of holes from the chemicals and she was covered in huge welts from the thrashing animal, but she said, 'Miranda was the light of my life.'[28] She even wrote a poem for her:

> *Me-ran-der is my little lamb*
> *She is a ewe and not a ram*
> *Me-ran-der, Me-ran-der,*
> *She has such lovely woolly fur.*

> *Soon we'll have to cut off her tail*
> *When we do she's sure to wail*
> *Me-ran-der, Me-ran-der*
> *But I'll love her just the same, Sir.*
>
> *Once I took her for a walk*
> *My only complaint is she cannot talk,*
> *Me-ran-der, Me-ran-der*
> *Soon to the butcher I must hand her.*

In the summer of 1926 to Decca's delight – she was always trying to get away from home – she was allowed to join dancing classes held in the homes of neighbours. Unity, who was more interested in her new pet goat, did not wish to go, and Debo was too young, so Decca, dressed in organza party frock and cashmere shawl, was taken to classes by Nanny every Wednesday. This pleasant occupation came to an abrupt end when she took the opportunity between dances to tell some of her contemporaries how babies were conceived and born. 'The telling was a great success,' she recalled, 'particularly as I couldn't help making up a few embellishments as I went along.' A week or so later Sydney sent for her, having received complaints from parents that their children were disturbed by what Decca had told them. 'Just ret-ribution,' Decca wrote, 'quickly followed. It was clear to everyone, even to me, that I couldn't be considered fit company for nice children after that. The enormity of my ill-advised act . . . was such that years later, when I was a débutante of sev-enteen, I learned from an older cousin that two young men of the neighbourhood were still forbidden to associate with me.'[29]

That year Diana was sixteen and in her final year of education before her début. David's dream house was in the final stages of building and Asthall was to be sold. In the autumn Sydney took all the girls to Paris on an 'economical trip' for three months accompanied by Nanny and Miss Bedell, while David finalized the sale of Asthall, organized the move to Swinbrook House, and purchased a town house, in a leafy cul-de-sac, distinguished by two tall white pillars guarding its entrance and overlooking Hyde Park. It was situated in that exclusive triangle bordered by the Harrods end of Brompton Road, Kensington Road and Exhibition Road, and was Sydney's *quid pro quo* for the sale of Asthall. It was not a mere whim on her part, although the money she had inherited from her father perhaps entitled her to more of a say in the matter than she would previously have had. With five younger girls to bring out, and the probability of 'doing the Season' for at least another fifteen years it made sound financial sense not to continue renting houses in London, and for David – who spent days at a time working at the House of Lords – a home in London would be convenient. For Nancy's first Season they had rented a house in Gloucester Square, which was not only expensive but 'dead money'; furthermore, a house in London at that time – in 1926 the year of the general strike – was nothing like the drain on resources that it would be today.

The Victorian house, 26 Rutland Gate, was – and is – elegant, tall, cream-stuccoed, and on the first of its six storeys it boasted a ballroom for those all-important coming-out dances. David was especially proud of the passenger lift, which he had installed. He was not in London a great deal – he was far too busy at Swinbrook overseeing the finishing off of the new house. The family teased him about his obsession, Nancy especially, addressing letters to him from Paris to 'Builder Redesdale, The Buildings, South Lawn, Burford, Oxfordshire'. South Lawn had been the name of the old farmhouse on the site but David had decreed the new house would be called Swinbrook House. It was a good tease to refer to it innocently as 'South Lawn', which never failed to annoy him.

The main purpose of the visit to Paris was to establish Diana in a day-school to 'finish' her education and improve her French. Pam had done the same thing and it had worked well for her.

Sydney had written in advance to the Helleus asking them to suggest suitable establishments and the result, after an interview, was that Diana was accepted by the Cours Fénelon in the rue de la Pompe for a year. Having accomplished her mission Sydney and the others were free to enjoy the remainder of their holiday.

They stayed in a modest hotel, Les Villas St Honoré d'Eylau in the avenue Victor Hugo, close to the Helleus' flat, and within a short time of their arrival Sydney took her family along to meet her old friends. Diana was already exhibiting the classical beauty for which she would become renowned. One friend, James Lees-Milne, wrote in his diary that Diana was the most beautiful adolescent he had ever seen: 'Divine is the word, for she was a goddess. More immaculate, more perfect more celestial than Botticelli's seaborne Venus.'[30] This blossoming allure was not lost on Helleu, either: 'Voici la Grèce,' he remarked, taking her by the hand to lead her in and introduce her to his family. Although it was generally acknowledged in the family that Diana was 'the only one of us who had a face', any pretensions were firmly squashed by the sensible Sydney, or Nanny Blor, whose famous put-downs, chiefly intended to spare self-consciousness, ran along the lines of 'Don't be silly, darling, *nobody*'s going to look at *you*.' Helleu became almost obsessed with Diana's small, neat head and cool, classical features, which exactly matched a stylized ideal for beauty in the twenties and thirties, and he made a number of portraits of her. 'He was even a bit in love with me, which complicated things,' Diana wrote, many years later to a friend, '[but] he was the first grown-up . . . who treated me on an equal footing and not as a silly little fool.'[31] It was heady stuff to an impressionable teenager.

'I learned more at the Cours Fénelon in six months than I learned at Asthall in six years,' Diana wrote. Each morning the class of a dozen or so girls did 'prep' and in the afternoon they were lectured to and questioned by professors from the

Sorbonne. The afternoon classes were larger, for some girls who were taught at home by governesses attended the lectures and question periods. They came mostly from rich backgrounds and were accompanied by footmen who sat and waited all afternoon for their charges. Diana felt very grown-up in being allowed to walk back unattended to the hotel, which was close to the school, but to her annoyance she was still lumped with her younger sisters when it came to experiencing Paris Society.

While Diana was at school the younger ones were given daily lessons by a French governess. After lessons they would go for a walk in the *bois* and bowl hoops along the gravel paths. Nancy and Pam were allowed to spend time sightseeing, shopping and were even allowed to go and stay at a château with a family whom Pam had met during her year in Paris and of whom Sydney approved. She would not have been so sanguine had she known that Nancy spent some of her time flirting outrageously with a fellow guest whom she described as 'the most seductive young man in the country'. One of Nancy's best friends was Middy O'Neil, granddaughter of Lord Crewe, the British ambassador in Paris, so she and Pam went frequently to the embassy where they met interesting company. Even Diana was allowed to go there occasionally because she would be returning to Paris alone in the new year and Sydney wished her to be introduced to suitable young people. More often, though, Diana had to share tea with Nanny, Unity, Decca and Debo, and for these three the biggest drama of the trip revolved around the temporary escape of their pet hamsters which they called 'desert rats'. The children feared that if the loss was discovered they would be asked to leave the hotel, and Sydney would be angry at their carelessness. A round-the-clock watch system was established by the sisters, including Diana, during which they sat near the small hole in the floor through which the furry delinquents had escaped, holding out tempting titbits until they were all recovered.

For Nancy, Paris increasingly became the *beau idéal* of life. She found there an elegance, glitter, warmth and freedom that were lacking in London. One could be uninhibited there without drawing clucks of disapproval, 'I have often danced all down the Champs Élysées,' she wrote to Tom, 'and no one notices they are so used to that sort of thing . . . Oh I am so excited.'[32]

When the Cours Fénelon term ended in December Sydney returned with her brood to London and moved into Rutland Gate. The house was furnished with French furniture brought from Asthall: Louis XVI commodes and secretaires, and white chairs covered with needlepoint. Sydney splashed out and bought new curtains and soft furnishings, and the effect was light and elegant with the exception of David's business room, which he had furnished himself. He had chosen as curtain material 'a frightful sort of sham tapestry covered in dingy leaves and berries', Diana wrote.[33] When the children groaned at its ugliness he told them he imagined he saw birds and squirrels peeping through the foliage, which made him feel nearer his coverts at home.

David was generally down at Swinbrook but Sydney, always happiest in London, busy with her family and running Rutland Gate, never bothered to go down to see what he was up to. Perhaps in view of his taste in curtain material it was unwise of her to allow him a free hand with the new house. But that, surprisingly, is what she did. He told his family he intended it to be even better than their beloved Asthall: there was a bedroom for each member of the family instead of the girls having to 'double-up', and even tennis and squash courts. There were garages, staff cottages, greenhouses and gardens. Uncle Tommy, the brother next in age to David, recently married, had seen it all and when he paid a visit to Rutland Gate he assured them, rubbing his hands, that David had provided 'the best of everything for everybody'. They all missed Asthall but they had every reason to expect that when Swinbrook was completed it would be a marvellous place to live.

During that Christmas holiday Diana was invited to stay at Chartwell, home of the Winston Churchills. At least at Chartwell, Diana noticed with gratification, she was no longer treated as a child. She admired 'Cousin Winston' enormously and was always thrilled when she was seated next to him, hanging on his words as he talked politics incessantly. Churchill called her, affectionately, 'Dina-mite'. Clementine, whom Diana adopted as a role model of elegance and beauty, told her 'just pull his sleeve to start him off'.

In the new year of 1927 Winston and Randolph were due to leave for Rome to visit Mussolini, and when Diana returned to Cours Fénelon in early January she travelled to Paris in their company, which obviated the need for Sydney to arrange a chaperone. At the Gare du Nord, she parted from the Churchills and was met by an old woman, one of two sisters who made a living by taking in English girls who were attending finishing schools in Paris. Their boarding-house was close to the hotel where the family had stayed, the school and the Helleus'. Consequently, Diana was allowed to walk alone to school, to her music lessons and to visit the Helleu family. Even this limited freedom was intoxicating.

Life in the boarding-house was not exactly comfortable. There was no bathroom and twice a week a small tin bath was filled with an inch or two of hot water so that the young residents could bathe. When Sydney sent Diana a small amount of money to enable her to go to the hotel and take a proper bath occasionally the two old ladies considered it not only personally insulting but highly extravagant.

Diana settled in well at the school and found that as her French improved she could cope easily with the work. Immediately she arrived in Paris she had contacted the young friends made through Nancy and Pam, and used the limits of her freedom to the utmost. Just as Nancy had once used her visits to Eton to cover meeting with her Oxford friends, so Diana invented extra music lessons in order to go to the cinema with a young man, and even – occasionally – to a tea dance.

And there was Monsieur Helleu, admiring and uncritical, who would take her for a sandwich or coffee, to visit fellow artists, or to walk in the wintry gardens at Versailles, or to Rouen to see the exquisite rose window in the cathedral. As he was a friend of Sydney, this was perfectly allowable. But when Helleu became ill and Diana called at the flat, his daughter Paulette refused to let her see him, which indicates that she was aware of her father's obsession with Diana and was probably jealous. Diana reciprocated Helleu's admiration but their relationship was innocent. 'Monsieur Helleu is terribly ill,' she wrote to James Lees-Milne. 'I don't know how I can write it, coldly like this . . . a man whom I have almost worshipped, and who has worshipped me for three months is going to die. I shall never see him again, never hear his voice saying, "Sweetheart, *comme tu es belle*," never ring at his door and hear him come to open it with a happy step. How can I bear it?'[34] She had never experienced such gaiety, liveliness and enthusiasm in any man she had ever met. Within a few days Helleu had died and Diana wrote to tell Lees-Milne: '. . . Nobody will ever admire me as he did. He called me "*beauté divine*" always, and said, "*Tu es la femme la plus voluptueuse que je n'ai jamais connu.*" This from a man who has known all the lovely women of his day in Paris, London and New York, and had the most amazing *vie amoureuse*. He didn't believe in God, but he believed in beauty . . . He loved the wind, and clouds, and leaves, and statues, and above all very young women.'[35] She returned sadly to London for the Easter recess, taking with her one of the portraits he had made of her, which had been reproduced in the magazine *L'illustration* and brought her considerable cachet at school. The entire family sympathized at the loss of her friend and she was comforted.

Shortly before she was due to return to Paris Diana was out walking in the park with Pam one morning when she suddenly realized she had left her diary lying open in the drawing room. She had been writing in it after breakfast when someone had telephoned and she had forgotten to return to it. She returned home hastily but as soon as the door was opened she knew there was trouble. 'Her Ladyship wants to see you,' said Mabel, the parlourmaid. She heard her mother calling her to come at once, and the dreaded 'Diana!' From that she knew things were bad. She was never called Diana in the family: Sydney called her 'Dana', David called her 'Dina', Nancy 'Bodley', Pam and Unity 'Nardy', Decca called her 'Cord', and Debo called her 'Honks'. 'Diana' meant she was in deep trouble. 'Useless to protest the harmlessness of what I had done; to have been to the cinema alone with a young man, in Paris, even in the afternoon, was a frightful disobedience and an almost unforgivable crime.'[36] Of course, if she had written of all the things that Monsieur Helleu had said to her, her parents might have been even more upset.

It was the worst Mitford row in years. After the initial explosion David and Sydney did not speak to her for several days, and at first her sisters were sympathetic. But the tense atmosphere in the house persisted while their parents decided what to do about the matter and soon her sisters were all affected by the tension and gloom, and by the inevitable tightened restrictions on their own freedom. They became irritated with Diana, calling her a fool for leaving her diary lying about in the drawing room – 'How could *anyone* be so stupid!'

There was no question of her being allowed to return to Paris: telegrams were sent cancelling all her arrangements there. Neither, since she was in disgrace, could she simply be detained at Rutland Gate. The Season was just about to begin with lots of plans already made for Nancy and Pam; she would be in the way and she certainly did not deserve any treats. Nor could she be sent to Swinbrook, which was not yet ready for habitation. At last a decision was reached. She was to spend the summer with 'the little ones', Nanny and Miss Bedell, the current governess, at

Bucks Mill, a seaside cottage at Clovelly in Devon belonging to a great-aunt, Lady Maude Whyte. There, Diana suffered the terrible agony of boredom. Only Unity at twelve and Decca, nine, were of schoolroom age. Debo was taught by Sydney when she was at home, and now, on holiday, was in Nanny's sole charge. There was nothing to capture Diana's interest: she had nothing to read, no money to buy books, no one of interest called on them, and the three long months limped by with an agonizing slowness. She 'ached' at the waste of time. In Paris she had been so close to everything that was worth living for, and the wonderful opportunity to learn, to use her brain. That summer at Bucks Mill was a truly awesome punishment.

At the end of the holidays Nanny took them home, not to lovely Asthall but to the newly completed Swinbrook House. They claim to have been horrified. With the exception of seven-year-old Debo, who came to love it, and David, the family hated it. Everything was wrong: the design, the materials, the very newness of it. Instead of Asthall's weathered old stone, encrusted here and there with lichen, they found a huge, square, three-storey, new stone building, which the family described as looking like 'an institution'. Nancy called it Swine-Brook.

For the older children the worst aspect was its lack of a bolt-hole. One of the best things about Asthall had been the privacy of the library, situated away from the main part of the house. The grand piano had been in the library at Asthall, and Tom had practised there for hours; he was an excellent pianist and might easily have become a professional musician. At Swinbrook, though, the piano was in the drawing room, so Tom hardly bothered to play it because he could never do so without being disturbed. More often at Swinbrook it was Sydney who played the piano, and the family and visitors gathered round to sing old parlour favourites, like the stirring 'Grace Darling' or sentimental Victorian ballads such as 'The Last Rose of Summer'.

True, the girls each had their own bedroom, but they were on the top floor, and fires were never allowed there unless they were ill. Sometimes in the winter they found their sponges and face-cloths solid with ice. Sydney especially hated the rustic look of rough-hewn beams and local stone fireplaces. The green elm of the new doors warped and shrank, and made the house draughty. Situated on the top of a hill, on the site of the original old Georgian farmhouse, Swinbrook had wonderful views but it was exposed to the worst of the weather, and with its draughts, and the damp chill from plasterwork that had still not dried out, it always seemed cold. A guest who visited there, however, describes it as a cheerful, light house. The drawing room was especially comfortable with its brilliant white walls and chimneypiece of rough stone, while the tall french windows provided long views across the valley. It was 'lavishly provided with books and flowers' – a typical Sydney touch.

David was hurt by the family's rejection of Swinbrook: it even affected his enjoyment of his fishing, and shooting in his own coverts. He had never felt about Asthall as his family did, and one of his nieces thought he was always troubled by the ghosts at Asthall and was 'jolly pleased to leave it'. At Swinbrook he closeted himself gloomily in his study, which he had made child-proof by fitting an oversize mortice lock to the door. His plan was not only to lock out his children, but sometimes to lock them in for a telling-off. 'However,' Nancy wrote, 'we children usually managed to effect an escape.' The family called it 'the closing room', after Decca pointed out that since he spent virtually all his time in there, often with his eyes closed while he was 'thinking', it was almost inevitable that one day he would close his eyes there for the last time. Even the servants began to use the term: 'Miss, His Lordship wants you in the closing room . . .'

While David tolerated such teasing – and far more – with remarkable equanimity, he also began to spend an increasing amount of time away from home at his London club, the Marlborough, since the house at Rutland Gate had been let. He had given up his committee work at the Lords to oversee the building of Swinbrook but although he was less than interested in politics he took his seat in the upper house and even, occasionally, got up to speak, especially when the subject under discussion touched a nerve. Such an occasion occurred when the Lords debated whether to allow peeresses in their own right to sit in the upper house. David opposed the bill and Nancy maintained that his reason was a practical one. There was only one lavatory close to the chamber, and David thought that if women were allowed to attend the upper house they might want to use it. (If only we could so clearly see the basis of *all* our legislation.) In recess, and during the Season, he went shooting in Scotland, leaving the family to settle in at Swinbrook.

The children congregated on the second floor, where could be found the schoolroom, nursery and living quarters for the governesses and Nanny, all painted in 'Redesdale blue', the colour for the indoor servants' uniforms. The rooms were generous and separated from the rest of the house, just as the servants' quarters were, by a green baize door. The schoolroom, described by Decca as 'large and airy' with bay windows, had a coal fire and chintz furniture. It does not sound unwelcoming but it lacked the cosy familiarity of beloved Asthall. The younger girls took to sitting in the warmest place they could find: the linen cupboard through which ran some hot-water pipes. Squeezed in among heaps of crisply ironed linen sheets and pillowcases, towels and bath mats, neatly stacked on slatted racks, they spent hours hatching plans and working out new rules for their 'Hons Society'.[37]

Many years later Decca would recall the cupboard's 'distinctive stuffy smell and enchanting promise of complete privacy from the grown-ups'. Decca and Unity, the two Bouds, spoke fluent Boudledidge, which the other sisters understood well enough to know what they were talking about. The older ones were allowed to join them there for giggles, Mitford jokes, stories and teasing. Here, Nancy produced poems and stories to entertain them. A typical one impersonated the governess in residence Miss Broadmoor's elocution, a tortured diction that passed for refined ('refained') speech: 'Ay huff a löft, and öft/as ay lay on may ayderdown so soft/(tossing from sade to sade with may nasty cöff)/ay ayther think of the loft/, or of the w-h-h-h-heat in the tröff of the löf', though some might say this was a bit rich coming from someone who pronounced 'lost' and 'gone' as 'lorst' and 'gorn'. Nancy immortalized the linen closet as 'the Hons Cupboard', but it was not, as is generally believed, a part of her own childhood, and even Unity was only allowed in there occasionally. The Swinbrook linen cupboard belonged to Decca and Debo, the two Hons. There was another Hons Cupboard, a disused bread oven in the wall of Old Mill Cottage at High Wycombe, just large enough to hold three small children (Unity was always too large for that one), but the one Nancy described in her novels is that at Swinbrook House.

Miss Broadmoor was not the only governess to come in for 'attention', for governesses came and went with tedious regularity, which the children liked to claim was due to their relentless naughtiness. A few lasted only a school term or two, but ten stayed for a year or more between 1910 and 1936. The best of these, Diana feels, were Miss Mirams and Miss Hussey (who was called variously by the children Steegson or Whitey) and who tutored them for two separate periods of several years. Like Miss Mirams, Miss Hussey had been trained at Ambleside to teach the PNEU system mentioned earlier, and was recruited by Sydney in 1922. One of her ambitions was to travel to India and in early 1925 she heard of a family who needed a governess to go there with them. 'So of course she had to take it,' said Diana.[38] Miss Hussey returned to Swinbrook in 1931 to teach Decca and Debo, and stayed this time for just over two years. She thought that in the intervening years some of the governesses had let the girls down badly, but that their English was better than hers.

In *Hons and Rebels* it was 'Miss Whitey' who was the hapless

governess made famous for having been subjected to a prank.
Decca records how Unity's pet snake was left 'wrapped around
the lavatory chain' so that the unwary woman, having locked the
door of the WC, suddenly spotted the snake, fainted and had to
be rescued with crowbars. This incident, however, is open to
considerable doubt, for although something of the sort occurred,
the snake was not Unity's but Diana's ('It was just a little grass
snake; I bought it at Harrods'), and the governess at the time of
the alleged incident was Miss Bedell, not 'Miss Whitey'. Diana
recalls the incident less dramatically than Decca. It occurred
during that dreadful summer at Bucks Mill when nothing of
any note happened. On the day in question, 'Nanny came in and
said to me, "Diana, your snake has escaped and is lying in the
corner of the lavatory."' Ordered to go and rescue it before it got
out, 'I put it out of doors, set it free,' Diana recalled. Perhaps it
took only a small leap of imagination from reality to the amusing incident recorded by Decca; perhaps the children plotted
such a scenario to pass the time.[39] It was some years later that
Unity bought Enid, *her* snake, which she took to débutante
dances with her. 'In any case the governesses were all used to our
various pets and wouldn't have been frightened by a little grass
snake,' Diana said. The anecdote would hardly bear refuting,
she said, were it not for that the story in Decca's book was widely
believed, and later used by the writer and literary critic Rebecca
West as evidence of Unity's 'cruelty'.[40]

Then there was Miss Bunting, the governess who, Decca
claimed, taught the two youngest girls the gentle art of shoplifting. Diana bridled at this story, too, doubting its veracity.
However, she was not under the aegis of the schoolroom when
shoplifting was part of the curriculum. Debo was, and she also
recalls the governess, Miss Dell, introducing it – 'Like to try a
little jiggery-pokery, children?' It was just small things – some
postcards, a packet of razor-blades – in a small post office in
Devon. 'My mother found out but thank goodness the

shopkeepers didn't, and Miss Dell disappeared.'[41] Another governess taught them the card game Racing Demon, and was liked by the children because she was lax about lessons. 'We just played Racing Demon the whole time, Debo recalls.' It seems, when one also recalls the head-banging Nanny, that Sydney's interview techniques may have been in need of revision.

Debo, now twelve, felt safe and secure at Swinbrook and never had the urge to flee the nest as her sisters had. Her parents were always there, the dozens of pets and farm animals were considered as important as humans, and there was a nucleus of long-serving staff whom she considered her friends. 'My best friend was our old groom, Hooper,' she said. 'He was the human end of the horses and ponies . . . I adored, and of the stables. One of the jobs Hooper had to do was to drive the eggs in a horse-drawn float from my mother's chicken farm to the station . . . It was six miles to the station at Shipton-under-Wychwood, and nice and hilly so it took a lovely long time, and I was allowed to drive the horse. A dramatic and strange thing happened on one of these journeys. It was the eleventh of November 1927, nine years after the end of the Great War. Everything stopped for two minutes' silence then, all traffic and factories . . . Hooper got out his watch and exactly at eleven, he stopped the cart, got down to hold the horse's head and took off his cap. No sooner had he done this than the old mare swayed and fell dead, I suppose of a heart attack. Since she had been bought out of the Army at the end of the war, having seen service in France, her death during the silence made a great impression on us children.'[42]

Diana missed most of these schoolroom excitements. Having served her allotted penance she was permitted to spend time later in the summer of 1927 at Chartwell with the Churchills. Here, in addition to Randolph and Diana Churchill, of whom she was very fond and who had stayed at Asthall on a number of occasions, she was exposed to the company of some interesting fellow guests: Walter Sickert, the artist, and Professor Lindemann,[43] one of the finest scientific brains of his generation. During the First World War he worked at Farnborough, then in its infancy as an aviation experimental unit. In those days the biggest threat to young airmen was not the enemy but the involuntary spin. No one had been able to work out how to recover from a spin, although one pilot who survived one suggested that pushing the stick forward seemed to have made a difference. This defied logic, so Lindemann set to work and proved mathematically that pushing the stick forward was the correct manoeuvre. No one was keen to test his theory so he learned to fly and tested it himself, at great risk, and subsequently saved many lives.

At Chartwell over dinner one evening Lindemann put his brain to the onerous task of calculating with a slide rule how much champagne Churchill had consumed during his lifetime (enough to fill a railway carriage, apparently). And it was the German-educated 'Prof', as Diana called him, who, on learning that she was bored, suggested to Diana that she might learn German so that she could read some of the German classics. He was not a man who suffered fools gladly and he must have recognized something unusual in the teenage Diana to bother with her. Coincidentally Tom was in Vienna learning German, so when she returned home she asked David if she, too, might take German lessons. He refused, and when she pointed out that Tom was doing so, she received the inevitable quelling answer, 'Tom's a boy!' She complained that her father could hardly have been more annoyed by her request if she had asked to learn the can-can, seeming to forget that she had already demonstrated that she was not to be trusted when sent abroad to learn a foreign language.

Tom, beloved of everyone, and especially of David, seems never to have put a foot wrong. He was handsome, bright, talented, charming, and sympathetic with his sisters. He was sometimes accused of arrogance, even by friends, but perhaps it was only the arrogance of youth. Although as a young man in London he was something of a ladies' man – his various girl-friends thought the world of him – it is known that he had several homosexual relationships at school. What is surprising about this, perhaps, is that he confided in his sisters. On one occasion when he had an Eton friend to stay the house was already full of guests. When Sydney innocently asked Tom if he would mind sharing his room with his friend she couldn't imagine why the girls doubled up with silent mirth and one by one fled the room.[44] On leaving Eton he could not make up his mind whether he should become a musician or a barrister. Little of the real Tom can be gleaned from his letters for he wrote few and they are so brief that one can imagine he counted each word.

Germany was still crushed by the terms of the Versailles Treaty, and had not yet begun the resurgence of the next decade, but Tom fell in love with the country, the land, the culture, the music, the literature. For part of the time he stayed as a paying guest with the family of Janos von Almassy, a Hungarian count he met through a mutual friend, in an ancient Gothic castle called Schloss Bernstein. It had originally been in Hungary but when Tom was there it was considered to be in Austria, as 'since the war . . . they moved the border a few miles'.[45] The family was almost as eccentric as Tom's own and Janos, a highly intelligent man, was interested in the supernatural and horoscopes. Many evenings were spent in holding séances and casting horoscopes. Later Janos became a close friend of other members of the Mitford family. In the following year Tom decided to study law in Berlin.

When Diana attended her first ball at Oxford's Radcliffe Infirmary in the autumn of 1927, Clementine and Diana Churchill stayed at Swinbrook and went to the ball with the Mitfords. Next day Professor Lindemann rang Diana to see how many proposals she had received. It was his little joke, but Diana's beauty guaranteed that she would be a sensational débutante and, although she was watched extra carefully by Sydney, she took London by storm in the following spring when she was presented to the King and Queen. In a diary entry written many years later, when he was happily married, James Lees-Milne recalled coming across the golden-haired seventeen-year-old Diana sitting on a low wall at Swinbrook: 'I think she is the most flawlessly beautiful woman I have ever seen; clear creamy complexion, straight nose, deep blue eyes . . . Her figure is so slim. Is spare the word?'[46] Not everyone concurred, of course: the journalist Michael Burn, who met her a few years later, thought her loveliness 'cold'. Diana herself felt that she was less beautiful than her cousin, Clementine Mitford, Uncle Clement's posthumous daughter.

Nevertheless, within weeks of making her début in the spring of 1928 Diana had captured a prize, and fallen in love. Bryan Guinness, heir to one of the greatest fortunes in the country, proposed and she accepted. Described as 'a quiet, gentle youth with a vague, almost haphazard, manner, which was utterly beguiling', Bryan was 'a writer at heart and was happiest in the company of artists and writers'.[47] More than anything this, rather than his fortune, appealed to Diana. Sydney was appalled. 'How old is he?' she asked her daughter. On being told he was twenty-two her verdict was that they must wait two years to announce their engagement, although later she relented and reduced the waiting period to a year.

Meanwhile the couple considered themselves secretly engaged and Diana went on the offensive – quietly. Decca later described her sister's method of obtaining her objective: it was to 'pine away' and she sulked around the house for months looking pale and interesting. It was, Decca wrote,

> perhaps the only [method] that could have succeeded
> short of elopement . . . She stayed in her bedroom a great
> deal of the time, and came down to the drawing room
> only to sit in stubborn silence, looking vacantly out of the

window. This strategy for getting one's own way was not
entirely unknown to us. Some years earlier Debo had
successfully pined away for a Pekinese, causing suspension
of an ironclad family rule that no one under the age of ten
could own a dog . . . As prisoners confined to their cells
manage to communicate to each other their restless,
intolerable anxieties, creating the conditions for a mass
riot, Diana managed to communicate boredom.

The sisters were wholeheartedly with Diana and the forbidden
romance with 'Bry-inn'[48] and against the predictable attitude
of their parents. But Diana was only just eighteen; a few years
earlier, at twenty, Nancy had caused furious family rows by
cutting her hair short without permission. That a young
American aviatrix had shown that a woman could perform
feats previously regarded as a wholly male preserve cut no ice
with David and Sydney. Amelia Earhart had just flown the
Atlantic in twenty-eight hours and spent the end of the Season
in London being escorted by the great and the good. But just
as Tom was 'a boy', Earhart was 'an American' so it didn't
count.

During Diana's long sulk Decca fell ill, and was not convinced
by Sydney's airy pronouncement that she had simply eaten too
much breakfast. She waited until her mother went out to see to
the chickens and telephoned Dr Cheatle in Burford, asking him
politely if he would 'mind coming over to take out my appendix'.
An investigation showed an appendectomy to be appropriate
and it was duly carried out in the nursery, with everything eerily
swathed in white sheets. David was summoned from the closing
room to supervise while Decca was anaesthetized by chloro-
form-soaked handkerchief. Dr Cheatle gave his patient the
offending organ in a jar of alcohol and the object became one of
fascination for Debo. 'Oh, you *are* so lucky to have a dear little
appendix in a bottle,' she cried longingly. Decca sold it to her for

a pound, but soon afterwards the appendix began to smell and had to be washed down the loo by Nanny.[49]

By the time Decca had recovered, several important things had occurred in the family. Pam had become engaged to Oliver Watney, known as 'Togo'. He was a member of the Watney brewing family who were neighbours of the Redesdales so he was acceptable to David, though not unreservedly for poor Togo suffered from chronic tuberculosis, for which there was then no cure. He apparently proposed to Pam under pressure from his father and when she accepted he gave her a ring that was a replica of 'King Alfred's jewel' in the Ashmolean Museum in Oxford. Found in Athelney in 1693 the original is made of translucent enamel set in beaten gold. Nancy commented cruelly that it 'looked like a chicken's mess', which must have taken away Pam's joy in it. And Nancy must have known this for she used the incident in *Pursuit of Love*:

> Linda, whose disagreeableness at this time knew no bounds, said that it simply looked like a chicken's mess. 'Same shape, same size, same colour. Not my idea of a jewel.'
>
> 'I think it's lovely,' said Aunt Sadie, but Linda's words had left their sting all the same . . .[50]

Following the death of his father later that year Togo went on an extended cruise for his health, during which his mother talked him out of the engagement. When he returned he called to tell Pam, who was unconcerned for she, too, had had second thoughts. The Redesdales were furious with Togo, but no harm was done. The requisite announcement was placed in *The Times* – 'The marriage between . . . will not now take place' – and all the wedding presents had to be returned, mostly by Tom, 'driving round London in his little car'.[51] Years later Pam was asked what had become of the chicken's mess. 'I gave it to Bobo.' 'And what did Bobo do with it?' 'Oh, she gave it to Hitler.'[52]

Next Nancy announced that she was unofficially engaged to arch-sewer Hamish St Clair Erskine who was four years younger than she, and thoroughly unsuitable in various ways, not least of which that he was an obvious (though unadmitted) homosexual. A friend described him as having 'the most enchanting looks though not strictly handsome, mischievous eyes, slanting eyebrows. He was slight of build, well dressed, gay as gay, always, snobbish however, and terribly conscious of his nobility . . . he loved being admired and he was . . . shallowly sophisticated, lithe of mind [and] a smart society figure.'[53] He was also intensely amusing and could make his friends laugh until tears ran down their faces, which was his chief asset as far as Nancy was concerned. David was livid, and so was Hamish's father, the Earl of Rosslyn. The two men conspired together to break up the relationship, but the parents were not the only ones who frowned on it. Tom had enjoyed a brief homosexual relationship with Hamish at Eton and although he had now transferred his sexual attentions to women, his experience of Hamish enabled him to see what Nancy could not: that Hamish would never return her romantic devotion and that he was not marriage material.

Faced with these upsetting situations, and Diana's sulk – and despite certain aunts pointing out what David and Sydney already knew, that Diana was only eighteen and 'barely out of the schoolroom' – David and Sydney suddenly capitulated and allowed Diana formally to accept Bryan's proposal. Both the London house and Swinbrook were already let in anticipation of the parents' latest prospecting trip to Canada. The younger sisters were packed off with 'the gov' (governess) to the seaside for a few months, Nancy went up to Scotland to stay with relatives of her friend Middy O'Neil, Pam went with David and Sydney to the shack at Swastika to help recover the family fortunes after the expense of the building of Swinbrook (she was the only Mitford child who ever visited Swastika), and Tom, who had left Eton in the previous year, returned to Vienna to continue his German language studies.

Diana, accompanied by Nanny, was allowed to visit her future in-laws on the coast in Sussex, and when Bryan introduced her to his mother he broke staggering news: 'And she can cook, Mummy.' Lady Evelyn, a delightful eccentric who only ever spoke in whispers, was dumbfounded. 'I've never *heard* of such a thing. It's *too* clever,' she said faintly. Diana was modestly self-deprecating, and explained she could only fry eggs. 'Anyone can do fried eggs,' she said lightly. But it was too late, the word went round and soon even the nursery staff at Bailiffscourt had taken up the refrain: 'To be able to cook – *too* wonderful.'[54]

In the late autumn the Mitford family was reunited at Swinbrook where Bryan paid his return visit of a week, accompanied by Robert Byron, a leading Swinbrook Sewer and good friend of Nancy. 'Bryan is grotesquely in love with Diana Mitford (who is very beautiful) and goes red whenever she comes into the room,' Byron wrote to his mother. 'The house is modern, built in fact the other day, square, of Cotswold stone, commanding, as they say, lovely views.'[55] Diana wrote that she 'glowed with pride' every time Bryan did something 'uncountrified', but he had a great love of horses and although he, like Pam, had had polio as a child,[56] he rode well. The week went by satisfactorily without David exploding, though it was a near thing as Bryan tended to wave the porridge spoon around to illustrate some point he was making while he helped himself to breakfast. His audience held their breath but he never spilt or splashed anything. Following his visit the usual announcement was sent to *The Times* and the Mitfords moved *en masse* to London to prepare for the wedding. Inconveniently, 26 Rutland Gate was still let so they moved into 'the garage' – the family name for the chauffeur's cottage in a mews behind the house.

The wedding reception was to be held at the Guinnesses' London house at Grosvenor Place.

The younger girls always loved staying in London, though for Decca any time spent there was marred because she was not allowed to take Miranda. 'She'll be no trouble,' she said on this occasion, adding, 'The dear thing would so love it. She's never been to London.'[57] But the parents were cruelly adamant: London was no place for a sheep. There was compensation: the games about white slavers took on a heightened intensity, for Nanny had warned that London was the headquarters of the white-slave trade. They might be sitting quietly at a matinée in the cinema, and feel nothing but the slightest prick in an arm, and they would wake up from a morphine-induced sleep, in chains, in Marseille, bound for South America. Decca and Unity were fairly sure that Nanny was right for they had been able to identify a white slaver who lived close to them in Rutland Gate. Each morning as they walked the dogs he hurried past them in his pinstriped suit and bowler hat, and he always said, 'Good morning.' Since he was not in uniform and he spoke to them even though they did not know him, it was obvious to Decca that he was a white slaver. 'Don't answer him,' she cautioned Debo, 'or you'll wake up in Buenos Aires and be distributed.'[58] It was a significant disappointment to discover after some months that the man they watched so carefully was a friend of Nancy and was married to Mary Lutyens (later Mary Sewell).[59]

But even white slavers were forgotten in the weeks leading to Diana's wedding, for living in London was even more thrilling than usual. Decca and Debo lived for the wedding day, relishing the fittings for their cream and gold bridesmaids' dresses, glorying in the drifts of satin and lace, boxes frothing with tissue, the constant planning of guest lists, menus and the trousseau; an atmosphere of joyful anticipation pervaded the house. Diana was carried away with exhilaration. She remembered joking with pseudo-sophistication at the vulgarity of some of the presents, but her father reminded her quietly and gravely, 'It is so kind of people to give you presents.' Debo chiefly recalls the joy of it because, as the youngest of six girls with a thrifty mother, she 'never had a new dress. Those jerseys and skirts and straight cotton frocks are engraved on my mind.'[60] So the excitement was intense and only Unity, now fourteen and large-framed, though not fat, with very straight fair hair that stuck out in an unflattering manner, did not look forward to the wedding. Self-conscious about her looks she chafed at being cast in the role of bridesmaid and was persuaded only with difficulty to submit to fittings. 'Oh dear, poor Boud, she *is* rather enormous,' Sydney sympathized, which can only have added to Unity's discomfort.[61]

When the great day dawned, 30 January 1929,[62] Decca and Debo, the two sisters who had most looked forward to the wedding, were confined to the sickroom with a contagious disease that would probably never have affected them had Sydney allowed them to be injected with 'disgusting dead germs'. Decca recalls that they had scarlet fever, and flushed red faces. Diana thought it was whooping cough, but whatever it was they could not attend the wedding of the year – as the newspapers referred to it in acres of coverage. The absence of her bright, funny little sisters 'spoiled the wedding for me,' Diana wrote. 'I could have spared anyone more easily than them.'[63]

5

BRIGHT YOUNG THINGS
(1929–30)

Diana and Bryan left in a cloud of confetti for Europe. There was no sense of anticlimax for Diana because marriage meant freedom to pursue the things that mattered to her. Chief among them was meeting interesting new people without having to face the disapproval of her parents, good conversation, books, pictures, music and travel. Some of these, clearly, were available to her at home but perhaps she had felt too constrained there to enjoy them. From being treated as a child to be sent hither and thither, always with a nanny or governess, always chaperoned, and subject to the will of one or both of her parents she was suddenly transformed into a grown-up, married woman with a handsome, kind husband whom she loved in a romantic sense, leading a glamorous life. The sense of liberty was blissful. Every day was like a new kind of heaven to her, especially when the long honeymoon took them south towards Sicily and she first saw the Mediterranean, with its Greek temples among almonds in blossom, and olive groves. 'I would willingly have stayed there forever,' she wrote; adding naïvely, 'It seemed to me a mystery why anyone who is not obliged to do so by work should choose to live anywhere else.'[1]

When the couple returned to London they moved into 10 Buckingham Street (now Buckingham Place), Buckingham Gate. It was a pretty Lutyens house but the furniture had been chosen by Bryan's generous parents and was not to Diana's taste. Not that it worried her unduly for in a sense the eighteen-year-old Diana was still only playing house. She made a brief attempt at keeping household accounts in the book Sydney had given her, bound in dark blue leather with her initials tooled in gold, but when Bryan's eccentric mother, Lady Evelyn, discovered Diana bookkeeping she was horrified: 'How *barbarous* of Bryan,' she whispered, assuming her son had decreed the practice. Diana never again kept accounts.

Decca claimed in her memoir that Sydney's chief objection to Diana's marriage was not her age but that Bryan was so rich, but Diana says she never realized, and neither did Bryan at this stage, that they *were* rich.[2] Probably they never gave it any thought. When Diana had visited Bryan's people at Bailiffscourt on the south coast, they were living in what she regarded as a substantial beach hut while a new house was being constructed to Lady Evelyn's requirements. The other Guinness houses Diana had seen were furnished with eccentricity and there was no evidence of great wealth or grandeur. But by the time she was twenty Diana found herself mistress of the house in Buckingham Street, of Biddesden, a country estate in north Hampshire, of Pool Place, a small house on the south coast that was permanently loaned to them by Bryan's mother, and of Knockmaroon, a rambling property adjacent to Phoenix Park in Dublin. No wonder the practical and prudent Sydney had had reservations. Diana, though, rose to the challenge. Robert Byron wrote to his mother, 'They are setting up housekeeping with innumerable servants, chauffeur etc. Nancy says he has £20,000 a year settled on him already. I don't know if it's true.'[3] It was close enough: Bryan eventually found out that a huge amount had been settled on him from the Guinness Trust, founded by his grandfather. 'My father was a Trustee,' he wrote. 'It was very much his subject.'[4]

Decca, who was eleven when Diana married, missed her elder sister and at first, like Unity and Debo, she scoured the Society pages of the daily newspapers to learn about Diana's activities, but this soon palled. In the aftermath of the wedding 'a suffocating sense of the permanence of [my] surroundings, family, and way of life . . . the unvarying sameness suddenly became unbearable,' she wrote, although she admitted also to a guilty realization that 'outward circumstances were not altogether responsible for my obscure malaise, because objectively life was extremely varied'.[5] Sydney did her best to ensure that the three younger girls received as rounded an education as was possible, with far more treats than the older girls had enjoyed. There were more trips to London, seaside holidays, and more trips abroad: they were taken to Switzerland for winter sports, especially for ice-skating at which the whole family was proficient. She took fourteen-year-old Unity and eleven-year-old Decca to Sweden, where they saw the amazing City Hall in Stockholm, 'a sort of 7th Wonder of the Modern World,' they thought.[6] Unity chose this trip to begin the fits of prolonged sulking moodiness that lasted until she was eighteen.

Despite what Decca wrote in her delightful memoir *Hons and Rebels* about her unhappy childhood, her sisters, cousins and contemporaries remember her as a normal, happy, curly-haired little girl until the time of Diana's marriage, though this point of reference is probably coincidental rather than connected. Shortly after Diana and Bryan returned from honeymoon Decca and Debo went to stay with them in Sussex and Decca wrote to thank David for some postal orders he had sent. 'You absolutely *Marvellous* old Lord,' she wrote, '. . . how I absolutely *adore* you. Oh thank you, thank you . . . thank you, thank you, thank you . . . [it] did save my life and reputation among the motorboat and donkey people. You, and life, are so ABSOLUTELY MARVELLOUS, so absolutely marvellous . . . love from your Very Affec Daughter (doubly so since the 5s[hillings] arrived).' Several letters from her to her father survive and they are lively, happy and teasing, demonstrating a close and loving relationship.

Bryan Guinness recalled that during his visits to Swinbrook shortly after his marriage to Diana, Decca seemed a happy child in a happy environment; he remembered the recitals given by her in Boudledidge, and her games of 'slowly working away', and 'hure, hare, hure'. These were curious games: the winner was the person who could stand the longest being scratched with a fingernail ('working away' at one spot of skin) or being pinched, 'really hard'.[7] Then there were her demonstrations of her double-jointed arm, and the mock battles she organized between the Hons (Decca and Debo) and the Counter Hons (Unity and Tom, when the latter was at home), both sides armed with toy spears. He remembered David as a kindly man with an ironic sense of humour. 'The parents seemed to me to devote much of their lives and thoughts to the education of their children . . . and [providing] an unworldly background.'[8] No one pretended David did not have a quick temper over small things; he barred Gladys, Duchess of Marlborough, from Swinbrook because on her first visit she had left a paper handkerchief on a hedge.[9]

One of the cousins blamed Decca's teenage angst on 'Nancy's clever friends,' who made the younger children feel discontented and 'that their home was rubbish'.[10] Whatever its cause, the bored malaise of which Decca wrote, and which Sydney dismissed at the time as teenage gloominess – possibly she had suffered from it herself – would, within a few years, find a cause, and burgeon into burning resentment, turning Decca into a serious rebel. Initially she became 'naughty' and Nanny was forced to commission a bed-time prayer for the three youngest Mitfords: 'God bless Muv, God bless Farve . . . and make Decca a good girl, Amen.' When Decca considered running away she quickly realized that she would soon be brought home as she would not be able to look after herself. So the first practical effect of her dis-content was the 'running-away' account, which she opened at Drummonds, the bankers, in 1929, a few months after Diana's marriage. 'Dear Madam,' an understanding bank manager replied, 'We are pleased to acknowledge receipt of your ten shillings to open your Running Away account. Passbook no. 437561 enclosed. We beg to remain, dear Madam, your obedient servants, Drummonds.'[11]

At the heart of Decca's misery, she wrote, was desperation to go to school. She had a secret ambition to be a scientist for which she would need to go to university, but she knew that unless she had some formal education she would never achieve this. Her parents' refusal even to consider school became a source of bit-terness in Decca that lasted well into middle age. Nancy had longed to go to school for the interaction with other people. Diana passionately wanted to use her brain and yearned for a more challenging education but without going away to school. Decca simply had

> a certain conviction . . . that one had to get away from that dread place at all costs . . . I biked into Burford and rather shudderingly went to see the headmaster of the Grammar School. He said I could be admitted to the Grammar School (which had a scientific laboratory, that's why I wanted to go) if I could pass a fairly easy exam, which I could learn to do by reading a list of books he gave me. I was very excited over this and rushed home to ask Muv if I could get the books, take the exam and bike to school each day. A cold 'NO' was the only answer, no reason given. After that lessons with the gov. seemed totally pointless, although I admit I could have learned more than I did.[12]

The point-blank refusal 'burned into my soul,' souring her adolescence, and Decca was far more affected by the transition from child to young adult than any other of the Mitfords. Rebelliousness coloured her youth and laid down the attitude of her adult years. Meanwhile she cast about for support from her siblings. When Diana had been agitating against their parents she had been a Favourite Sister for Decca to be proud of. Indeed it had been easy to side with Diana in hot defence of her secret engagement. Now that Diana was married and in charge of her own destiny, she ceased to be a role model for a budding rebel. Nancy had only rebelled to obtain the specific things she wanted: to go to boarding-school, cut her hair, choose her own friends, wear slacks. Tom now stepped in as favourite elder sibling/mentor and, realizing that Decca was suffering from a lack of mental stimulation, he introduced her to Milton, Balzac and Boswell's *Life of Johnson*.

Unity, too, had developed a scowling discontent but hers was more a dumb insolence that alternated with the occasional mischievous prank, such as climbing out on to the roof at Swinbrook through an attic window, or throwing slates off an outhouse roof, or eating all the ripe strawberries in the greenhouse just before a luncheon party.[13] Although she went hacking on a big roan horse, she did not hunt like Nancy, Diana and Debo, so lacked the framework to the week that regular hunting fixtures provided. A study of her life as a teenager suggests that she was, quite simply, bored stiff. Perhaps recognizing this, Sydney gave in to Unity's pleas for a private sitting room at the top of the house, which quickly became known as the Drawing from the Drawing room or DFD. Although initially Unity wanted it as a private space in which she could work on her 'paintings', which were a mixture of collage and paint, Decca gradually took over a 50 per cent share of it. Debo, a remarkably well-balanced child, was more an outdoor girl, living for riding and Saturday hunts, and to walk the pheasant coverts with her father.

In the summer of the year following their marriage Bryan and

Diana visited Tom, who had just begun reading law at Berlin University. He told her all about life at the university and the fights between politically opposed students. For the first time Diana heard the word Nazi used to describe those in favour of Fascism. 'Do you take sides?' Diana asked. 'Oh no,' he replied. 'It's their own affair. But if I were a German, I suppose I would be a Nazi.' When pressed by Bryan he said there was no question about where his sympathies lay, for there were only two choices, Fascism or Communism, and the latter was totally unacceptable.[14] Although later Decca would dispute this leaning in Tom, there are extant letters to friends in which he repeats the same statement.[15] However, it is important to recognize that in 1928 Tom was speaking without the benefit of hindsight: then 'Nazi' merely described supporters of a right-wing political movement. There was no hint of the horrors that would be perpetrated a decade and more later.

In 1928 Nancy had managed to persuade her parents to allow her to attend the Slade School, then under the directorship of Professor Henry Tonks, to study art. Despite the titanic arguments she endured to get there, she lasted less than a month: Tonks told her baldly that she should learn to cook for she had no talent as an artist. 'I wept,' she said,[16] but she could not resist teasing Decca by telling her she had given it up because she found it impossible to look after herself in her bed-sitter. Decca was furious. 'Oh, darling, but you should have seen it,' Nancy drawled. 'After about a week it was knee-deep in underclothes. I literally had to wade through them. No one to put them away.'[17]

In order to earn some additional pocket money Nancy began submitting items of gossip to *Vogue* and *Harpers Bazaar*, and from this graduated to writing the occasional article. The first known to be published was 'The Shooting Party, Some Hints for the Woman Guest' by the Hon. Nancy Mitford. She earned twenty-two pounds for each one, which she spent on gifts for Hamish. Her romance with him was going nowhere, although she longed to marry him. Whenever she could she stayed in London, chiefly with Middy O'Neil who had been so helpful in Paris, and Evelyn Gardner, whom she had known for many years. When it was not let, she was occasionally allowed to stay at, and even entertain from, 26 Rutland Gate. She had given a smart little party there for Evelyn Gardner when the latter became engaged to Evelyn Waugh ('who writes, I believe, very well') in 1928.[18] After the two Evelyns married, the complication of their names was resolved by the simple expedient of referring to them as He-Evelyn and She-Evelyn. The marriage could never have worked: Waugh had homosexual urges and was not able to give She-Evelyn the emotional security she needed; as a writer he needed quiet and isolation, while She-Evelyn craved social life.

That social Season – which heralded the Wall Street Crash and a world depression – and the one that followed it were arguably the most hectic ever known in London. For the privileged few there was a party every night, mostly in costume: clown parties, baby parties, bath and bottle parties, heroes and heroines parties, Roman orgy parties, Russian parties, wear-almost-nothing parties, ancient Greek parties, subject-of-a-book parties. A party where guests attended in ordinary evening clothes was just plain unsmart.

Diana and Bryan were the acknowledged leaders of London Society. They were rich, young, intelligent and beautiful, and a focal point for various sets: the aesthetes, such as Roy Harrod, Henry Yorke, Harold Acton, Robert Byron and Brian Howard; the pre-jet jet-setters, such as Emerald Cunard, Margaret Mercer-Nairne (Lady Margaret Myddleton, daughter of Lady Violet Astor), and Duff and Diana Cooper; the more cerebral world of Lytton Strachey and his lover Dora Carrington, John Betjeman and Professor Lindemann; and the theatre world of Noël Coward.

As for the Bright Young People, Diana and Bryan knew many of them, but regarded them as too frivolous. Diana, still not twenty, preferred grand balls especially because Bryan was a wonderful dancer: 'I loved dining out and dancing . . . we never went to all those [Bright Young People] "parties" except Brian Howard's Greek party in fancy dress. We had many parties at Buckingham Street, some in fancy dress though the house wasn't big.'[19] One of these was an 1860s party that was grist to Evelyn Waugh's literary mill. That summer, in ten days, he wrote twenty-five thousand words of a novel about it all: 'It is rather like a P.G. Wodehouse,' he wrote to a friend, 'all about bright young people. I hope it will be finished by the end of the month.'[20]

Earlier, in May, She-Evelyn had invited Nancy to move in with her at the Waughs' house in Canonbury Square, Islington, because He-Evelyn wanted to go away to the country to work on his book. Nancy had been there only a matter of weeks when She-Evelyn bolted with a lover, leaving a note for He-Evelyn breaking the news. Clearly Nancy could not stay with He-Evelyn alone so she had to return home, which at that juncture was High Wycombe, Swinbrook having been let to provide extra income. Leaving the rarefied company of Diana's social whirl and London's literati for Old Mill Cottage with its singular delights of 'the children', Sydney's collection of Leghorns and bantams, Unity's goat, Decca's sheep and Debo's guinea-pigs was like an emergency stop in a vehicle that had been racing along deliciously at maximum speed. Nancy was morose and teased everyone more than ever. Friends thought she was just 'spinsterish', following Diana's marriage: it was considered something of a blow to have a younger sister marry first.

Later that summer Diana and Bryan went to Paris and stayed at the house of Bryan's parents in rue de Poitiers. Bryan had known Evelyn Waugh at Oxford and wrote asking him to come to stay with them while he completed his novel. Waugh had attempted reconciliation with She-Evelyn but, having at last admitted that divorce was inevitable, accepted the invitation.

Later Nancy went over to join them. All her sympathies were with He-Evelyn, and before the Paris trip they had taken to lunching together at the Ritz, where she dispensed emotional sympathy, and he provided advice about her writing after she began working on a novel called *Highland Fling*.

Waugh had taken the world of the Guinnesses as the setting for his novel *Vile Bodies*, a world he knew intimately, though often he must have been more observer than participant. 'It is a welter of sex and snobbery,' he wrote of his novel to a friend, 'written simply in the hope of selling some copies.'[21] For those in the know it was scattered with private jokes, like plums in a rich fruitcake. He even managed to insert one of Decca's favourite expressions. Because of her love for Miranda she would say, 'It's perfectly sheepish' to describe something that Nancy and Diana would have called 'divine', and 'goatish' to describe a horror. Waugh wrote, 'He left his perfectly sheepish house in Hertford St . . .'[22] Nancy based her principal character on Hamish, and Bryan, who wrote a novel as tit-for-tat for Waugh's plot, took as his subject the marriage of a young writer whose wife runs off with a lover, leaving her husband to find out about it in a note. While the three worked at their respective novels, Diana, who was pregnant, sat in bed reading contentedly and making occasional comments on their progress.

Diana's first child, Jonathan, was born in March 1930. Unlike Sydney who had dismissed most of her babies as 'too ugly for words', Diana was a natural mother, worshipping all her children as babies and as they grew. Evelyn Waugh and Randolph Churchill stood as godparents, and the Churchills' old nanny, Nanny Higgs, was recruited for the nursery. Despite the world depression Diana returned to Society. The Season was more frenetic than ever with non-stop entertainments every night, if not a dinner, dance or fancy dress ball then a 'treasure hunt' in which guests were provided with a list of items they must retrieve, such as a policeman's helmet or a lamppost or street sign, kidnap a dog, or collect a duck from St James's pond. There were other pranks too, such as a pretend exhibition of modern works by a fake artist called Bruno Hat, who was in reality Tom Mitford in bohemian clothes and false whiskers.

Waugh, who spent a lot of time with Diana and Bryan, became curiously disapproving of Diana's desire to return to the social whirl after Jonathan's birth. Increasingly he tried to persuade her not to go out, but to stay at home and enjoy quiet conversation. But Diana, just twenty that summer, longed to dance again, and meet clever new people, and thought he was being 'boring'. It was not that he had suddenly developed a sympathy with those who wrote to the newspapers deprecating a disgraceful flaunting of wealth and privilege in the face of growing unemployment and real poverty, nor with the older generation, like David and Sydney, who could not stomach the frivolity demonstrated by the Bright Young People, with its inconvenience to innocent bystanders. Many years later, he admitted that he had been jealous: he had fallen in love with Diana and wherever they went she was surrounded by a court of adoring young men. While she was pregnant he had her to himself, sharing long hours with her, 'just sitting with him all day, and dining in bed – I had a table in my room for Evelyn and Bryan . . . which of course was very cosy. But Evelyn didn't much like *new* friends such as Lytton Strachey who stayed with us in Ireland . . . Evelyn refused to come.' During a visit with the couple to their south-coast property, Pool Place, he picked quarrel after quarrel with Diana and left abruptly, sending her only a brief note to apologize for being 'unfriendly . . . Please believe it is only because I am puzzled and ill at ease with myself. Much later everything will be all right.' In fact, it marked the end of their friendship and they were only to make contact again in 1966, shortly before his death, when he admitted the true cause of his boorish behaviour. By the time he left Diana had begun to find his behaviour 'so horrid . . . that one didn't miss him at all'.[23]

As the weeks went by she found she missed his conversation and tried to bring him back, but he refused all invitations.

In January 1930 when Waugh published *Vile Bodies*, the novel he had been working on during the previous year, and which portrayed so graphically the almost demented partying by the young of the upper classes, he dedicated it to Bryan and Diana 'without whose encouragement and hospitality', he wrote, 'this book would not have been finished'.[24]

THE STAGE IS SET

(1930–32)

While Evelyn Waugh was launching V*ile Bodies* to wide acclaim, Nancy's manuscript of *Highland Fling*[1] was with the printers. She hoped to make some money from it because David had virtually halved her allowance owing to financial pressures stemming from the depression. Fortunately she managed to talk herself into 'a job' with the *Lady*, writing a weekly column on subjects such as 'The Chelsea Flower Show', 'The Débutante's Dance' and 'The Shooting Party', at a salary of £250 a year.[2] Her contributions are not in the same league as her later bestselling novels but they are pithy and observant. In the following excerpt she advises how to behave during a visit to the photographer.

> People about to be photographed are always at great pains to explain that their motives are both noble and unselfish. They never say, 'I wanted a picture for myself,' but imply that countless friends and relations are clamouring for one and that it is for their sakes alone that an unpleasant ordeal is being faced . . . Don't bother to be very natural; it is not an informal snapshot, but a carefully considered portrait . . . and a little affectation often helps to secure a

good result. This is why it is important never to take a
friend with you. They are so apt to spoil a really good pose
by giggling or saying, 'Darling! What a soulful
expression!'[3]

Meanwhile the rest of the family went to Switzerland. Skating
had become a virtual obsession with David, who skated regularly
at Oxford, and packed his skates whenever he went up to
London. Various members of the family skated almost to professional standard: Tom was able to partner Sonja Henie without
disgracing himself, Unity won a bronze medal, and Debo was so
good she was invited to join the British junior team, but
Sydney – realizing the commitment required for international
level competition – vetoed this. The Mitfords usually stayed at
Pontresina, close to but less expensive than its fashionable neighbour St Moritz, where they skated on the rink in front of the
glitzy Suvretta House Hotel.

   Uncle Jack, David's favourite brother, but better known as
the debonair *éminence grise* of the International Sportsman's
Club, was also a fine skater, but he was more interested in the
Cresta bobsleigh run, which attracted a racy international
crowd. That year he had brought along an unusual guest.
Sheilah Graham was a bright working-class girl of quite extraordinary beauty and at that time was one of 'Mr Cochran's Young
Ladies'.[4] She was married but had been forced to keep the marriage secret (even from Jack) for the sake of her stage career.
Years later, when she wrote her bestselling memoir, *Beloved
Infidel*, and recalled that holiday, it was not Jack whom she
described but David, whom she likened to a Saxon king: 'a
blond, blue-eyed giant of a man with a striking head, great
shoulders, and a hawk-like look to his finely chiselled face'.
Sheilah met Tom there and they remained friends for some
years; 'Tom Mitford, a youthful edition of his father and, at
twenty-one, one of the handsomest men I had ever seen,' she

recalled. 'Outrageous fantasies danced through my head. I had always wanted children. And I had not been successful. Perhaps I could found an aristocracy of my own. And I would choose Tom Mitford to be the father, and my sons would look like Saxon Kings . . .'[5] As she sat listening to the Mitford family chatting over meals, even the children joining in as the conversation changed effortlessly from English to French, Italian to German, she felt ashamed of her ignorance. Subsequently she began a programme of self-education that changed her life and led to a career as a Hollywood journalist and a love affair with Scott Fitzgerald.

Although Tom was not rich he received a good allowance from David, and made it work for him for he travelled extensively, dined in the best places, was seen in the best company. He was particularly friendly with Winston Churchill, and in one of the longest letters he ever wrote he described a weekend spent at the home of Philip Sassoon. The party, he wrote to Sydney, consisted of Clementine and Winston Churchill, Sir Samuel and Lady Hoare, Tom's cousin Venetia Stanley and Brian Thynne, 'and Aircraftsman Shaw [T.E. Lawrence]'.

> I am a little disappointed with Shaw. He looks just like any other private in the Air Force, is very short and he's in his five years of service become quite hardened. He isn't a bit like the Sargent portrait of him in his book.
>
> Last night I sat next him at dinner and he had Winston on the other side. Winston admires him enormously. He said at one moment 'If the people make me Prime Minister I will make you Viceroy of India.' Lawrence politely refused and said he was quite happy in the Air Force. When asked what he would do when, in five years time he has to leave, he said simply 'Join the dole I suppose.' It is curious that he should enjoy such a life with no responsibility after being almost King in Arabia. Some

say it is inverted vanity; he'd have accepted a Kingship, but as he didn't get it he preferred to bury himself and hide away.

This morning we flew over to see Colonel Gunnes at Olympia, about 80 miles away. We had a 7 man unit and flew in perfect formation over Brighton and the other resorts – very low to frighten the crowd. Lawrence was thrilled at flying; he said Ministry had stopped him flying a year ago.[6] Winston drove his machine a little way. I hadn't realised he had done a lot of piloting before the war.

We flew in arrow-head formation:

Philip

Winston   Sam Hoare

Me   Lawrence

Venetia   Bryan Thynne

(each with a pilot)

and landed in [a] field . . . It took about an hour getting there and ¾ hour back, as we didn't return in formation. It was very amusing flying *very* low over the edge of the sea and jumping the piers at Brighton and Littlehampton, to the astonishment of the people there.[7]

That spring Decca realized her dearest wish. The family was living at Old Mill Cottage in High Wycombe when Sydney appeared to have a change of heart about schools. In an attempt to get Unity interested in something, and stop her sulks, which goaded David into bad tempers, she allowed Unity to attend a day school at Queen's Gate near their London house. This experiment lasted only a short time before she was expelled and Decca thought that was that. But Sydney persisted and found Unity a

place at a boarding-school, provoking the often-heard cry of the
Mitford children, this time from Decca who *ached* to be allowed
to go to school, 'But it's not *fair*!'

After Unity had successfully completed two terms, the unbe-
lievable happened: Decca and Debo were suddenly allowed to
attend a small local private day school for by the daughters of
upper-middle-class families in High Wycombe. It was no treat
for Debo: she fainted in a geometry class because it was so difficult, and the blackberry pie and custard made her sick. After
'three days of hell' she was allowed to leave.[8] But Decca revelled
in it. She was brought up short, however, when after some weeks
she asked Sydney if she could invite her 'best friend' home to tea.
'Oh, no, darling,' Sydney replied. It wasn't possible because
Decca would be invited back to the girl's home and Sydney 'did
not know' her mother. Decca knew instinctively that there could
be no appeal, and though it seems an insignificant incident it
helped to form her personal convictions about class and privilege.
At the end of the term she was withdrawn from the school and
once again thrown upon autodidactic study to expand the
PNEU curriculum available at home.

Her personal research began to take a direction unsuspected by
Sydney: social politics. 'By the time I was thirteen,' Decca wrote,
in an unpublished manuscript, 'major storms were brewing outside the Swinbrook fortress. Whole population centres were
designated "distressed areas" by the Government. I read in the
papers of the great hunger marches, the great depression of the
early 30s hit the country and police and strikers fought in the
streets.'[9] Her single term at school was not responsible for, but
coincided with, the dawning of self-consciousness that her home-
life was exceptional:

> The discovery of other people's reality – more than fifty
> million in England alone! – is one you can grasp from
> time to time, only to find it eluding you again, its vastness

proving too much for you to handle. You discover suffering – not just your own suffering, which you know is largely of your own making, nor the childhood suffering over *Black Beauty, David Copperfield* or Blake's *Little Chimney Sweep* – but you catch disturbing, vivid glimpses of the real meaning of poverty, hunger, cold cruelty.[10]

Prior to this Decca and Unity had squabbled a great deal, and the childish battles between Hons and Counter Hons had been semi-serious at times,[11] but when Decca reached adolescence the two became Favourite Sisters.[12] Although she was thrown more and more into the company of Debo as the elder girls left home, Debo's clear enjoyment of her life at Swinbrook made her an unsympathetic confidante for Decca and her newly awakened social conscience. Now in the Hons Cupboard when they talked about what they wanted to be when they were grown-ups, Unity would say, 'I'm going to Germany to meet Hitler,' and Decca would say, 'I'm going to run away and be a Communist,' where-upon, so Decca wrote, Debo would state that she was going to marry a duke and become a duchess.[13]

Undoubtedly Unity's anti-parent stance attracted Decca just when she wanted to expand her personal horizons beyond Swinbrook with its apparently petty restrictions to which she would be subject for 'years and years', stretching far off into the future, until that happy day when she finally grew up and could run away. She described Unity as 'a huge bright glittering personality, [she had] a sort of huge boldness and funniness and generosity – a unique character that is hard to explain to anybody who did not know her in those days. She was tremendous fun to be with. She wasn't at all interested in politics [then] and she would go off into a dream world . . . of Blake, Edgar Allan Poe and Hieronymus Bosch . . . Oddly enough it was I who first became interested in Politics.'[14]

In fact Decca became so interested in what she read in the

newspapers that she even 'grudgingly' spared some money from her running-away account to buy leftist books and pamphlets, and pro-pacifist literature. But the defining moment of her burgeoning political interest came when she read a book by Beverly Nichols. *Cry Havoc* detailed the worst horrors of the First World War and was an eloquent plea for world disarmament. It appealed strongly to sections of a generation growing up in a world where the existing political systems seemed not to be working, and it gave Decca a focus for what were then no more than rags of political ideas. As she read about the growing social and fiscal problems across Europe she began to define her personal ideology, and a new element was added to her running-away plans. She realized that by instinct she was a socialist, and began to understand why she wanted to run away, what she was running away for and from. What she did not yet know was where she was running to. However, 'I felt as though I had suddenly stumbled on the solution to a vast puzzle which I had clumsily been trying to solve for years,' she wrote. Her first reaction was to appeal to Nancy and her pro-socialist friends, but she was disappointed in their reaction: they were thinkers not activists. Moreover, they were too busy attending parties every night to take seriously what Decca began to call 'the class struggle'.

Unity spent just over a year boarding at St Margaret's, Bushey (SMB, as it is known to its pupils) in Nicholson's house. The school was chosen presumably because her first cousins Robin and Ann Farrer, and Rosemary and Clementine Mitford were also there, so she was unlikely to be lonely. But she was remorselessly naughty and was expelled just before Christmas 1930, or rather her mother was invited to remove her – a nice point of distinction to which Sydney adhered stoically – because of her unsettling influence on the other girls. In later years Unity liked to claim that the reason for her expulsion was a single act, on Speech Day when she had to read aloud a quotation that included the line, 'A garden is a lovesome thing God wot . . .' to which she claimed she added the word 'rot'. However, her biographer discovered that this joke was used throughout the school before Unity's expulsion and one of Unity's friends at St Margaret's stated, 'What she got the sack for was a fine disregard of the rules of the school.'[15] Later, when Unity became infamous, pupils at St Margaret's were forbidden to mention her name and she was, as it were, expunged from the school records. Strangely, Unity was upset at her expulsion: even years later she told new friends how sad it had made her.

The Farrer girls who were at school with Unity were daughters of Aunt Joan, the third of David's four sisters. Joan had married Major Denis Farrer, a distant Redesdale kinsman who had been David's companion during his long-ago attempt at tea-planting in Ceylon. The Farrers had five children but it was the three girls who played a major part in the lives of the Mitford sisters. The eldest, Barbara, was the same age as Pam, while Ann and Joan (called Robin by her parents) were contemporaries of Unity and Decca. Major Farrer and David often shot together and there were exchange visits between Asthall and the Farrer home, Brayfield, on the Bedfordshire–Buckinghamshire border. Miss Hussey took some of the girls to Brayfield on several occasions, so it is something of a surprise to read in a letter between Decca and Ann that they 'never really met' until 1930 when Ann and Robin were invited to Swinbrook for the summer holidays.[16] Ann became known as 'Idden' and Robin as 'Rudbin' (their names in Boudledidge),* but after seeing Humphrey Bogart in *The Petrified Forest* in Oxford, Idden and Decca took to calling each other 'Sister' in correspondence.[17] They became instant best friends, and Idden was Decca's first real confidante outside her immediate family.[18]

---

*Because Idden and Rudbin are more memorable names (than Ann and Robin) I have referred to them by these nicknames throughout the book.

Two or three times they walked together to Chipping Norton – ten miles each way – to a shop where they could buy home-made sausage rolls (strictly forbidden under Sydney's Mosaic regimen) and fizzy lemonade (also forbidden at Swinbrook). It was to Idden that Decca revealed her concern about the have-nots in society. In return Idden told Decca about their Romilly cousins. The Mitford children had never met Esmond and Giles Romilly. Sydney disapproved of their mother, Nellie, because of her reputation and feckless nature, although Nellie was David's first cousin, and sister to Clementine Churchill. The two boys were not much welcome at the Farrers' home at Brayfield either, and they spent most of their summer and Christmas holidays at Chartwell with the Churchills. The Farrers had met them at Chartwell a couple of times and it seemed that no matter how naughty the Mitfords were, and it was inevitable that bright children thrown so much on their own devices would be mischievous, Esmond outdid them by miles. He held the head of Mary Churchill[19] under water until she conceded that there was no God, he smoked in his bedroom, and – a cardinal sin – he dared to appear once at dinner without a black tie.[20]

Although, according to Decca, it was her interest in politics that stimulated Unity's, the surviving evidence tends to show that Unity, three years older than Decca, had already become interested in pseudo-Fascist literature in 1930 a year or so before Decca's first political stirrings. Unity's biographer, David Pryce-Jones, came across a book she had owned. Autographed by her and dated 1930, it was a copy of *Jew Süss,* the novel by Leon Feuchtwanger about an eighteenth-century Jewish financier-adventurer. Because of its stereotypical Jewish characters, it was used in Germany to fuel and unify disparate elements of anti-Semitism. Pryce-Jones, whose father had been a Swinbrook Sewer at roughly the same time that Unity would have been reading this book, thought it an unusual choice of reading matter for a fifteen-year-old girl[21] and it set him on a course of research that led to the only biography written about Unity, whom he described enigmatically as 'a comet, blazing a trail too erratic to be charted'.[22]

But no matter which of the two came to politics first, it was typical that although Unity and Decca became emotionally close to each other at this time, they opposed each other ideologically. Decca was toying then with socialism before becoming, as Farve would have put it, 'a Bolshie', and Unity had an initial slight interest in Fascism. 'When Boud became a fascist I declared myself a Communist . . . thus by the time she was eighteen and I was fifteen we had chosen opposite sides in the conflict of the day' was how Decca put it.[23] As they egged each other on and their interest grew, a line was drawn down the centre of the DFD, and it became a miniature battleground of contradictory political fervour with the respective literature of each side crowding every surface, posters of Hitler and Lenin adorning opposite walls, swastikas, hammers and sickles scratched into the glass of the windows.

Yet if Decca was truly unhappy, as she claims to have been, it was not obvious to her family. Her letters sparkle, almost as much as Nancy's, with fun and enjoyment of her life, especially her friendship with Idden, and her beloved pets, the spaniel, Spanner, and Miranda, who loved chocolate. Her relationship with her father is nowhere better illustrated than by letters she wrote to him in 1932 from holiday on the Isle of Wight containing a series of spoof newspaper articles about him, illustrated with pen-and-ink drawings. David took these letters in great good humour, but apart from the closeness of Decca's relationship with her father these 'articles' also showed a basic understanding of the journalism for which in later life she would become renowned:

Peer Had up for Murder – and Rightly

Lord 'Sheepbrain' Redesdale, well known to all committee frequenters such as the skating committee . . . was had up yesterday for assaulting and injuring Mr Adolphus Jones who afterwards died of shock.

He is to be hung tomorrow as soon as possible [inset: 'his daughter's remarkable spaniel who has got mange']. The Hon. Nancy Mitford, another daughter, whose engagement to P. Rodd was announced in these columns, is being married in the prison chapel so that her father can give her away before the hanging . . .[24]

One illustration shows David, dressed in a suit decorated with arrows with a rope around his neck, escorting Nancy, dressed in flowing bridal clothes, to the altar. Her next letter contained a home-made four-page newspaper:

Man with Glaring Eyes Caught

Lord Redesdale is to be tried in the House of Lords for the unnecessary murder of Miss Belle Bathe, a bathing Belle of Totland Bay.

Lord Redesdale was interviewed today by our special correspondent. 'I was imagining myself in a skating rink' he [said] . . . when this damn girl came up and tried to hire out a towel. So I unfortunately trampled her underfoot with my skates.' Lady Redesdale, when interviewed, merely replied, 'Ohrrr, poor [darling]', so we expect she will be tried for being an accessory after the fact.

Miss Jessica Mitford was also interviewed by our correspondent. 'I always expected something of the sort', she said. 'You see he really is a subhuman and a pathetic old throw-back, so what was one to expect?' We also learn that Lord Redesdale is a great admirer of Hitler, 'The fellow has fair hair. Really almost yellow' he told our correspondent, 'so of course I admire him.' Lord Redesdale has narrowly escaped arrest for cruelty to children; loud shrieks have often been heard to come from his house . . .

[Headline]: Lord Redesdale hanged – last words: 'Take care of my skates . . .'[25]

The letters to David, which accompany these extracts, are alive with love and laughter, and appear to show a child confident in her father's affection. They are not in any sense demonstrative of an unhappy child. However, Decca did record that Sydney withheld her pocket money on one occasion when she referred to her father as 'a feudal remnant'. 'Little D, you are not to call Farve a remnant!' Sydney ordered. In fact, it was only one of countless names that all the children bestowed upon their parents and which were generally taken with good humour. Sydney became 'the poor old female', shortened to TPOF, and 'the fem' in conversation, while David was 'the poor old male', TPOM, and often 'the poor old sub-human'. Letters are scattered with references to the parents as 'the birds' and 'the nesting ones'. No one escaped a nickname in the Mitford household.[26]

Unity came out in the spring of 1932 and, economically, Sydney brought out Rudbin at the same time, irritated because David's sister Joan seemed unprepared to 'do anything' to launch her daughters into Society. A fellow débutante recalled that as she and Unity were both nearly six feet tall they were made to bring up the rear of the procession.[27] Dressed in white and with the regulation ostrich feathers in their hair, they felt ridiculous and rebellious, which created an instant bond of friendship. Invited to stay at Swinbrook, Unity's new friend was surprised and impressed by the sophisticated and free manner in which the

Mitfords talked about their parents. Unity, she said, was quite unlike anyone else, but it was her behaviour rather than her character that was different. Her clothes were outlandish and she brightened up the requisite débutante wardrobe approved by Sydney by adding dramatic flourishes such as velvet capes and flashy jewellery hired from a theatrical costumier.

Where Nancy enjoyed teasing, Unity liked to shock, though in her teenage years her manner of shocking people was often startling or funny rather than truly shocking. As a débutante she drew attention to herself by taking her pet white rat Ratular to dances and even to a Palace garden party. She would sit stroking it, almost daring young men to speak to her. Sometimes Ratular was left at home in favour of her grass snake, Enid, who performed as an unusual neck ornament. When either of these pets escaped – which was whenever Unity felt that things needed to be livened up – there was a huge amount of shrieking and commotion. Unity was not unattractive; someone said that looking at her was like looking at Diana in a slightly distorted mirror, and she had her own little court of admirers, but no one 'stuck'. She was too unusual: all photographs of her show her with a sullen expression, but friends say she smiled and laughed a great deal. 'She was fun,' one said. 'She used to giggle and giggle, but in photographs she looks severe because Diana had said that smiling wrinkled the skin, so she put on her photography face.'[28]

When she was presented in May she discovered some Buckingham Palace writing-paper in a waiting room and immediately pocketed it to use as 'jokey' writing-paper for thank-you notes. Sydney was aghast, but Unity needed to stand out, to draw attention to herself, to be accounted as someone in her own right, not simply one of the middle Mitford girls. She felt awkward about her appearance, and had endured a full complement of sisterly taunts about her size, but her character and behaviour made her what Decca called a *sui generis* personality. Her originality made a deep impression on many who were introduced to her then for the first time. Diana's neighbour, Dora Carrington, for example, met her in the summer before she came out while the Mitfords were visiting Biddesden, home of Diana and Bryan. 'Dear Lytton,' Carrington wrote afterwards, 'I went with Julian to lunch with Diana today. There found three sisters and Mama Redesdale. The little sisters were astonishingly beautiful and another of sixteen (Unity) very marvellous or Grecian. I thought the mother was remarkable, very sensible and no upper class graces . . . the little sister [Debo] was a great botanist and won me by her high spirits and charm . . .'29

Despite the seemingly ceaseless round of parties, and the trips to Venice, Greece and Turkey that Diana and Bryan made, Bryan must have found time to work for in 1930 he was admitted to the bar. To his disappointment he was offered few briefs and only discovered the reason for this by accident: the clerk considered that others in the chambers were in greater need of the three-guinea fee than Bryan. After that he more or less gave up. In 1931 the couple moved from Buckingham Street to 96 Cheyne Walk in Chelsea, overlooking the river. Formerly it had been the house of the artist James McNeill Whistler, and was two doors away from the old London home of Diana's grandparents, where David had been born. Some time earlier Bryan had purchased Biddesden, a Queen Anne house in the baroque style, set in rolling chalk downland near Andover in north Hampshire. It was a comfortable old property of mellowed red bricks with stone coining, originally built for General Webb, one of Marlborough's generals. A portrait of the first owner on his battle-charger hung, two storeys high, in the entrance hall. It went with the house and Diana was warned that if it was moved the general's ghost would make a nuisance of itself by riding ceaselessly up and down the stairs in protest. Her childhood memories of the Asthall ghost made her especially sensitive to this legend and she made no attempt to alter the decoration of the hall, though she stamped her own youthful taste on the remainder of the house.

That summer Diana was twenty-one and pregnant again, with her second son, Desmond, who was born in September 1931, so she did not travel abroad. When Bryan went away with friends, Sydney and the three youngest girls stayed at Biddesden to keep her company. Even so, and with a veritable army of servants, Diana lay awake at night, frightened of the darkness and listening for footsteps on the paving outside the house – presumably those of General Webb keeping a watch on his portrait. She confided her fears to their neighbour and close friend Lytton Strachey, whose reaction apparently cured her of her apprehensions once and for all. '[He] raised both hands in a characteristic gesture of despairing amazement. "I had hoped," he said, "that the age of reason had dawned."'[30] Nevertheless, the portrait of General Webb remained *in situ*.

With a real talent for entertaining and love of good conversation, Bryan and Diana encouraged an eclectic circle of friends from the worlds of politics, literature, art and science to stay at Biddesden for extended periods. John Betjeman was there almost every other weekend, with Augustus John, Lytton Strachey and Dora Carrington. Prof [Lindemann] was another frequent guest, as were the Sitwells, the Acton brothers, Harold and William, and the Huxleys. 'Randolph Churchill almost lived with us,' a member of the staff recalled.[31]

Biddesden had a 350-acre dairy farm and a herd of fifty cows. Bryan was only too happy to agree to Pam's suggestion that she manage it and run the milk round for him. There was a farm manager's cottage built of brick and flint on the property and Pam moved in, but she was often invited to Biddesden for dinner. The farm workers called her 'Miss Pam' and had a healthy respect for her as she worked alongside them, invariably dressed in riding breeches and boots, even when, in the early days, she made a few mistakes. For example, she bid at market for what looked to her like a very fine cow, only to discover when it arrived at the farm that 'the brute was bagless'. She always had an acute sense of humour about her own limitations and was quite unaware of her beauty, which endeared her to everyone who met her.[32] Since her broken engagement two years earlier she had formed no emotional attachments, but John Betjeman, who had been a friend of Bryan since 1927 at Oxford when they were successive editors of the magazine *Cherwell*, became a founder member of what he called 'the Biddesden Gang' and fell instantly in love with her. Betjeman, or 'Betj', as Pam called him, was on the rebound from a frustrated love affair but his affection for her ran deep. In a letter to Bryan he admitted that all his thoughts were of Pam. 'I hope I am not a bore. Possibly.'[33] Although quieter than her sisters Pam had the same physical beauty of open, regular features and attractive cheekbones, fair hair, with startling blue eyes, the same colour as David's.

John Betjeman and she 'walked out' for a while. 'He was mad on kite-flying at the time,' Pam would tell Betjeman's biographer. 'He used to bring his kite down for the weekend.' Sometimes they drove around Hampshire and Wiltshire together, exploring old churches and villages, picnicking on the downs, visiting his (hated) old school, Marlborough. On Sundays they always cycled down to the old church at nearby Appleshaw for matins, with the glorious ancient liturgy and hymns that David had insisted on at Swinbrook. Once Pam persuaded Betjeman to ride, putting him on a reliable old pony and sending him off into the woods behind the house where he would be 'safe'. Unfortunately, the local hunt was drawing there: at the sound of the horn the reliable old pony reared with joy, and happily decanted its passenger before galloping off to join in the fun.

Betjeman was too shy to advance his suit aggressively but he persisted quietly for over a year. 'My thoughts are still with Miss Pam,' he wrote to Diana in February 1932 from a hotel in Devon. 'I have been seeing whether a little absence makes the heart grow fonder and, my God, it does. Does Miss Pam's heart still warm towards that ghastly Czechoslovakian [*sic*] Count? . . . I do want . . . to hear whether this severe test has improved my chances and done down my rival. I have written a confession of my tactics to Miss Pam today. Was that wise?'[34] Diana encouraged him, and Betjeman continued as a frequent weekend visitor. He recalled that after dinner Bryan did conjuring tricks and guests used to gather round the piano for parlour songs, and 'rounds', but the absolute favourites were the old evangelical hymns. Diana's parlourmaid, May Amende, disapproved thinking that they were mocking them, but they were not, Betjeman insisted, 'We sang them in the car, too.'[35] Unity's favourite was also Sydney's, the old Moody and Sankey hymn about the lost sheep, which was almost prophetic.

> *There were nine and ninety that safely lay*
> *In the shelter of the fold*
> *But one was out, on the hills away,*
> *Far off from the hills of gold . . .*

Betjeman proposed twice. Pam turned him down flat the first time but on the second occasion he asked her to take some time to think it over. A month later, however, he was writing to an old friend, 'I suppose you have heard about the death of poor old Lytton Strachey [of cancer] and how about a fortnight later [*sic*] Carrington borrowed Bryan Guinness's gun and shot herself down at Biddesden. You may have heard too that I fell slightly in love with Pamela, the rural Mitford. I don't know whether I still am . . .'[36] Later still, with no favourable reply from Pam, he added a light-hearted PS in a letter to Nancy: 'If Pamela Mitford refuses me finally, you might marry me – I'm rich, handsome and aristocratic.'[37] Finally he wrote to Diana that Pam's fondness for the Austrian count, Tom's friend Janos von Almassy, 'that "Austrian Betjeman" about whom I am continually hearing, and about whose success I have had little reason to doubt' had killed his love for her and that he was now interested in 'another jolly girl'.[38] Years later Pam told Betjeman's daughter, 'Betj made me laugh. I was very, very fond of him, but I wasn't in love with him . . . He said he'd like to marry me but I rather declined.'[39] The future poet laureate, first person to use the term the Mitford Girls – in print, at least – consoled his disappointment by writing a ditty 'in honour of The Mitford Girls, but especially in honour of Miss Pamela':

> *The Mitford girls! The Mitford Girls*
> *I love them for their sins*
> *The young ones all like 'Cavalcade',*
> *The old like 'Maskelyns'*[40]
>
> *SOPHISTICATION, Blessed dame*
> *Sure they have heard her call*
> *Yes, even Gentle Pamela*
> *Most rural of them all*[41]

Betjeman and the girl who subsequently became his wife, Penelope Chetwode, were frequent visitors to Biddesden over the years that followed despite the effect of the house on him. Like Diana, he was affected by the supernatural ambience and on one occasion had a disturbing dream in which he was handed a card inscribed with a date. He declined to reveal the details but said he was convinced it was the date of his death.

To celebrate Diana's twenty-second birthday in June 1932 the Guinnesses held a party at Cheyne Walk. She was then at the height of her beauty, had been painted by half a dozen leading portrait artists and her face – which had become virtually an icon for the era with its classical planes – carefully composed, so as not to encourage wrinkles, appeared in newspaper Society columns regularly. She was the woman who apparently had everything: youth, riches, a happy marriage, a charming husband who worshipped her, and two healthy children. For her party she dressed in pale grey chiffon and tulle, and wore 'all the diamonds I could lay hands on'.[42] Their guests included Winston Churchill, Augustus John, first-time visitor Oswald Mosley, and 'everyone we knew, young and old, poor and rich, clever and silly'. It was a still, warm summer night and dancing went on until the glassy surface of the river was gilded with the pink and orange of sunrise.

There was a singular significance to this one party out of all the others for Diana, which is no doubt why she recalls it so graphically. A short time earlier, during the spring of 1932, she had met the dashing and dangerous Sir Oswald Mosley and had fallen madly in love with him. It was the real thing, a love that would triumphantly defy the world no matter what the cost, and endure for the rest of her life, but she could not have known that then, only wonder, perhaps, at the intensity of her feelings.

They met first at a dinner party, and little could the hostess have realized the part she was playing in history by seating them next to each other. Diana was not especially impressed with him that evening, but she found what he had to say interesting. Although he had not been previously introduced to her, they moved in the same circles and he had certainly noticed her on several occasions. The first time had been at a ball given by Sir Philip Sassoon at his magnificent Park Lane home. 'She looked wonderful among the rose entwined pillars,' Mosley wrote of Diana in his autobiography, '. . . as the music of the best orchestras wafted together with the best scents through air heavy laden with Sassoon's most hospitable artifices. Her starry blue eyes, golden hair and ineffable expression of a Gothic Madonna seemed remote from the occasion but strangely enough not entirely inappropriate . . .'[43] He spotted her again during a visit to Venice but they did not meet then either. At the back of Diana's mind was the knowledge that Mosley had a reputation as 'a lady-killer', which did not dispose her to favour him.[44]

It was only a matter of time, however, for soon the popular princess of London Society was completely under the spell of the man who was rapidly earning for himself a reputation as the *enfant terrible* of British politics. They met everywhere, trying to discover which function the other was attending – such as the coming-of-age party thrown by the Churchills for Randolph – seeking each other out at every opportunity, trying to suppress their feelings but unable to draw back from the delicious thrill of being in each other's company. As the attachment deepened they were both aware of the need for discretion, and of the furore there would be if word of their attraction got out. Also, Diana genuinely cared for Bryan and was mindful of how she could wound him. But when she compared what she felt for Mosley with her affection for Bryan it was as the sun to a candle. At her birthday party Mosley declared for the first time to Diana that he was passionately in love with her. On the following morning Diana's parlourmaid, May Amende, answered the phone. With his customary impatience, Mosley paused long enough only to identify the voice as female before he asked, 'Darling, when can I see you again?'[45]

Prior to meeting Mosley, Diana had been miserable following the deaths of Strachey and Carrington; Carrington's upset her particularly, because she had innocently loaned her the shotgun. Diana has a good mind, and during this period she began to use it. On the face of it she had everything, just as the papers simpered, but she concluded that, with the exception of the birth of her babies, her existence since her marriage to Bryan had been trivial and that there *must* be more to life. She began to recognize dimly that much of what her parents had said was right, and that she had really married 'in order to escape the boredom, and sort of fatal atmosphere that families make when too cooped up together'.[46] She also began to notice the world outside her cosseted existence.

Top: 1. Sydney and Dorothy ('Weenie') Bowles in their ubiquitous sailor suits, *c*. 1892.

Above: 2. Sydney the newlywed, Cowes, Isle of Wight, 1904.

Right: 3. David and Sydney with three-year-old Nancy, *c*. 1907. (Nancy used this image on the cover of her book *The Water Beetle*.)

4. David Mitford worked his mine in Swastika, Canada, for years but never struck gold. September 1913.

5. The Mitford family in 1912: Nancy, David, Tom, Diana, Sydney and Pam. Note the bloodhound with which David 'hunted' the children.

6. Batsford House, which David inherited in 1916.

7. The library at Batsford. A grand house but the Redesdales could not afford to keep it.

8. Seaside holidays at Hastings. *Left to right*: Diana, Tom and Pam.

9. Diana, Nancy, Pam and Tom with the chickens whose eggs paid for the governess.

Top left: 10. Nancy aged nine.

Top right: 11. Nanny 'Blor', much loved by all the Mitfords.

Bottom left: 12. Unity and Decca (seated), 1922.

Bottom right: 13. Decca aged four.

Clockwise: 14. Unity aged seven; 15. Tom at Eton; 16. Nancy (before she cut her hair) and Debo, 1923. There were sixteen years between Nancy and her youngest sister and Sydney asked her to be Debo's godmother.

Below: 17. Annual family photo call at Asthall in 1922. 'When one looks back at that time, it seems to have been all summers,' Sydney wrote.

18. Debo skating at St Moritz. She was invited to join the British junior team, but Sydney would not allow it.

Bottom left: 19. Nineteen-year-old Diana's marriage to Bryan Guinness on 30 January 1929, at St Margaret's, Westminster, was the 'society wedding of the year'.

Bottom right: 20. Diana and Bryan on honeymoon in Sicily.

21. Diana in fancy dress, photographed by Cecil Beaton in 1932 – the year she met Oswald Mosley. Her silver foil wig was made for her by theatre costume designer Oliver Messel.

22. Nancy by Cecil Beaton, 1932.

The teenage Decca was not alone in the Mitford family in recognizing that there were unacceptable aspects to Society, 'although,' Diana wrote, 'it was not necessary to have a particularly awakened social conscience to see that "Something must be done." The distressed areas, as they were called, contained millions of unemployed kept barely alive by a miserable dole. Undernourished, overcrowded, their circumstances were a disgrace which it was impossible to ignore or forget. The Labour Party had failed to deal with the problem, the Conservatives could be relied upon to do the strict minimum, yet radical reform was imperative.' More than most Diana realized that, for the rich, life had gone on as before the depression had struck, and would continue to do so. 'Nothing will stop young people enjoying themselves,' she continued.[47] Unlike Decca, Diana did not accept that axiomatically the rich had to be brought down in order to raise the poor: she felt instinctively that there must be a way of resolving the conundrum. She was seeking some sort of answer that she had not yet identified. When she met Mosley, and listened to his stirring ideas, the missing piece seemed to fall into place.

To anyone who lived through the Second World War the name Oswald Mosley has a sinister ring. During those years he became – after members of the German Nazi regime – public enemy number one. But a decade before the war Mosley was admired, fêted and listened to with respect. Arguably one of the most brilliant young politicians of his time, in the late twenties and early thirties he was widely regarded in political circles as a prime minister-in-waiting. It was simply a matter of time, and of him finding his place. By the time Diana met him, Mosley had already begun to take the bold steps that would sever him for ever from conventional politics.

The eldest of three sons, Mosley came from a similar background to Diana's. He graduated from Sandhurst on the outbreak of the First World War at the age of seventeen. He served gallantly in the trenches and in the air, but was badly injured in a landing accident and was invalided out of the forces, with a pronounced limp, before he was twenty. With a military career denied to him he turned to politics and was elected Conservative MP for Harrow in the so-called 'khaki election' of 1918, becoming the youngest member of the Commons. Thus began his meteoric rise. Confident, rich, darkly good-looking, he was over six feet tall and athletic: he rode well, played tennis and fenced at international level. Above all, he was charismatic; he excelled in debate and was a polished performer on the hustings. In those pre-television days political meetings were attended in numbers only dreamed of by present-day politicians and he thought nothing of addressing a crowd of thousands. With his impassioned speeches, delivered in a powerful, if unusually pitched, voice he found it easy to carry his audience with him when he called for political reform to 'get the unemployed back to work'. His speeches were as full of stirring phrases as were Churchill's: '. . . the tents of ease are struck, and the soul of man is once more on the move' and 'Supposing people had stood on the shore when Drake and Ralegh . . . set out to sea and said, "Don't go. The sea is very rough and there will be trouble at the other end . . ."'[48] During the 1931 election the *Manchester Guardian* wrote:

> When Sir Oswald Mosley sat down after his Free Trade Hall speech in Manchester and the audience, stirred as an audience rarely is, rose and swept a storm of applause towards the platform – who could doubt that here was one of those root-and-branch men who have been thrown up from time to time in the religious, political and business story of England.[49]

Two years after being elected, impatient for office and disillusioned by, among other things, Conservative inactivity to help former servicemen, Mosley crossed the floor of the Commons and joined the Labour Party. Nine years later, still only in his early thirties, he was made Chancellor of the Duchy of Lancaster in Ramsay MacDonald's government, and was one of a quartet of ministers given responsibility for dealing with unemployment, which had then reached the unheard-of level of two and a half million. The memorandum he produced on the subject was described several decades later by a political pundit as 'brilliant . . . a whole generation ahead of Labour thinking',[50] but his recommendations were rejected, and in May 1930 he resigned in protest, 'slamming the door with a bang to resound through the political world'. It was, wrote one respected political commentator, 'an amazing act of arrogance'.[51] Frank Pakenham met Mosley at a dinner party at the Astors' house, Cliveden, soon afterwards. 'It was a Conservative household but they entertained politicians of all persuasions there,' he said. 'I sat next to Tom [Mosley] and he looked at me with that odd look with which he seemed to transfix women . . . he had very dark, mesmeric eyes. Anyway, he said to me, "After Peel comes Disraeli. After Baldwin and MacDonald comes . . .?" And he left the question hanging in the air. "Who comes next?" I asked him. "Comes someone *very* different," he growled.'[52]

At this point Mosley had reached the pinnacle of his career in conventional British politics. 'He had become a major political personality in his own right,' his biographer stated, 'with a wide, and almost unique, range of support and goodwill across the political spectrum.' Churchill himself proposed Mosley for membership to the Other Club, which Churchill had founded with F. E. Smith, later Lord Birkenhead, in 1911, as a dining club for men prominent in political life. Shortly after Mosley's resignation from the Labour Party, the government fell, caught by the effects of the world depression. Mosley could easily have gone back to the Conservative Party and they would have welcomed him, but he could see no radical thinking there, and a radical solution was – he insisted – the only way to deal with the worsening economic situation.[53]

Instead, he charted a courageous course. Prompted by George Bernard Shaw, and with the financial backing of Sir William Morris (later Lord Nuffield), who donated fifty thousand pounds, he formed his own party, which he called, rather unimaginatively, the New Party, and campaigned in the 1931 election. The result was a Tory landslide. Not one New Party candidate was elected and Mosley lost his own parliamentary seat. The handful of notables who had supported him, such as Oliver Baldwin, Harold Nicholson, John Strachey and Alan Young, quickly faded away, but Mosley was far from defeated. Over the next twelve months the New Party evolved into the British Union of Fascists (BUF), which was officially launched on 1 October 1932. It proposed a totalitarian concept of government, uniforms for its active members, and support of European Fascist parties, although Mosley was nothing if not strongly nationalistic.

There is an informed and objective portrait of Mosley during this period. At the request of a favourite aunt, James Lees-Milne spent a fortnight during the election canvassing and performing menial tasks for Oswald Mosley's party. What he saw of Mosley, from his subordinate position, made Lees-Milne uneasy: 'He was in those days a man of overweening egotism. He did not know the meaning of humility. He brooked no argument, would accept no advice. He was overbearing and over-confident. He had in him the stuff of which zealots are made. His eyes flashed fire, dilated and contracted like a mesmerist's. His voice rose and fell in hypnotic cadences. He was madly in love with his own words,' Lees-Milne concluded, after noting '. . . the posturing, the grimacing, the switching on and off of those gleaming teeth and the overall swashbuckling'. This was written many years later when Mosley was in a political wilderness, and Lees-Milne added, 'I believe Mosley is no longer like this. He has acquired tolerance and wisdom which, had he only cultivated them forty years ago, might have made him into a great moral leader.'[54] A number of people made similar observations to me while I was researching this book.

Mosley continued to campaign with his ideas at public meetings and paid ministerial-style visits to Mussolini. Unlike the two main parties, the BUF had no major newspaper as a platform, although initially Lord Rothermere's *Daily Mail* gave Mosley some limited support. His meetings were often rowdy, indeed he encouraged hecklers for he was so confident and clever that he found it easy to turn interruptions to his advantage. The *Daily Worker* printed constant encouragement to its readers to break up Mosley's meetings, and as matters began to get out of hand, he appointed 'bouncers' from within his ranks of supporters. They rapidly evolved into silent and sinister-looking bullyboys, presenting BUF meetings in a light guaranteed to be unappealing to the average British voter. It is surprising that Mosley, with his political acumen, did not grasp that this was a major error of judgement.

From the start, once he struck out on his own, Mosley promoted Fascism as the answer to the global collapse of the economic order. Capitalism, he argued, had shown that it could not resolve the current problems of poverty and mass unemployment, while Bolshevism was to be avoided at all costs. Some of the horrors of the Bolshevik administration were known, though not by any means the true extent, and there was an undercurrent of fear among the upper classes and British middle-class Conservatives that the proletariat masses might seize power and 'ruin' the country. If one was to be radical in that period there were only two directions in which to travel, far right or far left: Fascism or Communism. It is important to recall that at that time Fascism, as a political model, was unmarred by the horrors we now associate with Nazism. Indeed, there was practical contemporary evidence in Europe that right-wing radicalism worked well, and did not necessarily lead to abuse of power.

Mussolini, whom Mosley admired, claimed that Fascism was the *only* alternative to Communism and, unlike the Bolsheviks, he did not seek to change the monarchy or the Church or confiscate private property. He seemed to offer action without revolution, and Mosley needed to point no further than Italy's economic resurgence during the late twenties under Mussolini. In addition there were the exciting ideas of Adolf Hitler, the leading National Socialist in Germany, tipped as the next chancellor. What he had done in Germany was apparently a miracle: he had taken a nation with five million unemployed and put men to work building roads and factories. To the British voter Mosley might have had extreme ideas, but he was then untouched by the bogeyman image that history has since applied.

In Mosley's book *The Greater Britain*, upon which he was working when he and Diana met and which he published a few months later through the BUF press, he unashamedly advocated totalitarian government: freedom for the individual but within complete state control; a democratically elected government headed by an authoritarian leader, who, he insisted, could not be described as a dictator as long as an elected parliament retained the power to dismiss the government. Unlike Hitler's *Mein Kampf*, in which Jews are specifically mentioned as the enemy of the people, Mosley's book made no reference to Jews but – paradoxically one might think upon the most cursory examination of his own lifestyle – he regarded decadence as the real adversary. His vision included a nation of citizens living 'like athletes', working wholeheartedly towards the common goal of a nation made great again, 'shrinking from no effort and from no sacrifice to secure that mighty end'. The political commentator Beatrice Webb's reaction was that he was merely imitating Hitler, whose policies were degraded because they followed primitive values 'of blood lust, racial superstition, [and] blind obedience. As for Mosley,' she wrote, 'he has not even Hitler's respectable personal character nor Mussolini's distinction . . . he [is] dissolute and unprincipled, without common sense in every sense of the word.'[55]

At this point Mosley had been married for twelve years to Cynthia 'Cimmie' Curzon, second daughter of Lord Curzon, a former viceroy of India and, during the war years and until his death in 1924, one of the outstanding figures in British political history. Mosley first saw Cimmie on Armistice Night in 1918 when, swathed in the Union Flag, the sweet-faced twenty-year-old had climbed on to one of the lions in Trafalgar Square to lead a rousing chorus of 'Land of Hope and Glory'. A year later they were formally introduced. Curzon was then Foreign Secretary, and though the wildly ambitious Mosley clearly fell in love with the personable and intelligent young woman, her father's position, and her own personal wealth (through trusts settled on her by her millionaire American grandfather),[56] undoubtedly affected his decision to marry her.

After a fashion the marriage worked well. Soon after their marriage, Cimmie, no slight politician herself, was elected Labour MP for Stoke-on-Trent. When she was not pursuing her own career she was Mosley's staunch supporter and campaigned strongly for him. They were an unlikely pair to represent socialism: members of the élite upper class, with a serious side to their lives but living an unashamedly luxurious and highly privileged lifestyle. Mosley made no secret of his 'almost-unlimited appetite for fun', and the single significant problem in the marriage was his sexual incontinence. Even prior to marrying Cimmie, he had a reputation as a womanizer, and his marriage vows did not change what was a virtual obsession. Cimmie soon learned about his serial affairs, and her misery was increased by his expectation that she accept them. As time went on she tried hard to 'look the other way', sometimes even bringing herself to tease him about it in her letters to him. The unwritten rules of upper-class society accepted that liaisons outside marriage were inevitable and, though regrettable, were allowable provided they were conducted with discretion. Divorce, of course, was unthinkable and amounted to social suicide.

Mosley was happy to abide by the rules and was usually reasonably discreet. His infidelities were trivial, he insisted to Cimmie, and would never affect the deep and meaningful love he felt for her. Their son Nicholas wrote that when his father met Diana he continued to love Cimmie deeply, though probably he had ceased to find her sexually attractive.[57] Mosley's London flat in Ebury Street, ostensibly necessary for his work, was by unspoken agreement off-limits to his wife. There seems to be a general belief that it consisted of a single palatial room with a large bed on a raised dais, and that it was clearly unsuitable as a place to entertain political contacts. However, Diana remembers that 'The bed was upstairs and invisible from the big room, which had a sofa and chairs, and was very suitable for serious politicians to visit.'[58]

In that spring of 1932, when Mosley and Diana were falling in love, Cimmie had recently given birth, by Caesarean section, to her third child. She had not been in full health for over a year, suffering from a mild kidney infection after a fall but complaining over a prolonged period of backache, headaches, weight gain and a general malaise. Today such symptoms in an intelligent and apparently healthy young woman who appeared to have the world at her feet would immediately invite suspicion of an unacceptable level of stress.

In July 1932, a month after the birthday party at Cheyne Walk, Mosley attended a ball at Biddesden held by Diana to celebrate the end of Unity and Rudbin's first season. There Unity met Mosley for the first time, and she, too, fell under his mesmeric influence, though for her it was an ideological surrender. He became her ideal of a political leader – indeed she referred to him thereafter as 'The Leader' – and her allegiance to Fascism became as deep, fulfilling and enduring as was Diana's emotional attachment to Mosley.

Diana and Bryan had arranged to spend the hot summer months touring southern Europe, culminating in Venice. The Mosleys made similar plans, travelling separately so that Cimmie could make the journey in comfort by train. Diana and Mosley arranged to meet, apparently accidentally, at Arles or Avignon but the plan went awry when Diana became ill at Avignon with diphtheria. She and Mosley were writing to each other virtually daily, and fearful that his letters, addressed to await her arrival at various points on her itinerary, might be innocently intercepted and opened by Bryan during her enforced isolation, Diana had to take her friend Barbara Hutchinson, at whose house she and Mosley had first met, into her confidence to avert discovery.[59]

Within weeks Mosley and Cimmie, Bryan and Diana were all together holidaying on Venice's Lido as part of a British contingent that included Tom Mitford, Randolph Churchill, Bob Boothby, Emerald Cunard and – the love of her life – Sir Thomas Beecham, Edward James and his wife Ottilie (the Viennese dancer Tilly Losch, with whom Tom was still half in love despite her marriage), and Doris Castlerosse, who was not only one of Diana's closest friends at the time but also a girlfriend of Tom before her marriage to Viscount Castlerosse. In telling Barbara Hutchinson about Mosley, Diana had opened Pandora's box, and the mere fact of being away from England in a holiday environment perhaps led to a lack of normal reserves. The lovers lost all sense of discretion and were always at each other's side laughing into each other's eyes. It was patently obvious to everyone, especially Cimmie and Bryan, that Mosley and Diana were seriously involved with each other. They disappeared for hours at a time, and everyone knew that they were together somewhere; Mosley openly borrowed a room from Bob Boothby on one occasion. The discomfited Bryan and Cimmie could only hope that at the end of the holiday the affair would have run its course. Cimmie cried a good deal of the time.

But back in England matters merely candesced. At a *fête champêtre* at Biddesden in September, Diana and Mosley danced together the entire evening. They made a striking couple, he with his black eyes, black hair and black moustache, dressed in stark black, she with her blond hair and fair skin in white. They had eyes only for each other and hardly even spoke to anyone else, although at one point she had a short conversation with Henry Lamb, the artist, who was working on a portrait of her and was consequently spending a lot of time at Biddesden. She noticed him frowning in Mosley's direction, and said to him, 'You're thinking what a frightful bounder he is . . .'[60] Cimmie wrote letters full of hurt to Mosley in London, agonizing openly at the knowledge that he entertained Diana at his Ebury Street flat: 'Bloody damnable, cursed Ebury – how often does she come there?' she asked bitterly. She knew that he lied to her when he stayed away from home, she wrote, and that when he was being sweetest to her he was really 'trying to get away with something'.[61] Mosley was experienced at dalliance and could handle this. He wrote loving replies, ridiculing her fears, full of 'lovey-dovey, baby-talk', using their pet names for each other, dismissing Diana and other liaisons as part of his 'frolicsome little ways' and declaring continued undying devotion to Cimmie, insisting that she was 'the one' for him. Cimmie wanted, needed, to believe him and so the game went on.

It was far more difficult for Diana to live with the deception as she was, and is, congenitally unable to lie.[62] Furthermore she had time in which to think about it all, while Mosley was always frenetically busy, his mind and his life filled with matters other than their affair. *The Greater Britain*, which defined his policies, and acted as a manifesto for his party, sold rapidly and went into three editions. He was a member of the British fencing team that year, which involved not only the dedicated training demanded of any international athlete, but bouts of *epée* around the country. He represented Great Britain several times up to 1937, even though surgery after his flying accident had left him with one leg several inches shorter than the other, and he had to wear special shoes to counteract this disability.[63] But, more importantly, Mosley had worked that year to form the BUF, which demanded the majority of his time and attention for many months. There was always an aura of excited energy about Mosley that transmitted itself to those with whom he came into contact, and it is difficult to avoid the analogy that Diana was like a moth drawn to a flame. 'The fact that Mosley was so busy in a variety of ways,' Diana wrote, 'was one of his great attractions for me. I wanted more freedom than Bryan was prepared to give me.'[64]

The opening rally of the BUF was held on 15 October in Trafalgar Square, and as usual the devoted Cimmie was there to support and help Mosley win the popular vote, even though she was personally undecided about Fascism. A week or so later there was a well-attended meeting in a hall in Farringdon Street. In Italy and Germany Fascist meetings were quiet, respectful and nationalistic. In England every shade of political opinion wanted its say and Mosley's meetings were characterized by noisy barrages. In fielding questions from a small group of hecklers in the gallery Mosley referred to them facetiously as 'three warriors of [the] class war, all from Jerusalem'. This was the first time he had made any public reference to Jews and though it would not then have been considered universally the racist remark it would be today it was a major error and enabled his opponents to charge him with anti-Semitism. Another mistake, with hindsight, was his decision to uniform active members of the BUF in black shirts designed on the same clean, classic lines as Mosley's fencing jacket; within weeks of their introduction the shirts had become a symbol, were slashed with razors and torn off the backs of wearers. Somehow Mosley did not recognize that his methods, and his rousing speeches, attracted to his standard every working-class tough spoiling for a fight, the 1930s equivalent of skinheads and soccer hooligans.

After the Farringdon Street function Mosley went to Rome to see Mussolini, ostensibly to attend the tenth anniversary celebration of the dictator's accession as leader of the Italian Fascist Party, but more importantly to try to persuade him to back the BUF with financial support. But before he left he visited Diana at Biddesden to discuss their relationship. She had already decided that she had to leave Bryan, even though Mosley made it clear that he could not leave Cimmie for her. She knew that divorce would mean social ostracism, and that was bad enough, but she was proposing not simply to divorce a thoroughly nice and popular man but to live openly as the paramour of a man in public life who had a wife and three young children. Curious as it may seem now, Mosley's political stance was not a significant factor in the equation for at that time Fascism was 'still on the edge of being respectable'.[65] She also understood that because of his hectic political schedule, and the time he needed and wanted to devote to his family, Mosley could spend only limited amounts of time with her. She would have to be satisfied with the dregs. Furthermore, all the principals of this drama were young and ostensibly healthy: Diana was looking at, and fully prepared for, a lifetime commitment in which she gave everything for little in return. But the strength of her love for Mosley, and her confidence in his love for her, gave her the courage to decide that, no matter what difficulties would result, it was what she wanted. Mosley accepted her decision.

While he was away Diana told a devastated Bryan that she was leaving him, though there seems to have been some sort of agreement that she would postpone it until after Christmas – probably for the sake of the children. Perhaps Bryan hoped that given time he could persuade her to change her mind. But there were frequent quarrels between them over Mosley. Diana was aware that she was behaving badly, but there was no turning back.

Eventually she confided in Tom and Nancy, who were shocked at her decision, and deeply concerned for her; 'Mitty [Tom] and I spent the whole of yesterday afternoon discussing your affairs,' Nancy wrote on 27 November, 'and we are having another session in a minute. He is horrified, & says your social position will be *nil* if you do this. Darling I do hope you are making the right decision. You are SO young to begin getting in wrong with the world . . .'[66] Two days later she wrote again:

> I feel convinced that you won't be allowed to take this step, I mean that Muv & Farve & Tom, Randolph, Doris [Castlerosse], Aunt Iris, John [Sutro], Lord Moyne & in fact everybody that you know will band together and somehow stop it . . . Oh dear I believe you have a much worse time in store for you than you imagine. I'm sorry to be so gloomy darling . . . Mitty says £2,000 a year will seem tiny to you & he will urge Farve, as your Trustee, to stand out for more . . . if you want me at Cheyne Walk I'll come of course. Only I think I can do more good down here.[67]

A few days before Christmas David and Lord Moyne (Bryan's father) went together to see Mosley.[68] It was a difficult interview for all concerned, but Mosley refused to be lectured or intimidated into giving Diana up, just as she had when her parents and, indeed, all her relatives attempted to pressure her. She listened to all the arguments, persuasions, impatient anger and pleading – she was only twenty-two, she hardly knew her own mind, she was throwing her life away, she was ruining the children's lives, no one, including the family, would ever speak to her again, she would be an outcast and, even worse, her actions would rebound on the reputations of her sisters – but she had taken it all into account before making her decision. The only disapproval she really minded, she said, was Tom's, for he sided with his old friend. 'He was fond of Bryan,' Diana wrote. 'He also thought that for a temporary infatuation I was ruining my life and that I should bitterly regret it.'[69]

At this point, having extracted from Diana her word that she would not invite Mosley to their house, Bryan agreed to go away to Switzerland for three weeks, to give her some time for reflection. He had spent several holidays there with David and enjoyed winter sports, which Diana did not. Their agreement did not, however, prevent Diana attending a New Year's Eve party at the house in Somerset that Mosley and Cimmie had rented for the holidays. Also present was Cimmie's younger sister Alexandra ('Baba' to her family and soon to be known in the press as 'Baba Blackshirt'), together with her husband Major 'Fruity' Metcalfe, equerry to and close friend of the Prince of Wales.

When Bryan returned home to Cheyne Walk in mid-January Diana moved out, leasing a small house at 2 Eaton Square for herself, her two sons and their nanny. The Guinnesses' marriage was over. In the same month Adolf Hitler came to power in Germany.

SLINGS AND ARROWS
(1932–4)

Highland Fling was not a bestseller but it went into a second impression within weeks of publication, which Nancy found gratifying. She told her friend Mark Ogilvie-Grant, who designed the cover, that it was selling at the rate of thirty a day, 'which I'm told is definitely good for a first novel'.[1] It earned her ninety pounds, which was soon swallowed up by a trip to the Côte d'Azur, where she stayed with friends. By the following autumn she was stuck at Swinbrook bewailing the fact that she could not afford to be in London because of the cuts in her 'already non-existent' allowance.

If anyone flourished among London's smart set it was Nancy, but at least she was occupied for her few months of enforced imprisonment in the country as 1932 drew to a close. She hunted twice a week with the Heythrop, and began work on a new book. Decca recalls her sitting by the drawing-room fire giggling helplessly as her pen flew across the lines of a child's school exercise book while she wrote *Christmas Pudding*. She maintained the same bright style used in *Highland Fling*, drawing on friends and relations for characters, and places she knew well as settings. 'It is all about Hamish at Eton,' she reported to Mark

Ogilvie-Grant. 'Betjeman is co-hero.'[2] Sometimes she read extracts out loud. 'You *can't* publish that under your own name,' Sydney said, aghast at Nancy's thinly veiled caricatures.[3]

But while the literary side of her life was progressing reasonably well Nancy's informal engagement to Hamish Erskine had not prospered. Indeed, she appeared to be the only person who ever thought it might. She was obsessed with him and her letters to friends are peppered with comments about him that are invariably witty but often leave the impression of hurt. Both sets of parents were implacably opposed to the match and Hamish dithered about announcing an engagement, though at one point he gave Nancy a ring 'from Cartier'. He was sent down from Oxford because of his dissolute lifestyle there, shortly afterwards. Without allowing him to go to London where Nancy was staying with friends, his parents shipped him off to America where they had lined up a job for him.

The news of his departure came as a body blow to Nancy and she wrote to him, breaking off their informal engagement. Though she put on a brave face for most of her friends ('I don't mind at all,' she wrote to several), she confided in Mark Ogilvie-Grant that she had made a half-hearted attempt at suicide by switching on the gas fire in her room without lighting it. 'It is a lovely sensation,' she wrote, 'just like taking anaesthetic . . .' Fortunately she remembered in time that her hostess, who was pregnant, might find her body and miscarry: 'so I got back to bed and was sick . . . I am really very unhappy because there is no one to tell the funny things that happen to one & that is half the fun in life don't you agree? . . . How can I possibly write a funny book in the next 6 months, which my publisher says I *must* do. How *can* I when I've practically got a pain from being miserable and cry in buses quite continually?'[4]

A new admirer soon appeared on the scene, Guards officer Sir Hugh Smiley, who was far closer to David's idea of 'the right sort'. He proposed and Nancy replied that she couldn't even think about it until her book was finished. When he persisted she accepted, then changed her mind. At home she quarrelled with Sydney and, in a fit of misery, she rounded up Decca and the two went on a long damp country walk during which Nancy confided her woes. 'I can almost hear the squelch of gumboots,' Decca recalled forty years later, when she reminded Nancy of the occasion. 'The rain seemed like one's inner tears of bitterness because of boredom, and the inner futility of that life. You told me how Muv had given you a terrific dressing down for not being married, having turned down yet another proposal of marriage, & that you would be an old maid if you pursued this hopeless course . . .'[5] Nancy replied, 'I was telling lies if I said Muv wanted to marry me off . . . I think I was probably in a blind temper about something else and talked wildly. One of the reasons for my respect is that she never did urge marriage without inclination and I hardly think she knew who was rich and who was not. I would have liked to marry Robert Byron but he was a total pederast . . .'[6]

A few weeks later Hamish returned from America, drinking heavily because, he said, his bulwarks (Nancy) had gone. Sir Hugh proposed twice more before Nancy gave him a firm refusal at the Café de Paris where he was wooing her with orchids while Hamish sat giggling at the next table. After that Sir Hugh turned cool and a few months later married another Nancy, Cecil Beaton's sister. The unsatisfactory relationship with Hamish, but not the engagement, was back on, and life for Nancy went on much as before with parties, nightclubs, lunches at the Ritz and dinners at the Café Royal. She had earned several hundred pounds from her books and articles by then: 'I'm just so rich I go 1st Class everywhere and take taxis,' she enthused, boasting that she had even refused an offer of ten pounds a week to write gossip for the *Tatler*. 'I'm having a perfectly divine time, it is certainly more fun not being engaged.'[7] She did not mention to anyone how 'deeply distressed' she had been at a conversation during lunch with Cynthia Gladwyn when she was told what she had apparently never realized: that Hamish was homosexual.[8]

Hamish knew that marriage to Nancy would never work because of his sexual predilections, and he confided this to several friends, but his emotional attachment to her was important to him so he allowed things to drift. He was not sexually promiscuous, in fact 'not very sexy',[9] but eventually he realized he must make it clear to her, finally, that while he valued their friendship it could never progress further. He did this by inventing an engagement to another girl, Kathleen 'Kit' Dunn, sister of Philip, who was engaged to Hamish's sister, Mary. Kit was apparently a wild and eccentric character, whom Hamish and Nancy had chuckled over together, but presumably she was prepared to play along with the charade.

Nancy had spent a good deal of the spring of 1933 staying at Diana's house in Eaton Square in open defiance of David and Sydney's decree that 'the Eatonry', as the Mitford children referred to the house, was out of bounds. And Nancy was not alone in defying David. On 14 June, the day before the Guinness divorce proceedings were to be heard, there was a gathering of the elder sisters. Pam was there, and Unity, who had just finished a term at art school, called in too to offer sisterly support.[10] When the butler announced that Hamish was on the telephone and wished to speak to Nancy, she left the room and went to the phone. She was completely unprepared for what Hamish was about to tell her and she returned, minutes later, white-faced with distress and told them about his engagement.

Hamish called round later that day and there was 'a dreadful scene' for which Nancy apologized in a letter:

But darling you come and tell me you are going to share your life with Kit Dunn. *You* whom I have always thought so sensible & so idealistic about marriage, you who will love your own little babies so very, very much, it is a hard thing for me to bear that you should prefer *her* to me. You see, I knew you weren't *in love* with me, but you are in love so often and for such short spaces of time, I thought in your soul you loved me & that in the end we should have children & look back on life together when we are old . . .[11]

Three weeks later Nancy announced her engagement to Peter Rodd, a friend of her and Hamish. At Oxford his friends had made up a ditty about him:

> *Mr Peter Rodd*
> *Is extraordinarily like God*
> *He has the same indefinable air*
> *Of Savoir Faire*

According to Diana, Peter proposed only a week after Nancy and Hamish broke up. He had taken Nancy to a party and had had – as usual – a good deal to drink. Nancy was the third girl to whom he had proposed that week. In a letter dated 31 July he hinted to her that he had only intended the proposal as a joke,[12] but Nancy was not in a mood for jokes. She had spent almost five years in an unsatisfactory relationship and now, at nearly thirty, she felt perilously close to becoming the old maid of Sydney's prediction. She felt hurt and humiliated at Hamish's treachery, she wanted a home, children and some sort of financial stability, and perhaps she wanted to prove to Hamish that she was desirable to others if not to him. She would have done better with the besotted Guards officer, no matter how dull she thought him, for in the event Peter Rodd, or 'Prod', as he quickly became known to the Mitfords, proved a poor provider in all departments.

His reputation at the time was poor anyway. At Oxford he

regarded college rules as being for everyone but himself, and he was eventually sacked from Balliol for entertaining women in his rooms after hours. While travelling in Brazil he had worked at a succession of jobs, in banking and journalism, found for him by his father, the multi-talented diplomat Baron Rennell. An arrogant and pedantic know-it-all, Prod had either been dismissed or resigned in the nick of time from all of them. He ended up destitute, and under arrest, and had to be bailed out by his unfortunate father. On the credit side he could be amusing, was undeniably clever, and certainly good-looking. According to one biographer, he preferred to admire his talents as works of art, rather than use them, and he spent his life avoiding making achievements that were well within his grasp. Perhaps his character was best captured by Evelyn Waugh who used him as the model for his comic fictional hero Basil Seal.[13]

Prod was willing to go through with his commitment to Nancy, but for her it was a classic rebound situation: she could not perceive his faults through her rose-tinted delight. David, who lunched his prospective son-in-law at Rutland Gate while the requisite paternal permission was sought, announced that 'the fella talks like a ferret with his mouth sewn up' but he agreed to the marriage anyway. By now even he had begun to grasp that, as far as his elder daughters were concerned, his edicts had little effect.

Prod spent a week at Swinbrook, talking until the family reeled with boredom. No matter what subject was brought up, it seemed he was the world expert. 'I know, I know,' he would interrupt. 'I know, I *was* an engineer and I . . .' or 'I know, I know, I *am* a farmer . . .' The sisters swore he once said, 'I know, I know, I *am* the Pope . . .' One of his lectures, delivered to the haplessly captive Decca and Debo, was a detailed account of the tollgate system in the eighteenth and nineteenth centuries. Their dazed reaction can be imagined, and from then they referred to him as 'the old Toll-Gater',[14] which Nancy inevitably converted into a *bon mot*: 'For whom the Gate Tolls . . .'

Almost overnight the tone of Nancy's letters changed from misery to sheer delight as she began the customary visits to introduce herself to members of her fiancé's family. 'Well, the happiness. Oh goodness gracious I am happy. You *must* get married darling,' she advised Mark Ogilvie-Grant, writing from Highcliffe Castle, Hampshire, which was the home of one of Peter's aunts.[15] 'Everybody should this minute if they want a receipt for absolute bliss . . . *And remember true love can't be bought.* If I really thought it could I'd willingly send you £3 tomorrow.'[16] Prod, too, wrote letters expressing his happiness, to Nancy herself, and to Hamish, apologizing for taking Nancy away from him. It was a polite fiction between friends. 'I know it is hell for you and I wish it wasn't [but] I am so much in love with her that I can understand how you feel.'[17]

Pre-wedding activity now absorbed the Mitford household for the marriage, originally planned for October but eventually held on 4 December at St John's Church in Smith Square, with Diana's two small sons as pages.

While Nancy had been switching fiancés, and the scandal of the Guinness divorce was on everyone's lips, tragedy had befallen the house of Mosley. In April 1933 Mosley and Cimmie had gone to Rome where he played a major role in a huge rally during which the Italian Fascist Party presented him with a black banner containing the Union Flag and Fascist symbols as the BUF standard. The couple returned at the end of April and Mosley immediately resumed his visits to Diana. Absolute discretion was essential. Bryan had 'behaved like a gentleman' and offered fake evidence of infidelity so that Diana would not have to appear in court, but with the proceedings in the offing it was imperative that the department of the King's Proctor was given no evidence to indicate 'collusion'. 'The King's Proctor haunted us all,' Diana wrote. If there was any suspicion that the divorce was 'arranged' the courts were obliged to deny the petition; and even in the year after a divorce was granted, evidence of an affair by the petitioner could make the divorce invalid. Under cover of darkness Mosley could walk the short distance between his Ebury Street flat and Diana's house in Eaton Square in about five minutes. When he tapped on her windows with the walking-stick he had carried since the flying accident in 1918, she would be waiting to let him in.

During the first weekend in May Mosley went to his country property, Savehay Farm in Denham, Buckinghamshire, where he had arranged to spend the weekend with Cimmie. On the Saturday night they had a terrific row about Diana, and Mosley slammed out of the house. Cimmie spent the night crying, which was not unusual for her at that time. The following morning, she wrote to Mosley, apologizing for behaving unreasonably to him, and explaining that she had been feeling particularly unwell 'with sickness, and crashing back and tummy pain'.[18] Later that day, within a few days of the Mosleys' thirteenth wedding anniversary, Cimmie was rushed into hospital with a perforated appendix. She was operated on and Mosley dashed to her side. This did not, however, prevent him going straight from the clinic to the Eatonry that night. Appendicitis was not in itself considered dangerous, but in the days before antibiotics there was always a risk of infection, and within three days it was clear that Cimmie was critically ill with peritonitis. The doctors felt that if she fought hard she might win through, but on 15 May she died at the age of thirty-three, without, her surgeon announced, 'both mentally or physically ever lifting a finger to live'.[19]

It was a devastating blow to all concerned, and Mosley, who had unquestionably loved his wife, according to his lights, spent 'hours and hours' sitting by her flower-bedecked coffin. When it was removed to the chapel at Cliveden, home of Nancy Astor, who had befriended the young Cimmie (whose own mother had died when she was eight),[20] Mosley spent hours pacing endlessly about at their home in Denham, in the garden Cimmie had created. Cimmie's two sisters were so concerned about his demeanour that they had his revolver removed from his bedroom and hidden from him. They knew that when Mosley had walked out after the row on that last Saturday night before Cimmie was taken ill he had gone straight to Diana Guinness. 'God, what a terrible doom for Tom [Mosley]!' Cimmie's elder sister, Irene Ravensdale, wrote in her diary. 'And to think that Cim has gone and that Guinness is free and alive . . . where is any balance of justice!'[21] Upon one matter, Mosley was absolutely insistent: his three children must have no further changes in their lives. They must continue to live at Savehay, the old house at Denham that Cimmie had decorated to her taste, surrounded by the same nursery staff, himself, their grandmother and aunts. It was the best he could do to give them a sense of security.[22]

For Diana, of course, it seemed like absolute disaster. She had not disliked Cimmie, and had certainly not wished her ill. She knew that Mosley had had affairs with at least a dozen women before her, and she had supposed that Cimmie accepted his behaviour. Now, with the papers full of eulogies for Cimmie, opinion hardened against Diana. Plenty of people gossiped that Cimmie had died of a broken heart, rather than infection. From being the darling of Society a year earlier Diana became a social pariah, as her parents had foretold.

She saw Mosley only for very short periods. Several times a week he would drive to London in the early evening from Denham and be back there by 1 a.m. 'Who could it be but Diana Guinness?' Irene Ravensdale wrote in her diary. 'Baba and I were sick with terror.'[23] The sisters could see that Mosley was genuinely ill with grief, that he was doing his best to be a good father to the children and was always sweet with them. But, equally, they thought it hurtful to Cimmie's memory that Mosley should wish to go on seeing Diana at such a time. How could they know, since he did not tell them, that his relationship with her (they referred to Diana as 'the horror' between themselves) was any different from those he had shared with other women in the past? They bearded him about it and he told them frankly that he felt he had an obligation to Diana and he could not 'shirk' it. They saw danger signals, too, in that Unity had recently joined the BUF and was keen to become a serious activist. They suspected that in some way Unity was spying on Mosley on Diana's behalf. With the summer just beginning it was decided between them all that Irene would take the two elder children on holiday, the baby, only a year old, would go with Nanny to the Isle of Wight, and Baba, having cleared it with her husband 'Fruity' Metcalfe, would accompany Mosley on a motoring trip in France.

One evening Mosley visited Diana at her request. Afterwards, according to Irene Ravensdale's diaries, he told his sisters-in-law that he had asked Diana, referring to the divorce proceedings, 'Have you jumped your little hurdle yet?' She had been wounded that he should take so lightly the enormous sacrifice she had made, crying, 'It's my whole life!'[24] There was a terrible row, he reported, and he left after telling her that he was going on holiday to France with Baba. Diana refutes this. 'He did not say, "Have you jumped your hurdle?" Nor did I say, "It's my whole life." We always understood each other perfectly.'[25] It appears, then, that either Mosley or Irene Ravensdale invented the incident. Nevertheless, Diana cannot have been happy to hear that Mosley was going on an extended holiday with Baba and it is probable that hot words were exchanged.

All this had occurred between Cimmie's death and the gathering of the elder Mitford sisters at Diana's house a month later, on 14 June, on the eve of the divorce hearing, when Hamish told Nancy of his fake engagement. If ever Diana had been in need of sisterly support it was then. She was just twenty-two with two small children. At a time when she might have reasonably expected strong support from the man for whom she had broken up her marriage, he was involved with his own crisis and was available only occasionally. Worse, she had just learned that he was going on holiday with another woman. Although she is too loyal to Mosley to have ever said so, she must have felt utterly alone and defenceless. One or two friends, having overcome their initial disapproval, had begun to invite her to dinner parties, and mutual friends told Cimmie's sisters that Diana was looking grim, with her face 'dead-white'.[26]

Perhaps Diana already suspected that Mosley's interest in Baba was more than platonic or strictly familial for, astonishingly, Mosley began a long-standing affair with her that summer. It was an open secret within the family: Irene Ravensdale, who had enjoyed a brief, unimportant romp with Mosley before his marriage to her sister, wrote, 'I pray this obsession with her will utterly oust Diana Guinness.'[27] With hindsight Diana says she did not mind about Mosley's affair with Baba, because 'I was somehow always confident that he would come back to me', though she admits to periods of jealousy.[28] At the time, however, she was more deeply in love with Mosley than ever, and though she and Mosley quickly patched up their quarrel, it must have been a difficult period for her. One surprising thing happened: through Unity Diana was advised that she might visit Swinbrook for the weekend of 6 June. She and Unity spent most of the time sitting in the garden for David refused to speak to her, but it was 'the thin end of the wedge' in his parlance.

In the following week Unity was admitted to the BUF as a member, and she was thrilled to receive, on that eventful day of 14 June from the hands of 'the Leader' himself, a BUF coat badge, which Mosley removed from his own lapel. Her membership was known to her siblings and to others outside the family, but was kept secret from David and Sydney.

What of Decca and Debo during this turbulent period? They

were living quietly at Swinbrook doing much the same things that the four elder sisters had done, with perhaps a little more freedom, although never enough for Decca. Still, the rebellious unhappiness that she details in her memoir is nowhere in evidence in her contemporary correspondence. Nor did her friends regard her as unhappy. One, who met her for the first time in 1932, was fourteen, about a year older than Decca, when he was taken to Swinbrook by his mother so that she could discuss Women's Institute matters with Sydney.

> I sat quietly and covertly looked about me while the ladies talked [he recalled]. Then the door opened and with what seemed a single swift movement Jessica was in the room, closing the door behind her, standing straight, feet together, smiling. She was wearing a print frock and a black patent leather belt tight to the waist. Her brown hair was short and thick. Her eyes full of amusement, and also friendliness, as they took me in. She shook hands, and sat down, feet together, back straight, the very picture of *une jeune fille parfaitement bien élevée*, but with such an expression of intelligence and humour as I had rarely seen in a girl her age . . . Decca at that time would have been thought of as a child by most elders . . . nevertheless there was nothing childish about her, in any sense implying weakness or silliness or inability to hold her own in her own world. That first summer afternoon I swiftly came to know that my first impression of originality had been quite correct; here was a spirit both lively and adventurous, a keen mind fed by a highly varied diet of reading, a sparkling sense of humour and all allied to a delicious appearance . . .[29]

If Decca had been as deeply unhappy as she claims, it was never obvious to her new friend. It seems more likely that the discontent with her life at home was something that flowered in the years that followed and was so traumatic that it coloured all her early memories.

As Mosley was touring in France with Baba, Diana decided to go to Europe that summer on holiday too. Unity asked if she could go with her, rather hoping, she confessed later, that Diana would choose to go to Italy or France. But Diana chose Bavaria, partly because Tom was there and spoke so glowingly about it, and partly because she wanted to find out more about the regime, especially about the new German chancellor, Adolf Hitler, in whose activities the newspapers took such an interest.

In the immediate aftermath of Hitler coming to power there were outbreaks of violence against anyone who had opposed his election, or who 'did not fit' an accepted profile. Those rounded up were imprisoned in hastily erected concentration camps such as Dachau outside Munich. Then the camps resembled conventional prisons rather than the places of systematic murder they became less than a decade later. The improvements in the German economy were the envy of other European governments and most people accepted the unpleasantness – extreme as it was – as an almost inevitable cost of a new, radical regime.

Although Germany had not been her first choice, Unity was immediately mad keen on Diana's proposal. She was just nineteen and with her increasing interest in the BUF she wanted to see for herself how the system worked. Unity was not yet wholly committed to Fascism – indeed, John Betjeman, who knew her reasonably well, thought she was more interested in film stars and the cinema. But that trip to Germany, Diana wrote in her autobiography, unquestionably 'changed Unity's life'.[30] The streak of obsessive behaviour in Unity's character, which might have made her ultra-religious had she leaned towards the Church, fastened instead on Nazism.

Earlier in the year, before Cimmie's death and her divorce, Diana had met a German called Putzi Hanfstaengl at the house of one of Bryan's relations. Hanfstaengl was the Harvard-educated son of a rich Munich family of art dealers, and an old friend of Hitler. When the National Socialist putsch of 1923 failed, Hitler was wounded and several of his comrades-in-arms were killed. Hanfstaengl took Hitler into his home and hid him for a while, and after Hitler's arrest he continued to support him throughout the two years of imprisonment that followed, during which Hitler wrote *Mein Kampf.* In the period of political wilderness after Hitler's release, Hanfstaengl remained loyal to his friend, and when things improved he obtained hard currency from the United States (his family had a gallery in New York) to help fund Hitler's return to politics. His donation of a thousand US dollars during the financial chaos of Germany's years of hyperinflation was a lifesaver to Hitler, so it is not surprising that when the Nazis came to power Hanfstaengl was rewarded with a senior appointment as Hitler's public relations adviser, and he made it clear that he worshipped the Führer.

At the party where Diana first met him, Hanfstaengl was annoyed. All one read about Germany in the English newspapers, he complained, was of the regime's attitude towards the Jews. 'People here have no idea of what the Jewish problem has been since the war,' he told his listeners hotly. 'Why not think of the ninety-nine per cent of the population, of the six million unemployed? Hitler will build a great and prosperous Germany for the Germans. If the Jews don't like it they can get out.'[31] Recalling this meeting, Diana was certain that if she called on Hanfstaengl in Munich, he would introduce them to Hitler, but at first the trip consisted of sightseeing with some of Tom's friends. Eventually, however, Diana made contact with Hanfstaengl.

He was hospitable, providing the two young women unexpectedly with tickets to privileged seats for the first Parteitag in Nuremberg, and finding them scarcely obtainable accommodation near by. The rally, which began on 31 August and lasted four days, had a major effect on both young women. The carnival atmosphere was vibrant with enthusiasm as crowds milled about and revelled to the sounds of oompah-bands playing old favourites along with regular insertions of the popular '*Horst Wessel Lied*' that had become the Nazi anthem. Some four hundred thousand people attended the event. 'The old town was a fantastic sight,' Diana wrote. 'Hundreds of thousands of men in party uniforms thronged the streets and there were flags in all the windows . . . the gigantic parades went without a hitch. A feeling of excited triumph was in the air, and when Hitler appeared an almost electric shock passed through the multitude.' It was, she decided, 'a demonstration of hope in a nation that had known collective despair'.[32]

It was difficult for those present not to be emotionally affected and, indeed, Diana and Unity were not the only visitors impressed by the showmanship of Hitler's party. Many young Englishmen who visited Germany in the first part of that decade were moved to support Hitler's regime, even though later some came to despise it. In a recent television documentary examining the attraction of Hitler to the youth of Europe at that time, Nigel Nicholson was just one who stated that he was thoroughly hooked: 'The catchy "*Horst Wessel*" song, the marching, the torches, the singing and tramping of boots – I *was*, at that moment, a Hitler youth,' he said. Michael Burn was another: 'I wrote home, "I cannot think coherently – it is so wonderful what Hitler has brought this country back to . . ."' He recalls that he was 'stunned and excited by the cohesion of Germany after the political disunion in Britain. Then there was the theatre of Nuremberg: 'great lights in the sky, moving music, the rhetoric, the presentation, timing, performance, soundtrack, exultation and climax. It was almost aimed at the sexual parts of one's consciousness.'[33] Over the years that followed most of these young people recognized the true nature of the Nazi movement and defected from it, becoming leaders in the wartime fight against

Hitler, but for the moment all they felt was excitement and admiration. For Diana and Unity the only regret of the holiday was that they did not meet Hitler in person. Although with their blonde, tall, slim appearance they were the physical personification of Arian womanhood, Hanfstaengl told them that he did not dare to introduce them as they wore so much lipstick, which Hitler abhorred. They were used to this; Farve felt much the same way.[34]

When they returned to England Diana had to face her father's anger: she was still in semi-disgrace over her divorce, and when Unity gaily told them about the Parteitag David erupted. 'I suppose you know without being told,' he wrote to Diana, 'how absolutely horrified Muv and I were to think of you and Bobo accepting any form of hospitality from people we regard as a murderous gang of pests. That you should associate yourself with such people is a source of utter misery to both of us – but of course, beyond telling you this . . . we can do nothing. What we can do, and what we intend to do, is to try to keep Bobo out of it all.'[35]

Mosley was still touring France and the children were staying at Biddesden with Bryan, so Diana left almost immediately for Rome where she spent six weeks at the luxurious house overlooking the Forum, owned by her great friend Lord Berners. Gerald Berners, a homosexual, was a quintessential eccentric; had he possessed no talent at all, he was rich enough to indulge himself as a dabbler in the aesthetic disciplines he so enjoyed, but he was also clever and exceptionally well read, an able musician, composer, artist and writer. He had been posted to Rome as a junior diplomat but while Diana was there he seemed to spend more time working on the score for a Diaghilev ballet. Nancy would later use him as the model for her colourful character Lord Merlin in *The Pursuit of Love*, a compliment that Berners rather enjoyed. At his country home, Faringdon, he kept a flock of doves, which he dyed in pastel shades so that when they rose into the sky it looked as though someone had flung a handful of confetti over the rooftop, a pretty nonsense amusingly described by Nancy. Berners was one of the few friends who accepted Diana's decision to divorce Bryan without critical comment, and Diana valued him because he was clever, witty and made her laugh – a quality that was especially welcome at that time – but also because he was her mentor: she once said that her relationship with Berners had been the equivalent of reading arts at university.

A sense of humour is an ethereal quality that is difficult to describe but Diana explained Berners' wit beautifully. She wrote of how, when they drove back to England together in October, they stopped over in Paris where they met Violet Trefusis, notorious as the lover of Vita Sackville-West. Her mother was Mrs Keppel, the favourite of King Edward VII. Violet and Berners decided to pretend they were engaged and in November this was announced in London gossip columns to the astonishment, presumably, of everyone who knew either of them. Violet phoned him to say she had had dozens of congratulations. Berners was delighted; he had received none, he said. When Mrs Keppel insisted that a denial must be made as the joke had gone far enough, he suggested announcing in *The Times*: 'Lord Berners has left Lesbos for the Isle of Man.'[36]

Unity passed the time at Swinbrook working at her collages and painting, and, unknown to her parents, made regular trips into Oxford where she dropped in at the BUF offices and helped to sell copies of the *Blackshirt*. By comparison Nancy's innocent tea parties with undergraduate friends in Oxford cafés, which had provoked David's fury a decade earlier, seem tame. Sydney saw to it that Unity did the Season again, so that her social life continued as it had during her débutante year. But whenever she was in London during the run-up to Nancy's wedding, or during secret visits to the Eatonry after Diana's return, Unity attended BUF rallies or Mosley's meetings, proudly sporting a black shirt and her unusual badge, which identified her as someone special in the party ranks. At Swinbrook visitors during that period report that hardly had they set foot in the entrance hall before they were besieged by Unity and Decca demanding, 'Are you a Fascist or a Communist?' When one young man answered, 'Neither, I'm a democrat,' they retorted in unison, 'How wet!' and lost interest in him.[37]

Unity was not alone in attending Mosley's meetings: the elder sisters all turned up occasionally, out of loyalty to Diana if nothing else, but they were all interested to a greater or lesser degree in politics. In November Nancy wrote to Diana about a meeting in Oxfordshire, within striking distance of Swinbrook, so of course she and Unity found a way of attending. 'T.P.O.L.'s [the Poor Old Leader's] meeting was fascinating, but awful for him, as the hall was full of Oxfordshire Conservatives who sat in hostile and phlegmatic silence – you can imagine what they were like. I think he is a wonderful speaker & of course he is better still with a more interesting audience . . .'[38] Even Pam attended one or two meetings, but there is no record of her opinions.

Although Diana would never construe it in such a light, her long uncomplaining absence during that summer and autumn brought Mosley to heel. When he became ill that winter with phlebitis, from which he had suffered previously, he was advised to spend some time in a warmer climate. After Nancy's wedding, following which the newly-weds went to Rome for their honeymoon, Mosley asked Diana to accompany him to Provence where they lived near Grasse in a rented house for a month or so at the beginning of 1934. Despite his illness, they were happy. It was the first time they had been free to be together without attracting disapproving looks or worrying about the King's Proctor, or lectures from friends and family. Although Diana was now in touch with her parents again, they regarded Mosley as 'that man' and it was tacitly understood that he was not to be introduced into the conversation. David even went so far as to write Mosley's name on a slip of paper and lock it away in a drawer: he believed strongly that this practice would bring an enemy to grief.

In the meantime, Decca finally achieved a taste of the freedom for which she so longed. In the autumn of 1933 Sydney arranged for her and Cousin Idden to spend the customary year abroad – a year in Paris to be 'finished' and improve their French before their coming-out year. Sydney took them to France to settle them in but while she was with them the girls' hearts were in their mouths as they attracted admiring glances from young men, even the odd pinch (and once in the cinema, a groper, but Decca made sure Sydney did not find out for fear she would refuse to leave them). Sydney, more used to English restraint in ogling, was irritated at the attention the girls attracted and with Diana's experience still fresh in her mind made cross little threats every now and again: 'If this continues I shall have to take you both home.' At last, to Decca's heartfelt relief, she left them and went on a short cruise, before returning home to see Nancy married to Peter Rodd.[39]

A few weeks later there was some rioting on the streets but it died down quickly, too quickly for Decca who found it rather diverting. Nor was she especially sorry that she missed Nancy's wedding for there had been a coolness between her and Nancy since the latter had joined with Mrs Hammersley in teasing her about being 'a ballroom Communist, a cut below a parlour pink'.[40] The truth stung, for the closest Decca had been able to get to Communism before her departure for Paris had been on those occasions when she had slipped away from Nanny during a walk in the park. Then she was able to join the groups gathered round the Communist orators at Hyde Park's Speaker's Corner, which inevitably included a stirring rendering of the anthem 'The Internationale' and an opportunity to demonstrate solidarity with the clenched-fist salute.

In Paris, free of parental control for the first time in her life,

Decca had no intention of behaving herself in the way her mother expected – nor, probably, would many teenagers in those circumstances. On the other hand, she was careful in her letters home to be circumspect and she did not repeat Diana's mistake in keeping an incriminating diary. She told Sydney as little as possible about the riots, but quoted a good deal from the Communist newspaper *L'humanité*.[41] In the evenings, telling Madame, their guardian – who seems not to have cared much what they did – that they were going to the opera, they visited picture-houses, nightclubs and even the Folies Bergères with various boys, and accepted numerous invitations to dinner. Decca 'fell in love' with a married man called Émile, who was too passionate for her comfort, but the relationship soon ended with no harm done. Idden fell in love with a poet called Maurice and smuggled him into their room, causing Decca to worry that they might throw her out.[42] In the event he was too shy even to kiss Idden so that relationship did not last either. For one date with a much older man Decca wore a tight satin suit, the chief attraction of which was that she knew Sydney would not have approved of it. After dinner, instead of going on to a nightclub as Decca expected, her companion steered her to a bordello. She pretended nervously that this was all quite normal for her, but when he showed her a salon '*pour les sadistes*' she felt anxious and Nanny's warnings came back to her. She could almost *hear* Sydney say, in a dampening manner, 'Not at *all* a nice place, Jessica, I shouldn't think,' and after a brief struggle with her companion, she made a hasty exit. It was all very daring and even though they were still attending school (the Sorbonne) – which in itself was *wonderful* – Decca felt very much a woman of the world and even her handwriting, which had formerly been the neat, stylized script of the schoolroom, changed into the hasty scrawl that characterized her letters for the rest of her life.

The two girls went home for Christmas, and during the holidays Unity began a determined campaign to persuade her parents to let her spend her 'year abroad' in Germany. All the other sisters had gone to France to polish up their French, which Unity had refused to consider. Her trip with Diana in the previous year, though, had made her want to learn German, she said, as Tom had, and she wanted to go to finishing-school in Munich. Since Sydney had spent some years trying to get Unity interested in anything, one can only sympathize with what she probably regarded as a new and positive attitude in this lovable but difficult daughter. She did some investigation and learned of a Baroness Laroche who had a house at 121 Königinstrasse, which operated as a sort of informal finishing-school where English girls could study German under a governess. Mary St Clair Erskine, sister of Hamish, and other English girls of 'the right sort' from families known to Sydney, had stayed with the Baroness. Sydney therefore approved her daughter's request.

Looking back, it seems that 1933 was a pivotal year for the Mitford family. By the start of 1934 Sydney probably believed that the worst of their problems were now behind them. Although she and David still disapproved of Diana's affair with Mosley, the initial scandal, which had caused them extreme distress and embarrassment, seemed to have died down. Nancy was married and wrote home of her ecstatic happiness; Decca was successfully established at school in Paris and would come out at the end of the year. Tom, who never gave any trouble, had recently qualified in law; Pam was still working at Biddesden for Bryan. Only Debo, a reasonably contented child apart from an occasional adolescent outburst, was still in the schoolroom at Swinbrook. Miss Hussey had given a term's notice and Sydney reasoned that it might be easier to send Debo to school for a year rather than recruit a new governess. Even Unity had found an interest.

No one could have foreseen the tragedy that resulted from the Redesdales' decision to allow Unity to go to Germany.

8

UNITY AND THE FÜHRER

(1934–5)

In the spring of 1934 the Rodds, back from their honeymoon,
attended several BUF rallies, and even bought black shirts. 'Prod
looked very pretty in his black shirt,' Nancy wrote years later to
Evelyn Waugh, 'but we were younger and high-spirited then and
didn't know about Buchenwald.'[1] Prod had flirted briefly with
Fascism at Oxford, before transferring his political allegiance to
the Labour Party, and for a few months early in their marriage he
and Nancy supported Mosley's movement by paying a subscrip-
tion. With hindsight, however, and bearing in mind Nancy's
lifelong support of socialism, it is more likely that they were
actually supporting Diana, though they must have been interested in hearing what Mosley had to say. Equally importantly,
Nancy was gathering material for another book. Later that year,
from her small house at Chiswick, she began working on *Wigs on
the Green*, probably the least known of her novels. This time the
leading character was Unity. One cannot say it was 'Unity to the
life' because Nancy's characters were always larger than life,
unmerciful caricatures, but it was clearly Unity to everyone who
knew her, despite Nancy's disclaimer that 'all characters in this
book are drawn from the author's imagination'.[2]

'BRITONS, awake! Arise! Oh, British lion!' cried Eugenia
Malmains in thrilling tones. She stood on an overturned
wash-tub on Chalford village green and harangued about
a dozen aged yokels. Her straight hair, cut in a fringe,
large pale-blue eyes . . . well-proportioned limbs and
classical features, combined with a certain fanaticism of
gesture to give her the aspect of a modern Joan of Arc . . .[3]

This was guaranteed to make the sisters, at least, scream with
laughter, for to their merriment, and to the astonishment of the
postmistress, Unity had taken to appearing in Swinbrook's only
shop (Chalford *was* Swinbrook to the life) and throwing up her
hand in a smart Nazi salute before ordering a twopenny chocolate bar.

'The Union Jack Movement is a youth movement,'
Eugenia cried passionately, 'we are tired of the old . . . We
see nothing admirable in that debating society of aged and
corrupt men called Parliament which muddies our great
empire into wars or treaties . . . casting away its glorious
colonies . . . And all according to each vacillating whim of
some octogenarian statesman's mistress—'
   At this point a very old lady came up to the crowd . . .
'Eugenia, my child,' she said brokenly. 'Do get off that
tub . . . Oh! When her ladyship hears of this I don't know
what will happen.'
   'Go away, Nanny,' said Eugenia . . . The old lady again
plucked at Eugenia's skirt. This time, however, Eugenia
turned and roared at her, 'Get out you filthy Pacifist, get
out and take your yellow razor gang with you.'

It was all there, TPOM and TPOF, the insults that Decca and
Unity hurled at each other in pseudo-earnestness, a brilliant
parody of the BUF anthem sung to the tune of '*Deutschland,*

Deutschland Über Alles'; and sly little digs at Fascism. '"I really don't quite know what an Aryan is." "Well, it's quite easy. A non-Aryan is the missing link between man and beast. That can be proved by the fact that no animals, except the Baltic goose, have blue eyes . . ."'[4]

When Decca came home from Paris for the Easter break she was fascinated to hear the grown-ups tut-tutting about the latest prank of one of the unacceptable Romilly cousins, Esmond. A year younger than Decca he had run away from Wellington College where he had been running a left-wing magazine called *Out of Bounds* and because of his relationship to Winston Churchill the newspapers were on to it. 'Mr Churchill's 15 year old Nephew Vanishes' ran a typical headline; others referred to him more luridly as 'Churchill's Red Nephew'. It was said that he was under the influence of a group of London Communists, but his mother told reporters coolly, 'We are not worried about his safety. We have a good idea where he is . . .'[5] There was a great deal of family sympathy for his parents for having to put up with such appalling behaviour, but Sydney blamed Nellie for it.

Listening to the conversation of the grown-ups, Decca thrilled to the exploits of this swashbuckling cousin whom she'd never been allowed to meet, although once she had missed him by only days, when she had gone to stay at Chartwell and found the Churchill nannies agog with stories of his wickedness. In the previous autumn, while she was settling herself in Paris, Esmond had declared himself a pacifist and had wrecked the Armistice service in the school's chapel by inserting pacifist leaflets in the prayer books. Diana has sometimes been held responsible for indirectly setting Decca on a left-wing path, by steering Unity towards her right-wing allegiance. But it was Nancy who was the biggest influence in Decca's life. 'Watching her,' Decca wrote, 'all through her engagement to Hamish, and [seeing] how she loathed Swinbrook and longed to be free of Muv etc, *her* fate — to be stuck in that life because she hadn't any way of escape being without money even after she started writing – was a huge influence on me, then and ever [afterwards].'[6] She was determined not to be stuck at home like Nancy, obliged to marry to escape.

There was one last sitting for the annual family photograph taken in front of the house, with everyone in their usual position, Unity with Ratular on her shoulder, Diana, Debo and Nancy clutching dogs, David looking handsomely serious with his thick hair now turning white, Sydney expressionless but revealing that the girls took their beauty from both sides of the family, and Tom in a bright lumber jacket. It was the last time they would all gather like this for a ritual photograph. Then Sydney departed, taking with her Decca, Idden and Unity. Decca and Idden were about to embark on their final term at the Sorbonne, but before leaving them Sydney spoke firmly with Madame Paulain, making it clear that her daughter and niece required their bedlinen to be changed more often than once every three weeks. Then she departed with Unity for Munich, to oversee the settling-in process at Baroness Laroche's.

The Baroness, whom Diana remembers as a charming woman, took her girls *en pension*. They joined her for lunch and dinner at which the food was always delicious, and all conversation was conducted in German.[7] They were given formal German lessons by a governess, Frau Baum, and when Unity made her first appearance in May she had already missed the first few. She wore her black shirt and BUF badge to classes but these emblems had no power to shock as they did in England as Nazi emblems were common everywhere. Her fellow students were a year or two younger than Unity, and were being 'finished' prior to coming out. Indeed, one or two were already discreetly dating young 'storms', as they called the storm-troopers. Because she was already out Unity did not have to attend the deportment classes, but she did not waste her free time; she worked hard at her German for she had a good incentive to do so. Within weeks of her arrival she had conceived a plan, and begun what was to be her daily programme for the next year or so. She discovered from Frau Baum, a keen Hitler supporter, that Hitler sometimes took lunch in a restaurant called Osteria Bavaria. Unity's objective was to meet him, but she had discovered that to communicate with him she would need to speak German for he spoke no English. So she concentrated on her studies, and made a few exploratory sorties to the Osteria, and to the Carlton tearooms, which Hitler also patronized.

In June, she finally got to see him. Derek Hill, a young English painter who was visiting Munich, was an old friend of Unity and was in the Carlton tearooms one evening with his mother and aunt when the Führer arrived. There was no pomp when he attended a restaurant, except that he was always accompanied by several henchmen, or members of his inner circle, and the inevitable bodyguard. The party simply came in unannounced and sat down quietly, keeping themselves to themselves. Derek Hill immediately phoned Unity, who jumped into a taxi and sped to the tearoom. 'I went and sat down with them [the Hill party] and there was the Führer opposite,' she wrote to Diana. Hill noticed that Unity was trembling so violently with excitement that he had to steady her cup.

Three weeks after Unity's first sighting of Hitler the Night of the Long Knives took place, when Ernst Roehm and over a hundred officers of the brown-shirted SA (Sturm Abteilungen, storm-troopers) were brutally assassinated on Hitler's orders. Some were shot on their front doorsteps, others were formally executed or hacked to death in secret, some – thinking the attack was part of an anti-Hitler plot – died screaming, 'Heil, Hitler.' Like many of those killed, Roehm had been an old comrade of Hitler's since before the 1923 putsch and had helped him to power. But the SA had been a problem for some time, with Roehm refusing to accept Hitler's right to give direct orders to SA troops. It seems unlikely that he was guilty of plotting against

Hitler, as was claimed at the time, but was disposed of because he posed a threat to the more disciplined black-shirted SS (Schutz Staffeln, Protection Squad) troops, whose leader, Heinrich Himmler, made his rival's death the price of future co-operation. Hitler called personally on his former friend to arrest him, saying that he alone could arrest a chief of staff. Unity wrote breathlessly to Diana about the massacre, which had shocked Munich burghers to the core.

> I am terribly sorry for the Führer – you know Roehm was his oldest friend and comrade, the only one that called him 'du' in public . . . it must have been so dreadful for Hitler when he arrested Roehm himself and tore off his decorations. Then he went to arrest Heines[8] and found him in bed with a boy. Did that get into the English papers? Poor Hitler.[9]

The words said to have been used by Hitler when he arrested his old friend became a catchphrase among the girls at Baroness Laroche's, '*Schuft, du bist verhaftet* [Wretch, you are under lock and key],' but Unity was unable to see the funny side of this, and was upset that her beloved Führer had been in danger.[10]

It was a subtly changed Unity who returned to Swinbrook for the summer. Photographs show that she had a poise and a singular beauty, where since the age of thirteen she had merely looked fair and awkward. She and Decca squabbled as usual about politics, but they were loving squabbles, and they sat down cheerfully afterwards to discuss what they would do should either of them be placed in a position where they had to give orders for the execution of the other. Only one thing marred Unity's summer: she received a postcard from Tom, who, having grown up with six sisters, had learned a thing or two about teasing. He was in Bayreuth, he wrote, and he had been invited to supper with Hitler and Goering. She believed him and was miserably jealous for days, until she heard that it was untrue. But she was so enthusiastic about her life in Munich that Sydney decided to take Decca and Idden there for a short holiday in September after the beginning of Unity's autumn term.

Unity went back early, in August, so that she could attend the 1934 Parteitag and Diana joined her there a few weeks later. Putzi Hanfstaengl refused to help them, saying that their excessive make-up embarrassed him and, besides, there was not a ticket to be had for the rally. If they went to Nuremberg, he warned, they would find every bed reserved and would end up spending their nights sitting in the railway station. The sisters decided to go anyway and found it, just as he had predicted, crammed. They sat in a café and Unity was thrilled simply to be there. '*Do* be glad we came,' she kept repeating happily to Diana. But luck was with them: an old man with whom they shared a table in a beer garden was wearing an unusual emblem. Unity engaged him in conversation, curious about his badge, and it turned out that he was one of the first members of the Nazi Party and his card bore the number 100. It entitled him to various privileges and, impressed with the enthusiasm of the English girls, he arranged accommodation and passes to the stadium for them.

Diana's motive for visiting Germany at this point was not simply to attend the Parteitag. She had already begun to do what Professor Lindemann had suggested and was learning to speak German. It was not possible for her to be away from Mosley or her two boys[11] for extended periods, to learn as Unity was learning, so she took some Berlitz courses in London and was now looking to improve on this base. She enrolled in a short course at the university run for foreigners, due to begin in November, and returned home in the meantime. In November she moved into a flat that Unity had found just off the Ludwigstrasse. It was full of Biedermayer furniture, centrally heated and the rent included a good cook. Unity was no longer staying with the Baroness and had taken a room at a hostel, a *Studentheim*, for women university students, which she always referred to as 'the heim'. She left it and moved in with Diana.[12]

With the help of Putzi Hanfstaengl Diana obtained a press card, which enabled the sisters to get into meetings at which Hitler was to speak. Whenever her classes allowed she joined Unity at the Osteria. Otherwise Unity went there alone. Initially she persuaded friends to accompany her, but after a while she was content to eat a light lunch on her own and read a book to pass the long hours of waiting. She was rewarded and saw Hitler on a number of occasions, which was always a terrific thrill for her. When she was not waiting for Hitler she and Diana were fond of visiting the Pinakothek (Munich's Museum of Art, now the Alte Pinakothek, one of the leading art galleries in the world), the palaces, museums and parks such as the Englischer Garten, and they wandered around the old and new parts of the city, the 'new' parts designed by King Ludwig I over a century earlier in the neo-classic style. Ludwig bankrupted himself and the city to bring about his ideals, and eventually lost his throne because of his affair with the dancer Lola Montez. Diana had enjoyed the city in the summer, but found it just as attractive in the winter: its proximity to the mountains made it possible for many of its citizens to be on the ski slopes in under an hour, and at weekends there was almost a holiday atmosphere. 'The icy air out of doors had a special smell so that had one been set down there blindfold one would have known at once it was Munich. Possibly the smell was of brewing, combined with the little cigars the men smoked.'[13]

But whatever they did their timetable was subject to any possibility of seeing or hearing Hitler. The two young women have been referred to in recent years, crudely, as 'Hitler groupies' and because of what Hitler subsequently became those who admired him were inevitably to be reviled. Then, however, he was not universally regarded as a monster, but as a statesman in whom *everyone* was interested, leading an administration with a new and radical form of government that appeared to be working well. Few intelligent English visitors to Germany in the thirties would have turned down an opportunity to see or speak to Hitler. Numerous visitors who would become pillars of the British establishment or distinguished in the fields of literature, art, entertainment and politics tried every possible method to meet him, including courting Unity and Diana when it was known that they had access to him. And Diana, because of her allegiance to Mosley and the British Fascist movement, had reason to be more interested than most.

In September Sydney, Decca and Idden joined Unity. It was Sydney's first visit to Germany and she wanted to see things for herself, and also to try to moderate Unity's passionate enthusiasm. She was agreeably surprised to find, instead of the heavy, dark, ugly buildings and furnishings that everyone had told her to expect, great beauty and charm. She thought that nothing could have been lovelier than the small baroque theatre in Bayreuth, and the gilded, pastel-coloured churches of Bavaria seemed to invite the worship of God. However, in her written account of that visit one of her chief memories was of an almost daily squabble with Unity. Outside the Feldherrnhalle a plaque commemorated the 1923 putsch when several of Hitler's closest comrades had been killed. Two SS men stood guard beside it and everyone who passed this spot saluted as a sign of respect. It soon became obvious to Sydney that no matter where she and the girls went, they always seemed to pass it, whereupon Unity would throw up her hand in an almost theatrical Nazi salute. Sydney was slightly embarrassed by this, and as a foreigner she certainly did not feel obliged to salute. When she insisted that they avoid the building Unity simply went off on her own, leaving her to find her own way back to the hotel. If it proved unavoidable Sydney would take the opposite side of the street, leaving Unity to make her salute, but there was no animosity about this. 'We met at the other side [of the building], with great laughter,' Sydney wrote.[14]

We do not know Decca's reaction to Munich for although photographs of the visit survive, she never mentioned it in her memoirs, or in any surviving letters and papers. She did say in *Hons and Rebels* that in 1935, the year after her visit to Germany, it occurred to her 'over and over again' to pretend to be a convert to Fascism, so that she could accompany Unity to Germany and meet Hitler face to face. 'As we were being introduced,' she fantasized, 'I would whip out a pistol and shoot him dead.'[15] But that was after she had read *The Brown Book of Hitler Terror*,[16] one of the first testaments to the horrors lurking at the heart of the Nazi regime. Like *Cry Havoc*, Beverly Nichols' indictment of the First World War, it had a major impact on Decca. It explained the new anti-Semitic laws in Germany, and how they were being implemented, while pictures showed the effects of treatment meted out to Jews by storm-troopers. At that stage it was beatings and brutal handling, but the book also prophesied what would happen if the regime continued unchecked. There was little demand for such works in England and they were largely distributed through left-wing bookshops and Communist channels.

Decca, now as strongly aligned to the Communist movement as Unity was to Fascism, read the book carefully, accepted it absolutely and was consumed with righteous anger. She brought it to the attention of David and Sydney, who told her what the majority of the population would have told her at that time: that they believed the book to be Communist-inspired propaganda and an exaggeration. That she could not make them see the dangers that to her were so evident made her sick at heart. Every day she read more about such horrors in the *Daily Worker* and in her left-wing pamphlets, and increasingly she spent a lot of time crying in her room from frustration that she could do nothing constructive, or even make the family see the dreadful problems. Much later she stated in an interview, 'People say they didn't know what was happening to the Jews until after the war, but they did know because it was all there.' She referred to the books *Cry Havoc* and *The Brown Book of Hitler Terror* which had made such an impression on her. But by this yardstick, those who supported Communism should have known about the millions of people being murdered by Stalin in the thirties. Vague reports of those atrocities also filtered into England only to be regarded by supporters of the regime as anti-Communist propaganda.

On days when she felt more cheerful, although she still experienced pangs of guilt because such activities were contrary to the class struggle, Decca looked forward to being a débutante. She imagined it would be a sort of extension of her experiences in Paris, and at the end she would be regarded – finally – as 'grown-up' and therefore free to run away. But the reality of being a débutante was less exciting than the anticipation: Decca found that Sydney still treated her as a child, and chaperoned her carefully from Rutland Gate to a seemingly endless series of lunches, tea parties, cocktail parties, dinners and dances. None of the 'chinless wonders' or 'debs' delights', as the young men were known, interested Decca in the slightest. There is a picture of her in her presentation gown with extravagant train and court feathers; the dress is white satin with a row of pearl buttons down the front, which are twisted to one side and caught in the sash. She has made little effort with her appearance for the occasion and looks frumpily and balefully at the camera. There was an explanation for this disarray: recalling that Unity had grabbed some writing-paper when at the Palace, Decca felt she should do *something*. At the buffet following her presentation, she took some chocolates to eat later, and hid them in her bouquet. Sydney took her and Nancy, who was being presented again 'on her marriage', straight from the Palace to the photo studio. To Decca's dismay when she picked up her bouquet to pose, the chocolates tumbled out all over the floor just as the photographer was about to shoot.

However, the event that most coloured Decca's Season as a débutante – she had only one – concerned her wicked younger cousin, Esmond Romilly, who had been in the news again. Having been expelled from Wellington he was now ensconced in a left-wing bookshop in Bloomsbury from where he was editing and publishing his *Out of Bounds* magazine, distributing it to public schools. He had not always been a Communist: he had recently converted from ultra-Conservatism. This had come about when he was asked to attack the Russian government in a school debate. He wrote to his uncle Winston, who replied that he was too busy to give detailed information and advised that the point to stress was that the Russians had murdered millions of people during the revolution. After blundering around for a while, confusing pacifism with Communism, Esmond came across the *Daily Worker* on his way to Dieppe on holiday. That put him on track and he became a daily subscriber. From this source he learned 'that there was another world as well as the one in which I lived'. His own magazine was bright, informative and cheeky. The fact that it was banned in many public schools gave it a considerable cachet and he triumphantly emblazoned the names of those establishments on the front page. But he was clever enough to realize that he would not gain new readers through political editorials alone, and to increase circulation he included articles on subjects that were of primary importance to public-school boys . . . bullying by masters and older boys, the fagging system, and obscure hints at masturbation and homosexuality. In an article on how a thirteen-year-old new boy might expect to be warned by masters of what lay in store, Esmond wrote from his own experience: his housemaster had lined up the 'wet bobs' and explained incomprehensibly, 'Men! There are men here who will try to take advantage of a man because a man is a new man. That's all I have to say to you.' There was even an article on that most shocking of subjects, co-education.[17] Needless to say, underground copies of the magazine were soon to be found in every public school in the land and, once again, the national newspapers got to hear of it.

Through gossip about his exploits, Esmond became a sort of hero to Decca. Although a year younger than her, he was an open rebel doing all the things that – had she the courage – she would have liked to do. She wished that somehow she could contrive to meet him. She might not have expected the apparition who greeted Philip Toynbee, though, who on 7 June 1934 ran away from Rugby School to join Esmond, fired with enthusiasm for the Communist cause by *Out of Bounds*. 'At this point,' Toynbee wrote of Esmond, 'he was at the height of his intolerant fanaticism, a bristling rebel against home, school, society . . . the world.' He had been living semi-rough in the basement of the shop on what he could earn from his magazine sales, sleeping on a camp bed, and smoking endless Craven A cigarettes. Nellie had washed her hands of him, unable to cope with an ideology that was opposed to everything in which she believed. 'He was dirty and ill-dressed, immensely strong for his age and size; his flat face gave the impression of being deeply scarred, and his eyes flared and smouldered as we talked.'[18]

After the 1935 Season ended, Decca hung around at Swinbrook, thoroughly miserable, waiting for mealtimes. Now she *was* depressed and unhappy, and everyone could see it. Sydney put it down to a late attack of adolescent misery and was sorry for her daughter, but any attempt to offer sympathy resulted either in floods of tears or in loud recriminations from Decca that she had not been allowed to have a proper education and therefore could not go to university. Being 'grown up' seemed to have no particular advantage at Swinbrook, and having had her year in France, and made her début, without attracting an 'eligible', Decca had nothing to do, and nothing whatever to look forward to. She had almost fifty pounds in her running-away account but she could not see the best way of using this to give herself a future. It seems that her boredom and unhappiness at this point coloured all memories of her earlier life at Swinbrook. This is the only possible explanation for differences between extant papers and the testimony of her contemporaries, and what she wrote of her childhood in *Hons and Rebels*.

Sydney, though by no means won over to the Nazi regime by her visit, was enthusiastic about what she had seen in Germany, which prompted David to visit the country of his old foe, the Hun. In January 1935 he took Unity back after the Christmas break. She had stayed with Diana in the flat until the end of the previous term, but now she returned to 'the heim', and David stayed at a hotel. One day while they were lunching at the Osteria, Hitler put in an appearance. Unity was overjoyed. They did not speak, of course, but David was impressed. 'Farve has been completely won over by him,' she reported to Diana, after David left for home, 'and admits himself to being in the wrong until now.'[19]

Meanwhile, Unity had made progress towards her dream scenario, and in February 1935 she met Hitler face to face at last. Her Führer-watching had become more scientific by then: she scanned the newspapers for his movements. If he was not in Munich, or if he had a specific appointment during the afternoon, then it was pointless wasting time at the Osteria. She made friends with some of the guards at the Brown House (the Nazi Party headquarters in Munich), where she was a regular caller, and there she received odd snippets of information about when Hitler was expected. When he appeared she made small attempts to be noticed, such as dropping her book. Eventually this paid off. Hitler became used to seeing the tall, Nordic-looking girl – often alone – sitting in the same seat every time he visited the Osteria, and saw that her attention was fixed constantly on him. To her huge delight he began to nod to her sometimes as he passed her table. Eventually he became curious enough, exactly as she had hoped, to enquire of the restaurant owner, Herr Deutelmoser, who she was.

The day of 9 February 1935 was, Unity wrote to David, though she claimed she was still almost too shaky to write properly, 'the most wonderful and beautiful of my life.' About ten minutes after she arrived at the Osteria, she wrote, Hitler spoke to Herr Deutelmoser and the two men glanced across at her. Deutelmoser walked to her table and said, 'The Führer would like to speak to you.' Unity continued, in an 800-word letter,

> I got up and went over to him, and he stood up and saluted and shook hands and introduced me to all the others and asked me to sit down next to him. I sat and talked for about half an hour . . . I can't tell you of all the things we talked about . . . I told him he ought to come to England and he said he would love to but he was afraid there would be a revolution if he did. He asked if I had ever been to [a Wagner festival at] Bayreuth and I said no but I should like to, and he said to the other men that they should remember that the next time.[20]

Then they spoke of London, which he felt he knew well, he said, from his architectural studies. They went on to discuss films (Hitler said he considered *Cavalcade* the best he had ever seen), the new road systems being constructed all over Germany, the Great War and the Parteitag. He signed a postcard to her, writing in German: 'To Fraulein Unity Mitford as a friendly memento of Germany and Adolf Hitler'. Then he pocketed the slip of paper on which she had written her name for him to copy, and left after instructing the manager to put Unity's meal on his bill. 'After all that,' Unity continued in her letter to her father, 'you can imagine what I feel like. I am so happy that I wouldn't mind a bit dying. I suppose I am the luckiest girl in the world . . . you may think this is hysterical. I'm sure Muv will, but when you remember that for me, he is the greatest man of all time, you must admit I am lucky even to have set eyes on him, let alone to have sat and talked to him.'

Several days later she wrote to her mother of Hitler's pleasing simplicity: he had been 'so ordinary that one couldn't be nervous . . . I still can't quite believe [it] but I have my signed postcard as proof'.[21] Nothing Hitler could say or do would subsequently destroy Unity's admiration of him. She had swallowed the Nazi bait whole: waving banners, emotional anthems, torchlight processions, and anti-Semitism.

There must have been some extraordinary quality in Unity that not only attracted Hitler's attention but caused him to establish a deeper relationship by continued invitations to her to join his table. Other people regularly visited Hitler's known haunts in the hope of catching a glimpse of him, but he never noticed them. Unity wrote of how some congratulated her after that first meeting, and she was amazed that they were not jealous of her, a foreigner, for having been singled out for notice.

Two weeks later she was having tea at the Carlton tearooms with a fellow student when Hitler spotted her and invited both girls to join him. In the following week she was there with Michael Burn, who later became well known as a journalist, writer and poet. Burn had known Unity since he attended a Rutland Gate party during Unity's year as a débutante and, like Derek Hill, he was struck by Unity's extreme reaction when Hitler appeared. As Hill had witnessed, she trembled. 'Hitler passed our table and spoke to her,' Michael Burn recalled, 'and then he went on to his table in the garden. One of his adjutants came back and said Hitler had invited her to join them. She rushed off after him. I might not have existed . . .'[22] A week after that a similar invitation was extended to her at the Osteria; this time Unity was introduced to Goebbels. Her diary reveals that between their first meeting in June 1935 and her penultimate meeting with him in September 1939, on the eve of war, she and

Hitler met and talked on 140 occasions – an average of about once every ten days, remarkable when one considers what Hitler's schedule must have been like in those four years leading up to the war. Can one even imagine Churchill or Roosevelt behaving like this with a foreign student? But so quickly did Unity find a place as a friend of Hitler that, within months, when Diana, Tom, Pam and Sydney visited her, she introduced them to him without any difficulty.

Was this purely because of Unity's 'presence', the unique quality that Decca wrote about in her memoir yet which she could not quantify? Or might it have been that Nazi intelligence sources had connected her with Diana Guinness, mistress of British Fascist leader Oswald Mosley, which led in turn to the even more surprising information that the twenty-one-year-old English student was a close relative of Winston Churchill? However, it is doubtful that any connection would have been made initially with the divorced Mrs Guinness, and it is reasonably certain that, whatever happened subsequently, those first meetings occurred as the result of Unity's own personality.

That April, when she had met him three times, Hitler invited Unity to a luncheon party. To her surprise, Unity discovered when she arrived that it was in honour of Mosley, who was paying a private visit to Hitler. It was the first meeting between the two men, and they met only once more. Neither spoke the other's language, and neither was especially impressed with the other. Besides an obvious interest in meeting the man whose name was on everyone's lips, Mosley possibly hoped to obtain financial support from Hitler: funding for the BUF from Mussolini (which Mosley always denied receiving) was drying up, the organization was rapidly eating up the donations of major supporters in England, and was in danger of draining Mosley's own fortune. In the event it is doubtful that Mosley even broached the subject of finance in the short time allowed for discussion, after which they joined the ladies in the dining room of Hitler's comfortable apartment. As well as Unity, two other women had been invited: Winifred Wagner, the brilliant English-born widow of Richard Wagner's son, Siegfried, and the Duchess of Brunswick, only daughter of the Kaiser and a great-granddaughter of Queen Victoria. These English connections were intended as a graceful compliment to the guest of honour. Hitler, apparently, was not aware of the relationship between Unity and Mosley,[23] for he appeared taken aback to find that his young English student friend knew Mosley so intimately. Later, he asked her who her father was. Hitler was unfamiliar with the customs of the English peerage, and when Unity said he was Lord Redesdale, not Mitford as Hitler had expected, he assumed she was illegitimate, patting her hand and murmuring sympathetically, 'Ah, poor child!'

The meeting between Hitler and Sydney, which occurred soon afterwards, was something of an embarrassment to Unity. They joined him for tea at the Carlton tearooms, and Unity had to translate her mother's lecture about the value of wholemeal bread. 'Whenever I translated anything for either of them,' she complained to Diana, 'it sounded stupid translated . . . I fear the whole thing was wasted on Muv, she is just the same as before. Having so little feeling, she does not feel his goodness and wonderfulness radiating out like we do . . .' In fact, Hitler was something of a health-food fanatic and probably agreed with Sydney about the bread.

Unity found Pam little better than Sydney as a potential fellow worshipper of the Führer. Pam had given up managing the farm at Biddesden in the previous autumn and spent the rest of the pre-war years travelling extensively, visiting parts of Europe by car that after the war were behind the Iron Curtain. In June 1935 she called on Unity with Wilhelmine 'Billa' Cresswell [later Lady Harrod]. Billa was an old friend of all the girls and lives on in literature as Fanny, the narrator of Nancy's most famous novels *The Pursuit of Love* and *Love in a Cold Climate*, and the major

character in a subsequent book, *Don't Tell Alfred*. It was during
Pam's second visit that autumn that she met Hitler. She and
Unity were lunching at the Osteria and had just finished eating
when there was a flurry of activity, which Unity knew meant that
Hitler's black Mercedes, with a similar car containing members
of his party, had been spotted arriving outside the restaurant. She
told Pam to go and stand by the door if she wanted a good view
of him. As Hitler passed her, he looked straight into Pam's eyes,
the most strikingly blue of any of the sisters'. A short time later
Schaub, one of Hitler's adjutants, came over and asked Pam if she
was Unity's sister. On receiving a positive answer he said that the
Führer had invited both of them to move to his table. The sisters
cheerfully ate a second lunch with Hitler. When she returned to
England and was asked about him, Pam described Hitler vaguely
as 'very ordinary, like an old farmer in a brown suit'. But she
recalled every detail of the food they ate and was rhapsodic over
some of it, 'Oh, the new potatoes . . . they were absolutely delicious,' she said.

Tom's reaction was more to Unity's satisfaction. He paid several visits to her while staying with his friend Janos von Almassy.
That summer he and Unity argued hotly about the Nazi regime
for although Tom had conceded the transformation in Germany
that the Party had brought about since coming to power, he was
opposed to the racial creed it espoused. Nevertheless, he was
interested in seeing Hitler for himself, which caused Unity to
worry that if she introduced him he might say what he felt to
Hitler, which would rebound on *her*. She therefore took Tom to
the Osteria very early, knowing that Hitler never arrived before
two o'clock and often later than that. On this particular day,
however, Hitler arrived early and Tom was duly introduced. To
Unity's relief, 'Tom *adored* the Führer,' she wrote to Diana. 'He
almost got into a frenzy like us. But I expect he will have cooled
down by the time he gets home.'

But if Unity felt irritated by the casual demeanour of Sydney and Pam in the presence of her earthly god, then she soon gave her entire family every reason to feel aggrieved by her own behaviour. In June that year she wrote a letter to a publication owned and edited by the notorious Julius Streicher. Copies of *Stürmer* were displayed in bright red boxes all over the Reich. It was less of a newspaper than a propaganda organ, but it carried stories of a popular nature and had a circulation of 100,000 copies. Streicher was an old acquaintance of Hitler – indeed, Hitler made few new friends after 1930; most of those with whom he surrounded himself were from the *Kampfzeit*, the years of struggle, or *die Altkampfer*, the old fighters. Streicher's membership card in the Nazi Party was number two and Hitler's was number seven. Soon after Hitler came to power Streicher was made Gauleiter of Franconia, a region he purged not only of Jews, but of all non-Aryans without mercy. It was Streicher, for example who made a party of Jews clear a meadow by tearing out the grass with their teeth, an incident that evidently caused much amusement in the higher echelons of the Nazi Party.

It was Streicher who initiated the Nuremberg rallies and promoted the Nuremberg decrees against the Jews. We now know from surviving correspondence that he became a great liability to the Nazi regime and was detested by Goebbels and hardly ever saw Hitler except at Nuremberg. Unity would not have known this: when she wrote to Streicher's newspaper her motive was almost certainly to make Hitler and his immediate circle aware of her unqualified support, in a tone that she could hardly adopt in conversation. She was now playing with very big fish indeed, and the letter haunted her for the rest of her life.

Dear *Stürmer*, [she wrote in German]
As a British woman Fascist, I should like to express my admiration for you. I have lived in Munich for a year and read *Der Stürmer* every week. If only we had such a newspaper in England! The English have no notion of the

Jewish danger. English Jews are always described as 'decent'. Perhaps the Jews in England are more clever with their propaganda than in other countries. I cannot tell, but it is a certain fact that our struggle is extremely hard. Our worst Jews work only behind the scenes. They never come into the open, and therefore we cannot show them to the British public in their true dreadfulness. We hope, however, that you will see that we will soon win against the world enemy, in spite of all his cunning. We think with joy of the day when we shall be able to say with might and authority: England for the English! Out with the Jews! With German greeting, Heil Hitler!

    Unity Mitford.

PS: If you find room in your newspaper for this letter, please publish my name in full . . . I want everyone to know that I am a Jew hater.

The hysterical tone of this letter sounds remarkably like Nancy's character Eugenia in *Wigs on the Green*, and if it was a deliberate ploy by Unity to ingratiate herself with top Nazis, then it worked. Streicher was intrigued enough to ask her to do an interview for the *Münchener Zeitung*, in which she spoke just as freely about the BUF and her hopes for Germany and Britain to be united in Fascism. He prefaced Unity's remarks with the information that her father was a *Graf* and that she was related to Winston Churchill, so that there could be no doubt in the minds of potential readers that this was a young woman of status whose views should be regarded with respect.[24] Next he invited her to the midsummer festival at Hesselberg, near Nuremberg, where, dressed in a military-style black shirt, and her favourite gauntlet gloves, she was treated as an honoured guest and asked to give an impromptu speech. It was widely covered in the British press under headlines such as 'The Girl Who Adores Hitler' and 'Peer's

Daughter is Jew Hater,' illustrated with photographs of Unity giving a Nazi salute. The Redesdales were appalled to be contacted by reporters from the national daily papers, and asked to comment on their daughter's pronouncements. In the aftermath one reader from Kingston-on-Thames wrote, via the correspondence columns of a daily paper, to ask what Unity Mitford would do if she were put into a kindergarten 'with a score of beautiful Jewish four-year-olds, and then given a gun and told to wipe out that much Jewry'.

David and Sydney had been about to join her in Munich but now they cancelled their trip and ordered her home for the summer instead. Realizing how angry they were, and since they had yet to find out about the *Stürmer* letter, Unity thought she had better comply. She told them the Hesselberg incident had been 'unavoidable'. She couldn't have refused to go, for the sake of politeness, she wrote to Sydney, and once there she couldn't wave away the bouquet presented to her, or refuse to take the microphone.[25] But friends of Unity in Munich saw no signs of regret over any of the notoriety she subsequently attracted.[26] In a sense she had achieved the ultimate success. All her life she had obtained pleasure from shocking people, now she had shocked so absolutely that people *had* to sit up and notice her. She was, at last, notable as someone in her own right. She had even begun to create her own legendary persona, building on the coincidence of her conception in Swastika and always calling herself Unity Walkyrie.

At home, she was soon brought down to earth. From Mill Cottage in High Wycombe on the evening of 26 July, she wrote to Diana that David was in a vile temper with her, 'mainly because of the letter in the *Der Stürmer*'. Its contents were reported in the *Evening Standard* that afternoon, and on the following day it was carried in the daily national press. She received a huge postbag of letters, some from people who were opposed to her views and some from people who supported them. Nancy wrote teasingly, 'We were all very interested to see that you were Queen of the May this year at Hesselberg. "Call me early, Goering dear/For I'm to be Queen of the May." Good gracious, that interview you sent us; fantasia! Fantasia!'[27] But by then Unity and Nancy were scarcely on speaking terms. It was far more important to her that Decca wrote from a holiday in Brittany to say that she hated what her Boud had written but that she loved her nevertheless.

Later in the month Unity went to visit friends at Hayling Island. They were out sailing when she arrived and Unity was greeted and welcomed by their father, an 'old-style *Times* correspondent and a great Liberal'[28] who, having left Unity to unpack and settle in, went off to do some work. Hearing the sound of gunfire in the garden he went to investigate. Unity was firing at targets with her pistol. When he asked her what she was doing she told him she was practising to kill Jews. Her friend reported, 'Father almost left the house at once.'

Unity's pistol was a pearl-handled 6.35 Walther, which she sometimes wore in a small holster. Her biographer was unable to verify whether Hitler had given it to her, as Paulette Helleu claimed Unity had once told her,[29] or whether she had simply purchased it to wear for effect with her Nazi regalia. One friend thought she had bought it during a trip to Belgium and this seems more likely. Although Hitler was keen that women should be able to defend themselves and know how to handle guns and shoot properly, a few years earlier he had suffered a significant personal loss when his half-niece, Geli, generally believed to have been the love of his life, committed suicide by shooting herself with his gun.

To escape the censorious atmosphere at home Unity went to stay with Diana, but she made no attempt to keep a low profile while in London. There were several incidents during which she deliberately antagonized small crowds gathered around socialist speakers at Speaker's Corner, calling out '*Heil, Hitler*' and giving the Nazi salute.[30] She was furious when Nancy teased her that she had done some research into the family history and had discovered a great-grandmother Fish, who made them one-sixteenth Jewish.

During a visit to Swinbrook with Diana, Unity produced an autographed photograph of Julius Streicher, which she proposed to display prominently in the DFD to offset a bust of Lenin that Decca had recently installed. This was too much for Decca, and she objected violently, referring to Streicher as a filthy butcher. In her autobiography she made much of the argument: "'But, *darling*,'" Diana drawled, opening her enormous blue eyes, "*Streicher* is a *kitten*.'"[31] Diana's short response to this, when asked about it some sixty years later, was 'A *kitten*? Rubbish!'[32]

9

SECRET MARRIAGE

(1935–7)

In the autumn Unity was allowed to return to Munich, but David insisted on chaperoning her. There, he called on the British consul and asked, 'Can't *you* persuade Unity to go away from here?' To others he would say mournfully, over a cup of tea, 'I'm normal, my wife is normal, but my daughters are each more foolish than the other. What do you say about my daughters? Isn't it very sad?'[1] The wife of the consul thought it *was* very sad. She remembers seeing both the Redesdales in Munich and recalls that they were 'distraught parents', very nice and quite unable to cope with Unity's obsessive behaviour.[2] Yet surely David had the means to ensure that Unity could not stay in Germany. She was only able to live there because he provided her, as he did his other daughters, with an allowance of about £125 a year. This was hardly a fortune, but there was a special rate of exchange for sterling, which made it sufficient for her to enjoy a reasonable standard of living.

When Unity became ill with tonsillitis, David insisted on staying on to look after her. His English self-confidence coupled with his bumbling manner both endeared him to her and irritated her. The ice rink was closed and he could not skate, which made him determined to dislike the entire trip. 'He refuses to take the least interest in anything and pines for home,' Unity complained to Sydney. 'He had much better let me come alone, like I planned. I must say one thing, he is very good-tempered.' Most of the waiters and hotel staff in Munich spoke a little English, but David had only to hear one word of English, she said, before addressing them exactly as he would a waiter in London. 'On the train he suddenly said to the dining car man, "I don't think much of your permanent way, but the rolling stock is pretty good going on. These cigarettes are killing me by inches!" Then he fires questions at them,' she continued, 'like, "Do they sell Brambles [a type of country hat] here?" or talks about her ladyship and expects them to know it's you. The poor things are so confused. I think they think he's cracked.'[3]

After her contretemps in June Unity had no option but to submit to her father's presence with good grace. Her brief notoriety had upset her parents badly and she was fortunate to have been allowed to return to Munich at all. The situation had not been helped along by the publication of Nancy's *Wigs on the Green* at the end of June, just as the papers got wind of Unity's interview. Unity took her cue from Diana: it was not acceptable to mock either Mosley or Hitler.

Nancy was well aware that the timing was bad and contacted both sisters, writing to Diana (firmly): 'A book of this kind *can't* do your movement any harm. Honestly if I thought it could set the Leader back by so much as half-an-hour I would have scrapped it . . .'[4] and to Unity (winningly):

Darling Head of Bone & Heart of Stone,
    . . . Please don't read the book if it's going to stone you up against me . . . Oh dear do write me a kind and non-stony-heart letter to say you don't mind it nearly as much as you expected . . . Oh dear I'm going to Oxford with Nardie [Diana] tomorrow, our last day together I suppose

before the clouds of her displeasure burst over me . . . oh
dear, I wish I had called it mine uncomf now because
uncomf is what I feel every time I think about it. So now
don't get together with Nardie and ban me forever or I
shall die . . . oh dear, OH DEAR!⁵

Perhaps it was asking too much of Diana, who had pinned
her colours so positively to Mosley's mast, to see the book in
quite the gleeful way Nancy intended, and realizing this, albeit
late in the day, Nancy had tried to soften the blow by fore-
warning her sister while she was writing: 'Peter says I can't put a
movement like Fascism into a work of fiction *by name* so I am
calling it the Union Jack movement . . . & their leader Colonel
Jack . . . but I don't want to Leadertease,' she wrote appeasingly,
'as the poor man could hardly have me up for libel under the circumstances!'⁶ Diana was allowed to read the manuscript and
although she suggested a rash of edits, which for the most part
Nancy agreed to, both she and Unity had told Nancy they
would never speak to her again if she published it. But Nancy
had little option as Prod was not working and their only income
besides her tiny allowance was the royalties from her books. She
was unable to make their funds meet their outgoings and she
had become used to visits from the bailiffs and receiving hand-
outs from her father-in-law. 'I really couldn't afford to scrap the
book,' she told Diana.

One problem was that the game had changed somewhat
between the time that Nancy conceived *Wigs on the Green* and its
publication. From being 'almost respectable' eighteen months
earlier, Mosley had become, as Bernard Shaw put it, 'ridiculed as
impossible'.⁷ Since the infamous BUF Olympia rally in 1934, a
scene of unprecedented violence in British politics (though worse
was to come), Mosley had lost all chance of leading a conventional party. On the other hand, the active membership of the
BUF had reached ten thousand with, Mosley's biographer

estimated, a further thirty thousand non-active members and supporters.[8] Mosley pointed out that Fascism in Britain had grown faster than anywhere else in the world, and there was evidence of a significant amount of support for it as a political ideal from uncommitted voters. When one of the first Gallup polls asked interviewees to choose which they would prefer, Fascism or Communism, 70 per cent of people under thirty chose Fascism. In the upper echelons of society there is plenty of proof that the Cliveden set and a large slice of the upper classes, while not actively pro-Mosley, were supportive of a Fascist style of government because they were all terrified of the threat of Communism.

Then there was Mosley's style of dressing, which had hitherto been a neat black shirt under a well-cut dark suit. Suddenly, for marches and rallies, he and his lieutenants adopted a uniform that was distinctly military in design. The black jacket had brass buttons and epaulets, and was worn with a Sam Browne-type leather belt, and an officer's peaked hat. Brown riding breeches were tucked into gleaming riding boots. It drew some pejorative comments from onlookers: 'They look like Nazi jackboots' was one obvious remark. 'More like King Zog's Imperial Dismounted Hussars' was the retort. And, increasingly, BUF marches and grandiose rallies, apparently based on European models, became an excuse for aggressive and vicious thuggery. Bands of Communists and some who were simply anti-Fascist would begin by heckling or throwing missiles, and eventually order would deteriorate with the exchange of blows. Mosley never openly advocated anti-Semitism, but plenty of his supporters were willing to act against East End Jews in the name of the BUF. In the event the uniform was short-lived, for the wearing of it was banned by the Public Order Act of 1936, but it was not forgotten by the public.

News of the treatment meted out to Jews in Germany was filtering through to the United Kingdom: national newspapers ran small reports of how Jews were increasingly being stripped of possessions, their shops and businesses closed and looted, and how they were being generally humiliated. German towns put up signs boasting that they were 'Jew free', park benches were marked 'Aryan' and 'Jew', shops proclaimed that Jews would not be served. Such news items were tucked away, a forerunner of what was to come. Those of the silent majority who read the reports did not know how seriously to take them, or decided that it was 'not our business', so there were no demonstrations of public anger, but some opprobrium inevitably clung to Mosley's movement and – whether it was true or not – he was widely perceived as anti-Semitic. When questioned about the Nazi regime's attitude to Germany's Jewish population, he replied, 'Whatever happens in Germany is Germany's affair, and we are not going to lose British lives in a Jewish quarrel.'[9]

Because of her affection for Diana, Nancy had accepted Mosley up to a point, had even casually joined the BUF with Prod and been present at the Olympia fiasco, but her allegiance soon waned. The Rodds decided that they did not like the direction in which British Fascism was moving. When they received an invitation, written in German, from Joachim von Ribbentrop to a function to celebrate his appointment to the London embassy, Prod declined for them both – in Yiddish.[10] But Nancy had never really taken to Mosley; her book was the equivalent of a modern television satire and lampooned what he stood for. Mosley took himself very seriously, and though he never minded opposition, derision was a different matter.

The publication of *Wigs on the Green* caused a serious rift between Nancy and Diana. In November, almost six months later, in a letter to a friend, Nancy wrote: 'I saw Diana at a lunch . . . 2 days ago, she was cold but contained & I escaped with my full complement of teeth, eyes, etc.' But even had Diana forgiven her, Mosley would not have done so. For the next four years he refused to allow Nancy to visit Diana at the house they acquired in early 1936. Indirectly, this rift led to more serious repercussions. Unity, too, was unforgiving, telling people she met in Munich that she was never going to speak to Nancy, so that Nancy could only reply affirmatively to John Betjeman's query on reading the book: 'I suppose it will be all up with Unity Valkyrie and you?' Years later, when she had become a distinguished writer, Nancy refused to allow *Wigs on the Green* to be reissued, saying that too much had happened for jokes about Nazis to be considered as anything but poor taste, but one suspects that the problems it caused within the family were just as likely to have been the reason.

Unity attended the 1935 Nuremberg rally with Tom and Diana. On the eve of the event they met Hitler and Streicher at the opera; on the following day when they found their reserved seats they had been seated prominently, next to Eva Braun who had recently become Hitler's mistress. There are many photographs of the trio of Mitfords in newspaper archives because by now the British press thought the Nazi rallies important enough to cover, and both Unity and Diana made good copy. So, there are photographs of Tom and Diana flanked by Nazi banners, of the two women against a backdrop of marching storm-troopers, of Unity giving the Nazi salute, and any number of poses that would later compromise them.

Diana and Mosley had been together for more than three years. Their initial passion had stood the test of time and out of this a remarkably close intellectual friendship had also grown between them. They remained very much in love; and they wrote to each other, and often spoke to each other in the baby talk of lovers.[11] As Mosley's son, Nicholas, attests 'There was an aura around her and my father such as there is around people who are in love.'[12] Mosley, it is true, still flirted and continued to have casual affairs with other women. He was still sexually involved with Baba Metcalfe and there were numerous other infidelities during the thirties that are a matter of public record. There was even a bizarre court action brought by one woman for slander after she had initially alleged 'breach of promise'.[13] In view of his unquestionable love for Diana it is difficult to explain away his infidelities but many powerful men share the unattractive characteristic of sexual incontinence – Palmerston, Lloyd George, John F. Kennedy and Bill Clinton among them. One thing is for sure, neither Mosley nor Diana was ever wholly happy when they were apart.

Diana tended to treat Mosley's philandering as he had once advised Cimmie to do, as a tiresome 'silliness' that he somehow could not help. In 2000 she wrote that she was sometimes jealous, but 'I was so confident about him. I knew he'd always come back to me.'[14] But to very close friends at the time she admitted that she suffered 'agonies of jealousy',[15] and during 1935 there is evidence of at least one major row between the two, concerning his relationship with Baba. That summer Mosley was staying with two of his children, Nicholas and Vivien, on the Bay of Naples; he had bought a thirty-foot motor yacht, which was moored below their rented villa[16] and used for day trips to the islands and swimming. The arrangement was that Baba would spend the first half of the holiday with them, and Diana the second.

Diana had been injured recently in a car accident, and needed quite extensive plastic surgery to her face. While she was convalescing in a London clinic, Mosley wrote to her: 'Hurry up and get well as this place is lovely – 1,000 steps down to the beach – soon get used to them – we run up and down them now – saying, "Won't they be fun when Diana arrives!" I feel so badly being away while you are so bad . . .'[17] The letter, with its promise of recuperation in the sunshine and Mosley's company, was too much for Diana: with her face still in bandages she discharged herself at five-thirty one morning, a week earlier than her surgeon recommended. With David's help – he hired a car and booked her plane ticket – she drove straight to Croydon airport and flew by seaplane to Naples. It is interesting to reflect that although this was only two years after her divorce David was prepared to assist her to get to Mosley.

She arrived at the villa four days earlier than planned – during a dinner at which Mosley and Baba were entertaining the Crown Princess of Italy – at almost the same time as the cable she had sent advising Mosley that she was coming. Diana recalls that she was 'half-dead and only wanted to sleep'.[18] Vivien remembered hearing a row between the grown-ups that night, and Nicholas recalls doors banging, and being prevented on the following morning from going into one of the bedrooms. 'Do not go there,' a servant warned him. 'Eet ees Mrs Guinness.'[19] With hindsight, Nicholas wrote that the situation was 'a social and a personal challenge worthy of the mettle of someone like my father – on his tightrope, as it were, juggling his plates above Niagara!'[20]

After breakfast Mosley left with Baba and the children for Amalfi, where the adults booked into a hotel and the children slept on the boat. Diana was left alone with the servants at the villa, sitting in the shade and enjoying the peace until Mosley and the children returned on the date originally fixed for her arrival. She soon recovered from her injuries, and took boat trips with them, sitting on the prow with 'an air of stillness about her like that of the sphinxes and classical statues that looked out over the sea from the terraces of the villas on Capri'.[21]

If she was annoyed with Mosley, Diana was quite likely to close the Eatonry and go abroad to stay with a friend in luxury and sunshine. She knew that the removal of her loyal support and love was effective punishment. Her beauty gave her a sort of invulnerability, for she always attracted admiring men wherever she went, and at a personal level this must have been the proverbial double-edged sword for Mosley. He was 'apt to be jealous', said Nicholas, when he was apart from Diana.

As well as the row in Italy that year, Diana became pregnant and had a termination. In those days illegitimacy was a serious stigma, not something to inflict lightly upon a child, and had Diana borne Mosley a child at this point the old scandal would have reopened, with all the resultant bad publicity for him, and hurt for the Redesdales. But the abortion provided some sort of catalyst in the relationship, for Diana loved her babies. Although by modern standards she spent little time with them, and even when she was at the Eatonry they were cared for by Nanny, rather than her, this was not unusual in their circle. Her son Jonathan insists that he and his brother saw as much of their mother as did any of their acquaintances. Diana is on record as saying, 'Marriage meant nothing to me, yet three years after his wife's death we did marry, because we wanted children, and in those days it was supposed to be better for children to be born in wedlock.'[22]

In the early part of 1936 Diana and Mosley decided to marry, but for various reasons that would become obvious – Baba for one, presumably – Mosley did not want news of this to leak out, so they had to find a way to do it in secret. At first they thought it would be possible to marry in Paris but discovered that the banns would have to be posted at the British consulate. Meanwhile there was the question of where to live. The Eatonry was too small: they needed a family home in the country.

Mosley's two sisters-in-law were still running his home, Savehay Farm, and looking after the children with the help of dedicated and loyal staff. Diana occasionally visited there, always to a cool reception, and Nicholas recalled being instructed by his nanny that he must 'never speak to Mrs Guinness'. Although Cimmie had been dead for nearly three years, Mosley knew it would have caused ructions if he had tried to move Diana in, so Diana set about looking for a suitable home, where they could accommodate all the children of their respective earlier marriages. It had to be convenient for Mosley's campaigning, which continued unabated, especially in the Midlands and industrial north. She found Wootton Lodge in Staffordshire.

Wootton has been called 'one of the most beautiful houses in England', and is vast, magnificent, romantic, if somewhat impractical as a family home. It was built in 1610 and had been a Royalist stronghold during the civil war. Its architecture is reminiscent of the more famous Hardwick Hall ('more glass than wall') with huge mullioned windows, which give it an ethereal appearance. The estate agent openly regarded it as a white elephant – for in the prevailing economic climate it seemed unlikely to be taken off his hands – but Diana fell in love with it and persuaded the owner to lease it to her 'for almost nothing' with an option to buy later. Mosley paid the rent and installed a heating system, but they agreed that Diana would have to be responsible for the upkeep and staffing. Bryan had made her a generous settlement but she was not rich and she knew that living at Wootton would mean sacrifices. Fortunately for her, David chose this moment to have one of his regular 'furniture sales' Swinbrook was to be sold and already he, Sydney, Decca and Debo were living more or less permanently at Old Mill Cottage in High Wycombe. Diana was able to buy some of the best pieces of furniture and family paintings to furnish her beloved Wootton at a discount.

It was not quite so fortunate for Sydney: 'From Batsford *Mansion*, to Asthall *Manor*, to Swinbrook *House*, to Old Mill *Cottage*' was the derisive chant coined by Decca and Debo to describe the decline of the Redesdale family fortunes. Despite Sydney's financial prudence, David's various moneymaking schemes – the gold mine, and investments in ventures such as diving to a sunken galleon to raise gold bullion – ate into the Redesdale inheritance. He turned down schemes that subsequently made money, such as the first ice-cube-making machine to be introduced to England. Even worse, he seemed to have an uncanny knack for investing at the top of a market, and selling at the bottom.

As before, when David was selling their homes, Sydney took

herself well out of the way. She, Decca, Debo and Unity, whose year of study was now over, went on holiday. After a week in Paris the party boarded the Donaldson-Atlantic Line's SS *Letitia* on a 'cultural cruise' of ancient sites and places of architectural and archaeological interest such as Napoleon's house in Corsica and the Parthenon in Athens, and there were a number of public-school parties on board. But there were enough passengers of the right sort to create some interest, and when Decca wrote to Nancy telling her 'there is a Lord on board called Ld Rathcreedon, he's rather nice too. His brother is travelling also . . .' Nancy replied inimically:

> There is a Lord on board,
> A Lord on board, poor Decca roared,
> But the Lord on board is a bit of a fraud,
> 'Cause the Lord on board has a wife called Maud,
> There is a Lord on board . . . [23]

For the first time in years the three younger Mitford sisters were all together on holiday and Unity and Decca behaved like schoolgirls, giggling and misbehaving. It must have been wearing for Sydney for their cavorting began in Paris and seems to have lasted the entire holiday. In Paris they met Dolly Wilde, daughter of Oscar Wilde's brother and a noted lesbian. Attractive and witty, she was a leading light in the rich, artistic crowd who peopled Paris Society in the thirties and knew everyone worth knowing. Nancy had provided introductions, and Unity and Decca deliberately irritated Sydney by pretending to be 'in love' with Dolly, fighting to sit next to her in a taxi, stroking her fur collar and accepting gifts of frilly nightgowns from her.[24] Aboard ship they teased 'the Lord on board' and his pale-looking brother, and sang rude songs about sixteen-year-old Debo's innocent holiday flirtation with 'Red' Rathcredon. 'On the good ship Lollipop,/It's a night trip, into bed you hop,/With Ld Rathcreedon/All aboard for the Garden of Eden.'[25]

They peppered their conversation with their favourite talk of white slavers; they teased other passengers with practical jokes, convincing one young man that Unity said her nightly prayers to Hitler while giving the Nazi salute. Even Decca joined in this one but in general all three followed Unity's lead as they set out to shock while appearing models of innocence. It was common-room stuff: 'Did you see the Canon's balls today?' one would enquire loudly of the others at dinner after a visit to a crusader castle. At one point following a tour of a *haramlek* in a palace in Istanbul Sydney summoned them to her room and looked so grave that they feared there had been bad news from home. 'Now, children,' she said, 'you are *not* to mention that eunuch at dinner.'[26] Unity even managed to put across her political message when one passenger, the noted left-wing Duchess of Atholl, gave a lecture on 'Modern Despots'. Unity insisted on the right to reply, and did so. A few months later, when word of this debate, and in particular Unity's platform, was being belatedly discussed in newspapers, Sydney wrote to the *Daily Telegraph* pointing out to the Duchess that 'Nazism is from every point of view preferable to Communism.'

But the fun between the sisters came to an abrupt end when in Spain, just before the cruise ended, they went ashore to visit the Alhambra. As they got out of the cars in Granada's town square, a small crowd gathered to see the tourists and Unity's Fascist badge was spotted. It was a gold swastika, a special one presented by Hitler, and was engraved on the back with his signature. She was hugely proud of it. Before anyone realized what was happening she was surrounded by hostile Spaniards, trying to tear off the hated symbol. Other members of the party rescued her and the Mitfords were put back into a car and returned to the ship. On the journey Decca and Unity began a physical fight in the back of the car, scratching, hair-pulling and arguing. Sydney separated them, gave them 'a good talking-to' and confined them in separate cabins for the remainder of the trip. Decca spent the time mulishly plotting how she could escape and run away.

Following the cruise there was an uneasy truce between Decca and Unity, which was tested every so often by news of the advance of Fascism across Europe. That spring, 1936, Abyssinia fell to Mussolini's forces and was annexed by Italy, and Hitler's army marched into the Rhineland to be greeted rapturously by the inhabitants. To Decca's dismay the British press began to echo her parents' opinions, that Hitler and his Nazi troops were a bulwark for the rest of Europe against the threat of Communism. Even Beverly Nichols, whose book *Cry Havoc* had played such a pivotal role in Decca's developing ideology, seemed to have changed his tune: in the *Sunday Chronicle* he admitted that Germany had 'moral strength . . . There is so much in the new Germany that is beautiful, so much that is fine and great . . . all the time we are being trained to believe that the Germans are a nation of wild beasts who vary their time between roasting Jews and teaching babies to present arms. It is simply not true.' In July Franco launched his attack on the Popular Front government in Spain and long-sighted commentators began referring to it as a rehearsal for a second world war. Shortly afterwards Decca heard on the family grapevine that Esmond, *lucky thing*, had run off to Spain to join the International Brigade. Then there were rumours that the King was involved with a married woman, an American for heaven's sake, and she was to get a divorce – but was it in order for her to marry the King? The question was on everyone's lips and swept the subject of Germany off the pages of newspapers.

But Unity was seldom at home while these things were coming to pass: she spent most of her time in Germany. Even before the cruise she had squeezed in a short trip, visiting the Goebbels family in Berlin in February, and joining Diana in Cologne for the general election held in April when Hitler was returned to power by 99 per cent of the electorate (there was, of course, no opposing candidate). They checked into the Dom Hotel and were having lunch when Hitler walked in, his face set, arm raised in a Nazi salute. Then his eye fell on the Mitford sisters and his face broke into a smile. 'What, you two here?' he said, and invited them to join him for tea. In the jubilant atmosphere that prevailed following his victory he invited them both as his personal guests to the Olympic Games to be held in Berlin in July, and to the Bayreuth Festival afterwards.

When she returned to England Diana received an invitation to lunch from the Churchills whom she had not seen since she threw in her lot with Mosley, although she had once been a frequent guest at Chartwell and numbered Randolph and Diana among her best friends. As an artist Churchill is generally known for his landscapes and still lifes, but Diana was among the few people he painted.[27] Churchill wanted to hear Diana's opinions on Hitler, and the others present – Lord Ivor Churchill and Sarah Churchill – were 'simply fascinated' as she told them about him. Earlier Hitler had asked her about Churchill, and it is worth noting that Diana was one of the very few, if indeed there were any others, who knew *both* Hitler and Churchill well at a personal level. She suggested that they should meet, convinced that the two great men would get on, though it was clear they already regarded themselves as rivals. 'Oh, no. No!' Winston replied.

It is tempting to wonder what might have happened had Diana been able to arrange a meeting. Might the war, which tore Europe apart, have been prevented? Hitler was pro-England, and had made a study of its culture and history. He was especially fascinated by the ability of such a small nation to control and apparently subjugate a vast empire containing millions of people. He regarded this as evidence of the superiority of the Aryan race and it is widely considered that this was what saved the United Kingdom from precipitate invasion. When Nazi chiefs of staff were poised and ready to strike, at a time when Britain was at its most vulnerable, Hitler hesitated to give the order until the moment was lost. Churchill, on the other hand, is a heroic figure to us now, but in the mid-1930s he was not regarded in that light. Most people in his own class, in his own party, in the government and in the establishment regarded him as an adventurer and a warmonger, with a great failure in his past. The disastrous First World War campaign at Gallipoli had been his initiative, and he had lost his post as First Lord of the Admiralty because of the huge loss of life there in 1915–16.

After the cruise Unity shot back to Munich, where she was living more or less permanently now, in a flat in the Pension Doering. She had her two white pet rats there and even a dog, a black Great Dane, called Flopsy as a puppy, but later Rebell. At the end of June she went to stay with Janos von Almassy in Austria for a week. Her time in Munich was spent in a ceaseless circle of waiting to be invited by Hitler to join him for lunch, tea or dinner – sometimes in his flat. 'The greatest moment in my life,' she told a friend, 'was sitting at Hitler's feet and having him stroke my hair.'[28] She gave alcoholic parties in her apartment for her friends from 'the heim', and her favourite storm-troopers. One of the SS men, Erich Widemann, she regarded as a boyfriend for some years, but it is unlikely that there was any sexual activity between them. If she was 'in love' with anyone it was Hitler, in her naïve, adolescent way.

When they went to the Olympics later that summer, Diana and Unity were invited to stay with the Goebbels at their country house Schwanenwerder, just outside Berlin on the Wannsee Lake. The party was taken each day to the stadium by limousine, and, fortunately, Diana felt, she and Unity were not given seats next to their hosts – they found it boring to sit and watch track events for hour after hour: they preferred to get up and walk around. In the evenings there were social events, state banquets, and parties at which leading Nazis vied with each other to provide the best entertainments: von Ribbentrop gave a decorous 'embassy-style' dinner party; Goering held a dinner for eight hundred guests who were entertained by a ballet company, dancing in the moonlight, followed by a vast *fête champêtre*. Two days later Goebbels entertained two thousand guests on an island on the lake: guests reached the site across pontoons strung from the shore, guided by the light of torches held aloft by lines of Nazi maidens (the girls' equivalent of the Hitler Youth movement).

When the Games ended Diana and Unity were driven to the Wagner Festival at Bayreuth, in a Mercedes provided by Hitler, for performances of *The Ring* and *Parsifal*. The latter was Diana's least favourite of Wagner's works and she said so to Hitler when he asked how she had enjoyed it. 'That is because you are young,' he told her. 'You will find as you get older that you will love *Parsifal* more and more.'[29] She states that his prediction was accurate.

The relationship between both women and Hitler had now progressed to a stage where they could even hector him gently. At one luncheon party at Goebbels' home, he sat with Unity on one side and Diana on the other while they 'attacked' him for appointing Ribbentrop as ambassador to London. Ribbentrop was absolutely the wrong man for London, they told him. Such *lèse majesté* did not go down well with Nazi officials who were always on their guard in the presence of Hitler. No one *ever* contradicted him. For these two 'over made-up British women' to dare to do so did not make them popular. Increasingly Unity found them blocking her access to Hitler. Meanwhile Hitler appeared to enjoy their company, and there is one eyewitness account of them, both dressed in powder-blue jumpers, blonde and striking, sitting on either side of him while they all discussed the reason for the Mitfords' peachy skin. The English rain was responsible, they told him. In their presence Hitler could be tempted into one or other of his party pieces, either an elaborate pantomime of himself carefully rolling and smoking a cigarette, or an impersonation of Mussolini strutting and bellowing and receiving the gift of ceremonial sword which he drew from its scabbard and flourished dramatically. Hitler usually finished this mimicry by saying in a self-deprecating manner guaranteed to draw good-humoured applause, 'Of course I'm no good at that sort of thing. I'd just murmur, "Here, Schaub,* you hang on to this."'[30]

But despite appearances, a more serious purpose than mere junketing lay behind Diana's four visits to Germany in 1936.[31] The BUF required huge sums of money to run its headquarters with full-time staff, its advertising and promotion, and the cost of Mosley's hectic programme all over the country. Its revenue, which consisted of the combined income from BUF subscriptions and donations from wealthy sympathizers, were proving insufficient. Eventually, Mosley used virtually all of his own fortune propping up his party, but in 1936 he was confident he could find some way to provide for the necessary shortfall in income. Several schemes were floated but Mosley settled on the only really serious one, which, if it could be brought off, was the equivalent of a licence to print money.

In essence it was to start a commercial radio station, based in Germany and broadcasting in Britain. The BBC held a monopoly on radio transmission for the UK in the thirties, and there were no commercial stations. There were, however, two overseas radio stations that provided what the audiences wanted, and which the BBC staidly refused to offer: evening programmes offering popular music. The most famous of these, the foreign-owned Radio Luxembourg, which played modern recordings hour after hour, interspersed with advertisements, was the only commercial station available in most of England and Scotland, and even though reception was patchy at times it was extremely

---

*Hitler's adjutant.

popular until well into the 1960s. The other station was owned and run by Captain Plugge, a Tory MP, who had obtained a wavelength from the French government. He called his station Radio Normandie and though it could only be received in southern England he made a small fortune from it. Bill Allen, a senior figure in the BUF, was in the advertising business and knew all about Radio Normandie. He backed the idea enthusiastically for he knew that large national companies were looking for alternative advertising platforms to the traditional ones of newspapers and magazines, and the huge success of radio advertising in the USA had pointed the way.

What was required was a medium-band wavelength, powerful enough to reach most of the United Kingdom, so Diana, whose German was by now fluent, was asked to use her friendships and contacts with top Nazis to try to secure permission for the establishment of such a radio station. Apart from the much-needed revenue that would be generated from advertising commercial products, Mosley and Diana planned a range of own-label cosmetics and other domestic items. And despite the station's declared aim of being strictly commercial, and relaying only sport, sweet music, beauty hints and similar domestic delights, the opportunity for covert propaganda to the mainly young audience that such a station would attract was incalculable, though Diana refutes this was ever on the agenda. As bait Diana offered payment in hard currency to aid the Reich's serious balance-of-payments deficit.

To ensure that advertisers would not be put off advertising on a station that was so firmly allied politically, no mention of Mosley's name was ever made in connection with it. However, the directors of the company, Air Time Ltd, formed to float the idea were senior members of the BUF. The secrecy over Mosley's involvement was not mere paranoia: in the previous year Lord Rothermere's *Daily Mail* complied instantly when a Jewish industrialist threatened to withdraw all advertising from the newspaper if it continued to support Mosley. For this reason absolute confidentiality concerning Diana's mission was maintained, and even Unity – perhaps especially Unity, who was a chatterbox – was not party to the plan.

Immediately Diana ran up against a major hurdle. Her friendship with Joseph and Magda Goebbels might have led her to assume some support from the propaganda minister who was the person who most mattered in the scheme, but Goebbels was implacably opposed to any broadcasting from Germany over which he did not have ultimate control. Diana knew, however, that the right word from Hitler could change Goebbels' mind and she was working to this end, while at the same time cementing other friendships that might prove useful. But although her friendship with Hitler was now a matter of record, 'occasionally . . . we dined and watched a film or talked by the fire. We did not discuss the radio project,' Diana wrote. 'It was the sort of thing that bored him and was left to his ministers.'[32]

She did not get far with the radio station project in 1936, but one positive thing for her came out of the series of visits. Diana got on well with Magda Goebbels, and the two women spent a good deal of time together and were close enough for Magda to confide her unhappiness in her marriage. The women had something in common: Goebbels was a notorious womanizer and at one point the marriage almost ended in divorce over his affair with the beautiful Czechoslovakian film star Lida Baarova. On that occasion Magda appealed to Hitler asking for a divorce, but Hitler insisted the couple remain married and that Goebbels give up his lover. Press photographs of the apparently happily married couple with their six beautiful blond children projected too powerful an image of a perfect German family to be discarded. Furthermore, as Hitler had no wife, Magda occupied the position of 'first lady' in the Nazi administration. She complied on this occasion as on others, the chief reason, she said, being her children. In turn Diana told her about the problems she and Mosley had experienced in keeping their marriage ceremony secret from the British press. Here, Magda was able to help: she invited Diana to hold her marriage ceremony at her Berlin home. When this proposal was put to Hitler he agreed to ensure that no news of the ceremony would reach the German press, and furthermore that he would attend as guest of honour. Goebbels was less than enchanted by the arrangement, especially when he found that Mosley proposed Bill Allen as his witness. Allen was one of the directors of Air Time Ltd and Goebbels did not trust him (probably he was aware that Allen was an MI5 agent). He did not like or trust Mosley either, and quarrelled with Magda about the forth-coming wedding,[33] but with Hitler's sanction the plan went ahead

Diana and Mosley were married in the drawing room of the Goebbels' apartment on 6 October 1936. In her autobiography Diana recalled that she wore a pale gold silk tunic dress.

> Unity and I, standing at the window in an upstairs room, saw Hitler walking through the trees of the park-like garden . . . the leaves were turning yellow and there was bright sunshine. Behind him came an adjutant carrying a box and some flowers . . . The ceremony was short; the Registrar said a few words, we exchanged rings, signed our names and the deed was done. Hitler's gift was a photograph in a silver frame with [the initials] A.H. and the German eagle.[34]

Apart from Hitler, Unity and their hosts, the only people pres-ent at the ceremony besides the bride and groom and the registrar were Mosley's witnesses, Bill Allen and Captain Gordon-Canning, an officer in the 14th Hussars. The British consul had been advised of the marriage, for the sake of legality, but was asked not to publish information about the wedding, which he was not obliged to do since it was not performed under British jurisdiction. He was also invited to attend but declined owing to a previous engagement.[35] The small party went straight from the ceremony to a wedding feast organized by Magda Goebbels, and there was no time for Mosley and Hitler to speak privately as Diana had hoped there would be. Afterwards they attended a meeting at the Sportsplatz where Hitler addressed a crowd of twenty thousand. Although Mosley spoke no German Diana thought it would be interesting for him to see Hitler's technique. Hitler then left on a special train for Munich and the newly-weds went to their hotel, the Kaiserhof. It had been a long day and they were both tired. What should have been a romantic occasion was spoiled by a quarrel, 'of which, try as I will, I cannot remember the reason,' Diana wrote, 'and we went to bed in dudgeon. Next day we flew home to England.'[36]

Apart from Unity, only David, Sydney and Tom were told of the marriage, under a strict vow of secrecy. Although David was not reconciled to Mosley, both the Redesdales were relieved that at least Diana was no longer living in sin and the rule that he must never be mentioned was relaxed. However, Sydney realized shortly afterwards that the world still thought Diana was living in sin, and that therefore she could still not allow Debo to visit Diana at Wootton. 'The poor thing was quite distraught about it,' Unity wrote to Diana, 'and . . . did hope you would understand.'[37]

There was still no change in the relationship between Nancy, Diana and Unity. And the singular thing about this quarrel is that Nancy, the queen of all teasers, was deeply hurt by Diana's continuation of the 'non-speakers' rule, and from this hurt grew an increasing bitterness. Perhaps she was not even aware of it herself, but it shows in waspish comments in her correspondence. During the summer she and Prod had taken Decca on holiday to

Brittany. Decca enjoyed herself, especially as they treated her as a grown-up and took her to nightclubs, but it was traumatic for Nancy because Prod was in the middle of a love affair, one of many but this one seemed more serious than the others. The girl-friend, Mary Sewell (née Lutyens, she was married for a short time to Unity and Decca's 'white slaver'), lived a few doors from Rutland Gate, and the Sewells and the Rodds used to meet regularly to play bridge together. Mary followed the Rodds to Brittany and stayed in the same hotel, causing an aura of emotional tension to pervade the holiday. The Rodd marriage, which had started off so well, was already a sham whose front was wholly maintained by Nancy. She might have accepted the infidelity, for she saw so much of it in the circles in which she moved, but Prod had also started to drink heavily, which made him unpleasant and aggressive. Also Nancy desperately wanted a child, and tried for years. It was altogether an unhappy period for her as the Rodds moved from their first married home, Rose Cottage, at Strand-on-the-Green, into a small Victorian house at 12 Blomfield Road in Maida Vale. The tiny garden backed on to the Grand Union Canal, which was 'enchanting' and the saving feature of the otherwise poky little house.

It could not have helped that Diana and Mosley had moved into beautiful Wootton Lodge earlier in the year. It was tranquil indoors and out: bluebell woods surrounded the house and clothed the valleys that were dotted with trout pools. Diana had made there 'an atmosphere of extraordinary beauty and stillness,' Nicholas Mosley recalled. 'Whenever [my father] became exhausted or ill – such as the time he was hit by a brick at Liverpool – he would return to Wootton as if it were his fairy castle and Diana his princess.' They were so happy there that they spent all their holidays at home in preference to going abroad. When they were apart they sent each other loving notes: 'Today,' wrote Diana, 'as my heart is full of love I shall write what is always in my thoughts; and that is, that I love you more than all the world and more than life. Thank you my precious wonderful darling for the loveliest days I could possibly imagine . . .' And Mosley wrote in kind, 'Tried to ring you Saturday night but told no answer – nothing special – just love!'[38] In Diana's diaries during their time at Wootton the same entries occur over and over. 'Perfect day with Kit [her name for Mosley],' and 'Wonderful day.'[39]

Romance was in the air, it seems, for Pam, the 'most rural' Mitford, had at last fallen in love. For some time she had been seeing Derek Ainslie Jackson, the thirty-year-old good-looking son of Sir Charles Jackson, founder of the *News of the World*.[40] He had married Poppet John (daughter of Augustus John) in 1931 but a divorce was in progress when he and Pam began their relationship. Derek and his identical twin Vivian had been orphaned while still teenagers at Rugby, and were inseparable. They took scholarship examinations for different universities because it was thought best for their development that they were split up (Derek applied to Trinity, Cambridge, and Vivian to Oxford), and when they parted company at Bletchley Junction[41] it was believed to be the first time in their lives that they had been apart. Although their guardian cheated them by selling blocks of their shares in *News of the World* at rock-bottom market price and then bought them back himself, they were gleefully aware that they would be millionaires when they reached their majority. They had a highly developed sense of fun and were great teasers. They could be bombastic and arrogant, but they were also lively, charming, generous, funny and devoted to animals.

They had first-class brains and read science subjects. When Derek graduated with a first, as anticipated,[42] he was contacted by Professor Lindemann, who offered him laboratory facilities of his own at the Clarendon Laboratory at Oxford to work on his doctorate. Later Derek would say that Professor Lindemann had 'bought' him, 'just as you might buy a promising yearling. But this particular yearling was a spectacular winner, for at the age of only twenty-two his specialist research in the field of spectroscopy led to a leap of thought considered so brilliant that no book on physics could ever be written again without including his findings.[43] He would go on to become a world-renowned physicist, and a professor at Oxford, and although his life outside his work was filled with activity and pleasurable pursuits, science was always what mattered most to him, ultimately taking precedence over everything else: nothing was so sacred that it could not be shelved or cancelled if he happened to be at a crucial point in his research.

Second only to his love of science was Derek's love of horses. He rode with significant success and great bravery as an amateur in National Hunt races, including several times in the Grand National, and he hunted like a hawk with the Heythrop hounds two or even three days a week in the season. Compared to the Mitfords he was not tall at five foot eight; compactly built, he could hunt thoroughbreds when most men needed a heavy-weight hunter – thus he had an incomparable advantage when following hounds across fast country. His riding, jumping and off-the-cuff quips (an important part of hunt social life), as well as his eccentricity, became the stuff of Heythrop legend. He once came off into a ditch and was soaked through but, undaunted, he dashed home, changed, and returned to finish the day. To sixteen-year-old Debo he had been a hero-figure for some time. She considered herself in love with him, and was delighted when Pam began going out with him, for it meant she got to see him at home. In the autumn of 1936, however, Pam moved into Derek's home, Rignell House, anticipating his divorce by a few months, and the couple drove over to High Wycombe to announce their engagement to her family. On hearing their news the infatuated Debo 'slid gracefully onto the flagstones in a dead faint'.[44]

That December saw the abdication of Edward VIII that most

people had been hoping would somehow be avoided. James Lees-Milne recalls in his diary that he stayed overnight at Wootton with Diana and listened to the broadcast with her. 'We both wept when Edward VIII made his abdication broadcast. I remember it well, and Diana speaking in eggy-peggy [baby talk] to Tom Mosley over the telephone.'[45] Christmas carollers that year invented new words to add to the old favourite: 'Hark the herald angels si-ing/Mrs Simpson's pinched our King . . .'

Three weeks later, just two days before the end of 1936, Derek and Pam (the latter 'laden with jewels, which her generous bride-groom had showered upon her'), were married at the Carlton register office. In the formal wedding picture, the small group of Mitfords and family friends are muffled in furs and dark winter clothes. No one is smiling, but this is probably because it was no more customary, then, to smile for formal photographs than it was when sitting for an artist for a portrait. The posed annual family photographs of the Mitfords are equally serious. Diana and Nancy, apparently with hatchets temporarily buried, stand shoulder-to-shoulder behind Pam, Derek and Sydney. Tom is half hidden behind David. Unity, Decca and the heartbroken Debo are not in evidence.

The newly-weds left for Austria on honeymoon. On arrival at their hotel in Vienna in early January the manager came out to meet them and asked Derek quietly if he could speak to him alone. Derek spoke fluent German and it was from this complete stranger that he received the news that his twin Vivian had been killed in St Moritz. A horse-drawn sleigh he was driving had overturned after hitting a telegraph pole. Pam told Diana that Derek was never the same again. 'Part of him died with Vivian, who meant more to him than any other being on earth ever could.'[46]

10

ELOPEMENT
(1937)

Hardly had the Redesdales recovered from the news of Vivian Jackson's tragic death, and worry over the inevitable unhappiness this meant for Pam at the start of her marriage, when another crisis was upon them.

During the autumn of 1936, prior to Pam's wedding, Sydney had been conscious of Decca's unhappiness. It was for this reason that the Redesdales took her up to Scotland with them in December to visit David's Airlie cousins, but she seemed even more bored there than at home despite the pre-Christmas festivities. Racking her brains to try to bring her daughter out of the doldrums Sydney came up with the idea of taking her, Debo, and a friend of theirs on a world cruise departing in March. Debo was due to make her début the following year and a cruise would be as good as a period at finishing-school, which in any case Debo did not want. But nothing could please Decca at that time and in her autobiography she admitted that 'even the exciting planning of the trip was marred by my bad temper'. There were arguments about every stop on the itinerary, which usually ended with Sydney saying in the languid drawl that came from the top of the back of her throat, 'You're *very* silly, Little D.' After these rows Decca was always angry with herself because she recognized that her mother was only trying to help her. But the source of her misery was that she felt trapped, living a life of luxury, provided by 'the very people' who upheld the non-intervention policy that allowed the barbarous war in Spain to escalate. So it was probably somewhat to Sydney's relief when an invitation arrived for Decca that was greeted by its recipient with unusual enthusiasm.

In the third week of January 1937, Decca went to stay with Dorothy Allhusen at Havering House, near Marlborough in Wiltshire. Renowned for her hospitality, 'Aunt Dorothy' was credited with being the Edwardian instigator of weekend house-parties – 'Do come Saturday to Monday' – and her house was famous as a haven of comfort. Fires blazed in all the rooms throughout the winter, and no expense or detail was spared to make guests feel pampered. Those who accepted her generous hospitality included Lord Beaverbrook, Winston Churchill and Somerset Maugham. Also among their numbers was Esmond Romilly, for Aunt Dorothy had a soft spot for her wayward young kinsman. She was a widow, and having lost her only son to a childhood illness had informally adopted Esmond. After he ran away from school he had been sent to a remand home when his mother told the court she could not control him. Aunt Dorothy had stepped in at this point and offered to be his guardian. Knowing all this, Decca thought she might hear some news of Esmond at Havering, but on her arrival it was even better than she hoped. Her fellow guests were an American couple called Scott, and Esmond, who was expected later that day. Decca felt faint with anticipation.

Esmond had recently returned from Spain, where he had gone within weeks of hearing of the Falange rebellion to join the International Brigade. With fifteen other Englishmen he joined a unit of miscellaneous volunteers from France, Germany, Italy, Belgium and Poland who, after the briefest of training, were sent to the front at Cerro de Los Angeles. In December 1936 he was involved in the battle of Boadilla del Monte from where he sent several dispatches, which appeared in the pro-loyalist *News Chronicle* under headlines such as 'Winston Churchill's Nephew Sends Graphic Message'. Twelve days earlier, Esmond reported, his company of men had numbered 120. Following the battle their number was reduced by death and injury to thirty-seven. There was no field discipline and they were sometimes shelled by their own side; there were no supplies, and no medical aid. Eventually he, too, succumbed to the conditions, and was invalided home in early January with dysentery. Later he wrote that that he hardly recalled the hardships of that period; all that remained in his memory was an impression of

> a wild Russian-filmish scene of endless singing of the
> 'Internationale' and wine-drinking in romantic cafés with
> tough Russian drivers and frenzied cheering and rushing
> around in romantic corduroy trousers with romantic belts
> of hand grenades and sleeping on the romantic stone
> floors of churches and all the rest – that was all there . . .
> but a more truthful account would have to include also
> the continual Army slogan – 'We're being f——ed again',
> and that the personal struggle for an extra square foot of
> space on a truck or train and the attempt to avoid tasks
> like carrying boxes of ammunition did in fact loom larger
> than 'No Paseran'.[1]

After several weeks' treatment in King's College Hospital, Aunt Dorothy told Decca, Esmond was now recovered. He had been spending a couple of days visiting the parents of young men who had been killed beside him in the fighting (he was one of only two English survivors), and he was probably already on his way to Wiltshire by train.[2] Decca had been trying for months to find a way of meeting Esmond. Before she was dragged off to

Scotland (her description) she had arranged through a mutual friend, Peter Nevile, to meet Giles Romilly at a Lyons Corner House, 'a place where you are hardly likely to run into anyone you know', and asked him if he could help her to run away and join the International Brigade. Nothing had come of this, but during his spell in hospital, Esmond had learned from Giles and Peter that Cousin Decca, 'the ballroom pink' of the Mitfords, had been making detailed enquiries about him, and wanted to get to Spain to help in the fight against Fascism. He then suggested to his doting aunt that Decca might be an interesting house guest.

In an interview in later life Decca admitted that she was already half in love with Esmond before she ever met him. 'There was a marvellous photo of him in the front of his book *Out of Bounds*, at which I used to gaze wistfully . . .'[3] She dressed that evening with special care in a mauve lamé ankle-length dress. It was very fashionable but uncomfortable to wear, and she worried about its tinny smell. She sat in her pretty room agonizing about what he would think of her, and wondering about possible rivals for his affection: sophisticated London women, brave Spanish freedom fighters, 'all of them beautifully thin, no doubt'. At last, gazing at her reflection in the flattering pink glow lent by the dressing-table lamp, she decided she didn't look *too* disgusting, and steeled herself to go down to join the others. Over sherry she talked to Mr Scott and watched Esmond out of the corner of her eye. He was not quite as she had imagined him. He was shorter than the Mitford men, thin with bright eyes fringed with long lashes. Energy seemed to flow from him and he had a manner of standing with his head held on one side, listening to what anybody said as though it were the most important thing he'd ever heard in his life. Spain had changed him, according to his friends: he had gone out a romantic and come back disillusioned, though not embittered. He was serious that night, quiet and full of admiration for the

Communists who alone, he said, had saved Madrid.[4] After they went into dinner things moved fast.

Aunt Dorothy had thoughtfully seated the two cousins together and taking advantage of a moment when the others were deep in conversation Decca furtively asked Esmond if he was returning to Spain. He said he was. 'Well – I was wondering if you could possibly take me with you?' she asked. Esmond needed no time to think over this bold proposition. He replied immediately and easily that he would. Decca, prepared to counter any number of depressing arguments, was taken aback. Could it really be this easy? No cavilling about her being too young or a girl? He suggested they went for a walk after breakfast to discuss it, and carried on talking to the others. That was all it took for Decca to fall in love with Esmond but in her defence it must be said that many contemporaries recalled him as a highly charismatic personality.

Next morning Decca was first down, and after breakfast Esmond extricated them from the party expertly. 'We won't be long,' he said firmly, as they left the room with his hand under her elbow. Walking in the freezing muddy lanes of an English midwinter, Esmond outlined a plan he had concocted during the night. He had an advance of ten pounds from the *News Chronicle* to return to Spain as a war correspondent, which would enable him to get the necessary visa. He suggested that Decca should go as his secretary, which should allow her to obtain a visa too. He brushed aside as irrelevant her concern that she could not type: he did all his own typing anyway, and he was impressed when she told him about her running-away account which had been painfully accumulated from saved pocket money, sales of valued objects such as the appendix and windfall half-crowns from uncles and aunts at Christmas and birthdays. Fifty pounds would make things *much* easier, he said. Quickly they laid their plans and less than twenty-four hours after they met everything was in place. At last, Decca was about to achieve

her childhood ambition to run away, *and* with the adored
Esmond. All her dreams coming true.

So much changed for her over that weekend that when Decca
arrived back at Rutland Gate three days later, she was amazed to
find everything unaltered. There was Sydney drawling, 'Hullo,
Little D, did you have a nice time at Cousin Dorothy's?' and talking about clothes for the cruise and typhoid injections.
Household routine went on as ever. No one seemed to notice
that Decca was no longer bad-tempered and bored. Next morning she made sure that she was standing by at nine-thirty to pick
up the small pile of post, into which she slipped a letter she and
Esmond had concocted together at Havering. It purported to
come from her friends the Paget twins, who she knew were in
Austria for the whole winter. She opened and read the letter in
front of Sydney so that she could make appropriately enthusiastic noises. 'Darling Decca,' it began:

> Twin and I are so anxious to see you before you go off
> around the world. Now I have a suggestion to make.
> Sorry it's such short notice, but do try and fall in. We
> have taken a house in Dieppe, that is, Auntie has taken
> it. We mean to make it the centre for a motor tour to all
> the amusing places round. We are going there from
> Austria on Wednesday and would love you to join us
> next weekend . . . or two weeks . . . there won't be much
> of a party, just two boys from Oxford, us three and
> Auntie . . . our address is 22, rue de Gambetta, Dieppe.
> So perhaps you could send a telegram to me there if you
> can come . . . we shall be so disappointed if you can't . . .
> Our house in London is successfully let, hope yours is
> too.[5]

It was something of a masterpiece of composition. It told Sydney
that there was no point in trying to contact the mother of the

twins at the London address to confirm the story. It told her that the holiday was to be a touring one so that there was no way of getting in touch with Decca to check on her. An added bonus was that, if she was allowed to go, Decca's running-away expenses would be met by the Redesdales as far as Dieppe. Sydney not only sanctioned the trip but even agreed to a thirty-pound advance on Decca's dress allowance for cruise clothes. Decca was amazed by how easily it all worked. Although Sydney insisted on her shopping for cruise clothes, and getting a typhoid injection before she left for Dieppe, she agreed Decca might go, 'although you might not be able to spend the whole two weeks, Little D,' she said. Decca's biggest problem was losing the others during a shopping trip so that she could get to the bank to draw out her running-away money and meet Esmond to apply for her visa. She did feel a pang of guilt, however, when Sydney splashed out three guineas for a solar topee that Decca knew she would never wear.

On Sunday 7 February both parents took Decca in a taxi to the station. As they settled her into her seat in the train they fussed about her comfort, and forwarding addresses, and last-minute instructions and hoped she'd enjoy herself. Her stomach was churning with apprehension but she caught a glimpse of Esmond hanging around at the end of the platform, which stiffened her. She hardly dared think of what would happen when her parents discovered she had left home for good. But by now she felt that, whatever happened, Esmond would sort it out. She was so much in love with him that he had achieved something of a god-like status. It seems extraordinary that Decca would jettison her entire life and family for a young man whom she had known for only a weekend, but that is what happened.

For the next ten days everything seemed well to Sydney. She went ahead with preparations and packing for the cruise and received several postcards from Decca and a letter.

9 Feb, 1937 Dieppe

Darling Muv,

. . . the weather is pretty bad here so we shan't be doing much motoring till Thursday. We are just back from Rouen, the Cathedral is lovely . . . the Pagets send their love . . . I called on Aunt Nellie Romilly this morning and was told she was expected here next week . . . Love Decca.[6]

Two further letters followed from stopping points on the imaginary tour, chatty with details of the holiday and the weather, sending love from the twins, and advising that she would not be home before Sunday 21 February. But even before these last two letters were received Sydney sensed somehow that something was not right. She cabled the twins' mother at the address in Austria given in the forged letter, 'DO YOU KNOW WHERE DECCA IS?' and contacted a Paget aunt in London. Within hours she learned that the story of the holiday with the twins had been an invention. To say that the Redesdales were worried at this discovery would be a gross understatement. They had grown so used to Decca's childish threats to run away that it never occurred to them that she would finally do it. Where could she have gone? Her allegiance to the Communist Party caused them great concern — to whom might she have gone? Had she tried to get to Russia? For almost three days they had no idea where she was, or with whom, and when two cheery letters arrived from her they knew them to be fabrications, so they were no comfort.

Esmond told Decca that he had fallen in love with her on the day after they arrived in France. Thereafter, since they intended to marry eventually, they saw no reason to pay for two hotel rooms as they journeyed south. Decca's letters were designed to keep her parents' minds easy until a letter (forwarded by Esmond to Peter Nevile on the thirteenth), had been delivered to Nellie Romilly in Dieppe on Saturday 20 February. Esmond thought that by then, two weeks after their elopement, they would be married and 'in the clear', but they soon found that a marriage was not possible because they were both under age. Esmond was eighteen and Decca was nineteen; as minors they both needed parental permission. Meanwhile, they waited in Bayonne for Decca's Spanish visa. For Esmond, who was anxious to get to Spain, it was frustrating, but for Decca everything was new and exciting. Only one incident marred her enjoyment and it led to their first quarrel.

They were sitting drinking in a café one evening when a large rough man came in with a dog, muzzled and on a leash. After a while the man began to beat the dog across the face with a switch and as it yelped and whined the other diners laughed and cheered. Decca became frantic and shouted to Esmond, 'Tell him to stop . . . the cruel brute, can't you do something?' Esmond pulled her up out of her seat and said, 'Come on, let's get out of here.' Outside the café he told her furiously,

> What right have you got to impose your beastly upper-class preoccupation with animals on these people? You're behaving like a typical British tourist. That's why English people are so hated abroad. Don't you know how the English people of your class treat people, in India and Africa, and all over the world? And you have the bloody nerve to come here – to their country, mind you, and . . . telling them how to treat their dogs . . . I can tell you when you get to Spain you'll see plenty of horrible sights, bombed children dying in the streets. French people and Spanish people don't give a damn about animals and why should they? They happen to think people are more important. If you're going to make such an unholy fuss about dogs you should have stayed in England, where they feed the dogs steak and let people in slums die of starvation.[7]

Decca refused to admit that it was necessary to ill-treat animals in order to care for people, and they quarrelled all night. Next day they made up but what Esmond said made her think more deeply about her commitment to his brand of politics. It is interesting that the first disagreement between these two firebrand radicals was over a point unconnected with ideology. However, as she recalled later, she and Esmond felt they could do anything, achieve anything, and that they were not bound by any rules. Years later she attributed this to a special brand of self-confidence due to their upbringing: they enjoyed 'a feeling of being able to walk through any fire unscathed'.

Nellie received Esmond's letter on the twentieth, in Dieppe, too late to reply the same day, but the following morning she contacted Dorothy Allhusen, and asked her to contact the Redesdales immediately to tell them the startling news she had just received from Esmond: '. . . When I met Decca Mitford at Cousin Dorothy's the other weekend,' he had written, 'we both more or less fell in love with each other . . . then we arranged that she should come to Spain as my secretary. I expect by the time you get this we'll have been married in Spain, as of course we've been unofficially so, since we left, and we're intending to have three children . . . her family loathe the name of me . . . so pour some white wash on me.'[8] Any attempt to get Decca back, he warned, would result in his leaking to the papers the truth about Unity and Hitler: 'It wouldn't be a very nice thing to have that advertised.'*

By this time Peter Nevile had called at Rutland Gate with the unenviable task of telling the Redesdales that their daughter had eloped with a young man whom for years most of the family had thought would have been improved with a horsewhipping. He also told them that the couple were presently living as man and

---

*This was either a bluff or some nonsense of Decca's.

wife in a cheap hotel in Bayonne and that by now they might be married. Having worried for days that Decca might have run off to join a Communist cell, or even that she had been taken by white slavers, Mitford legend says that David sank into a chair muttering, 'Worse than I thought. Married to Romilly!'

Sydney wrote immediately to Decca at the address in Bayonne: 'My darling, we have been in such agonising suspense . . . please come home. I cannot do more than *beg* of you to return. We shall be here as we are not, of course, going on the cruise.'[9] On the same day Sydney received a seven-page letter from Nellie Romilly, which must have made her want to scream. Nellie began by saying that she and her husband, Bertram, were proud to have Decca as a daughter-in-law, even though they were concerned that Esmond had taken such a step when he was in no position to keep a wife. She was surprised, Nellie continued, as before he left she had asked Esmond if he had any romantic entanglements and he had replied that he was in no position to fall in love as he could not support a wife. 'I know only too well that he cannot appeal to any mother as a husband for her child . . . his attitude has always been one of defiance to law and order,' she wrote. She only hoped, she said, that 'the children' were in northern Spain where there was no fighting.[10] When Nanny Blor was told about this all she said was, 'Good gracious, she didn't take any clothes to fight in.[11]

The couple *were* in Spain by this time. Decca had finally been granted a Spanish visa and after a rough three-day voyage in a small cargo boat across the Bay of Biscay, she and Esmond arrived at Bilbao. Whenever she stopped to think about what had happened it seemed like a dream to her: here she was, in Spain, with Esmond, the embodiment of years of fantasizing. As members of the accredited press corps they were given free board and lodging in the Hotel Torrontegui in the centre of the town which, although it was some distance from the fighting, showed all the signs of a war zone. Food was scarce; meat, eggs, butter and milk were unobtainable. Every meal, breakfast, lunch, supper, was the same, and they existed on beans and coarse grey bread, with an occasional treat of fish, all washed down with the thick chocolate drink of the region. Utility services were spasmodic and garbage was piled up in the nearly deserted streets.

After a few days they were taken by jeep to the front where a representative of the Press Bureau explained the various battle positions to the assembled reporters. Decca, looking out of place among the contingent of hardened war correspondents, was asked if she would like to shoot a rifle. At that moment she must have wished that she had gone out shooting occasionally with her father for the recoil knocked her off her feet and the bullet embedded itself in a tree. This was Decca's sole experience of front-line fighting in Spain, and it seemed 'unreal'. After that, she and Esmond settled quickly into a routine in Bilbao, checking each day with the Press Bureau for war news and spending a few hours each afternoon preparing and typing dispatches for the *News Chronicle* such as 'One Night on the Spanish Front: by Esmond Romilly'.[12] But she was fidgety and anxious about what was happening at home, half worried that her parents would find a way of bringing her back. She wrote to her mother with pretended insouciance: she and Esmond were quite safe, she said, and they were not to worry about her. She told of how they had been taken to see a prisoner-of-war camp where she thought the prisoners were rather too well looked-after – 'when you think how the fascists treat *their* prisoners . . .'[13] Often, at night she could hear the heavy guns as war raged an hour's drive away.

At Rutland Gate the Mitford children had soon clustered round the distraught and bewildered Redesdales. Unity had 'scrammed back' from Munich as soon as she heard the news of the elopement, and by the time she arrived they had heard via the consul in Bayonne that Esmond and Decca were now in Spain. Prod was well to the fore when legal options were being discussed, with plenty of 'I-know-I-*am*-a-lawyer' suggestions and it was agreed that he and Nancy should go out to Spain and bring Decca home. 'Prod was boring about the whole thing,' Unity wrote later. 'Right from the beginning he wanted to arrange everything and he was dying to be the heroic brother-in-law who rushed out . . . (expenses paid by Farve) to bring you back. Also it was his silly and expensive idea to make you a ward in chancery. I don't suppose, either, that you loved his piece in the *Daily Mail*, in which he said that you only became a communist to get even with me.'[14] Meanwhile she told of the sad spectre of their parents sleepless for nights on end, with David clumsily making pots of tea for Sydney.

Through Churchill, the Foreign Office had become involved ever since the Redesdales realized that Decca was missing. Now, Foreign Secretary Anthony Eden agreed to allow the Rodds to travel aboard a naval destroyer just leaving for the port of Bermeo (thirty miles from Bilbao) to take off British subjects and refugees trapped by the fighting. Eden also sent a personal cable to the consul in Bilbao: 'FIND JESSICA MITFORD AND PERSUADE HER TO RETURN'. Meanwhile the family solicitors, Hasties, were instructed to cable Esmond: 'MISS JESSICA MITFORD IS A WARD OF COURT STOP IF YOU MARRY HER WITHOUT LEAVE OF JUDGE YOU WILL BE LIABLE TO IMPRISONMENT STOP HASTIES'.[15]

The same day the British newspapers got on to the story when the *Daily Express* headlined its front page: 'Peer's Daughter Elopes to Spain'.[16] This was the sort of romantic episode that reporters could make something of: the pretty teenage daughter of a peer of the realm, eloping with a younger cousin who also happened to be the notorious and rebellious 'red' nephew of Winston Churchill. What was more, the girl came from a family with two already newsworthy daughters: Diana, who supported (they dared not go further) Sir Oswald Mosley, and Unity, who had already made her position on Hitler and the Nazis well known. The story, with considerable embellishment, made headlines in all the British papers, and many European ones, for weeks: 'Another Mitford Anarchist', 'Consul Chases Peer's Daughter', 'Mixed Up Mitford Girls Still Confusing Europe'. Unfortunately, despite their scoop, the *Daily Express* got the sisters mixed up and stated that it was the Hon. Deborah Freeman Mitford who had eloped. Debo subsequently sued for libel because of the damage to her reputation, and settled out of court for a thousand pounds, which she spent on a fur coat. Esmond, who felt that he and Decca had undergone all the hardships and were desperately short of money, never got over the injustice of Debo's windfall.

Now that her whereabouts were known, Decca was besieged with mail from home. Nanny was frantic about her wardrobe and whether she had enough underclothes – 'We shall have no peace while you remain in Spain. Darling, how could you do it?' she wrote. '*Do please come.*' On the eve of what should have been the departure of their world cruise Sydney wrote,

> Darling beloved Little D;
> I am writing this for Peter to take to you . . . I think I am living in the most frightful nightmare and half expect to wake up and find it never happened and Little D is here . . . Nannie's heart is broken . . . Bobo and Debo miss you all the time and the house is so sad . . . I beg you to listen to Nancy and Peter and do as they say . . . It is something to know where you are, I nearly went mad when it seemed you had quite disappeared . . . I can't help blaming myself terribly for it all . . . I knew you were unhappy, but the cause of it all was beyond me, except that like many girls you had nothing to do. I ought to have been able to help you more . . . Farve is better now but it was frightful to see him so down, I have never seen

him like that . ... Tom & Diana & Bobo have been
wonderful and helped so much . . .[17]

Tom, Diana and Unity had all sided with Decca, provoking
uproar at Rutland Gate. Two weeks later Unity wrote from
Munich that when she arrived home she found Aunt Weenie
announcing that it would be better if Decca were dead, 'but I
know she thinks that about me and Diana, too'. Unlike her gen-
tler older sister Sydney, Weenie was all for sending Tom to give
Esmond a good thrashing, and accused Diana of causing all the
problems of Decca and Unity by 'setting a bad example'. But
futile threats to horsewhip Esmond were all that David could
manage. Coming on top of Diana's divorce and marriage to 'that
man', and Unity's obsession with Hitler, Decca's defection had a
devastating effect on him and what was to be a rapid physical
decline appears to date from this point. The 'poor old Fem and
Male' were utterly miserable, Unity continued. At first they had
suggested that Unity went out to get Decca, but then they
decided that,

as Esmond is by way of hating the idea of me . . . it might
do more harm than good. So I came here instead, in the
new car Farve gave me . . . four-seater and black. I stayed
two days . . . at Nuremburg on the way [and] met the
Führer by great good luck last Tuesday . . . he asked me to
go to tea with him and I followed his car to his flat and sat
with him for 2½ hours alone, chatting. He wanted to hear
all about you and what happened since I saw him last. He
had forbidden it to appear in the German newspapers
which was nice of him wasn't it – at least perhaps you
won't think so as Nancy says Esmond adores publicity.[18]

Rudbin wrote to advise that 'Your elopement has caused the
biggest stir since the abdication . . . but darling, you never

would have done it if you'd known what misery you'd cause here . . . poor Aunt Sydney seems absolutely broken and wretched, and poor Debo's eyes filled with tears . . .'[19] Idden wrote as well, and confessed that when she first heard the news she really thought Decca had run off to fight, 'and I kept thinking of you dead or in screaming agony, and no food or baths. It is absolutely true about Muv and Farve and all the family being broken by it, really sist, what else could you have expected? You must have known the agony it would cause them . . . Uncle Jack [David's brother] is more wildly against you than all the rest put together. He thinks you ought to be flogged till your nose bleeds!! But I must say he giggled at your letter this morning . . .'[20]

The distress of the Redesdales was predictable, but Debo was also deeply affected. The sale of Swinbrook some months earlier had been a great sadness to her, for alone of her siblings she loved the house and considered her childhood there to have been idyllic. Furthermore, Decca had been the nearest sister in age to her: Unity at six years older was virtually grown up by the time Debo was ten. The sight of her parents and Nanny in anguished despair, the absence of Decca on top of losing Swinbrook, and the cancellation of the cruise to which she had been looking forward, hit her hard. Even now she regards this period as one of the unhappiest times in her life.[21] However, when she told Decca this, in a letter fifty years later, Decca was truly astonished, apparently never realizing how deeply her running away had affected her youngest sister.[22]

But there was no turning back for Decca, any more than there had been for Diana when she made her decision to leave Bryan for Mosley, or for Unity once she had met Hitler. The British consul at Bilbao had gone out of town for a few days and his secretary spoke limited English, so Esmond composed the reply to the Foreign Secretary's cable for him. The wording of this cable is perhaps a measure of this extraordinary young man and his

attitude to authority: 'HAVE FOUND JESSICA MITFORD STOP IMPOSS-
IBLE TO PERSUADE HER TO RETURN'.

Within days, however, Hasties' cable was delivered to Esmond
by the vice-consul, Arthur Pack, who had been sent to the town
to deal with the impending emergency of refugees.[23] He spelled
out the full legal implications of Decca's being made a ward of
court. His warning was reinforced when the British ambassador,
Sir Henry Chilton, called Esmond and Decca to his temporary
embassy in a hotel. Chilton was renowned as a problem-solver,
but one can imagine his irritation: he was in the midst of a real
crisis, plagued by hundreds of anxious people wanting assurance
that they would be rescued by the Royal Navy, his staff had
hardly enough to eat, and now his attention was diverted by this
frivolous young couple who appeared to be under the personal
protection of the Foreign Secretary.

He told them that the Basque government was relying on the
assistance of the Royal Navy to evacuate women and children
refugees, as the battlefront moved towards the coast. Unless
Decca boarded the destroyer, he said, the British government
would refuse all further co-operation in the evacuation programme; furthermore if they chose not to comply he would
notify the Press Bureau of the reason why British co-operation
was being withdrawn. It was a no-win situation, for even if
Esmond and Decca called the ambassador's bluff, and Esmond
was pretty sure it was a bluff, their Spanish visas would almost
certainly be withdrawn. Esmond won one concession: he and
Decca would board the destroyer, he said, but would travel only
as far as St Jean de Luz, where Nancy and Peter had disembarked
a few days earlier as they had no visas to enter Spain.

Twenty-four hours later Nancy and Peter, surrounded by
British reporters, were waiting for them at the end of the dock.
Decca, convinced that she could count on Nancy 'to be on my
side through thick and thin'[24] had looked forward to seeing her
elder sister, though Esmond scowled every time she said this. As

far as he was concerned the entire Mitford family were Nazis. 'Nancy, tall and beautiful' waved her gloves at them and a fusillade of flashbulbs went off as Decca walked down the gangplank. Hours of intense argument followed, Nancy – no doubt hoping to save Decca from making a similar mistake to her own (and Diana's) by marrying in haste – argued hotly that Decca should come home and 'do things properly', not live with Esmond as she was doing. It was not respectable and Society could 'make things pretty beastly to those who disobey its rules'.[25] Decca was mortified to find that Nancy had 'ganged up with the Grown Ups' against her. Prod told Esmond that if Decca went back to England he felt sure Lord Redesdale could be persuaded to give her an allowance, but the implication that he wanted money out of his proposed marriage to Decca, and from such a tainted source as Lord Redesdale whom he referred to as 'the Nazi Baron',[26] infuriated Esmond. Next morning Nancy and Peter left, somewhat to the surprise of Decca and Esmond, who had expected them to put up more of a fight.

It was not so much success for the runaways as stalemate, for the British consul made it clear that Esmond's application for a renewal of his Spanish visa would not be sanctioned as things stood. Yet the couple could not marry. Furthermore their finances were critical. They had spent Esmond's original advance and two or three sums sent to him by Peter Nevile for the *News Chronicle* articles. Decca's running-away money, the thirty-pound dress allowance and an extra ten pounds that David had given her for spending money were also long gone. They now had nine shillings between them,[27] so Esmond walked round to the Reuters office and talked himself into a job, translating and transmitting what was being reported by radio from both sides in the Spanish war. This paid two pounds a week, which was exactly the cost of a double bed and board at the Hôtel des Basques. Esmond did not speak Spanish well enough to translate the excitable transmission so the manager of the hotel did it for him each night, refusing however to listen to or translate Falange broadcasts. Esmond made that part up based on what he gleaned from that of the republicans. The couple decided to remain at Bayonne until they could see a way out of the present situation, and meanwhile there was a rapid-fire exchange of letters between Sydney and Esmond, in which he, still livid at Prod's implied charge that he was after money, was coolly offensive and advised that they considered themselves married so that any letters addressed to *Miss* Jessica Mitford were being returned unopened.

Decca had replied to Unity's chatty letter that she didn't think Esmond would be very keen on her keeping in touch with a Fascist and Unity's response was matter-of-fact:

> About Esmond's feeling for Fascists (actually I prefer to be called a National Socialist) . . . I hate communists as much as he hates Nazis . . . but I don't see why *we* shouldn't personally be quite good friends, though political enemies . . . I do think family ties ought to make a difference. My attitude towards Esmond is as follows – and I rather expect his to me to be the same. I naturally wouldn't hesitate to shoot him if it was necessary for my cause, and I should expect him to do the same to me, but in the meantime I don't see why *we* shouldn't be quite good friends.[28]

Esmond, of course, could see every reason why they should not be friends and his reaction is probably best summed up by a single paragraph in *Boadilla*:

> I am not a pacifist, though I wish it were possible to lead one's life without the intrusion of this ugly monster of force and killing – war . . . And it is not with the happiness of the convinced communist, but reluctantly, that I realise that there will never be any peace, or any of

the things that I like and want, until that mixture of profit-seeking, self-interest, cheap emotion and organised brutality which is called fascism has been fought and destroyed forever.[29]

Sydney now decided to see Decca. She travelled out to Bayonne with the aim of talking her daughter into going home with her. Perhaps if she had gone in the first place, instead of Nancy and Prod, she might have been saved a good deal of heartache, although there was never any chance that she would change Decca's resolve. Sydney's calm manner and ability to laugh at most things won Esmond's grudging respect, while the Rodds had made him bitter and intractable against the entire Mitford family, an attitude he was fast transmitting to Decca. When Sydney left, she had realized that Decca could not be talked out of marrying Esmond and – since Decca had admitted to her in confidence that there was a strong possibility she was pregnant – she said she would see what she could do to help them. Esmond contacted Peter Nevile to say that there was no change in their plans and that Lady Redesdale had left after two days of amicable discussion. On the other hand they were in urgent need of more cash so he suggested leaking the latest position on the runaways to the *News Chronicle* – 'It can't do any harm, provided it's not presented with too many details as though a "story" sold to the press. Then we can combine the proper attitude to this "hateful publicity" with a little more filthy lucre.'[30] The resultant 'interview with the runaways' appeared on 12 March. 'Unfair tactics on behalf of the British Government – diplomatic blackmail, if you like – are responsible for the fact that Decca and I are [here] . . . I am hoping to return to Spain to continue my journalistic work, and I hope to take Decca with me . . .'

Esmond and Sydney then engaged in a series of letters in which he bluffed that he was beginning to think that there was not a lot of point in marrying at all. And, when Sydney wrote to say she had persuaded the judge to consent to the marriage and that she would like to attend the wedding, he wrote saying that since the Redesdales had such a low opinion of him he did not want anyone from Decca's family present. Perhaps this was due to the fact that the same post that brought Sydney's placatory letter also brought a furious letter from David saying that Decca would never get a penny from him while she remained with Esmond, married or unmarried. The couple now conveniently forgot that they had acted badly and caused distress. They began to regard themselves as victims and it was the start of a long period of acrimony between Decca and various members of her family.

In the event, both Sydney and Nellie Romilly attended the civil wedding on 18 May. It was, the newspapers said, 'the wedding that even a destroyer could not stop' (for by now it was accepted by the press that the Foreign Secretary had sent the destroyer solely to find Decca). After a ceremony of a very few words at the British consulate, Esmond Mark Romilly, bachelor and journalist of the Hôtel des Basques, and the Hon. Jessica Lucy Freeman Mitford became man and wife. Lady Redesdale took the small wedding party to lunch at Bayonne's smartest hotel. It was all she could do to make a celebration of the day but she regarded it as an ineffably sad rather than happy occasion. It was difficult to accept that her darling funny 'Little D', the natural clown of her children, had chosen to marry in such a hole-in-the-corner manner, with no friends or jovial family group to support her. She had not even a wedding gown, just a simple summer dress, bought by Sydney in Bayonne, with a sufficiently relaxed shape to accommodate the slight bulge in the bride's waistline.[31] There were a few gifts to unwrap, which Sydney had carried over with her, and which provided a brief degree of festivity: a portable gramophone from Unity, a pearl and amethyst necklace and earrings from Diana and some books Decca had asked for.

On the following day, with many misgivings, Sydney left the

newly-weds to the life they appeared to enjoy, in an untidy and, she thought, a rather squalid hotel room. Although she had wanted her girls to be comfortably married within their own class, she had never wanted them to marry for money, and they had all grown up believing that love was the most important ingredient in a marriage. Sydney's initial objection to Bryan Guinness had not only been Diana's age but his excessive wealth, and she must have felt that if Diana had had to budget and work hard at running a house, as she herself did, that the Guinness marriage might not have come under such pressure. But Decca's marriage seemed to be starting out with everything against it: she and Esmond were hardly more than children, without any prospects whatsoever, no home to go to and no income. Decca knew nothing about the practicalities of running a house, as was obvious from the untidiness in which they were living. Furthermore, their ideology seemed destined to alienate them from everyone who might be persuaded to help them. Her only reassurance was that they were, clearly, very much in love and Esmond appeared protective of Decca. They talked a lot about earning their living and were fine, intelligent young people if, in her opinion, misguided. So she clung to a hope that it would eventually work itself out. She had arranged a touring holiday for Debo to compensate for the disappointment of the cancelled world cruise, and when she left Bayonne she went to Florence where they were to meet.

Esmond then landed a job of sorts. He became an interpreter between the Basque government and the captains of several merchant vessels who were trying to land vital supplies at Bilbao, despite a reported blockade. This provided him with a number of reporting scoops for which the *News Chronicle* paid him an extra five pounds a story, through Peter Nevile who was acting as his agent. When not writing his dispatches Esmond worked doggedly at his book *Boadilla*, his brown head bent over his typewriter and the hotel-room floor littered with pages of typescript. With its historical perspective, and its reasoned argument, it is a remark-able book, by any standards, for an eighteen-year-old to have written. Decca teased that he was the only person she had ever heard of who had written two biographies before he was nineteen. She felt proud, but also sad and guilty, knowing that it was because of her that Esmond could not get to Spain, which he really wanted to do. In the event he never returned.

Most days he finished work by early afternoon, after which they had lunch and went to Biarritz to bathe in the sea.[32] These pleasant visits almost came to an abrupt end when Esmond was caught in an undertow and nearly drowned. Decca could see that he was struggling but the person she begged to go to his rescue was a poor swimmer and sensibly refused.[33] She was in despair, but Esmond somehow fought his way back and sat exhausted on the beach, with Decca in floods of tears at his side. They had decided to stick around in Bayonne for the July fiesta, a carnival which emulated the famous bull-run of Pamplona except that in Bayonne cows were released on to the streets. It was a few days of drunken revelry, providing respite from the miserable news from Spain during the interim weeks. Between Guernica – Franco's first experiment in 'total war', in which the town was mercilessly bombed until nothing remained standing – and the eventual capture of Bilbao on 19 June there had been a remorseless stream of bad news.

The only comfort was that, with a few wedding-present cheques, Esmond's earnings and an advance for his book, their exchequer was boosted again to something over fifty pounds. With the confidence of a wealthy man Esmond came up with a brilliant idea to resolve all their financial problems permanently, inventing a system that would 'break the bank' at the local casino. Like all such gambling systems it could not fail, and when he explained it even Decca was convinced that in a night they would become millionaires. Predictably, within two hours they had lost everything. In desperation and in secret Decca wrote to Sydney to ask for help. Although she could not resist an uncomfortable dig about their spending, Sydney sent three pounds as a gift, and a ten-pound dress allowance, explaining that she had been obliged to reduce the allowance for both Decca and Debo from £140 a year to £120 because of a rise in income tax, which had reduced her salary from the *Lady*. In future, the dress allowance would be paid into their accounts at Drummonds in monthly instalments of ten pounds. Clearly, there were to be no more lump-sum advances large enough to finance elopements.

After the fiesta the Romillys spent several months touring France in a car borrowed from a fellow reporter who had returned to England, and camping in a two-man tent. They lived on small sums sent over by Peter Nevile. Eventually, in Dieppe, where they had spent a few weeks as Nellie Romilly's guest, the car seized up as they had forgotten to put any oil in it. The weather was turning too cold for camping and Decca was becoming increasingly ungainly, so they decided to return to England, where another friend had offered them a flat in his house at Rotherhithe in south-east London.

11

FAMILY AT ODDS

(1937–8)

Debo was seventeen on 31 March 1937 but her moment of
metamorphosis was overshadowed by the elopement crisis. Her
coming-out ball was postponed for a year and she left London
after a birthday party for a visit to Castle Howard as a welcome
break from the tensions at Rutland Gate. With no children left at
home, Nanny Blor – who had also been badly upset by Decca's
elopement – took a long holiday with her family at Hastings, followed by 'doing the rounds', visiting Nancy and Diana, before
going to stay with Pam who was recuperating from gynaecological surgery. It was hoped this would enable her to have a child,
but it was not successful and she never carried a child to term.

For her birthday Debo was given a car and a course of driving
lessons. It looks as if Sydney was taking no chances of her becoming bored, and bolting. But there was never any real danger of
that for, in general, Debo enjoyed her life at home. On the other
hand, this youngest of the Mitford sisters had every right to feel
aggrieved by the actions of some of her siblings. Not only had
Decca's elopement upset her emotionally, it dampened her birthday celebrations. Even worse, the notoriety of Diana, Unity and
Decca inevitably cast a blight on her prospects. What mother of

an eligible son could have felt unalloyed pleasure in a connection with a family where three elder sisters had already demonstrated such contempt of Society's values? Sydney realized this and was ultra-careful on Debo's behalf. But Debo was never affected with the jealousy from which Nancy suffered or with Decca's inexplicable bitterness. She was uncomplicated, like Pam, although far more lively and everyone liked her.

While Sydney went to Bayonne for Decca's wedding, Debo – somewhat cross at not being allowed to see her sister married – travelled with a friend to Italy and waited in Florence for her mother. There, she was closely watched by her temporary guardians: 'I wasn't allowed into town so I couldn't send you a telegram on the wedding day,' she explained to Decca.[1] When Sydney joined her they toured northern Italy together, and stayed in Venice before travelling north to join a party at Janos von Almassy's *Schloss* in Austria, which, since the Anschluss a few months earlier, was now in Hitler's Reich. Janos was an ardent supporter of Hitler but it was not simply from this partisan source that Sydney and Debo received their impression – so different from that reported by the British press – that the Austrians were overjoyed at this development: everyone they met seemed truly pleased with it.

Prior to the Anschluss, having read about his anti-Hitler speeches, Unity had written to Winston Churchill setting out a number of facts for him about Austria and telling him of her own experiences. She received a kindly worded but firm reply that 'a fair plebiscite would have shown that a large majority of the people of Austria would loathe the idea of coming under Nazi rule'.[2] It must have seemed to Unity that Churchill was wrong, for on 14 March she was able to witness for herself the scenes of wild jubilation, German troops pelted with flowers, and the deafening chant of '*Sieg Heil! Sieg Heil! Sieg Heil!*' And '*Heil, Hitler!*' that rang joyously through Vienna when Hitler appeared on the balcony of the Hotel Imperial. What Unity did not witness, of course, was the brutal treatment of anyone opposed to the new regime: the beatings, the arrests, the deportations to concentration camps.

From Austria Sydney and Debo went on to stay with Unity at Pension Doering.

12 June 1937,

My darling Little D, We are leaving for home tomorrow . . . and it has been great fun touring around with Bobo . . . of course the little car has been a real comfort . . . yesterday we went out to Nymphenburg [and] I am hoping to go round one of the girls' work camps before we go. I think the others told you of our tea party with the Fuhrer. He asked after Little D. I wished I could speak German I must say. He is very 'easy' to be with and no feeling of shyness would be possible, and such very good manners . . . All love, darling, and to E, Muv.[3]

Decca and Esmond were not at all amused to learn that her name was on Hitler's lips, but they decided that it was all that could be expected from Decca's 'Nazi family'. Sydney kept Decca *au fait* with all family news, writing every week while Decca was in France. David and Tom, she reported, had joined them in Munich for a few days, but Tom had gone on to visit Janos von Almassy, and David had returned home and rented 'the fishing cottage' (also, confusingly, called Mill Cottage) at Swinbrook for the summer, so that they could all go there for weekends if they wanted. While they were together in Munich, the Redesdales had been given a tour of the city by one of Hitler's adjutants and years later, in *Hons and Rebels*, Decca would state that they were driven round in Hitler's car. 'Not true,' Sydney pointed out, 'you wouldn't catch Farve in anything but his own Morris.'[4] News of her father from other members of the family was the closest Decca would ever get to him. The day he put her solicitously on the train for Paris, tucking the travelling rug around her legs and handing her ten pounds as spending money, was the last time she ever saw him, although he lived for another twenty years.

Debo, meanwhile, was thoroughly enjoying her tour and looking forward to her début as a Grown-Up when she returned home. 'I think Munich is no end nice . . . if I had to live anywhere abroad I should certainly live here,' she wrote to Decca. The Hitler tea party had been fascinating: 'Bobo was like someone transformed when she was with him and going up stairs she was shaking so much she could hardly walk. I think Hitler must be very fond of her, as he never took his eyes off her. Muv asked if there were any laws about having good flour for bread, wasn't it killing?'[5] They spoke about the Anschluss and Hitler told Sydney, 'They said England would be there to stop me, but the only English person I saw there [Unity] was on my side.'[6]

Sydney was happy to get back to her bread-making at High Wycombe: 'We had lovely times abroad but it is very nice to be at home,'[7] she wrote, telling Decca that Debo was looking forward to attending Royal Ascot in the following week, and had received invitations to a number of smart dances including one given by the American ambassador for which she had bought a dress of white tulle. One cannot avoid wondering if, when relaying this sort of detail, Sydney hoped to make Decca regret what she had done, even at this late stage. 'Tom spends all his time with the Territorials and will be going to camp with them. He is nearly every weekend shooting at Bisley or doing something of the kind. You know how thorough he is when he does anything.' Tom, like David before him, had discovered a real enjoyment of military life and would subsequently go to Sandhurst with a view to making the Army his career. 'Woman [Pam] is coming over to see us tomorrow,' the letter concluded, 'and Nancy has gone to Scotland to escape the hay fever.'[8]

Decca now advised her sisters that the doctor had confirmed the anticipated date of confinement was 1 January: 'Do you remember poor Lottie's agonies [a pet dog] and I expect it's much worse for humans . . . I do hope it will be sweet and pretty and everything. Goodness I have been sick but I'm not any more.'[9]

'My darling Little D,' Sydney wrote from High Wycombe, 'Bobo tells me you have told her about the baby . . . No one else except Farve knows because I didn't tell anybody, not even Nanny, but will now. She will be pleased. I wonder if you would like to have this cottage for 3 months from 8 December when we will be at Rutland Gate.'[10]

Debo was staying with her parents at Mill Cottage, Swinbrook, by the time she wrote to Decca to congratulate her on the baby. 'It is more than ever like a Russian Novel here, because Farve has taken terrific trouble to buy things he think Muv will like and she goes round putting away all the things that he has chosen. The worst of all was when she went up to her bedroom for the first time and saw two wonderfully hideous lampshades with stars on them and said, "I certainly *never* bought those horrors," and Farve's face fell several miles.' However, despite the cold, she said, they were enjoying being back at Swinbrook and the trout fishing was good.[11]

Debo was now embarked upon a round of débutante dances, two or three a week, and her Grown-Up status required her to be sophisticated about these:

I must say they exactly are as you said – perfectly killing . . . Luckily for me Tuddemy has been to all the ones I have. He is simply wonderful and waits around until I haven't anyone to dance with and then comes and sits on a sofa or dances with me. I must say it's terribly nice of him. My conversation to the deb's young men goes something like this:

Chinless horror: *I think this is our dance.*

Me (knowing all the time that it is and only too thankful to see him, thinking I'd been cut again): *Oh yes, I think it is.*

C.H.: *What a crowd in the doorway.*

Me: *Yes, Isn't it awful.*

(The C.H. then clutches me round the waist and I almost fall over as I try to put my feet where his aren't.)

Me: *Sorry.*

C.H.: *No, my fault.*

Me: *Oh I think it must have been me.*

C.H.: *Oh no, that wouldn't be possible* (supposed to be a compliment).

Then follows a dreary silence sometimes one or other of us says, 'sorry' and the other 'my fault,' until . . . the end of the dance and one goes hopelessly back to the door to wait for the next CH.

Besides her social life, she continued, 'nothing has changed much, Farve goes off to the *Lady* and the House of Lords, and Muv paints chairs and reads books like *Stalin, my Father*, or *Mussolini, the Man*, or *Hitler, my Brother's Uncle*, or *I was in Spain*, or *The Jews, by one who knows them.*'[12] Debo's letters, Decca said, made her 'roar'.

With the exception of Decca the entire family attended the Coronation of George VI, and Unity and David had places of honour aboard a royal escort vessel for the fleet review at Spithead. At her first ball Debo was presented to the King and Queen: 'He looks a changed man since he was King, so much happier looking and alert,' Sydney wrote to Decca. '*She* looks more serious.'[13]

After the Coronation, Unity drove back to Germany, taking her cousin Clementine Mitford back with her for a short holiday.

Munich was also *en fête*, she reported to Decca, and looked so gay that by comparison the Coronation decorations appeared insipid. Her friendship with Hitler went from strength to strength and her letters were full of incidents where he chanced to 'spot her' in the midst of a crowd and called her out. Often, now, he would invite her back to his flat: 'We sat for hours, chatting, quite alone' and 'The next night I went with him to the opera to see *Aida* done by the Milan Scala company. It was lovely to be able to go as all the tickets had been sold out 3 months before and it was a *wonderful* performance.' He invited Unity and Clementine to accompany him to the Bayreuth Festival, and sent his long black Mercedes to collect them. 'We were there ten days,' Unity wrote, and then they returned on Hitler's special train, watching delightedly as loyal Germans lined the track waving swastika flags and saluting Hitler. 'I have seen the Führer a lot lately which has been heaven, but now he has gone back to his mountain for a bit.'[14]

Although she was only twice invited to Hitler's mountain eyrie, the Berghof overlooking Berchtesgaden, which was the domain of his mistress, Eva Braun, Unity was now a frequent guest at gatherings of Hitler's inner circle, and sometimes she saw him alone in his quarters. Some of Hitler's senior officers regarded her naïve prattling with the Führer as potentially dangerous, and were concerned about the niche she had established for herself in his life. She now signed her name 'Unity Walküre', in the German manner, adding a small swastika underneath. She told people that she been named 'Unity' at the outbreak of the Great War because her pro-German family hoped that England and Germany would soon be at peace again. Probably she had even begun to regard this exaggeration together with the curious fact of being conceived in Swastika as evidence of her destiny. True, she saw Hitler only in his off-duty moments when – as the memoirs of those close to him testify – he could be immensely charming and jovial, especially when he was in the company of women. Diana, who also saw him in his off-duty periods, was never witness to the aggressive outbursts, megalomania or cruel humour that those who knew him for many years at a personal and professional level have catalogued. Unity saw him lose his temper twice, but she was so obsessed that she regarded the incidents with awe rather than disgust. 'He got angrier and angrier,' she wrote to Diana, 'and at last he thundered – you know how he can . . . "Next time . . . I shall have him arrested . . . and sent to a concentration camp; then we shall see who is the stronger; Herr Gurtner's law or my machine guns!" . . . It was wonderful. Everyone was silent for quite a time after that.'[15]

Unity chatted to Hitler as she would to any member of her family, unselfconsciously bright, always seeking to amuse, entertain or impress. No one else in his life dared to treat him in the casual manner that Unity adopted. His adjutants and lieutenants were always aware that a chance remark made in fun might cause him to take fast, bitter retribution, and were guarded. Eva Braun, according to contemporary observation, was apparently cowed for much of the time and few people outside of the inner circle knew about her. Even during the time that Diana spent alone with Hitler, which was far more than most people realize, she was always aware of his position, and her radio-station agenda, and she addressed him accordingly.

It has never been proved that Unity's intimacy with Hitler damaged anyone, though there are accusations that – wittingly or otherwise – she denounced various people to their serious disadvantage. Whether it is true or not, it is clear that her apparent naïvety in such a situation made her potentially dangerous. Her letters show that she discussed Mosley's activities with Hitler, for she wrote to advise Diana that Hitler thought Mosley had made a mistake in calling his movement Fascists or Blackshirts instead of something more acceptable to the British. When she asked him what he would have done in Mosley's place, he told her he would have emulated Cromwell and called his followers 'Ironsides'.[16]

Albert Speer, another inner-circle member, recalled that 'even in the later years of international tension,' Unity – or Lady Mitford as he called her – 'persistently spoke up for her country and often actually pleaded with Hitler to make a deal with England'.[17] Increasingly, Unity regarded some form of alliance between the two countries as a personal mission: *this* was her destiny, to prevent war between the two countries she loved. And it was just this sort of conversation that worried and irritated Hitler's chiefs. Nor did it go unnoticed by the British ambassador. On a number of occasions he reported back to London conversations he had had with Unity in which, he wrote, she was as open in telling him what Hitler had said to her as she undoubtedly was in telling Hitler what the British ambassador thought. The ambassador met Unity at the railway station when he went to greet the exiled Duke and Duchess of Windsor in September 1937. While they waited, she told him that Hitler disliked Mussolini but thought the Italian dictator's forthcoming visit was useful in demonstrating to other countries the strength of the Berlin–Rome Axis. 'Miss Mitford . . . said that she had heard it stated that HM's Government had asked Herr Hitler not to receive the Duke of Windsor. Hitler had replied that he knew nothing of this and would gladly receive the Duke of Windsor.'[18] He pointed out that he could not guarantee the accuracy of Unity's statements, and he thought that she was so obsessed with Hitler that it was possible she sometimes put words into his mouth, 'but I know that Herr Hitler is on familiar terms with her and talks freely to her . . . [and] subject to certain reservations I have little reason to doubt the accuracy of what she occasionally tells me of her conversations with the Chancellor'. As the situation deteriorated towards war, there were further conversations with Unity that the ambassador reported back to London.

These vignettes underline Unity's unique position among

Hitler's suite but there has always been speculation about her private, i.e. sexual, relationship with Hitler, and this was discussed at the time even in the Mitford family, judging from Esmond's letter to his mother at the time of his elopement. Further research indicates that if there was ever any sexual element to this relationship, it was never fulfilled by physical intercourse. Diana also believes this is the case. She spent many evenings alone with Hitler, but she was an acknowledged beauty who had been courted and flirted with all her life; unlike Unity, she was experienced in assessing the motivations of men. She told me she thought Hitler was not very interested in sex, and she was convinced that Unity had never slept with him. 'He enjoyed her company and it ended there, I think,' she said. Had he asked Unity to sleep with him, would she have agreed? 'Oh, yes,' she replied unhesitatingly.[19] That Unity was in love with Hitler is borne out by the testimony of many people who saw her over a period of years in his presence. One of these was another remarkable woman who had the ear of Hitler, Leni Riefenstahl.

On one occasion she asked him about Angela 'Geli' Raubal, the half-niece he had loved, who had committed suicide. Geli had not been his only lover he told her frankly, but, he said, 'my romances were mostly unhappy. The women were either married or wanted to get married.' He did not mention Eva Braun in this conversation, although Leni knew about his secret mistress hidden away in the mountains.

> He was bothered, he told me, when women threatened suicide in order to tie him down, and he repeated that he could have married no one but Geli. I asked him what he thought of Unity Mitford, the pretty Englishwoman who, as the whole world knew, was so in love with him. His reply surprised me. 'She's a very attractive girl, but I could never have an intimate relationship with a foreigner, no matter how beautiful she might be.' I thought he was

joking, but he assured me, 'My feelings are so bound up with my patriotism that I could only love a German girl.' Amused, he said, 'I can see you don't understand. Incidentally . . . I would be completely unsuitable for marriage for I could not be faithful. I understand great men who have mistresses.' The tone of this was lightly ironic.[20]

That Unity wielded influence with Hitler is evident from her part in a matter involving Putzi Hanfstaengl, who suffered directly when Unity repeated a private conversation they had had while sailing his yacht on the Starnberg Lake. He told her that he had hated being stuck in New York during the 1914–18 war, and said it was a pity there was no fighting anywhere now except in Spain. He said he envied those fighting for Franco. He went on to criticize Goebbels, whom he thought was 'schizophrenic and schizopedic',[21] and even criticized some things Hitler had done. 'I may have gone too far,' he said, in his autobiography.[22] Clearly he had, for Unity turned on him and told him, 'If you think this way you have no right to be his foreign press chief.' He countered, saying it was bad for the Führer to be surrounded always by yes-men, and thought that that was the end of the matter. Shortly afterwards, however, Unity wrote to Diana that Hitler planned to play a 'wonderfully funny joke on Putzi' to repay him for some remarks that she had passed on.[23]

Unity regarded what followed as a practical joke, a Nancy-style tease. History does not relate what Hitler intended, though it seems a curious way to treat a man who appeared to have been consistently loyal to him through bad and good times.[24] Hanfstaengl certainly did not find it amusing. He was ordered, quite normally, to report to an airport to carry out a project for Hitler. Once in the light aircraft he opened sealed orders, which advised that he was to be dropped behind the lines in Spain on a secret mission. He had no trouble making the connection with his conversation with Unity, and guessed that she had probably repeated his wild criticisms of Goebbels and Hitler. Knowing a good deal of how Hitler's machine worked he immediately suspected that he was to be assassinated and his death written up as an accident. He begged the pilot, a fellow Bavarian, to put down somewhere. The pilot, who was puzzled by the whole affair, pretended that the aircraft had developed technical problems and made an unscheduled landing, whereupon Hanfstaengl made his escape and fled to Switzerland. Many years later he met the pilot, who told him that his orders had been to fly him round Potsdam for a few hours then await further instructions. He had been given to understand that Goering was entertaining high officials from overseas, and that the highlight of the military display was a demonstration of how they would shoot down a dummy on a parachute. 'It still does not sound like a joke to me,' Hanfstaengl wrote in his autobiography.[25]

Unity subsequently contacted Hanfstaengl in London on several occasions, dismissing the affair as a joke as she tried to persuade him to return to Munich. Even Diana got involved, and tried to win from Hitler a pension for his old friend, and a personal guarantee that it was safe for him to return to Germany. Subsequently, Hanfstaengl received a letter from Goering, which told him: 'I assure you that the whole affair was intended as a harmless joke. We wanted to give you an opportunity to think over some rather over-audacious utterances you made. Nothing more than that was intended . . . I consider it vitally necessary that you come back to Germany straight away . . . forget your suspicions and act reasonably. *Heil Hitler!* Herman Goering.'[26] But Hanfstaengl dug into his intimate knowledge of Hitler and, having got his son out of Germany to the USA (though his sister Erna remained in Munich), he decided that he was safer where he was. The irony of this episode is that Hanfstaengl was incarcerated as an enemy alien in England during the Second World War. So, indirectly, Unity probably saved not only his life but also his way of life. After the war he and his family returned to Munich and lived out their lives in his old family home, which would scarcely have been possible had he remained an active member of the Nazi hierarchy.

That September the Redesdales joined Unity for the annual Parteitag. It was the year of Speer's famous 'Cathedral of Light', which received a great deal of attention in the British and US press. The party included David's sister-in-law, Aunt Helen, mother of Clementine and Rosemary Mitford. Randolph Churchill was also present, but it was the Redesdales the British papers noticed, and they began to ask just *why* Lord Redesdale's family were so interested in the Nazi regime.

Diana made a number of visits to Germany that year, almost all for the purpose of furthering the Air Time Ltd project. She timed her visits to match periods when she knew Hitler would be in Berlin, and she would check into the Kaiserhof Hotel and send a note to let him know she was there. Quite often he would reply through an adjutant, inviting her to the Chancellery after he had finished his day's work. When he had had a full day, and especially after an important speech, he found it difficult to sleep, so he welcomed the opportunity of a long chatty conversation to wind down before retiring. They used to sit together by an open fire in his private rooms in the Reichskanlei, and talk. 'I got to know him fairly well,' Diana states in her autobiography. 'Sometimes we saw a film, sometimes we talked . . . in conversation he was quick and clever, and, of course, very well informed, and he had that surprising frankness often found in men at the top, in contrast with mystery-making nonentities.'[27] Diana is good company, as were all the Mitfords: it can have been no hardship for Hitler to spend time with a sophisticated and beautiful woman who happened to share his taste in art and music. She told Mosley's son, Nicholas, that they spoke of what was happening in England, what was happening in Germany, of Mosley and the BUF, and the state of the world.[28]

Although it took a long time, her calm persistence in the matter of the radio station paid off. Back in October 1937 she had been advised formally that 'the greatest objection was raised from the side of the appropriate military authorities' to the idea. 'The Führer regrets that under these circumstances he is not able to agree to your proposal.'[29] Most people would have given up at that point, but Diana continued with her patient strategy. It was no hardship for her, either, to maintain her friendship with Hitler as she enjoyed their *tête-a-têtes*. In the spring of 1938 she was told by a German contact that Hitler had asked for the radio-station files and had taken them away to read. In June she was advised that he had approved a form of joint venture based in Heligoland, in which Air Time Ltd would share the profits with a German radio station.[30] By any standards the obtaining of this concession at such a time was a remarkable achievement by Diana.

It was at about this time that William Acton drew all six Mitford sisters in works that have since become well known. He had made a pencil sketch of Diana earlier in the year, at the same time as he had made a huge Wagnerian-type oil painting of her, part of a series he did of many of his friends. Sydney liked the sketch so much that she commissioned him to draw the other girls, too. It seemed unlikely that she would see them all together again for a long time (they were *never* all together again). He worked from photographs, though it is possible that Nancy and Debo also sat for him. Sydney had them mounted in red brocade frames and hung them in her sitting room. Nancy told her that it looked like Bluebeard's chamber.[31]

From early October Decca and Esmond were ensconced at the rented house at 41 Rotherhithe Street. It was tall and thin, linking two of the great warehouses that lined that stretch of the southern bank of the Thames. With its dark wharves and teeming slums Rotherhithe was one of the most deprived areas of

London, and when Philip Toynbee first visited he got hopelessly lost. 'When I asked a muffled stranger the way, he said, "What ship do you want, mate?" and I knew I was in authentic Esmond territory.'[32] It was the first time Toynbee had met Decca, and he was impressed not only with her beauty and her cheerful whole-hearted support of Esmond, but her upper-class voice, 'a curiously cadenced sing-song which would have been grotesquely affected if it had not been even more grotesquely natural'.[33] Esmond could be all things to all men and his voice though cultured was not obviously so, whereas the Mitford girls are renowned for the manner of their speech. Decca did not try to change this for some years, and Toynbee recalled her once asking a burly working man, 'Could you be absolutely *sweet* and tell us where we can get some delicious tea?'[34]

Esmond was keen to save so that they could travel to Mexico, so he got a job at five pounds a week, at J. Walter Thompson's advertising agency on the Strand, writing copy for Radio Luxembourg commercials. Even Decca got a job for a few weeks, while she could still work, as part of a market-research team employed by the same agency. She travelled, ate and shared rooms with a group of women who conducted the surveys and it was the first time she had met anyone who was truly working class. Formerly her socialist and Communist contacts had all come from the upper classes, which was Esmond's chief objection to the Communist Party in England: he felt that it was over-loaded with young intellectuals and was therefore unrealistic. The local branch of the Labour Party was closer to his ideology. The coarse attitude towards their menfolk, and to life in general, of the other women in Decca's group was a great shock to her and depressed her. Surely these were not the working classes for whom she had battled with Unity in the DFD? Occasionally she and Esmond would row about her 'upper-classishness', but they were so much in love with each other that all disagreements were quickly made up. And she was young and resilient enough to accept the hardships of the life they shared. The freedom from all restrictions and restraint, so utterly different from life with her parents, made it acceptable and enjoyable – a fulfilment of rebellion.

Occasionally the couple made plundering sorties to the homes of the rich, in response to any casual invitations that came their way, teased right-wingers and filled pockets and handbags with cigars, cigarettes, and any small knick-knacks that took their fancy. Esmond claimed he once had to restrain Decca who had her nail scissors poised above a set of bedroom curtains she fancied for the sitting room at Rotherhithe.[35] The young Romillys regarded this behaviour as amusing and acceptable, for in their persistent war against the upper classes no holds were barred. However, when the stories got out their behaviour was regarded with shocked disgust.

Esmond had some other novel ideas about making a profit from well-heeled friends. The Romillys held parties to which guests were invited to 'bring a bottle', but any wine or spirit that appeared was carefully stashed away in the grandfather clock and only beer was served.[36] Then there were the gambling parties. Esmond seems to have been an eternal optimist when it came to gambling and most weeks spent the best part of his earnings from the agency at the greyhound track, always certain that he was going to make their fortune. When he found he could not win as a punter, he had the brilliant thought of becoming 'the bank' so he acquired a roulette wheel and set up a casino in the sitting room. Any idea he had of fleecing their connections to recoup losses was bound to failure if the single experience of Bryan Guinness is anything to go by.

Bryan had remarried, very happily, and he and his wife had a child a few months old. Relations between him and Diana were friendly again and remained so for the rest of their lives. He also maintained contact with other members of the Mitford family but he was surprised when he and his wife were invited to lunch at Rotherhithe with Decca and Esmond. He soon realized why for 'They told us in all frankness,' he wrote, 'of their intention to make a little money by organizing some gambling for their friends.' Subsequently the Guinnesses played roulette in the homespun casino. Bryan was well aware that he was expected to lose and he was perfectly willing to do so – indeed, he looked on it as a form of charitable giving to help Decca, of whom he was fond. But the evening did not go as planned: 'The stakes were low, but we determined to lose a little to our kind hosts,' Bryan recalled. He staked recklessly, and to his growing despair found that he had won large sums of money. Much more, he realized, than Esmond and Decca could possibly afford. In desperation he continued to play for long hours after he and his wife wanted to go home to bed, and it was almost dawn before he had managed to make a small loss and felt he could retire with honour. 'It was fortunate I think', he wrote, 'that the Romillys did not adopt the profession of croupiers.'[37]

This sort of contact was rare, however, for Esmond was absolutely opposed to Decca seeing any of her family, and although she did meet some of them, she did so in secret to prevent an argument. Tom was the exception. He went to Rotherhithe often, the only member of the family allowed to visit there. Despite his written statements to friends that he supported Fascism, and that had he lived in Germany he would be a Nazi, he somehow convinced Decca and Esmond that he supported them. 'Tom was pure Cudum [Boudledidge for Communist] when he used to come to see us at Rotherhithe Street,' Decca wrote later. 'Esmond adored him (the only one of our family he did) ... but of course *he* adored the Boud [Unity]. In some ways I always thought she was his Favourite Sister.'[38] One is forced to the conclusion that Tom Mitford was not deeply politically committed in any direction and was happy to be whatever was necessary to be allowed to visit his sisters.

When Unity came home in October she and Decca met in

Harrods without Esmond's knowledge. He was apparently incapable of understanding that the affection between the two sisters could survive their political differences. They used to drive around London, shopping for the baby's layette or visiting friends, and when Esmond was not there Unity sometimes took Sydney out to Rotherhithe, a journey of about an hour from the West End. Unity was at the height of her relationship with Hitler, and she was even considering becoming a German citizen. The newspapers had somehow discovered that she had enquired about this, and rumours swirled about that she and Hitler planned to marry. There is no denying that Unity enjoyed all the attention. She drove around in her MG with a pennant on the bonnet emblazoned with a swastika, and that she had become a personality in her own right, not simply the sister of Diana or Decca, pleased her. It was at about this time that Sydney made her famous remark, 'Whenever I see a headline beginning with "Peer's Daughter" I know one of you children has been in trouble.'

A few friends ventured out to Rotherhithe. One, Debo's friend Christian Howard,[39] of Castle Howard, went in the spirit of friendship to a social outcast. 'I was so scared to come into the slums,' she told Decca, 'that I wore my oldest clothes.' Decca was seared by the patronage. 'You don't need to worry,' she said hotly. 'Nobody would know, as your best clothes look like other people's oldest.'[40] It was the last time Decca ever set eyes on her.

Sydney had hoped that Decca's baby would be born late as first babies often are. Early January, with the possibility of calling it premature, would be the best that could be hoped for, and she had instructed the other girls to say, if asked, that Decca's baby was due 'in the spring', which caused much scoffing from the mother-to-be. Decca was something of a lost cause, but Sydney had Debo to think of, and she was undoubtedly thinking of the baby, too, for stigma clung to a child and arbiters of social niceties had long memories. In any case the lusty full-term infant did not oblige. Julia Decca Romilly was born on 20 December[41] in the Rotherhithe flat, and three days later Unity drove Sydney there with her car loaded with presents for Christmas and the new baby. Esmond was at work.

Decca had no idea about housework, and now, with a new-born baby, things got out of hand. It was fortunate, therefore, that the brand of extreme socialism practised by the Romillys did not prevent them from hiring a housemaid. Rose cost them £1 1s 3d a week ('The odd one shilling and threepence is insurance,' Decca told Debo).[42] Decca wrote movingly of the first months of little Julia's life, of the two doting parents gleefully watching as the baby grew, 'learned to smile, wave her feet, and catch them with an unsteady hand'.[43] Sydney, however, was always concerned about Julia's appearance, and thought she was 'too thin' and pale, with none of the pleasing chubbiness of her own children as babies. When Unity returned from Germany in early March, she saw Julia for the first time since she was a few days old, and reported to Diana that she was 'absolutely sweet, but her legs are like Marlene Dietrich's'.[44] Sydney offered to send Nanny Blor, who was eager to help out, but Esmond would not allow it. For the same reason Decca returned Diana's gift of baby clothes.

Baby Julia was four months old when a measles epidemic struck Rotherhithe. Concerned, Decca took her baby to the local clinic for inoculation but the nurse assured her that this was unnecessary as a breast-fed baby was immune to the disease. In giving this information she assumed, of course, that Decca had already had measles and would confer immunity, and who could blame her? It was inconceivable that any child brought up in the docks of London would have escaped the disease. But Decca had never had measles, and had never been inoculated, and within days both she and baby Julia succumbed. Childhood diseases are always more serious in an adult and most of the time Decca was barely conscious. In desperation Esmond engaged nurses to look after them both round the clock, and Decca finally surfaced to the agony of watching her baby fight for breath in an oxygen tent. Julia died on 28 May of pneumonia.

Decca and Esmond were stupefied with grief, 'like people,' she wrote, 'battered into semi-consciousness in a vicious street fight'.[45] Esmond drew out all their savings and made reservations, and the day after the funeral the couple 'fled'. They went to Corsica for three months, during which time Decca recovered her health, protected by time and distance from family sympathy that she could not have borne. Not everyone *was* sympathetic. Philip Toynbee, who had *entrée* to all social events despite his dedication to Communism, was shocked when Julia's death was discussed at dinner parties in Kensington and Mayfair and people said callously that it was more or less to be expected since the baby had been raised in a slum, neglected by its feckless parents.[46] There was a spitefulness, Toynbee considered, out of all proportion to the irritation inflicted by Esmond's pranks. Like most radicals he seems not to have realized that people who quietly conform may feel as deeply about their ideology as those who aggressively try to inflict an opposing one. The remarks about the Romillys were cruel and tasteless, but so was Esmond's behaviour.

The Mitford family was now sadly fragmented with most of them not speaking to at least one other person. Nancy was not allowed to visit Diana at Wootton, or Decca at Rotherhithe, although she and Decca maintained an occasional correspondence. Diana could now visit her parents, but Mosley was still forbidden, and even when Sydney let Rutland Gate it was with the proviso to the tenants that Oswald Mosley must never be allowed to set foot in the house. Nor was Diana allowed to visit Decca, for her support of Mosley made her 'the enemy'. Unity was able to write to Decca but not allowed to visit while Esmond was at home. Debo was forbidden by her parents to visit Decca, but she did so secretly a few times and recalls Esmond as being 'very charismatic – sort of lit up inside'.[47] She wrote frequently to

Decca giving news of the wider family: 'The other day there was a wonderful family gloat, a cocktail party given by Aunt Helen[48] for a farewell for Rosemary who is going to New Zealand for three years.'[49] Pam – who had suffered a miscarriage – was away travelling a lot with Derek. Only Tom was welcomed everywhere.

12

SLIDE TOWARDS CONFLICT

(1938)

By the summer of 1938 war was looming as a distinct possibility. Indeed, pundits said that it was no longer a matter of 'if', but 'when'. However, most people in Britain still preferred to ignore this. After all, public opinion reasoned, why should a central European war affect Britain? So what if Hitler's armies were threatening to overrun Czechoslovakia? The Czechoslovakian state was not an ancient country, but had been cobbled together by modern politicians who, when the boundaries were drawn up for the Versailles Treaty, had placed 3.5 million Germans – formerly subjects of the old Habsburg empire – inside Czechoslovakia's border facing Germany and Austria. Perhaps the Germans had a genuine grievance concerning 'self-determination' – and look how the Austrians had welcomed the Anschluss. Hitler, as shown on Pathé Pictorial news, might sound disagreeable, with his ranting oratory, and look comical, with his little moustache, but what he said made a sort of sense. 'I am in no way willing that here in the heart of Germany a second Palestine should be permitted to arise. The poor Arabs are defenceless and deserted. The Germans in Czechoslovakia are neither defenceless nor are they deserted, and people should take notice of that fact.'[1] As for Kristallnacht, yes, it had been objectionable, but all this was someone else's fight. Let them get on with it. The new slogan that Mosley had adopted had an undoubted appeal to many who feared another all-out war: 'MIND BRITAIN'S BUSINESS'.

Yet for thinking people it was difficult to ignore what was happening in Germany. Czechoslovakia had been the last democracy in central Europe and now only force could prevent Hitler from establishing a German nation stretching from the Ural mountains to the French coast. In 1938, also, there was a marked change of attitude in Germany towards its Jewish citizens. For the previous five years German Jews had lived under the constant threat of physical abuse, but from 1938 their persecution became a relentless legal reality. On Kristallnacht, 276 synagogues were burned to the ground and over 7,500 Jewish businesses were burned, looted and vandalized. The government impounded the insurance money claimed by the dispossessed, stating that the Jews had brought the horror upon themselves. From that point no Jew was allowed to own a business or to run one. It became difficult to keep up with new legislation concerning what civil rights remained to them. They were not allowed to own or drive a car or motorcycle, and were barred from public transport. They were not allowed to attend theatres, cinemas or art galleries, and were banned from beaches, swimming-pools and gymnasia. They were banned from owning a radio. Their children were not allowed to attend schools where there were Aryan children. Sex or marriage between an Aryan and a Jew became a criminal offence carrying a prison sentence. And so it went on: the slide towards genocide. Reading the newspapers of that time now, it is hard to believe the scale of anti-Semitism being perpetrated in Germany could attract such little comment in the world press.[2]

Esmond was one of those who made it his business to know what was going on, and when he and Decca returned to England in August they flung themselves into activism. A rebel by nature, he now had a genuine cause, and for Esmond this meant physical action against Mosley's Blackshirts and other British Fascist organizations. In his memoir *Friends Apart*,[3] Philip Toynbee details the fist fights with knuckle-dusters and even razors used on both sides to inflict as much damage as possible, and vividly portrays the raw hatred of the opposing factions. For Decca, activism meant raising money for the Spanish fight against Fascism, helping to sabotage Mosley's marches, or participating in Labour Party and trade-union marches for better conditions for the working classes.

In *Hons and Rebels* Decca recalled one such march: it was a May Day march to Hyde Park and the entire community of Rotherhithe turned out in a holiday atmosphere, waving a forest of banners that read, 'United Front against Fascism'. They linked arms and sang songs, 'Ohhhh! 'Tis my delight of a dirty night to bomb the bourgeoisie . . .' and a bowdlerized version of 'The Red Flag', 'The people's flag is palest pink, it's not as red as you might think . . .' as they marched. They had been warned that the event would probably be disrupted by Mosley's supporters, Decca said, 'and sure enough there were groups of them lying in wait at several points along the way . . .' There were several skirmishes, and at one point, 'I caught sight of two familiar, tall blonde figures: Boud and Diana, waving Swastika flags. I shook my fist at them in the Red Front salute, and was barely dissuaded by Esmond and Philip who reminded me of my now pregnant condition, from joining in the fray.'[4] Diana has no memory of this incident, and points out that Decca claimed she was pregnant when the reported May Day incident occurred: 'she was still in Spain in May 1937,' she states. 'She wasn't pregnant in 1938, and by May 1939 she was in the USA.'[5] Furthermore Diana states that she 'never possessed such a flag' and never went to any marches, either Communist or Fascist, because Mosley did not wish her to. 'I greatly doubt Bobo being there,' she wrote, 'but I am certain I was not.'[6]

But Unity was active for the Fascist cause and there is photographic evidence that she attended marches as a bystander. She was now so notorious that she hardly had to make a protest; her mere presence was enough to upset bystanders and an objective witness of one incident was shocked at the reaction she provoked. One day in April 1938 Joe Allen, who owned a bookshop and publishing company near by, was standing listening to Sir Stafford Cripps who was speaking at Hyde Park Corner when a fight broke out between some Communists and Fascists from the Imperial Fascist League (not part of Mosley's organization). Unity was standing close to Allen and turned, as he did, to watch. Almost simultaneously someone spotted Unity's swastika badge, reached out and tore it off her lapel. She retaliated, striking out and kicking her assailant. When the crowd around her recognized her some turned ugly, shouting, 'Why don't you go back to Germany?' and made rude remarks about Hitler. Then there was a sort of crush towards her with shouts of 'Let's duck her.'

Allen assumed they meant to throw her in the nearby Serpentine. Together with another gentleman,[7] and a police officer, he helped form a shield around Unity to protect her from the blows that were landed on their shoulders, and stones that were thrown. Even so, someone managed to kick Unity before her protectors got her to a nearby bus stop, where she boarded a bus and quickly got away. Joe Allen and the policeman had to restrain people from following her on to the bus to continue the affray. 'I was very concerned for her safety,' he said. 'People were just beginning to think they didn't like Herr Hitler very much.'[8] The press got hold of the story and coverage of the incident was anti-Unity, with headlines such as 'Hitler's Nordic Beauty Beaten Up By London Mob' and 'At it Again, the Mad, Mad Mitfords'. Unity did not mind: she later said that she wasn't at all frightened, just excited.[9] She seems to have enjoyed all the publicity and was pleased at the postbag that resulted from the Hyde Park scuffle. After attending Debo's coming-out ball, she returned to Munich, where a sympathetic Hitler, who had learned of the affair through the newspaper reports, replaced the lost badge with two new ones, each engraved with his signature on the back.

Within weeks she was in the newspapers again, photographs of her and Julius Streicher (whom Decca described as 'a filthy butcher') splashed under headlines such as 'Unity Mitford – Detained in Czechoslovakia' and 'Stay at Home, There's a Good Girl'.[10] She had been arrested in Prague on 31 May, hardly surprising since Germany and Czechoslovakia were on the brink of war and Unity persisted in strolling around the city 'flaunting' her gold swastika badge. She was instantly recognizable with her tall, blonde good looks, and the confident air that made even her manner of walking an aggressive statement. Nor could she claim that she was unaware of the delicacy of the situation for in her letter to Diana she wrote of the Czechs' scorched-earth policy in Sudetenland, of seeing railways, bridges and important buildings mined against the coming of the German army, of the 8 p.m. curfew, and of tanks and machine-guns on the roads leading to Prague.[11] She was travelling with two Fascist companions and a Sudeten MP, Senator Wollner, and her car had been stopped several times at roadblocks. Although Wollner was a citizen of Czechoslovakia, Unity had been advised at the frontier, as 'a known Nazi', not to proceed. Her arrival, in the face of these warnings was, said a dispatch from the British consulate, 'a clearly provocative act'.[12] She was soon released, but her passport and other items were withheld for a further forty-eight hours. Diplomatic reaction from the British legation was that she had asked for trouble and got what she deserved.

It seems as though her actions were a natural progression from her lifelong urge to shock and gain attention. Where she had once been content to release Ratular into a flock of débutantes, her actions now seemed designed to court physical danger; perhaps she hoped that Hitler would notice and that such incidents would prove to him her absolute loyalty. There is no evidence to prove the growing rumour that she hoped to marry Hitler, but it cannot be discounted either, since her behaviour was obsessive. And Hitler *did* know of these incidents. The Czechs refused to return Unity's camera but a few days later Hitler presented her with a new Leica, which, she wrote to Diana, 'cost £50' – ten weeks' wages to a white-collar worker in England.

That the relationship between Hitler and Unity was considerably more than that of an adoring fan and a superstar is proven by small incidents rather than great sequences. She began referring to him as 'Wolf' and he called her 'Kind' – Child. They exchanged gifts. As well as the camera, he gave her a framed signed photograph of himself, and at Christmas he sent her a tree complete with decorations. Unity made up one of her collages for him, of Hannibal crossing the Alps, and she gave him the 'chicken's mess' ring.[13] They were close enough to share private jokes. When Unity had been disparaging of Italy and Mussolini, and was ticked off by one of Hitler's adjutants, Hitler came to her defence, albeit without agreeing with her comments. Subsequently, even the slightest discussion of Italy would cause him to catch her eye and 'blither' (Boudledidge for giggle). When one guest at a Hitler luncheon said that the Osteria was just like an Italian *trattoria*, but cleaner, Hitler looked at Unity out of the corner of his eye, and the two began to giggle 'quite uncontrollably'. When he had mastered himself sufficiently Hitler pointed at Unity and said to the astonished guest, 'She likes to hear that.'[14] The thought of Hitler giggling at all, let alone 'quite uncontrollably', is difficult to imagine, and suggests that Unity brought to his life an uncomplicated form of friendship in which laughter played a significant part. Judging from biographies of him – there have been about a hundred – it was the sort of relationship he had never known elsewhere.

In August Hitler invited Unity to accompany him on a trip to Breslau, a city situated in the tongue of German land lying between Czechoslovakia and Poland. Although she was feeling unwell with a head and chest cold, Unity could not refuse such a wonderful opportunity to be with him, especially at such an exciting time, though it is clear from her letters to Diana and Sydney that she was forcing herself by willpower to stay on her feet throughout a daunting programme. She sat 'just behind' Hitler as 150,000 men paraded past him in unbearable heat. Wollner sat behind her and she was pleased that he was 'frightfully impressed' that she had travelled in Hitler's party. At one point Sudeten marchers broke ranks and surrounded Hitler, holding out their hands and crying, 'Dear Führer, when are you coming to help us?' Unity was very moved: 'I never expect to see such scenes again,' she wrote to Diana. In reply Diana agreed that it must have been an unforgettable experience: 'Even in *The Times* one could see how wonderful it must have been. I was frightfully jealous,' she wrote.[15]

Hitler's contingent left Breslau and flew to Nuremberg in two planes, and continued on by car to Bayreuth. By now Unity was feeling so ill that she chose to fly in the second plane, fearing that she might infect Hitler. On arrival at Bayreuth she collapsed with pneumonia and was admitted to a private clinic. Hitler instructed that all medical bills were to be sent to him and before he left for Berlin he sent Unity flowers and ordered his personal physician to remain in Bayreuth to care for her. Sydney flew out immediately, and was horrified to find that instead of relying on the natural healing processes of 'the good body', Unity was submitting to ten or fifteen different injections each day from Theodor Morrell. She was very unhappy about this, but as Hitler – who trusted the doctor implicitly, even though it was later discovered that Morrell's treatments caused him harm – had sent a telegram begging Unity to do everything the doctor ordered, she realized that any protests were pointless.[16]

Ten days later David flew out to take over as bedside-sitter while Sydney returned to England. On the day Unity was discharged David discovered that Hitler had already paid her bill and sent signed photographs of himself to her nurses.[17] There were no circumstances under which David would have been prepared to allow another man to foot the expenses of his unmarried daughter. However, his immense old-fashioned charm ensured that no feelings were ruffled when he reimbursed Hitler, and during Unity's convalescence the two men met several times. With the exception of Derek Jackson, whom he scarcely understood, David seldom liked the men his daughters liked, and referred to his sons-in-law as 'the man Mosley, the boy Romilly and the bore Rodd'. Somewhat to his surprise, however, he found that he rather liked Hitler. 'Farve really does adore him in the way we do,' Unity wrote to Diana, grossly exaggerating this, 'and treasures every word and expression.'[18]

Considering the state of European politics in August 1938, one might be forgiven for assuming that Sydney left because she was in danger of being trapped in a war zone. However, she flew home because Nancy had had a miscarriage; within three weeks she was back again for the Nuremberg Parteitag. The Redesdales stayed at the Grand Hotel where, a witness recalled, they seemed out of place. Lady Redesdale was always to be found sitting over her needlework in a corner of the lounge while Lord Redesdale helped her find her needles or wandered around 'with a bewildered air as though he were at a rather awkward house party where (curiously enough) nobody could speak English'.[19]

In the interim Dr Morrell's injections, or perhaps the Good Body, had done their work and Unity was well enough to attend the rally with her parents. Nancy's friend Robert Byron joined them, using the ticket Unity had obtained for Tom, who at the last minute found he could not attend. Byron was vehemently anti-Fascist and attended out of curiosity to compare Germany with his experiences on a recent visit to Moscow. Unity's party was seated in the front row, so close that Byron found he could meet the eyes of 'Hitler and his henchmen'. Not surprisingly, Nuremberg was the focal point of the international press corps that year, and over tea one day Unity found herself sharing a table with freelance correspondent Virginia Cowles, who had earlier noticed the Nazi hierarchy 'bowing and scraping' to Unity, and kissing her hand. 'She seemed rather embarrassed by their attention,' she wrote. Hitler took his reserved table with Lord Stamp, Lord Brocket, Ward Price and Herr Henlein. He looked grim and his eyes swept the room but when his gaze lighted on Unity he suddenly smiled and saluted her. She saluted back, and shortly afterwards an orderly came over and invited her to Hitler's suite in the Hotel Deutscher Hof after tea. When Cowles saw her a few hours later she asked Unity what Hitler had said and if she thought there would be a war. 'I don't think so,' Unity replied ingenuously. 'The Führer doesn't want his new buildings bombed,'[20]

But Hitler's closing speech on 12 September, in which he 'promised' the Sudeten Germans his help, made conflict in some form inevitable, and Byron left immediately to avoid being trapped.[21] Three days later, in a last-ditch attempt to prevent war, sixty-nine-year-old Prime Minister Neville Chamberlain made the first flight of his life, arriving in Germany for what would be a series of high-level talks at Hitler's mountain home. In all, Chamberlain made three visits in two weeks. Meanwhile, the Redesdales departed to England, unable to persuade Unity to accompany them, though she promised to fly home for Christmas.[22] In the meantime she went to Austria to Janos von Almassy's home and the two went on to Venice. Members of the Mitford family, who have read her diaries at the time of this holiday, are 'fairly sure she had a brief love affair' with him.[23]

Diana's statement about Decca in connection with the May Day parade was only partially correct. She was not aware of it but Decca *was* pregnant in 1938. The exact dates are not known but

Decca wrote that she was 'twenty-one . . . when I had my one and only abortion', which, if strictly accurate, would place the event after her birthday on 11 September. To have been pregnant during the 1938 May Day march means she conceived soon after Julia's birth so she must have had the abortion between the May Day march and Julia's death on the twenty-eighth of that month, after which the Romillys 'ran away' to Corsica. And it raises questions. By her own admission both Esmond and Philip Toynbee knew of the pregnancy. Why did she need to terminate it? Perhaps the thought of two tiny babies within a year was too much for her to countenance, or for the Romillys to finance. Yet it must have happened then if Decca's recollection in *Hons and Rebels* is accurate. If not, she must have run several incidents together: her acute memory of the huge May Day rally, and of seeing her sisters protesting on another day.

Most likely Decca had the termination some weeks after she and Esmond returned to London from Corsica. There are no further details and speculation is pointless, but it is known that she found it a traumatic experience. Twenty years later she wrote about it during a campaign to legalize abortion in the USA. By then she was a leading civil-rights campaigner and had recently tried to help a young woman who needed a pregnancy terminated. She was appalled to find that in California in the 1950s there was still one rule for the poor, the back-street abortionist, and another for the rich, the private clinic that didn't ask too many questions. Just one. 'Tell your friend,' the Californian doctor instructed Decca, 'that if she's had the merchandise for more than three months it can't be returned.'

When she decided to have her abortion in 1938, Decca wrote, it was not only an illegal act but the subject was taboo. Clearly she was not aware of Diana's terminated pregnancy some years earlier for she stated that she did not even consider consulting anybody in her family because they 'wouldn't have been likely to have useful ideas on the subject' and furthermore she was 'estranged' from them. Instead she sought advice from a friend, a woman older than herself who was 'a Bohemian', and was given an address: 'There's no telephone,' her friend said. 'Just go there, and take five pounds in cash.' This represented a week's wages for Esmond, as Decca indirectly pointed out. She took a bus and a tube to where the abortionist lived 'deep in the East End slums', rang the bell and announced nervously, while holding out five one-pound notes, that she had an introduction from a friend:

> She wasn't what I had expected – a hard-bitten Dickensian crone. No, just an ordinary middle-aged Englishwoman plying her trade . . . At her direction I undressed and lay on a bed. I was a bit surprised that there was no sign of sterilization of the instruments, which she fished out of her underclothes drawer . . . Her method was injection of soap into the uterus, which would in about five hours induce labour. The procedure was horribly painful, hardly ameliorated when the abortionist cautioned just as I was leaving, 'If you get sick, don't call in the doctor, because if you should die, I'll swing.' [A reminder that the death penalty was in force] . . . I did get sick, I did call a doctor – and I survived. Years later I read in a magazine that abortion by soap injection was by far the most dangerous of all methods, resulting in a huge number of deaths . . .[24]

Because Diana was also pregnant through the summer of 1938, her presence – even accidentally – at any march after August (when Unity was in Germany) is questionable. She certainly felt that her pregnancy was too advanced to attend the Parteitag and was taking things easy at Wootton. That month Debo had paid her a surprise visit accompanied by two young men, one of whom was Lord Andrew Cavendish, younger son of the 10th Duke of Devonshire. The couple had met a short time earlier in a restaurant off Curzon Street. 'I first saw her at Eton, when she was fifteen or sixteen, and stunningly beautiful,' he recalled in an interview. 'Then we met at a dinner party . . . and if it wasn't love at first sight it was certainly attraction at first sight.'[25] For the moment, however, they were keeping this to themselves. Debo had been expressly forbidden to visit Wootton and her companions were clearly nervous when Diana introduced Mosley, who had been fishing in the lake with Diana's two sons from her first marriage. 'They all looked as if they had seen a ghost,' Diana reported to Unity. 'Debo said they were frightened they might be shot at.'[26]

Diana's third child, Alexander, was born in November. Mosley had given up his flat in Ebury Street for a house in Grosvenor Road. It was a five-minute walk from the Houses of Parliament and the windows overlooked the Thames. It was here that Diana had her baby. 'From my bed I could see across the black November water to the wharves on the far bank: they were blanketed in snow,' she wrote.[27] Later, she took the baby home to Wootton, which became for her, for the first time, a real family home. Nanny Higgs, who had formerly looked after Jonathan and Desmond, ran the nursery.

Alexander's birth obliged the Mosleys to make public the fact that they were married. Following a year of concentrated networking in Germany, Diana was advised shortly after the Anschluss, when Germany acquired all the Austrian wavelengths, 'You have your wavelength, and a very nice one too.'[28] The contract was signed and sealed three weeks before Alexander's birth and work began immediately to construct a transmitter on the island of Borkum in the North Sea. The secrecy felt to be essential in 1936 was no longer a major issue, but Mosley's name did not feature in the contracts. However, there was a price to pay. The news of the two-year-old marriage was a sensation, and filled the front pages of newspapers with stories trumpeting (incorrectly) that 'Hitler Was Mosley's Best Man at Secret Wedding', and articles such as 'The Family That Mosley Has Married Into', which detailed the colourful histories of Diana's divorce, Decca's elopement and Unity's close friendship with Hitler. The Redesdales were upset: they seemed never to grow hardened to publicity about their daughters. But their reaction was tame compared to that of Mosley's family connections. Nobody in his family knew of the marriage, not even his mother who had supported him and filled the role of 'first lady' of the Blackshirt movement since the death of Cimmie, or his eldest son, fifteen-year-old Nicholas, who was then at Eton. They found out about the marriage, and the new baby, from the newspapers.

Mosley's Curzon sisters-in-law could scarcely believe it was true. Initially, one reporter got the detail wrong and asked Mosley outright whether it was true that he had been married secretly in Munich a year earlier. Mosley denied the story cleverly, stating simply that he had not been in Munich for the previous two years, and there is a strong suggestion here that even at this late stage he would have preferred that the marriage remained secret. But it was soon evident that there had been a marriage, and it was confirmed in the BUF newspaper *Action*. Baba, who was on a train between London and Paris when she read the news, was understandably distraught since her relationship with Mosley had continued unchecked since the summer following Cimmie's death. Later she stated that she would not have allowed the affair to continue, had she known that Mosley and Diana were married. Since she was married herself this seems a curious morality, but that is another story. Mosley claimed to journalists that the reason for secrecy was that he was concerned Diana would suffer abuse and even personal danger were it known she was married to him. Diana was confident that the real reason was the secrecy necessary to establish the radio station without any traceable link to Mosley. But Cimmie's sisters, Irene Ravensdale and Baba Metcalfe, and Nicholas Mosley, always believed that the real reason was that Mosley did not want his affair with Baba to end.[29]

Irene Ravensdale was in America when the news broke, and she wrote in her autobiography that she nearly fainted when she was told. There had been a vague rumour a year earlier about a marriage, but Mosley had categorically denied it to her. Now it appeared the story had been true, and 'that Hitler had been the best man [sic] and Goebbels the chief witness'. She claimed to have found this shocking,[30] but she wrote this twenty years later, after Hitler and the British Fascist movement had been thoroughly discredited. Irene Ravensdale was a keen supporter of Mosley and the BUF throughout the thirties, and her latterday statements seem designed to distance herself from that. She knew all about Mosley's affair with Baba, and sanctioned it as a means of weaning him from Diana, so her remark that she felt Mosley's 'excuses of the need for secrecy . . . were pretty sordid'[31] sounds much closer to the truth.

That summer Nancy had also discovered, to her great joy, that she was pregnant. Like Pam she had been trying unsuccessfully to have a baby for some years and the conventional treatment, dilation and curettage (also used for legal abortions), was, no doubt, why she referred to foetuses as 'the scrapage'. Having submitted to this treatment in the spring of 1938 her pregnancy was confirmed in July. She was advised to remain in bed for the first four weeks and thereafter to rest as much as possible. In August, when Sydney flew home from Munich, leaving Unity in hospital, she took Nancy to stay with her friend Helen Dashwood at West Wycombe. After this Nancy went to the cottage to look after Debo, while Sydney returned to Munich for the Parteitag.

After a week the two sisters moved to Rutland Gate, where Nancy kept up her chatty teasing correspondence to amuse herself during the tedious 'resting' stage. As usual the Rodds were desperately short of money, and could scarcely afford to live themselves, let alone raise a child. 'Of course it is *lunatic* really,' she wrote happily to Robert Byron, 'I quite see that but one must never be deterred from doing what one wants for lack of money don't you agree?' An aunt had written and hoped it would be a boy so that it could inherit from Lord Rodd, but Nancy said, 'If I thought for a minute it would be a boy I'd go for a bicycle ride here & now – 2 Peter Rodds in 1 house is unthinkable.'[32] By the time David and Sydney arrived at Rutland Gate from Munich, on 17 September, Nancy was in bed recovering from the miscarriage that had occurred a day or so earlier. Nancy never wrote about her loss, but it seems that she felt it deeply. She was thirty-four, and although her doctor had told her there was no reason why she should not conceive again it seemed unlikely to her as Prod had embarked on yet another of his serial love affairs. Added to which he was out of work again. She blamed her inability to conceive on her mother: apparently, as a small child, she had suffered from an infection of the urethra and, of course, Sydney had refused to call a doctor. Nancy always felt that the damage this caused was the reason for the gynaecological problems she suffered as an adult.[33]

Decca was taking part in a market-research survey in Southampton when the Prime Minister returned from Munich in apparent triumph but, of course, having given in to all of Hitler's demands over Czechoslovakia. A visitor who called on the Romillys at this point recalls that, although Decca was young, her 'intellectual brilliance in matters of political vision made her almost clairvoyant: she predicted the Nazi attack on Poland and on the Soviet Union, and . . . the incredible period of suffering for the British people'.[34] Decca firmly believed, and did so for a long time, however, that it was just her 'class', people like her parents, uncles, aunts, and the suited members of the Cliveden set 'with their furled umbrellas, so symbolic of furled minds', that was the cause of Britain being swept into war, because of their acceptance – or even active support – of Fascism in Europe. Perhaps this view was hardly surprising

23. Oswald Mosley with Swedish fencing partner, *c.* 1932.

24. Unity, Diana and Nancy attending the wedding of a cousin in 1932.

25. Family photo call, Swinbrook House, 1934.

26. Nancy's marriage to Peter Rodd in 1933.

Below left: 27. Diana on Mosley's motorboat during their Mediterranean holiday in 1935.

Below right: 28. Mosley driving his boat.

29. Julius Streicher presents Unity with a flower.

30. Unity at Hesselberg, 1935.

NEWS REVIEW ★ NOVEMBER 18, 1937. Vol. IV. No. 19   SIXPENCE

NEWS
Review
The First British Newsmagazine

NAZI-LOVER THE HON. UNITY FREEMAN-MITFORD
But for "certain difficulties," a German . . .
(See "Women.")

Registered at the G.P.O. as a Newspaper   Member of the Audit Bureau of Circulations

31. Unity on the front cover of a magazine in 1937. It was widely rumoured that she might marry Hitler.

Right: 32. Tom at the Parteitag in 1937. Although in sympathy with Fascist political ideology, he was opposed to Nazi anti-Semitism.

Below: 33. Unity and Diana, posing at the request of writer Ward Price. He wanted pictures for his book, *I Knew these Dictators*.

Bottom: 34. Unity with Hitler. One of a series of pictures she and Diana had taken with the Führer.

35. Sir Oswald Mosley takes salute of his BUF ranks, October 1935.

36. Decca with Unity's storm-trooper 'boyfriend', Erich Widemann, in Munich, September 1934. Curiously, she made no mention of this trip in her memoirs.

Left: 37. Decca, the reluctant debutante, 1935.

Above: 38. The elopers. Decca and Desmond at the Hôtel des Basques on the day of their wedding in May 1937.

39. Esmond and Decca at Rotherhithe, 1937.

40. Esmond and Decca running their bar in Miami.

41. Diana in April 1939, aged twenty-nine, at the height of her beauty.

42. Diana and Mosley, taken the evening before his arrest in 1940.

when half of her family was in Germany that month, enjoying Hitler's hospitality.

But Decca was astonished when Chamberlain returned, clutching his furled umbrella and waving his bit of paper, to find that the working people she spoke to were overjoyed. 'But it's peace,' they told her, 'peace in our time. That's good, isn't it?' More than anything she wanted to finish her work and get back to London and Esmond, for surely, she thought, there this capitulation to Fascism would have made people sit up and take notice. But she found Esmond profoundly depressed: the storm of public indignation he had anticipated over Czechoslovakia had simply not materialized.[35] In a sense this put an end to what Philip Toynbee referred to as 'the wild and comical capers . . . cut by Esmond and Decca'. People suddenly woke up to the fact that war was now a strong possibility, despite Mr Chamberlain's signed contract with Hitler, and the government began to take the measures to prepare for conflict that Winston Churchill had advocated for several years. What Diana calls 'war fever' now affected everybody in Britain. Gas masks were issued to every citizen, trenches were dug in London parks, conscription was to be brought in, and armament production speeded up.

Esmond was no coward, as later events proved, but he realized that if he stayed in England he would be among the first to be called up. He had no objection to joining the fight against Fascism, but until war was declared he had no wish to be sucked into the maw of British Army life, which would condemn him to the sort of discipline he considered pointless and against which he had always fought: the Army bull, the shined boots, and 'salute everything that moves' attitude of his boarding-school's OTC. Yet what could he and Decca do? They had no money and were incapable of managing on what was considered a reasonable white-collar income. Following their return to England in August they had spent a good deal of their time dodging a writ-server.

No one had told Decca that electricity had to be paid for so she left lights, heaters and stoves burning all day and night at Rotherhithe, and the huge bill was still unpaid.

Since their return from Corsica they had lived in a small bed-sitter in a street off the Edgware Road near Marble Arch. They had decided that it was too traumatic to return to the place where Julia had died, and their new accommodation was more conveniently situated for Esmond's job on the Strand. But the Electricity Board tracked them down, and an unfortunate young man was sent to serve them with a court order. They either disguised themselves with dark glasses and false moustaches and slid past him in the communal doorway before taking to their heels down the street or stayed in bed while he rapped at the door. 'Sometimes we stayed in bed for as long as two days,' Decca wrote, '[but] though enjoyable to us, these lost days were becoming a source of irritation to Esmond's boss.' At this period, Philip Toynbee recalled, there was little evidence of the careless optimism normally displayed by the independent and 'fanatical Decca',[36] and Esmond, with his peculiar blend of intellectual idealism, mulish pugnacity, boyish charm and 'irresistible horse laugh'[37] was unusually depressed.[38] Enthusiasm was at a low ebb in the Romilly household.

Shortly after Decca's return from Southampton, however, things miraculously changed for them. Three weeks earlier, she had celebrated her twenty-first birthday, in those days the legal coming-of-age. When each of her children was born, Sydney had opened a savings account for them. Every week she paid a small amount into each account, to be given to them when they reached twenty-one. Decca had either forgotten about this nest egg, or perhaps thought that in the circumstances her mother would not give it to her. But when she met Sydney for lunch in London in early October, she found herself the recipient of a hundred pounds. These undreamed-of riches provided Esmond with the answer to all their problems: they would emigrate to

America and work there until war was declared. They would make a fortune from lecturing before he joined up.

Immigration visas were in great demand, and difficult to obtain without demonstrable means of support. The three hundred dollars with which the Romillys would have been left after paying their steerage passage would not last long, but Esmond and Decca appeared before the American consul with sincerity and enthusiasm for the American ethos shining out of their handsome young faces. They laid it on pretty thick, stressing how they were impressed by the freedom of the people and 'the land of opportunity', and it worked. At about the time that the papers were full of Diana's marriage to Mosley, the Romillys heard that they had been granted visas and the all-important green-card work permits.

Before they sailed for New York aboard the SS *Aurania*, in mid-February, they spent time calling on friends. During a trip to Oxford they detoured to Swinbrook as Decca wanted to say goodbye to Miranda before she left. She went to the field where she had discovered that Miranda was kept, 'walked over to the flock of sheep and called out, "Miranda." She came hobbling out to me – her feet all full of foot rot. I was in floods of tears,' she wrote to Nancy.

Following that, the couple planned a final salute to Esmond's *Out of Bounds* period. It was a raid on Eton College, with Philip Toynbee acting as gang member. Decca knew the layout because of her many family connections who were Old Etonians, and she took them to the anteroom of the chapel where they relieved the hat pegs of all the top hats they could carry away. They returned to London flushed with victory and thirty hats, 'gallant symbols of our hatred of Eton, of our anarchy, our defiance,' Toynbee wrote.[39] Later, Toynbee lost his girlfriend over the incident for when he told her about it she turned huffy and said it was stealing. And it is difficult, with hindsight, to put any other interpretation on it. Had the trio repaired in good humour to a

Thames bridge and cast the lot into the river, it might have been viewed as a prank, and a snub to a society they abhorred. But instead Esmond sold the hats to a second-hand clothes dealer and pocketed the cash. Which seems to smack as much of opportunism as any form of idealism.

13

NO LAUGHING MATTER

(1939)

Decca and Esmond spent their first few weeks in the United States in New York, wallowing in unaccustomed luxury at the Shelton Hotel, which Peter Nevile had recommended to them. At $3.50 a day it was rather more than they could afford but Peter had told them that they should put on a 'good front' if they wished to impress the natives. He was right. Within no time at all, the letters that they wrote on Shelton writing-paper introducing themselves ('My good friend Peter Nevile suggested that I should contact you . . .') brought results and they were able to move out of the hotel and go visiting real Americans. At one grand house Decca met Katharine – Kay – Graham, daughter of Eugene Meyer, who owned the *Washington Post*. Kay was Decca's age, and even then an ardent Democrat and 'New Dealer'. The two women were destined to be good friends, and both Decca and Esmond liked the Meyers because, although they were rich Republicans, they were also anti-Fascist.

To Esmond's chagrin the lecture circuit was uninterested in them, and his English style of copywriting failed to impress Madison Avenue advertising agencies. They told him his British experience was a positive handicap, so Decca helped the exchequer by inventing a history in the fashion trade and landing a job in a dress shop. It gave her a real thrill to take home a wage. Her former occupation as a market researcher had brought in occasional sums of money through Esmond's agency, but this was a real job that she'd found for herself, and she was proud of it. Among the upper classes in England the term 'shop girl' was used pejoratively, and Decca was probably the first woman in her family ever to work for a living. To Decca these were plus factors. In the meantime the couple were welcomed open-handedly by New York society for the bubbling enthusiasm they carried around with them: they were lively, good talkers, entertaining company and they *loved* America. Decca found a second-hand clothes shop where she bought a couple of evening dresses at six dollars each, but it cost more to outfit Esmond: his dinner jacket alone cost them $6.50.[1]

When they moved out of the Shelton they rented a room in the walk-up apartment of two actors in Greenwich Village. It was, said a visitor, as untidy as a schoolboy's bedroom but always 'gloriously happy'. Esmond juggled with apples while Decca cooked supper and chided him for scuffing his shoes. He pretended contempt at being told off, but he was noticeably attentive and would dart across the room to light her cigarette.[2] Interviewed by the *New York Daily Mirror* and *Life* magazine, Esmond said he was going to become an American citizen as soon as possible, but he was anxious to correct any impression that he had left England to avoid fighting and pointed to his experience in Spain: 'I wasn't a Communist, I am not now, and I never will be, but in the beginning Madrid was a symbol to me. If England is drawn into a war now I shall go back and fight – because of all the things that are dear to me and Decca will be drawn in . . . but I have no illusions about England fighting for democracy.' Since Munich, he told them, the last democracy in Europe, Czechoslovakia, had fallen. 'It is imperial England against imperial Germany now.'[3]

Decca was making contacts who would become lifelong friends. The most important of these was a tall Southern belle who wore white broad-brimmed hats and huge skirts that rustled when she walked. Virginia Durr spoke in a 'soft scream' with a marked Southern accent, which fascinated Decca. At first she did not like Virginia, who seemed loud and bossy. Nevertheless, since it was their policy 'to swoop down . . . on a circle of people, become part of them for a brief time, glean what there was of interest and be off again', she accepted an invitation for her and Esmond to visit the Durrs at their sprawling white farmhouse about seven miles from Washington, DC. There they met Virginia's husband Clifford who worked for the Federal Communications Bureau, which controlled broadcasting, and the couple's noisy, happy family. By the end of the evening they were fast friends and Decca marvelled at how quickly this had occurred. In England, she reflected, it would have taken years of 'getting to know someone' before they reached such a stage of friendly intimacy.

Apart from Esmond's determination to join up as soon as any fighting began in Europe, there was only one problem in Decca's life at that time. Besotted as she was with Esmond she could not admit him into one part of her life, and that was her love for Unity. Along with Esmond she bitterly denounced her family in general as 'Nazis', including the rabidly anti-Nazi Nancy, the Conservative Pam and even the apolitical Debo. But she could never bring herself to extend it to Unity, though Unity was arguably the chief offender. This, surely, tells us something about Unity who, despite the publication of an excellently researched biography, remains an elusive personality. 'Although I hated everything she stood for,' Decca wrote, 'she was easily my favourite sister, which was something I could never have admitted . . . to Esmond. I knew I could never expect Esmond, who had never met her, to feel anything but disgust for her, so by tacit understanding we avoided discussing her.'[4]

A month earlier the London *Daily Mirror* had given Unity an entire page to express her views and ideology under the headline 'WHAT MISS MITFORD WOULD LIKE TO SEE'. It is a surprisingly reasoned and well-written argument, which states that England and Germany had too much in common to be enemies; and that the two countries ought to be allies with Germany as the greatest Continental power and Britain the great colonial power. But her premise is undermined by her insistence on the importance of racial superiority: too much for most readers to swallow even in the less enlightened 1930s. 'One of the foundations of Nazi ideology is the racial theory,' she wrote. 'They believe that the future of Europe stands or falls with the Nordic race . . .'[5]

Curiously, despite the part that Unity had played in Putzi Hanfstaegl's sudden exit from Germany, she remained on good terms with his sister Erna. So much so that in the spring Unity, always short of money, moved out of her flat and in with Erna. 'It is lovely staying here with Erna,' she wrote to Diana, 'but she is very strict and makes me wash the bath out . . . The only boring thing is that she [complains] as much as ever and shrieks at me as if I were responsible for it all [her brother's defection].'[6] If only Unity could talk personally to Hitler, Erna believed, she might get Putzi reinstated. Unity was only too willing and she waited her moment to raise the subject with Hitler. 'Last week I was lunching with W[olf],' she wrote to Diana, 'so I summoned up all my courage and asked if he would see her. He was perfectly sweet and said yes.'[7] Erna had not seen Hitler since he had been a fugitive after the failure of the 1923 putsch, when he hid at her home. They met alone and Unity waited outside the room, joining them afterwards for tea. Everything appeared to have gone well, she thought. A few days earlier she had introduced Erna to Randolph Churchill, who was visiting Munich, and Erna told him she intended to visit her brother in London. Randolph said she must visit his father while she was there. Erna told Hitler this and asked him what she might say to Churchill. He replied casually, 'Use your own judgement.'

Ten days later Erna handed Unity a letter addressed to Hitler and asked her to give it to him. Apparently it was a request that Putzi's back pay from the Nazi Party be conveyed to her in the form of a cheque signed by Hitler, which she would take with her to England. Hitler read only a few sentences then flushed with anger he tore up the letter. The Hanfstaengls, he told a startled Unity, were money-grabbers, and she had 'been living on a dung heap'.[8] He burned the letter and forbade Unity to see Erna again, not even for one day. This presented her with a problem since she was living with the woman, but it was no problem to Hitler. He said he would find her a flat, and even help her to furnish it. In the meantime Unity moved into an hotel and Janos von Almassy, who was staying in Munich with a friend, went to see Erna and collected Unity's luggage. On 5 June Unity wrote to Diana that she had found an apartment. 'Wolf told [Gauleiter] Wagner that they were to look for one for me . . . So today a young man from the Ministerium took me round to look at some . . . At last we found the *perfect* [apartment] in Schwabing . . . It belongs', she wrote, 'to a young Jewish couple who are going abroad.'[9] Subsequently she saw the couple again and, apparently amicably, purchased some furniture from them.

It was the acquisition of this flat that essentially placed Unity forever over a line from which there could be no historical rehabilitation. She was not a fool: her own writings in newspapers, particularly her *Stürmer* article, show that she had an excellent grasp of the situation concerning the Jews. She cannot have avoided seeing the treatment already inflicted on Jews in the streets of Munich – even irregular visitors witnessed scenes where Jews were infamously humiliated. We know she thought that Streicher's act in making Jews crop grass with their teeth was amusing, and that she approved when a group of Jews were taken to an island in the Danube and left there to starve.[10] She told a friend, Mary Ormsby Gore, how an old Jewess, heavily laden, had approached her in the street and asked the way to the railway station. She deliberately sent her in the opposite direction, and thought it an amusing thing to have done. Even if one is pre-pared to give Unity the benefit of the doubt, and accept that she could not have known what would be the ultimate fate of the majority of Germany's Jewish population, it is difficult to write of these things without a cold hand upon the heart. It is hardly conceivable that Unity would not have known what lay behind the statement that the young couple with the apartment were 'going abroad', and, as Diana said, sadly, 'It is impossible to defend Unity . . . she condemned herself out of her own mouth.'[11] And knowing what she knew, Unity accepted the req-uisitioned apartment in Schwabing and loved it right from the start. Her enjoyment was not dimmed by the manner in which she had acquired it, only by Hitler having forgotten his promise to help her furnish it. Perhaps, in that summer of 1939, he had too much on his mind to worry about sideboards for Unity.

A week later Unity was in England. She was in good spirits and saw many members of her family. She also saw Hanfstaengl and told him what had happened with Erna, and with Diana and Tom attended Mosley's huge peace rally at Earl's Court. Here, Tom – by now an officer in the Territorials – greeted his brother-in-law with the Fascist salute as he walked past them. The newspapers took it amiss that a serving officer in His Majesty's Forces should behave like this. Tom's commanding officer was interviewed by reporters, who were clearly hoping to stir up trouble, but the colonel merely told them he wasn't going to be deprived of one of his best officers over the matter of a salute.[12] Afterwards Unity went back to Germany, her car laden with small items of furniture, lamps and curtain material. Larger items that she had appropriated with Sydney's permission from Rutland Gate were shipped out to Germany with the assistance of a friend in the diplomatic corps.

The Redesdales spent the summer of 1939 on a remote island in the Inner Hebrides. David had bought this island, Inch Kenneth, complete with an austere three-storey house, cottage, and a ruined chapel in 1938 after a friend at his club had brought the property to his attention. He, Sydney and Unity had gone to view it and loved it on sight. Because of its windswept isolation and the fact that there was no shooting it was not worth a great deal, and David paid for it with what remained from the sale of Swinbrook. Thereafter, everybody who visited fell in love with Inch Kenneth's stark beauty and pristine beaches, though it was difficult to get to, and hardly a sound prospect as a potential retirement home. From London it involved travelling to Oban by an overnight sleeper train, followed by a ferry trip of several hours to the island of Mull, a fifteen-mile drive across Mull to the hamlet of Gribun, then a short boat trip to the island. On calm days this last stage of the journey was a pleasant half-hour excursion, but in inclement weather with a lumpy sea it could be long and uncomfortable. The Redesdales employed a couple, who lived in the cottage; the wife helped Sydney with the house, and the husband was responsible for maintaining and operating the small motor-boat called the *Puffin,* and a rowing-boat. These vessels ferried the family and visitors to and from the island and collected supplies sent over from the mainland. At Gribun, the nearest civilization, the Redesdales kept an ancient Morris in a shed, for the journey across Mull to the Oban ferry. Immediately Sydney set to work to ensure that the kitchen garden was planted with as much produce as it could support, and the 'farm' supported a few dozen chickens for eggs and a couple of cows for milk. Once on the island the only contact with the outside world was the news over the wireless. As the long hot summer of that last year of peace continued, the news worsened and the Redesdales grew more and more concerned about what would happen to Unity if and when war was declared.

At the end of July Unity and Diana had attended the Bayreuth

Festival at Hitler's personal invitation. On arrival Unity was greeted with two large bouquets, one from Herr Wagner of Munich, the other from the Mayor of Munich. Neither, apparently, was immune to the gossip in Munich, which ran along the lines of: 'did Unity Mitford and Hitler sleep together or not?' On 2 August, the final day of the Wagner Festival and a day before they were due to leave Bayreuth, the sisters lunched with Hitler. Diana remembers that he told them he believed England was determined on war, and that if this was so, it was now inevitable. Diana said that Mosley would continue to campaign for peace, with the British Empire remaining intact, as long as it was legal for him to do so, and Hitler warned her that he risked assassination, 'Like Jaurès in 1914,' he said.[13]

Remarkably, we have Hitler's version of a similar conversation. 'Churchill and his friends decided on war against us some years before 1939,' he said, in a recorded conversation. 'I had this information from Lady Mitford [Unity]; she and her sisters were very much in the know, thanks to their relationship with influential people. One day she suddenly exclaimed that in the whole of London there were only three anti-aircraft guns! Her sister [Diana] who was present stared at her stonily, and then said slowly, "I do not know whether Mosley is the right man, or even if he is in a position, to prevent a war between Britain and Germany."'[14]

His report of Diana's reaction to Unity's casual remark is interesting for it suggests that she was either shocked or displeased by its naïvety. But whether Unity's statement was accurate or not is unimportant, for Hitler had a huge embassy in London, and the information about armaments provided by his intelligence service would have been far more informed than anything Unity could tell him. Diana thinks that the three anti-aircraft guns remark was the sort of joke then prevalent in UK newspapers and points out that Unity spent little time in England in 1939 so would not have known anything of any value. 'I often disapproved *strongly* of things Unity said . . . but she was incapable of disloyalty to England.'[15]

When the sisters were alone together after luncheon, Unity told Diana for the second time that if war was declared between England and Germany she would not live to see the tragedy unfold: 'She simply felt too torn between England and Germany to wish to see them tear themselves apart.' Diana was not the only person to whom Unity made this statement or others like it: she had also told Tom, Debo and Decca that she intended to 'commidit' ('commit suicide' in Boudledidge) rather than choose between England and Germany in a war. Diana never saw Hitler again, though Unity had lunch with him on the first two days following her return to Munich.

Despite what Hitler had said to them, Unity did not seem to accept that war was so imminent for when Diana left on 3 August, she still hoped that her sister might be able to return on the eighteen with Jonathan and Desmond for the Parteitag. But Diana was pregnant again and, anyway, events unwound far more rapidly than anyone had anticipated. Within a month of her return to England it was already too late to travel to Germany. Instead Diana was at Wootton making the preparations for war that were suddenly obligatory for all householders. Blackout curtains had to be made for the numerous massive windows.

Irene Ravensdale, together with Mosley's children from his first marriage, joined the Mosleys there, so it could not have been a comfortable period for anyone concerned, given Lady Ravensdale's much-aired antipathy towards Diana. Nor did it help relations, Irene Ravensdale wrote in her autobiography, that Diana prominently displayed in her drawing room the large autographed photograph of Hitler that had been his wedding gift to her. In fact, Diana had purposely removed this photograph before Irene's visit because she was aware it might cause offence. 'I wrapped it in brown paper and put it in a cupboard,' she recalled. In June, shortly after Mosley was arrested, she deposited the brown paper parcel at Drummonds bank and has never seen it since.[16]

Meanwhile, Unity amused herself by decorating her apartment. Janos von Almassy came to stay with her for a few weeks in early August, during which he bought her a dining table and chairs. When he left, the Wrede twins, half-Spanish princesses who had served as nurses in the Spanish civil war, stayed with her for a few days. It was only towards the end of the month that she began to feel isolated. Hitler was in Berlin, occupied with affairs of state, and the British consul summoned Unity and ordered her to return to England. She refused, and was told that she would forfeit British protection if she did not leave with the few remaining British subjects. She retorted that she had far better protection than that: Hitler's. But she was miserable: most foreign journalists had now been withdrawn, and all her friends had pulled out, too. Even her German friends had retreated to their homes. Food was already rationed and becoming scarce, although Hitler sometimes remembered her and sent supplies to her flat. The few friends she did manage to see were frightened by the idea of war, and were also made uneasy by Unity's assertions that if war was declared she would have no alternative but to shoot herself.

On 22 August she wrote to Diana that she was thrilled to hear about the Nazi–Soviet pact for surely, she wrote, this would make Germany so strong that England would never dare oppose Hitler. A few days later she was writing that she was not so sure the pact had helped: war seemed even more certain. The worst thing was that she had not seen Hitler for nearly three weeks. 'I wish he would come,' she said plaintively. By now it was obvious to her that Diana could not fly out to Germany and all the borders were closed. 'On thinking things over,' Unity wrote, 'I might disappear into the mountains in the Tyrol perhaps, if war is declared. Of course the other way seems the easiest way out, but it seems silly not to wait and see how things turn out, it might be all over within a week.'[17] On 30 August she received two last letters from Diana and her parents. It seemed a miracle that they had got through for the city was now on full alert for war with mandatory blackout after dusk, and the postal services were spasmodic. David had sent her 1,500 German marks that he had left over from his last trip 'for emergency'. She replied thanking him and telling Sydney about her idea of going to the Tyrol, and to Diana asking that 'if anything was to happen to me and the English Press try to make some untrue story out of it against W[olf], you will see to it that the truth is known won't you . . .'[18] Her biggest fear, though, was that 'I shan't see the Führer again.' These were the last letters that got through.

While Unity idled away the last few weeks of August, working on the decoration of her apartment and sunbathing on its balcony, hoping against all hope for a reconciliation between Germany and England, Pam and Derek Jackson were in New York. He was engaged on a high-level mission for the Air Ministry, but they made time to call on Decca and Esmond at their flat in Greenwich Village. They just knocked on the door, without prior announcement. 'I was amazed at Woman turning up here,' Decca wrote to Sydney.[19] As usual it was the meal that Pam most recalled about their visit. Forty years later she remembered that they ate roast chicken, which Pam cooked and carved. It was a 'boiling hot day', she reminded Decca, and even the effort of carving the chicken had brought her out 'in a muck sweat'. The other thing she remembered was that Decca showed her where they hid their money, between the leaves of books. Pam worried for weeks that they would forget where it all was, or leave some behind when they left. It was pleasant for the sisters to meet, and Decca enjoyed telling them about her work and how they were managing. Derek and Esmond did not hit it off, though, and this made the occasion 'uncomfortable and stiff'.

Decca had just left her job at the dress shop, having been offered a better one at Bloomingdales. In the meantime she was working on a trade stand at the New York World Fair. The Jacksons went to the fair several times to see her there without Esmond. When it was time to leave the United States, they invited the Romillys to dinner at their hotel and Esmond was fascinated to learn that they proposed to fly back to England. The Americans had been operating a transatlantic service since June, which carried up to seventeen civilian passengers. On 4 August a British service was inaugurated and Derek arranged for them to be on the second trip. So unusual was the mode of transport that just before they took off the Jacksons were interviewed by journalists, who asked why they had chosen to *fly* to England. 'Well, you see,' Derek explained, 'tomorrow is our little dog's birthday so we are in rather a hurry to get home . . .' He had in reality been allocated seats because he was carrying top-secret papers. 'The embassy had asked him to give them to them for transmission in the diplomatic bag,' Diana recalled. 'Derek refused. He said later, "If I'd accepted, the Russians would have had them next day."'[20]

Almost the last thing Pam did before leaving New York was to arrange a singing telegram for Decca's twenty-second birthday in September. Then they set off for England. Three years earlier, a transatlantic flight of any kind was still deemed worthy of a tick-ertape parade but aviation in the thirties represented the exposed cutting edge of technology. Aircraft evolved in that decade from flimsy club biplanes through classic racers and record-breaking fuel carriers, to the sophisticated fighting machines of the Second World War. The Jacksons went home in a Caribou flying boat. 'Our flying journey', Pam wrote to Decca, 'was wonderful, but rather frightening when we took off. The plane seemed far too small to battle all across the Atlantic. We came down at Botwood in Newfoundland, and were able to go for a walk while the plane was being filled with petrol. The next stop was at Foynes in Ireland. The whole journey only took 28 hours!'[21] Pam was probably among the first hundred women to fly the Atlantic, and although she is always regarded as 'the unknown sister, who never did anything', this flight in 1939 represented a quiet act of courage. No fuss, no nerves: it was typical of the daughter who most resembled Sydney.

Other members of the Mitford family besides Decca, Unity and Diana were now taking up partisan positions. David had swung round in a U-turn and for him the Germans had once more become 'the beastly Hun'. Sydney was having none of this: she had met Hitler and liked the man; she had seen for herself the 'marvellous' things that his administration had done for a country brought to its knees by the previous war, and she continued to support him. Hitler's arguments about encirclement by unsympathetic neighbours made perfect sense to her and, in her opinion, if a war was impending it was Churchill and the British government who were the cause for they had it in their power to stop it. For Debo, the only child left at home, this was a traumatic time. She was the only witness of the effect on her parents of Decca's elopement, the worry over Unity, and the continuous disagreement between them about Hitler and the looming conflict. With the exception of Pam, whom they hardly saw, her family seemed to have become somehow totally enmeshed in politics.

Even Nancy became actively involved. In the late spring of 1939 she travelled to Perpignan where Prod was working as a volunteer with international charity organizations in the Roussillon region near the Spanish border. The area was inundated with half a million supporters of the previous Spanish government who had fled across the border to escape retribution under Franco's regime. The French could not cope and herded the men into wire-enclosed camps. The women and children quartered wherever they could. It was left to international organizations such as the Red Cross to feed, clothe and care for them.

The plight of the refugees was a shock to Nancy: there were

few frivolities here and she was genuinely affected by the plight
of the dispossessed families.

> If you could have a look, as I have, at some of the less
> agreeable results of fascism in a country [she wrote to
> Sydney], I think you would be less anxious for the
> swastika to become a flag on which the sun never sets.
> And whatever may be the *good* produced by that regime,
> that the first result is always a horde of unhappy refugees
> cannot be denied. Personally I would join hands with the
> devil himself to stop any further extension of the disease.
> As for encirclement, if a person goes mad he is encircled,
> not *out of any hatred* for the person but for the safety of
> his neighbours & the same applies to countries . . . if the
> Russian alliance does not go through we shall be at war in
> a fortnight, & as I have a husband of fighting age I am
> not particularly anxious for that eventuality.[22]

Nancy joined the volunteers, working ten hours a day and
more to help the refugees find food, clothes, accommodation,
medication and, ultimately, transportation to Mexico, Morocco
or other parts of France. The biggest logistical problems concerned the loading of refugees on to the ships, and sometimes she
and Peter could not find time to go to bed or even talk to each
other for days at a time. When the departure of one ship was
delayed by a hurricane Nancy worked among the women
refugees stranded on the quayside, helping where she could.
There were two hundred children under two who had to be fed,
many with bottled milk, and changed every four hours. Some
women were in the last stages of pregnancy. But amid the chaos
and despair Nancy could spot a joke: 'Peter said yesterday one
woman was really too greedy, she already had 4 children and she
wants 3 more,' she told her mother. 'I thought of you.'[23] At last
the ship was able to dock and the men were allowed to rejoin

their families. 'None of them had seen each other since their retreat . . . you never saw such scenes of hugging. The boat sailed at 12 yesterday, the pathetic little band on board played first God Save the King for us, and then the Marseillaise & then the Spanish National anthem. Then the poor things gave three vivas for an Espana which they will never see again. I don't think there was a single person not crying. I have never cried so much in all my life.'[24] By the time Nancy returned to England she was a fully committed 'rabid anti-Nazi',[25] but though a socialist by inclination she never tipped over the edge into radicalism. 'There isn't a pin to put between Nazis & Bolshies,' she wrote that autumn to Mrs Hammersley. 'If one is a Jew one prefers one & if an aristocrat the other, that's all as far as I can see. *Fiends!*'[26]

On Saturday 2 September Unity telephoned Rudi von Simolin (later Baroness von St Paul), a friend of Janos von Almassy and Erna Hanfstaengl. Rudi was visiting her father at Seeseiten, about an hour's drive from Munich, when Unity rang, and there followed a long conversation. Unity said that she had heard from the British consul that there would now be war within days. All her efforts of the past two years, to persuade Hitler that there could not be war between their two countries, had been in vain, she said, and she intended to shoot herself when war was declared. 'I was terrified for her,' Rudi told Unity's biographer.[27] She urged Unity to do nothing until Monday when she would return to Munich and they could work out what should be done for the best. The war might not last long, she said, and there was no need for her to shoot herself. She reminded Unity of their plan for an autumn riding holiday. All the same, when she put down the phone Rudi had the feeling she had not got through to Unity and tried to ring back, but the receiver was off the hook.

On the following morning Unity received a message that there was a telegram for her at the British consulate. She walked round to collect it and was informed that Britain had declared war on Germany that morning. Immediately she went home and wrote to her parents: 'This is to say goodbye . . . I send my best love to you all and particularly to my Boud [Decca] when you write. Perhaps when this war is over, everyone will be friends again and there will be the friendship between Germany and England which we have so hoped for . . .'[28] She hoped that they would see Hitler often when the war was over and that Tom would be safe. It was light, matter-of-fact, final. The consul would deliver the letter for her, which was guaranteed to chill the heart of a parent.

Her next act was to go to Gauleiter Wagner's office and ask if she was to be interned as an enemy alien. He assured her that she was not, and even offered to obtain some petrol for her car. Despite his reassurance she seemed distracted and she requested him to ensure, should anything happen to her, that she was buried in Munich with her signed photograph of Hitler and her Nazi Party badge. He was concerned enough about her demeanour to order that she should be discreetly followed, and she was next observed calling on the wife of her singing teacher. She had paid some outstanding bills from the money David had sent her, but a thousand marks remained and she gave this to the woman, saying she had no need of it. She also gave her an envelope containing keys and asked if they could be delivered to Rudi the following day. Then she walked back to her flat.

A little later she returned to Wagner's office in her car and handed him a large, heavy envelope. Her former agitation had disappeared but nevertheless she bade him goodbye in something of a hurry. Wagner was half persuaded that there was no need to worry and it was not until he had dealt with the matter in hand that he opened the envelope Unity had left with his name on it. In it he found a suicide note saying that she was unable to bear the thought of a war between England and her beloved Germany, a sealed letter for Hitler, and her two most precious belongings: the signed framed photograph of Hitler which she took with her even when she travelled back and forth to England, and her special Party badge. He made enquiries, but no one had seen her drive off or knew which direction she had taken. All he could do was alert the police.

Unity drove to the Englischer Garten, the beautiful three-mile-long park beside the swiftly flowing River Isar, just east of the Schwabing district. It was familiar territory, one of Unity's favourite places in Munich and quite close to her flat on Agnesstrasse. She had often walked her dogs along the winding paths under willow trees between the flower-beds, and exercised them on the open grassy spaces, before finding new homes for them a few months earlier. She even knew of a secluded little glade where, on occasions, she had sunbathed naked, giggling helplessly at the thought of what Sydney would say if she knew. She was not laughing on 3 September and she did not seek seclusion. Just inside the park, a few yards from the Königinstrasse, and close to the Haus de Kunst, an art gallery built under Hitler's direction, she took her pearl-handled pistol from her handbag and shot herself in the temple.

For her it was a warrior's exit, an honourable departure from a situation she regarded as intolerable. Metaphorically, she fell on her sword. 'She put her life and ambition into avoiding a war,' Rudi told Unity's biographer. 'She had been on a pedestal and therefore was mistaken into thinking that she had influence. She was too loyal to her beliefs.'[29]

A Frau Koch and her two sons were out walking in the Englischer Garten a little after noon on that fateful Sunday. Unity had just passed them when the shot rang out. The elder of the two brothers turned at the sound and caught Unity almost as she slid to the ground. With his mother's help he carried her from the pavement and laid her on the grass. Blood was streaming down her face.[30] Just across the road there was a military establishment and Frau Koch ran over to appeal for help. Within a short time a Luftwaffe car drove out, picked up Unity and drove off with her. Later, the Kochs were questioned by the police and told not to talk about the incident with anyone. They only learned Unity's identity a few days later.[31]

On the following day Rudi returned to Munich. She called first on Unity's music teacher whose wife handed her the envelope Unity had left. She said she had heard that a young woman had shot herself in the Englischer Garten. The envelope was found to contain the keys to the Agnesstrasse apartment so the two women hurried off there together. They found the apartment sealed off by the authorities, so Rudi called on Gauleiter Wagner. He told her what had happened, that Unity was alive, but in a coma and not expected to regain consciousness. Rudi went immediately to the hospital and was told that the bullet had entered Unity's right temple, and was embedded at the back of the skull from where it could not be removed. Later a doctor said that had he tried to follow the track the bullet had taken with a scalpel even with his years of experience he could not have done so without killing the patient. It was something of a miracle that Unity had survived.

Rudi spent the next weeks visiting the hospital daily, having been given a petrol allowance for the purpose by Gauleiter Wagner. She also wrote or cabled Janos von Almassy daily to keep him advised of the situation. Hitler visited Unity on 10 September before she regained consciousness. A day or so later she came round, although she was deeply confused and paid no attention to her visitors, her carers, or the banks of flowers that had been sent in by Goebbels, Ribbentrop, several gauleiters and Hitler. Hitler sent roses. On 13 September, ten days after the shooting, Unity managed to say one or two words to Hitler on the telephone. He did not visit her again until 8 November; by then she could understand better, and even hold a short conversation. He asked her what she wanted to do. She said she would like to go back to England for a few weeks, then return to Munich.[32]

According to Julius Schaub, Hitler's adjutant, Hitler was 'deeply shaken' by Unity's appearance and manner, as was everybody who saw her over the next few months. She seemed to have no memory of the suicide attempt (although she made a further attempt to kill herself by swallowing her swastika badge which had to be removed from her stomach with a probe), only a limited ability to speak, and she was partially paralysed. Her face was badly swollen due to the wound in her temple and there was little resemblance to the beautiful, alert and lively girl she had been. Instead, she had the empty fixed stare of someone who had suffered a stroke.[33] Hitler asked Frau Schaub if she would watch over Unity by visiting each day, and went off to discuss her case with her doctors. Subsequently he set in motion an arrangement to get her to Switzerland as soon as it was feasible for her to travel. Once again he made himself personally responsible for her hospital bills. Her suicide attempt was declared a state secret, and after the first report of the anonymous woman, it was never mentioned by the German media. It is difficult to know whether Hitler did this out of consideration and affection for Unity, or whether he felt uncomfortable that yet another young woman with whom he was connected had attempted suicide. Two other women who were sexually linked, by rumour or fact, with Hitler, committed or attempted suicide with varying degrees of success: Geli, his half-niece, and Eva Braun, who made two attempts.[34]

The Mitford family knew nothing of this, although Gauleiter Wagner told Rudi they had been notified, and that all frontier checkpoints had been advised that Lord and Lady Redesdale and Mrs Diana Mosley would be permitted to cross.[35] In the early days of the war, however, there no way in which they could have been contacted, and the German press silence meant that the news was confined to those most closely involved with the incident. Tom and Diana were in no doubt that Unity would have shot herself, as she had so often said she would. Her hint about the Tyrol gave a spark of hope, but in their hearts they feared the worst.

Sydney, David, Debo and Nancy were at Inch Kenneth when war was declared. Nancy immediately left for London and Sydney drove her to the Oban ferry. During the journey Nancy made a rude remark about Hitler, and Sydney told her to shut up or get out and walk. Realizing that her mother was worried and wretched about Unity, Nancy chose to shut up. There was no talking to Sydney about Hitler: her high regard for him had been borne of a genuine fear of Communism and nurtured over tea-cups in Munich when Unity had translated polite conversations between the two. During September they had no news of Unity, only rumours. On 15 September Nancy wrote to Mrs Hammersley: 'Bobo, we hear on fairly good authority, is in a concentration camp for Czech women which much as I deplore it has a sort of poetic justice.'[36] She also referred to an interview in the *Daily Mirror* in which David had 'publicly recanted like Latimer' and said he had been wrong about Hitler.

It was not until 2 October that the Redesdales heard from Teddy von Almassy, brother of Janos. He was in Budapest, which was neutral so had postal communications with England and Germany, and he wrote to say that Unity had been ill but was in hospital and was now recovering. Sydney and Debo left David at Inch Kenneth and travelled down to live at the mews cottage in London. It was a curiously changed London with sandbags everywhere, windows criss-crossed with brown paper, barrage balloons, hardly any traffic and almost everyone, it seemed, in uniform. But even there, pulling strings, Sydney could not get any reliable news of Unity, so she busied herself by closing Rutland Gate 'for the duration' and putting the furniture into storage. Most of this was lost in a warehouse fire within a few weeks but as Sydney wrote to Decca, '*Things* don't seem to matter much when one thinks of the terrible world conflagration.'[37] They had another brief communication, this time by cable from Teddy von Almassy, advising that Unity was making good progress, but no further explanation of what was wrong with her. 'It is a terrible and continual worry,' Sydney wrote to Decca. 'One cannot bear to think what agonies of mind she must have been through as she never believed a war could happen between the two countries.'

There was considerable animosity between Nancy and Sydney now. Following the declaration of war Nancy was furious at Sydney's open support of Hitler. 'She is *impossible*,' Nancy wrote to Mrs Hammersley. 'Hopes we shall lose the war and makes no bones about it. Debo is having a wild time with young cannon fodder at the Ritz etc. Apparently Muv said to her "*Never* discuss politics, not even for 5 minutes, with Nancy." Rather as some devout RC might shield her little one from a fearful atheist!'[38]

Nancy, working in an underground casualty depot in Praed Street, was already bored with the degree of sacrifice and discipline demanded for no apparent reason throughout the months of the Phoney War. She was telling everybody she had been given an indelible blue pencil with which to write names and other details on the foreheads of the dead and injured, and asking what she was supposed to do 'if a coloured person was brought in'. Derek Jackson was away on a mission for the RAF, Tom, Prod and the Bailey and Farrer brothers were all in the Army, Debo was planning to work in a canteen. Ten days after they first met Randolph Churchill married Pamela Digby, to whom he had become engaged within twenty-four hours of setting eyes on her. 'She's rather a friend of Debo's – pretty with red hair and lovely colouring,' Sydney wrote to Decca.

Both Sydney and Pam kept Decca updated with the latest news. Aunt Iris had become an all-night telephone operator and Uncle Jack had joined the auxiliary fire brigade. 'Coal was rationed and though food was not rationed yet, it soon would be,' Pam wrote. Everyone was busy making blackout curtains, the barrage balloons over London were very pretty and some

London refugees had been billeted on them at Rignell House. 'Fortunately they spent only a few nights before deciding it was too far from the pub and returned to the East End.' Sydney wrote that London was 'much less gloomy than it was in the first weeks and there is a lot of entertaining in restaurants, all of which, and all the nightclubs, are full'.[39]

The Romillys were still enjoying America; making the most of what time they had left before the fighting began. Shortly after Pam and Derek's visit they had moved to Washington, DC, where Esmond got a job selling silk stockings, door to door. It was a high-pressure sales job and Esmond learned the patter fast: 'Mrs Robinson, have you ever felt a bit of *real fresh silk*?' he would begin, producing a skein that looked like tangled horse-hair. He wound it around the potential customer's wrist and tugged hard. 'That would certainly have a hard time breaking, wouldn't it?' Then he would invite the hapless victim to take a pin and make a hole in a piece of printed silk, 'woven exclusively for the discriminating woman, almost impossible, isn't it?' But he withdrew the pin quickly for it had been known to happen. 'Your big toe would have a hard time trying to go sightseeing through that, wouldn't it?' By a process of flattery and smooth-talking he invariably came away with an order, leaving a flustered housewife wondering how she had parted with eighteen dollars for enough stockings to last twelve months. In fact, he was so good at it that he exceeded his sales quota and proudly carried home to Decca the prizes that he was awarded as gifts for his 'little woman': a Snugfit Supersoft Shortie Housecoat and a Brushrite brush and comb set. He never achieved the fifty dollars a week that had been glowingly advertised when he applied for the job, but he earned enough to pay their expenses.[40]

At weekends they relied on invitations to grand houses, where they were wined and dined, and in return entertained their fellow guests with stories of Decca's upbringing and their elopement. On one occasion when she phoned to accept an invitation to a mansion in Virginia, Decca was asked, 'You ride, of course?' 'Oh yes,' Decca said blithely, unwilling to forfeit a weekend of lavish hospitality, and giving only momentary thought to those frequent falls in the paddock at Swinbrook. 'Do bring your riding things,' said her hostess. Decca's riding things consisted of a pair of old trousers and a rough shirt. The other guests were clad immaculately in gleaming boots, well-cut breeches and hacking jackets. Nor was Decca able to handle the thoroughbred she had been allotted. It was a disaster.

In early November the Redesdales heard through the American embassy that Unity was 'in a surgical hospital in Munich' and making a good recovery from an attempted suicide. At least now they knew the worst and when, a few weeks later, a reporter rang in the middle of the night to ask if it was true that Unity had died in hospital, Sydney was confident enough to hang up on him. Suddenly the newspapers were full of a story that 'The Girl Who Loved Hitler' had shot herself following a massive row with Hitler and had died in a Munich hospital. In other versions she had been shot on the orders of Himmler, and buried in an unmarked grave. Blor, who was in London for Christmas shopping ('It didn't take long,' she said, 'the shops were empty'),[41] saw a news-vendor the next day holding a poster with headlines announcing Unity's death. 'She went up to the man and said, 'THAT'S NOT TRUE!' Sydney wrote. 'He was astonished . . . Debo is terrifically gay and goes out to lunch and dinner every day. I suppose there is a great dearth of girls in London and the young men come up quite a lot . . . The cottage at Swinbrook is presently housing Diana's nurse and baby and is to be let for a month at Christmas to friends of Debo; Andrew Cavendish and another boy. I do hope they won't break it up completely.'[42]

Debo and Andrew Cavendish had been secretly pledged to each other for some months having been in love since shortly after they met in the previous year. Debo thought it was pointless asking for permission to marry; they would only be told they were too young. Sensibly, they decided to wait for a more propitious moment.

Hearing the latest reports, Decca wrote anxiously asking for news. The Romillys were now in Florida, and she had been mobbed by reporters offering her money in exchange for a story but she didn't know what to make of the assertion that Unity was dead. Sydney cabled her enough information to set her mind at rest.

David came down from Inch Kenneth to spend Christmas at the mews cottage and it was while he was there, on Christmas Eve, that he and Sydney received further news about Unity. It was the best Christmas present they could have received, for it was Janos calling and, after explaining that he was with Unity in Switzerland, he handed the phone to her. 'When are you coming to get me?' Unity asked plaintively.

14

IRRECONCILABLE DIFFERENCES

(1940–41)

Although in the brief telephone conversation Unity sounded normal it was obvious from what Janos told them that she was far from well. The family learned that Hitler had arranged for Unity to be taken to Berne in a specially fitted out ambulance carriage attached to a train. As well as Janos, she was accompanied by a nursing nun, who had been with her since the shooting, and a doctor who was the ex-husband of a friend Unity had made when she first went out to Munich to learn German. The doctor had now returned to Germany but the nun and Janos would wait until the Mitfords arrived.

Somehow, although it was Christmas, David acquired the necessary travel papers in three days, and on 27 December Sydney and Debo set off for Switzerland. David was to remain in England 'to organize things from that end' and to meet them with an ambulance when they returned on the cross-Channel ferry. Debo was nineteen and thinks that Sydney might have had some special permit from the Foreign Office to present at the inevitable checkpoints and borders. It was one of the most harrowing and strangest experiences of her life. It was midwinter, grey, freezing cold, and none of the trains ran to schedule, but at

least there was no fighting yet. She and Sydney were both anxious to get to Berne and on 29 December they arrived at the
clinic. Nothing had prepared Debo for the shock of what they
found.

Unity was still bedridden, propped in a sitting position with
pillows since she suffered from severe vertigo and could not
remain upright without help. She looked frail and very thin,
having lost over thirty pounds, and her dark blue eyes seemed
enormous in her yellowy white face with its sunken cheeks. 'She
was *completely* changed,' Debo recalled. 'Her hair was short and
all matted. Because of the wound I expect they couldn't do much
about washing or combing it, and her teeth were yellow; they
had not been brushed since the shooting. She couldn't bear for
her head to be touched. She had an odd vacant expression . . . the
most pathetic sight. I was very shocked and I can't begin to imagine what it must have been like for my mother seeing her like
that . . . But it wasn't just her appearance; she was a completely
changed person, like somebody who has had a stroke . . . Her
memory was very jagged and she could remember some things
and not others. She recognized us though.'[1]

Just to be reunited with Unity was an enormous joy to Sydney,
and Unity was thrilled to see them and asked after the others.
'We were all three so happy,' Sydney said later.[2] As they talked,
Unity's problems became more obvious. She frequently confused
words, calling the sugar 'chocolate' or the salt 'tea' – typical symptoms of brain damage. Janos, who had already stayed longer than
planned in Berne, was anxious to get back to his family, so
exchanged pleasantries then left. The nun, who had nursed Unity
for four months, remained with her patient until they left Berne
on New Year's Eve. She passed on the details of Unity's clinical
treatment, explained that the medical bills had been met by the
Führer, and that he had arranged for Unity's furniture to be
packed and placed in storage at his expense. Altogether this was
a remarkable sequence of events, and it is curious that none of

Hitler's many biographers has attempted to explain either the relationship or his many small kindnesses to Unity.

The ambulance carriage was now hooked on to a train heading for Calais. Presumably Sydney enlisted the help of British diplomats in Switzerland for it seems unlikely that she could have dealt with the matter on her own. The journey to the French coast was a nightmare, according to Debo, and what should have taken two days took three or four. 'It seemed to go on for ever,' she said. 'Every time the train jolted, stopped and started, it was torture for her. It was a long, dark and cold journey, and Unity was *so* ill. My mother worried it would be too much for her.'[3] Worse was to come. The press were waiting for them at Calais. Unity's activities had featured in the newspapers for a long time now, and the attention her return stimulated in journalists was a forerunner to the intense press interest associated with modern celebrities. It took them all by surprise. When they reached Calais they found they had missed the sailing and had to stay overnight in the hotel near the terminus. Here, Sydney received a note from a *Daily Express* reporter offering three thousand pounds for an interview with Unity. As if she was declining an invitation to tea, Sydney replied courteously that Unity was too tired, having been very ill, although she was now much better for she had been well cared-for in Germany. This was seen by the reporter as an invitation to trade. He increased his offer to five thousand. Sydney declined again and asked the hotel staff to keep the press away.

Next morning Unity was carried on to the ferry where they encountered problems with the Customs officer and a doctor. Rudi had packed all she could of Unity's personal belongings from the Agnesstrasse apartment into fourteen containers.[4] The Customs officer insisted on searching each one, and when he came across some tablets that Unity could not identify he seized them. The doctor said they were cocaine and brusquely accused Unity of being a cocaine addict. Sydney insisted he took them away and had them analysed. They turned out to be some old pills that had been prescribed for Rebell, the Great Dane. At last the boat reached Folkestone where David was waiting anxiously with the ambulance. As Unity's stretcher was carried down the gangway in the failing light, he rushed up and kissed her.

The press corps had been kept out of the port, a restricted area, but after the ambulance passed through the gates the Redesdale party was followed by about twenty cars containing reporters and cameramen. A few miles outside Folkestone the ambulance began to make ominous clanking sounds. A spring had broken and they decided to return to the hotel David had used while he waited for them. They arrived unexpectedly and there was nobody to carry Unity, so David supported her as she walked unsteadily inside while flashbulbs popped and reporters shouted questions. The foyer of the hotel was a blaze of light and crammed with journalists. Sydney tried to calm the frenzy by asking, in wonder, 'Are you all *quite* mad? What is it all about?'[5] That they were inside the hotel made her suspect that the broken spring had been sabotage. 'At the time I was not sorry,' she said later. It had been so difficult driving in the dark of the blackout with pinprick lights, and Unity was worn out. They all were. Before she was carried upstairs the press managed to get a few words from Unity. 'Are you pleased to be home, Miss Mitford?' someone called. 'I'm very glad to be in England, even if I'm not on your side,' a newspaper report claimed she replied. On the following day David hired another ambulance and the party drove to the cottage at High Wycombe without further interference.

That week cinema-goers were treated to a newsreel film of Unity looking startled and puzzled, as David helped her from the stretcher to her feet outside the hotel. Sydney had washed and combed Unity's hair while they travelled, which improved her appearance, and that she was able to walk made it appear as though there was not much wrong with her. With little else to write about the incident, journalists made a story of the fact that Unity had been brought home in a first-class carriage with a special guard's van at a cost of £1,600 to her parents. A good three-bedroom house could be bought for three hundred pounds in 1939. Perhaps it is not surprising that the newsreel was greeted by scathing jeers and catcalls from largely working-class audiences, earning perhaps four or five pounds a week. Opposition – hatred, even – was understandable for 'the girl who loved Hitler', but so unusually aggressive was the press coverage of Unity's arrival that questions were asked in the House of Commons and, later, some newspapers had the grace to admit that their reporters had 'gone too far' in their treatment of a young woman who was, clearly, still gravely ill. For some months afterwards the cottage at High Wycombe was given police protection. This led to the assumption that they were being 'watched' by the authorities.

When she had rested for a few days Unity was admitted to hospital in Oxford but the doctors told the Redesdales that everything that could be done had already been done in Germany.[6] Only time could help Unity now, they told Sydney. Unity kept repeating, 'I thought you all hated me but I don't remember why.' She asked Nancy, 'You're not one of those who would be cruel to somebody, are you?'[7] And 'Am I mad?' This was an occasion when Nancy was kind. 'Of course you are, darling Stonyheart,' she said gently, 'but then you always were.'[8] Initially Unity appeared to think that her doctors had made a hole in her head, which had caused her illness. Later, though, as her memory returned she asked Diana privately if she thought it 'very wicked to die by one's own hand'. Diana believes that 'to that small extent man must be the master of his own fate. He did not ask to be born; if his life becomes too tragic or unbearable he has the right to die.'[9] She told Unity this, but told her also that as she had been saved, she must now concentrate all her energy on recovering her health.

Nancy sometimes stayed with her parents during this period,

and to pass the time she worked on *Pigeon Pie*, a novel based on her experiences in the first-aid post. As usual it was peopled with her friends and connections: 'You are in it,' she wrote to Decca, 'as Mary Pencill.' After it was published Nanny Blor wrote to Decca to say she'd read it, but hadn't enjoyed it. Everyone who wrote to Decca said how Unity continually asked after 'my Boud' and said how wonderful it would be if she were to walk in the door. Tom and Nancy wrote that they had to leave the room to cry when they first saw her, but that there was a gradual improvement.

The combined effort required to bring Unity home had created a temporary lull in the growing discord between Sydney and David about Germany. With Unity safely home, their differences surfaced again. For a short time in 1938 David had gone along with Unity's line that the Treaty of Versailles had been unfair to Germany, and that it was only right that the former German colonies should be restored. Like most of the upper classes David had been deeply concerned about the spread of Communism, and feared it. Fascism appeared to be a possible alternative. And Hitler had behaved like a gentleman over Unity's illness. But by 1939, in common with practically everyone else in Britain, David viewed Hitler as a threat as great as Communism, and someone to be strenuously opposed. Sydney, however, still regarded Hitler as the charming music-lover who had entertained her to tea and, what is more, had looked after Unity so kindly. She recalled the tidiness of German towns, the cleanliness of its hotels, the magnificent *autobahns*, the feeling that everyone was happy and working together for the greater good of the country, under the beloved Führer. '*When* the Germans have won,' she said to David, 'you'll see, everything will be wonderful and they'll treat us very differently to those wretched beastly Poles.'[10] By mid-February 1940 the couple were 'absolutely at loggerheads', as Nancy put it, quarrelling bitterly. Eventually David confided in Nancy that he did not think he could continue to live with Sydney for much longer. And when Nancy wrote to Mrs Hammersley she said that he 'is more violent now against Germany than anyone else I know, and against any form of peace until they are beaten . . . I really think they hate each other now.'[11]

Initially the Redesdales intended that after Unity was discharged from hospital, they would take her to sit out the war in the quiet and solitude of Inch Kenneth. But the island was made a 'protected zone' like many coastal areas, and when David applied for permits to travel there he was turned down. Unity might be British and she might be an invalid, but she was no more trusted than an enemy alien. Lady Redesdale had made her views on the Germans clear, and she was not allowed to go, either. Lord Redesdale was permitted to go there, of course. He blamed Sydney for this, believing that had she told the truth about the extent of Unity's brain damage, and not aired her pro-Nazi views so forthrightly, there would not have been a problem. Sydney could hardly admit to herself that Unity might have brain damage, so perhaps it was not surprising that the rest of the population did not know the facts, and it did not help matters when Sydney was quoted as having stated firmly that Unity was 'recovering well . . . My daughter must not be made into one of history's tragic women,' she insisted to a reporter.

The old David, tall, strong, funny, fiery and the inspiration for 'Uncle Matthew', had almost disappeared. The events of the last few years, Diana's divorce and remarriage to Mosley, whom he detested, Decca's defection, Unity's suicide attempt, and now the quarrel between himself and Sydney, had broken him. Although he was only sixty-two his health was failing. His eyesight was poor because of cataracts and, white-haired and stooping, he looked a decade older than he was. Where once he had thundered, his tempers were now mere flashes of irritation. When Unity came out of hospital an added and unforeseen problem presented itself: the brain damage had made her clumsy and incontinent – when eating she frequently spilled or dropped her food and David could not stand the sight of her at the table. Eventually it all became too much for him: he went alone to the island, taking the under-parlourmaid, Margaret Wright, as his housekeeper. She was also a trained nurse, which was an advantage with his failing health. David and Sydney wrote to each other almost every day, and often their letters – from David anyway – were tender, always beginning, 'My darling'. In future the couple were together occasionally for special family occasions, and they sometimes stayed at each other's houses, but it was the end of their marriage as such and they never again lived as husband and wife. For the remainder of the war David spent six months of each year at Inch Kenneth and the other six, in the winter, at the mews cottage at Rutland Gate.

Sydney decided to return to Swinbrook, reasoning that everyone in that remote area had known Unity from childhood so she was unlikely to be attacked or harmed. She rented the old 'fishing cottage' next door to the pub for the summer, and took on a Mrs Timms as a daily. Soon she had acquired some hens and a goat, which gave birth to twins within weeks of purchase. Unity was thrilled, and wrote to Decca about the kids in wavery childish handwriting with grammatical errors. It must have brought a lump to Decca's throat when she compared it with Unity's letters before the shooting. Blor came to help with the nursing and after she went home to her family Sydney looked after Unity alone. With dedicated and loving care Unity made limited progress but she remained childlike for the rest of her life. For Sydney it was an unremitting job: Unity's incontinence meant that her bedlinen had to be washed every day, and as she recovered her mobility she wandered further from home, which, given her trusting simplicity, was often worrying. Old friends and cousins, such as Idden and Rudbin and the Baileys, visited along with Tom and all the sisters except Decca.

Decca had been very anxious. Like the Redesdales in England, she had been badgered by American reporters offering a thousand dollars and more for 'the inside story' on Unity. Poor as the Romillys were, and in some ways unscrupulous, and much as they loathed Fascism, Decca's love for Unity prevented her speaking to the press. One magazine she turned down ran a story anyway: 'I see they have an article about the "fabulous mansion at High Wycombe",' Decca wrote to Sydney, 'and pointing out that Farve is one of Princess Marina's closest friends and talking of Winston Churchill as Bobo's uncle. One journalist wrote that I had said, "Unity was always a wild youngster,"[12] (I hadn't even seen him) and next day it was in headlines in every US paper.'[13]

From Sydney she learned that six months after the shooting the doctors expected Unity to go on making limited progress for up to eighteen months but that she would never recover completely. She was stuck at a mental age of eleven or twelve. Sydney tried to remain optimistic, treating the injury like concussion, and reminding everyone how long Tom had taken to recover from concussion caused by a car crash some years earlier. However, she admitted that Unity's personality was changed: 'That old insouciance has rather gone,' she wrote, 'and she is so much more affectionate and sweet to everyone and there is something really so pathetic about her, poor darling.'[14] At Unity's request, Sydney arranged for her to see a Christian Science practitioner. From this point on Unity displayed the obsessional fixation on religion that can often be a characteristic of mental illness. The *Daily Express*, however, chose to link Unity's interest in Christian Science with the Nazi movement, pointing out that 'several of the leading Nazis' were strong Christian Scientists. But Unity was interested in many religions and swung from one to another, depending on whom she had last spoken with.

The papers continued to run stories on Unity almost weekly and David was often bothered for 'a statement' and referred to in reports as a supporter of Hitler. Finally he could bear it no longer and on 9 March he wrote to *The Times*:

My only crime, if it be a crime, so far as I know, is that I
am one of many thousands in this country who thought
that our best interests would be served by a friendly
understanding with Germany . . . though now proved to
be wrong, I was, at any rate, in good company . . . I
resent . . . the undoubted undercurrent of suspicion and
resentment caused by publicity to which there is no right
of reply . . . I am constantly described as a Fascist. I am
not, never have been, and am not likely to become a
Fascist.[15]

To spare Unity potential hurt the newspapers were hidden away
from her, even though, Sydney wrote to Decca, she could only
read a few lines if she found them, for she had the limited attention span of a child, her concentration was gone and she suffered
blackouts.

The old life in England seemed far away to Decca and
Esmond. He wrote a series of brilliantly simple, though obviously subjective, essays on the political situation and the
Cliveden set, for journals such as the *Commentator*, but though
he frequently criticized England and its administration, he never
wavered from his intention to join up when it became necessary.
His brother Giles was already serving in the British Army and
had been sent with the British Expeditionary Force (BEF) to
France, but while everybody waited for the Phoney War to end,
he and Decca were determined to enjoy what they knew was a
limited period of freedom.

Driving to New Orleans they made a mistake in navigation
and ended up in Miami. There, by virtue of invented backgrounds, Decca found a job on a *faux*-jewellery counter in a
drug store at fourteen dollars a week, and Esmond, 'known for
his inability to carry a teaspoon from one room to the next', was
employed by a restaurant based on his 'long experience' as a
waiter at the Savoy Grill. He lasted one evening, during which he

soaked his customers with wine, dripped tomato sauce on their clothes and ended up crashing spectacularly into a heavily laden fellow waiter leaving the kitchen with a tray of food. He was asked to leave but such was his personal charm that he talked the owners into letting him open a cocktail bar at a wage of five dollars a week plus meals and tips.[16]

The bar was an immediate success but the Miami police called round and closed the restaurant down because, they said, the bar was being operated illegally. To reopen the owners needed a liquor licence, which would cost a thousand dollars for the season. The Italian family who owned the Roma restaurant were crushed by what seemed the end of their livelihood, but Esmond struck a deal with them: he would raise the money, he said, in exchange for a full partnership in the restaurant. They agreed, probably thinking he was mad. If he could raise that sort of money why would he work for five dollars a week? Even Decca doubted Esmond in this case, especially when he told her his plan. He would use their small savings to fly back to Washington, DC, and see Eugene Meyer and talk him into lending them the money. In Decca's experience rich people got that way by not lending money without equity so she wrote immediately to Tom asking him to transmit to her the three hundred pounds in her account at Drummonds, proceeds of the sale of some shares David had given her. This, she thought, would pay off Mr Meyer if he agreed to the loan, but Tom could not comply with the request due to currency regulations.

Esmond's interview with Eugene Meyer was brief. He described the venture and launched into an explanation of the exchange rate between English pounds and American dollars, which Mr Meyer cut across with the remark, 'Yes, Esmond, I happen to know about the exchange rate.' Then he leaned back in his chair and said, 'A thousand dollars. Yes, I think I can lend you a thousand dollars.' Esmond was so bemused at not having to trot out his brilliant arguments that all he could think of to say was, 'Oh! Well, I hope it won't leave you short.' Collapse of stout party: Mr Meyer thought the remark hilarious and wrote out a cheque on the spot.[17]

Decca resigned from her drugstore job to help Esmond run the bar. They became part of the Italian family and if Decca thought, What would *Muv* think? when she had to eject a drunken woman from the restaurant powder room, it was all part of the fun of building their business. It seemed never to have crossed their minds that ownership of a business might carry a whiff of capitalism, and they cheerfully quizzed customers about their politics while always strongly espousing the left. It was an enormously happy time for them: young, bright and successful they managed to put the war out of their minds. 'We spend the mornings on the beach,' she wrote to Sydney, 'and the rest of the time eating up the delicious Italian food.' To her great surprise she met Harry Oakes in Miami, the man who had made his millions at Swastika. She had heard of his good fortune all her life, whenever David talked about the gold mine. To meet him was, she thought, an *extraordinary* coincidence.

The Phoney War ended suddenly, in May 1940, as Hitler's troops swept victoriously through the Low Countries and crossed into France. On 10 May Chamberlain announced his resignation and Churchill was asked to form an all-party coalition government. The BEF was forced to retreat until there was only the English Channel at their backs, and were rescued by the miracle of a massive fleet of small boats ferrying back and forth from Dunkirk.

Decca believed that Esmond changed a lot during the eighteen months they spent in the USA, that he had outgrown his automatic adolescent rebellion against any form of authority. He was steadier and more serious. There was only one aim in his life now, and that was the permanent defeat of Fascism. News from home was bad. Esmond's father died suddenly on 6 May. His brother Giles was missing in the fighting, believed to have been taken prisoner at Dunkirk. Nellie wrote to tell him that Aunt Clemmie had come for the funeral, and that Uncle Winston rang her to say that Holland and Belgium had been invaded. 'Esmond,' she wrote, 'if it is your own sincere conviction not to come home there is nothing more to say – but if Decca is holding you back from your country in her hour of anguish remember Uncle Winston's words, "If Britain lives a thousand years . . . this will be her finest hour."'[18] Suddenly Europe loomed over them again.

They sold the bar, making a small profit after settling the loan, and set off for Washington, DC, where Esmond intended to join the Canadian Royal Air Force and volunteer to serve in Europe, even though, as he told Decca, 'I'll probably find myself being commanded by one of your ghastly relations.'[19] He suggested that she should enrol in a stenographer's class while he was away. They both knew it was going to be tough and lonely for her with him gone. Learning shorthand and typing would be occupation for her and enable her to earn a living, as typists were always in demand. As for accommodation, Esmond had this worked out, too. They called on the Durrs and, while Decca was engaged in heated conversation with Cliff, he slipped into the kitchen to ask Virginia if Decca could stay with them after he left. 'I'm sure she will be so lonely. If you could just keep her for the weekend I can't tell you how much I would appreciate it.'[20] She told him she was going away that weekend to a Democratic convention but agreed that Decca should go with her, to take her mind off Esmond's departure for an RCAF training depot at Halifax, Nova Scotia. 'Within days,' Virginia wrote, 'we had become devoted to Decca.' They referred to her jokingly as 'our refugee' and she fitted very well into the untidy mêlée of the extended family, pets and stray visitors that peopled the farmhouse. Decca wrote to Esmond, 'Virginia has very kindly – entirely due to you, you clever old thing – asked me to stay as long as I want, but of course if there's any chance of seeing you I could scram North in a second.'[21] In the event Decca ended up living with the Durrs for two and a half years, and Virginia always said that Esmond had had the whole thing worked out from the start.

On the journey to Washington the Romillys had stopped off at New Orleans for a two-week holiday. They had wanted to visit the city since they had taken the wrong turning that led them to Miami. Arriving after dark they found a small hotel in the French quarter, which offered rates that were half what was asked by other hotels. A few days later they discovered the reason for the low price: it was a brothel. This discovery amused rather than worried them for they were on a second honeymoon and it was a romantic interlude, emotions heightened by their imminent parting. 'Actually while the rate-per-room was listed as per night, one was expected to get out after a couple of hours,' Decca explained, 'to make room for the next people. However we stuck it out for the 2 weeks, much to the annoyance of the nice Madame . . .'[22] The only thing that spoiled the interlude for Decca was the 'vile' attitude of the white population to the blacks: 'I found them extremely depressing,' she wrote.[23]

Although Esmond was not aware of it, Decca had plans of her own. She knew that Esmond would consider it foolhardy to encumber herself with a child at such a time, but she was determined to conceive before he left her. Within a month of Esmond's departure for Canada, Decca knew she had been successful. Her baby was due early the following year. During the summer the Romillys wrote to and telephoned each other several times a week. Their letters, preserved today in the library of Ohio State University,[24] not only reveal the deep love they felt for each other ('Darlingest Angel . . . I have missed you so much . . . it's been like a prolonged dull kind of stomach ache,' Esmond wrote), but also that Decca could be as funny and sparkling as Nancy. Telling Esmond how she and the Durrs had played 'the Marking Game', where players allot marks out of ten to the subject under discussion, she wrote: 'Va [Virginia] fell on it as a tiger on a piece of juicy meat. I can see we'll be playing it constantly . . . In spite of the fact that Virginia, Ann and Mrs F were marking Cliff 10 for nearly everything, and Ann was trying to sabotage you and me with low marks, you came out top for Brains, Force and Sex Appeal. We tied with a low of 18 out of a possible 40 for Sweetness.'[25] She referred to Esmond's camp as 'Camp Boredom' and her letters were sprinkled with Mitford-speak.

Here, too, are Esmond's acute perceptions of how the war was going, and his own shift in mood. He had entered the Canadian Air Force in the ranks. Before long he had applied for a commission as a pilot officer. 'There are a great many advantages in every way in being an Officer in England now,' he explained. He could justify his change of attitude because commissions were awarded based on performance in the courses, not on one's background, and an added incentive was increased pay. Decca, however, was not to regard this as 'the Price of Principles', it was simply that he was 'absolutely using every particle of the good in the situation and none of the bad'.[26]

As summer turned into autumn he was moved to Saskatchewan for advanced training before being sent to Europe. His mother, Nellie Romilly, wrote that she was thrilled to hear he was to be in London and Decca forwarded it, remarking gloomily that it seemed Nellie could hardly wait to apply for a posthumous VC for Esmond. Meanwhile, she had found a job in an exclusive dress shop, Weinberger's, which paid well (if one discounted the 'damages' she was always having to pay for because she was clumsy), and through her work ('Weinbergering', she called it) she met members of 'the rich set' in Washington. By now Esmond knew about the baby, but her employer did not and Decca was slightly concerned when Mrs Weinberger drew attention to the fact that 'Mrs Romilly's waistline appears to be rather thick'.[27] Decca took to wearing a corset, until she fainted one day and Virginia made her leave it off. Esmond, too, could be very funny: on 11 September he wired Decca with a standard message that he had chosen from a book of templates: 'On this occasion of your birthday may we offer our congratulations and express our pleasure at having been allowed to serve you in the past together with the hope that we may continue to do so in the future. Romilly.'[28]

The couple saw each other occasionally. Once, Decca bussed up to Montreal to meet him and he parked their old car in the street outside the boarding-house where she was staying. Next morning they found that the trash collectors, who thought it had been abandoned, had cleared it away. She found him deeply concerned that his application for a commission might be turned down because during his medical it had been discovered that he had suffered a mastoid in his childhood. Here, for once, Nellie proved helpful to him. She personally contacted Beaverbrook and Churchill to see if anything could be done. At first it seemed hopeless: 'Experience has shown that those who have suffered from mastoid cannot stand heights,' Beaverbrook wrote. 'I am told the regulations are severely adhered to . . . it seems he must seek a ground job.'[29] But with these big guns firing on his behalf Esmond was cleared to fly, having proved in a practical manner that he could stand flying at great heights, but only as a navigator, not a pilot. Almost as an afterthought Nellie mentioned to Esmond that his cousin Diana Churchill had told her that Lord Lothian had seen Decca in Washington and reported that she was pregnant – Esmond had forgotten to tell his mother this news.

Meanwhile Max Mosley, Diana's fourth child, was born on 13 April. The Mosleys had given up Wootton a few months earlier and moved into Savehay Farm at Denham, Buckinghamshire, the house Cimmie had loved and left to Mosley. Cimmie had been dead six years, and Mosley's Curzon sisters-in-law had drawn further away from him, though remaining in contact because of Cimmie's children. Mosley needed a base nearer

London and, anyway, it had become financially impossible to continue to run both establishments; indeed, there was even talk of letting Savehay. When the German radio project folded due to the outbreak of war Mosley was virtually ruined. Diana estimates that he put £100,000 of his own money (well over £2 million today) into the BUF. He was now reliant on family trusts, under the supervision of his sisters-in-law, to pay the school fees for Cimmie's two sons, and even to bring out his elder daughter Vivienne.[30] This caused significant bad feeling, because the sisters were determined not to allow Mosley to use any money from the trust fund to finance the ailing and unpopular BUF and were suspicious of him.

As Diana had said to Hitler, Mosley continued to campaign for peace between the two countries until the declaration of war, after which he argued for a negotiated peace. It was not until 9 May 1940, a few weeks after Max's birth, when Hitler squashed any remaining doubt of his intention to dominate Europe, that Mosley made a statement to the effect that the BUF was at the disposal of the British armed forces. He then advised members that he expected them 'to resist the foreign invasion with all that is in us'. He also attempted to join his old regiment. None of this did anything to change the public perception of Mosley. He was by now the most hated, and even feared, figure in public life in England. Although he never actively supported Hitler – it was Mussolini whom he, along with Winston Churchill in the early 1930s, had always regarded as 'the most interesting man in Europe' – neither had he condemned him. He was regarded by the majority in Britain, including most politicians, as a dangerous Hitlerite who, should Germany be successful in invading Britain, which looked ominously possible in May 1940, would end up as a Germano-British puppet dictator reporting to his Nazi masters.[31]

Although Mosley's two sole contacts with Hitler had been through Diana, her frequent visits to Germany to further the radio project, her meetings with Hitler and Hitler's presence at the Mosleys' marriage ceremony harmed Mosley because these events appeared to the British public to demonstrate a close relationship between him and Hitler. We now know that such a relationship never existed, and Mosley always insisted that the puppet-dictator scenario was never a possibility. He wished to be Britain's leader all right, but not under Hitler. He saw Fascism strictly in terms of its application in Britain as a political expediency, not subject to Germany or Italy. Without straying into the details of a repulsive ideology, or the fact that Mosley preached the overthrow of one of the oldest successful forms of democratic government in the world, according to his own lights Mosley was a patriot who sought peace with all Britain's sovereign possessions intact. His biggest fear was that war with Germany would cost Britain the Empire and, of course, history proved him right. Years later Diana told her stepson Nicholas Mosley that her relationship with Hitler had ruined her life. 'And', she added, 'I think it ruined your father's.'[32]

We do not know precisely what Hitler had in mind for Britain if his invasion plans had been successful, but we know what he thought of Mosley: in May 1940, at about the time when the BEF was trapped on the beaches of Normandy, Hitler spoke of him to an adjutant. 'After our meal,' Gerhard Engel wrote in his diary, 'a long conversation and dialogue from Hitler about Mosley, [he said that] Mosley might have been able to prevent this war. He would never have become a populist leader, but he could have been the intellectual leader of true German–British communication. He [Hitler] is convinced that Mosley's role hasn't run its course yet.'[33] Although Diana is adamant that this was never what Mosley intended, and that 'Mosley would never have accepted such a role',[34] had the Germans successfully invaded Britain it is possible that Mosley would have been a prime candidate for the position of Fascist overlord.[35] Diana disagrees. At forty-three he was too young, she said. A more likely candidate, she feels, would have been Lloyd George, a much older man who had been a great figure in the First World War, 'like Pétain in France. Also Lloyd George greatly admired Hitler and they got on extremely well together, which Hitler and Mosley never did.'[36] Lloyd George's admiration of Hitler is historical fact. As late as 1936 he regarded Hitler as 'the greatest leader in the world', and even told him so during a visit to Germany.[37]

On 23 May the Mosleys drove to their London apartment. Mosley had given up the house in Grosvenor Road and bought a flat in a modern building a short distance away, in Dolphin Square. As they drew up they saw a group of men waiting near the entrance. They were plain-clothes policemen and produced a warrant for Mosley's arrest. Although Mosley must have recognized that he was deeply unpopular he had never done anything illegal and both he and Diana thought that the matter would be quickly resolved, that a trial would exonerate him. But there was no charge, and there was never a trial.

In the previous summer, when war was known to be imminent, an Emergency Powers Act had been rushed through Parliament. An amendment to Rule 18B of this act, made in the following months, enabled the Home Secretary to arrest and detain without trial anyone of 'hostile origin or association' if this was believed necessary for the defence of the realm. In May 1940, when Hitler's troops advanced clear across Europe and there was justifiable fear of an invasion, 'a wave of fifth-column hysteria swept the country'.[38] Churchill's new National Government decided to arrest and detain enemy aliens, Fascists and Communists, on the grounds that they were a potential security risk, and also for their own safety. During the First World War German nationals had been badly treated by angry British citizens. Accordingly, Rule 18B was amended, and under Rule 18B(1a) the government was now empowered to imprison indefinitely, without trial, any member of an organization which, in the Home Secretary's view, was subject to foreign control, or whose leaders were known to have had association with leaders of enemy governments, or who sympathized with the system of government of enemy powers. This may be regarded as poetic justice by some, for although Mosley argued hotly that his arrest and incarceration were against rights laid down in Magna Carta, there is good reason to believe that had his party ever come to power those rights would have been sacrificed by him for expediency. He had, after all, proposed similar legislation in 1931 to combat mass unemployment.[39]

The following day Diana visited Mosley in Brixton Prison, and found, with some difficulty, a solicitor willing to represent him. Many of the BUF officials had been arrested with Mosley, and Diana agreed to perform a few tasks for the party, such as paying outstanding wages. When she returned to Denham and her children, the police were hard on her heels, with a warrant to search the house. From documents at the Public Record Office we now know that Diana was not arrested at the same time as Mosley because the security services wished to keep her under surveillance. Her phone was tapped, her mail intercepted, her movements and contacts recorded during the entire time that she was at liberty. Within a short time she was informed that Savehay was to be requisitioned for the war effort, and she began to pack.

Sydney and Unity, who were frequent visitors to Savehay Farm, came on the bus from High Wycombe, and Lord Berners, another frequent visitor, also called to cheer her up. Pam came to the rescue, offering to take in Diana, the babies and Nanny Higgs at Rignell House until things had sorted themselves out. Meanwhile Diana visited Mosley once a week and took in books and old country clothes at his request. Not wanting to worry her, he told her that everything was fine, and it was a long time before she discovered that the cells allotted to BUF prisoners were infested with bed-bugs and lice. On 29 June, Diana was also taken into custody and government records show that it was always intended that she should be. Any doubts that might have existed were swept away when several members of her own family freely advised officials that Diana was at least as dangerous as Mosley, if not more, for it was she who was the friend of Hitler, not he.

Nancy, who knew nothing of the reason for Diana's frequent visits to Germany – to obtain an airwave – was one of those who informed on her sister. On 20 June, nine days before Diana was arrested, Nancy admitted this to Mrs Hammersley: 'I have just been round to see Gladwyn[40] at his request to tell him what I know . . . of Diana's visits to Germany,' she wrote. 'I advised him to examine her passport to see how often she went. I also said I regard her as an extremely dangerous person. Not very sisterly behaviour but in such times I think it one's duty.'[41] Lord Moyne, Bryan Guinness's father, wrote to Lord Swinton to inform him 'of the extremely dangerous character of my former daughter-in-law'.[42] He submitted as supportive evidence a two-page memorandum based on the testimony of his grandsons' (Jonathan and Desmond) governess, who recounted statements and opinions that she claimed to have heard or overheard Diana making. Irene Ravensdale wrote to the Home Secretary saying virtually the same thing: that Diana was as dangerous as Mosley.

As a result of surveillance of and information-gathering on Diana, the head of MI5, Brigadier Harker, recommended that 'this extremely dangerous and sinister young woman should be detained at the earliest possible moment'.[43] He understood that she had been the principal channel of information between Mosley and Hitler, had been deeply involved in the radio project from which 'all the profits were to go to Mosley [sic]', and not least because she clearly approved of Unity Mitford's disloyal behaviour and friendship with Nazi leaders such as Hitler and Streicher.[44] Clearly, the government knew everything about the radio project, and of Mosley's involvement, probably through Bill

Allen. Diana states that Mosley was aware of Bill Allen's involvement with the Secret Service. 'He always told us that he was an agent. Mosley never minded. He said he had nothing to hide. The secrecy about the radio station was only to prevent the press from knowing.'[45] Nevertheless, every movement of Mosley and Diana, for many years previous to the outbreak war and since, had been reported and, notably, Bill Allen was not among the eight hundred members of the BUF who were imprisoned under Rule 18B.

Although she was still breastfeeding her baby, Diana opted to leave him with his nurse. She was told 'to pack enough clothes for a few days' and in turn she left instructions to her staff to continue packing for their planned departure for Rignell House. She was then driven to Holloway Prison. Perhaps unsurprisingly, given the hatred felt for Mosley and the date of her arrest, she was treated badly. Her reception was rough and on her first night she was given a dark, dirty basement cell containing a thin, worn mattress placed upon a bare damp floor. The only window was blocked with sandbags. She could neither eat the food nor drink the tea, and was too cold, even though it was midsummer and she had not undressed, and was in too much pain, since her breasts were full of milk, to sleep. In short, life was made as uncomfortable as possible for her, and far more so than was necessary. A mutual friend had once told her of a conversation with Churchill. The two men had been visiting the slums of Liverpool and Churchill was moved by the misery and degradation. 'Imagine,' he said. 'Imagine how terrible it would be, never to see anything beautiful, never to eat anything savoury, never to say anything clever.' These words often came back to Diana during her years in Holloway.[46]

Later she was given a better cell, better in that it was dry. It was six feet wide by nine feet long and contained a hard single bed with harsh calico sheets that felt like canvas and stained blankets. There was a hard chair and a small table. Under the chair was an enamel chamber-pot and on a three-cornered shelf was a chipped basin and jug. From the ceiling hung a single dim light. There were other Fascist women there, and innocent women of Italian and German origin who were married to British men but who came within the scope of Rule 18B. The support of these women helped Diana to cope with her imprisonment, though she never lost her anger at those who imposed it, and she never became accustomed to the unnecessary filthy squalor in which the prisoners were obliged to live. One inmate, a German Jew who had been a prisoner at Dachau before 1939, when it was a concentration camp rather than an extermination centre, and had escaped to England, complained that Holloway was dirtier than Dachau. But Diana's worst deprivation was, naturally, being parted from her babies. In view of the conditions in Holloway, she had been wise to leave the eleven-week-old Max in a healthier environment, but she suffered all the anguish of any mother parted from her baby and her two-year-old toddler. Her only consolation was in knowing that they were safe. Pam took in the Mosley babies and Nanny Higgs at Rignell House where they remained for the next eighteen months. After that Sydney arranged for them to board with the MacKinnon family at Swinbrook House where she could see them every day.

With Diana's children and the farm animals, the war years for Pam were busy and not unhappy, although Derek was away a great deal of the time. With his scientific ability Derek Jackson would have been of huge value to the war effort as part of Professor Lindemann's team at Oxford, but he demanded to be allowed to join the RAF during 1940. Lindemann fought to keep him, but a direct intervention by Churchill freed Derek to join the fighting, and he quickly demonstrated his ability in this field as in others. Posted to a night-fighter squadron as radio operator and gunner he brought to this work the same fearless attitude that he always displayed when hunting or racing. Within months he had been awarded the DFC and during the course of the war was responsible for bringing down at least five enemy air-craft, and several others that were 'unconfirmed'. He also earned the AFC, an OBE and the American Legion of Merit.

For Diana the time dragged interminably, for the BUF women lived in far worse conditions than their male counterparts. Although the men suffered from bed-bugs and were locked up for twenty-one hours a day in Brixton, conditions at Holloway were almost Dickensian. When a bomb fell and hit a main sewer the ground floor of the prison was awash in urine for three days as the lavatories overflowed. There was no water for washing or cleaning and almost immediately the women went down with food poisoning. Convicted prisoners were evacuated to a safer location since it was recognized that Holloway would be badly affected by bombing raids on London. Initially, Diana and her fellow Rule 18B inmates were locked into their cells at night, lights out at five o'clock, and the distant sound of nightly air-raids made the long, freezing winter nights a hell of noise and apprehension. What sustained Diana through the early days was her belief that her incarceration was temporary. Had she known it would last three and a half years, she feels she would have pre-ferred to die. The cells were unlocked as soon as the local air-raid siren sounded so that prisoners would not be trapped in the event of a direct hit, and the women huddled together and chat-ted to while away the time when noise made sleep impossible. Diana was popular because she could always make them smile, and inevitably she became a sort of leader because she could articulate their problems. Also they sympathized with her over her separation from her babies. Usually during air-raids Diana went to sit with a woman who had a ground-floor cell.

One consolation during these long months of misery was pro-vided by a German woman, who had been given permission to bring with her a wind-up gramophone and dozens of records: Beethoven, Schubert, Bach, Handel, Debussy and Wagner. She held concerts in a room across the yard. 'Despite the tiresome pauses while the gramophone was wound up,' Diana recalled, 'these concerts were heavenly. There is nothing like music for transporting one a thousand miles from hateful surroundings into realms of bliss.'[47] But throughout her imprisonment the highlight of her week was a letter from Mosley, who she learned had grown a beard, 'Guess what colour it is – red!! At least quite a lot of it – silver threads among the gold.' Mosley used his time in prison as an opportunity to study literature and languages. In his autobiography he would write, 'Plato's requirement of withdrawal from life for a considerable period of study and reflection before entering the final phase of action was fulfilled in my case, though not by my own volition.' His letters kept Diana informed of his daily life, his studies, his love for her. He called her 'my precious darling', and 'my darlingest one'. On the few occasions when the letters were held up for a day or two, Diana plunged into near despair.

As months went by she was allowed occasional visits from members of the family. Even Nancy visited after a year or so, never letting Diana know that she had 'shopped' her, but as usual it was Sydney who was to the fore in offering support. During the entire period of Diana's imprisonment, no matter how difficult it was to travel, Sydney was a regular visitor to Holloway for the weekly quarter of an hour with Diana when she would impart news of the children and the family. Sydney spent four to six hours travelling and was generally obliged to wait for up to an hour in the damp, grimy prison waiting room before Diana was fetched. Sydney also visited Pam and the Mosley babies whenever possible. Later, she took all Diana's children to the prison, but she was expecting sympathy from the wrong quarter when she wrote to Decca about the conditions: 'They have no water and no gas, so can't cook, they get 1 pint of water a day each for washing cooking and drinking, and there is none at all for the lavatories. Diana says the smell is terrible.'[48]

Nancy was unrepentant that her intervention had helped put

Diana – to whom she referred in contemporary correspondence as 'Mrs Quisling' – in prison. Though she loved Diana she had seen hardly anything of her since the publication of *Wigs on the Green* four years earlier, and she clearly felt that her sister deserved punishment for supporting and encouraging a regime that had turned Europe upside down and endangered millions of promising young lives. Soon London was under blitz bombing and this alone seemed sufficient justification. Diana and her fellow prisoners were in the thick of it, too, of course, and Holloway suffered a direct hit on B wing, belying the rumour that the prison was protected because the Germans knew Diana was in there. But Nancy's house in Blomfield Road was especially vulnerable: it was in the sightline of German bombers aiming for Paddington Station. Her reports of the bombing, once it began in the late summer of 1940, make baleful reading even though she sprinkled her letters liberally with merriment. Prod had survived Dunkirk and his regiment had performed well, but he was mostly away, leaving her alone through the air-raids. She wrote to Violet Hammersley after one raid:

Ten hours is too long of concentrated noise and terror in a house alone. The screaming bombs . . . simply make your flesh creep, but the whole thing is so fearful that they are actually only a slight added horror. The great fires everywhere, the awful din which never stops & wave after wave of aeroplanes, ambulances tearing up the street and the horrible unnatural blaze of searchlights all has to be experienced to be understood . . . in every street you can see a sinister little piece roped off with red lights round it, or roofs blown off, or every window out of a house . . . People are beyond praise, everyone is red-eyed and exhausted but you never hear a word of complaint or down heartedness . . . Winston was *admirable* wasn't he, so inspiring . . . [49]

A few weeks later she had become so accustomed to the bomb-ing that she could write, 'People here pay no attention whatever now to the bombs and if somebody does take cover you can be sure they are just up from the country.' She had changed her job at the first-aid post and now looked after evacuees and those bombed out of their homes. David came down to London for the winter and as the mews was having some essential repairs car-ried out – when builders could be found – Nancy opened up 26 Rutland Gate and moved in with him, taking some of her own furniture from Blomfield Road. Like many people with spare rooms, they took in homeless people for a short period, while accommodation was found for them. From October 1940 they had a Jewish refugee family billeted on them. Nancy liked them. 'On the day after they arrived,' she wrote, 'Farve . . . got up at 5.30 to light the boiler for them and charming Mr Sockolovsky who helped him, said to me, "I did not think the Lord would have risen so early." Wasn't it biblical?'[50]

Shortly afterwards, all the empty rooms in the house were requisitioned for other Jewish families evacuated from the East End.[51] When Sydney arrived in London after a bomb dropped in Swinbrook and damaged the roof of the cottage, she could see no humour in the situation and was 'beastly' to David and Nancy. Although it had already been decided that the house must be sold as soon as possible because they could no longer afford to keep it on, Nancy wrote, 'she says if she had all the money in the world, she would not ever live in the house after the Jews have had it'.[52]

What had actually caused Sydney's outburst of anger was that her once immaculate house was so unkempt. In mitigation Nancy had only one maid to help her while Sydney had run the establishment as a family home with half a dozen loyal staff. Nancy admitted that the house *was* rather dirty, 'but it's only floor dirt which can be scrubbed off'. Even had she been able to afford staff it was impossible to find anyone: all the young women who had once gone into domestic service were now in the services or munitions factories. Nevertheless, the incident caused a chill between mother and daughter for some time. And after a winter living with David, and trying to cater to his requirement of a main meal containing meat every evening, and putting up with his irascibility, Nancy was pretty fed up with her father, too.

Like all other families, the Mitfords each had their own worries, which the war somehow made harder to shoulder. Nancy, tired from working and trying to run the house, and fully aware of Prod's serial adultery, was depressed that her marriage was a failure, David, increasingly ill and lonely, was missing Sydney but was unable to live with her ridiculous support of the enemy. Sydney was worried about all her children and grandchildren: Tom in the Army, Diana in prison, the babies staying with Pam, Decca in the USA, Debo who was now unhappy even at her beloved Swinbrook, and, of course, the full-time care of the incontinent and mentally impaired Unity. It is not surprising that tempers flared occasionally. But despite her disagreement with Sydney even Nancy saw how unfair it was that the burden of caring for Unity should fall entirely on her mother. 'Muv has been too wonderful with her and has absolutely given up her whole life,' she reported to Decca, while their father was being simply beastly about Bobo. 'He hardly ever goes near her, and has never been there to relieve Muv and give her a chance to have a little holiday.'[53]

As the bombing worsened, Tom wrote advising Sydney to prepare for invasion. Nancy's version of Sydney's reaction to the Jews occupying her house must be compared with Sydney's own letters at the same time. On the subject of evacuees she wrote to Decca, 'we have about 70 at Rutland Gate . . . about 50 of them Jews, but it's not very comfortable [for them] as there is no furniture but straw palliasses on the floor. The families have a room each to themselves which they go into during the day time but they all troop down to the basement at night . . . it is really sad to see the plight of the homeless . . .'[54] Nancy was so fanciful in her letters, and sometimes in her speech, that it is difficult for the researcher to know what is fact and what is invention but in this case Sydney's own mild reaction appears more likely to be the accurate version of the incident. As Sydney was wont to say, 'There is a small knife concealed in each of Nancy's letters.'[55] As soon as the mews was habitable Nancy returned there and together with Mabel, the parlourmaid, two or three friends and a cook from the Women's Volunteer Service, she looked after the constantly shifting residents of 26 Rutland Gate.

It was a chance request from a friend in the War Office, at this point, that changed the course of Nancy's life, although this is only evident with hindsight. She was asked to 'worm' her way by any means possible into the Free French Officers Club and find out what they were up to. 'They are all here under assumed names,' she wrote to a friend, 'and all splashing mysteriously large sums of money about and our people can't find out anything about them and are getting very worried.'[56] With her social contacts it was only a matter of time before Nancy was able to comply with the request and as a result she met André Roy,[57] a thirty-six-year-old 'glamorous Free-Frog', with whom she fell in love and had a light-hearted affair lasting into the following year. Nancy had never complained about Prod's infidelities though she was deeply hurt and often lonely. During her relationship with André Roy, she came into her own again, sparkling, shimmering and wittily ornamenting London Society.

Sydney, Debo and Unity returned to life at the cottage at Swinbrook, and although they were away from the terror of London bombing raids, life was anything but idyllic. As Unity recovered her strength she became as irrational and as temperamental as David had once been, but without his fun and charm. Debo was the one most affected by this, just as she had been the most affected by the disintegration of her parents' marriage. On one occasion when David visited them for a weekend Debo wrote to Decca graphically describing the tensions in the house. 'Muv and Bobo are getting awfully on my nerves. I must go away soon, I think. There was a dreadful row at breakfast this morning and I shouted at Muv in front of Mrs Timms. Farve shook me like he did you after you'd been to Mrs Rattenberg's [*sic*] trial.'[58] Despite this, she admitted, 'I hadn't seen him for ages . . . he was heaven. He was bloody at the scene where he shook me, but otherwise very nice.'[59] Unity had commandeered two large tables in the small sitting room for her collage work, Debo wrote,

> and if I so much as put my knitting on one of them she hies up and shrieks BLOODY FOOL in my ear which becomes rather irksome . . . She absolutely HATES me . . . She is completely different to what she was and I think the worst thing . . . is that she's completely lost her sense of humour and never laughs . . . Muv is fairly all right but awfully bitter and therefore it is sometimes very difficult. I must say she's wonderful with Bobo and never loses her temper or gets impatient even when she's being maddening . . . if you ever come across the Kennedys (the Ambassador here) do take note of Kick, she is a dear girl and I'm sure you'd like her.[60]

Kathleen 'Kick' Kennedy had fallen in love with Andrew Cavendish's elder brother, Billy, Lord Hartington, who was heir to the Duke of Devonshire, the massive Chatsworth estate, land and properties in Yorkshire, Sussex and Ireland, and an income of a quarter of a million pounds a year. Kick was eighteen and Billy was twenty when they first met but while Billy's antecedents were so impressive that he had been suggested as a possible future husband for Princess Elizabeth, the Kennedys, despite Joseph Kennedy Senior's ambassadorship, were still regarded by many Americans as upstart Boston Irish who had made good only within living memory. But it was neither the age of the couple nor even their cultural differences that cast doom upon the relationship. The Cavendish family were staunch Protestants and ferociously anti-Catholic. 'I am a black Protestant,' the Duke of Devonshire was wont to say, 'and I am proud of it . . . Papists owe a divided allegiance, they put God before their country.'[61] The Kennedys were bitterly entrenched Catholics. The couple knew from the start that there was no future to their courtship because of irreconcilable religious differences, and Billy described it as 'a Romeo and Juliet thing'.[62] Kick was heartbroken when her father insisted she return to the USA in 1939 and by the time Debo wrote her letter to Decca, Kick was already working for the *Herald Tribune* in Washington.

By now Debo and Andrew Cavendish had announced their engagement, and to make things easier at the cottage Debo often went to visit friends or family, and spent some time with Andrew's parents at Chatsworth. Andrew was at Sandhurst before he joined the Coldstream Guards, but the couple were able to meet occasionally.[63] Their wedding was scheduled for the following spring when they would both be twenty-one. In the meantime Debo worked in the garden, for which she developed an interest that surprised her, and rode a four-year-old piebald horse that she had bred from her old hunter. She trained it to pull a pony cart, which she painted blue and red – 'It is very useful now there is so little petrol,' Sydney wrote to Decca.[64] Everyone was pleased about the engagement: Nancy wrote, 'He is a dear little fellow & I am sure she will be happy. Also it will be easier for Muv as she [Debo] and Bobo get on so badly.'[65] In December Debo moved out of Swinbrook when she was loaned a cottage at Cliveden, where she had agreed to work in the canteen of the Canadian Military Hospital.

In this darkest time of the war, when Britain was fighting for its life, little thought was given to the appalling conditions suffered by those imprisoned under Rule 18B. Indeed, large segments of the population would have been heartily in favour of making things as uncomfortable as possible for internees. Diana's scorn of the dirt, poor food, filthy lavatories and inadequate washing facilities helped her to rise above the horror of it all. She ignored the noise of the nightly bombs that fell terrifyingly close, shaking the walls of the prison and setting her fellow inmates screaming or whimpering, because she hardly cared whether she lived or died. But when Jonathan was taken to hospital for an appendectomy and she was refused permission to visit him, she found her situation almost unbearable. All day and all night, she paced the floor of her cell, worrying about her child lying seriously ill, and probably asking for her. In that first winter in prison she began to suspect that her imprisonment might be intended to last for the duration of the war. This was the nadir of Diana's life.

As 1940 drew to an end, things were tough for the rest of the Mitford family too, but not as gloomy as they might have been. None of them had been bombed out or injured, and they had Debo's wedding to look forward to. Debo and Andrew were to live in a small house in Stanmore, Middlesex, close to where Andrew was to be stationed. Pam and Derek had a house near by. 'I expect we will be terrifically poor,' Debo wrote to Diana, 'but think how nice it will be to have as many dear dogs and things as one likes without anyone saying they must get off the furniture. I *do* so wish you weren't in prison, it will be vile not having you to go shopping with, only we're so poor I shan't have much of a trousseau.'[66]

15

GAINS AND LOSSES

(1941–3)

On 9 February Decca gave birth to a six-pound ten-ounce girl in the Columbia Hospital in Washington. She had a bed in a five-bed charity ward,[1] and was inundated with flowers, fruit and gifts for the baby. Virginia Durr, an indefatigable networker, had introduced Decca to everyone in Washington worth knowing, including Virginia's 'kissin' cousins' Lyndon and Lady Bird Johnson ('I looked up Lady Bird in the Peerage,' Sydney is said to have written to Decca, 'but could find no trace of her'). At innumerable Washington cocktail parties Decca had been introduced as 'the wife of Winston Churchill's nephew', which, she told Esmond, while it made her cringe, she had to admit was very effective.

Even so, considering she had been such a short time in the country and had no background there, the flood of visitors she received in hospital seems to testify to Decca's personal charm and energy. When Eugene Meyer sent a photographer to take a picture of Decca and the baby for the *Washington Post*, it caused a sensation in the ward and the nurses suddenly became 'very deferential'. Typically, Decca saw the humour in the situation, writing to tell Esmond how a rather coarse woman in a bed at the end of the ward, whom she heartily disliked, had announced loudly to no one in particular, 'Why're they taking her picture? Was her baby born with teeth?'[2]

Initially Decca wanted to call the baby Esmé, after Esmond, but then suggested Constancia because she had been reading a book about Constancia de la Mora.[3] Esmond agreed but then panicked and wrote saying he thought Carol was better as the baby would undoubtedly be called 'Connie'. Decca countered that she didn't see why, since no one ever called her 'Jessie'. So Constancia it was, though to her family and friends she was always the Donk or Dinkydonk (and is still known universally as Dinky). This stemmed from that July weekend when Esmond left for Canada and Decca attended the Democratic Convention with Virginia Durr. Decca was already suffering badly with morning sickness and Virginia suggested that it was the Democratic Donkey, symbol of the Democratic Party, kicking up its heels. Thereafter Decca always referred to her bump as 'the Donk'.

In England the family celebrated another happy event with Debo's marriage to Lord Andrew Cavendish, on 19 April at the church of St Bartholomew the Great, Smithfield. There had been heavy bombing and many of the windows and the curtains of 26 Rutland Gate were damaged, and there was glass everywhere. But the mews cottage remained intact and the Mitfords were virtually the only family in their circle who could still live in their own home. 'The Airlies, Wernhers, Jack and Iris and the Devonshires are all bombed out, and we have even got gas!' Sydney reported. The refugees had all left No. 26 so it was decided to hold the wedding reception there. 'Of course it is empty and looks hideous with so many broken windows, but it seemed the best place. The caterers will bring tables and chairs . . . We have asked such a lot of people, the Devonshires asked nearly 500 . . . everyone seems to like a party in these days when there aren't many.'[4] Sydney got hold of several rolls of heavy wallpaper and made 'curtains' with it for the large drawing-room windows.

My darling Little D,

Debo's wedding was on Saturday and all went off well and happily. It was a pouring wet morning, which was rather horrid as of course there was so much coming and going . . . The poor old house (No. 26), quite empty with all the ball room windows blown in (the last came in on Wednesday night), looks slightly dreary, but Aunt Sport [Dorothy – wife of Uncle Tommy] had sent up some lovely spring flowers and great branches and so with these on the mantelpieces the places where the pictures used to hang looked less bad. And about 100 huge blooms of great red camellias had come up from Chatsworth from the tree planted by Paxton 100 years ago. I put them in an enormous washbasin and they were lovely.

My curtains made of wallpaper in grey and gold really looked just like brocade, and pelmets were tacked on in the same paper. Those huge windows looked so ugly without any curtains. The ballroom I had to leave, just sweeping away the glass. The Mayfair Catering Co. did the party – the last in the old house. I wonder really that they can still do it. They brought tables, chairs, linen and silver and crockery etc, and of course the food, of a plain variety. The wedding cake was one they had made some time ago, of course, no icing as that is not allowed, but they put on a white cardboard casing which looked quite nice and was taken off to cut it.

Debo's dress was all white tulle . . .very pretty and she had a bouquet of white orchids. Nancy and Peter were there, and the Woman (but not Derek) and Tom, who showed people to their seats . . . The party lasted quite a bit and Debo went to the Mews to change her dress . . .

they had quite a lot to do after they left Rutland Gate as
they had to get Debo's identity card and ration card
altered to her new name, and then go on and register for
National Service as she was born in 1920 . . . They have
taken a tiny mews cottage near Regents Park and hope to
go straight there after their honeymoon [in Eastbourne] in
about a week . . .

All greatest love, darling,
Muv.[5]

Photographs of David arriving at the church with Debo show an
old man. Dressed in his Army greatcoat over his old uniform, he
looks grim and wretched. One wedding guest described him as 'a
broken man'.[6] Among the wedding telegrams were messages
from Diana and Mosley, Joe, Jack and Kick Kennedy, and Decca,
who hinted that Debo had nearly got her duke. 'A very counter-
hon remark,' Debo commented.[7] Considering the reduced size
of newspapers the wedding and going-away of 'Lord and Lady
Cavendish' were covered in surprising detail.

The life of the story was extended when journalists noticed
that Unity appeared 'quite normal'. Why, since she was able to
attend her sister's wedding, they asked, was she not in prison like
Lady Mosley? But no one seeing those photographs and com-
paring them with Unity before the shooting could regard her as
'normal' – even her eyes were not properly co-ordinated. The
matter was brought up in Parliament when a Labour MP asked
the same question. Home Secretary Herbert Morrison answered
coolly that he was aware of Unity's medical condition and the circumstances in which she was living. At present, he said, there
were no grounds that made it necessary, in the interests of
national security, to take her into custody.

In the eighteen months since the shooting Unity had made a
recovery of sorts. By 1941 she was able to take the bus into
Oxford and she even advised Decca that she had applied for a

provisional driving licence to take driving lessons. In Oxford she had lunch at the British restaurant, where meals were fixed at a shilling, and Unity used to rejoin the queue to get another shilling's worth, which was greatly disapproved of as she was recognized.[8]

By the time Decca received all this news she was staying in Hamilton near Toronto, having taken Baby Dinky up by train. She rented a small flat near the military camp for a few weeks. 'Esmond comes home to dinner every night,' she wrote to Sydney, 'but next week I am going back to Va's because he goes west for final training.' It was marvellous for them both to be together with the baby. In late June Esmond flew down to see them for a few days before shipping out for England. They spent a week at Martha's Vineyard with friends. When someone asked him if he was nervous about flying on raids over Germany he replied, matter-of-factly, that he had no misgivings. 'I have no doubt at all,' he said, 'that I will survive this war whether shot down or not.'[9] On 27 June Esmond left to take a ship to England.

Letters from the Mitford family were mostly about food shortages in England and the huge prices charged for what food was available. Sydney was grateful that she hardly ate any meat and that she no longer had a large family to cater for. However, she could still get good flour for bread, she made cheese from goat's milk, which she sold in Burford 'off the ration', and they had unlimited eggs, which was lucky as 'they are only allowed 1 egg a week in towns'. She had embarked on a project to provide 'school dinners' for the children at Swinbrook and Asthall as both schools were crammed with evacuees and she felt that they should get at least one nourishing hot meal a day.

Pam, with plenty of fresh produce from Rignell House farm, was more concerned about the shortage of labour for the farm and the house, and clothing coupons: 'We only get 66 a year and a new Mackintosh is 14,' she wrote. She told Decca about the

Mosley babies, who had been living with her for a year now, and
that cattle feed had become so expensive that she could no longer
afford to keep the herd of beautiful Aberdeen Angus she had
built up. 'The bull, "Black Hussar", has already gone to the
butcher. Poor Black Hussar!' Derek was now flying operations at
night over Germany as gunner and navigator and had been
awarded a DFC for bringing down a bomber among other
things. He had just been home for six days' rest, badly needed
after eight weeks of 'ops'.

Debo, now Lady Andrew Cavendish, was pregnant. She could
hardly keep it secret like Decca, she wrote, because she kept
being sick. But there was compensation for, she joked, as it was
'work of national importance' she did not have to work for the
war effort. She could not imagine Andrew as a father. It was
hard when he went away, for she could hardly go to Swinbrook
as Bobo still hated her.

Esmond cabled from England in early August that he had
arrived safely, a relief to Decca in view of the danger of U-boat
attack in the Atlantic. He could be contacted, he said, at the
Savoy, not that he was staying there but it was a good address to
use and he could call in every few days for his mail or ask them
to forward it when he had to go out of London. He knew he
did not need to worry about Decca and the baby for Virginia
Durr wrote to him to say how much they loved having her, and
how well she was doing. 'She misses you dreadfully of
course . . . but she is "all the rage" . . . we might let her out by
the day or week since she is so superior to most. "Strictly high
class English refugee with good connections. Best Mayfair
Accent". All our acquaintances are green with envy . . .
Seriously Decca is splendid, in fact we think you outmarried
yourself . . .'[10]

By the same post came a letter from Decca, telling him
matter-of-factly that she had 'a good chance of getting a place
on a lend-lease bomber and coming to England'. It would

have to be fairly soon, she told him, as she was pregnant again. By the time she received his reply, Decca had miscarried and the plan to fly to England was temporarily shelved. Instead, when she recovered she enrolled for the stenography course she had planned several months earlier, because, she added, she wanted to get out of 'that salesgirl – refined-type-English-upper-class-lending-tone – rut'. The business school was 'huge and busy . . . people making out schedules, high schooly and college girls all over the place rushing when the class bell rings'.[11] She teased that her shorthand textbooks looked exactly like his handwriting. 'I don't mind a bit about [losing the baby] any more,' she wrote, 'and I hope you don't. The Donk is so frightfully nice and companionable, she is really all I need.'[12] There was a lot about Dinky that reminded her of Pam's 'womanly' qualities.

Esmond's letters to Decca and to Philip Toynbee demonstrate that the sheer fatigue of nightly operations over Europe was wearing him down. His brother Giles had been captured at the start of the war, had tried to escape and was recaptured. When his relationship to Churchill was discovered he was transferred to Colditz, as a special-category prisoner. In one month six members of Esmond's squadron were killed. Twice he found himself spending the entire day flying over the North Sea searching for survivors of aircraft reported to have 'ditched'. He allowed himself to sink into a depression, which he only overcame after a visit to Philip Toynbee.

When Decca wrote that, although there was no hope now of her hitching a lift on a plane to England, she had put her name down for a place on a boat, he was pleased. Earlier in the year he had been mildly discouraging about her plan to join him but now 'I wish tremendously that I'd taken a different line right away,' he wrote. 'But I didn't know how things were going to work out. Now it isn't only that I can see you will be really happy over here, despite all the factors I've mentioned . . . it is also that

I am being utterly selfish, and want to be with you again more than anything in the world.'

He went on to explain that four of his 'closest friends' had been killed and that 'I have been through rather a bad spell – but am now right through it. Two were people I did not have a lot in common with – it was a friendship based simply on a sharing of the same experiences combined with adaptability and agreeableness of manner . . . as a result we had developed quite an affection . . . on a fairly humorous basis of joint boastings and "line shootings" about our trips.' He described how they used to meet in his room, discussing books and politics and life in general and the changes they hoped would be made after the war. Their loss, he felt, was 'a cruel blow from something against which it is impossible to strike back, it is so huge and powerful and at the same time so vague and shadowy'. He continued:

This whole business has made me realise one thing very deeply – i.e. that this sort of thing is infinitely worse for the wives etc, of the people concerned than it is for themselves. The thought that when people are missing, it is of course a very long time before any definite news can be reached of them, i.e. as to whether they have landed anywhere and been captured. In a very large number of cases this turns out to be the case. You may say, of course, that I don't seem to have taken this attitude in the case of my friends – but that just proves what I am trying to say, i.e. one always imagines the worst somehow, which is utterly irrational.

Incidentally, if, which I certainly think is an inconceivable improbability, I should ever find myself in this sort of situation, I have absolutely determined to escape in some way or another, and I'm sure that if you are sufficiently determined of anything you can achieve it.

However I'm equally sure the need will never arise, so
please don't attach any sort of significance to the above, or
imagine it indicates a resigned or nervous frame of
mind . . .

>Very much love, darling angel,
>Esmond.[13]

Esmond wrote again, two weeks after the above letter, full of
suggestions and plans for what they would do when she came to
England, where they would live, how it would be, the pros and
cons of bringing Dinky or leaving her with the Durrs, but Decca
had still not received this when she cabled him joyously on
Monday 1 December: 'LEAVING FRIDAY SO TERRIFICALLY EXCITED
DARLING STOP DECIDED BRING DONK DO WIRE THAT YOU AGREE HOW
SHALL I CONTACT YOU JOURNEY WILL BE VERY COMFORTABLE LOVE=
ROMILLY'.[14]

She was full of enthusiasm for the forthcoming voyage. The
Durrs had gone to New York and she was to leave Washington
on Wednesday 3 December to join them there for two nights and
then they would see her and Dinky off. With luck she would be
with Esmond at Christmas. On Tuesday 2 December, she
received a telegram, which she assumed was a reply from
Esmond. It read, '2 DECEMBER 1941, MRS E. M. ROMILLY . . . REGRET
TO INFORM . . . THAT YOUR HUSBAND PILOT OFFICER ESMOND MARK
DAVID ROMILLY MISSING ON ACTIVE SERVICE NOVEMBER 30 STOP
LETTER FOLLOWS'.[15]

The shock, of course, was dreadful. The last letter she had
received from him, only a few days earlier, had been that message telling her not to give up hope if he was reported missing.
It was an uncharacteristic letter, so different from all his others
to her, and in her distress it must have seemed to her that when
he wrote it he had been reaching out, that in some way he had
known what was going to happen and had written to forewarn
her. She decided not to go to England and the Durrs came

rushing back to Washington to find her with her feelings icily in check, aloof with suppressed fear, but resolute. She was absolutely convinced that Esmond was still alive, she kept telling them, she would have sensed it if he was dead. She thought he had been picked up by a passing trawler, or even a German submarine. It was merely a matter of waiting for news.[16] The Durrs pulled strings in Washington everywhere they could think of: the British embassy, the US Air Force, but there was no further information.

Decca cabled Sydney and Nellie Romilly, asking them to try to find out anything they could from their end, and a flock of cables and letters winged back from England. Some merely expressed sympathy, others begged her to 'come home'. After ten days she received a letter from Esmond's commanding officer, which gave her more details. Esmond had been navigating an aircraft to Hamburg on Sunday the thirtieth and failed to return to base. Nothing was heard from his aircraft following a radio contact, which gave a position of approximately 110 miles east of the Yorkshire coast, 'well out in the North Sea'. From the start, the CO wrote, he knew there was little chance of Esmond being found, and now, 'as they have not been seen or picked up although aircraft searched for them the day after, I am afraid there is little or no chance of their survival. The area where they were last heard of is some considerable distance from normal shipping lanes so I think the chance of being picked up by some ship must be ruled out.' Esmond had done some fine work on operations since joining the squadron, he wrote. 'He was very happy and I think enjoyed the life. We shall all miss him a great deal.'[17]

Even this did not shake Decca's conviction that Esmond was alive, was probably a prisoner-of-war, and that he would escape or find a way of getting news to her. She knew this, absolutely, because he had told her in that penultimate letter. She received his final letter in due course, a normal chatty one. She felt she had to hang on to her conviction of his survival: it was all she had.

On 7 December the Japanese attacked Pearl Harbor and launched assaults on the Philippines, Malaya and Hong Kong. On the following day Britain and the USA declared war on Japan. Three days later Germany and Italy declared war on the USA. Isolationists there who had campaigned for 'schools not tanks' might not have been happy, but Churchill recorded in his diary that on that night 'I went to bed and slept the sleep of the saved and thankful.'[18] On 12 December he left London for the USA for the first of his wartime meetings with President Roosevelt in Washington. He need not have hurried. HMS *Duke of York* took ten days over the voyage due to relentless storms, and instead of steaming up the Potomac, as intended, Churchill was so impatient to see Roosevelt that he jumped ship at Chesapeake with his valet, doctor and Lord Beaverbrook, and flew on to Washington, telling the remaining entourage to follow by train when they could.

During the first two days that Churchill spent at the White House he had no free time, but as soon as he could he contacted Decca. He already knew, of course, that Esmond was missing. On Christmas morning Roosevelt had arranged to take Churchill to a local church 'to sing hymns with the Methodies'.[19] Two Secret Service men were dispatched to the Durrs' house at Seminary Hill, with a message asking Decca if she would join him at the church, and spend some time with him at the White House after the service. Decca had gone out to call on some friends, and having listened to the message Virginia drawled, 'Waaal, it'll take more than two men to get Decca into church, even for the Prime Minister of England and the President of the United States.'[20] When Decca returned and was told about the message she telephoned the White House immediately. Though she had no particular fondness for Churchill she knew that through him she could get the information she wanted about

Esmond. She explained who she was and was immediately put through to Eleanor Roosevelt, who made an appointment for her to see Churchill the following morning.

She took Dinky with her, ten months old, fair and chubby, and dressed in a white woollen suit.[21] Churchill was in bed, hard at work on a speech to be delivered to Congress later that day, and which famously began 'I cannot help reflecting that if my father had been American and my mother British, instead of the other way round, I might have got here on my own.'* Decca recalled that 'He looked marvellous . . . like some extravagant peacock in his bright silk dressing gown.'[22] He was affectionate in his manner, and warmly sympathetic about Esmond. She listened attentively to what he had to tell her, and it could not have been an easy task for him.

He told her that, at Nellie Romilly's request, he had already made enquiries about Esmond and had learned that there was not the slightest chance that Esmond had been taken prisoner. His aircraft had left the base at 4.45 p.m. as part of a nine-plane raid of Hamburg. The crew were reported to be in good spirits. Shortly after 8 p.m. a radio message advised that due to low oil pressure in the port engine the captain had abandoned the mission and was returning home. At 8.30 p.m. another message was received, 'Give bearings immediately.' Bearings were taken on the radio signal, and a navigational course was plotted and relayed back. Twelve minutes later the aircraft put out an SOS signal, but no further contact could be established.

The position had been confirmed at about 110 miles east of the Yorkshire coast, over the North Sea, but searchers could only guess at how much further the aircraft might have flown before ditching. On the following morning a thick fog prevented a search until almost noon, when three air-sea rescue aircraft set off

---

*Through his mother Churchill could trace unbroken descent through five generations from a lieutenant who served in George Washington's army.

and searched throughout the remaining hours of daylight. It was intensely cold and there was a lumpy sea. A large patch of oil was observed about thirty miles south-west of the assumed position, but there was no sign of a dinghy, and no wreckage was ever found. On the 2 and 3 December thick fog lasted all day and prevented any further search so the rescue operation was abandoned. Churchill was 'quite sure that Esmond had been drowned'. Even had the crew survived a landing at sea, he told Decca, the temperature of the North Sea in late November was such that no one could survive more than twenty minutes in the water.

Decca was devastated and Churchill was deeply affected at the distress of the young woman who, he wrote to Nellie, 'looked very lovely'.[23] To mask the awkwardness of the moment, and give them both an opportunity to recover, he cleared his throat and changed the subject. He began to talk about Decca's family, hoping to comfort her. She hardly took in most of what he was saying, but when he talked about Diana, and explained what he had done to try to make things more comfortable for her, including arranging for some of the convicts to clean the prison, she came to life. A sudden and uncontrollable anger swept over her at the thought of Diana being pampered by servants when Diana's 'precious friends' had just killed Esmond. She exclaimed hotly that Diana and Mosley should be put up against a wall and shot. Churchill had had no idea of her feelings about Diana, and listened quietly while she raged. Then he brought the subject back to Esmond and Giles.

As small children the brothers had spent many Christmases, and most of their summer holidays, at Chartwell with the Churchills. He felt he knew them well. Decca realized that Churchill's affection for Esmond was genuine, and his regret at Esmond's loss was not simply assumed. He told her he was full of admiration for Esmond and that he had died a hero's death. He advised Decca to remain in the USA for the duration of the war[24] but offered to arrange for her to return to her family if she wanted to do so. She said she had not made up her mind what to do. As she was leaving he called in his secretary, and Decca was handed an envelope addressed to Mrs Esmond Romilly. When she looked inside it she found five hundred dollars.

Later a rumour went round London about this gift. It was not secret and a number of people seemed to know about it, possibly through Nellie. It was said that Decca had thrown it in his face. This is not true. She recognized that the gift was kindly meant, to help her in a difficult time, and – as she said in her papers – '$500 was a great deal of money.' But she did come, after a while, to regard it slightly as 'blood money' so she gave some to the Durrs' elder daughter to buy a pony, and donated the rest to a Communist Party fund. When Churchill saw Tom Mitford in Libya some months afterwards, he told him of the meeting. She was not just angry about Diana, he said, for on hearing that she had just completed a stenography course and was looking for a job, Churchill offered to get her one on the staff of the British ambassador, Lord Halifax. She snapped, 'I wouldn't touch him with a barge pole.' Churchill told Tom that he felt very snubbed, and sighed that Decca was as fanatical a Communist as ever.[25]

Now, Decca began to accept that Esmond was dead. Cliff and Virginia Durr often heard her weeping at night. Sometimes Virginia would go to her room and Decca would sob on her shoulder. That the invincible Esmond had perished in the icy waters of the North Sea was a terrible thing for her to bear.[26] The image of him drowning in that cold water haunted her. Decca could be 'cool and aristocratic' when she chose, but Virginia Durr wrote that as one of the few people who had ever seen her with her defences down she knew that Decca was a very emotional and vulnerable woman. After the desolation and weeping came the natural anger of grief, which was focused on the Mosleys, especially Diana, for despite Unity's history she was never accorded a share of the blame for Esmond's death. Decca felt sorrow for Unity, never anger. But she never ceased to blame Diana for Esmond's death, and she was a good hater.

Virginia Durr was deeply concerned about her, and wrote secretly to Sydney, saying Decca would 'be furious and send out her porcupine quills at me' if she found out about the letter. From Decca's descriptions of her family in England, Virginia wrote, she had formed

> a high opinion of your loyalty to your children and your strength of purpose . . . The situation here is very simple. I think Decca wants to come home to England but she feels she has no place to come. She receives from the Canadian Government about $65 a month as a dependant's allowance, and W. Churchill as you know gave her $500. The allowance from the Canadian Government will stop after 6 months if Esmond is not found and she will receive a very small pension . . . it may be that it is too dangerous for her to make the trip to England but at least she should not have the feeling that there is no place she can go in England . . . she is very welcome here, but . . . she is so essentially English, and so bound to England by her affection that she could never be anything else. She has been hurt so much both by circumstances and her own fierce pride that I cannot bear for her to have the further hurt of feeling unwanted.[27]

Immediately Sydney wrote, begging Decca to return home. Decca's cousins, Rosemary (daughter of the late Clement Mitford) and her husband Richard Bailey (son of Sydney's sister Aunt Weenie), were in Washington at the time, and it was suggested that she return home with them.[28] Sydney heard from Decca before her letter could have reached Washington. Worn out by sleepless nights and crushed by alternate hope and despair, Decca wrote on 22 February, almost three months after

Esmond was reported missing, that she was still convinced he was alive, a prisoner of war, and that she thought she might not hear anything from him until the end of hostilities.[29] She had decided, she continued, to remain in the USA, was continuing with her stenography lessons and had a part-time typing job with the RAF delegation. Decca's mettle now made itself apparent. The easy option for her would have been to return to England with her baby. There she would have been welcomed, fussed over and cared for. She would hardly have had to think. Instead she was determined to carry on the fight that she and Esmond had begun, against Fascism in all its forms. And she felt she could do that more effectively in the USA, starting with nothing.

At the end of 1941, while trying to support Decca from afar, Sydney had plenty of problems at home. Debo's baby, a son, was stillborn. Unity was sent off to stay with friends so that Debo, who was very depressed, could come to the cottage for a while. It was tragic for Sydney that her daughters all seemed at odds with each other. She could never understand it. Nancy, too, had a crisis. Her lively relationship with 'the charmer' André Roy had resulted in an ectopic pregnancy in which her Fallopian tubes were found to be damaged beyond saving and so were removed. She was told that she could never have children. Perhaps it was not surprising that in the circumstances Peter's parents were not sympathetic, but Nancy clearly expected them to be. Her mother-in-law was told by the surgeons that Nancy would be 'in danger' for three days. 'Not one of them even rang up to enquire let alone send a bloom,' Nancy wrote to Diana. 'I long to know if they looked under R in the death column . . . Muv was wonderful. She swam in a haze between me and Debo. When my symptoms were explained to her she said, "Ovaries – I thought one had 700 like caviar." Then I said how I couldn't bear the idea of a great scar on my tum to which she replied, "But darling who's ever going to see it?" Poor Debo must be wretched, the worst thing in the world I should think – except losing a manuscript of a book which I always think must be *the* worst.'[30]

Friendly relations had been re-established between Nancy and Diana, and occasionally, when Diana got permission for her elder children to spend a day with her in Holloway, Nancy had twelve-year-old Jonathan and ten-year-old Desmond to stay with her overnight at Blomfield Road to make things easy for them. 'They are bliss,' she told Diana, 'so awfully nice & thoughtful and tidy. The nicest guests I ever had. Jonathan is so funny . . .'[31]

In March 1942 Nancy got a job at three pounds a week managing Heywood Hill's bookshop at 17 Curzon Street.[32] George Heywood Hill had been called up, so Nancy ran the shop helped by his wife, Anne. She enjoyed her job, had always loved being surrounded by books, and here her wide knowledge of literature was put to a practical use. She had no objection to the administration side of a bookshop, packing and unpacking, sorting and placing the books in their correct categories, and her friends popped into the shop for a chat whenever they passed. It became a meeting place, with knots of Nancy's friends standing around 'roaring' so that at times other customers might have been forgiven for feeling they were intruding on a private cocktail party. Nancy always had a new story to make droppers-in laugh, such as the one she told of the wife of the American millionaire who met a parson's daughter wearing a necklace of lapis lazuli. 'Oh,' said the American, 'I have a staircase made of those.'[33] She usually walked the two and a half miles to work every morning, and sometimes back again in the evening, so she became fit. The only thing she disliked was the drudgery of working hours. Once she decided to catch a bus and was accosted by an American serviceman who grabbed her round the waist. Nancy rounded on him. 'Leave me alone, I'm *forty*!' And he did.

James Lees-Milne was surprised to find that the rebellious Nancy had become rather conventional. 'It is clearly our duty,' she lectured him, 'to remain in England after the war, whatever the temptation to get out. The upper classes have derived more fun from living in this country since the last war than any other stratum of society in any other country in the world. No more foreign parts for *us*.'[34] And she hissed the final sibilant, almost turning it into a joke. But she was deadly serious about 'doing her bit' for the war and she demonstrated it by walking to work, saving electricity by not turning on the water heater, sticking to a four-inch depth of water in her baths, and refusing to attend a ball thrown by Debo 'because the news was so bad'. Her first love, Hamish, had been taken prisoner, as had Tim Bailey – the only survivor of the four Bailey cousins.[35] Tom was in Libya and Prod was in Ethiopia. While they were dancing in London, she said, the men might be fighting for their lives.

This was a somewhat inconsistent view, for Nancy hardly lived like a nun and had an active social life, which included throwing parties regularly. To fill lonely evenings she had begun work on what she called 'my autobiography' but, she told friends, she would not be able to publish it until her parents were dead because it would hurt them.[36] Like Decca, Nancy was bitter that her parents had denied their 'clutch of intelligent daughters' an education, and it showed when her book was eventually published, making the Mitford family a household name. She had changed her mind about waiting until her parents were dead and they *were* hurt, but disguised it because they were so pleased by Nancy's success. 'There is a vein of callousness in her which almost amounts to cruelty,' James Lees-Milne once observed. 'All the Mitfords seem to have it, even Tom.'[37] Nevertheless, her wit endeared her to a wide circle of friends.

In the summer of 1942 Nancy was still involved with André Roy and when Unity turned up 'looking a mess' for a party at Blomfield Road, it was the 'adored Capitaine Roy' who took her upstairs to apply make-up and fix her hair so that she looked pretty. But fate was waiting in the wings for Nancy. Her relationship with Roy was a light-hearted, affectionate friendship, which provided emotional and social relief from her half-life as Prod's wife. The Rodds' marriage had been over before the war but Nancy's pride had not allowed her to admit it; her friends said her remarkable stoicism over the bombs was the result of her 'steeling herself to an indifference to Peter's misbehaviour'.[38] In September 1942 Nancy met Gaston Palewski and, for her, life began.

Palewski, or 'the Colonel' as Nancy always called him, was the right-hand man of Charles de Gaulle, leader of the Free French forces, in London. The relationship between these two men was strong for it had been Palewski, then a rising young diplomat and politician, who had first brought de Gaulle to the notice of Paul Reynaud, Minister of Finance in the Daladier government of 1934. Thereafter, both men had absolute trust in, and respect for, the other's abilities. At the outbreak of war Palewski volunteered for the French air force and was mentioned in dispatches for his valour in the battle for Sedan.

When France fell, he contacted de Gaulle offering his services to the Free French in London. Palewski spoke English fluently, having done a year's postgraduate study at Oxford, and he had well-honed diplomatic skills. He spent six months in London from August 1940, acting as interpreter and go-between, but by the spring of 1941 he had become irritated and disillusioned by the constant quarrels and jealousies among the Free French as de Gaulle tried to organize an efficient resistance movement. Feeling he could be of more value in an active role, he asked for a posting to Africa and subsequently commanded the Free French forces of East Africa in Ethiopia until de Gaulle summoned him back to London in 1942 to be his *chef de cabinet*.

Where de Gaulle was austere and absolutely single-minded in his quest, Palewski embraced every pleasure life had to offer. And though the fight against France's enemies was, for the time being, the most important thing in his life, he was easily able to incorporate this aim into his considerable *joie de vivre*. He was forty-one, charming, intelligent and a brilliant conversationalist; he loved the arts, good food and wine, beautiful women and clever talk. He was a welcome addition to London's café society, and before long was seen everywhere at smart parties, such as those of Emerald Cunard and Sybil Colefax, both of whom he had known for some years.

While Palewski was in Ethiopia he had met Peter Rodd in Addis Ababa and when the subject came up at a dinner party, Palewski was told that Nancy Rodd would welcome first-hand news of her husband. As a result he arranged to meet her at the Allies Club in Park Lane, a short walk from the bookshop, and they talked of Ethiopia, Peter and France. Although she had lost the bloom of youth Nancy had presence, while her chic appearance, despite wartime clothes rationing, and brisk wit interested the Colonel immediately. In his diaries James Lees-Milne provides some vivid vignettes of Nancy at this time. On one occasion he noted her running down South Audley Street to get warm. 'She made a strange spectacle, very thin and upright, her arms folded over her chest, and her long legs jerking to left and right of her like a marionette's. I really believe she finds it easier to run than to walk.'[39] On another he describes her wearing a 'little Queen Alexandra hat, with feathers on the brim, pulled down over her eyes, and looking very pretty and debonair'.[40]

Gaston Palewski was neither handsome nor patrician in appearance; he had none of the aesthete's effeminacy that had been characteristic of the men to whom Nancy had hitherto been attracted. On the contrary, he was shortish and stocky, with features that owed more to the Polish roots of his grandparents than his innate Frenchness. He had dark hair and a moustache, and his olive skin was pitted with acne scars, yet he was unmistakably distinguished; he dressed well (Savile Row), exuded self-confidence, magnetism and infectious joviality, and Nancy found herself 'powerfully attracted. He charmed and flattered her; he gossiped, joked and made her feel that she was the centre of his undivided attention.'[41] Within weeks they were lovers, and for Palewski love-making was an art form.

Nancy fell headlong, obsessively, in love, as Diana had with Mosley, as Decca had with Esmond. It would last throughout her life but though Palewski was 'in love' with Nancy for a time, he never loved her in the sense that she was the only woman in the world for him. She was for him a light-hearted affair, such as Nancy had enjoyed with Captain Roy, a pleasant diversion from the everyday dreariness of war. He liked her tremendously, and she remained one of his dearest friends into old age, but for him she was not the great love and he made this clear to her from the first. In the heady grip of an intense and passionate emotion for the first time in her life, Nancy felt that she could win him eventually. She laughed at the way he parried her declarations of love, telling Diana Cooper, 'I say to him, "I love you colonel," & he replies, "That's awfully kind of you."'

They were discreet for the sake of Nancy's reputation, and also for Palewski's, for he told her that de Gaulle would not have approved of him having an affair with a married woman. They were caught out on only one occasion. After dining at the Connaught Hotel they were on their way upstairs to Palewski's room when they were stopped by a disapproving receptionist who pointed out that ladies were never allowed to visit the bedrooms of male guests. The mere mention of this incident was enough to make Nancy's cheeks glow with embarrassment, and sometimes, to tease her, the Colonel would end his letters, 'P.S. Connaught Hotel!'

Eight months after they met, Palewski went to Algiers with General de Gaulle where he remained for just over a year. He and Nancy kept in touch by letter and when he returned in June 1944 their affair resumed. Because of Nancy's writings we know how she felt when he reappeared. In *The Pursuit of Love* Palewski is instantly recognizable as the character Fabrice de Sauveterre. The heroine, Linda, although a mixture of Diana, Debo, Decca and Nancy at various times in the plot, is pure Nancy when the telephone rings and she hears Fabrice's voice, after a long absence during the war, saying he will be with her in five minutes. In his absence London had been grey and cold, but now 'all was light and warmth . . . sun, silence and happiness'.[42] One biographer likened Nancy to Scheherezade,[43] using her gift as a storyteller to keep her lover amused and entertained with anecdotes of her childhood and her family. Indeed, it was Palewski's endless delight in hearing these recollections that made Nancy recognize their potential as material for a book that would set her on a course for undreamed-of fame.[44]

16

WOMEN AT WAR
(1943–4)

During the first year of Diana's incarceration she had been allowed a weekly visitor. Usually this was Sydney, who made the journey no matter what the conditions. In winter months the weekly treks were especially tiring, for petrol rationing meant that she could rarely drive there, even though she got a small extra petrol ration for producing her goat's cheese. So she travelled on a series of packed, chilly trains and buses, returning home long after the blackout. Sometimes Nanny or Pam went along instead. The children's occasional visits could be traumatic and once two-year-old Alexander had to be torn away from Diana after soaking her clothes with his tears.

With the exception of Diana, all the BUF women with children were released by Christmas 1940. Following this, the Mosleys' lawyer campaigned vigorously for Diana's release but it was never a possibility: constant hostility to the Mosleys in the newspapers had made her the most hated woman in England. He was told that public opinion against her was too strong. Churchill still had a soft spot for Diana, though, and on hearing of the atrocious conditions in which she was held, he tried to help. In December 1940 he sent a memo to Herbert Morrison asking why the Rule 18B prisoners could not have daily baths, and facilities for exercise and games: 'if the correspondence is censored, as it must be, I do not see any reason why it should be limited to two letters a week . . . what arrangements are permitted to husbands and wives to see each other, and what arrangements have been made for Mosley's wife to see her baby from whom she was taken before it was weaned?'[1] He wrote to the Home Secretary on 15 November 1941 asking why the BUF couples could not be interned together. 'Sir Oswald Mosley's wife has now been eighteen months in prison without the slightest vestige of any charge against her, and separated from her husband. Has the question of releasing these internees on parole been considered?'[2] The response was that it was simply not possible to cope with married prisoners living together, but he was able, at least, to insist that Diana be allowed to take a bath each day. Diana was sent for by the Governor and told that a message had come in from the government saying that Lady Mosley was to have a bath every day. 'I looked at him,' Diana wrote in her autobiography. 'He knew, and I knew, that it was not possible. There were two degraded bathrooms in the wing, and enough water for four baths. We took turns and got a bath roughly once a week. It had been a kindly thought of Winston's who had I suppose been told that this was one of the hardships I minded.'

The Mosleys appeared separately before an advisory committee set up to hear their appeals against the injustice of their imprisonment. By the time Diana appeared before Norman Birket, the committee's chairman, she was already deeply prejudiced against him. Mosley had been questioned for several days by Birket, three months earlier, and there was no movement towards his release. Both the questions and Diana's haughty responses were hostile and somewhat pointless, as in this exchange concerning Hitler:

Q: How many times do you think you have seen him between 1935 and 1940?

A: I do not know.

Q: Is he still a friend of yours?

A: I have not seen him for some time.

Q: Absence makes the heart grown fonder. Do you still entertain the same feelings for him?

A: As regards private and personal friendship, of course I do.

Q: The history of Hitler in recent years has not affected your view about that?

A: I do not know what his 'history' has been.

Q: . . . Did you hear the bombs last night? That is Mr Hitler as we suggest. Does that kind of thing make any difference to you – the killing of helpless people?

A: It is frightful. That is why we have always been for peace . . .

And so it went on. For Diana the issue was that she was locked in a filthy prison, parted from her four children, merely for seeing Hitler. Yet, she reasoned, many other people, including Churchill's niece Diana Sheridan, had visited Hitler – it had not been *illegal* to visit Hitler. Upon what grounds had she, Diana Mosley, been singled out? Mosley always said that he had been grossly misrepresented and misunderstood by critics who made no allowances for the fact that he detested war; that he had fought in the First World War and had campaigned ceaselessly for peace. It is clear that neither Diana nor Mosley was in tune with 'the man on the Clapham omnibus' who wanted peace, too, but not under a regime where basic freedoms were not available to all. Nor did the Mosleys ever seem to recognize that the thug element attracted to the ethos of the BUF was deeply offensive and even frightening to decent-thinking people. The cleverness, and often the validity, of Mosley's oratory was missed because of the alien posturing and what looked remarkably like Nazi-style exhibitionism. At least during the first years of the war, there was never any chance of their release and the advisory committee had been a sop to the Mosleys' lawyer.

Diana grew painfully thin because she could not bear to eat the food she was offered, perhaps wisely in view of the number of food-poisoning cases among her fellow prisoners. The BUF prisoners 'enjoyed' the same status as prisoners on remand, in that they were not convicts. This entitled them to some off-ration treats if they were prepared to pay for them and they were available, such as a bottle of beer, or half a bottle of wine per day. Because Diana had an account at Harrods she was able to send gifts to friends and family at Christmas, and Mosley sent her a whole Stilton cheese. To augment this she ordered some bottles of 'grocer's' port, which were doled out to her one at a time. She lived for months on a small portion of cheese and a small glass of port every evening. Somehow, the newspapers got hold of this and blew it up into a story, claiming that while the rest of the country was suffering austerity conditions, the Mosleys were living in idle luxury in prison. 'Every morning his paid batman delivers three newspapers at the door of his master's cell,' the *Daily Mirror* advised its readers. 'Breakfast, dinner and tea arrive by car. After his mid-day meal Mosley fortifies himself with alternative bottles of red and white wine daily. He occasionally asks for a bottle of champagne . . . his shirts and silk underwear are laundered in Mayfair . . .' It was laughable, but since Mosley had never requested any wines he decided to sue the newspaper for libel.

The suit itself was irrelevant, but there was a chance that if they both gave evidence the Mosleys might see each other in court. And this was what happened. They were allowed a few minutes together in the robing room in the presence of their barrister. 'Looking forward to this meeting and thinking about it afterwards kept me happy for several days,' Diana wrote. Mosley looked very thin and had grown a beard, but he argued his case well and won a small compensation and costs. The money was passed to Sydney who used it to buy Diana a shaggy fur coat, which was not elegant but warm. Diana wore it all day and it covered her bed at night. She became intensely grateful to the reporter who had invented the story.

As a concession, in the spring of 1941, the husbands and wives imprisoned under Rule 18B were allowed to see each other for half an hour once every two weeks. Mosley and Admiral Sir Barry Domville, a senior member of the BUF, were brought to Holloway in a police car for these treasured meetings with their wives. One day, shortly after Germany attacked Russia in 1941, when Diana went to see her weekly visitor she found Tom, who was on leave. He told her he was dining with the Churchills that night. 'Is there anything you want me to say?' he asked. She asked him to say to Churchill that, if she and Mosley must remain in prison, could they not at least be together.[3] Tom was not the only person lobbying on behalf of the Mosleys: Baba Metcalfe and other influential friends, such as Walter Monckton, had worked for months to improve the conditions in which they were imprisoned. However, soon after he had dined with Tom, Churchill ordered the prison officials to find a way to cut the red tape and make it possible for the few Rule 18B husbands and wives still imprisoned to be interned together. This was almost certainly due to Tom's intervention.

After eighteen months of separation the Mosleys were reunited in Holloway. 'Our joy was such that, unlikely as it may seem, one of the happiest days of my life was spent in Holloway Prison,' Diana wrote.[4] Even in the worst days Diana could cope, as long as she was with her beloved husband, and it amused him, even many years later, to recall a morning when they were lying in bed discussing a particularly unpleasant and unattractive wardress. Diana had capped the conversation by stretching luxuriously and declaring, 'Well, anyway, it's so lovely to wake up in the morning and feel that one is lovely *one*.'[5]

They were lodged in a small 'house' within the prison walls called the Preventative Detention Block, which they shared, initially, with three other couples, but two were soon released and eventually it was used only by the Mosleys and Major and Mrs de Laessoe. Each couple had three rooms and use of a kitchen and bathroom (dubbed 'a suite' by newspapers). The men stoked the boiler and grew vegetables in a kitchen garden. All their rations were provided raw for them to cook for themselves, and thus they began to have reasonable meals instead of prison food. Two convicts were recruited to wash down the stairway and passages; sex offenders were chosen for this, Diana was told, 'because they are clean and honest'. It was the provision of these convicts that Churchill had mentioned to Decca, and which had so infuriated her.

The Mosleys spent a further two years in Holloway before their release in 1943. 'He was so marvellous in prison,' Diana recalled. 'It's rather incredible to be locked up like that with somebody for two years and we hardly ever quarrelled. He used to laugh so much over me and the wardress, and he was so incredibly good-natured when you think what an *active* person he'd been, rushing about, and we'd both been abroad so much. And there we were locked up like animals in a cage. He was really wonderful and always ready to laugh.'[6]

Mosley's eldest son, Nicholas, was now a serving officer so was granted extended visiting rights beyond the fifteen minutes of Sydney and the others. His arrival heralded a minor celebration and he usually managed to smuggle in a small bottle of spirits, or a tin of ham, and some books in his Army greatcoat. He described how a wardress would escort him across a cobbled yard into a door in the high inner wall, beyond which Mosley would be waiting. They would walk past a piece of ground like a railway embankment where Mosley grew aubergines and Diana's favourite *fraises de bois* with cabbages and onions. The building where they lived was like a deserted cotton mill, he said, high, austere and dingy, yet Diana had managed somehow to give their rooms a slight aura of elegance, 'like that of some provincial museum for shells . . . There was Diana's old gramophone with its enormous horn that contained tiny sounds like those of the sea . . . Diana would prepare one of her legendary dishes from . . . my father's vegetables . . . on the gramophone there would be "Liebestod" or "The Entry of the Gods into Valhalla".'[7]

Six months after Esmond's death, Decca left her part-time job with the RAF delegation at the British embassy in Washington, and went to work for the Office of Price Administration (OPA), a government agency responsible for price control, rent control and wartime rationing policy. Her starting salary as a 'sub-eligible typist' was $1,440, but she expected this to be increased soon: 'It's about £500 a year, which is swell,' she reported to Sydney who might possibly have run across 'swell' at the cinema.

Decca explained that she had now moved out of the Durrs' house and into an apartment in Washington close to her workplace, and that Dinky was being cared for by a black neighbour who had twelve children of her own and twenty-four grandchildren, 'so she knows about children'. She had taken in two boarders to help pay the rent. 'I call us the three Boards,' she wrote. 'One is a Bawd, the other an ordinary Board and I am just Bored (by them). Actually they only sleep here and don't have meals with me, thank goodness. [The Durrs] are amazed by . . . the Bawd, as being very respectable people they haven't seen any before.' Virginia Durr was now quite famous in Washington, as her bill to abolish poll tax in the Southern states had recently gone through the House. Esmond's intuition had been spot-on: if he had searched the length of the USA he could hardly have found anyone better to look after Decca than the politically minded and sound Durr family. They had seen her through the dark days and by midsummer she had begun to accept the likelihood that he had not survived.

Although still grieving, and irritated by the preoccupation of most Americans with material comforts, Decca enjoyed her work, seeing it as the front line in the fight against major business interests, which she equated with Fascism. The majority of employees at the OPA were left-wingers and New Dealers, and she felt comfortable there. Her intelligence and zeal earned her rapid promotion to the post of investigator, which – she discovered to her dismay – required her to be a college graduate. Recalling her long-ago language course in Paris, and realizing that no one could check since Paris was in the hands of Germans, she resolved the problem by writing in the appropriate box, 'Graduate, Université de Sorbonne'. To Sydney's repeated requests that Little D come home, she wrote that she had made up her mind to remain in the USA.

> America is a much better place to bring up children,
> people are so much nicer to them here & the free
> schools are better. Also I doubt if I could earn enough
> for us to live on there. I know you realise that I couldn't
> ever come and live with the family. After all I was told
> once [by Farve] never to come home again, which I
> know wasn't your fault, but it still means I never
> shall . . . Of course I do hope one day I'll see those
> members of the family I'm still on speakers with;
> probably after the war.[8]

As part of her job Decca was sometimes assigned to assist senior members of staff on surveillance operations. One of those she worked with was a clever young Harvard-educated Jewish lawyer, Robert Treuhaft. After one successful case in which they had apprehended the Norwegian ambassador using petrol for 'pleasure driving' (the ambassador and his wife had driven to a nightclub, in defiance of regulations), Bob Treuhaft delighted Decca by sending her a poem.

> *Drink a drink to dauntless Decca*
> *OPA's black-market wrecker.*
> *Where there is no violation*
> *She supplies the provocation.*
> *Smiling brightly she avers*
> *'Je suis agente provocateuse . . .'*[9]

It was only to be expected that Decca would catch the eye of many young men. At twenty-five she was at the height of her beauty, poised and independent, intelligent and supremely funny; her slender figure, wide blue eyes, soft curling hair and remarkable presence made her a head-turner. She was attracted to Bob as a friend, without in any way surrendering her feelings for Esmond, and after the first anniversary of Esmond's death she began to accept Bob's showered invitations to dinner. She enjoyed his company, not least because they had a shared sense of humour and were political allies, but also perhaps because he was so different in appearance from Esmond. Shorter, slim and black-haired with large black eyes that positively twinkled, she repaid his hospitality by inviting him to escort her to a series of Christmas parties, including an exclusive ball. She had made many friends in Washington Society through the Durrs but the attention paid her by Churchill had not gone unnoticed, either, and she was in demand once she began to accept invitations. At first she attended parties as a form of saving on her housekeeping bills, as taught by Esmond, and she could have eaten out most nights had she cared to. In general, though, she lived quietly, spending as much time with Dinky as she could.

On 28 December 1942, Bob Treuhaft wrote to his mother Aranka of the ball to which he had escorted Decca. It had taken place at

   a tremendous colonial mansion with white columns,
   footmen etc . . . all the women were seven foot tall and

looked down their noses. I was probably the only non-congressman, non-commissioner or non-delegate, and certainly the only non-Aryan.'

My sudden appearance on the Washington social scene – the ball was only the climax of two weeks of similar activities – is connected with my wild, uncontrollable and completely futile infatuation for the most terrific female the world has ever seen.

You've probably heard of Unity Mitford . . . and her sister. One of them is reputed to be Hitler's girl friend . . . and the other is married to Oswald Mosley, leader of the English fascists. Well, this is their sister, the only non-fascist member of the family and consequently disowned by them years ago as a radical.

She married Esmond Romilly, Churchill's nephew, and went to Spain to fight with the loyalists in the Spanish war . . . he joined the RAF and has been lost 2 years [*sic*], and she has a beautiful 2-year-old baby. I discovered her working here at the OPA . . . and we've become good friends. She's constantly sought after by the local aristocracy and diplomatic set, and she's constantly throwing them out of her house because she hates stuffed shirts . . . Besides being beautiful she is exceptionally talented and shines with a kind of fierce honesty and courage. All this will undoubtedly make you very, very sad, because it is another lost cause. But you shouldn't feel that, because I've never enjoyed anything so much in my life and . . . the situation is under control.[10]

Since Aranka knew that Bob was on the verge of an engagement to a young woman called Mimi, this letter called forth an anxious query as to what he thought he was playing at. 'Mimi went to Detroit and wants to come back in two months and marry me,' he replied soothingly, 'don't worry. Nothing rash will happen before I see you again.'[11] When Decca learned, at a New Year's Eve party, of Bob's understanding with Mimi, she was deeply shocked, not by the relationship but by her own reaction. 'For the first time in my life,' she wrote, 'I was assailed by the bitter, corrosive emotion of jealousy. I could not quite understand this myself, but it brought home to me what I had begun to suspect: that my feelings about Bob were in a hopeless muddle.'[12] She felt such pleasure in Bob's company and looked forward to seeing him more than anything else in her life except Dinky. Yet she was still grieving for Esmond, still had that tiny doubt in the back of her mind about his death, and she believed that she would never, could never, love another man. She told herself that she had 'no call over Bob's affections' or even the right to mind who he went out with. At this point, unable to handle the matter, Decca ran away for the second time. She learned of a vacancy in the OPA in San Francisco, which paid $1,800 a year, and she put in her application for a transfer.

In February she and Dinky set off for California. Bob offered to see her off but was taken aback when he came to help with her luggage, which consisted of a large suitcase, Dinky's tricycle, and a dozen bulging carrier-bags tied up with string. He commented that he hadn't expected matched luggage but he thought she might have tried at least for matched carrier-bags. He was unable to stand the thought of parting from Decca and stayed on the train with her for a few stops, before catching a bus back to Washington. They promised to write to each other. For the rest of the three-day train journey Decca had plenty of time to reflect that in running away from her feelings for Bob she had put three thousand miles between her and her American friends, and she was going to a place where she didn't know a soul. She tried to override the unusual diffidence that she experienced after Bob got off the train, telling herself that she had now left everything behind her, including the still bitter memory of Esmond's death. She was heading for a new life. It was exciting. Wasn't it?

During the first few days she found temporary lodgings (forty dollars a month, room and board) and someone to care for Dinky while she settled into her new job. It was important that there was not too much interruption in her income and, she told herself, there would be time later to look for a better home. For Decca the regional office was more interesting than Washington's for it was a hotbed of warfare between radicals and conservatives and there were fierce clashes over political issues. The radicals fought for the rights of government employees to join unions, and for rent and price controls. The conservatives were suspected of planting stool pigeons in the unions, and liaising with the Apartment House Owners Association and business interests generally to sabotage the work of the OPA. This sort of activity was right up Decca's street, yet she was listless and could hardly take an interest.

Then there were Bob's letters. They were not love letters: they were the letters of a dear friend who told her indirectly that he missed her and Dinky. 'It's no good Dec, having all those miles of Field between us.'[13] As the weeks wore on she found she missed him a good deal, and that the distance she had put between them had not put him out of mind as she had intended. She wrote to him once a week, telling him all the small details of her new life, and of incidents that she thought might amuse him such as when her landlady confided in her that her former husband had been a beast. 'He ruined my bladder,' Mrs Betts[14] told Decca mysteriously as they washed up the dishes after supper. Bob's response to this information delighted Decca. It was another poem set to the tune of a popular song: '. . . In a fit of depravity/He filled the wrong cavity/ . . . What's the madder, You ruined my bladder/You took advantage of me.' And Decca realized that 'more and more I found my only source of real pleasure and sustenance was Bob's letters'.[15]

The room that Decca and Dinky inhabited in Mrs Betts's boarding-house was at 1350 Haight Street near Ashbury. Two and a half decades later, in the Summer of Love of 1967, the Haight-Ashbury area would become the world centre of hippie culture. Now it is a trendy suburb where tourists shop and take coffee in sunny pavement cafés. In 1943, however, it was an area of run-down working-class homes, shops and cheap boarding-houses. Most important to Decca was that the motherly Mrs Betts agreed to look after two-year-old Dinky, along with her own two small boys, while Decca worked. A secondary factor was that it was convenient for her job, and was within her limited budget: she had still to save enough to buy furniture when she found an apartment. She trudged around the city following up rental advertisements but too many people were chasing too few apartments. When, after a few weeks, the occupant of the unfur-nished apartment below Decca's room moved out, she persuaded Mrs Betts to let it to her. It was the epitome of inconvenience: two small rooms, a minuscule kitchen and a boarded-up shop-front facing on to Haight Street. It could be reached only by going through the boarding-house and descending an outside wooden fire escape, or through a pitch-black alley and climbing up the fire escape. She bought second-hand furnishings and tried to make it a home.

Although by 16 March Decca had still not made up her mind whether to stay in San Francisco or to go to Mexico to fulfil an ambition of Esmond's, she adopted a defiant tone in her letters to Sydney. 'We love San Francisco . . . we have got an apartment in this building,' she wrote. 'It is $25 a month and Mrs Betts is going to look after the Donk and feed her for an extra $40. This is a terrific bargain as nurses here in SF are about $100[16] . . . You asked whether the Donk has Mitford eyes; no, she hasn't. In fact she doesn't bear the slightest resem-blance to any Mitford either in looks or character, but is exactly like Esmond.'[17] This was patently untrue: Dinky would have fitted into any of those annual Mitford photo-graphs at Asthall and Swinbrook, without raising any suspicion of being an interloper.[18] But Decca was truthful about her work and enthusiastic about the new friends she had made in the union. 'My job is heaven; tho unfortunately the reactionaries here are trying to prevent a lot of the things we want to do & it may even result in us all losing our jobs. If so, I can get another job; but I do love the OPA The FBI (like Scotland Yard) are investigating a lot of people in our division at the moment, including me. This is part of a red-baiting program. The Durrs were investigated, too.'[19] Her future, she thought, did not lie in England but in the USA 'I feel that in my job here, I'm working for the cause I always believed in – the destruction of fascism.'

In May 1943 she was sent to Seattle for two weeks to train some new OPA recruits, and as a result of one operation in which she successfully obtained a prosecution of a lumber company there, she was offered a permanent job in Seattle at $2,600 a year. It was a big temptation, she wrote to Sydney, especially as the government would pay all her removal expenses, and rents there were much cheaper than in San Francisco. She had not turned down the offer, but she wanted to wait until after the visit of a friend who was coming out from Washington in early June. 'By the way,' she finished, 'please don't put "The Hon" on the envelopes as when I get them at the office they leave them around on my desk and of course no-one knows anything about my family. If they did, it would soon get around to some beastly journalists and all that publicity would start again.'[20]

The friend she was waiting to see was Bob Treuhaft. He took a 'streamliner' train out to California and spent five days with Decca. During this time they spent a few days vacationing at Stinson Beach with Dinky, declared their love for each other, and Bob decided to move out to California as soon as he could arrange to do so. Fortunately there were vacancies for lawyers in the San Francisco branch of the OPA and within two weeks he had packed up his apartment, arranged to ship his furniture ('at government expense'), and pulled strings to get an airline seat. Tickets were limited and priority was given to official travellers. 'It was hard work but I finally persuaded the airlines how vital it was for me to get to see my old Dec in the shortest possible time,' he wrote to Aranka on 19 June from 'over Chicago'. 'I'm looking forward tremendously to life in a real earthy community, after the ivory tower campus atmosphere of Washington . . . Decca's in the swing already in local politics, clubs and unions and even in my short stay there I began to feel a part of it.'

Eight days later he wrote again:

> If I didn't say much over the phone it was only because
> the wonder and the beauty of it all just left me
> speechless . . . I came out here knowing that Decca loved
> me, but with little hope of persuading her to marry me.
> The second day here I asked her the question and she said
> yes before I had a chance to finish, because she had been
> thinking about this for months, and had already made her
> decision. When Decca makes up her mind she *never*
> changes it . . . We parked the Dinkydonk with some
> friends and went out to a beautiful resort [Guerneville,
> California] among the Redwoods on Russian River and
> got married by a lady justice of the peace the next day [21
> June]. I never dreamed that so much glorious living could
> be packed into one week. Aranka she is just magnificent
> in every way – and completely devoted. She is the only
> girl that I've ever known that I *know* I can be completely
> happy with, whatever may happen.[21]

Decca's best friends, Marge (Frantz) and 'Dobbie' (Doris Brin), were not entirely sure about the marriage. 'When he first arrived he was obviously nuts about her, but we thought he wasn't good enough for her,' one said.[22]

Decca also wrote home with news that dumbfounded her family.

> Darling Muv, you will be v. surprised to hear I am married to Bob Treuhaft. I know I haven't told you about him before, so I'll do so now. I have known him since last December . . . and since coming out here in February I was terrifically lonely without him. We are tremendously happy and all the bitter, horrible past months seem to have vanished . . . we are going to live out here and we will come on a trip to Europe after the war . . . The Donk adores Bob. I do hope you realise how wonderful everything is. I would have written you sooner about it except that it was so terrifically sudden . . .[23]

It was very fortunate, she wrote, that the whole thing had been done secretly and there had been no publicity in the papers.

> They would have made an awful stink, especially as Bob is Jewish and they would have brought out all the old stuff about our family . . . I really didn't mean to tease when I wrote about being turned out by the family. That's all a long time ago anyway. What I really meant was . . . that all our ideas and beliefs are so tremendously different and opposed that it would be impossible to go back to an ordinary family life. But I don't think anymore, as I once did, that this means one can't be on writers or even speakers if close enough.[24]

However, this policy was not to be universally applied. Later that year when writing to advise that Bob had been promoted and had a job at the magnificent salary of $4,600, and that she had applied for US citizenship, she added angrily that she was furious to hear about the release of the Mosleys and felt it was a betrayal of those engaged in fighting Fascism. Indeed, if she were to hear that Diana and Mosley were staying with Muv she had decided not to continue writing.[25]

Having read that there had been a mass demonstration of protest from forty thousand people, who marched on the House of Commons demanding 'Put Mosley Back', Decca went further. She wrote to Churchill ('Dear Cousin Winston') protesting that the release of her sister appeared to indicate that the government was out of touch with the will of the people of Britain to defeat Fascism in all its guises and an absolute betrayal of all those who had given their lives in the war to date.[26] She demanded that the Mosleys be kept in jail, and she felt so strongly that she broke her own rules. She made the letter public by giving it with an exclusive press release to the San Francisco *Chronicle*, thus ending her period as a closet Mitford.

The papers had been on to her anyway. The *Examiner* had run the story headlined, 'Sister of Nordic Goddess in OPA Job Here' after a journalist talked his way into Decca's office and – when he took her picture through a glass partition – was attacked by a furious Decca who knocked the camera out of his hands, kicked it and grabbed him by the throat. The other papers ran stories inventing facts where they could find none, and her own polite 'No comment' to journalists waiting outside her office building was construed in the press as 'a reluctance to discuss her presence in San Francisco'. This, she said, reminded her of a similar incident when she and Esmond were runaways in Bayonne and Esmond had threatened to punch a reporter if he continued to pester them. The reporter filed his story next day, quoting Esmond as saying, 'I am with the girl I love.'

For some days Decca and Bob hid in their apartment with the blinds pulled. The difficulty of access to it suddenly became an asset, as reporters had to knock on the door of the boarding-house whereupon Mrs Betts sent them packing. Fifteen years later Decca wrote that she regretted the tone of her letter to

Churchill, because with hindsight she found it 'painfully stuffy and self-righteous – and also, as Nancy pointed out in her under-stated fashion, it was "not very sisterly"' but, she said, when she wrote it she was feeling 'a deep bitterness over Esmond's death and a goodly dash of familial spitefulness'.[27] Her letter led to her being invited to join the Communist Party through her friend Dobbie Brin (later Walker), whom Decca had met during her first weeks in San Francisco.

There was a slight hiccup in Decca's application to join the party because the membership application form contained the ominous question: 'Occupation of father?' and she did not feel that 'Aristocrat' or 'Peer of the Realm' was acceptable. Fortunately she remembered her father's gold mine, and was able to answer 'miner'.[28] Her background and connections were known about, of course. And though there were a few dissenters she was elected to membership on the understanding that she would do all she could to 'overcome the handicaps of birth and upbringing'. To Decca, being elected did not mean simply being content to be a card-carrying member and attend meetings. It meant being an activist, and her enthusiastic participation in party activities was soon rewarded. 'Within a few months of joining the Party, Bob and I rose in the ranks.' Bob was elected to serve on the cam-paign committee for the party's municipal election platform. Decca became 'Drive Director', responsible for collecting a sort of monthly 'tithe' of a day's pay from party members. She excelled at this, and her enormous charm made her popular with almost everyone. Shortly afterwards she was nominated for the full-time job of county financial director.

The amount of publicity that the Mosleys' release provoked in San Francisco and throughout the USA was nothing to what was happening in England. Until the autumn, 1943 had been a rea-sonably quiet year for Sydney. In the spring David had undergone surgery to remove the cataracts which had made him quite blind. To everyone's relief this was successful, and though he now had to wear thick glasses he could see again. There was also great joy when Debo gave birth safely, in April, to a baby girl, Emma. Tom had been in Libya but was now in Italy; he wrote as regularly as the war allowed, short letters just to let Sydney know he was safe. Pam was happy with her country life. Unity was now able to travel alone and could spend short periods with friends and relations. Doctors said she had recovered as far as she was likely to, and although friends who had known her before she shot herself found her an uncomfortable caricature of her former self, she seemed contented enough. Then, in October, Mosley became ill and they were all pitchforked into front-page drama again.

Because of prison conditions, lack of exercise and inadequate diet, both Mosley and Diana had suffered from periods of illness during the two years they were in Holloway. Diana collapsed at one point with dysentery, which fellow prisoner Major de Laessoe treated, with some pills he found in his old first-aid kit that dated from a residence in Angola. She was unconscious for twelve hours and when the pills were analysed they were found to be opium, of which she had been given a massive dose. Mosley's was an old weakness: phlebitis caused by poor circulation in his right leg, which had been damaged in the First World War flying accident. He was unwell and in a lot of pain in June 1943, when the eminent doctor Lord Dawson examined him and concluded that the phlebitis would not clear up in prison. He advised the government that Mosley should be released. Prison doctors disagreed. In November 1943, the illness flared up again. This time Mosley's condition deteriorated rapidly, and so much so that the prison doctors were now inclined to agree with Lord Dawson's earlier opinion, although releasing him hardly seemed an option. Diana was worried that he might not survive the winter and decided that she must let Churchill know how seriously ill Mosley was, and appeal for better treatment. Tom was serving abroad so, much as she hated to do it, she asked Sydney to go and see Clementine Churchill for her.

Clementine had been a bridesmaid at Sydney's wedding forty years earlier, and both Redesdales had once been proud of their connection with Winston. Since 1939, however, Sydney considered that Churchill bore a major responsibility for causing the war ('a warmonger' was her description of him), and was certainly responsible for Diana's incarceration. For Diana's sake, however, she swallowed her reluctance to ask a favour of him, and went to see Cousin Clementine. It was a difficult interview. Clementine began by saying, 'Winston has always been so fond of Diana,' and telling her that the Mosleys were better off in prison as they would probably be lynched if released. Sydney said frostily that they were prepared to take the risk. 'I can picture her cold and proud demeanour,' Diana wrote in her autobiography.

Whether Sydney's appeal influenced the matter is not known, but shortly afterwards a medical report submitted by a Home Office doctor, sent to examine the invalid, worried the government enough to consider releasing Mosley forthwith. They weighed the fact that his death in captivity might confer on him a form of martyrdom and provide a new rallying point for English Fascists. The Home Secretary, Herbert Morrison, argued strongly against releasing the Mosleys but Churchill was in favour and he carried the cabinet on 18 November. The war rumbled on but England no longer stood alone: the alliance with Russia and the USA had made a tremendous difference, and Churchill's popularity as war leader was riding high. He must have anticipated a level of protest from Labour MPs, trade unions and Communists, but no one was quite prepared for the storm that broke. On 19 November he wrote to his wife, 'Today Mr Morrison is going to tell the House about the Mosleys. I hope it goes all right.'[29]

The Mosleys learned about the decision from their wardress, who heard it announced on the radio on 20 November, burst into tears and ran to tell them they were free. It was a restricted form of freedom: they were advised that they would be permitted to live only in locations approved by the Home Office, and under house arrest, 'for the duration'. They were not allowed to live in London, to own a car, or to travel beyond a seven-mile radius of their accommodation. Nor were they allowed to meet or associate with anyone in the Fascist movement, or to make any political speeches or announcements or put out press releases. The initial problem was where they were to go. Savehay Farm was still requisitioned by the War Office and the only other property they owned was the London flat, which they were forbidden to use. Diana got a message to Pam and Derek, who immediately offered to take them in at Rignell House.

During the three days it took to make the necessary arrangements a countrywide outcry grew. Newspapermen waited outside the prison gates on hastily erected press stands, newspapers filled their front pages with reports on the matter and protest demonstrations were organized. It must have been an agonizing three-day wait for Diana, with the fear that their release might yet fall through because of the protests. But finally they were smuggled out in pitch darkness some hours before dawn through a little-used side gate in the prison, which the reporters had overlooked. There, two police cars were waiting with engines running.

We were driven fast through the dark, sleeping city [Diana wrote]. The police kept looking behind them but we had given the journalists the slip. As day broke and revealed the frosty country landscape M[osley] and I thought that nothing so beautiful was ever seen by human eye. At Rignell a wonderful welcome awaited us. Derek had got leave; Muv used her month's allowance of petrol and came over with Debo. We had delicious food, beautiful wine, talk, and laughter, perfect happiness. Then, for the first time in three and a half years we slept in soft, fine linen, in soft warm beds.[30]

Neither Sydney nor Diana ever really gave Churchill credit for what he did on Diana's behalf. His papers now reveal that he had always been opposed to the Mosleys' imprisonment without trial, that he had a 'deep loathing' of Rule 18B, and that he had stuck his neck out on Diana's behalf to get better treatment for them and, ultimately, to allow them to leave the prison. He was in Cairo when they were released and it was left to Herbert Morrison to bear the brunt of the protests. Clementine reported to her husband what was happening in his absence. On 23 November twenty thousand union members and factory workers from all over the country (many undertook long, difficult train journeys) handed in a petition to Downing Street and stood in protest in Whitehall. The newspapers had a field day. Three days later another mass protest was held in Parliament Square and MPs were lobbied as they went in to hear Morrison defend the decision. There was a debate in which a backbencher asked why Lady Mosley had been released since it was her husband who was ill. 'Yesterday, Mr Morrison lunched with me,' Clementine Churchill wrote to Winston. 'He seemed battered by what he is going through in the Mosley affair. I felt very sorry for him . . . the crowds at various points of London have been quite large but good-tempered. I ran into hundreds [in] Parliament Square . . . rather like a football crowd.'[31]

Mosley was confined to bed but he and Diana were not allowed to remain long at Rignell House. Journalists soon discovered their whereabouts and pictures of Diana looking fit and glamorous – from a photo taken years earlier at Ascot with Randolph Churchill, though he had been cropped out – appeared alongside stories that the couple were living in a luxurious country mansion protected by baying hounds, though the only dogs were Pam and Derek's dachshunds, Wüde and Hamelin. Suddenly it was realized by someone at the War Office that Diana's sister Pamela Jackson was the wife of the eminent scientist Derek Jackson, who had been involved in top-secret scientific projects at Oxford.[32] Herbert Morrison telephoned Derek personally to explain why the Mosleys could not be permitted to remain at Rignell. Derek, the war hero who was afraid of nobody, was unimpressed: he replied that he needed no lessons in patriotism from a man who had spent the First World War dodging around in apple orchards.[33]

In any event the Mosleys decided that it was best for them to move, but houses were impossible to find. All country towns and villages were bulging with people who had fled the cities, or had been evacuated due to bombing. Sydney heard that the partly disused inn at Shipton-under-Wychwood was available to rent, and as it was only three miles from Swinbrook, it meant they could visit each other. It was called, somewhat bizarrely, the Shaven Crown, and the hotel had been closed since the beginning of the war though the bar still functioned as a village pub. The rooms were as cold, dirty and uncared-for as any building neglected for so long would be, but they moved in with Nanny and the two little boys – Alexander, now five, and Max, three. Diana set about turning it into a temporary home, and when Jonathan and Desmond came home from boarding-school for the Christmas holidays Diana had the joy of having all her children around her at last. It was their first Christmas together since 1939. They spent the day at Mill Cottage with Sydney and Unity, all crammed into the tiny dining room.

The Shaven Crown was intended only as a short-term solution to their housing problem and at once Diana set about looking for a suitable house. In January she found Crux Easton, 'the most delightful house one could imagine'. Meanwhile, Mosley was still very ill and the burden of caring for him, doing the housework and cooking for the family was hers. Feeding them all was the most immediate difficulty for rationing was at its height and she had no store of the basic provisions that most prudent housewives had built up. Sydney often gave her a few eggs, which were like gold dust, but, Jonathan recalled, everyone was obsessed with food. When Unity's dachshund was drowned in the Windrush Diana returned home and announced solemnly, 'There's terrible news I'm afraid.' Thirteen-year-old Desmond immediately assumed the worst: 'What,' he asked anxiously. 'No sausages at Hammett's?'[34]

Wisely, Sydney, did not mention the Mosleys in her next letter to Decca, for fear she would stop writing.

> We had a very cheerful Christmas, couldn't get a turkey or a goose but had a large, enormous chicken, almost as good. Very horrid not being with Farve and I greatly hope that next Christmas we may be together. I have not heard lately from Tom; he may be in Italy now . . . Debo spent Christmas with the Devonshires, her house is very cold and she was quite glad to go somewhere warm for a bit. She and Emma are perhaps coming here when I expect to go to Inch Kenneth for a month or more.

She said that what she had most enjoyed was organizing a Christmas party for fifty village children, evacuees and thirty old people. 'We had the Christmas tree and . . . I have still got all the old decorations & the old Father Christmas clothes, of course one can't buy anything of that sort, and I'm nearly at the end of the candles.' She had swapped two dozen eggs for a Christmas cake from a caterer: 'It is worth anything to have a few hens . . . if you depended on a shop you get one egg, per head, per month – perhaps.'

Debo, she reported, was expecting a second baby in May, Andrew was in Italy, Pam was alone, but Derek got leave occasionally and managed to get home to see her. It was now impossible to get any domestic help, she said,

> but no one minds a bit . . . I am sure most . . . would never go back even if they could to a house full of

servants. Things like carrying coals and keeping fires going and ordinary housework are *so easy* and quickly done. Of course we are completely spoiled having the good Mrs Stobie, but when she goes away for a bit I see to what there is to do. My outside work takes about three hours a day and because of this I am allowed an extra 10 clothing coupons for gumboots etc. I am so pleased.[35]

Sydney's chatty letter was not answered and when, after three months, she queried whether Decca had received it, Decca wrote on paper bearing the letterhead Joint Anti-Fascist Refugee Committee:

The main reason why I haven't written . . . is that you never answered my question about the Mosleys. I see in the papers that they are now living at Shipton, so I suppose you do see them. I was so disgusted when they were released, and so much in sympathy with the demonstrators against their release that it actually made me feel like a traitor to write to anyone who had anything to do with them. However I see that it is difficult for you, and not your fault . . .[36]

That year Decca's romance with Bob was not the only one to affect the family. Before she moved from Washington she met Kick Kennedy at just about the time that Billy Hartington became engaged to a niece of Lord Mountbatten.[37] Kick was still madly in love with him, and was convinced that he had proposed to someone else only because she had left England.[38] She felt sure that if she returned he would change his mind. Her parents objected when she resigned from her job on the *Herald Tribune*, and joined a Red Cross programme with the aim of returning to England to help the war effort. But Kick was more self-confident than she had been in 1939 and ignored their protests. In June she sailed for England aboard HMS *Queen Mary*, which had been converted to a troopship. She had been correct about Hartington's feelings: shortly after she arrived in London they became secretly engaged. The old stalemate, however, still existed: to her brother Jack she wrote, 'Of course I know he would never give in about the religion, and he knows I never would. It's all rather difficult as he is very, very fond of me, and as long as I'm about he'll never marry . . .'[39]

As the winter lengthened into spring and everyone waited for the invasion of France, which was now only a matter of time, the Devonshires, realizing how much the couple cared for each other, withdrew their opposition. Rose Kennedy, however, was implacable: no daughter of hers would marry out of the Church. Cardinal Spellman and Archbishop Godfrey (the English papal legate), and through him the Pope, were all involved in the heated exchanges that flew between London and Hyannis Port, in letters, phone calls and cables, in the vain hope of finding a resolution to the problem.

Eventually Kick realized that she could never hope to win over her mother, and her father had abdicated any say in the matter by embarking upon an affair with a married woman. Although she was warned that she would be excommunicated from the Church, and that her only hope of salvation was for Hartington to die first, Kick reached a private agreement about the religious education of any future children, and the couple decided to marry in a civil ceremony.

THE FRENCH LADY
WRITER
(1944–7)

On 27 April 1944 Debo gave birth to a son, Peregrine Andrew Morny[1] Cavendish. Three weeks later Decca gave birth to a son, Nicholas Tito Treuhaft, and Idden, now Mrs David Horne – Sydney wrote to Decca – was also about to produce.

Sydney had been able to spend two weeks with Debo after the birth, but Decca's announcement by cable of her new baby came as a complete surprise for she had not told them she was pregnant. She rectified her former reticence with enthusiastic descriptions of the birth, and the baby who was 'wonderful. He weighed over 9lbs . . . having him was no trouble at all . . . the actual birth took only 7 minutes, so Bob was able to stay with me till almost the end . . . We call the new baby "the Mong" because of his Mongolian eyes (Bob is part Mongolian).' Decca had left the OPA in December, she said, and within a few weeks would begin a new job as financial director of the California Labour School, 'which trains Union people in organising economics etc. My job is to raise funds to keep the school going, write publicity etc. I think it will be very interesting . . .' Dinky was growing up fast, she reported, and at three years old she could already dress herself and make her own bed. Furthermore, 'standing perilously on a high stool by the stove . . . she always cooks the bacon for breakfast . . . and is learning to cook scrambled eggs'.[2] She liked to wash the dishes and was very motherly with the new baby, and these 'Womanly' – as in Pamela – qualities in her small daughter were a source of amused surprise to Decca. But there were signs of Decca, too: 'She gets furious if you try to help her do anything and she has a habit now of threatening to run away if we scold her . . . the other day she got her little suitcase and packed her doll and nightgown and started for the door. We think she has running-away blood in her, and is bound to really do it one day.'[3] The family at home 'roared' at this.

The news of Nicholas' birth also prompted the offering of an olive branch from David, who wrote to Decca for the first time since she had run off with Esmond. In his neat, clear handwriting, he wrote, 'Just to send you my love and every good wish for him and his future. Some day, when things are in a more settled state, I greatly hope to see you all, and judging from all news and the look of things it seems to me there is some prospect that I may last that long – I should much like to. Much love, Farve.'[4] There was a slight improvement in his failing health, undoubtedly due to the fact that Sydney had received permission to visit Inch Kenneth, and the couple spent two and a half weeks together there. Writing from the island, Sydney told Decca,

Farve looks terribly thin and frail and very easily gets tired. He sleeps a lot in the day. All the same he sees to the farm and animals and boats etc. We are in the middle of a tiresome cut-off period, the sea is too rough to get across and we have had no letters or papers for 4 days. We can always manage for food as there's enough on the island, and of course the 'news' comes on the wireless. Tom is, I suppose, in this fighting in Italy. I heard from him . . . 1 May, [he was] living in a peasant's hut in company with

two Italian families and their cows! I left Debo . . . with all
the excitement of Billy's wedding . . . they really have been
so faithful over 5 years and would have married years ago
but for the difference in religion. To me it seems like *Old
Forgotten Far-off Things & Tales of Long Ago* and a
reversion to the days of Queen Elizabeth . . . Everyone
likes her enormously, Debo and Andrew especially . . .
you know her don't you?[5]

The wedding of Debo's brother-in-law Billy Hartington and
Kick Kennedy finally took place at the Chelsea register office on
6 May 1944. Joseph Kennedy cabled his best wishes and made a
generous settlement so that Kick would never be financially
dependent upon the Cavendish family, but Rose Kennedy
remained opposed to the union. As a result only one member of
the Kennedy family attended the wedding, Kick's eldest brother,
Joe. He was serving in the United States Air Force, based at
Dunkerswell in East Anglia, and attended the ceremony in defiance of his mother's wishes.

The newly-weds honeymooned at Compton Place,
Eastbourne, the same family property used by Debo and
Andrew for their honeymoon four years earlier. Then Billy
returned to his regiment to take part in the preparations for the
D-Day offensive. On 13 August the Kennedy family were devastated by the distressing news that Joe Jr had been killed on
the previous day, when his bomber exploded during a top-
secret mission. Kick wangled a place on a military flight to the
USA to attend her brother's memorial service. She stayed in
Boston with her mother, having sent word to Billy to say that
if there was any chance he might get leave she would return
immediately. On 13 September a person-to-person call came
through from London for the Marchioness of Hartington to
tell her that Billy had been killed. While leading his men in a
rush on German lines in Belgium he had been hit in the chest

by a sniper's bullet and died instantly.[6] Frantically, Kick cabled Billy's parents for information, but her cable crossed with one from them, telling her about Billy's death, and asking her to come back to England. To a close friend in Washington[7] she confided the gnawing pain of losing part of herself: 'The amazing thing about Billy was that he loved me so much. I felt needed. I really thought I could make him happy.' That she had not conceived a child during their short time together was an added misery.[8]

Churchill arranged a place on an RAF flight for Kick, and she turned up at Chatsworth looking small, pale and absolutely lost. Rose Kennedy had apparently done a good job of convincing her daughter that in marrying Billy she had committed a mortal sin, so in addition to her deep grief over the loss of her husband and her favourite brother, Kick was concerned about her immortal soul. She and Billy had spent only five weeks together as man and wife, and she could not help reflecting that so much of their time before their marriage had been overshadowed by discussions about the religion of any future children. She said bitterly to a friend, 'Well, I guess God has taken care of the matter in His own way, hasn't He?'[9] Lady Elizabeth Cavendish, sister of Billy and Andrew, said that in all her life she had never seen anyone so desperately unhappy as Kick at that time. The Cavendish family liked Kick a great deal and rallied round, supporting her as much as they could. The Duchess told her, 'All your life I shall love you – not only for yourself but that you gave such perfect happiness to my son whom I loved above anything in the world.'[10] Some months later Kick took up Red Cross work in London.

The obvious significance of Billy's death was that – as soon as it was established that Kick was not pregnant – Andrew now became heir to the dukedom. In that, there was no joy for Andrew and Debo and, indeed, it took years for Andrew to come to terms with the fact that he had inherited through a frightful incident. He was serving in Italy, and Debo, who was constantly fearful for him, was staying with Diana at Crux Easton when the news of Billy's death came. She took her two babies to stay with the grieving Devonshires. 'Poor little Debo is quite distracted,' Nancy had written to Sydney a short time earlier, 'all these deaths must terrify her for Andrew,' although Prod had assured her that the worst was over in Italy.[11]

Sydney and Unity stayed with Debo for two days in July on their way up to Scotland. Following the successful invasion of France a few weeks earlier, Unity had been given permission to visit the island and it was to be her first visit there since the outbreak of war. Debo had driven them over to Chatsworth in a flat farm cart pulled by her piebald horse. 'She puts a mattress in it . . . and you can sit propped up with masses of cushions. The whole thing looks very queer but really it is most comfortable and the horse goes at a steady trot up hill and down for miles and miles.' They had admired the gardens at Chatsworth but did not go inside as it was being used as a girls' school and Sydney could not face 'rows of hideous little iron beds everywhere'. Meanwhile, Nancy was coping well with the new and terrifying flying bombs in London, Sydney reported, and Tom had returned home for a few months having been promoted to major. He had to undergo a period of training at the Army Staff College but he had gone directly to the island to see her as soon as he landed.[12]

Nancy *was* coping with the flying bombs, as her mother said. Indeed, after the first few weeks of the war she had adopted a fatalistic attitude and more or less ignored the bombing, never going into an air-raid shelter. She coped so well that after one raid in which she helped to deal with incendiaries, early in the Blitz, she was thrilled to be asked to deliver a series of lectures to trainee fire-watchers. After the first lecture she was sacked: apparently her upper-class vowels irritated her listeners so much that they wanted to put her *on* the fire. But despite the insouciance of her letters, Nancy was less able to cope when her husband suddenly put in an unexpected appearance.

One morning Prod simply appeared in the shop, having come straight from an Italian beachhead. Within no time at all he was living up to his nickname of Toll-gater and regaling Nancy with boring diatribes. 'I felt quite faint,' she reported to Decca. '3 years he was away. So you can imagine there was some wonderful toll-gating. He is toll-gating round the place now . . . and completely blissful the dear old fellow – a *Colonel* . . . . "Is the Colonel in for dinner?" You must say it's funny.'[13]

James Lees-Milne came across the couple celebrating at the Ritz. Peter looked tough and bronzed, well, and slightly drunk. 'Even so,' he wrote in his diary, 'I expected he might lash out at Nancy at a moment's notice and on the slightest provocation. Nancy, apprehensive and solicitous, plied Peter with questions but he never answered any. Instead he talked incessantly in his boring manner . . . the sad truth is that one should believe only a quarter of what Peter says.'[14] Fortunately for Nancy, Prod had left again by the time the adored Palewski returned in June, but he was only there for a week, then left for France with de Gaulle.

'I must go. Au revoir, Linda.' [Fabrice] kissed her hand politely, almost absent mindedly, it was as if he had already gone, and he walked quickly from the room. Linda went to the open window and leaned out. He was getting into a large motor-car with two French soldiers on the box and a Free French flag waving from the bonnet . . . As it moved away he looked up. 'Navette – navette,' cried Linda with a brilliant smile. Then she got back into bed and cried very much. She felt utter despair at this second parting.[15]

After a short stay with Sydney at Inch Kenneth, Tom returned to London. A few days later as James-Lees Milne was walking past the Ritz he suddenly heard Nancy's voice calling him, and he turned round to see her with Tom 'back from the Mediterranean after two and half years' absence. He almost embraced me in the street, saying, "My dear old friend, my very oldest and dearest friend", which was most affecting. He looks younger than his age, is rather thin, and still extremely handsome.'[16] When the two men dined together a few nights later, Tom told Lees-Milne

> that he must marry and asked my advice which of his girls he should choose. I said, 'Let me know which are in the running?' So he began, ticking them off one by one on his fingers. He told me with that engaging frankness with which he always confides in me, the names of those he had already slept with, and how often, and those he rather loved, and those he merely liked, until I stopped him with, 'But all this sounds most unromantic to me. If I were one of those girls and knew how you were discussing me, I wouldn't dream of marrying you' . . . and he roared and roared with laughter.[17]

When Lees-Milne asked Tom if he still sympathized with the Nazis, 'he emphatically said Yes'.[18] He said he knew a lot of Germans and the best sort were Nazis, also that he was an imperialist by nature. Shortly after this conversation, Tom requested a transfer to Burma: 'He does not wish to go to Germany killing German civilians whom he likes,' Lees-Milne wrote. 'He prefers to kill Japanese whom he does not like. Tom makes me sad because he looks so sad.'[19]

The two men met often during Tom's leave and on one occasion drove to Swinbrook together, 'to see Muv and Bobo'. By 1944 Unity had become 'rather plain and fat, and says she weighs 13½ stone,' Lees-Milne recorded. 'Her mind is that of a sophisticated child, and she is still very amusing in that Mitford manner . . . she talked about the Führer, as though she still admired him . . . being with her made me sad, for I love this family, and I see no future for Bobo but a gradually dissolving fantasy existence.'[20]

Tom left for Burma (now Myanmar) at the end of the year.[21] Having come right through the war in Europe and Africa unscathed, he appeared to be charmed, and was popular with his men as well as his brother officers. Although he was initially posted to a position on Staff it is typical of him that he went immediately to see the general and requested a transfer to a fighting battalion. His exact words were, the general later wrote to David, 'To hell with the Staff.' He was subsequently attached to the Devonshire Regiment as brigade major commanding Indian troops. On 24 March 1945, he led a force from the 1st Battalion against a small group of Japanese who were occupying a wooded rise. The enemy had several machine-guns, and the company of men that Tom was leading were pinned down by rapid fire. Tom took shelter behind some sheets of corrugated iron but was hit in the neck and shoulders by several bullets from a machine-gun. He did not lose consciousness, and was taken immediately to the field hospital. Forty-eight hours later an operation was carried out, and a bullet was found to be lodged in the spine, causing paralysis. The surgeon decided against removing it, and on 26 March Tom was evacuated by light aircraft to company headquarters at Sagang where there were better surgery facilities. He was not in any pain, and – perhaps thinking of Unity's experience – he believed he was getting better. Unfortunately he developed pneumonia, which did not respond to treatment, and he died, aged thirty-six, on 30 March. He was buried in the military cemetery near Yangon (formerly Rangoon).[22]

'Beloved, handsome Tom,' Lees-Milne mourned when he heard, 'who should have been married with hosts of beautiful children; Tom, caviar to the general . . . but to me the most loyal and affectionate of friends. It is hell.'[23] The core of his grief lay in that Tom had been his first love at Eton. 'On Sunday eves before Chapel at five, when the toll of the bell betokened that all boys must be in their pews,' he recorded in his diary, 'he and I would, standing on the last landing of the entrance steps, out of sight of the masters in the ante-chapel and all the boys inside, passionately embrace, lips to lips, body pressed to body, each feeling the opposite fibre of the other . . . When Tom left Eton it was all over. He never again had any truck with me and turned exclusively to women.'[24] The war in Europe was over to all intents and purposes; if only Tom had not volunteered to go to the Far East, he wrote. The tragedy of it seemed overwhelming.

It was David who heard first. He was in London when, on 2 April, he received a telegram advising that Tom was badly wounded. Sydney was on the island in the most beautiful spring weather for many years when David got the news to her. 'As the days passed,' she wrote to Decca, 'we grew hopeful, and the shock was so bad when it came that I nearly went mad, being so far away at Inch Kenneth. I went to London by the next possible train as Farve was all by himself at the Mews . . . he is sadly down, and you can imagine what it is to us both, and in fact I know all of you, to lose Tom. He was certainly the best of sons and brothers and I think we all relied so much on him.' It was dreadful to think that all the time they were hoping for his recovery, she said, Tom was already dead, but she was consoled that in all his letters he had said how glad he was to be in Burma. 'Alas, we are only one family of thousands all over the world, and what a world it has become, all black and dark . . . I have to learn from you darling,' she wrote, obviously referring to the loss of Esmond, 'for your great courage was an example for anyone, but you always were such a brave little D.'[25]

The news had spread quickly and family and friends converged on the mews to offer what comfort they could to the bereft parents. Nancy and Peter, Pam – Derek was in America – Debo and Andrew, and Nanny all came as soon as they heard. Diana and her family were at Crux Easton. Mosley called

Whitehall but without waiting for permission to leave the seven-mile zone, Diana borrowed a Daimler and drove to London with Mosley and two policemen in attendance. Although Sydney and Unity often went to stay at Crux Easton Diana and David had not spoken for many years, and there was a sharp intake of breath when Diana walked into the room. But David greeted her affectionately and 'At once, like the old Diana,' James Lees-Milne wrote, having been told of the incident by Nancy, '[she] held the stage and became the centre of them all.'[26] It was David, 'in his sweet old-fashioned way', who remembered the two policemen sitting outside, and insisted on sending out cups of hot sweet tea, which he said policemen always liked best. Diana had not mentioned that Mosley was also sitting in the car, and took Nancy to one side to explain and ask for help in keeping David away. But when she got up to leave he insisted on taking her downstairs despite Diana's protests, saying that of course he must escort her to her car. Finally, she had no option but to explain gently, 'Farve, the Man Mosley is waiting in the motor for me,'[27] at which David smiled regretfully, and allowed her to go.

Soon afterwards when James Lees-Milne called into Heywood Hill's bookshop he saw a frail bent figure leaning heavily on a stick. It was David, waiting for Nancy. His face was lined and shrunken, his features twisted, and he wore round spectacles of the sort of thick glass that magnifies the eyes. 'Oh, the onslaught of age!' Lees-Milne wrote, of the man who had once been capable of reducing him to a quivering wreck. 'Last time I saw him he was upstanding and one of the best-looking men of his generation. I suppose Tom's death has helped hasten this terrible declension. I melted with compassion.'[28] David and Sydney never recovered from Tom's death. The great tragedy was that the ideological differences between them had made it impossible for them to live together and console each other.

Everyone felt for Decca, knowing how she had always adored Tom, and that she was unable to grieve with anyone else who had known him. Debo, Pam and Nancy wrote to her immediately. They were all amazed at how well their parents were taking the news. Perhaps for the first time they saw their real mettle. Decca was heartbroken.[29] 'I do wish I were there,' Decca wrote to Nancy. 'It seems like a lifetime since that day in 1939 when Tuddemy saw us off [for New York] at the station – he and Nanny . . . And he was one of the few people in England I was really looking forward to seeing again.'[30] All the old childhood memories were stirred, such as those Sundays in Swinbrook church when the girls had tried to make Tom giggle by nudging him whenever the word adultery was mentioned.

In Nancy's letter to Decca she had casually mentioned the book that she had once described as her autobiography. She had changed her mind about saving the material for her old age and had recently gone back to work on it: '[It's] about us when we were little,' she wrote. 'It's not a farce thing this time but serious – a novel, don't be nervous.'[31] Sydney also wrote about it, telling Decca that Nancy had left the bookshop for two months to work on her new book. 'It's about all of you as children, the heroine appears to be Debo, and you appear in it of course, and Farve and I, but I've only read a little.'[32] To her friend Evelyn Waugh, Nancy explained that although people might think she had copied from his recently published success *Brideshead Revisited*, in that she was relating the narrative in the first person, her book was 'about my family, a very different cup of tea, not grand and far madder. Did I begin writing it before *B'head* or after – I can't remember . . . I'm awfully excited. My fingers itch for a pen.'[33] As she recycled her youthful experiences she found the book almost wrote itself as the words flowed. Never before and never again would Nancy find it so easy to write.

The characters in *The Pursuit of Love* were all drawn from real life and easily recognizable despite the Nancyish distortions of David as Uncle Matthew, Sydney as Aunt Sadie, Hamish and Prod as several personalities and Palewski as Fabrice, le Duc de

Sauveterre. The heroines were amalgamations of herself and her sisters, but their experiences were unmistakable: here was 'Jassy' with her 'running-away money', and 'Linda' welling with hot tears over the little houseless match, and falling headlong for Fabrice. In June she showed the manuscript to Hamish Hamilton and was thrilled to be offered an advance of £250, the most she had ever received. Having only read a chapter or two Sydney was rather doubtful about it: 'This family again,' she wrote somewhat mournfully to Decca, unconvinced of Nancy's prediction that it might earn her as much as a thousand pounds.

In the event Sydney could hardly have been more wrong. The book was a success from the moment of publication and sold two hundred thousand copies in the first year. It has hardly been out of print since, is regarded as a classic of its genre, and spawned a crop of plays and films. Nancy had discovered her métier, at last, although it took her a little longer to realize this. For her the most important thing in her life was still her beloved Colonel. And before she knew that her book would be successful she made an attempt to get him back into her life. In the late summer of 1945, David somewhat surprisingly made Nancy a gift of three thousand pounds. Perhaps it was because he no longer had a son to provide for that he was sympathetic to her musings that she would like to open a bookshop of her own. She used some of the money in September 1945 to go to Paris, ostensibly to buy second-hand books for her shop, but really to see Palewski. Her letters home positively glowed with happiness and reflected none of the discomforts of post-war existence – the black bread and acorn coffee, or the fierce restriction of water for washing.

I am so completely happy here . . . I must come and live here as soon as I can. I feel a totally different person as if I had come out of a coal mine into daylight . . . Diana Cooper [wife of the British ambassador] is being too angelic. I am captivated completely by her beauty and charm . . . She gave a literary cocktail party for me and John Lehmann[34] & we met all the nobs, you must say it was kind. And she really persuaded me to stay on here . . . Oh my passion for the French. I see all through rose coloured spectacles . . .[35]

She borrowed a flat at 20 rue Bonaparte ('you must say it's dashing to have a flat in the rue Bonaparte'), close to where Palewski lived at number 1. He was deeply involved in the French elections and although Nancy saw him from time to time he was too busy to devote much time to their affair. 'What strikes me,' Nancy wrote to Randolph Churchill, '[is that] you never see attacks on General de Gaulle. All the attacks, and they are many and venomous, are directed against Palewski, who is presented as a sinister *Eminence grise l'ennemi du peuple*. G.P.R.F. (Government Provisoire de la Republique Francais) which is on all their motor cars is said to stand for Gaston Palewski Régent de France . . .'[36]

Nancy was back in London in December for the publication of her book. She was as surprised as anyone when it roared into bestseller status, and gratified that those who mattered in contemporary English literature, such as Evelyn Waugh, John Betjeman, Cyril Connolly and Rupert Hart-Davis, to name a few (although they *were* her friends), were fulsome in their praise not only in correspondence but in the all-important reviews. Betjeman wrote privately, 'You have produced something that is really a monument to our friends. It is exactly how we used to talk at Biddesden . . . It cannot be that the wonderful, unforgettable Uncle Matthew is really like Lord Redesdale, can it? He is my favourite character in the book . . . Oh you clever old girl.'[37]

Suddenly, for the first time in her life, Nancy had enough money to do the things she wanted to do. What she did not have was Palewski, and because of her book a small embarrassment lay between them. He was initially flattered and later worried that the book had been dedicated to him. Although she had killed off Fabrice and Linda at the end of the story he became concerned that French Communists would somehow make the connection between himself, Nancy and Unity. Furthermore, Nancy had committed a cardinal sin by using the real name of one of his lovers in the book.

> Diana says you're cross with me about the boring Lamballe woman [she wrote to him]. Don't be cross. I can't bear that . . . Tell her to write a book about *me* – I am very vulnerable. I hate her – hateful Lamballe who deserted you when you were a lonely exile and ran off with her own soul. It was a mean and shabby trick. All the same, I will take her out of the American edition if you think it worthwhile . . . Come soon to London dearest Col – don't be cross . . . you must be rather pleased with Fabrice really he is such a heavenly character and everyone is in love with him![38]

Palewski forgave Nancy – since he had encouraged her over the dedication he could hardly do otherwise – but as passion cooled for him, their relationship assumed a different character. For Nancy this meant years as a supplicant and having to be content with crumbs of affection from Palewski. He was always open with her about his feelings, and his relationships with other women, which were legion, were never deliberately concealed from her. It was a take-it-or-leave-it situation and it made Nancy miserable, but she recognized early on that if she could not look the other way she would lose him altogether, and she could not face that. In April 1946 she decided to live in France. Her book had made it possible financially and she was convinced that if she were always available then the Colonel would perhaps be more constant. She confided in Sydney her true feelings for Palewski and her sincere admiration for de Gaulle only to have Sydney ask in exasperation, 'Oh, why do *all* my daughters fall for dictators?'

Nancy would never live in England again. In the first months she was delirious with joy. Palewski had been ousted in the elections and was at a loose end; Nancy was available and entertaining, and her open adoration of him was balm to his wounded spirit. She had money to buy wonderful clothes and wore them beautifully. She was funny and good company, so in demand socially, usually on the arm of Palewski. Soon she had settled into the apartment that would become synonymous with her greatest literary successes: number 7 rue Monsieur. Here she began the sequel to *The Pursuit of Love*, which would secure her financial independence. The family began to refer to her as 'the French lady writer'.

The end of the war brought joy, of course, but it also engendered sadness when Sydney took stock of the cost to her family. There were the deaths of Esmond, four nephews who had been childhood playmates of her daughters, and Billy Hartington. And then, at the end of the war, there had been the death of her own beloved Tom. Several young relatives had been prisoners-of-war and were still trickling home in various degrees of ill-health. Unity's life had been ruined. Diana's children had been deprived of their mother during their impo tant formative years. And then there had been Sydney's own irreconcilable differences with David.

This permanent separation was not of Sydney's making; indeed, she found it 'sad and inexplicable' that David chose to live at Redesdale Cottage in Northumberland, so far away from his family. Like her daughters, she disliked Margaret Wright, who had assumed 'airs and graces', and was downright proprietorial to David's visitors. When anyone called, she insisted on acting as the lady of the house and pouring the tea. Had David been a younger man in good health one would have suspected a romantic liaison (Decca and Bob believed this probably *was* the case: 'He did that old-fashioned thing and ran off with the parlourmaid,' Bob said), but it seems unlikely given his poor physical condition and sad demeanour. Although crushed by Tom's death, Sydney made every effort to keep herself occupied by working the farm at Inch Kenneth, her regular bread-making, cooking and running her homes on the island and at the mews with minimal help. David had little to occupy him, or distract him from his unhappiness. He could no longer see well enough to shoot or fish, he could not skate, and he no longer cared to go to the House of Lords. His surviving children were dispersed far away from him, and may have been discouraged from visiting because of Mrs Wright, though Diana visited him every year, 'and always loved it, despite Margaret'. His letters were cheerful and he described himself as living in comfort, but he became increasingly bored and lonely. 'I never think he gets enough to eat,' said Sydney briskly.[39] Occasionally they attended family functions together, such as the wedding of the Churchills' youngest daughter Mary to Captain Christopher Soames.[40]

As 1945 drew to a close the aftermath of Tom's death caused yet another rift in the family. Only a month before Sydney had written to Decca,

Farve has made over the island to Tom, and I have come to manage the farm while Tom is away . . . It is not very ideal for Farve as he can't enjoy himself with the boats etc. But you know how he always gets tired of a place after about 5 years so perhaps it would have happened anyway . . . I must try to make the farm, if not pay, at least not lose too much. We have to have a boatman as well as a farm man & wife, and of course with wages very high and nothing coming in . . . I don't want to ruin poor Tom . . . The house is absolutely hideous . . . in no way beautiful, but comfortable inside, and the sea and rocks are so lovely . . . Bobo and I do the housemaiding, it takes no time at all.[41]

Somewhat surprisingly, in view of his legal training, Tom died intestate, and when his estate was being administered it was discovered that as the deed of transfer of Inch Kenneth had been made under Scottish law, ownership of the land and property now passed in equal shares to Tom's siblings, not to his next of kin (David and Sydney) as would have happened under English law.[42] The Redesdales inherited only the chattels. Nancy, Pam, Diana, Unity and Debo decided to hand the property back to Sydney for her lifetime.

Decca did not go along with this. She wrote that she would like to deed her share to the Communist Party in England, 'to undo some of the harm that our family has done, particularly the Mosleys, and Farve when he was in the House of Lords'. Sydney responded unemotionally that they would, of course, comply with her wishes, and Decca appointed Claud Cockburn as her power-of-attorney to see the matter through all legalities. Cockburn was then a journalist on the London *Daily Worker*. Decca and Esmond had admired him from afar in the days of the Spanish civil war for his essays on Spain and his 'muck-raking journal' (this description by Decca was intended as a compliment) called the *Week*. Decca first met Cockburn at the founding convention of the United Nations in San Francisco, just after the details of Tom's will had been relayed to her. She asked him to act for her in donating her share of the island to the Communist Party of Great Britain.

Cockburn was no fool: he could see that there was as much mischief in the gesture as romantic idealism, and he recognized that Decca envisaged a scenario where bands of jolly holidaying Communists might rattle the windows of the Redesdales' house with rousing choruses of 'The Internationale'.[43] It was the sort of practical joke that the pre-war Esmond might have thought up, but with apparently no thought given to the distress that Sydney, the island's inhabitant, was suffering following the recent death of her only son. Cockburn saw all this, and was already extremely doubtful as he approached the Communist Party leadership in London with Decca's offer. He was told: 'What the hell does anyone think we can do with a small little bit of a desolate island somewhere off the coast of Scotland. Who, in the name of God, goes there and what would they do there if they went?'[44]

Subsequently Cockburn met David at the House of Lords to discuss the matter. David had made a special journey to London for the meeting and pointed out that the island was very tiny. 'I don't know that any of us – I mean we or the Communists – would be happy under the circumstances' he said. Cockburn was inclined to agree, and there the matter foundered. When she found she could get no response from Cockburn, although the two remained lifelong friends, Decca revoked the power-of-attorney and agreed to sell her share of the island to the other sisters, who were willing to buy it at market value, to enable Sydney to spend her retirement there. Sydney volunteered to act as power-of-attorney to complete the legalities of a contract in English law. She did not tell Decca that everyone else in the family was so livid with her that no one else was prepared to act for her. In the event Decca's one-sixth was only worth five hundred pounds – a third of what she had anticipated (an independent surveyor valued the island and property at three thousand), but she saw the matter as a point of honour. 'To me, it seems that money is an important political weapon,' she explained to her mother, '. . . and that is the only reason why I'm interested in getting any of it, and also why I'm interested in getting the maximum . . . I don't know whether developments in the last ten years have yet proved to you what a criminal thing it was to have supported Hitler and an appeasement policy . . . but you know what I think about it, so therefore you can see the logic of my . . . using the money from the island in this way.'[45] In the event Decca kept her one-sixth share and the sisters unanimously agreed to Sydney's life tenancy.

David's reaction was never recorded and Sydney never responded to Decca's accusations that she and David (as well as Diana) had been major causes of the war; perhaps she was afraid that if she did so, she would lose touch with Decca altogether, and would never see her two American grandchildren. She never mentioned the matter, writing instead every few weeks, to keep Decca in touch with news of the rest of the family.

From her mother's letters Decca learned that Andrew Cavendish was now out of the Army and was going to stand as MP for Chesterfield in the forthcoming elections, that Pam had just suffered yet another miscarriage almost six months into her pregnancy, that Derek had left the RAF and was going to ride his own horse in the 1946 Grand National, that Sydney had to leave the cottage at Swinbrook as it was wanted by someone else. She had decided to return to High Wycombe but Unity loved Swinbrook and wished to remain there. They tried unsuccessfully to find a cottage for her, unable to afford the only ones available for rent. Nancy's book had gone into a second edition; she had given up her job and was now living permanently in Paris which she said was 'her spiritual home'. Neither Sydney nor Decca ever referred to Diana, of course. Sydney hoped that once the war was over Decca and Bob would travel to England. 'Some day,' she threatened lightly, 'I shall get into an aeroplane and arrive at your house, seven years is too long. You probably won't know who it is when I arrive.'[46] A year later that is exactly what she did.

Bob and Decca no longer lived at the inconvenient apartment in Haight Street. In September 1944 they had moved to a house about ten blocks away in Clayton Street, and shortly after they settled in Decca was granted US citizenship.[47] Three years later the Treuhafts sold the Clayton Street house and moved across the bay from San Francisco to its workaday neighbour, Oakland. There they purchased an apartment at 675 Jean Street, convenient for the law firm Bob had joined as a junior associate. Gladstein, Grossman, Sawyer and Edises, promptly renamed by Decca as 'Gallstones, Gruesome, Sewer and Odious', was the only left-wing law firm in the area, and they specialized in employment disputes, representing trade unions and civil-rights cases. Decca's friend Dobbie who had first introduced the Treuhafts to the Communist Party was also an associate. With Decca's assistance Bob was a pioneer in 'trying to deal with one of the worst police departments in the country. They were mostly whites who had been recruited from Southern police departments and they were extremely hostile and vicious towards the growing black population.' He engaged in lawsuits against the police, which no one had ever done before. 'It was not a very lucrative practice, I can tell you that,' he recalled.[48]

The Treuhaft household at Jean Street was happy, noisy and busy, if slightly shambolic. Decca, fulfilled by her work for the party, had no aptitude for housework and domestic occupations, though now and again a spurt of guilt would drive her to some unaccustomed activity such as polishing all the wooden floors in one evening, on her hands and knees. 'She had to learn from scratch,' Bob said. 'All the housework at her childhood home had been done by maids who got up early and were finished by the time the family came down.' Bob, who had grown up knowing what happened in a kitchen, was a better cook than his wife, and did most of the shopping and cooking. Decca had a few specialities, though – an English roast beef and Yorkshire pudding, a poached salmon, chicken paprika – that she would whip up for guests, and when she put her mind to it she could produce an excellent table for she adored entertaining and her house was always full of visitors. A succession of daily cleaners varied in competence, and six-year-old Dinky took on some household chores because she enjoyed them. 'She knows all sorts of housework things like cleaning the woodwork, which I have no idea of' Decca wrote to Sydney. On one occasion Dinky slipped in through the door after school to find her mother on the stairs with a dustpan and brush. She stood for a moment, watching the activity, then said witheringly, 'Decca, I think you're supposed to start at the top and work *down*.'[49] Decca much preferred to spend her time raising money for the Communist Party, at which she excelled. 'If you went to a function run by Decca,' a friend recalled, 'you paid the small entrance fee without realizing it was just a downpayment. There would be a twenty-five cents charge for getting your coat back, and another quarter for drinks, or to use the bathroom.'[50]

Nicholas was now almost four, and the apple of Decca's eye. Perhaps because he had several health problems, such as eczema, and because he never displayed the sort of independence that Dinky had shown from the start, he received a greater share of Decca's time.

Aranka, Decca's mother-in-law, was the sort of hands-on mother to which Decca felt she had been entitled and had missed out on, who was involved at a deep, emotional level and interested in everything her child did. Although there were differences between the two women they got on pretty well, and Decca's warm, chatty letters to Aranka, with sketches, jokes and detailed descriptions of the children's illnesses and development, are different from those to Sydney, except when she was writing about her children and lost her spiky tone: Nicholas was a wonder child if a little accident prone and 'He does the most awful things like falling out of the car when it's moving, eating quantities of sleeping pills (we had to rush him to the hospital to have his stomach pumped) and setting fire to the house with the electric stove . . .'[51] Sydney must have blenched at this, thinking of the ordered nursery routine of her own children under Nanny Blor.

In October 1947 Sydney received a cable telling her, as usual out of the blue, that Decca had given birth to another son, a 'nine-pounder called Benjamin'. A letter from Dinky shortly afterwards decided the matter. 'Granny Muv, could you come over here one day?' she wrote. 'Do you know that I do not have Esmond as my father now? I have a father called Bob, at least I call him Bob, and I like him very much . . .'[52] Debo had just lost another baby at eight months into her pregnancy and had gone to Africa to convalesce and recover from the inevitable depression caused by the experience. Sydney decided she would fly to San Francisco and meet Decca's family at last.

For years Decca had kept her family, friends and comrades amused with tales of her upbringing, and like most raconteurs she never worried about adding a little embroidery to make a good story even better. Dinky had grown up with these stories, with Bob and all their friends falling about with laughter, and now, when she heard that Granny Muv was coming to visit, she began teaching Nicholas to bow. 'She has a strange idea of our childhood,' Decca wrote to Nancy. But Decca was apprehensive about the visit. She had convinced herself that she disliked Sydney, and that her childhood had been deeply unhappy. Now, the thought of her cool, austere, disapproving mother arriving in California was almost too much for her to stand. 'I was in a state of near terror about her visit,' she wrote to Nancy. 'And then she tottered forth from the aeroplane (it was a rough trip and she was quite done for), and at once it became apparent that she had come to make friends at all costs.'[53] Any reticence was dispelled by Dinky, who sat in the back of the car listening to the awkward silence as they drove from the airport. Suddenly she piped up, 'Granny Muv, aren't you going to tell Decca off for running away?'[54]

However, the last vestiges of the ice chip that had lodged in Decca's heart had not yet melted. This occurred several days later when she and her mother were working in the kitchen and the touchy subject of Decca's childhood came up. Sydney knew Decca felt strongly about not being allowed to go to school and university because many of her letters over the years had contained short, barbed comments such as 'because you never let me go to school' or 'because I was never allowed to go to college'. Suddenly, the accumulated resentment, bottled up for years, burst forth, and with hot tears of rage streaming down her face Decca verbally lashed out at her mother for failing to educate her.[55] Although it was an unpleasant experience for Sydney, it was cathartic for Decca.

The chief purpose of the visit had been to re-establish family ties. 'I remember watching them,' Dinky said, 'my mother and my grandmother trying to negotiate some sort of relationship.'[56] And certainly Sydney's visit helped Decca to get her feelings for her family, or at least her mother, into perspective. She found that Sydney was not as she had remembered or anticipated: she did not mind the untidiness of the house, or her bedroom, which had no cupboards. 'It was really a sort of downstairs study, disused room, and she had to put her clothes on the piano which rather amused her . . .'[57] She was not standoffish or vague; rather, she was friendly and grandmotherly to the children, teaching Dinky to knit, and endlessly amused by Nicholas who answered, 'Okay,' to everything. 'My little Okay,' Sydney called him. And Sydney's childlike delight in the convenience of supermarket trolleys (which through a misunderstanding she called panniers, and wrote to *The Times* to recommend), and her genuine enjoyment in meeting the Treuhafts' circle of Communist friends, who were enchanted by her, touched Decca. When asked where she wanted to be taken it was not notable sights, such as the Golden Gate, that Sydney wanted to see but 'a supermarket, a women's club and a funeral parlour'. The first was understandable, for England was still in the throes of food rationing, and Sydney explained that her desire to see a funeral parlour was the result of reading Evelyn Waugh's *The Loved One*. By the time she flew back to England via New York, where she stayed overnight with Aranka, Decca had come at last to appreciate the more

remarkable qualities of her mother and to conclude, to her surprise, that 'I really rather adored her.'[58]

Decca's pregnancy and Benjamin's birth had made it necessary
for her to leave her job and stay at home for some months. This
proved convenient while Sydney was visiting, but in the longer
term her domestic ineptitude, she claimed, caused Bob to beg
her to go back to work so they could employ a cleaner-cum-
babysitter. The result was that Decca became involved in the
Civil Rights Campaign (CRC), a legal-defence arm of the
American Communist Party formed in 1945 with the aim of
establishing civil rights and civil liberties for blacks. With the end
of the war black workers from munitions factories and the armed
forces found themselves unable to get work, or when they did
found that they were paid lower rates than white workers. Long
before it became fashionable or politically correct Decca had
identified the implications of statistics and studies of racialism,
and was active in breaking through racial barriers. She met and
came to know black people, was accepted into their homes and
even went into their churches. It was the terrible unfairness that
spurred her to oppose the injustices. Soon she became secretary
of the East Bay CRC, and these activities, together with her
membership and former executive post in the Communist Party,
made her a prime target for the McCarthy witch-hunts, which
were just beginning to gather pace.

For Nancy, too, there were gathering problems. In 1947,
Palewski's fears over his connection to *The Pursuit of Love* had
been substantiated.

A heavy blow has fallen [she wrote to Diana], which I
must say I've been expecting for some time – a hateful
weekly paper here has come out with an enormous
headline 'Hitler's mistress's sister dedicates book to
Palewski'. I haven't seen it & the Col won't let me because
it is apparently too revolting – but he is in a great-to-do

about it and really I think I shall have to go away from here for a bit. You see he is such an ambitious man & you know how the one thing that can't be forgiven is getting in their way politically. Of course it was madness, the dedication, and what I can't tease him with now is that it was entirely his own doing . . . he insisted on having his entire name . . .[59]

There is a mystery here. The left-wing paper to which Nancy referred had indeed planned to run the story but a strike by printers prevented publication for three months and the piece never appeared. Surely Nancy must have known about the strike. But if she believed what the Colonel told her, it implies that he lied to her. 'It is bizarre,' Diana wrote recently, 'Colonel *invented* it, and why didn't she ask to see the article?'[60]

One can only assume that Palewski wanted Nancy out of the way for, whatever lay behind the matter, Nancy went to England for a few months, apparently at his request. Her letters show that she missed him, but she was kept busy as she was now in great demand, working on film scripts, writing articles and seeing family and friends.

18

TRUTH AND
CONSEQUENCES
(1948–55)

In early May 1948 Sydney arrived back in London. Unity had been staying with friends while her mother was in America, and it was arranged that on her return they would both go immediately to Inch Kenneth for the spring and summer months. David was now living permanently at Redesdale Cottage in Northumberland, where his mother had spent her final years.

The two women had only just arrived on the island when they heard from a distressed Debo that Kick Kennedy Hartington had been killed in an air crash in France. After her husband's death Kick had settled in England, and had made a new life for herself. A few people, including her brother Jack, who had spent some time in England, knew that she had fallen in love again during 1947, and they were happy for her, although once again there were difficulties; the man she chose, war hero Peter Fitzwilliam, was married. His wife was an alcoholic and the marriage was unhappy, but lawyers advised him that divorce was out of the question.

On 13 May 1948 the couple chartered a twin-engine De Havilland Dove to fly to Cannes for the weekend. In the Rhône Valley they flew into a storm and were advised to turn back.

Fitzwilliam decided to continue and the plane crashed into a mountain near the town of Privas.[1] There were no survivors. Kick had quarrelled with her mother again, for she was determined to marry Fitzwilliam if he could divorce his wife. At their last meeting Rose Kennedy told her that if she did so the family would disown her. The matriarch's reaction when she heard of her daughter's death was 'That airplane crash was God pointing his finger at Kick and saying no!' The Devonshires organized Kick's funeral and buried her at Chatsworth. The Duchess chose her epitaph: 'Joy she gave/Joy she has found.'

Unity was a good deal improved physically by 1948. Indeed, it had now become a source of concern to Sydney that Unity might outlive her, for although Diana and Pam had both told her they would always look after their sister, Sydney doubted that they were prepared for the amount of personal care involved. Unity led a reasonably active life, visited her friends, went to the cinema and shopping in High Wycombe or London, and while at Inch Kenneth travelled to Mull or even the mainland for concerts and ceilidhs.* But she was still incontinent, and her temper was unreliable: she was liable to burst into fury at the slightest provocation. Her chief consolation was a restless pursuit of religious activities. In England she attended church services of all denominations; on the island she conducted her own services in the old ruined chapel. She enjoyed planning her own funeral, choosing the hymns that would be sung.

Three weeks after they arrived on the island Unity developed a feverish chill and was put to bed. There was no telephone but there was a crude signalling system. At Gribun the postmaster would hang a large black disc on Sydney's garage door to signal that mail or parcels were awaiting collection, and Sydney scanned for signals every day with her binoculars. There was a similar

---

*Gaelic: informal gathering for singing, dancing and story-telling.

device on the island to summon help in an emergency, but although the doctor was called, high winds and a rough sea prevented him from reaching Inch Kenneth for several days and during this time Unity's condition worsened. She complained of severe headaches and had attacks of vomiting. One morning she suddenly looked up and announced loudly, 'I am coming.'[2] Sydney said that her heart sank. When the doctor came across Unity was treated with Sulphathiazole and improved but her temperature stayed obstinately high. On the third day, the doctor noticed that the scar on Unity's right temple was bulging and tender; by this time Unity could not tolerate any disturbance, or answer questions.

Suspecting a cranial abscess or meningitis, the doctor called in a consultant, who diagnosed meningitis, and Unity was transferred from the island to the mainland. The journey was traumatic for Sydney and she could never bear to talk about it afterwards. They arrived at the West Highland Cottage Hospital in Oban at midnight on the evening of 27 May and Unity was treated with penicillin. Arrangements were made to move her to the neurosurgery unit at Killearn Hospital on the following morning, but before she could be loaded into the ambulance she had an epileptic fit. She remained unconscious until she died at ten o'clock that night.[3] It was concluded that she had died of pneumonococcal meningitis, caused by an infection in the site of the old head wound.

When Sydney left California she had asked Decca if she had any message for Unity, and Decca said, after some hesitation, 'Just give her my love.' The sisters were no longer in regular contact but in one of her last letters Unity wrote of how she had asked her father who he would best like to see coming through the door, and he had answered at once, 'Decca.' On hearing of Unity's death Decca wrote, 'Of course, I mourned for my Boud years ago when I first realized we couldn't be friends any more.' (Dinky, however, recalled that her mother had been 'heartbroken' when Unity died.[4]) Sydney replied that Unity had mourned Decca in exactly the same way. 'She knew you would probably never meet again, but her love for you was quite unchanged. She was always going back in her mind to when you were both young and m'Boud was a constant topic of conversation . . . when I gave her your love when I came back she knew it was with one part of you. I could see by her face. I think you both understood each other.'[5] Unity had been Sydney's life for eight years and her death so soon after Tom's was a cruel blow. Her only consolation, she wrote to a friend, was something Unity had said to her while she was ill: 'No one ever had such a happy young life as I did up to the war.'[6]

David came up to Oban from Northumberland, and he and Sydney accompanied the coffin on the long journey south, by train, to Swinbrook. Unity was buried on 1 June, close to the church, and with the hymns she had planned. Most of the family attended, including the Mosleys. Although there was sadness, most felt, as Decca did, that the old Unity had died on the morning war was declared. She was one of the first casualties of the war, they were wont to say, just as Tom had been one of the last. On the tombstone Sydney had ordered the epitaph, 'Say not the struggle naught availeth,' a line from the work of nineteenth-century poet Arthur Hugh Clough, and said to be Winston Churchill's favourite poem during the war years. At the funeral David and Mosley did not speak to each other, but a few weeks later Diana received a touching letter from her father, apologizing for this, and saying that it had been inadvertent on his part. It was a welcome hint at reconciliation.

The Mosleys had been living for some time in Crux Easton, a small country house near Newbury. Having found it, Diana – hungry for beauty after the bleak years in Holloway and the temporary lodging at the Shaven Crown – wasted no time in turning it into a comfortable home with her usual flair. She got the Wootton furniture out of storage, and employed a cook and a gardener. To supplement the war rations they bought a cow, which gave them butter, milk and cream, and they had fresh vegetables and fruit from the eight-acre garden. 'I had the joy of the children,' Diana wrote, 'and of seeing Mosley get better day by day.' Although they remained under house arrest until the end of the war in August 1945, with fresh air, good food and a sort of freedom, the immediate horrors of Holloway receded. They used bicycles to get around the countryside, and from the house they had wonderful views over Berkshire and Hampshire. Diana's two younger sons were seven and five now, and she taught them to read and write and do simple arithmetic.

Their education caused their parents considerable concern for no school could be found to take them. The name Mosley was like poison. It was John Betjeman who eventually found a prep school for them. 'You really are an *angel*,' Diana wrote to him, 'to have found a school which might accept Alexander and Max as pupils – or should I say a genius . . . Thank you so, so much for all the trouble you have taken. I was beginning to despair, as I had so many furious refusals. Isn't it odd in a way? If I had a school I should welcome reds, in the hope of converting them.'[7] Although the Mosleys could not travel until the end of the war they received visitors, and Tom had spent several periods with them while he was at Sandhurst before being shipped to Burma. 'I was so thankful,' Diana wrote, 'that we had him with us for his leaves that year . . . Muv came and Bobo who loved little Max.' The tradition of entertaining continued after the war: 'Randolph [Churchill] wanted to come and was indignant when we refused . . . Of course Gerald Berners came and stayed.'[8]

Unlike most people, Mosley foresaw that rationing of food and other necessities would continue long after the war ended. He decided that the only thing to do to mitigate this would be to farm. Although they loved Crux Easton, its eight acres were patently insufficient, so they bought the eleven-hundred-acre Crowood House estate, near Ramsbury in Wiltshire. It was beyond the seven-mile perimeter and they were forced to purchase the property without having seen it, but fortunately, when Rule 18B was lifted and they moved there they found the eighteenth-century manor house, built of grey stone, 'quite perfect'. The uprising against the Mosleys, prophesied by Clementine Churchill, never occurred. They were ostracized by some elements of local society but they also met with 'wonderful kindness' from others, 'mixed with curiosity no doubt,' Diana says.

This did not unduly worry Diana, for several old friends lived close enough for regular visiting. The Betjemans lived at Wantage, and Daisy Fellowes was in Donnington. Diana's old friend Lord Berners, who had visited her in Holloway, lived near by in his amazing house, Faringdon. Nancy described it in *The Pursuit of Love* as Merlinford, home of Lord Merlin. Betjeman also described life at Faringdon: 'on a sunny summer evening. The bells of Faringdon church tower are playing "Now the day is over" across the grass terraces. Pigeons dyed blue are still strutting about in front of the limestone façade . . . All day long from early in the morning, Lord Berners will have been at work either composing on the piano in the dining room – a piano with a huge gilt fish perched upon it – or he will have been writing in the drawing room where [are] . . . the early Corots, the Matisse seascape, the Constable paintings, the Dufy of the races. A third thing . . . would have been painting the lake from his terrace or . . . the willowy flat valley of the Upper Thames with the Cotswold Hills rising blue in the distance.'[9] This was the Mosleys' calling circle, and with this, and occasional visits by Diana's family and Cimmie's grown-up children, Vivienne and Nicholas, Diana was content. The prep school Betjeman found was not a success: Alexander hated it and lasted less than a term. Thereafter, an old recluse who lived near by taught the boys, and later Diana employed a tutor to teach them at home.

As soon as he recovered his health and vigour, Mosley began to write. While they were living at Crowood he produced two books, *My Answer* and *The Alternative*. No publisher would touch them but this did not deter the Mosleys: they set up their own publishing house called Euphorion Books. There was some difficulty in obtaining paper, and printer after printer turned them down as soon as the name Mosley was mentioned, but these difficulties were overcome. The woman who had persuaded the Nazi hierarchy to give her a radio airwave was not to be put off easily by a few rural printers.

Eventually they produced a list, which included reprints of classic works as well as Mosley's books. One new book even became a bestseller: Hans-Ulrich Rudel's *Stuka Pilot*, with an introduction by English flying ace Douglas Bader. The profits from this one book underwrote the costs of Euphorion. *My Answer* set out to explain and defend Mosley's policies. 'As well as a future to be gained, there was a past to be justified . . .' his biographer wrote, 'a past which Mosley recognized now constituted a new and major barrier between him and the British people.'[10] *The Alternative*, however, was clearly intended to launch his postwar political career. He worked up to this slowly, careful not to give the government any excuse to rush in any new legislation to prevent him speaking in public. Of one thing Mosley was always convinced: the war meant the end of the British Empire; therefore, the future for Britain now lay in Europe. A United Europe, he said, must become a power to match that of the USA and the USSR. This was his vision, and the nature of his work after the war. He was a politician by instinct: all that had happened during the war had not changed this. His reading during the years in prison had been focused on a European union, and he had also learned German, fluently enough to be able, several years later, to deliver a speech in that language without once referring to his notes.

From November 1947 he began to address meetings of a new

movement, which he called the Union Movement, based mostly in the East End of London. He was always willing to speak whenever he could get a hall, but most remained closed to him. Now his battle cry was that if a union of European countries was linked to the rich resources of a developing Africa, the two continents could form 'a force which equalled any power in the world'.[11] In the following year he returned to active politics, campaigning for 'Europe a Nation'. Had he remained in conventional politics during the 1930s who is to say what might have been his destiny?

But in the pre-war years the general populace had come to revile his ideas. Though extant papers tend to confirm his claims that he was never personally anti-Semitic and that the Jews formed no part of his doctrine, he was – and probably always will be – branded with the label anti-Semite to the mass of British voters. Once the full horror of Nazi rule became common knowledge there was never any chance of Mosley's restitution as a serious political leader. Astonishingly, neither he nor Diana seemed to recognize the finality of this, or if they did, they chose to ignore it in the hope of winning through in the long term. He battled on for a while, speaking where he could (a core of faithful old BUF members always turned up to hear him), fighting against print unions who refused to produce posters for his meetings and newsletters. Plans to launch a newspaper had to be cancelled when he was refused a newsprint quota but he was constitutionally unable to admit defeat. Years later, in 1956, he addressed a series of public meetings – his first in five years: 600 turned up in Kensington, 1,500 in Manchester. 'After all these years', a *Daily Telegraph* reporter wrote, 'I thought some of the fizz might have gone out of him. Not a bit of it. Alone, he held a packed proletarian audience – only a few velvet collars – for 75 minutes, pulverising each party in turn.'[12]

No matter what Mosley faced, Diana remained steadfastly

loyal. She and the children spent the summer of 1947 at Inch Kenneth, and loved it, but like many of her friends following the war years what she really longed for was to travel in Europe again. She hankered after sunshine and the carefree ambience of the Mediterranean, but this was impossible because the government refused to grant the Mosleys passports. 'Not allowing free travel is one of the typical features of socialism everywhere,' she wrote with chagrin,[13] but Decca and Bob had precisely the same problem in the USA: their membership of the Communist Party made them ineligible for passports.

As usual Mosley found an answer. He discovered that under Magna Carta any British subject has the right to leave his country and return to it at will. No passport was required *in law*, though in practice the shipping lines and airlines prevented travel by refusing to sell tickets to anyone without one. His answer to the Foreign Office was to purchase a boat, a sixty-ton ketch called the *Alianora*, complete with skipper and crew. It was not a smart, gleaming yacht but a strong, sea-kindly, ocean-going working vessel. The Mosleys made no secret of their plans, and mentioned them to many people; on the day before their departure in the early summer of 1949, their passports suddenly arrived in the post. Diana believes that the Foreign Office did not wish to look foolish, but she is, understandably perhaps, jaundiced.

Unlike her mother, Diana was no sailor and she was seasick, but as they sailed south to Bordeaux, Corunna and Lisbon she was thrilled to be free at last of petty restrictions. Max and Alex went with them and they all celebrated Diana's thirty-ninth birthday in Lisbon. From there they sailed to Tangier and Formentor. Then the two boys returned to the UK, as they were to spend half of the summer with Sydney at Inch Kenneth while the Mosleys went on to cruise the ports of the Mediterranean and meet up with many old acquaintances from pre-war days. They visited Nancy who was staying with friends near Marseille, and at the end of the summer Debo came to join them in Antibes. On the last night of their holiday the trio dined in one of the old grand restaurants frequented by Mosley a decade earlier. He wrote,

> Debo . . . was now a married woman of some years standing, but she looked so young in her diaphanous summer clothing that no one would have believed it. Waiters observed me dining magnificently in the presence of Diana, then at the height of her extraordinary beauty, and of this lovely child, enchanting and seemingly enchanted for to their astonishment she finally pulled a wad of notes from her pocket and paid the immense bill. An old waiter whispered in my ear, *'C'est Monsieur qui a la chance.'*

They left the boat in France for the winter and Debo drove them back, 'along that road,' Mosley wrote, 'more golden in our eyes than the one to Samarkand, back to England and politics'.[14]

They stopped off at Nancy's Paris apartment and memories of her sunny courtyard with its pots of geraniums provided a sharp contrast to the grey austerity that gripped England that winter. The Mosleys spent one further summer aboard the *Alianora* visiting Venice and all their favourite places, and then she was sold, having well served her purpose. Mosley had begun to feel that in order to become a true European it was necessary to leave England. In 1951 Crowood was sold and the Mosleys moved to Ireland, where they bought the former palace of Irish bishops, Clonfert Palace in County Galway.

Pam and Derek Jackson were already living in Ireland. They had left Rignell in 1947, driven out of England, like so many rich people, by 98 per cent super-tax. Initially they rented Lismore Castle, the Devonshires' Irish seat, but eventually, through Ikey Bell, one of the most famous names in foxhunting history, they found a house of their own, Tullamaine Castle, near Fethard in County Tipperary. Their life revolved around horses: Derek indulged his passion for foxhunting and steeple-chasing. Pam rode every day, though the weakness in her leg, resulting from the polio, prevented her hunting, and ran the farm. At first the life suited them admirably but after the delights of tax freedom faded, and unlimited horsy society paled, Derek became fidgety. His first love had always been science and he missed being able to pop into the laboratory at Oxford to use the facilities there or argue a technical point with Professor Lindemann, now Lord Cherwell. He was invited to Ohio State University as a visiting professor,[15] and began to spend several days a week in Dublin, where he had access to several laboratories at Dublin University and Dunsink Observatory. Pam did not object to his absences, but while he was working in Dublin he met and fell in love with Janetta Kee, a young divorcée. Pam gave Derek the divorce he requested, and remained at Tullamaine for a short time. Then she sold it and went to live near Zurich amid picture-book scenery. She used her house there as a base for the frequent travelling she enjoyed. Later she bought a cottage in Gloucestershire.

Derek married Janetta and they had a daughter, Rose, of whom he was immensely proud, but a child did not cement the marriage. After a few years the couple divorced and Derek married three times more. This flamboyant character, who was a major personality in the lives of the Mitfords, used his money to enjoy the lifestyle of a bygone age. He would stop trains by pulling the communication cord to complain about dirt in his carriage, would contemptuously toss a ten-pound note at Jockey Club stewards in payment of a fine for some riding misdemeanour, finished twice in the Grand National riding his own horses, and was a much-decorated war hero. His intellect was only just short of genius yet he would happily revise complicated travel plans to avoid 'hurting the feelings' of his beloved dachshunds. Pam's marriage to him lasted fourteen years, and was the only one of his six marriages – apart from the last, which ended with his death – to endure for more than a couple. Pam and Derek always remained great friends and saw each other frequently after he went to live in France, where he became a researcher at the Bellevue Laboratory near Paris.

Both Prod and Andrew Cavendish, who had become Marquess of Hartington at the death of his elder brother, had tried to get into Parliament after the war. Prod did not get further than the initial interview, which Nancy had forecast because, she said, married to a Mitford he hadn't a hope of being selected as a candidate. Nevertheless, she said, she 'egged him on' because candidates were given ninety extra petrol coupons. Andrew, however, following family tradition,[16] twice contested the constituency of Chesterfield in 1945 and 1950, both times unsuccessfully. A friend who canvassed for him was told by a voter, 'they like 'im, but they say booger 'is party'.[17]

In 1946, Andrew's father, the 10th Duke of Devonshire, made over the estate to him in an attempt to shelter the family's assets from the punitive new rate – up to 90 per cent – at which death duties were levied by the post-war Labour government. The assets were transferred into a discretionary trust, called the Chatsworth Settlement, the beneficiaries of which were Andrew and his family. As the inheritance laws stood Andrew's father had to live for five years after transferring the property to avoid paying duty,[18] and since the Duke was a healthy fifty-one-year-old, it seemed a pretty safe bet. Even so, he once told his son that every Sunday when he attended church he mentally ticked off another week of the five years. Meanwhile, there was a great deal for Andrew to learn. He had expected to have to earn his living after the war, and it was Billy who had received all the training appropriate to the duties of the head of the family.

A year later Debo, Andrew and their two children, Emma and Peregrine – called 'Stoker' by everyone, even today[19] – moved to the pretty village of Edensor (pronounced locally as 'Enzer'), which is part of the Chatsworth estate. Living at Edensor House, a fifteen-minute walk across the park, meant that they were able to get to know the great house and its land. But while the estate was in good heart, Chatsworth House was in a sorry condition.

The family had hardly lived in it for many years, and no decorating had been done at all since before the First World War. The plumbing was Victorian or worse, there were no modern bathrooms and hardly any hot-water supply. The 9th Duke and Duchess had preferred to live in other family properties. Andrew's father inherited in 1938, but he and his duchess lived at Chatsworth for only a few months that first winter. They held a lavish party there in August 1939 for Billy's coming-of-age, but a month later the house was turned over to Penrhos College for the duration of the war. The college's premises, safe in North Wales, had been requisitioned by the Ministry of Food and it was inevitable that Chatsworth would also be required for the war effort. The Duke wisely reasoned that three hundred girl boarders and teaching staff would do far less damage than a large number of servicemen so it became a boarding-school. The most valuable furniture and pictures were moved to the library, where Rembrandts, Van Dycks and Reynoldses were stacked against the bookshelves. The silk-covered and panelled walls were boarded over to protect them. When the school decamped in 1946 the great state rooms had taken on an institutionalized appearance after six years as dormitories, classrooms, dining hall, gymnasium and study rooms. The only staff employed to clean had been two housemaids left *in situ* by the family.

When Debo first saw it after the war she thought it 'sad, dark, cold and dirty. It wasn't like a house at all, but more like a barracks . . . careful tenants as Penrhos College and the girls were, the sheer number of them had made the house pretty shabby and worn when they left . . . It was very depressing.'[20] Her parents-in-law had lost heart after Billy's death but they organized the cleaning, the reinstatement of pictures and furnishings, and some redecoration, although the government limited the supply of paint to £150's worth. At Easter 1949 they reopened the house to the public. There was still a huge amount of work to do but this was planned to take place over years rather than months.

Like the Mosleys, Debo and Andrew travelled a lot in the post-war years, enjoying the South of France and Italy, which had none of the austerity of England. Debo often stayed with Prince Aly Khan at his fabulous villa Château l'Horizon where she met movie stars and other famous people, the food was delectable and every luxury supplied. Yet she enjoyed life at Edensor House too: she was and is a countrywoman, and was much at home there. She had suffered greatly from the loss of two babies, but 'Em and Sto' were plump, healthy and intelligent children and a joy to their aunts. To Diana, they helped to compensate for the years she had lost in seeing her own babies grow up. To Pam, called by Emma's generation Tante Femme, Emma and Stoker, Max and Alexander were the nearest she would come to having children of her own. Nancy, too, loved her nephews and nieces, recounting stories of them with unalloyed pleasure. When she visited them in September 1946, when Stoker was two and a half, she said to him, 'Can you talk?' He answered, 'Not yet.'[21]

On 26 November 1950, Andrew's father died suddenly of a heart-attack while chopping wood at Compton Place, his house near Eastbourne. He was fifty-five and had given every impression of being fit and healthy so it was a great shock to everyone. Andrew was in Australia studying farming methods and flew back immediately; Debo met him at London airport. The death of his beloved father was a stunning blow to Andrew in every possible way for he had lost in him a friend and mentor. Furthermore, the Duke had died fourteen weeks short of the vitally important five years. As a result death duties of 80 per cent were now due on all resources. It looked as though the estate would have to be broken up, and many of the treasures and works of art, collected by the family over four centuries, sold off to pay the horrendous bill. Andrew was now the 11th Duke, but it seemed that the title might be all that could be salvaged. From this moment Chatsworth became the centre of his and Debo's lives. It seemed unlikely that they could save it for their children and their descendants, but they were not prepared to give it up without a fight.

Meanwhile, Nancy was at work on a sequel to *The Pursuit of Love*. It did not 'write itself' this time and she struggled with it for several years. *Love in a Cold Climate* was published in July 1949 and was even more successful than its predecessor. Although Sydney was proud of Nancy's success she was less happy about being cast again as Aunt Sadie. Too many people thought that Aunt Sadie *was* Lady Redesdale in real life, and Uncle Matthew Lord Redesdale.

Though riding the crest of a wave in her literary career, Nancy's personal life was less successful. The Colonel was often too busy to see her, occupied with his political career or engaged in one of his other love affairs. To be fair to him, he did little to encourage Nancy's dependence: he would never sleep at her apartment, though he was happy to lunch or dine there. She became an emotional beggar: 'Darling Colonel,' she wrote typically, 'I know one is not allowed to say it, but I love you'[22] or 'I wish I were sitting on your doorstep like a faithful dog waiting for you to wake up you darling Col . . . *Do* miss me.' She wrote scores of letters to him that are almost painful to read, in consideration of who and what she was. Although she pretended to treat his casual neglect as a joke, and made light of it in correspondence to family and friends, she was deeply wounded. But she had no option if she wanted their relationship to continue. She could not give him up and she hated to leave him even to take a holiday.

Once, in the Louvre, she saw him wandering around hand in hand with a former resistance heroine who had been in love with

him for some time.[23] The Colonel looked so 'fearfully happy'
that Nancy was knocked sideways, and convinced herself he had
proposed marriage. She rushed home and in agonies of jealous
misery considered taking an overdose. At last she rang Palewski
who was delighted to hear from her:

> absolutely angelic. I kept saying but you looked so *happy*
> [Nancy wrote to Diana] . . . 'No, no, I'm not happy,' he
> said, 'I'm very unhappy.' So dreadful to prefer the loved
> one to be unhappy – I ought to want him to marry, I
> know. He did say, 'but *you* are married, after all,' & I
> know he really longs to be, & I feel like a villainess to
> make all this fuss . . . the fact is I couldn't live through it if
> he married & what is so dreadful is I know I can stop
> him – or at least I think so – and that condemns him
> to . . . loneliness and no children. Perhaps I ought to leave
> Paris for good . . . I must say this has plunged me into a
> turmoil – oh the *horror* of love. *Later.* I've just been to see
> him and told him about the pills, which I see to have been
> a great mistake, he's simply delighted at the idea. 'Oh you
> must, you must, what a coup for me.'[24]

But it is clear that Nancy would never have left Paris. Her
apartment was the epitome of elegance; living there was one of
the great pleasures of her life and with her earnings she was able
to indulge her passion for designer clothes. Her svelte figure
suited the New Look admirably and she wallowed in the luxury
of Dior and Schiaparelli outfits with tight waists and long, full
skirts, so feminine after wartime fashion. Only occasionally
was she driven to complain to Palewski about her situation: 'I
said "I've given up everything – my family, my friends, my
country," & he simply roared with laughter, & then of course
so did I.'[25]

One of Nancy's biographers said that the tragedy of Nancy's

life was that she never came first with anyone. From the moment of Pam's birth she always had to share affection. To the four loves of her life, Hamish, Prod, André Roy and, most importantly, Gaston Palewski, she was not their great love. This was sad for her, as was the lack of children, but it does not mean her whole life was tragic: one only has to read her letters to see that.

When Peter Rodd finally asked for a divorce on the grounds that he was tired of being cuckolded, her first reaction was 'Good'. Although she did not underestimate the social implications of being a divorcee, she had tolerated his womanizing for years, and now that Prod had access to her bank account in England he plundered it. Perhaps if she was free to marry, the Colonel might oblige, despite his protestations that he must marry a rich, single Frenchwoman for career reasons. But divorce was a protracted process, and there were tax considerations, bearing in mind Nancy's earnings and her domicile in France. In the event it was another seven years before Nancy was free of Prod.

When Palewski was too busy to see her, Nancy was not lonely – far from it. She had a host of friends and her work; she turned out books regularly. There were two further volumes in the style of *The Pursuit of Love* and *Love in a Cold Climate*, called *The Blessing* (1951) and *Don't Tell Alfred* (1960), in which Nancy's best female friend, Diana Cooper, was the basis for Lady Leonie, counter-heroine to the narrator, Fanny, who was modelled on Nancy's childhood friend Billa Harrod (née Creswell) – who was conveniently married to Cooper's replacement as ambassador to France. According to one visitor, 7 rue Monsieur was a cultural annexe of the British embassy, a congenial *salon* for the upper classes and literati of England and France. Nancy also became an eminent biographer, which she enjoyed even more than writing novels and which was just as financially rewarding. By the time the Duff

Coopers left the Paris embassy Nancy had a huge number of friends in the city. Eventually the Mosleys and Derek Jackson also went to live there, and Pam often called in as she passed through between her homes in Gloucestershire and Switzerland.

19

RETURN TO THE
OLD COUNTRY

1955–8

Looking back, the early fifties had been an extraordinary time for Decca. In 1950 she and Bob had intended to visit England but were denied passports owing to their membership of the Communist Party. There was some compensation: Debo visited them in Oakland, 'for a Honnish reunion', during which they entertained Bob with Honnish songs and stories, and Debo generally wowed the comrades who, to Decca's amazement, couldn't wait to meet a real live duchess, just as they had crowded in to meet Sydney. During the next half-decade the Treuhafts made several unsuccessful attempts to get passports. Decca 'longed' to go to England to see her mother and one or two others such as Nancy, Idden and Nanny Blor, and finally asked Sydney to appeal to Winston Churchill. 'Do see what you can do . . . it may be the only chance,' she wrote. 'But if you correspond with him, please send me a copy.'[1]

Sydney refused. 'I'm afraid there's nothing doing as regards asking favours, it would not be possible for me anyhow, and surely not for you either, as you are heart and soul against him.'[2]

Regrets were soon buried under a welter of work. For Decca, with the house and family to care for, there were hardly enough hours in the day as the CRC gathered strength. At first she was confined to the office, involved in mass mailings and the organization of protest meetings, but she became more personally involved with the case of a young black man, Willie McGee, who had been sentenced to death in Mississippi for raping a white woman. There was evidence that the plaintiff had been his willing mistress for several years and had accused him of rape only when he attempted to end their relationship. This, however, was not admissible in court and in McGee's home town no one dared speak out on his behalf for fear of retribution from the powerful Ku Klux Klan. No one, that is, except McGee's wife Rosalee, an uneducated twenty-eight-year-old, who left the town for the first time in her life and embarked on a nationwide speaking tour funded by the CRC. Her aim was to recruit sufficient national sympathy to persuade the Governor of Mississippi to commute the death sentence.

Decca met Rosalee in Oakland and was appalled when she heard how the family lived. Rosalee had already lost three close male relatives to white lynch mobs or a vicious justice. Decca talked three women comrades into joining her, and drove to Jackson, Mississippi, to take up the cause in person. She and her three-woman 'delegation' were unable to prevent McGee's execution, but Decca's self-confident aplomb – she thought nothing of telephoning the Governor at his home to discuss the McGee case – and the fact that she had ventured into the town during the row gave others the courage to speak out where before they had remained silent. When she organized a protest, other white women came from the northern states to join it. Hundreds of black people streamed in, too, in defiance of the Ku Klux Klan, to stand in silent protest. Decca's spark helped to light the fire that the fight for civil rights became during the next decade. During her time in Mississippi the McGee case was national news, and although most national newspapers presented the protests as a desperate ploy of Communists to further the cause of international Communism and foment racial strife, the case was groundbreaking in the history of civil rights in the USA.

In 1951 Decca was subpoenaed by the California State Committee on Un-American Activities. She had to present herself at a court hearing, bringing with her the membership records of the East Bay Civil Rights Congress. This caused consternation among her friends and comrades, for the records contained the names and addresses of anyone who had supported the organization, including most of the Communists in the Bay area. Bob could not help her: he was already in hiding to avoid being subpoenaed himself, and as their phones were tapped and she knew the FBI was watching her, she dared not contact him. Recently, numbers of people had been sent to prison and she was nervous. She contacted the CRC lawyer who insisted she must take the Fifth Amendment and refuse to answer, to avoid incriminating herself. 'What if one elected to testify about oneself, but refused to answer questions about others?' she asked. 'No good,' he replied. 'If you answer one single question, the committee will say you waived the privilege and insist you answer as to related facts, meaning the names of your colleagues and other details.'[3] So Decca learned her single statement: 'I refuse to answer on the ground that my answer might tend to incriminate me.' She took Dinky with her to the court, having obtained permission from the headmistress to absent her from school that day in case her classmates teased her.

The scenes in the court are familiar to us now from old newsreels of grim-faced bullying inquisitors such as Joseph McCarthy demanding loudly of Hollywood notables, 'Are you now or have you ever been a member of the Communist Party?' Decca was not called to the stand until after the lunchtime recess. All morning she had watched others undergo the trauma of examination, saw how some had fought back, causing uproar, how others had wilted under pressure, and how some had stuck to the Fifth Amendment and refused to answer anything, just as she had been told to do. She took the stand clutching her membership-records file and after she had taken the oath the questions she had rehearsed were asked: 'Are you now or have you ever been . . .? Have you ever heard of or read the *People's World*? Have you been a director of the East Bay Civil Rights Congress since May 1950? Do you maintain a bank account for the Civil Rights Congress? Is your husband, Robert Treuhaft, legal counsel for the Civil Rights Congress?' To each question she responded with the memorized incantation.[4]

But she began to grow irritated. She wanted to retaliate to the bullying, to play to her friends in the gallery and make them laugh, but she clenched her teeth and replied as rehearsed. Suddenly a curious question was asked: 'Are you a member of the Berkeley Tenants Club?' She was puzzled for a moment, never having heard of it and thinking it must have some connection with bad landlords. Then she began her answer: 'I refuse to answer that question on the grounds . . .' To her confusion the courtroom erupted in a roar of laughter. The question had been 'Do you belong to the Berkeley *Tennis* Club?' and was an attempt at heavy sarcasm by the prosecutor, goaded by Decca's plummy voice and the fact that the club was a bastion of conservatism. In the uproar the chairman rapped his gavel for order and dismissed Decca as being 'totally uncooperative'. As she stepped down from the stand her lawyer grabbed her arm and hissed at her to get out fast and go into hiding. 'Don't go home . . . or to any house that might be under surveillance.' The court had been so confused by the noise and laughter that the chairman had forgotten to ask for the CRC records.

Decca cast an agonized glance at Dinky in the gallery, and bolted for her car having insisted that the lawyer saw Dinky home. She hardly had a chance to get clear of the building before the mistake was realized and she was recalled. By then she was in her car driving blindly away from the courthouse, hoping she was not followed. She hid with friends for a few days as Bob was doing, until they knew that the hearings were over, then Decca telephoned Dinky, who was looking after Nicholas and Benjamin. 'Thank goodness,' the redoubtable Dinky said, when Decca announced that she was coming right home. 'I've been doing all the cooking and we're sick of scrambled eggs.'[5]

The next few years were spent subpoena-dodging, going into hiding whenever a friend was served with one. As their phone was tapped and they were under surveillance by the FBI,[6] Bob and Decca were careful never to mention the name of a friend or comrade unless they were in an open space and knew they could not be overheard. Bob appeared once before the commission and scourged them with clever oratory that made the evening papers. On another occasion he was so angry with the Attorney General over some unfairness that he kicked down the door of the District Attorney's office. One of his partners overheard a policeman at the courthouse say to another, 'Do you think Treuhaft really wants to overthrow the government?' 'Well, no,' was the reply. 'But I think he wants to get someone else to do it.'[7] The newspaper reports of these incidents, sent home to Sydney by Decca, were stuck into a great album, alongside the Redesdales' invitation to Westminster Abbey for the Coronation of George VI, and Sydney's authorization to visit Diana in Holloway.

Decca went on with her work, and wrote regularly to Sydney: news of the progress of 'Dinky, Nicky and Benj' was interspersed with details of her trips around the country on CRC business. She sounded fulfilled and happy, if occasionally downcast by what she regarded as pettiness and the inevitable 'persecution' by investigators for the Un-American Activities Committee. The Treuhafts had moved to 61st Street in Oakland, a larger house, which they liked very much. 'We'll probably stay here for ever,' Decca wrote happily to Sydney. There was still no news of their passports, and it seemed that the children would be fully grown by the time Sydney saw them again. Then suddenly, with no warning, this busy, happy life was shattered.

All three children did extra jobs to earn pocket money so that they could buy things they wanted and pay for Christmas and birthday presents. They did chores like ironing Bob's shirts, or taking out the trash. Ten-year-old Nicholas had a paper round, delivering the *Oakland Tribune*, after school. On the afternoon of Thursday, 15 February 1955, while riding his bicycle home, he was hit by a bus and killed. Dinky had been on her way to look for him as he was late for supper, and heard the sound of the crash. She ran to the corner of the road to see what had happened and was with her dying brother within seconds. He was probably dead before the ambulance arrived. By then a small shocked and hushed crowd had gathered at the scene. One neighbour voiced her opinion that if Mrs Treuhaft spent more time at home this wouldn't have happened. Dinky flew at the woman in a blind fury and had to be pulled off.[8]

Friends rallied round the family but the hurt was too deep for comfort. In the evening, when Decca and Bob returned from the hospital, Dinky remembers wandering around the house with Decca alone in one room and Bob in another, all unable to share their grief. They buried Nicholas in Guerneville, the town where Bob and Decca had been married, and from then on Decca, in the only way she knew how to cope, bottled up her feelings. By tacit agreement Bob, Dinky and Benjamin followed her lead and Nicholas was airbrushed out of their lives, but never their thoughts. Dinky always kept a photo of him on her dressing-table, but shut it away in a drawer when Decca came in. Benjamin lost the person who had been perhaps closest to him. Those who knew them at that time recall the two little boys endlessly play-wrestling on the floor of the living room, sparking each other off with funny remarks. After his brother's death Benjamin had problems at school, getting low grades and into scrapes. On one occasion, decades later, when Decca was lunching with Kay Graham, her old friend from Washington, Nicholas was mentioned. A few days later Decca wrote, 'Sorry I damn near blubbed . . . I should have supposed I had totally recovered, not to mention that we were brought up *never* to cry in front of other people . . . so forgive the unaccustomed lapse.'[9]

Sydney, desperately upset about 'my little Okay', as she called him, and knowing what it meant to lose a son, wrote inadequately to Decca, 'Your letter came. You are very brave, but I always knew you were that . . .'[10] Debo was the only other member of Decca's family who had met Nicholas, but she was on holiday in Brazil when he died and Sydney decided not to tell her until she returned. For Decca Nicholas's death, she once said, was the last of the four big losses in her life: Julia, Esmond and Unity were the others.

The aftermath of Nicholas' death was a grim time for the Treuhafts. Bob felt helpless to comfort Decca and, in any case, she was unable to accept any form of sympathy. Because she had been in charge on the day of the accident, Dinky inevitably felt responsible for what had happened: she had been almost a surrogate mother as well as elder sister to Nicholas, and suffered greatly because she could not talk to either parent. Also there was a shift in her relationship with Benjamin, for Nicholas had been the connecting link between them. Dinky felt that the death of her brother distanced them all in a way and life was never quite the same again.[11] At the age of sixteen she developed a gastric ulcer, more usually associated with middle-age executive stress than the carefree life of an American teenager.

Twelve weeks later, to their immense surprise, the passports for which the Treuhafts had applied with dreary regularity over the previous five years arrived in the post. Decca lost no time in arranging a trip to England for her, Bob and Dinky. She felt Benjamin was too young to appreciate the trip, so he was to stay with his grandmother Aranka, in New York. She was horrified to discover the cost of the journey but there was still some money in her old running-away account at Drummonds bank that they could draw upon while they were in London. They had tried unsuccessfully to have this transferred to them shortly after Sydney's visit, and at Decca's request Sydney had arranged a meeting with the manager, to see if there was some way round the currency restrictions, as they were desperately short of money. 'Now let me see, your ladyship,' said the accommodating manager, 'we are unable to send the money to the United States, unless there is some strong mitigating reason such as that the money is needed for school fees, or to pay hospital bills and so forth. What is the money required for?' He could hardly have given a stronger hint. 'Oh I think she wants to give it to the Communist Party,' Sydney answered truthfully.[12] Whereupon the manager assumed a stern expression and refused the application. It had annoyed Decca at the time – as well as spawning a dozen after-dinner stories – but now the money would prove useful.

The travelling party was to include Nebby Lou, the daughter of friends. 'They were black intelligentsia with connections in New York,' Bob recalled. 'They were desperate about Nebby, she was at Berkeley High and had no interest in politics. She seemed unaware that there were any racial differences and was friends with, and stayed with, mainly white girls, shopped with them for cashmere sweaters and so on, all that high-school scene.' They asked Bob and Decca if they would take Nebby with them to broaden her horizons, and the trip was the start of a long friendship between her and Dinky. The Treuhafts planned to spend several months touring the UK and Europe, but their first call would be at Inch Kenneth, to visit Sydney. Decca wanted to show the others the high points of the English Season, such as Ascot, Henley and Lords, 'But where are they?' she asked Sydney. She had forgotten. 'Also I long to show them the Widow [Violet Hammersley]. I had a very nice letter from her not long ago, all about plans for her death bed. Perhaps she could arrange to have it while we're there? . . . About Farve, I quite agree we should see him, only he will have to agree to be nice to Bob, Dinky and Nebby Lou and not to roar at them. Does he still?'[13] Sydney had been delighted that Decca would have this holiday to take her mind off the tragedy of Nicholas, but her relationship with David was just as important. She would never brook what she considered to be impertinence about him. Nebby Lou was very welcome, she replied firmly, but since Decca had chosen to lay down conditions about visiting her father, it was better that she didn't see him after all.

David was still living at Redesdale Cottage. Nancy, Pam, Diana and Debo visited him at least once each year, Debo more often than the other three who were living on the Continent. Once when Diana visited him, he asked if she would like the fire lit. When she said she would he took out his keys, opened the safe and took out a firelighter. 'Nothing else was kept in the safe,' she said, recalling that he had done the same thing at Asthall to prevent the children taking firelighters to make the damp logs burn on the schoolroom fire. 'It was a relic of the old days. At Redesdale Cottage there were no children to take his firelighters but the idea they might was ingrained. Farve's safe would have been a grave disappointment to burglars.'[14] David and Sydney still met occasionally at Rutland Gate, during his increasingly rare visits to London, and she sometimes went to visit him in Northumberland. Like Sydney he was never sure whether to be flattered or annoyed by his portrayal in Nancy's novels. 'It shows how savage I must have been,' he wrote to Sydney once, 'but without knowing it.'[15]

After a succession of jolly send-off parties from their friends, Decca, Benjamin and Nebby Lou set off by train for New York where they were to spend a week with Aranka. Dinky was already there and Bob was to fly to New York just before the ship departed. Dinky met them at Grand Central Station with terrible news. A cable had arrived, demanding that the passports be returned. They had apparently been granted by mistake and representatives of the State Department had been to the house at Oakland, to Bob's offices and Aranka's house, looking for Bob and Decca. By now skilled at evading officialdom, Bob had eluded them and was on a flight to New York, due to arrive at any minute. They drove straight to the airport and met him. During the flight he had made alternative plans. They would hide at his sister's house overnight. He had discovered that a ship was sailing for Europe on the following day, the SS *Liberté*. If they went straight to the agent they could try to get on that, pretending, if they were stopped, that they had not received the cable.

They spent an anxious hour at the travel agent's. The ship was fully booked but there was a last-minute cancellation in cabin class. They decided to take it. Then they found that the price of their original tourist-class tickets was not refundable unless the agency could sell on the tickets to someone else. Decca saw her trip disappearing, but Aranka came to the rescue and offered to pay for the cabin, then whisked Benjy away before Decca had a chance to say a proper goodbye to him. Next morning there were heart-stopping moments at Customs and during the boarding process; at every moment they expected to be recognized and stopped. They did not dare to go to their cabin but mingled on deck among the other passengers until the ship steamed out and they knew they were clear. After that they enjoyed five days of peace and unaccustomed luxury on the voyage to Southampton.

Bob spent his time reading a series of humorous books on how to survive in a Society environment, *Lifemanship*, *Gamesmanship* and *One-Upmanship*. When Decca asked what he was reading he showed her and told her he was going to practise on her family. 'Decca exploded with laughter. She knew what a dim chance I'd have; they wrote the rules,' he said.[16]

Debo met them in London with ten-year-old Emma and eight-year-old Stoker, and they travelled up to Inch Kenneth together. It took only slightly longer to get to the island, Debo told them, than it had taken her to fly to Rio de Janeiro. Sydney was waiting on the dock as the Oban ferry arrived. 'It was one of the happiest moments of my life,' Sydney wrote later.[17] She and her boatman had brought two cars to drive them across Mull to Gribun, where the launch was waiting for them. 'The drive was a bit terrifying,' Decca wrote. 'We went with Muv in her 1930 Morris, she has bad palsy but drives like a New York cab driver, honking like mad at anything and everything in sight.' At one point on the single-track road she made a truck driver reverse for over a mile so that they could pass. While they were being rowed over to the island Sydney said to Decca, 'You and Bob are to sleep in the tent.' They were aghast, but found later that it was a tented four-poster in a comfortable room. Decca had long been concerned that her mother was living on a bleak island, and had pictured her scraping a lonely living. She was quickly disabused of this idea, as she wrote to friends in California: 'Muv's lonely barren life here is relieved, we find, by six servants (a cook, a housemaid, a boatman and three others to take care of the sheep, cattle and goats). The house is large and comfortable (10 bed-rooms and four *modern* bathrooms).' As usual Sydney had furnished the house simply but with tremendous style, although Decca thought the French furniture out of place on the haunt-ingly beautiful island.

Sydney loved her island. To her it was the next-best thing to living at sea, and she was happy pottering with her farm, her ani-mals and her garden, helped by people she knew well and trusted. Although in her seventies she still swam most days in the icy Atlantic waters. 'I'm just going for a little *plonge*, dears,' she would say to guests, and off she would go to Chapel Beach for a health-giving dip. The guests shuddered at the thought.[18]

To Decca the whole thing, the trip, the sight of rolling green fields and pocket-sized gardens from the train windows, Cockney voices, seeing her mother and Debo again, all had a curious dreamlike quality about it. For the others it was merely the coming to life of the amusing and incredible stories that Bob had heard from Decca since they first met, and with which Dinky had grown up. When Sydney had visited California in 1948 she had been invited to give a talk to the children of Dinky's school and chose to talk about her life on the island. One of the children had asked about her neighbours. 'I don't have neighbours, only sheep and cows,' Sydney said. 'What do you do there?' 'Oh, we have the sheep to shear, and we make blankets from the wool . . . and we have the cows,' Sydney continued. 'They give us milk . . . and they go to market in Oban.' 'How do they get there?' 'They swim across. I just take them down to the water and say, "There you are – *in* you go!"' The children had been captivated: it was like a fairy-tale, but here were those *same* cows, and here was the sea they swam across to go to market, and the bull – tethered to the back of the *Puffin* – swam across to the island each spring to service the cows. At dinner there were no napkins – the penny-pinching peeress still saved money on those – yet she sent all the other linen to Harrods by train in a huge laundry hamper, just as she ordered her groceries from Harrods' food hall and sent dirty banknotes to Harrods' bank to be exchanged for nice crisp new ones. She even had her library books sent from London. It was all *true*.

The island was said to be haunted, but for Decca on that first trip the ghosts were childhood memories: everywhere she turned there were reminders of Swinbrook and Asthall, from the high-backed Jacobean chairs that used to inhabit the closing room, to the six drawings of the sisters by William Acton all in a line in their red brocade frames, from the old records to which they used to sing and dance, 'Isn't It Romantic', 'Dancing Cheek To Cheek' and Unity's '*Horst Wessel Lied*', to the great photograph albums kept religiously by Sydney where those early family groups full of hopes and dreams smiled or glowered at the camera according to whichever phase they were going through. She would never again see Tom and Unity, but she hoped to see Nancy and Pam during her trip. She had made up her mind, however, not to see Diana. She wrote,

> I could not have borne [it]. When I was a small child she, seven years older, was my favourite person in the whole world. She was in all ways marvellous to me; she took me riding . . . taught me to speak French, encouraged me in the forbidden sport of 'showing off' in front of grown up visitors, was my staunch protectress against the barbs of Nancy, my ally in fights with Boud. I could see her in my mind's eye, a radiant beauty of seventeen shrieking at my jokes. Teaching me, helping me through childhood, in general being the best of all possible elder sisters . . .

It might have been possible for her to meet Diana again, she thought, 'if I hadn't once, long ago, adored her so intensely. To meet her as an historical curiosity on a casual acquaintance level would be incredibly awkward, on a basis of sisterly fondness, unthinkable. Too much bitterness had set in, at least on my part.'[19]

From Inch Kenneth they all went down to stay with Debo and Andrew at Edensor House. Naturally they wanted to see Chatsworth, where an army of painters, plumbers and decorators had taken over prior to the proposed move there of Andrew and Debo, now the Duke and Duchess of Devonshire. 'Chatsworth is only slightly larger and grander than Versailles,' Decca wrote to her friends in California, '[with] 178 rooms and no baths. Because of the Death Duties the poor dears cannot afford to live in Chatsworth, so they live in "the lodge" (which they own) in the village (which they own) and they make do by opening the house to trippers . . . This year they had 250,000 trippers at 2 shillings and sixpence a head.'[20]

Joking apart, the death-duties question still exercised Andrew's mind. He plotted and planned and worked for years to resolve the conundrum of how to pay the tax bill while keeping the house and at least part of the estate in the family. Speculation, both at national and local level, about the future of Chatsworth had acted as a spur. There was talk in the newspapers that it should become a branch of the National Gallery. So many old estates and so much family wealth were affected by the new taxes; fine old houses were left to moulder into ruins because institutions had neither the knowledge nor the resources to care for them. It took decades for the public to recognize that in keeping these magnificent buildings intact, functioning properly as the living heart of a country estate, for the public to view, the old families were almost performing a public service. When families were turfed out – one newly inherited duke was reduced to living in a terraced house on the south coast – the best that could happen to a great house would be for the cash-impoverished National Trust to take it on, when so often it became a sterile museum[21] with many of the treasures sold off to pay the Treasury and fund maintenance, or it would be sold, converted into apartments and lost for ever to the public.

As part of Andrew's plan, sales of Cavendish land began immediately after the death of his father. The 12,000-acre estate in Dumfriesshire went first, followed by 42,000 acres in Derbyshire, woodlands and property in Sussex, and a house in London. All were all handed over willingly to save Chatsworth. The nine most valuable paintings and art treasures, works by Rubens, Holbein, Rembrandt and Van Dyck among them, also went to pay off part of the crippling debt, then 141 precious books, 60 of which had been printed before 1500. Two years before Decca's visit Andrew offered the house where the Cavendish family's fortune had been founded, and Bess of Hardwick's beautiful Hardwick Hall ('The most beautiful house in the world,' said Debo) was tipped into the maw of the Inland Revenue. Painful though this was, the sacrifice of Hardwick secured Chatsworth –

and the family could no longer have supported two great estates anyway. As it was, money that should have been used for the upkeep and repair of Chatsworth, now regarded as a national treasure, had been lost for ever, and the Devonshires still faced an uphill battle. Not until 1974, twenty-four years after the death of Andrew's father, were all Revenue debts settled. In addition, Andrew had worked to change the public perception of houses and properties like Chatsworth. In the early days the county council had wanted to drive a major new road through the estate. Today the destruction of such beautiful parkland, always open free of charge to the public, would be termed vandalism, but Andrew had to work hard to prevent it in the post-war years.

For Bob, the sense that he had fallen down the White Rabbit's burrow in Alice's Wonderland was heightened at Chatsworth. It was not just the sheer size of the house, for, as he said, if he had been invited to the White House he would have known how to behave: at Chatsworth he wasn't even sure which century he was in. On looking through the visitors' book he noticed that many of the guests had signed with their surname – 'Salisbury', 'Antrim', 'Denham' and he did the same, then wondered why this caused such an outburst of merriment.* Even away from Chatsworth there were surprises. Both Decca and Bob were amazed at the freedom and openness in which the Communist Party operated in England, 'so accustomed had we become to the semi-outlaw status of Communists in America,' Decca wrote. When he tried to get a telephone number from the operator, Bob couldn't make sense of what he was being told and had to hand the phone to Decca. 'What is the matter?' she asked him. 'She's saying perfectly plainly that the number is Steeple Bumpstead 267.' 'That's what I thought she said,' Bob answered miserably,

---

*For the benefit of overseas readers, it is customary in the UK for peers to sign only their surname.

'but I thought she was pulling my leg.' At the mews he 'discovered swastikas and hammer-and-sickles cut in the windows with diamonds when we used to live here. We did roar,' Decca told Sydney.

From England Bob and Decca went to Vienna as a staging post for a proposed visit to Hungary. Bob's family had Hungarian roots; he had visited the country in 1937 and spoke a little of the language. But they had no luck in getting visas from the consulate in Vienna until Bob mentioned that Nebby Lou was the niece of Paul Robeson. Instantly, visas were produced and everywhere they went in Hungary they were welcomed by fellow Communists in the Peace Committee and treated as VIPs. Robeson was not Nebby Lou's uncle, simply a close friend of her parents, and she was rather put out at the deception, although as Decca pointed out to her, 'You've called him Uncle all your life.' The connection opened endless doors, and Nebby was loaded down with gifts – 'They even gave her an instrument that had once belonged to Bartók,' Bob recalled.

The VIP tours impressed Bob and Decca – here was the epitome of the triumphant success of socialism – in much the same way, it must be said, as Sydney and David were convinced about the success of Fascism when shown the prescribed sights of pre-war Germany by Hitler's adjutants. In both cases the visitors saw only what they were meant to see, showcase exhibits. Bob and Decca were thrilled with the neat collective farms, a workers' rest home, a new steel factory. Only two minor incidents bothered them, and they could not quite explain them or get them out of their minds. One day they were dining in a restaurant when their waiter asked them, in an urgent whisper, if they would post a letter to America for him. When they asked why he couldn't post it himself, he became flustered and looked over his shoulder. 'He was evidently in great distress,' Decca recalled. 'However, we regretfully decided we could not perform his mission. What if he were a spy, or an opponent of the Government?'

A similar thing happened when a teacher invited them to her house only to send them an urgent message at the last minute. '*Nicht kommen*, Magda, teacher,' it read. 'We had naturally assumed there was vestigial opposition to the Communist Government, yet these two encounters coming . . . within a few days of each other would seem to point to a greater disaffection than we had supposed existed.'[22] They asked one of their guides, who told them that since they had accepted the hospitality of the Peace Committee it would be better if they avoided such contacts. Decca wrote an article about the visit for the *People's Weekly* when she returned to California. Although the remainder of the article was published intact, the stories of the waiter and the teacher were edited out, 'for reasons of space'.[23] A year later, reading about the remorseless suppression of the Hungarian uprising by Russian tanks, Decca and Bob remembered the waiter and the teacher and fidgeted unhappily.

The grand finale of their European tour was a trip to Paris to visit Nancy after they had dropped off the two girls at a school for a few weeks. Decca had looked forward to this with tremendous enthusiasm. Nancy was her socialist sister, and they corresponded warmly and regularly. Nancy was not at home when they arrived in Paris, having had reservations at the last minute about Decca's politics. She had told a number of friends about Decca's impending visit, describing her to Raymond Mortimer as 'my Communist sister . . . Eton crop, pince-nez & men's trousers. She is in London with husband and child. Child has been told that Debo's money comes from selling slaves. Debo says, "Goodness, if we had any slaves we wouldn't *sell* them." I don't die for her as much as I pretend to when I write.'[24] 'Decca arrives with her children end of the month. I'm half delighted, half terrified,' she wrote to Evelyn Waugh. 'Seventeen years . . .'[25]

In the end she decided she was more terrified than delighted and flew to England to stay with Debo, thinking that Decca would be put off. In the event Decca had lost Nancy's phone number and the Treuhafts made their way straight to 7 rue Monsieur, the address to which Decca had been writing for years. She was a little surprised when the maid said that Nancy had gone to visit her sister '*la duchesse*'. Nevertheless, when they explained who they were, the maid let them in, made them welcome and lit the fire. Relaxed after helping themselves to Nancy's whisky, they telephoned her. It was sixteen years since the sisters had heard each other's voice, and Nancy made her excuses, chatting easily until she asked, 'But where are you staying?' and Decca said, 'We're in your flat.' Whereupon Nancy flew into a rage, accused them of running up a huge phone bill and slammed down the phone. Decca and Bob found this behaviour so 'utterly mad' that they laughed until tears ran down their faces. After a while Nancy phoned back, and they had a long conversation. When Decca put the phone down and asked Bob what he made of it he pointed out that Debo was paying for the second call.

A few days later Nancy returned to Paris 'in the sunniest of moods', and quietly pressed fifty pounds on Decca, which she said was to pay for books and furniture that she had taken from their flat after Decca and Esmond left for the USA. Decca remembered those books: tattered old left-wing volumes not worth five shillings. The fifty pounds, then, was an outright gift, given in such a way as not to cause embarrassment or give the impression that Nancy was dispensing charity. 'Nancy's extraordinary contradictory attitude to money,' Decca wrote, 'her excessive small meannesses alternating with bursts of lavish generosity, never ceased to baffle me.'[26] After Decca left, Nancy wrote to Evelyn Waugh that, after all, she had enjoyed the visit. 'Decca is . . . unchanged and so sweet. Also her Romilly daughter . . . is a beauty. I very much hope she'll send her here in a year or two to learn French & then I must find her a French husband (recipe for happiness).'[27]

Decca and Dinky stayed on for a few weeks after Bob and

Nebby Lou returned to the USA, to see Mrs Hammersley, who was living on the Isle of Wight, and Pam, who was about to return from Switzerland. Bob wrote to warn Decca that despite a fight on his part, he had been forced to surrender his passport in New York, and she could expect the same thing. Decca's letter to Bob reveals that her relationship with her family remained fragile: 'Woman was here to lunch (second sight . . . calling her Woman, since she's become a you-know-what-bian)[28] . . . After lunch we tried to teach her Scrabble but she never scored more than 4 on any one play and even Muv got a bit restive with her when she said, "What does I-C-Y spell?" after I'd put it down for a score of 35.'[29] She reported a terrific argument which had occurred when she happened to see on Sydney's engagement pad that she had invited the Mosleys to lunch in the following week. Decca had said that she and Dinky would not eat with 'murderers' and Sydney had been furious that Decca would refer to her 'own sister' as a murderer. All things considered it was time for Decca to return to California.

The passports were confiscated in New York as Bob had warned, but there was a warmer welcome when they arrived in California. Virtually all their friends turned up to meet the train, complete with a mock brass band of children's drums, trumpets and homemade banners, 'The sort of thing they put on here for returning prisoners of war or football teams,' Decca wrote to Sydney. All their friends and even Dinky were fascinated by Decca's voice. For years, although noticeably English, she had allowed her accent to become more relaxed, like that of an upper-class American dowager. 'After our trip,' Dinky recalled, 'her accent became very British. Benj and I could hardly believe our ears.'[30] The return to crisp Mitfordian English remained, despite teasing by the family.

There was an anticlimax to the excitement of homecoming: Decca learned that during her long absence the FBI had staged a huge anti-Communist sweep of the area, visiting the employers of party members and anyone associated with the CRC, asking pointed questions about the person concerned. In many cases the employer did not know that the employee was a Communist or a Communist sympathizer. There were no charges, FBI officers said, but they would appreciate hearing that the person had changed his or her job. These surprisingly Gestapo-like tactics worked. Even those employers who considered that a person's political affiliation was a private matter were intimidated. Small businessmen could not afford bad publicity, or to court the disfavour of either those in government departments or their customers who regarded Communism as a threat to the country. As a result many family breadwinners lost jobs and were forced to go underground or resign from the party.[31]

A few months later, in March 1956, the transcript of Khrushchev's secret speech to the 20th Congress of the Soviet Communist Party was published, detailing Stalin's horrendous crimes. Ten million people had been killed in the thirties because they opposed him, from peasant proprietors who objected to their land being 'collectivized' to members of the right-wing intelligentsia, old Bolsheviks and members of the old officer corps. Anyone who stood in his way had been mercilessly eliminated in the way that the Nazis had eliminated the Jews and other non-Aryans. The transcript 'sent shock waves' through the American Communist Party and there were resignations *en masse*, but Decca wrote,

> I did not share this anguish to any marked degree. I had never been as thoroughly convinced as most comrades had of Soviet infallibility. Terrible as the revelations were it seemed to me that the very fact that Khrushchev had seen fit to lay them out before the world signified that the Soviet leadership was set on a course of fundamental

change . . . At least that was my view at the time,
although, as it turned out, I was grievously mistaken.[32]

She regarded her membership of the party as a way of combating
Fascism in the West, not as an implied alliance to Russia.

Even the unfolding of the Hungarian situation did not persuade her to resign from the party, though there was always at the
back of her mind a niggling question mark over the waiter and
the teacher in Hungary. It was two years before the Treuhafts
decided to leave ('Bob was never as committed as Decca,' one
friend remembered), but eventually they did so, having concluded that the American Communist Party was no longer a
force for democracy, peace and socialism in the USA, and that
instead of fighting Fascism it had become a self-serving organization dominated by Russia and out of touch with working
people. Meanwhile the CRC was disbanded, perceived as an arm
of the Communist Party rather than an organization campaigning for civil rights, and Decca found herself out of a job. It
seemed that everything for which she had worked since she and
Esmond arrived in the USA eighteen years earlier was coming
apart. Nevertheless, in later years she stated on a television programme that the years of work for the Communist Party and
CRC were 'among the most rewarding of my life'.[33] And once,
when asked in an interview about her politics, Decca answered
wryly, 'sort of old left. Or maybe just left-over.'

For a while she worked in the classified section of the *San
Francisco Chronicle*, selling advertising space. As a new employee
her name was listed in the union's newspaper, and she was tickled when a fellow employee came round with a few extra copies
for her, saying, 'I know what a thrill it is to see your name in a
newspaper for the first time.' The job didn't last. The FBI found
out where she was working, contacted the *Chronicle* and Decca
found herself a housewife once again. Dinky and Benjamin were
at summer camps and from being frantically busy she now had

time to kill. To relieve boredom she began to sort through old papers, including bundles of Esmond's letters, and correspondence with Sydney going back to 1938. Over the next weeks she showed interesting or amusing extracts to one of her best girlfriends, Pele de Lappe, and to other old comrades, who like the Treuhafts had become 'Ex's' (ex-members of the Communist Party). It was at these friends' suggestion that Decca began to write a memoir of her childhood, including all the hilarious Mitfordian anecdotes she had related over the years, and the story of her relationship with Esmond.

She had already achieved a miniature literary success with a home-printed booklet called *Life-itself-manship*, a sideways look at membership of the Communist Party. She made up five hundred copies and it sold like hot cakes to the comrades. Demand was so great, Decca wrote to Sydney, that it looked as if she was going to have to mimeograph and staple another batch – 'Nancy is so lucky not to have to bother.' The memoir, untitled at that point, was a full-length book, and a different matter altogether. It took her two years to write, aided and abetted by a group of friends she called her 'Writing Committee'.[34] Working as a veritable team of editors, the committee read it, offered helpful suggestions and reminded her of stories she had half forgotten. Bob, of course, was editor in chief ('Chairman,' Decca said) though he recalled, 'I hardly saw the manuscript until it was finished.' The committee acted as editors and prompters only, the text was pure Decca and it was her apprenticeship as a writer. She sent the completed manuscript to six publishers but it was rejected. Disappointed, she put it away.

As compensation, in 1957 Decca learned that she had inherited a large sum ('it's between £8,000 and £10,000')[35] from the estate of Esmond's mother, but there were problems: it was eighteen months before probate was granted, and the English banks were unable to transfer the money to America because of the still-trenchant currency restrictions. Meanwhile Decca could not go to England because she had no passport so she appealed to the Bank of England on grounds of domestic need. 'Please don't bother to intercede for me,' she wrote to Sydney hastily, 'because I know you'll tell them I'm giving it to the Communist Party and I won't be able to get it . . .' Two years later, when a Supreme Court ruling restored their passports, Bob and Decca immediately set off to England, with Benjamin. Decca also took the manuscript, thinking it might get a better reception in England. If not, she thought, she would forget about writing as a potential career.

Nancy's career had been well established internationally since publication of her two Radlett novels, *The Pursuit of Love* and *Love in a Cold Climate*. Consequently, *Pigeon Pie*, which had attracted only limited sales when first published in 1940, became an 'overnight' success when republished in 1951: '*Pigeon Pie* has had better notices in America than any of my books, isn't it unaccountable,' she wrote to Sydney. 'When I *think* how poor I was when it came out, almost starving (literally . . .) I feel quite cross though it's nice at all times to have a little extra money.'[36]

Three years later she published her first biography, *Madame de Pompadour*, and the reviews again were good. 'Miss Mitford . . . admires money and birth and romantic love,' her friend Cyril Connolly wrote, '. . . good food, fine clothes, "telling jokes", courage and loyalty, and has no time for intellectual problems or the lingering horrors of life.'[37] The eminent historian A.J.P. Taylor wrote that everyone who had enjoyed *The Pursuit of Love* would be delighted that its characters had reappeared, 'this time in fancy dress. They now claim to be leading figures in French history. In reality they still belong to that wonderful never-never land of Miss Mitford's invention, which can be called Versailles, as easily as it used to be called Alconleigh. Certainly no historian could write a novel half as good as Miss Mitford's work of history.'[38] Another friend, Raymond Mortimer, described the book as 'extremely unorthodox . . . it reads as if an enchantingly clever woman were telling the story over the telephone'. Nancy did not know whether to feel complimented or not. 'I was rather taken aback,' she wrote to Evelyn Waugh. 'I had seen the book as Miss Mitford's sober and scholarly work . . . he obviously enjoyed it though he says the whole enterprise is questionable.'[39] The book was apparently banned in Ireland as being a potential threat to happy marriage. Nancy said she was prepared to edit it but on asking for a list of the offending material was advised that there was nothing in the text that had irritated the censors. 'Then why is it banned?' 'Well, it's the title,' she was told.

Perhaps even more responsible for Nancy's remarkable literary success was a small book that she produced almost as a joke. It was called *Noblesse Oblige – an enquiry into the identifiable characteristics of the English aristocracy*, and was a compilation of essays by various writers such as Evelyn Waugh and John Betjeman, taking an ironic look at fashionable mores and manners. Nancy edited the book and included an article she had previously published in *Encounter* on the aristocracy, which had appeared with an article on upper-class speech by Alan S.C. Ross.

Professor Ross was a sort of latter-day version of Eliza Doolittle's Professor Higgins, a learned if somewhat eccentric philologist working at Birmingham University. He was introduced to Nancy at a luncheon given by a mutual friend: her exaggerated drawl to him was what Eliza's Cockney was to Higgins; a prime subject for study. He told her that he had written an article on sociological linguistics for the Finnish magazine *Neuphilologische Mitteilungen*, in which he had quoted *The Pursuit of Love* as a source for indicators of upper-class speech. Nancy was captivated and having learned that it was written in English begged for a copy. It was entitled 'Linguistic Class Indicators in Present Day English', and she found its serious presentation killingly funny. 'It has sentences like, "The ideal U-address (U stands for upper class) is P.Q.R. where P is a place,

Q is a describer (manor, court, house etc) and R the name of the County, But today few gentlemen can maintain this standard and they often live in houses with non-U names such as Fairfields or El Nido,"' she wrote, chortling, to Heywood Hill. 'To me it seems a natural for the Xmas market illustrated by O[sbert] Lancaster and entitled "Are you U?"'

Her lively confidence in this proposal owed much to reaction to her article in *Encounter* (September 1955), which had sparked furious debate about the half-teasing theory that one could iden-tify true members of the upper classes by manners, words and expressions; those who used fish knives and poured milk into a cup before the tea (MIF = milk in first), and who referred to 'note-paper', 'mirror', settee', 'serviette' and 'toilet paper' betrayed their lower-class origins. Those properly taught by Nanny spoke of writing-paper, a looking-glass, a sofa, napkins and lavatory paper. There was a lot more nonsense in this vein and the great British public took it seriously. As a result, Nancy said, she had practically to rewrite *Pigeon Pie*, which was about to be repub-lished. It was, she explained to Evelyn Waugh, '*full* of mirrors, mantelpieces and handbags, etc. Don't tell my public or I'm done for.'[40] Waugh provided a piece for the book: 'An open letter to the Honble Mrs Peter Rodd (Nancy Mitford) on a very seri-ous subject.' John Betjeman wrote a poem called 'How to Get on in Society'.[41] Professor Ross rewrote his original article.

But even Nancy was surprised at the book's success. It was a worldwide smash hit and no one could quite work out why. Surely, with the new emphasis on socialism, she reasoned, few people were interested in the aristocracy and old-fashioned man-ners. But the correspondence columns of national newspapers, even the weightiest, were full of letters on the correct or incor-rectness of the word 'lounge' as opposed to 'sitting room', and the social implication of calling pudding 'a sweet'. Bookshops could not keep *Noblesse Oblige* on the shelves: 'U and non-U' was the buzz phrase of the day. Decca wrote in bewilderment to Sydney that the *New York Times* had reported that ten thousand copies had sold there in a week. 'What's that about?' she asked. In fact, Nancy's comments, never intended by her to be taken seriously, made her the arbiter of good manners for several generations. Professor Ross, however, resented her making fun of his serious academic thesis. Nancy found it all hilarious, and told the Colonel that her favourite joke was the new lyric to the old song: 'I'm dancing with tears in my eyes, 'Cos the girl in my arms isn't U'. Diana found the book rather distasteful and vulgar. Prod called it 'decaying tripe' in a letter to the editor of the *Daily Telegraph*. But, like it or not, *Noblesse Oblige* made Nancy a cult figure.

There was another biography in 1957, *Voltaire in Love*, followed by *Don't Tell Alfred*, a Society romp through the diplomatic *salons* of Paris with Fanny (the narrator of *Pursuit of Love* and *Love in a Cold Climate*) as the main character. Uncle Matthew is revived, Diana Cooper puts in an appearance as Lady Leone, and characters from *The Blessing* otherwise populate the pages. Friends loved it – and members of Nancy's inner circle were best placed to appreciate the in-jokes. For example, when Nancy wrote of Fanny's mother, always known as 'the Bolter', those in the know were particularly tickled: 'The bolter', based on the delightful and much-married Angela 'Trixie' Culme-Seymour, had appeared in the previous novels, but since then Trixie had eloped with the husband of her half-sister – who just happened to be Nancy's former brother-in-law, Derek Jackson. It was all *too delicious*. Between producing her own books Nancy had also done several translations, *The Princesse de Cleves* (1950) and *The Little Hut* (1951), for which she was also involved in writing the screenplay for the film. In 1954, after endless trouble trying to get a visa, she made a trip to Russia. Decca was putrid with jealousy – 'It's not *fair*,' she wailed in a letter to Sydney.

Except in her relationship with the Colonel, and her lack of children, Nancy had everything she had ever wanted. In 1955

Palewski was offered a ministerial post in Fauré's government, which meant that he had even less time for Nancy. She compensated by spending her summers in Venice with an Italian friend, a contessa who owned one of the old palazzos and could offer the sybaritic life Nancy loved. In the quiet early mornings she could do a few hours' work on her biography of Voltaire ('Not a life of Voltaire,' she wrote to a friend. 'Just a Kinsey report of his romps with Mme de Châtelet and her romps with Saint-Lambert and his romps with Mme de Boufflers and her romps with Panpan and his romps with Mme de Grafigny. I could go on for pages . . .').[42] At eleven o'clock she would board the Contessa's sleek motor launch bound for the Lido to swim, sunbathe and gossip with friends, then eat a late luncheon served by the Contessa's white-gloved footmen. In the afternoons there was time for a siesta with the windows thrown wide open to passing breezes. In the evenings there were dinner parties at palazzos, or in the cafés and restaurants around St Mark's Square where, dressed in couturier creations, she met old friends and members of the international set. It was an idyllic existence.

In the summer of 1957 she heard from the Colonel that he had been offered, with the influence of General de Gaulle, the post of ambassador in Rome. It was said to be the only personal favour that de Gaulle ever requested of the French government in his time out of office. At the time Paris was hot, and seemed a little small to Palewski, for he was involved in a passionate affair with a married woman who lived just round the corner from Nancy. From this date Nancy and he saw each other far less frequently, although she remained convinced that he could not manage without her and all would come right in the end.

When Debo gave birth to a healthy daughter, Sophia,[43] after a series of miscarriages, everyone was thrilled for her, but then, six months later, in the spring of 1958, David died at Redesdale Cottage. Diana had woken one morning with a strong presentiment that she must join Sydney and Debo, who were going up to Redesdale to visit David for his eightieth birthday, which was just a few days away. David and Sydney were in constant touch by letter and they all knew he had been unwell. 'I shall never forget the expression on Farve's face when Muv appeared at his bedside, and his smile of pure delight,' Diana wrote. 'All their differences forgotten, they seemed to have gone back twenty years to happy days before the tragedies. She sat with him for hours, Debo and I going in and out. After a couple of days Muv and Debo travelled on to Scotland and I returned to London . . . A few days later he died.'[44]

'My darling Little D,' Sydney wrote to Decca, 'Farve died peacefully two days ago . . . Diana and Debo and I had been up to see him on his 80th birthday and he died 3 days later, we did so wish we had stayed. He was pleased to see us, dear old boy, and we were able to have a little conversation, but he was terribly deaf. He was in bed, and obviously very weak . . .' But he had been quite like the old David and said such characteristic things that they were all kept laughing. The last thing David said to Sydney was 'Are you going to the Oban Hotel?' She replied that she was. 'Oh,' he said, 'remember me to the hall porter.' Sydney left for Inch Kenneth and had just arrived when the news of his death reached her. 'I turned right round and came back,' she wrote to Decca.[45]

He was cremated at Redesdale, and a funeral service took place at Swinbrook. Nancy wrote to Decca that they were both 'tear-jerkers', with all his old favourite hymns: 'Holy, Holy, Holy . . . I was in fountains each time. Then the ashes were done up in the sort of parcel he used to bring back from London, rich thick brown paper and incredibly neat knots. Woman and Aunt Iris took it down to Burford and it was buried at Swinbrook. Alas one's life.'[46] Diana mourned the Farve of long ago, the huge towering man with tempers like an inferno, humour that often made family mealtimes like a scene from a farce, and eccentricities such as chub-fuddling, which somehow made him more endearing in retrospect. Once, when she had been the subject of one of her father's rages, Tom had consoled her with the sage remark that Farve would mellow as he got older. He had been right, but Diana found that with hindsight she preferred the unmellowed version.

The last time Decca had seen David was when she had set off for Paris to elope with Esmond. She might easily have effected a reconciliation. David had written several times to her, brief kind letters on the birth of Benjamin and the death of Nicholas, and she might have gone to see him in Redesdale, but she took umbrage at Sydney's comment, 'Since you have imposed conditions it would be better not to see Farve . . .' When his will was read it was found that she had been cut out in a marked manner: he had never recovered from her attempt to hand over part of Inch Kenneth to 'the Bolshies' and was fearful that anything he left her would be given away. In every clause where he left assets to be shared between 'my surviving children', he had added the words 'except Jessica'.

20

A COLD WIND TO
THE HEART

(1958–66)

The Mosleys lived at the graceful old Bishop's Palace at Clonfert in Ireland for only two and a half years. During that time Diana spent a good deal of her energy turning it into the lovely home in which she expected they would spend the rest of their lives. It stood on the edge of a bog and was approached by a long avenue of ancient yews called the Nun's Walk. For twelve-year-old Max, who loved foxhunting, it was a kind of heaven. Hounds met within reach of Clonfert several times a week and he would go off alone on his useful little pony, Johnny, who loved hunting as much as Max did, and could jump walls higher than himself. On frosty days, when Max followed hounds on foot, Johnny would stand in his stable and squeal with rage at being left when he could hear hounds hunting in the bog near by. In the first winter there Max was let off school for the entire season by his father, so that he could concentrate on hunting. After that he had to knuckle down and went off to school in Germany. 'We thought, as Europeans, our sons should know at least two languages,' Diana wrote. 'Alexander went to school in France and Max in Germany, but both were expelled. After that Max went to a crammer and then to Christ Church, Oxford, where he read physics. Christ Church said it would take Alexander just on his A level results but he utterly refused to go and went instead to Ohio State University where he read philosophy. Their languages have been very useful to them.'[1]

Just before Christmas in 1954, Mosley and Alexander were alone in the house while Diana was in London. During the night a chimney fire set the house alight. The horses whinnying in the stables raised the alarm, but there was no telephone and a member of staff was sent by car to fetch the fire brigade. In saving the life of the cook, who had been safely evacuated but returned to an upper room to rescue her savings, Mosley and Alexander had no time to control the blaze, which, by the time the fire brigade arrived, had taken hold. It consumed the old house, which had been as dry as tinder since Diana had installed central heating, and many of their most treasured belongings, including most of their pictures. In the morning Mosley and Max drove to the airport to meet Diana, and break the news to her before she heard it from anyone else. 'The aircraft landed and she came across the tarmac waving and smiling happily,' Mosley wrote, '. . . then came to me a strange sense, heavy with the sorrow of things: for . . . we were in the sad position of the fates of classic tragedy, aware of what is coming to happy mortals who themselves are unconscious of . . . destiny.'[2]

> As I approached [Diana wrote], I noticed that he was unshaven. He took my hand and said gently, 'Sit down here on this seat. Everything is all right, nobody is hurt.' 'Hurt!' I said, and my heart missed a beat . . . For many days afterwards, my hands trembled so that I could not hold a pen . . . The losses I minded most were a drawer-full of letters . . . three studies in sepia ink that Tchelichew had done of me and the boys . . . A drawing by Lamb of Jonathan . . . photographs of M and the

children, the irreplaceable things with which one
surrounds oneself.[3]

They bought a house near the Devonshires' Irish seat at
Lismore where they lived until 1963, but by then they also
owned a small property at Orsay about twenty miles from Paris.
It was a delightful little jewel of a property, a *pavillon*, built in the
exaggerated classical Palladian Directoire style, in 1800, to celebrate General Moreau's victory at Hohenlinden by the architect
of the Madeleine. It was called Le Temple de la Gloire, and
potential buyers were told they were not allowed to change this;
it was the only thing about it that Mosley did not like. Even years
later, as an elderly man, he suffered twinges of embarrassment
when asked by a fellow Englishman for his address. On giving it
he sensed polite restraint, and somehow knew that his questioner was thinking, 'He was always a little *exalté* and now is right
round the bend.'[4] Diana adored everything about it. They purchased it as an empty shell in 1950 when it needed complete
restoration, having stood empty for a number of years. They had
no furniture, and because of currency restrictions Diana had a
limited amount of francs, but she haunted the salerooms and got
tremendous bargains as the Empire style she liked was temporarily out of fashion. Shortly after they bought the Temple,
David had visited Paris – his last trip to France – and given
Diana five hundred pounds to buy curtains. He met Mosley
then, and to Diana's delight the two men got on well together.

From now on Diana's life was a kind of reverse of Nancy's.[5]
Where Nancy had great professional success and an unhappy
personal life, Diana and Mosley enjoyed the sort of happy relationship where each partner was an exact half of a loving and
interdependent union; the sort of marital relationship everyone
would choose. But both Mosley and Diana wasted their considerable abilities in attempting to revive his career. He had
mellowed: his actions, speech and even his appearance were

somehow less theatrically threatening, but his post-war political aspirations were doomed to impotence.

This is not to say the Mosleys achieved nothing after the war. Between 1953 and 1959 Diana was the editor of an intellectual magazine they founded, called the *European*, and demonstrated that, like Nancy, she was a natural writer. Eventually it folded because its limited circulation meant it could not support itself, but it attracted many respected writers. In the years that followed she became a noted reviewer for *Books and Bookmen* and also for the London *Evening Standard*.

In 1959 Mosley stood for Parliament in North Kensington as the Union Movement candidate, espousing a united Europe and opposing non-white immigration. Although he insisted that his policies were economic, not racist, most people regarded him as being 'anti-black'. Nevertheless, he received almost 10 per cent of the vote, and although this was insufficient to win the seat he was heartened that he had achieved a notable result without party support. He was never able to capitalize on this base, however, and during a series of meetings of the Union Party, held around the UK in 1962, he was the target of several physical attacks. The worst of these occurred on 31 July in the East End of London when he was thrown to the ground, kicked and punched before his supporters could help him. So serious was that attack that it was believed there might be a plot to kill him. He was still loathed by the general public, and his meetings were always portrayed as rowdy in the newspapers, though in reality they tended to be tame and quiet compared with his pre-war rallies. In private, however, the Mosleys were not only accepted but welcomed whenever they appeared in London, even by former enemies. On one occasion when they were lunching with Frank Pakenham, now Lord Longford, at the Gay Hussar in London, the arch-socialist Michael Foot was at the next table. 'I saw Mosley look at him uneasily,' Lord Longford said. 'After Foot had finished his meal he stopped at our table and said, "What a pleasure to see you again, Sir Oswald." After he left Mosley said softly, "How English. How English. Only in England could that happen.'"[6]

Mosley continued to attend Fascist meetings in Europe, though one scheduled in Venice while Nancy was there was cancelled after Communists rioted about it. Nancy declared that she was 'outraged that Mosley is still going about lecturing as if the war had never happened', although the lectures were about a united Europe. Nancy and Diana were once again on friendly terms, but Nancy had never taken to Mosley: she considered that he had irreparably damaged Diana's life, and that because of loyalty to him Diana could never say so. Mosley did not like Nancy much, either, regarding her as silly, frivolous and disloyal to Diana. They tolerated each other because they both loved Diana, but they realized that politics was a subject to be avoided.

In 1968 when Mosley's autobiography *My Life* was published Nancy wrote to Decca, 'Have you noted all the carry-on about Sir Os? He says he was never anti-Semitic. Good gracious! I quite love the old soul now but really –!'[7]

Time had done nothing to lessen Nancy's attachment to Palewski and she was badly shocked when she learned that he had been involved in a long-term liaison with a married woman who had a son by him. Even this did not affect her love for him. Gradually she became resigned to the situation but she was unhappy that she was 'no use to you. When things go badly you don't need me, when they go well you turn to other, prettier ladies,' she wrote to him. 'So I seem to have no function . . . we are both trapped and frustrated in our different ways – I must say we take it well, neither of us shows a sad face to the world nor are we specially embittered.' She had sat by the telephone for three long days waiting for him to call, she told him, only to hear he had called a mutual woman friend 'for a chat. It was too much to bear.'[8]

When David's will was published his treatment of Decca created more headlines: 'Redesdale Will Cuts Out Madcap Jessica' and 'Red Sheep Cut Out Of Will' were typical ('It did so remind me of Miranda,' said Decca). Nancy was intensely irritated by her father's 'mad' will, considering it unjust. After thinking it over for a few weeks, she decided to give her share of the island to Decca by way of compensation. 'It seems to me the very least after the way Farve treated her,' she wrote to Sydney. 'What does she want it for? She doesn't say. Atom base I suppose; you'll probably see Khrushchev arriving any day.' It was yet another of Nancy's amazing acts of kindness, and Decca was touched. She had taken no umbrage against her father: as far as she was concerned they had parted ways long ago and she was astonished, while on holiday in Mexico, to be tracked down by journalists and asked to comment. 'I simply told them I wasn't expecting to be left anything,' she wrote, 'and couldn't see why it was such staggering news.'[9]

Nancy's gift meant that Decca now owned two-fifths of Inch Kenneth, with Diana, Debo and Pam owning the remainder. After David's death, Sydney thought she could no longer afford to go on living there and that the island would have to be sold. However, Decca's Romilly inheritance had now been announced at £11,400, and Dinky begged her parents, with tears in her eyes, to buy the island and let Granny Muv live there. And this is what happened. Because of Nancy's gift Decca was able to buy out her sisters' shares,[10] and the legal arrangements were finalized during her visit to England in 1959. It was to be a momentous, even life-changing, visit for her in more ways than one.

Dinky had just started as a freshman at Sarah Lawrence College[11] and did not accompany Decca and Benjamin, who travelled to England by ship, leaving Bob to fly over some weeks later, after he had completed a particularly important case. A month before Decca sailed, Blor died, a great sadness to Decca because Blor had always represented the one fixed star of her childhood. She had longed to see her again and show her the manuscript. Sydney met Decca and Benjamin at Paddington Station 'tottering' down the platform, 'palsieder than ever,' Decca wrote to Bob, knowing how he loved to hear Mitford stories. 'She told me later she had arrived at 1.30, only to find that we couldn't arrive until 3.30. She wondered how to fill the time and noticed some public baths so decided to have a bath while waiting . . .' They had driven straight to the mews where Nancy was waiting and they had laughed so much that her face ached.[12]

Decca's family and childhood friends were all convinced that Esmond had been the love of Decca's life and that her marriage to Bob was a friendly but far less passionate relationship. Her letters to him during this trip and over the years that followed disprove that view. Here were all the same loving phrases she had used in her letters to Esmond: 'darling angel' and 'I so long for you to arrive' and 'Goodnight darling . . . do remind me not to plan these long trips without you any more, as I miss you fearfully.'[13]

A few days after her arrival in London, while visiting the offices of the Communist Party, she asked one of the lawyers there if he knew of a good literary agent. He recommended James McGibbon at Curtis Brown. She made an appointment and went to see him. They chatted pleasantly until suddenly he floored her with the question: 'Oh, by the way, were you a member of the American Communist Party?' From an American this would have been an extremely hostile question, and the precursor to having the manuscript returned across the desk. Decca's heart thumped, and she flushed, but she looked at his friendly expression and decided to be open about it. 'Yes,' she answered, and explained that she had left a year earlier and why. 'Oh, *so* was I,' he said nonchalantly. 'I left for the same reason.' Decca thought the conversation 'superbly un-American'.[14]

She left the manuscript with him and expected to hear nothing for about six weeks, the length of time it had taken to hear back from publishers in the USA. But within days McGibbon had sold the book to Gollancz. Furthermore Lovell Thompson of Houghton Mifflin in New York happened to be in London and he bought the American rights. By then Decca was staying with one of her Farrer cousins, Rudbin – Joan Farrer, now married to Michael Rodzianko, whom Bob and Decca disliked intensely. She returned from a freezing outing with Benjamin on the Thames to find Rudbin jumping up and down screaming that the book had been sold in the UK, with a £250 advance, and in the USA for $1,500. 'You've got to go round there tomorrow and sign the contracts.' Decca had hoped for five hundred dollars if the book was accepted, and scarcely able to believe it, she cabled Bob. Back came his teasing reply: 'QUITTING JOB HOLD OUT FOR $2000'.[15] Later she wrote that she was so excited her knees buckled and Rudbin had more or less forced a whisky down her throat. 'To my sorrow Rudbin had to go out,' she wrote to Bob, 'but Benjy was a very satisfactory co-celebrant. He really was decent and rushed out then and there to the corner flower stand to buy me a dear little fivepenny orchid! The awful thing was that I had a date with Woman for dinner, so had to bottle all during dinner as of course I didn't want any of *them* knowing about it till 'tis actually out.'

Now, she wrote, there was a lot of work to be done on the manuscript and Benjamin had been invited to stay on with Rudbin while she went to the island to visit her mother. Hearing of this arrangement Diana had sent a friendly message via Sydney saying that she would love to meet Benjy, and would be glad to have him to stay with her while Decca was at Inch Kenneth. Decca refused this offer as she had refused other attempts by Diana to effect a rapprochement.[16] She reported to Bob that she intended to finish work on her book while on the island, 'if I can hide the ms. from Muv, which shouldn't be too hard . . . I won't really be in a mood to enjoy anything until you come, so do hurry up.'[17]

But she couldn't keep it to herself. As soon as she had signed the contracts she wrote to Nancy and Sydney to tell them about it. 'What exciting news,' Sydney wrote. 'I believe you all have much talent for writing . . . I thought a lot of yours so good, that you sent me.' 'How THRILLING,' Nancy wrote. 'What publisher? If I'd known I'd have forced you to go to mine who is a literal saint. You'll make a lot of money I'm sure.' Decca's weeks on the island were busy with fine-tuning, and interrupted only by ghostly noises. 'Muv . . . told me she had heard distinctly the ring of an anvil. I *was* terrified,' she wrote to Bob. 'There's also a lady in a white skirt who has been seen in the dressing room. I wouldn't stay here alone all day for anything in the world. I have spoken to Muv about having them exorcised (often done in these parts) but she seems to like the idea of them . . .'[18]

The title was giving her some concern; she rather preferred 'Red Sheep' over 'Revolting Daughters', but eventually settled on *Hons and Rebels*.[19] 'Hons comes from Hens, not Honourables,' she explained to Sydney, who was upset that too much was being made of the family status. 'James McGibbon thought it up,' Decca wrote to her friend Pele de Lappe, a professional artist, who at her suggestion was commissioned to design the cover in the USA.

I don't think it's at all bad, and only rather fear that Nancy will think I'm cashing in on her stuff . . . There is a tremendous speculation as to what it will be like (I'm not letting any of them read it . . . except Muv who read the first few chapters and swore not to discuss it with the sisters) . . . Debo keeps saying, 'Oh Hen, I *do* hope it's not going to be *frank*' . . . And the other day . . . in Heywood Hill's bookshop . . . Heywood told us . . . that

Debo, Nancy and Diana were all in his shop twittering
and wringing their hands about it . . . We have bought
the island. Are you amazed? Nancy has given me her
share . . . because I got a raw deal in Farve's will. As the
old saying goes, 'It's an ill will that brings nobody any
good.' Muv will continue to live there for as long as she
wants. We had lunch with John Betjeman yesterday. He
was one of the major 'damn sewers' and 'What-a-set-ers'
of Swinbrook days. Hadn't seen him since I was about
15 . . . he is now the highest paid poet in England . . .
some pewter beer mugs arrived on our table . . . full of
champagne . . . we went through two bottles ere lunch
was over. Betjeman is really quite a fascinator and a
terrific roarer. He has a lot of Red friends and seems
quite L[eft] himself, unlike most of the ex damn-
sewers.[20]

Decca stayed on after Bob returned, to see the book through
various stages of pre-publication, and complete the transfer of the
island. While she was there Sydney was diagnosed with
Parkinson's disease, which Decca had long suspected from the
palsied shaking and the increasingly tottering gait. 'She will never
get really weak, not able to dress herself, etc., or become a charge
on people because of the shaking,' the consultant had told Decca.
'No danger of loss of mental processes memory, etc.'[21] By August
she was longing to return to the USA, hanging on only because
of some delay in signing contracts for the island. She was dis-
missive of the family solicitors, Hasties, who were taking an age
and whom she had taken against ever since they had written to
Esmond in 1937 advising him that Decca was a ward of court.
'All the solicitors seem to have been chosen by horse lovers,' she
commented to Bob. 'Pam's is called Withers and Debo's is Curry.
Muv was on at me again for making her out to be a snob [in the
book], it really rankles it seems.'[22]

Sydney felt, among other things, that having mentioned the unheard-of medical treatment meted out 'by your eccentric parents, in fairness you ought to [explain] that these methods are now in general use and are the most modern medical treatment for those troubles'. Decca had already removed some references from the book at Sydney's request, after she read part of the galley proofs; 'the translation of the nickname for Tuddemy [Decca said it was Boudledidge for adultery] not the name itself of course, but the translation of it, because it seems to give him a bad character'[23] was one of these. She said she could not recall the 'dead silences at meals', only the great laughter at Farve's funny sayings and 'the picture of him always in a rage is not a bit true, but it does make a funny book'.[24] Nor was she pleased at the picture that Decca had painted of her – she felt that she was being made a figure of fun. It seemed to her, several nieces recalled,[25] as though all those years of bringing up her family, working for them, living for them, were now regarded as a mere joke. She was both hurt and annoyed, though she said nothing at the time to Decca for she was always afraid that Decca would cut herself off again and – despite her anguish – she was pleased for her. By the time the reviews appeared she had decided on the line to take: 'I read a very disagreeable review,' she wrote to Decca, 'asserting that Farve and I were both arrogant and dull. I really could not help a hearty laugh . . . the author of it must be such a dreary object. He could not see that the book is not meant to be taken seriously.'[26]

Sydney was not the only one vexed by *Hons and Rebels*. Many relatives refused to read it, but when they gathered together they discussed it interminably, and commented on the fairness or unfairness of what Decca had written. Idden was tackled by Aunt Joan, who said she had been shocked by what Decca had written about the behaviour of the two girls during their finishing year in Paris. 'I told her you hadn't put in the half of it,' Idden wrote. 'Answer: "Oh?!!?"' Rudbin wrote to say she was 'sorry to see

Farve has emerged . . . as a near Moron instead of one of the last giants of originality'. The aunts shouted it down, the uncles huffed that it was 'greatly exaggerated nonsense'. Before Decca left for California Sydney's sister, Aunt Weenie, had called round at the mews for tea. After chatting with Sydney and studiously ignoring Decca for an hour, Weenie demanded that she see her to the door with the statement, 'I want a word with you.' Decca said she felt about ten years old. At the door Weenie turned on her 'in a fury. "I for one will never forget the savage cruelty with which you treated your mother and father. And now, you filthy little cad, you come back and write a lot of horrible things about your mother and come and sponge on her . . ." Time I left, I think,' Decca wrote to Bob. 'I am longing, panting, sighing, fainting, dying for California & you.'27

Nancy, whose opinion Decca most wanted and most nervously awaited, wrote to her: 'I think it's *awfully good*, easy to read and very funny in parts. A slightly cold wind to the heart perhaps – you don't seem very fond of anybody but I suppose the purpose is to make the Swinbrook world seem horrible, to explain why you ran away from it . . . Esmond was the original Teddy Boy wasn't he, a pioneer of the modern trend and much more terrific than his followers?'28

To her correspondents Nancy was more scathing: 'She has quite unconsciously copied from my book instead of real life, & various modifications of the truth demanded by novel form are now taken as true,' she wrote to Heywood Hill. But Nancy was wrong in her supposition when she wrote:

> I believe her husband has re-written it, or helped a good deal as it is his voice if you know them both. My mother stood by her through thick and thin . . . my sisters mind more than I do . . . It is rather dishonest for an autobiography because she alters fact to suit herself in a way that I suppose is allowed in a novel. (But as I have

43. Pam, the 'most rural' Mitford, according to John Betjeman.

44. Pam's marriage to Derek Jackson. (*Front row*) Sydney, Derek, Pam, David. (*Second row*) Diana Mosley, Stella Jackson, Nancy Rodd, Aunt Weenie (Dorothy Bailey), Tom Mitford.

45. Debo aged seventeen.

46. David, still prospecting his gold claim in the mid-thirties.

47. Debo and Andrew at their wartime wedding in 1941. David (standing behind Debo, wearing his LDV uniform), broken down by family traumas, 'looked like an old, old man'. (*Left to right, standing*) Sydney, 10th Duke of Devonshire, David, Andrew, 'Billy' Lord Hartington, Duchess of Devonshire.

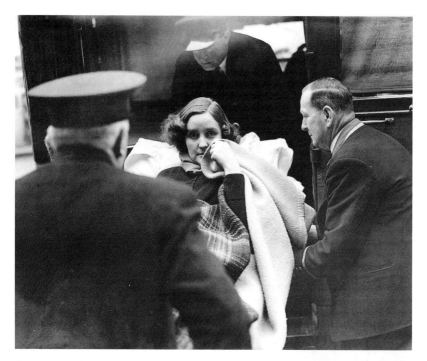

48. Unity on her return to England after her attempted suicide, January 1940.

49. Diana with Alexander on holiday at Inch Kenneth, 1947.

Above left: 50. Nancy, 'the French lady writer' in her Paris apartment. A portrait by Mogens Tvede in 1947.

Above right: 51. Gaston Palewski, Nancy's beloved 'Colonel' and de Gaulle's right-hand man in the Free French Army.

Left: 52. Visit of Princess Elizabeth and Prince Philip to Debo and Andrew at Edensor House (Emma and 'Stoker' in foreground), 1948.

Below: 53. Decca, Dinky and Bob, *c.* 1944.

54. Debo riding Grand National winner Royal Tan at the Devonshire's Irish castle, Lismore, in the mid-fifties.

55. Diana at the Temple, Paris, 1954.

56. Diana and Mosley with their sons Alexander and Max in Venice, 1955.

57. Nancy and Decca at rue Monsieur in 1962.

58. Sydney with her goats at Inch Kenneth *c.* 1958.

59. Diana and Mosley in the early sixties. The body language here says it all.

60. Diana with her youngest son Max; Mosley in the background. London, 1962.

61. Four of the sisters in 1967. (*Left to right*) Cecil Beaton, Nancy, Debo, Pam, Diana and Andrew at a dance after the wedding of Debo and Andrew's son.

62. Decca in front of a plaque commemorating Tom at Swinbrook church. The pews were donated by David, purchased by a win on the Grand National.

63. Bob and Decca at a testimonial dinner in Oakland, 1993.

taken full advantage of that I can hardly blame her I suppose!). She is beastly about aunts & people who used to give us huge tips & presents & treats. Diana is outraged for my mother – I had expected worse to tell the truth – & of course minds being portrayed as a dumb society beauty. Altogether there is a coldness about it which I find unattractive, but of course made up for by the great funniness.[29]

To Evelyn Waugh, she explained that she couldn't review it:

What I feel is this. In some respects she has seen the family, quite without knowing it herself, through the eyes of my books – that is, if she hadn't read them hers would have been different. She is absolutely unperceptive of my aunts and uncles, Nanny, and Dr Cheatle [the doctor at Burford] & the characters whom I didn't describe & who could have been brought to life but simply were not . . . Esmond was the most horrible human being I have ever met . . .[30]

In general, my research for this book tends to support some of Nancy's comments that Decca *has* exaggerated certain facts. Some of these are a matter of written record, and others have been confirmed by a number of surviving family members and friends who remember how things were at Asthall and Swinbrook. Decca was distanced from her family for so long, at a vulnerable time, when she was totally obsessed with Esmond, and subjected to his critical hard-boiled dislike of them. 'From what Decca told me,' Bob Treuhaft said, 'Esmond was completely devoid of sentimentality of any kind. I don't know about a sense of humour, but he would not have understood Decca's residual fondness for her family. They were "the enemy" . . . It's quite clear he kept her from visiting Unity.'[31] It appears that

Nancy's myths and half-facts had become genuinely inter-
changeable with real memory in Decca's mind. Then, too, she
was such a good storyteller and a natural clown, and after telling
exaggerated versions of Mitford stories for years to appreciative
listeners in California, the jokey versions probably became what
she remembered.

Despite this fluttering in the family dovecote, however, *Hons
and Rebels* was a resounding hit. Decca showed that she could be
as funny, ironic, deft – and waspish – as Nancy, and that she had
huge ability as a writer. It seemed that people could not get
enough of the eccentric Mitfords, and pre-publication sales in the
UK alone netted more than double Decca's advance. As any
author with a first book, Decca was nervous about the reviews,
but on the whole they were amazingly good. In interviews she
enjoyed playing to the gallery, and pulled no punches when
asked about Diana: 'I haven't seen her since I was nineteen. We're
completely on opposite sides of the fence. Her husband stood for
Parliament in the last election and I'm glad to say lost his deposit.
His programme was to send all the coloured people to Africa and
then divide Africa into two parts, the northern part white and
the southern part black. My idea was to form an organisation of
"In-laws against Mosley", led by my husband who is Jewish.'
Her mother, she told one interviewer, was especially fond of her
because, unlike most of her sisters, she had never been divorced
or to jail. Her sister Pam, she said, 'used to be married to a
jockey'.[32]

With ten thousand dollars assured within a month of US publication, the Treuhafts moved to a new house at 6411 Regent
Street, still in the 'old-fashioned neighbourhood' that they so
enjoyed in Oakland, but with plenty of space and a garden. At
the age of forty, somewhat to her astonishment, Decca found
herself successfully launched on a new career with offers flooding
in for articles and lectures – *Life* offered her five hundred dollars
for five hundred words and *Esquire* offered six hundred dollars

for a piece on civil rights in the South. She used the opportunity to go to Montgomery, Alabama, to hear Martin Luther King speak at a Baptist meeting and she became trapped in the church overnight while the Ku Klux Klan and a mob of 1,500 whites hurled tear gas through the open windows. The uproar had been caused by the surprise appearance at the event of the Freedom Fighters, a sort of flying squad of black youths on motorcycles, who were much feared by whites in the Southern states. Next morning when Decca was finally able to leave she found that her car had been burned out. Needless to say the article she turned in after this experience, cleverly titled 'You-all and Non You-all', was rather more controversial and interesting than the one she had originally intended to write.

To achieve a sudden 'respectability' after years of being almost a pariah was a heady experience. She began her second book almost immediately. It was a bit ghoulish, she said, but it had important social connotations. It was about the funeral industry in America and for the next few months she regaled her correspondents with gruesome bits of information on embalming. 'Hen, I'll bet you didn't know what is the best time to start embalming, so I'll tell you: *before life is quite extinct*, according to a text book I've got. They have at you with a long pointed needle . . . with a pump attached.'

In 1961 Debo visited America ('for a *tête-à-tête* with your ruler,' Nancy wrote to Decca); she admired the President a good deal and it was to be the first of five visits she would make to the White House over a couple of years. President Kennedy made one visit to Chatsworth to visit the grave of his sister, as did his brother Robert. Nancy could not resist writing to tell Debo that the *on-dit* at the Venice Lido was that if JFK didn't have sex once a day he got a headache, and to Decca to say, 'Andrew says Kennedy is doing for sex what Eisenhower did for golf.' Andrew had recently been appointed Under-Secretary of State for the Commonwealth. There was a row about this in Parliament since his uncle Harold was Prime Minister. The arch anti-royalist and anti-aristocrat MP Willie Hamilton asked a question about nepotism in the Commons. Macmillan replied blandly, 'I try to make the best appointments I can.'[33]

In the following year Dinky showed that she really did have running-away blood in her, and quit college to work for the civil-rights movement. Decca was furious. She travelled immediately to Sarah Lawrence College, just north of New York, and convinced the Dean to give Dinky, who was regarded as an excellent student, an 'honourable discharge' that would enable her to return to college at a later date. Then mother and daughter, so much alike in many ways, returned to California. 'We were on that train together three days and three nights and we barely spoke a word to each other,' Dinky said. A few months later Decca played at being 'Lord of the Isle' (as suggested by Debo) and went to Inch Kenneth for the first time since becoming its owner. 'Muv was asking me what is to be done with the Isle when she no longer comes here . . .' Decca wrote to Debo from there. 'I said, "Where will you be going?" and she went into gales of laughter, saying, "To the next world I expect." But to my great relief she really doesn't seem to be departing at the moment.'[34] But death was on Decca's mind for she was taking the opportunity to research her book about the funeral industry, she said, and had just come across a fascinating editorial entitled, 'Children's Funerals – a Golden Opportunity to Build Good Will'. 'Do admit, they are a lark,' she wrote.

While Decca was staying with Sydney, Nancy published a little book called *The Water Beetle*. It was a collection of her essays, including a sketch about Blor, the best description we have of the woman who was so important in the lives of the young Mitfords, but Sydney was also portrayed:

> My mother has always lived in a dream world of her own and no doubt was even dreamier during her many

pregnancies . . . when she was young she never opened a book and it is difficult to imagine what her tastes and occupations [were]. My father and she disliked society, or thought they did – there again, later they rather took to it – and literally never went out. She had no cooking or housework to do. In those days you could be considered very poor by comparison with other people of the same sort and yet have five servants . . . Even so she was perhaps abnormally detached. On one occasion Unity rushed into the drawing room, where she was at her writing table, saying, 'Muv, Muv, Decca is standing on the roof – she says she's going to commit suicide!' 'Oh, poor duck,' said my mother, 'I hope she won't do anything so terrible,' and went on writing.[35]

This was the so-called straw-that-broke-the-camel's-back as far as Sydney was concerned. She and Decca had a blistering row about *Hons and Rebels*, the education of the Mitford girls, and Decca and Nancy's literary portrayal of her as a dilettante mother leaving the upbringing of her children to nannies. Sydney wrote in a similar vein to Nancy, deploring the piece. But although Nancy wrote a conciliatory letter saying that she realized that their education had been the product of received wisdom at the time, rather than any whim of their parents, Sydney was not to be pacified and told Nancy what she had already said to Decca: 'I wish only one thing,' she said firmly, 'that you will exclude me from your books. I don't mind what you write about me when I am dead, but I do dislike to see my mad portrait while I am still alive.'

As usual Sydney spent the winter months at the mews. To save costs, the island was virtually shut down each autumn, the animals sold off and the house closed except for an occasional cleaning and airing done by her faithful couple, the McGillvrays. When she returned to the island in the spring of 1963, she was accompanied by Madeau Stewart.[36] Madeau, who had trained at the Royal College of Music, had stayed on the island for weeks at a time over several years and loved being there. 'Sydney played the piano and I played the flute; we used to play Victorian ballads, they were very expressive,' Madeau said. 'And there were lots of books to read and so much to talk about.'

Diana was less enthusiastic about visiting. On one occasion when she travelled back with Sydney they were stuck at Gribun for forty-eight hours in a storm, and finally boarded the *Puffin* in a grey and troubled sea. Sydney, in her eighties, still loved the sea. Wrapped in her oilskins against driving rain and spray, she shouted back to her daughter, 'Great fun, isn't it?' The lack of news, mail and table-talk also bothered Diana, although she conceded that the beauty of the island was some compensation. During those years she and Debo had a pact to write to each other every day while either was on the island, so that they could be sure of at least receiving some mail while they were there. Often the only visitors were picnickers, whom Sydney spotted through binoculars, and she used to send McGillvray as an emissary to invite them to tea. 'Such a haphazard choice of guests was, to me, strange taste,' Diana wrote. 'It must have been the gambler in Muv which made her positively enjoy . . . the luck of the draw at her tea parties.'[37]

About that journey in 1963, Madeau recalled that Sydney was 'very tottery. We had dinner and a bottle of wine on the train, and we got to Oban. I remember there were screams of laughter when I tried to put on her shoes and got them on the wrong feet. Anyway, the crossing was a bit rough and she said she'd like to lie down. That was unusual. When we got to the island she said she wasn't feeling very well and she thought she might call the doctor on Monday.' Alarm bells rang and Madeau decided to get the doctor immediately. She sent for Dr Flora MacDonald, whom Sydney liked. Dr MacDonald recognized that Sydney's condition was serious: having suffered from Parkinson's disease for many years she was now in the terminal stages of the illness and her condition was deteriorating rapidly. Madeau alerted the sisters, and Nancy, Pam and Diana came rushing up to the island. Debo could not leave immediately but Nancy kept her up to date until she could join them. Two nurses came in to help them with round-the-clock nursing, and though there were several periods when it seemed that Sydney was fading she rallied each time. Curiously, for she had been very deaf for some years, her hearing returned in the last days: they kept a fire burning in her room and she could hear the logs crackling and spitting.

'It is so poignant,' Nancy wrote to old Swinbrook-sewer Mark Ogilvie-Grant. 'She feels so ill . . . two days ago she said, "Who knows – perhaps Tom and Bobo?" . . . She laughs as she always has . . . We long for her to go in her sleep, quietly.'[38] A week later Sydney had a minor stroke and slipped into unconsciousness. 'Before that it was dreadful,' Nancy wrote. Sydney had been unable to swallow anything but sips of liquid because of throat constriction and was starving to death. Nancy had often claimed that she had never loved her mother but now she found that her feelings for her were stronger than she had suspected. 'Now she is slipping away and feels nothing . . . the sadness comes and goes in waves. I have a feeling nothing really nice will ever happen again in my life. Things will just go from bad to worse, leading to old age and death.'[39]

Sydney died on 25 May, just after her eighty-third birthday. A carpenter travelled over to the island and made her coffin, and a neighbour said prayers over her body. After a period of fearful storms there was a sudden calm, enabling the coffin to be ferried across to Mull as the sun was setting. The *Puffin*, flying her ensign at half-mast, was escorted by a small flotilla of local boats, and a lone piper played a lament during the short journey over to Gribun. Friends Sydney had known for many years met them and carried the coffin from the little launch to its overnight resting place before it was driven down to Swinbrook. It was all very moving, Pam wrote to Decca. Sydney had wanted to be buried next to David at Swinbrook where, on what was the first warm day of spring, the Mitford clan gathered. Debo wrote,

> Swinbrook looked perfectly magical. The birds singing so loud, and the churchyard was full of cow parsley and brilliant green grass. The sight of Choops,* Mabel . . . and all the aunts, so ancient now, and Honks [Diana], Woman and Nancy in deepest black . . . the feel of the pews, not to mention the taste when licked (do you remember) . . . When 'Holy, Holy, Holy' started Honks and I were done for; it was too much. We had 'Jerusalem', as well. Afterwards we thought we ought to have had 'For Those in Peril on the Sea' . . . Hen it was all fearfully upsetting and sad. The beauty of the place and the day and the flooding memories of that church and village . . .[40]

Decca, who was inexpressibly sad, for in latter years she had learned to value her relationship with Sydney, sent a subdued answer: 'I should have felt very lonely if it hadn't been for your letters (and Nancy's) . . . Thanks *so* much for sending flowers from me. (By the way my new book is all about the ridiculous waste of money on funeral flowers and an attack on the Florist Industry for inducing people to send flowers. But I can see not, in this case).' Decca was nothing if not irreverent.

In the aftermath of the funeral another Mitford story emerged. Weenie and Geoffrey were the only survivors of Tap's four children as George had died before Sydney. ('What did he die of?' Decca had enquired. 'A nasty pain,' Sydney replied.) When she returned to London from Swinbrook Weenie telephoned Geoffrey. 'George is gone and now Sydney is dead, don't you think we should meet?' 'But we *have* met,' he replied, puzzled.[41]

---

*Their old groom, Hooper.

That summer Dinky was invited to Chatsworth for the wedding of Emma (Debo's eldest child) to Toby Tennant, the youngest son of Lord Glenconner. To Dinky's horror everyone kept telling her she looked just like Diana, a compliment in any other branch of the Mitford family but Decca's. 'Silence was the only possible response,' she decided. Like Bob, she was unsure of herself in the big house, though not overawed; if anything her reaction was one of amusement. Invisible hands unpacked her luggage and her laundry was whisked away and reappeared looking fresh and new. 'They keep referring to Kennedy as Jack,' she wrote to her parents, 'and there is an autographed portrait of him in Debo's drawing room.' She found Nancy 'cold and aloof' and Diana 'trying to pretend there was no reason for there to be any unfriendliness between us'. Pam was 'relaxed and ordinary' and Debo 'so sensitive and welcoming'. In an odd sense, because she knew so much about the sisters, she felt like one of them, rather than a niece.[42] By the end of her trip she had reassessed some of her first impressions and thought Pam somewhat uninteresting, but she felt sorry for the way the sisters teased her, constantly making fun of her lack of sophistication and 'basic non-fascination'. Dinky thought this 'cruel – it was as though Pam came from a different family from the rest of you,' she told Decca. She was scared of Nancy at first until she realized that she was meant to be scared: it was Nancy's shell. Andrew's sister told her later that Nancy was actually quite shy.

Decca's book on the funeral industry was published in the summer of 1963; she had worked on it, on and off, for five years. It was Bob who had sparked her interest initially, before the publication of *Hons and Rebels*. He handled the estates of trade-union members and noticed, to his great irritation, that the hard-fought-for union death benefit, intended for widows, often end up in the coffers of undertakers. It didn't seem to matter whether the benefit was a thousand or three thousand dollars, the amount always seemed to be the exact cost of the funeral. As part of his job he attended fortnightly meetings of the local Funeral Society and Decca used to tease, 'Off to meet your fellow necrophilists again?' Having made a few enquiries he suspected that funeral directors used the natural distress of the widows, and their desire to 'do something' for the loved one, by persuading them into buying caskets, flowers and services they could not afford and which, in normal circumstances, they would probably not have considered. Decca, in sore need of a cause and sensing here not just one underdog but a whole pack, took up the matter with alacrity and began her lengthy research. Later she would say that at her age it was easier to sit down at the typewriter and work at being a rebel than going out into the streets and getting her head beaten in by police. An article, which she provoked, was published in the *Saturday Evening Post* in the late fifties, titled 'Can You Afford to Die?' It brought in more mail than any other in the magazine's long and distinguished history.

Realizing from this reaction that there was probably a good book in the subject, she had initially contacted James McGibbon and her American publisher, and suggested that she and Bob would write it. The book was commissioned, but on the condition that it appeared as a work by Jessica Mitford not a joint work on the grounds that 'co-signed works' never sold as well as one by a single author. Bob was a practical man and had no literary ambitions, having already achieved a successful reputation built on his legal career. However, he took a leave of absence from his law firm to work with Decca since the project was so huge and Decca did not feel she could cope with it alone. They shared the research: Bob went off to the San Francisco College of Mortuary Science to learn about the technical side of the industry, such as embalming processes. Decca posed as an about-to-be-bereaved relative with a limited budget, and set out to find how the industry operated in general terms. She was fascinated to see how she could be talked up from the cheapest pine coffin to an elaborate bronze casket, from simple flowers to great floral tributes, to embalming, even when there were no facilities for the family to view the dead body, the hundreds of extras such as Ko-zee shoes (open at the back to allow them to be fitted easily) and cosmetic enhancements. One young sales-man advised Decca seriously that they recommended silk for the coffin lining, 'because we find rayon so irritating to the skin'. A grieving widow who absolutely insisted on the least expensive casket was told, 'Oh, all right, we'll use the Redwood, but we'll have to cut off his feet.'[43]

Nothing was too grisly, sacred or funny for Decca: the cost of dying, she said, was rising faster than the cost of living. Her investigation was savagely incisive and for half a decade she rol-licked through funeral parlours opening wide her large blue eyes and asking innocently droll questions that trapped her victims like flies on sticky paper, without their even realizing they'd been had. She used her family as unpaid researchers in England and France, sending them questionnaires to answer about their expe-riences of funerals. Debo complied willingly, but Nancy balked, writing to explain that she was unable to call on the local *pompes funèbre*. 'I walk past there every day,' she said, 'but I fear I have the superstitious feeling of an old horse passing a knacker's yard.'[44]

Bob also shared the writing process, and the couple had tremendous fun choosing the title, oscillating between such gems as 'The High Cost of Leaving', 'Remains to be Seen' and 'A Funny Thing Happened on the Way to the Mausoleum'. Eventually they settled on the harder-hitting *The American Way of Death*, and despite its subject the book soared effortlessly to number one in the bestseller charts, as Decca's savage yet hilari-ous analysis of the practices of America's funeral industry both shocked and struck chords with the public. Decca dedicated the book to Bob, 'with much gratitude for his untiring collabora-tion', and it earned her a place in a publication called *Women Who Shook the World*.

The American Way of Death was a publishing phenomenon, holding the number-one position in the bestseller charts for months. The publishers were amazed, and so were Decca and Bob. But it was not simply a well-written and interesting read: it made a genuine impact on the way in which Americans regarded funerals. So much so that when President Kennedy was assassinated in November that year, Robert Kennedy chose the least expensive classically designed coffin on offer for his brother's funeral because he had read *The American Way of Death* and had been impressed by what Decca had to say.[45] 'Of all my writings,' Decca once said in interview, 'I'm most proud of *The American Way of Death.*'

Within the first year the book had netted over a hundred thousand dollars in royalties. From now on, like Nancy, Jessica Mitford was a media personality. That is not to say she was popular with everyone: America's funeral industry regarded her as a sort of Lucifer sent to torment them, and they paid her the compliment of referring to her simply as 'Jessica' in their trade papers. They made strenuous attempts to damage her credibility by dredging up her political affiliations, intimating that by damaging the funeral industry she was helping to destroy the American way of life, that she was trying to substitute the American funeral service 'with that practised in Communist countries such as the Soviet Union'. But too many people had been stung and there was enormous support for her demand that some federal controls be instigated to protect vulnerable people. To her amusement Decca found that clergymen were among her staunchest supporters in this.[46]

In the years that followed Decca took on other crusades, such as the Famous Writer School, which advertised for new members with the slogan, 'Would you like to become a writer?' and asked large up-front fees for tuition by mail. Although this was a publicly traded company Decca soon saw off the organization, pointing out in articles, interviews and lectures that so far it had pulled in millions of dollars from students without creating one famous writer. A chic Manhattan restaurant, which added a service charge to a bill she considered already inflated, was demolished in one of her articles. When she investigated pornography she described at a lecture a film she and Bob had watched during research: 'There was a man with an enormous penis perched on a motorbike with a woman. I said to Bob, "That looks dangerous."' A follow-up book, *The American Way of Birth*, spotlighted the huge cost of giving birth. Her signal failure, she thought, was a book about the American prison service: *Kind and Usual Punishment*. She felt strongly about the many injustices she had discovered during this research and, indeed, she made some progress in restricting the use of convicts by drug companies for experimental research. But the book did not sell in huge numbers, perhaps because the book-buying public did not personally associate with the subject as they had with death and birth. But Decca loved taking on controversial topics that no one else would touch and there was no matter into which she would not delve, from racism to venereal disease to the 'sale' of honorary college degrees.

In *Poison Penmanship – The Gentle Art of Muck-raking*, she wrote that in her repertoire she had something to offend everyone. The title was chosen after she was told by a television interviewer that an opponent had referred to her as 'the Queen of Muck-rakers'. She replied, 'If you're going to be a muck-raker it's best to be a queen, don't you think? . . . Of course, the whole point of muck-raking, apart from all the jokes, is to try to do something about what you've been writing about. You may not be able to change the world but at least you can embarrass the guilty.' Afterwards she rushed to the library to look up 'muck-raker' in the *Oxford English Dictionary*. It said 'often made to refer generally to a depraved interest in what is morally "unsavoury" or scandalous', and Decca concluded comfortably, 'Yes, I fear that does rather describe me.'[47]

21

VIEWS AND REVIEWS
(1966–80)

Decca and Bob visited Europe regularly throughout the sixties and seventies, Decca travelling over at least once a year, either with Bob or on more extended trips without him. Before Benjamin left school he often accompanied her on tours of Italy, Spain and France, the pair making an eclectic set of new friends as they travelled. By the end of the decade Benjamin had grown up and started work as a piano tuner. Dinky, who spent the 1960s and 1970s working for the civil-rights movement, parted from the Black Power leader James Forman, by whom she had two sons, and became an emergency nurse working in hospitals in Detroit, New York and Atlanta. To Decca's satisfaction Dinky was to remarry very happily.[1] There was no time in her busy life for her to accompany her mother, so Decca often travelled to Europe alone, but was seldom lonely.

In Paris Nancy took her to Society parties where she revived old friendships with Derek Jackson and others, including, to her amusement, Mr Whitfield, the former consul at Bayonne who had attended her and Esmond's wedding, and in London among leftist literary circles she made new contacts such as Sonia Orwell, widow of George, who became an important friend to her over the next two decades. Nancy insisted on taking Decca to Dior where she introduced her to the *vendeuse* as her 'very rich sister'. For years Decca had quipped that Nancy was dressed by Dior while she was dressed by J.C. Penney, but on this occasion 'I ended up with a dress that cost seven hundred dollars,' she said. Twenty years later she was still wearing it. Occasionally she saw Pam, who made her laugh by threatening to write a book based on the papers she had saved from her years with Derek, since she noted that Decca and Nancy had become 'so rich' by cashing in their memories. Sometimes she stayed with Debo in Ireland or at Chatsworth, or with Desmond, Diana's second son, of whom she and Bob became very fond. Still, she could never bring herself to see Diana and would go out for the day if Diana happened to be calling wherever she was staying. Nancy teased her by telling her that Diana habitually wore a baroque brooch that Decca had given her before eloping with Esmond. 'She says it is her great treasure . . . I hope your hard heart is touched! Sisters, Susan, Ah Soo!?![2] (Confusingly Nancy and Decca always called each other Susan in their correspondence. No one can remember why.)

The downside of these enjoyable trips for Decca was being parted from Bob. She missed the laughter she shared with him, and he was equally affected by their partings. 'Never, never will I let you leave again,' he wrote typically. 'The days drag on and on and it's not even June. Oh Dec I miss you . . .'[3]

In 1966 Bob ran for the office of District Attorney in Alameda County. He knew from the start that he would not be elected, no one with a past rooted in Communism could be, and he was also the first person to challenge the incumbent for fourteen years ('Clear the way with a new DA'). But he received a creditable share of the vote, which was a tribute to his personal local popularity.

As their lives became busier the Treuhafts decided that they had no time to use or look after the island, and put it on the market. Before they sold it, however, they spent a month there, celebrating Bob's fiftieth birthday with a day-long party attended by scores of visitors, including Sydney's old neighbours from Gribun, and Philip Toynbee and Rudbin. The crew of a yacht who put in to get fresh water were bemused to find numbers of jolly people in party clothes (and some in their cups) wandering around the tiny island. Philip Toynbee greeted them: 'If you decided to kill your children because of nuclear attack how would you do it?' he asked, with the careful enunciation of one who had imbibed generously.[4] In the evening there were Highland dancing and parlour games, such as Scrabble, until guests reeled off to bed in the small hours. Two of them decided to swap partners but were discovered *in flagrante*. 'Next morning there was a bit of a frost,' Decca reported to a friend in California. 'Only the innocent really enjoyed the usual kipper.'

The island was finally sold in 1966, and Decca visited for 'one last look' in the following summer. While in London she was introduced to Maya Angelou at a party at Sonia Orwell's home. Maya had just finished writing her bestselling memoir *I Know Why the Caged Bird Sings*, and in the following days she brought sections of the manuscript for Decca to read. The two women were to become the closest of friends, and Bob stated that one of the greatest moments in Decca's life came when Maya began calling her 'Sister'. Decca knew a thing or two about sisters. At about this time she was contacted by a friend of mine, *Sunday Times* journalist Brigid Keenan, who was writing a piece on Nancy and wanted Decca to comment on Nancy's statement that 'Sisters are a shield against life's cruel adversity.' Decca replied, 'But sisters ARE life's cruel adversity!'[5] Her relationship with Maya, however, was supremely important to her. 'It was as close – or closer – than a blood relationship . . . As sisters they went through many good and bad times together,' Bob said, 'and I was sometimes lucky enough to join in.'

While Decca's career was taking off during the last half of the

1960s, Nancy's life was also changing. Fretful in Paris, now that she saw so little of the Colonel, she decided to move from rue Monsieur. She found a house in Versailles, at 4 rue d'Artois, which suited. It was small but it had half an acre of garden, which enchanted her; she thought it was like living in the country. She hated the idea of a lawn and wanted only roses and wild flowers – poppies, valerian, irises, orchids, buttercups, marsh marrow, daisies and harebells. The effect she wished to create was a '*champ fleuri*' and, indeed, in the spring it resembled a country bower: 'My garden looks as though 1,000 Edwardian hats had fallen into it (roses).' By midsummer, however, it was more like an overgrown hayfield. She had as pets a cat, a hen bought for market who won her affection, and a tortoise who crawled out from under the shrubbery in the spring. She spent a lot of time in the garden watching hedgehogs and birds, bees and butterflies. The Colonel visited her sometimes, always her happiest days.

It was on a day in March 1969 that Nancy's world came apart. When the Colonel called to see her he gave her the worst possible news. Knowing how upset she would be, Palewski had found it difficult to tell her he was getting married – indeed, he had called twice and left without broaching the subject because she was feeling unwell. But at last he had to tell her, for on the following day the marriage was to be announced in *Figaro*. Nancy knew his bride quite well: she was rich and titled, and Palewski had been in love with her for many years but her husband had refused to give her a divorce. That alone was a deep wound; for one of the most frequent excuses Palewski had used when Nancy had asked him about marriage was that he could not afford to marry a divorcée without ruining his career. Now he had retired from politics, and he had chosen a divorcée after all, but not Nancy. The newly-weds were to live in the bride's chateau, Le Marais, forty kilometres outside Paris and regarded by many as one of the most beautiful chateaux in France. To her friends Nancy was matter-of-fact in announcing the news ('The Colonel (married) has just been. He makes that face – "it's all too silly" . . .'),[6] as though she had known about it all along and was pleased for him, but the hurt was like a knife.

Shortly afterwards she became seriously ill. Later, she made the link between the terrible shock of learning about the Colonel's marriage and the real onset of her illness, although it is clear that she was unwell weeks before Palewski broke his news. It began with obscure back pains that were written off as lumbago. When the discomfort persisted for two months, doctors investigated and found a lump in her liver. A tumour the size of a grapefruit was removed, and doctors advised Debo and Diana that it was malignant. Nancy was not told of this, as everyone thought it would be too much for her to bear, although when Decca heard, she strongly disagreed. 'I feel it is verging on wicked not to tell Nancy,' she wrote, 'because don't you see, it's awful enough to get such news when one is feeling fairly OK & strong; but if delivered very late in the thing and in much pain, harder to bear I think.'[7] She wrote immediately to Nancy offering to fly to Paris as soon as she could get a flight, and received an enthusiastic reply dated 9 May, which said, 'Oh yes, *do* come.' Decca postponed a planned holiday with Bob in the South and booked her flight. Next day a letter, dated 10 May, arrived in which Nancy said, 'I'm afraid it will be so dull for you as I want to work.' The following day, a further letter, dated 11 May, said point-blank that Decca should not bother: 'My maid is too tired to cope with visitors and I want to work . . . and please don't offer to help [with the housework] as there's no point.'[8] Decca was not only hurt by the apparent rejection but did not know what to do. Then it occurred to her that Nancy's indecision might be related to Diana, who called in on her each day: perhaps the problem of how to keep them apart was worrying her, or perhaps fear about the fall-out when these two estranged sisters met again – as Decca recognized was inevitable.

She consulted Debo, who advised her to go a little later in the year, and Decca did so, after writing that she would be careful to avoid any friction with Diana and hoped Diana would agree. Diana, of course, as mentioned earlier, had made several attempts over the years to reconcile with Decca, all rejected. Decca stayed at a small hotel round the corner from Nancy's house and spent her days sitting with Nancy, trying to entertain her when she was awake. When Diana called in, Decca usually went off to do the daily shopping or performed small tasks to keep out of the way. She spent hours 'removing whole continents of clover from the beds of parsley and lettuce, or anything Nancy asks. Thus I feel useful, in fact indispensable,' she wrote to Bob. There were times, though, when she and Diana were alone together when Nancy was sleeping after an injection. And Decca was usually scrupulous to be well behaved, as she had promised, for Nancy's sake. It was curious, meeting Diana again after thirty-four years: 'She looks like a beautiful bit of aging sculpture (is fifty-nine), they don't have this thing of wanting to look young here, her hair is almost white, no makeup, marvellous figure, same large, perfect face and huge eyes,' she wrote to Pele de Lappe. 'We don't of course talk about anything but the parsley weeding and Nancy's illness. God, it's odd. I thought it must have given her a nasty turn to see me, [I was] aged 18 when last seen by her. But she told Nancy I hadn't changed except for my voice.'[9] Diana's recollection is that they stayed off the subject of politics but often sat on the sofa together, laughing and chatting about the old days quite normally. However, one day while Diana was visiting Decca asked Nancy if there was some little job that needed doing. Nancy asked her to weed a clump of iris and she went off meekly to do so, returning to say mischievously, 'I've given them *Lebensraum*.'* The bitter

---

Lebensraum = 'room to live': Hitler's defence of his attacks on neighbouring countries.

little joke, at which Nancy choked, would not have been lost on Diana, but she did not react and the matter passed quietly.[10]

For a while the worst symptoms retreated and, although it was merely a remission, Nancy thought she had recovered and began work on what was to be another bestselling biography, *Frederick the Great*. The research took her to East Berlin, accompanied by Pam who spoke German, which Nancy did not. There, Nancy had a similar experience to that of Bob and Decca in Hungary: she was approached by a personable young man who told her of his desperate longing for freedom to travel. 'You know, how *can* Decca go on believing in it all?' Nancy wrote to Debo. 'I shall tell her it's all right being a commy in our countries but wait until you are nabbed by the real thing! For ten days we haven't moved without a policeman. I must say it suited me because I loved being looked after . . . still, it's a funny feeling . . . Checkpoint Charlie is *gruesome*.'[11]

Decca was not the only sister to feel concern that Nancy had not been told the truth about her condition: Diana also felt pangs of guilt. 'N. says she has got on so well with the book [*Frederick the Great*] that there is absolutely no hurry . . . this kills one with guilt, in case she reproaches & says I *could* have gone quicker & finished if I'd known.' Her solution was to confide in Nancy's publisher and ask them to press for an earlier delivery date, which worked as Diana had hoped. After the biography Nancy planned to write her autobiography, but the illness overtook her again. For a further three years she suffered increasingly agonizing bouts of illness and pain, offset by shorter and shorter periods of remission. She spent periods in hospital in France and England while her symptoms were investigated until even she suspected cancer, yet despite the malignant tumour the doctors were unable to diagnose the exact nature of her illness so she always had the hope that they would discover the cause and she would be cured. Meanwhile, with each session of illness, the pain grew relentlessly worse. By the time she took up her autobiography it was too severe to allow her to concentrate on writing and she got no further than mentioning it in a few letters to friends and family.

Towards the end she could hardly bear visitors except her sisters, and a few very close friends. Decca went to be with her three times, on each occasion for about a week. Debo and Pam stayed as often as they could, and Diana called almost daily. A few very close friends who could amuse Nancy were allowed to visit, and of course her beloved Colonel. On better days she continued to write her wonderful letters, usually managing to find a joke despite expressions of fearful pain. To her great joy she was awarded the Légion d'Honneur, which was conferred in person by the Colonel. And then, shortly afterwards, she wrote to Decca cheerily:

> It's a deep secret until announced but I've been given the CBE [Companion of the British Empire] which is next decoration after Knight or Dame – quite good for a pen pusher . . . I suppose it's sour grapes but I don't think I could have accepted Dame, on account of being called it, but I do see in my little book that Hons need not use it [the initials CBE on an envelope] because Hon is so much higher in the hierarchy, Good . . . But it may be withdrawn. I've had a furious growl from Downing Street saying too many people know. The reason is that Diana Cooper was sitting with me when I got the intimation – of course you can guess the rest!![12]

In mid-June 1973, warned by her sisters that she should spend some time with Nancy before it was too late, Decca made a final trip to Versailles. While desperately anxious to please, she found that being sister-in-residence was no longer the pleasant task it had been on previous visits. In desperate pain a good deal of the time, Nancy had the querulous air of the acutely ill and had fits of complaining about everything Decca did, from organizing her bedpan to arranging the flowers. When reporting to Debo one day Decca's despair at not being able to do anything right was obvious:

> Her eyes filled with tears & she said 'everyone says there are masses of roses in the garden, *why* doesn't anyone bring them up here?' So I said I'll dash and get some . . . and raced back with three more vases. So N, in cuttingest tones said, 'I see your life does not contain much art and grace.' Too true perhaps, but *Hen*! So I got lots more and put 'em round. Nancy: 'I can't think why you didn't get them earlier, you've nothing else to do.' In other words I think she's rather taken against me . . . of course as Diana pointed out, she's not exactly herself, which I do see . . . Isn't it *extraorder* how utterly preoccupied one is with this horror scene, everything else fades such as Watergate, hubby and kids, all one's usual interests.[13]

To Bob she wrote of wishing to be home: 'As you know we've always been slightly arms-length in contrast with Nancy/Debo, Nancy/Diana or even Nancy/Woman, so it's one of those things where, most likely, one can't do anything right . . . it is all deeply depressing – I rather hope to be fired, in fact.'[14] Before she left Nancy told her during a quiet time that she was 'ready to go', and she even pleaded with the doctor, in Decca's presence, to help her die: '*Je veux que vous me dépêcher* [*sic*].'[15]

Nancy died on 30 June 1973. By then Decca was back in California and Debo sent her a telegram. 'By a quirk of time I didn't get it,' Decca replied to her, 'until I'd seen the news in the paper, "Author Nancy Mitford Dies". A chill, yet blank message since the actual mourning for her has been going on so long.' Indeed, those who had loved Nancy could only feel relief for, if ever there was an occasion when the overused expression 'happy release' was apt, Nancy's death was it. She had suffered harrowing torments, and when the condition was finally diagnosed as Hodgkin's disease[16] she was not surprised to be told by her doctors that the pain was known to be one of the worst. 'The very worst is something on your face called *tic douloureux*,' she wrote in her customary jokey way. 'Bags not having that as well!' Her weight had fallen to under seven stone and her nurses had difficulty finding anywhere to inject morphine. Apart from the fact that the injections hurt, she always held off having morphine as long as possible because she dreaded losing control: 'I have got a little spot of grey matter & I don't want to spoil it with drugs or drink or anything else,' she said. 'My horror of drugs is the greatest of all my many prejudices.' But then came the times when she screamed with pain and had to give in; and in the end only morphine, and the quiet ministrations of Pam, with her loving womanly qualities, could really provide comfort. Just as she had with Sydney, it was Pam who saw Nancy through the worst times towards the end. 'Woman [was] such an utter trooper,' Decca wrote. 'Somehow it looked as though she really came into her own re appreciation of her efforts and rare qualities.'[17] One of the last things Nancy said to Debo was that she recalled hunting as a teenager. If there was one thing she would like to have done, she said, it was to have one more day with hounds.

To James Lees-Milne Nancy had written, 'It's very curious, dying, and would have many a droll, amusing & charming side were it not for the pain . . . the doctors will not give one a date, it is so inconvenient they merely say have everything you want (morphia).'[18] And to her beloved Colonel a few days before the end, her last letter: 'I'm truly very ill . . . I suffer as I never imagined possible; the morphine has very little effect and hurts very much as it goes in. I hope and believe I am dying . . . the torture is too great. You cannot imagine . . . I would love to see you.'[19] He did visit her sometimes, and then, on 30 June, while he was walking his dog, he suddenly had a strong presentiment that he must go to see her. Although she appeared to be in a coma when he arrived, she seemed to smile as he took her hand and spoke to her. The hearing is the last of the senses to fail and it is almost certain that she was aware of his presence. He was the dearest person in the world to her. Soon afterwards she slipped away. 'Nancy was the bright star of our youth,' Rudbin wrote to Decca, 'a gay butterfly fluttering through attainable territories – quite the wrong person to be ill and suffer. A gossamer personality.'[20] Diana wrote, too, and her short note survives in Decca's papers. 'Darling Decca, I'm staying with Woman. Nancy's funeral was yesterday. Swinbrook is looking wonderful . . . Debo will send obit from the *Times*. All love.'

The cremation was in Paris, and Diana took the ashes to Swinbrook for burial. She encountered typical bureaucracy, and a few days before the funeral service it looked as though the ashes would not be released to her in time. With arrangements already in hand Debo considered using a substitute box and burying the genuine ashes later. But it all worked out and Nancy's ashes were duly buried alongside Unity. Later, Pam had a headstone erected on the grave, bearing the heraldic device that Nancy had embossed on her writing-paper. It was a little golden mole, a creature included in the Mitford coat-of-arms. Unfortunately, Debo wrote to Decca, the mason concerned was obviously unfamiliar with moles and on the tombstone 'the result looked more like galloping baby elephants'. The sisters thought it irritating but, still, *rather* hilarious. Just as they roared when they heard that Nancy had told someone that her coffin ought to be 'a Mitford', so that Decca could collect a 10 per cent royalty. It had been a long-running joke between Nancy and Decca that the inexpensive basic coffin she recommended was called 'a Mitford', and that she collected royalties on every one sold. Decca did not attend the funeral but Debo told her all about it: 'green and summery . . . pink and yellow roses all over the grey-yellow stone . . . there were many friends and none of those ghastly people who crowd into Memorial Services'.[21] She sent a photograph of herself, Pam and Diana in 'deepest black', taken, she said, by a reporter hiding behind a wool merchant's gravestone. 'The result is enclosed, of 3 witches to make you scream.' It was one of those unfortunate pictures when all the subjects were caught off guard looking grim, but James Lees-Milne met Pam at a luncheon party shortly afterwards and she was, he wrote in his diary, 'looking more beautiful than words can say. Her face radiates light.'[22]

The middle years of the seventies were busy and fulfilled for Decca, with curious twists of fate intervening to change the direction of her life. One morning, to her gratified amazement, she opened the mail to find she had been offered the post of 'Distinguished Professor' by the Department of Sociology at California State University at San José, on the strength of *The American Way of Death*. Initially she did not intend to take up the offer, and was content to send copies of the letter triumphantly to her family and friends, but the more she thought about it, the more attractive it sounded. She was offered an honorarium of ten thousand dollars and a faculty house on campus to lecture to 'a small class of honours and/or graduate students' between the end of September 1973 and the end of January 1974. 'We seem to be in a period of rather active intellectual ferment,' the chairman said seductively, 'which I suspect would be as exciting to you as it is to us.'[23]

Decca took on the task with her customary *élan* and within days had clashed with the university authorities for describing the college's loyalty oath as 'obnoxious, silly and demeaning'. Her refusal to have her fingerprints taken 'for records' became a *cause célèbre* when she instigated proceedings against the university after being told that she either gave her fingerprints or faced being locked out of classes. Her lectures were oversubscribed by many times and two hundred students showed up for the first one in a room designed for thirty-five. Though she treated the responsibility seriously her droll manner kept the students in stitches and she made her points as though regaling dinner guests with anecdotes. Deemed a huge success, despite the 'ruckus' over fingerprinting, her time at San José University led to other short-term academic contracts, including periods at Yale and Harvard. In 1974 she was awarded an honorary degree as Doctor of Letters by Smith College. This entitled her, she learned, to the letters D. Litt after her name. 'Wouldn't Muv be amazed to find that Little D. has been transformed into D. Litt?' she wrote to her sisters.

During a trip to Europe after the term at Yale, Decca and Bob spent a few nights at Debo's Lismore Castle. 'Bob's face when the butler came to the door to ask "Shall I lay out your clothes, sir?"' she wrote to Pele de Lappe, 'was worth the detour, as the *Guide Michelin* would say.' Debo tried hard to bring about reconciliation between Decca and Diana, but Decca felt she could not oblige: 'It's not exactly politics now (except for the feeling one must draw the line somewhere, and you know all that part),' she wrote. 'It's more that having adored her through childhood it makes it 10 times more difficult to have just casual meetings . . . Even our meetings over Nancy's illness (in which Diana was marvellous) were rather agony.'[24]

Still, apart from the coldness between Decca and Diana, the four surviving sisters were closer in the early seventies than they had been at any time since before the war. This happy state was brought to an abrupt end by a biography of Unity, written by David Pryce-Jones, whose father had been a 'what-a-setter' of the old Swinbrook days. Pryce-Jones had written several books, which Decca respected, and he had done a good interview with Nancy. He and the Treuhafts swapped homes one summer, when it suited Decca to have a long-term London base, and his interest was piqued by the items of Mitford memorabilia he saw lying around in the Oakland house, 'some of the Acton drawings of the sisters . . . Coronation chairs with blue velvet seats and the royal monogram, and Lady Redesdale's set of Luneville china'.[25] A copy of *Jew Süss* with Unity's signature and the date June 1930 especially intrigued him. Subsequently he approached Decca suggesting that he write a biography of Unity, and she gave him what she said was a noncommittal reply, but which he took to be her approval. 'It's not quite like that,' Decca told Debo later, 'I told him that while I was not averse to his having a go at it, the other sisters might be. And that I thought it would be hopeless to try to do it in the face of family opposition . . . After that I forgot about it.'[26] Debo considered it still too early for a biography of Unity, and that without having known Unity intimately 'he couldn't possibly get the hang of the amazing contradictions of her character, nor her great funniness, nor her oddness. Therefore it would miss the point and be Nazis all the way.'[27]

The biography went ahead, and was published in 1976. Though she wrote to Pryce-Jones saying that she thought the epilogue 'really terrific', Decca refused to allow it to be dedicated to her. Even so, her connection with the author caused a great deal of bother between Decca and her family and Mitford friends in England. Pryce-Jones did a huge amount of new research, tracking down childhood friends, people who had known Unity in Germany in the late thirties, and even medical staff who had nursed her after her attempted suicide. The result, which contained verbatim transcripts of interviews with Unity's German connections, and snippets of information gleaned from cousins and family connections, was poorly received by Unity's loved ones, who tended to blame Decca for its publication. It is true that she helped the author with advice and information, telling him on a number of occasions that he must keep her assistance confidential, as she knew her family would disapprove. She hated the thought of losing contact with her family in England ('I dread losing Debo for ever'), but that rebellious streak still ran strong and she gibed at the fact that Debo had made herself the 'self-appointed arbiter of all that concerned the family (especially as I am three years older than she is)'.[28] But not all the family information in the book came from Decca. Diana gave the author a very long interview telling him things of which Decca had not known. This, he told Decca, led him to believe that if he worked at it he could make Diana 'an ally'. He underestimated Diana. She was never in favour and wrote 'an extremely hostile review' in *Books and Bookmen*. Several people made a determined attempt to have publication stopped, the Devonshires, Lord Harlech and the Mosleys among them. This rebounded on them for, although undoubtedly upsetting to the author at the time, it nevertheless gave the book much valuable pre-release publicity. Diana states that she wrote to fourteen people who were interviewed and quoted in the book and received back thirteen replies claiming they had been misquoted. One interviewee, Paulette Helleu, daughter of the painter, was prepared to take legal action through French courts.

But the author's claims were only half the problem as far as the family were concerned. It was what was perceived as Decca's disloyalty that most offended. And when some photographs, which Pam recalled having last seen in Sydney's photo album, appeared in the plate section, she wrote to Decca in cold anger: 'I suppose you gave them to him, you could have asked us first. The album . . . that Debo always had in her drawing room is missing and can't be found anywhere. Did you borrow it perhaps, as I believe you are writing your own life? If so we would all like to have it back.'[29] Decca was livid and wrote a furious reply, which put her and Pam on 'non-speakers' for more than a year.

Decca had not provided the pictures, and it is clear from correspondence between her and Pryce-Jones that a cousin had supplied the items in question from her own collection. When her immediate anger subsided Decca wrote in hurt tones to Debo, the only sister with whom she was still in regular contact: 'I don't know where we stand . . . [and] I am terrifically sad to think that perhaps this means it's curtains for us.' Lots of old hurts were aired, including the fact that Decca had been totally excluded from any contact with Harold Acton when he was writing his biography of Nancy (published a year previously). 'He asked if he could quote from *Hons and Rebels*, & I said of course and he did, extensively, but only to contradict everything I'd said. You and Woman were closeted with him . . . but not me. I admit that at that point a certain stubbornness set in. I mean, why should you be the final arbiter of everything about the family?' On and on, the letter went, listing the hurts and slights. 'Not only didn't I steal your photo album, I sent you all the Muv letters from the island . . .'[30]

Debo was equally upset by the episode. 'For goodness' sake don't let's quarrel,' she begged. 'Here we are getting old, I couldn't bear it . . . I suppose what we must do is face the fact that we are deeply divided in thought about many things, but that underneath our ties are strong.' Nevertheless, she was deeply unhappy about the book, and felt she must state her case before the matter was shelved. She deprecated the Pryce-Jones portrait of Unity, and like Diana, Pam and the cousins she blamed Decca for co-operating in its production. Mainly, though, she said, she was deeply saddened that none of Unity's good qualities were revealed: 'her huge, bold truthfulness, funniness, generosity, honesty and courage'. She explained that, like Diana, she had been contacted by many of those interviewed, claiming to have been misquoted in the book, and particularly offensive, to those who had sight of the manuscript, had been a claim by one interviewee that Unity had performed a lewd sexual act. 'How can you, as Muv's daughter, condone such writing?' Debo asked sadly. In the event Andrew persuaded the publishers to remove this paragraph before publication.

An uneasy truce followed with Debo and Decca trying hard in their correspondence to act as though the accusation of theft of the scrapbook did not lie between them. Decca visited England in early December in connection with a television documentary. She and Debo enjoyed a pleasant dinner together but they did not touch on the subject of Unity; nor was the joint letter, which Pam, Debo and Diana sent to *The Times* on the eighteenth of that month, mentioned. The letter alleged that the book was at best an inaccurate picture of Unity, and stated that they held letters from a number of interviewees who claimed to have been misquoted. Also they had Unity's papers, including her diary, to which the author had not had access. Cousin Clementine, daughter of the long-dead Uncle Clement, David's elder brother, now Lady Beit, wrote to Decca to say that the biography, when it was released, 'did not cause as much fuss as the scrapbook! The hysteria about the PJ book was violent and did untold harm to the sisters' cause . . . It was difficult to be objective about the book when it appeared. It was as if Bobo just lay there inert, with mud flying and her tragedy totally misunderstood. The book, for me, started as a quest and turned into a witch hunt and I felt David [Pryce-Jones] grew to hate her . . . I felt he did not want to understand her.'[31]

Perhaps at the heart of the matter was that Decca had long ago crossed an invisible line of behaviour acceptable to her family in England. People of her parents' generation, and even most of her own, lived by a strict code that Decca never accepted, hardly recognized. By running away, by treating her parents as she and Esmond had done, by her active Marxism, by the hurtful, small exaggerations in her book, funny though they were, she had broken this code and although she was still loved and welcomed back, her loyalty was never entirely trusted.

The row rumbled on until, in December 1977, the scrapbook was discovered, unaccountably where it was always supposed to have been, in Debo's drawing room. No one knew how it had been missed in the searches. It was 'very *strange*,' Decca wrote pointedly in answer to Pam's explanation for 'it was the size of a table'. But she also noted that 'there was never a word of apology', for the inference that she had stolen it. Nevertheless, after relieving herself of a few home truths, she said she was prepared to forget the whole unpleasant matter. She was going to be in London for a few nights on her way to Egypt where she was to write an article on the tomb of King Mut ('an ancient forebear?' she joked). 'Perhaps we could meet on neutral ground? ("But we *have* met," as Uncle Geoff said to Aunt Weenie.)'

When she tried to pin people down about what so offended them about *Hons and Rebels* she was given nebulous answers about old annoyances. There was the grass snake round the lavatory-chain story that was 'a complete invention', the grave with railings at Swinbrook church in which Decca claimed she had left her pet lamb Miranda while attending Sunday services – 'impossible for the purposes of enclosing a lamb,' said her siblings. She had tried, she told Debo, 'to explain about Boud; a near impossibility to get her down as she really was, so no doubt I failed. To this day I dream about her, arriving fresh from Germany in full gaiety, with all her amusingness etc. but Hen, don't you see how *awful* it all was?' The trouble was that they could all see how awful it was, but they wanted the awfulness to be left to history and remember the bold, lively, inventive Unity in private; they did not want her life continually disinterred. Nor, since most of them had either actively fought or opposed Hitler from the grimness that was wartime England, did they especially care for Decca's general dismissal of them all as Fascists.

Despite all the squabbles and period of non-speakers Decca remained in touch, mainly due to Debo who, following Sydney's death, became the heart of the immediate family. Decca regarded Debo as 'over-protective' of the family story, without realizing, probably, that Debo had been the sister most affected by everything that had happened. As the youngest child, Debo's adolescence had been rocked by the scandals of Diana's divorce and remarriage, Decca's elopement, Unity's involvement with Hitler and her subsequent suicide attempt. At each crisis David decreed that the sister concerned must not be visited or contacted. The others all had homes of their own in the years when the ideological quarrel between Sydney and David was as its height; Debo was the only one left at home to watch the painful disintegration of the marriage. And during the war, Unity's behaviour made it impossible for Debo to remain with her mother in the year before her marriage to Andrew. It is hardly surprising that she was unhappy at having it all regurgitated. But it is clear that Debo's strongest desire was to keep the family together.

The correspondence between her and Decca kept them in touch with the pattern of each other's family life, the marriages of children, births of grandchildren, the deaths of old friends and the previous generation, the daily domestic trivia that was so different for each woman. 'Derek Jackson came and stayed [for the wedding of Debo's daughter, Sophia]. It is so queer that he still thinks of us all as his family after 5 [*sic*] wives since Pam,' Debo wrote. 'She said, "Hallo, horse," when he came in, as though nothing had happened.' Sometimes, letters would contain phrases in Boudledidge (confusing to a researcher) such as, '*Jaub, Dzdiddle no zdmudkung* [yes, still no smoking] – I long for a puff,' and a scribbled message on the outside of an envelope, '*Jegg engludzed* [cheque enclosed]'.

By now Decca had a well-established and large circle of friends in England, completely unconnected with the Mitford family, but still she felt the pull of blood ties and she and Debo usually met whenever she was in England. Because they wanted desperately to save their friendship the two sisters found a formula by which they were able to put aside their accepted differences, and this worked well except every now and then when Debo would mutter, 'All those lies, hen.'[32] But there was always restraint in Decca's relationships with the greater family, and even with Pam for a while. There was no relationship at all with Diana: the brief truce during Nancy's illness was never reinstated. Curiously, although Decca liked Diana's son Desmond enormously, she could not bear his elder brother Jonathan. She had not seen him since he was four years old when he offended her by giving the Nazi salute, and when he became chairman of the ultra-conservative Monday Club (1970–72), he was forever branded by her 'a dangerous neo-Nazi'.

Shortly after the row about the Unity biography, Diana published her autobiography, *A Life of Contrasts* – 'the truth,' she teased, 'but not necessarily the whole truth'. It was extensively reviewed, and generally accepted as having been well written, but it was slated all the same. Many reviewers used the same phrase: Lady Mosley, they said, was 'unrepentant'. In the main this referred to the fact that Diana wrote her memories of Hitler, the man she had liked and admired, as though none of the things he did later (and none of the things which he was doing at the time, and which came to light afterwards) had occurred. That subsequent historical perspective did not change her original memories rankled. She did not condone the horrors perpetrated by his regime, but merely stated what her own reactions had been at the time. In turn, she had been offended by the factual inaccuracies published about Hitler by journalists and successive biographers; the fact was, she wrote, that she had observed a charming, cultured man, who did not rant and foam at the mouth (as was frequently claimed), with well-manicured hands (not roughened and nail-bitten), a fastidious man who ate sparingly (rather than the cartoon character who stuffed himself with cream cakes). Her lack of criticism brought fury raging down on her head, and her account of her time in the filthy conditions of Holloway invited the comments that many millions of women were incarcerated in far worse conditions during the war, thanks to Hitler and his supporters. A recent biography of Diana suggests that although the book answered some questions and repaid some recent slights it was substantially a vehicle for continuing the campaign that Diana had waged for the past fifty years: that of supporting and defending Mosley.[33] As every author knows, controversy never hurts a book and *A Life of Contrasts* sold well. 'Diana's style is better than Nancy's,' James Lees-Milne wrote in his diary. 'It lacks N's debutante touch, and is confident and adult.'[34]

Despite the hostility of her reviewers, Diana decided to write another book and her subject was hardly less controversial. Quite close to the Mosleys' Temple de la Gloire was the Moulin de la Tuilerie. Nancy had once considered buying the property when it was an unrestored old mill, but at the time she could not bear the thought of moving so far from the Colonel. Subsequently it was purchased by the Duke and Duchess of Windsor and converted into a sumptuous home. Neighbourly invitations were exchanged and when the Windsors first went to visit the Mosleys at the tiny temple, the Duchess said, 'Yes, it's very pretty here, but where do you *live*?'[35]

The Windsors and Mosleys liked each other and got on well. Perhaps part of the reason lay in the fact that both couples suffered from a perpetual bad press, and that the lives of each, despite the happiness of a sound marriage, were tinged by the underlying waste of unfulfilled promise. The uncharitable, among whom was Decca, saw it as a natural friendship 'given their mutual support of Hitler', though the Duke of Windsor's so-called 'support' of Hitler's regime is even now far from being proven. But it would be surprising if there was no understanding between two women who had each devoted her life to supporting a man deprived of what he regarded as his destiny. Diana regarded the Duke's treatment by the Royal Family as unfair. It was monstrous, she thought, 'to stop him *doing anything* and then to put it about that he was frivolous and lazy'.[36]

After the Duke's death, when the Duchess had slipped into a long-term comatose state, Diana's old friend Lord Longford (formerly Frank Pakenham), who was a director of Sidgwick and Jackson, visited the Mosleys at the Temple. He persuaded Diana to write a biography of Wallis, to correct the many 'lies' that pro-liferated about her friend.[37] The result is an interesting review of an enigmatic personality, and could hardly be otherwise for Diana had known the Duchess well at a personal level for some years. But it was roughly treated by many reviewers, and con-demned as 'a hagiography', presumably because Diana did not subscribe to bringing down her subject, which more and more seems regarded as an essential part of a biographical study. Present-day Royal researchers, however, see Diana's treatment as an important book in the Windsor canon and it sold a respectable 23,000 copies in hardback.

Decca, predictably, deplored it, and dismissed it in her cor-respondence as '*Woman's Own* writing'. She always displayed a certain amount of *schadenfreude* when Diana was castigated in the press. In answer to one letter from her, Rudbin replied, 'Actually I'm rather enjoying it and Diana is forgiven all for me by the glorious quote: "Come, come, said Tom's father, at your time of life/You've no long excuse for playing the rake/It is time that you thought, boy, of taking a wife/Why, so it is father: But whose wife shall I take."'[38]

Some years earlier Mosley had been diagnosed with Parkinson's disease. He staved off the worst symptoms longer than is usual because he was so strong and fit, had an agile brain and quick manner. In 1968 he had been the subject of a prestigious *Panorama* programme on BBC Television. Over eight million people tuned in to watch his hour-long inter-view with James Mossman, at that time a record audience. Throughout his seventies he was always happy to be inter-viewed on television or radio, to argue his corner, to write articles, and shine at dinner parties, but from his eightieth birthday in 1976 there was a clear deterioration. The drugs he needed to take in increasing doses caused him to fall over from time to time.

James Lees-Milne found Mosley physically frail but in good

spirits when he visited the couple at the Temple in May 1980. Mosley was now, he wrote in his diary,

> a very old man. Shapeless, bent, blotched cheeks, cracked nose, no moustache, and tiny eyes in place of those luminous, dilating orbs. I sat with him after dinner on a sofa and talked for an hour . . . Sir O has mellowed to the extent of never saying anything pejorative about anybody . . . I asked boldly if he thought he had made a mistake in founding the New Party. He admitted it was the worst mistake of his life. [He said] the British do not like New Parties . . . that if he had led the Labour government he would have kept Edward VIII on the throne. He [the King] was eminently suited to be an intermediary between his country and the dictators. Said that critics of himself and Duke of Windsor never made allowances for the fact that they detested war, having experienced the horrors of the trenches. They wanted to avoid it happening again at all costs . . . He stands unsteadily, but assured me his head was all right. Held me by both hands and said I must come again. 'Why not come tomorrow? Come and stay.' Charming he was.[39]

It was the last time Lees-Milne saw him. Mosley died quietly and suddenly in bed in November 1980.

For Diana it was as though her own life had come to an end. She had been utterly devoted to Mosley during the whole of their forty-four years of marriage and now her family wondered how she would ever cope without him. And though it was a shock, in a sense they were not surprised when Diana suffered what appeared to be a stroke and partial paralysis within a year of Mosley's death.

Further investigation proved that it had not been a stroke, but a brain tumour, and just as Nancy linked the trauma of the

Colonel's marriage to the development of her cancer, Diana suspected that the development of the tumour in her brain was connected with her devastation at losing Mosley.[40] It was thought that she could not survive. She was flown to a hospital in London where the tumour was confirmed and an operation was scheduled to remove it. 'Oh, hen,' Debo wrote tearfully to Decca, 'she is a person one thought nothing could ever happen to. A rock like figure in my life and lots of other people's.'

Against all the odds – Diana was seventy-one and frail after Mosley's death – the surgery was a complete success. Her paralysis gradually diminished and she was able to get about. Visitors to nearby wards were startled by the shrieks and roars of laughter that emanated from her room as a constant trickle of old friends dropped in to keep her company. It was a reminder of the words of her former wardress at Holloway to a journalist: 'We've never had such laughs since Lady Mosley left.' Her doctor thought at one point that she might be hysterical and ought to be watched. But it was just typical Diana; like her sisters, she is simply so inherently funny that it is impossible not to be amused by her.

One of her most frequent visitors was Lord Longford, who had become a national figure, known, among other things, for his championship of lost causes in the British prison service. As a director of Sidgwick and Jackson, he was one of Diana's publishers, and he and the Mosleys had been in the habit of meeting for luncheon whenever they all happened to be in London, their political differences put to one side. But Diana was touched by his visits to her in hospital. 'Frank's so faithful, the way he comes all the time,' she told her son. And she paused for a moment, before adding, 'Of course he thinks I'm Myra Hindley.'[41]

22

RELATIVELY CALM
WATERS
(1980–2000)

After Nancy's death Decca remained implacable towards Diana, her antagonism too ingrained for her to make any concessions. Throughout the 1980s and early 1990s, the tenor of all the sisters' lives was occasionally interrupted by tensions caused either by Decca provoking her sisters to annoyance by something she said or wrote, or by her reacting to something they had said or written to which she objected. One of these was Diana's portrait of Mosley, contained in her book, *Loved Ones*, which she wrote while convalescing at Chatsworth from her brain-tumour operation. However, Decca contented herself with private criticism in her letters and did not break into print about it, out of consideration for Debo.

Decca's career as a journalist was now at its zenith, and she was a regular and respected contributor to organs such as the *Spectator*, the *Observer* and the *New Statesman* in England, and *Esquire*, *Life* and *Vanity Fair* in the USA. In addition she wrote scores of newspaper articles. Her income from her writing was substantial and despite her apparent indifference to it, one of her intellectual friends told me, 'Decca was financially *very* astute.'[1] Like Nancy, she had triumphed over what both sisters regarded as a lack of education, and had made her way in a tough profession with better than average success. An objective reader might be justified in thinking that the sisters placed more value on formal school education than it warranted, for the true test of Sydney's system was surely what her daughters were able to achieve. When the BBC made a documentary about Decca called *The Honourable Rebel*[2] and she was a guest on the BBC Radio programme, *Desert Island Discs*[3] some of her remarks about their parents, and her stories about the family, were again the cause of a temporary coolness between her and her sisters, even though by this time they had more or less come to expect her to be controversial.

Many readers of this book will be familiar with the BBC production *Love in a Cold Climate*, screened in the spring of 2001. But when, in 1980, Julian Jebb made a television documentary about Nancy, called *Nancy Mitford – a Portrait by Her Sisters,* he inadvertently stirred up what he described as a hornets' nest. His programme was intended to coincide with an earlier dramatization based on *Love in a Cold Climate* and *The Pursuit of Love*, and given access to Nancy's (then) unpublished letters he had been fascinated by the two sides of Nancy: her wit, liveliness and genuine warmth which co-existed with snobbery and the malice so often evident in her teases. Jebb interviewed and filmed Debo and Diana together. 'Lady Mosley and the Duchess loved each other, that was clear at once,' he noted. 'It was not immediately apparent how profound, intense and comical is the Duchess's protective instinct for those she loves, who include every member of the family, living or recently dead.'

As for Diana, 'It is hard to convey her charm, even more to defend her politics,' he wrote. 'The latter are neither flaunted nor evaded but when they come up in conversation they are defended or explained with a temperance of language equalled by a gentleness of tone.'[4] He was especially interested that this most beautiful woman was camera-shy. It seems that just as a plain

woman may have a love affair with the camera and appear a rav-
ishing beauty on screen, the reverse can happen too. It is certainly
true that there are few photographs that show Diana's real beauty
in the way that paintings of her do. 'As soon as we began to
film,' he said, 'her face lost all its customary animation and her
replies to my questions came as if from a mask with darting
eyes.' He concluded that she felt trapped by the camera.

He filmed Pam at her home in Gloucestershire in front of the
blue stove that really *was* the colour of her eyes,[5] and on location
at Swinbrook, standing by the River Windrush, reading Nancy's
description of 'Uncle Matthew and the chubb-fuddler'. Then he
flew to California to conduct his interview with Decca. It had
been set up in advance and he took to her warmth and sense of
fun immediately. Things only began to go wrong when she produced a form for him to sign. This made her co-operation
conditional on his including in the programme extracts of a
letter about Tom, written by Nancy in 1968, at the time of the
publication of Mosley's autobiography. 'Have you noted all the
fuss about Sir Os? . . . I'm very cross with him for saying Tud was
a fascist which is untrue though of course Tud was a fearful old
twister & probably was a fascist when with Diana. When with
me he used to mock to any extent how he hated Sir Os no doubt
about that.'[6]

Jebb was taken aback: 'The letter was bound to offend Diana
and might annoy the other sisters,' he wrote in an article for the
Sunday Times in the spring of 1980. 'First I thought it was wrong
of Decca not to have told me this condition before I had travelled
all the way to California . . . second I thought it ironic that the
great upholder of liberal principles should impose what
amounted to censorship, for it is just as restricting to be forced to
include something as it is to be forced to delete it.'[7] In the end,
though, Decca prevailed and he had no option but to include the
letter. Working with Decca, he was struck by her articulate pro-
fessionalism, but also by her 'intense sadness' at her long

separation from Nancy. Diana was not upset, but she insisted on stating during her interview that Tom had been a paid-up member of the BUF, a fact now historically confirmed and curious in view of his pro-Jewish sympathies.

The letter certainly caused more bother between the sisters in private than its inclusion in the programme merited, and following this incident Decca made a trip to England without contacting Debo or Pam. The public, however, was now so inured to the political rivalries of the sisters that the item about Tom failed to have any shock impact. Decca had felt she must make the point about her brother for he had been the only member of the family whom Esmond could bear. When the dust settled she wrote to Debo explaining that she simply didn't believe Tom had been a Fascist. 'Neither, apparently, did Nancy, so I wanted to be sure to get that in.' But it is clear from Tom's own correspondence with his oldest friend, James Lees-Milne (which, of course, Decca would never have seen), that he was sympathetic to Fascism if not Nazism. The real surprise of the programme was seventy-three-year-old Pam, for in it the 'quiet sister' emerged as a star performer. Giggling, pretty, funny and sometimes serious, she positively stole the show from her more famous sisters.

At this point the Mitford industry, as the sisters referred to books and articles about their family, was at its peak, and books, plays and articles proliferated. There was a light-hearted musical called *The Mitford Girls* based on their lives. When Diana, Debo and Pam attended a performance the manager of the theatre gave them badges to wear, which read, 'I really AM a Mitford girl.'[8] One of the most important of the books was arguably Nicholas Mosley's *Rules of the Game*, published in 1982, about his father. Nicholas was Mosley's son by Cimmie, and the book was candid about Mosley's prolific sex life and his mother's distress at his father's infidelity. Among other revelations he included private letters between his parents, written when

Mosley and Diana were lovers in the period leading up to Cimmie's death. Diana and her Mosley children were outraged, as were Nicholas's own brother and sister. Diana was motivated by a fierce protectiveness of the love of her life for whom she was still grieving. Nicholas' siblings and his half-brothers perhaps felt they had already suffered enough publicity because of their father. They all felt it was 'too soon' to make this sensitive material public.

Nicholas justified the book by explaining that his father had asked him to write it shortly before he died, and that Diana had given him the letters without reading them. This surely says a great deal about Diana, for how many second wives would hand over this type of correspondence without at least a glance at it out of curiosity? Max, Mosley's youngest son and Nicholas' half-brother, suggested that his father was not *compos mentis* when he gave permission for the book, but Nicholas pointed out that Diana had been present at the time. Diana attempted to have publication stopped, but once again the action merely resulted in publicity, which helped the book. It was hard for Diana to have this aspect of the personal life of the man she still worshipped spread out for public consumption, and from a source that gave it such authenticity. Predictably, Decca rather enjoyed the embarrassment caused and made quips about it in her voluminous correspondence.

A year later Jonathan and Catherine Guinness wrote *The House of Mitford*, in which the Mosley case was strongly argued. This time it was Decca who refused to co-operate by withholding permission for any quotes from *Hons and Rebels*, or indeed any of her books or letters. 'Leave me out,' she wrote to her nephew grimly, 'you'll have plenty of copy from the rest of the family.'[9] Her dislike of Jonathan had been bolstered recently at a meeting with his daughter Catherine who, when interviewing Decca for an article, showed her a letter from Jonathan in which he warned her about Decca:

She's a very tough cookie [he wrote], a hardened and
intelligent Marxist agitator who knows very subtly how to
play on her upper-class background so as to enlist residual
snobbery (on both sides of the Atlantic) in establishing
Marxism. But this leads to problems of identity; to an
ambiguity as to what is real and what is an act. All this
was very evident in her TV appearance here. Bob Treuhaft
came over better, at least he *is* what he is. He is one piece
so to speak, the bright Jewish boy with his ready made
'red diaper' principles, seeing (e.g.) Chatsworth from the
outside with the healthy irony of a social historian.[10]

Decca interpreted this letter as implying that she was 'a liar
and not to be trusted', though Jonathan did not use those words.
One friend of many to whom she wrote about the affair, wisely
counselled her: 'He probably doesn't understand the immensely
important help you have given by instinct and design, to a host
of people, for most of your life, and you will never understand
that the very rich and powerful, in their isolation, also need
succour.'

For fear of alienating Debo again, Decca refused to review
the book for the *Guardian*. Instead, she sent sheets of quotable
material to her circle of literary friends in England for them to
use in their own reviews of the book, which she described privately as 'a puff job for the Mosley faction'. Several reviewers used
extracts from these 'crib sheets' of Decca's, and at least one major
review was copied almost word-for-word from Decca's comments. Decca knew her way about the world of English
reviewing which she described as 'a small pond where people
scratch each other's backs – or bite each other's backs – and they
all know each other. At least in California if your book is
reviewed well you know it's because they like it.'[11]

She employed the same tactics two years later when Selina
Hastings brought out a biography of Nancy. Decca was surprised

to hear that Debo, Pam, Diana and some of their childhood friends and cousins liked the new portrait of Nancy. But her contemporary letters show that she had taken against the author even before she read the book, for quite another reason: in writing to Decca, and to a New York newspaper, the author had signed herself 'Lady Selina Hastings'. This irritated Decca: she regarded it as snobbish and she was determined not to like the book. When the biography was published it contained a derogatory remark about Bob (Treuhaft) and as far as Decca was concerned the gloves were off. She wrote a review, 'Commentary in Defence of Nancy',[12] which was a brilliant, scathing and, of course, amusing condemnation of the book, but unfair in that she based her criticism upon a few selected passages. She made no reference to the immense amount of fascinating new material about Nancy's relationship with Palewski, including their private correspondence, which even Decca privately conceded was 'amazing'. And, even accounting for personal taste, the Hastings biography was far more incisive than the previous one, written by Harold Acton shortly after Nancy's death, which Decca found unsatisfactory. In case they should miss seeing her review, Decca copied it and sent it to all her Mitford friends and connections, some of whom – to their credit – wrote to disagree with her opinion. 'Thank you for sending me your championship of Nancy,' James Lees-Milne wrote, while also advising that she had misquoted him in her review. 'The Redesdale motto should be "Decca Careth For Us", instead of God,* for whom I don't suppose you have much use. And I admire your loyalty but, alas, I'm afraid we don't yet agree even on [this] book.'[13]

What makes this review, and those Decca wrote of other books at the time, especially interesting to a biographer is what it reveals about Decca's tight and confident literary style. For all

*Redesdale motto: *God Careth For Us.*

the success of her first book *Hons and Rebels* (in the opinion of many, including me, her best book) Decca's literary voice then had been that of an apprentice compared to what it was to become. By the 1980s her irreverent flourish had developed a polish that placed her in a superior pantheon as a wordsmith. And although her books after *The American Way of Death* did not have the same massive success, they were generally profitable and, more importantly, because of them, she was in constant demand for nearly two decades as a journalist and speaker. A simple list of her published articles would cover a dozen pages and she never failed to be delighted when offered a huge sum of money for her words.

It was at this point, in the mid-1980s, that I came into contact with her. She was warm, kind, bubbling. In interviews for this book I learned from numbers of people of her generosity to friends in trouble. Indeed, some months after our first contact, when she heard that my partner had died suddenly she was both hugely sympathetic and practical. She was, in fact, pretty well irresistible. This was the side of Decca that her friends saw, but woe betide an enemy. As an opponent Decca transformed herself into a determined avenger, able to use the power of words and her celebrity status as weapons. Her letters to friends are as full of spicy gossip as were Nancy's.

In January 1984 Decca flew to Nicaragua with a group of writers concerned with press censorship there and in neighbouring El Salvador. Within a short time of her arrival she suffered a deep-vein thrombosis while getting into an elevator: 'It was a very odd experience,' she said later, 'first a hand went, then a foot . . .'[14] Fortunately, it was only a minor stroke and within a few months she had recovered and was back to normal, apart from a moderate limp. But it frightened her. For years she had been drinking and smoking heavily – when short of words she found drinking helped, and she had been addicted to cigarettes from her youth. Now, three years short of seventy, these indulgences began to take an inevitable toll. Warned to give up smoking at least, she promised to try, and took to chewing a brand of gum marketed in the USA as an aid to quitting, 'because I have been such a bore to Bob and everyone,' she wrote to Debo. 'He was a total saint this time but how can he be expected to be ditto if it recurs due to my own fault?'

Apart from a few months for recuperation from the stroke, her work was unaffected. Later in 1984 she wrote *Faces of Philip*, an affectionate memoir of Philip Toynbee, Esmond's oldest friend, and she followed this with a biography of her mother's heroine, Grace Darling. Both books required her to spend long periods in England researching, and *Grace Had an English Heart* was eventually published in 1987. Neither of these latter books sold in quantity and Decca became bored with Grace Darling long before she completed the work. 'Grey Starling is about to take wing,' she wrote to her correspondents, 'oh the amazing relief. *Decompression.*' She was far more interested in the fulfilment of a long-held ambition: a trip to Russia.

Bob and Benjamin, along with Dinky, her husband and two children, and her immense circle of friends in the Bay area, many of whom dated back to the days when she had first arrived in California in the early 1940s, were paramount in her life, but she relished any new controversy that reared its head in the news as natural fodder for her articles. In the spring of 1989 the Islamic *fatwa* was declared on Salman Rushdie for his book *Satanic Verses*. On the day this was announced Decca appeared wearing an outsize cardboard lapel badge upon which she had printed 'I *AM* Salman Rushdie'. Later the badge went into production and was worn all over the USA by those opposed to literary censorship, and subsequently Rushdie himself was absorbed into Decca's vast international circle of literary and media friends. 'About the Salman Rushdie badges,' Decca wrote gaily to Debo, 'I'd send you one, but I fear you don't look much like him.'

Some years earlier, in 1982, Debo had also broken into print with *The House*; it was part autobiography and part a contemporary history of Chatsworth. She had written it as a product for the Chatsworth shops but it sold well generally, both in the UK and the USA, and she suddenly found herself touring on the lecture circuit in its wake. 'Nancy once told me,' Decca wrote, 'that if you ever became a writer you'd put us both in the shade.' In response to frequent requests from visitors Debo also wrote *The Estate* in 1990 (and in 2001 was working on a revision of *The House* prior to its planned republication).

When Andrew and Debo celebrated their golden wedding anniversary in 1991, the Duke spoke of their years together: 'My wife and I realize how lucky we have been,' he said. On thinking how best to celebrate the occasion he had had the idea of a 'golden wedding party' to which he and Debo would invite not friends and dignitaries but other Derbyshire couples who had married in 1941. He thought that, with luck, a dozen or so marriages might have survived fifty years and made the announcement. To the Devonshires' surprise and amusement, nearly a thousand couples applied, not all from Derbyshire, and this resulted in a massive party, held in a marquee almost a quarter of a mile long, at Chatsworth. There are undoubtedly some who would dismiss this generous gesture as paternalism, but there is equally no doubt that the happy occasion gave pleasure to a large number of people, and the attitude of the Duke and Duchess towards each other at that event showed the depth of their affection for each other.

In the latter years of the 1980s, Diana and Pam, who was now increasingly lame in the right leg that had been weak since her childhood attack of polio – 'I'm a bit short in the offside leg,' she would say in answer to enquiries – spent a number of holidays together, in Switzerland and Italy in the summer, and several winters in South Africa. They had grown very close in the last decade and enjoyed each other's company. 'I do hate winters now I'm old,' Diana wrote to James Lees-Milne. 'I feel happy in the sun among flowers.'[15]

She had endeavoured, in the absence of Mosley, to fill her life with serenity and beauty, but in November 1989 she provoked national controversy merely by appearing as a guest on *Desert Island Discs*. The BBC had tried to air the programme on three occasions: the first date they chose, 8 October, was changed because someone rang in to say that it was the eve of Yom Kippur, which was surely inappropriate scheduling. It was then announced that the programme would air on 1 October but the schedulers were advised that this was Rosh Hashana (Jewish New Year). A third date announced, 19 November, was found to be the date of the annual memorial parade of Jewish veterans, so the programme was rescheduled for a fourth time to 26 November. To Decca, it did not matter when the programme aired: the mere fact of giving Diana an opportunity to speak in public proved that the BBC was 'deeply imbued with the deep-dyed anti-Semitism that pervades all England'.[16]

As always, Diana answered the presenter's questions frankly, calmly and without hedging or exaggeration. Hitler was, she said, 'extraordinarily fascinating and clever. Naturally. You don't get to be where he was just by being the kind of person people like to think he was . . . Of course, at that moment he was the person who was making the news and therefore he was extremely interesting to talk to.' He had mesmeric blue eyes, she recalled. She had never believed there would be war between England and Germany, 'I thought reason would prevail,' she said. 'Had I the slightest idea I would be imprisoned I would have given up going to Germany. My duty was to be with my children.' She minded very much that she had missed those vital years of her children's lives: they had all changed completely by the time she was released.

According to newspaper reports, many listeners were upset by what appeared to be Diana's defence of Hitler, but Jewish leaders were infuriated by her championship of Mosley. Denying that he was anti-Semitic, she said, 'He really wasn't, you know. He didn't know a Jew from a Gentile . . . But he was attacked so much by Jews both in the newspapers and physically on marches . . . that he picked up the challenge. Then a great number of his followers who really were anti-Semitic joined him because they thought they would fight their old enemy.' Yes, she admitted, he had referred to Jews as 'an alien force which rises to rob us of our heritage' in a speech in 1936. 'One of those things which horrified him,' she said, 'was that we had this enormous Empire and he did think that the Jews, and the City in general, had invested far too much in countries that had nothing to do with our Empire . . . They were attacked by Communists very often on peaceful marches through east London and in all the big cities, and when there is a fight people are injured of course.'[17]

It was undoubtedly insensitive of the BBC to schedule the programme originally so that it coincided with Jewish anniversaries, but equally one senses that the inadvertent clashes of dates merely added another card to the hand of those who opposed the Mosleys, and that Diana would have been attacked, automatically, no matter when the programme went out. A Jewish representative stated, 'The activities of Oswald Mosley in the 1930s were racial, discriminatory and blatantly anti-Semitic. He capitalized on the economic difficulties of the 1930s attempting to throw responsibility on world Jewry . . . There can be no whitewashing Oswald Mosley today . . . BBC listeners should not be exposed to apologia for Hitler and Oswald Mosley.'[18] A BBC statement said that they had received some complaints from Jewish listeners but equally they had received a positive response from people who had enjoyed the programme. Diana had been close to centre stage in world history for a while; therefore, what she had to say was of immense interest.[19]

On 12 April 1994 a devastated Debo telephoned Decca to advise that Pam had died from a blood clot after surgery for a broken leg. Although eighty-six, Pam had continued to lead a full life right to the end, having only to curtail somewhat her beloved trips abroad in recent years. As with her sisters, age had made little difference to the way she lived, thought or wrote, and only physical impossibility prevented her leading the life she had lived since she was a young woman. At her eightieth birthday party she had wowed her guests by appearing in a gold lamé coat, and sat radiant with pleasure, her eyes still that amazing shade of blue, which showed no signs of fading to octogenarian paleness.

The accident occurred during 'a jolly weekend in London'. She had spent the day shopping, and after dinner with friends was invited next door for drinks. Despite her usual care (she had written to Decca a short time earlier advising her to be careful about breaking legs or hips), she fell down some steep steps and suffered a clean fracture below the knee in her weak leg. She was taken to hospital where the bone was successfully pinned, and on coming round from the anaesthetic her first words were 'Who won the Grand National?' Within twenty-four hours she was sitting up in bed entertaining visitors, such as Debo's grand-daughter, Isabel, with her new baby, and several other callers, and being her usual 'terribly funny' self. Debo was in Ireland and spoke to Pam on the phone. She had just arrived in London when she received a message to go directly to the hospital. Pam died ten minutes before Debo could get there.

'But imagine how she, of all people, would loathe a life confined to a wheelchair with somebody to look after her,' Decca wrote. 'And – God forbid, to do the cooking! (how I'd hate to be that somebody, come to think of it).' The last time Decca had seen Pam was in the previous autumn when Decca was a guest speaker at the Cheltenham Literary Festival. She and Bob had taken several people to Pam's cottage ('neat as a pin'), which was near by, and Pam had cooked 'the most delicious 3-course lunch . . . completely single-handed'.[20] The scrapbook row, which Decca had not forgotten but had decided to overlook, was long behind them.

Hosts of friends attended the funeral at Swinbrook to sing the hymn sung at all Mitford funerals, 'Holy, Holy, Holy'. Today, a small oak planted by Pam on the village green is as much a memorial to 'the quiet Mitford sister' as is her headstone in that peaceful place, which held so many childhood memories. Although she had no children of her own Pam's many nieces and nephews were left feeling bereft: 'Tante Femme's' maternal and caring qualities were unique in the family, and of all Sydney's daughters she was the most like her mother. A friend who attended the funeral wrote and told Decca that Debo had forbidden the vicar to preach a sermon – 'So like Farve with his stopwatch set for ten minutes,' Decca commented.

In November that year Decca was staying at Dinky's apartment in New York. She tripped on the hem of her long skirt as she and Bob were leaving to go out to dinner and suffered multiple fractures in her ankle. After a cast was fitted she and Bob were able to fly back to California where she was cared for by Benjamin's Korean wife Jung Min. Decca wrote to Debo that she was well aware that the accident had been caused by clumsiness because she had had too much to drink. She had broken her wrist a year earlier in the same way. She knew she had become far too dependent on alcohol to get her through difficult times, to enjoy good times, and increasingly simply to get her started in the morning. She considered all this and made a decision to give it up, cold turkey.

Dinky was now a highly qualified nurse. At one point she had been appointed a director of the hospital but found she disliked being away from the bedside: her vocation was nursing, not administration. She asked to be returned to nursing, offering her resignation if this could not be arranged, and was subsequently responsible for establishing an acute-pain and palliative-care clinic where she still works. The caring characteristic that Decca had noted in her infant daughter, which had so reminded her of Pam, had never faded, and as a professional Dinky was intensely aware of how difficult it was going to be for Decca to give up drinking. She considered it could not be done without help. 'She drank heavily for years and I do want to mention it because the way in which she gave it up shows the strength of Decca . . . When she tripped on the hem of her skirt she had been drinking and had had too much. It wasn't unusual. She could be very mean when she'd had too much to drink. A different person altogether . . . I never preached to my mother, but she suddenly realized what it was going to mean if she continued drinking as she got older, for example if her drinking caused another stroke . . . she couldn't stand the thought of being alive and dependent.'[21]

Decca confounded Dinky, remaining calm and showing none of the usual symptoms of withdrawal distress. 'She is positively amazing,' Dinky wrote to Maya Angelou. 'She's now [gone] 18 days without a drink. She fired the substance abuse psychiatrist after he droned on about residential treatment, group therapy, AA etc. She just looked at me with her blue, droopy eyes, and said, "I've decided to give it up, that's all."'[22] Dinky said she had never been prouder of her mother than during those early weeks when Decca turned her back on drinking. When she was mobile again, Decca attended AA meetings and Dinky acted as her 'friend'. 'She only ever called me three times,' Dinky said. 'She did it by sheer will-power. Once she gave up drinking she became a different person. A new and softer Decca emerged. All the crossness and meanness disappeared.' Bob agreed with this: it was a return to the old Decca and the Treuhafts' relationship benefited.

Decca's smoking was another matter. She had given up years earlier, ostensibly. While she had even given a series of lectures on 'giving up smoking', her biggest problem during these lectures, she wrote to Debo, was finding the time to run to the ladies' room 'to have a quick puff every now and then'. She chewed nicotine gum at the rate of six packets a day. 'She was so fastidious and it was quite uncharacteristic of her to chew gum,' Bob reflected. He genuinely believed she had given up smoking. One day, however, she was discovered *in flagrante delicto*: 'Dinky caught me and told Bob,' Decca wrote to a friend. 'How *awful* of her . . . So I suppose I will have to give up for real now.' And she did so, though she never got over the craving for cigarettes. 'Oh how I should like a puff,' she wrote wistfully, in letters to her many correspondents.

Now in her mid-seventies Decca kept up a pace that would have punished someone twenty years younger. She was still in demand for lectures and public appearances, even appearing tremulously, on one occasion, side by side with Maya Angelou as they rode two elephants at the head of carnival procession. In June 1996 her broken ankle was giving her trouble; in compensating for it she had thrown out her hip, causing enough pain to make her consult a doctor. She also mentioned to him that she had been coughing blood for a few days. A series of X-rays and blood tests carried out subsequently provided a shock diagnosis: she had lung cancer.

'It's a bit of a facer, Hen,' she wrote to Debo, but she said that she and Bob had decided to go ahead with plans for a holiday in Cape Cod in August. It was a place she had always loved since her time there with Esmond. In recent years she and Bob had visited the resort every summer as guests of Jon Snow, the Channel 4 news anchorman who had become a close friend after helping Decca with some awkward packing after a long visit to London. Decca instantly bestowed upon him the soubriquet 'Packer' Snow. Meanwhile, she said, she was determined to finish her present commission. It was an up-to-date revision of *The American Way of Death* or – as she referred to it in correspondence – 'Death Warmed Up'. She also amused herself by writing to 'Miss Manners', a San Francisco newspaper column on matters of etiquette. Was it, she asked, contrary to the rules of etiquette for a dying person to exploit the pity of their friends to make them do what she wanted?

In July she went into hospital for further tests pending a course of chemotherapy, and the results were even worse than anticipated. The cancer had spread to her liver, kidneys and brain and was thus inoperable. The doctors recommended her to forget chemotherapy and to have radiation of the brain, to conserve its function for as long as possible. With her years of experience at the highest levels of nursing, Dinky was the family spokesperson,[23] and though the prognosis was difficult for the rest of Decca's family to take in, it was perhaps worse for Dinky, who knew precisely what it meant, clinically, for her mother. Decca took it in the way she had always taken bad news: on the chin. 'You're so brave, Little D,' Sydney used to say. Even so, Decca asked Dinky to pass on the news to Debo, Maya and the people closest to her. The one thing she had never been able to face was sympathy.

Writing on 11 July to Debo, to thank her for contacting Jon Snow, Decca said, 'The Packer wrote such a funny fax, saying he'd never heard a Duchess say *Bugger* so much . . .' Her situation was curious, she said. She was suffering no headaches or even malaise following the radiation, just some pain in her thigh. Meanwhile life was quite pleasurable with innumerable friends rallying round, bringing in food and gifts, and she was working on the book. Although she had been given a prognosis of only three months, she found it difficult to believe this could be correct and was half convinced that a major mistake had been made in the diagnosis.

There was no mistake. Within days of writing this letter Decca began to suffer paralysis in the right side of her body and was admitted to hospital. Though concerned, when they ascertained that she had not suffered a stroke, the doctors agreed that she could still go to Cape Cod in a few weeks' time. From then on, however, her deterioration was rapid. 'It seems that one of the cancer lesions in the brain may have swollen or bled a bit,' Dinky reported. A week later Decca was being fed through a tube but after a few days she asked for this treatment to be withdrawn. 'Yesterday she told Bob . . . she wants to come home to die,' Dinky advised Debo. 'She looks pale and tired . . . she wakes up and smiles and tries to talk. She's very clear about what she wants, knows who everyone is. Bob asked her if she wants you to come, and she says she doesn't see the point . . . Who could have imagined this would go so fast?'

Decca's last four days were spent at home: her hospital-type bed was installed in the spacious sitting room she loved, surrounded by her books and pictures, Mitford memorabilia, closest friends and members of her family. Maya Angelou came every day and while Decca could still laugh they laughed together. At the end 'Maya was the real doctor,' Bob said. 'Decca was not reacting to anything. She could hardly swallow and barely recognized people. Maya would come in each evening and stand by Decca's bedside and sing to her . . . bawdy songs, romantic songs and Decca would finally react and realize, "Oh, it's you." And she would even open her mouth and try to sing along. Her last words were really songs that Maya started her singing . . . I'll never forget Maya for that. It was one of the great moments of my life learning what true sisterhood is all about.'[24] Decca died on 22 July less than six weeks after being told she had cancer.

Her funeral was minimal. She organized it herself from hospital: a no-frills cremation with her ashes to be scattered at sea, at a total cost of $475. Yet her host of friends wanted to mark the memorial service with something more fitting to her huge personality. Once in an interview she had been asked what sort of funeral she had in mind for herself and she had replied wryly, 'Oh, I'd like six black horses with plumes, and one of those marvellous jobs of embalming that take twenty years off . . . The streets to be blocked off, dignitaries to declaim sobbingly over the flower-smothered bier, proclamations to be issued, that sort of thing . . .' In a remarkable tease on Decca, that is almost what happened at the memorial service. More than five hundred people attended the service at a hall in Delancy Street, San Francisco. Tributes from friends were interspersed with old hymns from Decca's childhood, and the service finished with a band playing 'When The Saints Go Marching In'. As they spilled out on to the street, those who attended were greeted by the sight of six black horses wearing plumes and harnessed to an antique glass hearse that had been drawn up outside the hall. Inside it were copies of all Decca's books and articles.

A few months later there was a memorial service in London. It was held in a theatre, for it would have been hypocritical to hold it in a church, although this is the more usual venue in England. Debo had intended to go, and to speak, but press reports that it was to be 'a circus' with 'sideshows' of funeral directors showing their wares worried her. At the last minute she decided not to attend. However, a huge number of media personalities did go. Packer Snow compèred and Maya Angelou stepped in to pay the main tribute in place of Debo. It was a warm occasion, full of laughter, in celebration of the life of a woman who was brilliant, feisty and surprisingly complicated.

Decca did not live to finish her revision of *The American Way of Death*, but Bob completed and published it, using Decca's notes. 'I tried to preserve as much as possible of Decca's inimitable way of putting things,' he said. He still lives in their family home in the pleasant traditional 'neighbourhood' in Oakland. The house is old-fashioned, shingled, and has a generous front porch. Scented red and white roses planted by Decca flourish by the front steps. At the rear is a small enclosed garden of Californian flora, alive with humming birds, and squirrels scampering across the rails of the decked patio. When I last saw him in October 1999 Bob had just taken delivery of a new computer after organizing a website for Decca's books. 'We've had 1,300 hits already,' he told me gleefully, and gave me some instruction on using e-mail, a technology that I had yet to tackle. 'Decca had no idea of technology,' he recalled, but she had been thrilled by the instant communications provided by her fax machine. Shortly after she started using it she came downstairs on Christmas Eve to find that the messages received overnight had a red border. It did not occur to her that this was a warning that the paper was running low: 'She thought it was a delightful festive touch provided by the manufacturers,' he said, smiling at the memory, 'so of course she let the paper run out.' One day he brought her home a packet of yellow Post-it notes, which he thought would be useful for her to mark references in books. Next evening, he asked how she was finding them but she said she couldn't make them work. 'Well, how are you using them?' he enquired. 'Well I lick them like this and stick them down . . . look,' she demonstrated, 'but they keep falling off.'

Dinky, whom he adores, flies regularly from the East Coast to visit him as he feels he could no longer tolerate East Coast winters. Just before I visited them they had had a rare disagreement. Bob had referred to her in conversation as 'my step-daughter'. Dinky took him to task: 'You're the only father I've ever known,' she pointed out.

In Dinky's generation other descendants of the sisters, too, have made significant successes of their lives. Debo's son 'Stoker' has been chief steward of the Jockey Club, while her elder daughter Emma is a talented artist and has been for many years the head of National Trust Gardens. Diana's second son Desmond has devoted his life, and financial support, to the Irish Georgian Society, which he founded and which has saved countless eighteenth-century buildings, architectural features and artefacts. He has lectured all over the USA for forty years on the subject. Her son Max is president of the international organisation which governs Formula One motor-racing, and Debo and Diana each has a granddaughter who is a supermodel.

Debo and Diana are the sole survivors of the sisters. Diana celebrated her ninetieth birthday in 2000. When the Temple with its large gardens became too much for her to cope with she sold it, and now lives quietly in her light, airy apartment in the heart of Paris. Her sitting room is at tree-canopy level and over-looks a huge walled garden that once belonged to Napoleon's mother. With the full-length windows open in the summer, it is hard to believe it is only a few minutes' walk to the roar of the Place de la Concorde. Although Diana is very deaf, state-of-the-art hearing-aids enable her to enjoy the regular visits of friends, whom she entertains with customary style and charm, and her large family of grandchildren and great-grandchildren are never far away. Looking back over her life when interviewed for this book she said, 'We all seem to have gone from disaster to disaster, yet I look back on my life, except prison, as being happy, and so lucky.'[25]

Debo is equally family-minded, but for her there is no hint of retirement although her stewardship of Chatsworth is a full-time job that would defeat many a younger person. She still appears to have all the energy and liveliness that so characterized the Mitford sisters, and recently Andrew said in the popular TV series *Great Estates*, 'My wife is far more important to Chatsworth than I am.' This modesty is typical of the Duke. In fact, all the important decisions concerning the running of the estate have always been taken by him, though in recent years he has been assisted in this work by his son, Stoker. In addition, Andrew has taken his position in the county very seriously. Apart from his time as Member of Parliament, he was for a time Mayor of Buxton, and there is scarcely an organization in Derbyshire, large or small, from village cricket clubs to the Mothers' Union and the boards of major public institutions such as hospitals, that has not benefited in some way from his personal support.

But 'the house', as Chatsworth is known locally, has been Debo's responsibility for over fifty years now. The building that had such a hangdog air when the war ended now looks glossy and well cared-for. This has not happened automatically, and the huge cost of running Chatsworth has to be earned by making the house and the estate pay their way. Chatsworth has always been among the leading stately homes in terms of annual visitors, but what impresses those who pay to see it is not just its grandeur – it is one of the great treasure houses of Europe – but the sense that it is a family home and not a museum.[26] Debo cannot understand this, saying that it is a mixture of hotel and museum and that, after all, 'The family do not live in the state rooms.' Nevertheless, she has created an unmistakable ambience of warmth and friendliness, based on what she learned from Sydney. This does not simply apply indoors: the sense of belonging that Andrew and Debo have engendered among the huge staff, some of whom are in the third and fourth generation at Chatsworth and feel they are part of 'the family', permeates everywhere, even to the car parks where Debo's flocks of chickens – especially the stately Buff Cochins – scratching about in the sun have now become almost as famous as the house itself.

With no business training Debo is now a seriously successful entrepreneur, not only overseeing the commercial activities of Chatsworth but for some years serving as a director on the board of an international company where her opinions were greatly valued.[27] From the start she and Andrew were determined to make Chatsworth self-sufficient and it is a matter of personal pride that they have never asked for any government grants. A long-term renovation programme costing half a million pounds per annum concentrates on a major project each year and the work is carried out during the winter months when the house and its hundred-acre garden are closed to the public. When the house is open the full-time staff is supplemented by a small army of local volunteers who enjoy the sense of history of the house and being associated with its treasures. The famous Chatsworth Archive is available to scholars and researchers, and the Duchess is generous in allowing charities to use the house for functions. Several major events, such as country fairs and horse trials, are held annually, attracting tens of thousands of visitors.

When the house was first reopened to the public in the 1950s staff were often asked where they could buy souvenirs so Debo and her housekeeper organized a trestle table to sell matches and postcards. From this small beginning sprang a sizeable trade in souvenirs, books and high-quality items for the home, such as cushions, knitwear, porcelain and hand-made furniture. The famous Chatsworth Farm Shop sells estate produce, and queues form early each morning for new-laid fresh eggs from the Duchess' free-range hens. In recent years a healthy mail-order business has been added, and in the summer of 2000 Debo opened a London branch of the farm shop, which is already as busy as the one on the estate. The half-dozen picnic tables and chairs, originally put out to serve cups of tea to visitors, have evolved into a series of cafés and restaurants, and a highly prof-itable commercial-catering concern. In the last decade the retail and catering business has increased fifteenfold and Debo now runs a substantial and extremely profitable business, 'And there is no detail of the organization in which Her Grace is not intimately involved,' a member of staff told me. The house, the retail and catering spin-offs now support the estate, rather than the other way round, and it all helps to secure the future of Chatsworth. Debo said recently that she and Andrew 'set out to leave Chatsworth in better heart than we found it'. Without doubt they have succeeded in this aim.

It is this remarkable energy, *joie de vivre* and self-confidence that enabled all the Mitford sisters to take up their own individ-ual causes with such fervour, making their lives so unique that they have now become almost creatures of mythology. If Hitler had never come to power we might never have heard of them out-side Society columns or book-review pages, for Nancy was always going to be a writer and Decca, too, was a born wordsmith. Debo and Diana are undeniably able to write well – well enough, cer-tainly, to produce bestselling books – but their writing was a side-dish to the main course of their lives. It was the opposing political forces of Fascism and Communism that lit the tinder of the girls' lives and set alight fires that propelled them from the ordinary to the extraordinary, and made them household names.

And despite the portrait of Sydney promoted by Nancy's books and Decca's account of her unhappy adolescence, it is clear that much of their attitude to life was engendered by their mother, who allowed them freedom to develop while always being there to support in moments of crisis. In reply to his letter of condolence after David's death, Sydney wrote to James Lees-Milne that she thought often of 'the happy days when you were all young and David and I had the children all around us. I was lucky to have those perfectly happy years before the war. Isn't it odd how, when one looks back at that time, it seems to have been all summers?'[28]

SOURCE NOTES

Abbreviations used in citations

CHP	Chatsworth Papers
DD	Deborah, Duchess of Devonshire
DM	Diana Mitford (later Mosley)
DR	Lord Redesdale (David Freeman Mitford)
ER	Esmond Romilly
JLM	James Lees-Milne
JM	Jessica Mitford
NM	Nancy Mitford
OSU	Ohio State University
PJ	Pamela Mitford Jackson
RT	Robert Treuhaft
SR	Lady Redesdale (Sydney Bowles Freeman Mitford)
TM	Tom Mitford
UM	Unity Mitford
VH	Violet Hammersley
YUL	Yale University Library (Beinecke)

Introduction

1   Interview with Lord Longford at the House of Lords, May 2000.
2   Nancy Mitford; Diana Mosley and Unity Mitford. See Bibliography.
3   See Chapter 19.
4   DM to the author January 2001.
5   He was full brother to Caroline Bradley's Cornishman.
6   Rene Wayne Golden, who represented Decca's interests on a number of occasions in respect of screen rights.
7   As a result the film rights to the book (*Straight on till Morning*) were sold but the proposed film was never made. Plans are now in hand by Warner Bros to make a film based partially on the book, with Beryl Markham's memoir *West with the Night*, and other biographical material.
8   Ohio State University, Columbus, Ohio.
9   By US writer/journalist Peter Sussman.

Chapter 1: Victorian Roots, 1894–1904

1   James Lees-Milne, obituary of Sydney, Lady Redesdale; *The Times*, 28 May 1963.
2   'Barty' was probably a contemporary pronunciation of Bertie, although in some contemporary diaries and letters he is referred to as 'Barty'.
3   Redesdale, Sydney, 'The Dolphin' an unpublished memoir, p. 1. Jessica Mitford Papers. OSU/1699.
4   Bowles, Thomas Gibson, *The Log of the Nereid* (Simpkin, Marshall & Co, 1889).
5   Guinness, Jonathan and Catherine, *The House of Mitford* (Hutchinson, 1984), p. 221.
6   Rita Shell, known as 'Tello'. Tello would have several children by Thomas Gibson Bowles. These children were given his name and looked after financially, although he never married their mother. After Sydney and Weenie grew up, and no longer needed

a governess, Tello worked in a senior position at the *Lady* for many years. Sydney was always fond of Tello and knew about her half-brothers.

7 Telephone interview with Julia Budworth, 31 August 2000.

8 *House of Mitford*, p. 186

9 Sydney and her brother George were both painted as children by Millais; it is thought that George was probably the sitter for Millais' *Cherry Ripe*, one of the most popular images in Victorian England and used on the top of many chocolate boxes in the early part of this century.

10 *House of Mitford*, p. 221.

11 *Ibid.*

12 Budworth, Julia, *Never Forget – A Biography of George F. Bowles* (privately published, 2001), p. 182.

13 JM in interview: *Chicago Tribune*, 23 October 1977.

14 Julia Budworth, conversation with the author, 31 August 2000.

Chapter 2: Edwardian Afternoon, 1904–15

1 Interview with Diana Mosley, Paris, 2000.

2 Diana Mosley, letter to the author, 1 August 2000.

3 Guinness, Jonathan and Catherine, *The House of Mitford* (Hutchinson, 1984), p. 230.

4 *Ibid.* p. 154.

5 In her father's book *The Log of the Nereid* (Simpkin, Marshall & Co., 1889), Sydney hardly warrants a mention, but every baby utterance of Weenie is pounced upon and included to illustrate the cleverness and humour of his youngest child. The dedication reads: 'To Captain Weenie (aged 3) whose splendid impatience of discipline and entire want of consideration for others, absolute contempt of elders, complete devotion to her own interests, endeared her to the crew of the Negroid, this book is dedicated by her doting father.' Sydney's grandson, Jonathan Guinness, who has written an excellent biography of his great-grandparents in *The House of Mitford*, told me, 'The key to Sydney is her father.'

6   Mitford, Nancy, *The Water Beetle* (Hamish Hamilton, 1962), p. 8.

7   *House of Mitford*, p. 166.

8   James Lees-Milne, 'Obituary of Sydney, Lady Redesdale', *The Times*, 28 May 1963.

9   OSU: NM to JM, 13 October 1971. Diana and Debo say they never heard this story, and think it 'unlikely'.

10 *House of Mitford*, p. 166.

11 *Ibid.*

12 Governor of the Bank of England from 1920–44, he wielded immense influence in international monetary affairs throughout those troubled decades.

13 See *House of Mitford*, p. 249; also, Mary Soames, *Speaking for Themselves* (Doubleday, 1998), p. 4.

14 *Ibid.*

15 For the full story of the romance between Elizabeth of Austria and Bay Middleton, see John Welcome, *The Sporting Empress* (Michael Joseph, 1975). Captain Middleton broke his neck steeple-chasing in 1892.

16 Blanche confided this secret to Lady Londonderry at Aix where she had gone to be confined. See Lees-Milne, James, *Caves of Ice* (John Murray, 1983), p. 129.

17 Interview with Constancia 'Dinky' Romilly, October 1999. Decca believed that Esmond was Churchill's son. When Giles had a mental breakdown and committed suicide in 1967, Decca said to Nancy that she hoped it didn't run in the family on account of Dinky's children. 'Don't worry about it,' Nancy told her. 'Everyone knows Esmond is Winston's son and the mad streak came from Col. Romilly.' See OSU/1568, JM to DD, 26 October 1995.

18 'Puma': Frances Mitford Kearsey, David's eldest sister, 1875–1951.

19 *House of Mitford*, p. 234

20 *The Water Beetle*, p. 13.

21 The cottage belonged to Lord Lincolnshire. Sydney Redesdale bought it from him shortly after the end of the First World War.

22 Interview with DD, May 2000.

23 David never had an entrenching tool. Diana recalls that they heard as children that Sir Ian Colquhoun had one over his fire which gave Nancy the idea.

24 Duchess of Devonshire, *My Early Childhood* (privately published, 1995), p. 3.

25 Rosemary Bailey and Julia Budworth.

26 Julia Budworth, telephone conversation with the author, August 2000.

27 DD, in conversation with the author, Chatsworth, 2 April 2000.

28 DD, The Mitford Glow', OSU 1710.

29 The late Pamela Jackson, in informal conversation with the author, *c.* 1986.

30 Mitford, Nancy, *The Pursuit of Love* (Hamish Hamilton, 1945), p. 11.

31 *My Early Childhood*, p. 7.

32 Mosley, Diana, *A Life of Contrasts* (Hamish Hamilton, 1977), p. 9.

33 Budworth, Julia, *Never Forget – A Biography of George F. Bowles* (privately published, 2000), p. 155.

34 *House of Mitford*, pp. 155–6.

35 That is, Mosaic Law.

36 The child was Unity. Interview with DD, Chatsworth, May 2000.

37 His grandson, the famous Dr Cyriax of Harley Street, used many of the same techniques.

38 Murphy, Sophia, *The Mitford Family Album* (Sidgwick & Jackson, 1985).

39 Leasor, James, *Who killed Sir Harry Oakes?* (Sphere, 1985), pp. 12–13.

40 OSU/1697, SR to JM, 8 August 1937.

41 *The Water Beetle*, p. 5.

42 Bournhill Cottage on the Eaglehurst Estate (at Lepe, Hampshire), which then belonged to the Marconi family.

43 'They looked identical but talked quite differently', OSU/1565, JM, sundry note.

44 OSU/1697, JM to her parents, September 1926.

45 Duchess of Devonshire, 'Hastings': article in an unidentified magazine.

46 Obituary, Lord Redesdale, *The Times* 26 March 1958, and a subsequent letter to the Editor from Brigadier H.H. Sandilands.

47 Soames, Mary (ed.) *Speaking for Themselves* (Doubleday, 1998), p. 122: Clementine Churchill to Winston S Churchill, 'Helen Mitford dined here 2 nights ago – her baby is 5 weeks old. She is heartbroken that it is not a boy. She is 23 & her hair is grey, which looks so odd with her young face.'

Chapter 3: Nursery Days, 1915–22

1 Last Will and Testament: the Rt Hon. Algernon Bertram, Baron Redesdale, GCVO, KCB.

2 Guinness, Jonathan and Catherine, *The House of Mitford* (Hutchinson, 1984), p. 251.

3 Obituary, Pamela Jackson, *The Times*, 19 April 1994.

4 Butler, Lucy (ed.), *Letters Home* (John Murray, 1991), p. 107.

5 DM, interview with the author, Paris, January 2000.

6 OSU/1701, JM to DR, 9 February 1932.

7 Duchess of Devonshire, *My Early Childhood* (privately published, 1995), p. 7.

8 *Ibid.*, p. 1.

9 *Ibid.*

10 *Ibid.*

11 OSU, MS of 'Mitford Country Revisited', July 1982, p. 3.

12 OSU/1637, JM to DD, 5 March 1990.

13 OSU/1697, PM to SR, 24 June 1925.

14 OSU, Lady Beit (formerly Clementine Mitford) to JM, 13 July 1973.

15 Interview with Rosemary Bailey, Westwell, April 2000.

16 In other words, the appointment of the clergyman.

17 OSU/1637, JM to DD, 28 February 1987.

18 The legend tells of a medieval wedding party where the guests played a game of hide-and-seek. The young bride went off to hide and could not be found though the poor frantic bridegroom tore the house apart. A century later her skeleton was found, clad in the remains of her bridal finery. She had hidden away, curled up in a heavy old wooden chest decorated with the wood of a mistletoe bough; the lid had slammed shut and locked itself.

19 OSU/1565, JM, sundry note, 1 June 1995.

20 See also Murphy, Sophia, *Mitford Family Album* (Sidgwick & Jackson, 1985), pp. 37–8.

21 OSU/1698, SR to JM, 16 May 1968.

22 Mitford, Jessica, *Hons and Rebels* (Victor Gollancz, 1960), p. 13.

23 *Mitford Family Album*, plate.

24 In *Hons and Rebels*, p. 13, Decca says Tom was given the name Tuddemy 'partly because it was the Boudledidge translation of Tim, partly because we thought it rhymed with "adultery"'.

25 *Ibid.*, pp. 13–14.

26 OSU/812, unpublished MS.

27 *Hons and Rebels*, p. 23.

28 DD, interview with the author, Chatsworth, June 2000.

29 *Hons and Rebels*, p. 14

30 Founded by Charlotte Mason in 1887, PNEU has been particularly valuable for military families and those travelling abroad. No matter where the child was taught they could always 'drop back' into the system at whatever level they had reached. Mason founded PNEU because of the widely held belief that 'it was unnecessary to educate girls' and her credo was that 'the child is more complex than the sum of its parts'. Christian ethics is at the base of the curriculum, which concentrates on English and includes maths, science and biology, history and geography, music, dance, art appreciation and play.

31 Mosley, Diana, *A Life of Contrasts* (Hamish Hamilton, 1977), p. 30.

32 *Hons and Rebels*, p. 25.

33 OSU/1928, JM to DD, June 1996.

34 Mitford, Nancy, *Love in a Cold Climate* (Hamish Hamilton, 1949), p. 114.

35 *Ibid.*

36 Lord Longford, interview with the author, House of Lords, May 2000.

37 OSU/1637, DD to JM, undated fax.

38 *Ibid.*, NM to JM, October 1971.

39 *Ibid.*, JM to NM, 13 October 1971.

40 *Ibid.*

41 PRO: Last Will and Testament, Thomas Gibson Bowles, probated 21 March 1922.

Chapter 4: Roaring Twenties, 1922–9

1 Mosley, Charlotte, *Love from Nancy* (Hodder & Stoughton, 1993), pp. 16–17.

2 Acton, Harold, *Nancy Mitford* (Hamish Hamilton, 1975), pp. 14–15.

3 *Love from Nancy*, pp. 16–17, NM to SR.

4 Mitford, Jessica, *Hons and Rebels* (Victor Gollancz, 1960), p. 36.

5 Leslie, Anita, *Cousin Randolph* (Hutchinson, 1985), p. 8.

6 Mitford, Nancy, *The Pursuit of Love* (Hamish Hamilton, 1945), p. 46.

7 YUL, DM to JLM, uncat., 2 July 1981.

8 Hastings, Selina, *Nancy Mitford* (Hamish Hamilton, 1985), p. 46.

9 CHP, Lady Redesdale's housekeeping book, 1934.

10 Lady Kathleen Stanley (née Thynne), married to Oliver Stanley, cousin to the Mitford sisters. Lord Henry Thynne (Viscount Weymouth, heir to Lord Bath, as his elder brother had been killed in the war) had just gone to Oxford. He was responsible for introducing Nancy and the Mitfords to Brian Howard 'and all the others who became our great friends'. DM to author, January 2001.

11 The Countess of Seafield. She stammered badly and was consequently very shy. Brought up in New Zealand, she inherited

several large estates in Scotland, including Cullen and Castle Grant.

12 Acton, *Nancy Mitford*, p. 22.

13 *Hons and Rebels*, p. 10.

14 The rich homosexual son of an industrialist. Later he founded the magazine *Horizon* and employed Cyril Connolly as editor.

15 Duchess of Devonshire, *My Early Childhood* (privately published, 1995), p. 5

16 *Hons and Rebels,* p. 38.

17 OSU/1700, SR to JM, 3 May 1960.

18 *Ibid.*

19 *My Early Childhood*, p. 5.

20 Obituary of Sydney, Lady Redesdale, James Lees-Milne, *The Times*, 28 May 1963.

21 James Lees-Milne, *Another Self* (Hamish Hamilton, 1970), p. 61.

22 *Love from Nancy*, p. 566: NM to Cecil Beaton, 14 May 1969. The unfortunate young man was Mervyn, Viscount Clive, who was killed in the Second World War.

23 *Love from Nancy*, p. 51, NM to TM.

24 OSU/1697, PM to SR, 24 June 1925.

25 *Ibid.*

26 DM, letter to the author, 14 August 2000.

27 CHP, JM to SR, undated, *c.* 1925.

28 OSU/1738, JM to Emma Tennant (niece), 16 October 1993.

29 *Hons and Rebels*, pp. 11–12.

30 Lees-Milne, James, *Ancestral Voices* (John Murray, 1975), p. 444.

31 YUL, DM to JLM, uncat., 2 June 1987.

32 Hastings, *Nancy Mitford*, p. 50.

33 Mosley, Diana, *A Life of Contrasts* (Hamish Hamilton, 1977), p. 47.

34 YUL, DM to JLM, uncat., 19 March 1927.

35 *Ibid.*, 25 March 1927.

36 *A Life of Contrasts*, p. 53.

37 These rules included: 'Must be able to turn two somersaults running forward; Frog jumps across the tennis court; Pass a set of

general knowledge questions etc'. OSU/1698, Book of Hon Rules, sent to JM by SR.

38 DM, interview with the author, Paris, May 2000.

39 *Hons and Rebels*, p. 17.

40 Note from DM to the author, June 2000.

41 *My Early Childhood*, p. 10.

42 *Ibid.*, also DD, interview with the author, at Chatsworth, 4 May 2000.

43 Frederick Lindemann, later Lord Cherwell, 1886–1957. A close friend of Winston S. Churchill, during the Second World War he played a significant role in developing new weapons, and scientific research generally. Later he would become one of the first experts in nuclear physics.

44 Guinness, Jonathan and Catherine, *The House of Mitford* (Hutchinson, 1984), p. 282.

45 *Ibid.*, p. 282.

46 Lees-Milne, James, *A Mingled Measure* (John Murray, 1994), p. 46 and other entries.

47 Lycett Green, Candida (ed.), *John Betjeman Letters* (Methuen, 1990), vol. 1, p. 19.

48 OSU/1633, Bryan Guinness to JM, 13 January 1995.

49 *Hons and Rebels*, p. 39.

50 *Pursuit of Love*, p. 56.

51 *House of Mitford*, p. 279.

52 DM to the author, 16 January 2001.

53 Lees-Milne, James, *Ancient as the Hills* (John Murray, 1997), p. 113.

54 *A Life of Contrasts*, p. 62.

55 Butler, Lucy (ed.), *Letters Home* (John Murray, 1991), p. 107.

56 Guinness, Bryan, *Dairy Not Kept* (Compton Press, 1981), p. 87.

57 *Hons and Rebels*, p. 43.

58 *Ibid.*, p. 44.

59 OSU/1637, JM to DD, 31 March 1982.

60 OSU/1710, DD, 'The Mitford Glow'. It is an exaggeration, of course: there are several letters in which she thanks her mother for new clothes, such as 'the lovely red jumper'.

61 *Hons and Rebels*, p. 16.

62 Like her parents, Diana was married at St Margaret's Church, Westminster. Among the guests were Winston and Randolph Churchill.

63 *A Life of Contrasts*, p. 68.

Chapter 5: Bright Young Things, 1929–30

1 Mosley, Diana, *A Life of Contrasts* (Hamish Hamilton, 1977), p. 70.

2 DM, letter to the author.

3 Butler, Lucy (ed.), *Letters Home* (John Murray, 1991), p. 115.

4 Guinness, Bryan, *Dairy Not Kept* (Compton Press, 1981), p. 89.

5 Mitford, Jessica, *Hons and Rebels* (Victor Gollancz, 1960), p. 48.

6 OSU/1566, JM to DD, 25 August 1990. Stockholm's City Hall was designed by Ragnar Östberg and completed in 1923. It is Sweden's foremost building in the National Romantic style.

7 Described in *Hons and Rebels*, p. 13.

8 OSU, Bryan Guinness file: 'Dichtung und Wahreit among the Mitfords'.

9 Guinness, Jonathan and Catherine, *The House of Mitford* (Hutchinson, 1984), p. 577.

10 Julia Budworth, telephone interview with the author.

11 OSU, Drummonds to JM, 3 July 1929. During research for this book several people have asked, 'Which sister was the one with the "running away account"?' This seems to have struck a chord with many young readers.

12 OSU/1709, JM to NM, 13 October 1971.

13 DM, interview with the author, Paris, January 2000.

14 *A Life of Contrasts*, p. 73.

15 Lees-Milne, James, *Ancestral Voices* (John Murray, 1975), p. 355.

16 *Réalités*, 1 June 1961, pp. 71–3.

17 *Hons and Rebels*, p. 35.

18 NM to TM, *c.* October 1928, quoted in Selina Hastings, *Nancy Mitford* (Hamish Hamilton, 1985). Evelyn Waugh had just published *Decline and Fall.*

19 DM to author, December 2000.

20 Evelyn Waugh to Henry Yorke, 20 July 1929, in Amory, Mark (ed.), *The Letters of Evelyn Waugh* (Weidenfeld & Nicolson, 1981), p. 36.

21 *Ibid.* Evelyn Waugh to Harold Acton, July 1929, p. 37.

22 *Hons and Rebels*, p. 14.

23 DM to NM, quoted in Hastings, Selina, *Evelyn Waugh* (Sinclair Stevenson, 1994), p. 219.

24 *Vile Bodies* was published in January 1930. In August that year Waugh published *Labels*, a travel book (the dust jacket was covered in travel labels). Although published after *Vile Bodies* it had been written some years earlier and it, too, was dedicated to Diana and Bryan Guinness.

Chapter 6: The Stage Is Set, 1930–32

1 Lady Redesdale suggested the title 'Our Vile Age' for Nancy's book, which not only reflected her own opinions of present mores, but cleverly made reference to the title of *Our Village*, by a famous eighteenth-century author with the name Mitford. This is a nice example of Sydney's droll humour.

2 Mosley, Charlotte, *Love from Nancy* (Hodder & Stoughton, 1993), p. 62.

3 *Lady*, 10 April 1930.

4 Sir Charles Blake Cochran was a hugely successful theatre impresario, who produced many of Noël Coward's most famous musicals, *This Year of Grace, Bitter Sweet, Cavalcade*, etc., in London. The dancers in his chorus line were known as 'Mr Cochran's Young Ladies', which conferred a distinct cachet. The girls were chaperoned; a high standard of personal behaviour was expected of them and they were subject to dismissal if they married or were suspected of a sexual liaison.

5 Graham, Sheilah, *Beloved Infidel* (Book Club, 1959), p. 115.

6   This is quite true. The Air Ministry imposed conditions for agreeing to Lawrence's wish to remain in the RAF under his assumed name of Shaw. These conditions were that he was not allowed to fly, and he must not speak to any important personages, i.e. 'Churchill, Birkenhead, Sassoon, Lady Astor'.

7   CHP, TM to SR, 17 August 1930.

8   Murphy, Sophia, *Mitford Family Album* (Sidgwick & Jackson, 1985).

9   OSU/155, unpublished MS by JM.

10 Mitford, Jessica, *Hons and Rebels* (Victor Gollancz, 1960), p. 50.

11 OSU/1642, JM to Idden (Ann Farrer Horne) 14 August 1980.

12 OSU/155, Decca on Unity, unpublished MS.

13 *Hons and Rebels*, p. 61.

14 OSU/155, unpublished MS.

15 Pryce-Jones, David, *Unity Mitford – A Quest* (Weidenfeld and Nicholson, 1976), p. 43.

16 OSU/1642, JM to Idden (Ann Farrer Horne), 14 August 1980.

17 *Ibid.*, 22 February 1980. Few people born after 1960 realize the huge impact films had on the previous two generations in terms of manners, dress and accents.

18 OSU/1642, JM to Idden (Ann Farrer Horne), 14 August 1980.

19 Now Lady Soames.

20 Ingram, Kevin, *Rebel* (Weidenfeld and Nicholson, 1985), p. 17.

21 On the other hand Unity was a very unusual girl: her reading was not prescribed and she had been used to the run of an important library since childhood. Perhaps it is not such an odd choice, after all.

22 *Unity Mitford*, pp. 1–2.

23 Mitford, Jessica, *A Fine Old Conflict* (Michael Joseph, 1977), p. 24.

24 OSU/1701.

25 *Ibid.*, various correspondence from JM to DR, 1932.

26 In *The House of Mitford*, Jonathan and Catherine Guinness listed many of the nicknames of the immediate family as a separate section. It covers one and a half pages. See pp. 7–8.

27 Elizabeth Powell (later Lady Glenconner) to David Pryce-Jones, quoted in *Unity Mitford*. Unidentified newspaper article in JM's papers at OSU.

28 Mary Ormsby-Gore, in *Unity Mitford*, p. 53.

29 Garnet, David (ed.), *Carrington, Letters and Extracts from her Diaries* (Jonathan Cape, 1970), p. 473.

30 Mosley, Diana, *A Life of Contrasts* (Hamish Hamilton, 1977), p. 83.

31 May Amende, former maid at Biddesden, in *Unity Mitford*, p. 47.

32 *Daily Telegraph*, 13 April 1994.

33 Lycett Green, Candida (ed.), *John Betjeman Letters* (Methuen, 1990), vol. 1 p. 88.

34 *Ibid.*, p. 101.

35 Hillier, Bevis, *Young Betjeman* (Cardinal, 1988), p. 300.

36 *Ibid.*, p. 102.

37 *Ibid.*, p. 104.

38 *Ibid.*, p. 107.

39 *Ibid.*, p. 95.

40 Maskelyns, a famous stage magician of the twenties.

41 *Young Betjeman*, p. 302.

42 *A Life of Contrasts*, p. 89.

43 Mosley, Sir Oswald, *My Life* (Thomas Nelson, 1968), p. 44.

44 Mosley, Diana, *Loved Ones: Sir Oswald Mosley* (Sidgwick & Jackson, 1983), p. 156.

45 May Amende, in *Unity Mitford*, p. 47.

46 DM to the author 16 January 2001.

47 *A Life of Contrasts*, p. 94.

48 Skidelsky, Robert, *Mosley* (Macmillan, 1981), pp. 338–9

49 *A Life of Contrasts*, p. 94.

50 R.H.S. Crossman, 1961, quoted in *A Life of Contrasts*, p. 96.

51 Webb, Beatrice, Diary *1924–1943* (London School of Economics, 1985), p. 239.

52 Lord Longford, interview with the author, House of Lords, June 2000.

53 *Mosley*, p. 236.

54 Lees-Milne, James, *Another Self* (Hamish Hamilton, 1970), p. 97.

55 Webb, *Diary*, p. 335.

56 Cimmie's mother was the former Mary Leiter, daughter of Levi

Leiter of Chicago. On her marriage Leiter settled £5 million on Mary, the capital placed in trust for her children.

57 Mosley, Nicholas, *Rules of the Game* (Secker & Warburg, 1982), p. 239.

58 DM to the author, January 2001.

59 *Rules of the Game*, p. 217.

60 Lady Pansy Pakenham, in *Unity Mitford*, p. 48.

61 *Rules of the Game*, p. 237.

62 DD, interview with the author, June 2000.

63 Richard Cohen, a present-day fencing expert, maintains that Mosley was able to overcome the handicap of his injured foot because 'he was very fit and strong'. Letter to the author, 1 October 2000.

64 DM to the author January 2001.

65 *Rules of the Game*, p. 246.

66 *Love from Nancy*, p. 81.

67 *Ibid.*, p. 82.

68 DM, interview with the author, Paris, 2000.

69 *Loved Ones*, p. 156.

Chapter 7: Slings and Arrows, 1932–4

1 NM to Mark Ogilvie-Grant, 28 March 1931, in Mosley, Charlotte *Love from Nancy* (Hodder & Stoughton, 1993), p. 74.

2 Hastings, Selina, *Nancy Mitford* (Hamish Hamilton, 1985), p. 71.

3 Mitford, Jessica, *Hons and Rebels* (Victor Gollancz, 1960) p. 30.

4 *Love from Nancy*, pp. 71–2.

5 OSU/1709, JM to NM, 13 October 1971.

6 *Ibid.*, NM to JM, 18 October 1971.

7 NM to Mark Ogilvie-Grant (undated), in Hastings, *Nancy Mitford*, p. 74.

8 Lees-Milne, James, *Ancient as the Hills* (John Murray, 1997), p. 158.

9 *Ibid.*, p. 113.

10 *The Times*, 16 June 1933: '. . . In an undefended suit Mrs Diana

Guinness . . . prayed for the dissolution of her marriage with Bryan Guinness on the grounds of his adultery with . . .'

11 NM to Hamish Erskine, 14 June 1933, in *Love from Nancy*, p. 85.
12 *Love from Nancy*, p. 87.
13 Sykes, Christopher, *Evelyn Waugh* (Collins, 1975), p. 41.
14 OSU/1637, JM to DD, 26 April 1985.
15 Violet, sister of Lady Rennell and wife of Edward Stuart Wortley.
16 *Love from Nancy*, p. 90.
17 Hastings, *Nancy Mitford*, p. 86.
18 Mosley, Nicholas, *The Rules of the Game* (Secker & Warburg), p. 248.
19 *Ibid.*, p. 250.
20 Mary Leiter Curzon died in 1906 aged thirty-six, two years after giving birth to her third daughter, Alexandra, from an infection following a miscarriage. Cimmie was aged eight at the time of her mother's death.
21 *Rules of the Game*, p. 252
22 Mosley, Diana, *Loved Ones: Sir Oswald Mosley* (Sidgwick & Jackson, 1983), p. 166.
23 *Rules of the Game*, p. 297.
24 *Ibid.*, p. 258.
25 DM to the author, January 2001.
26 *Rules of the Game*, p. 298.
27 *Ibid.*, p. 259.
28 DM, in conversation with the author, Paris, 2000, and letter, November 2000.
29 Buchan, William, *The Rags of Time* (Ashford, Buchan & Enright, c. 1985), p. 142.
30 Mosley, Diana, *A Life of Contrasts* (Hamish Hamilton, 1977), p. 106.
31 *Ibid.*, p. 107.
32 *Ibid.*, pp. 108–9.
33 BBC2, 2000: *The Age of Nazism – Tourists of the Revolution*.
34 JM to Marge Frantz, 25 May 1986: 'we were forbidden to shave legs (we did it anyway) . . . and wear lipstick . . . why? I suppose

that my parents . . . disliked the idea of trying to attract men by
these artificial means.'

35 DR to DM, quoted in Dalley, Jan, *Diana Mosley* (Faber and
Faber, 2000), p. 152, and Jonathan and Catherine Guinness, *The
House of Mitford* (Hutchinson, 1984), p. 361.

36 *Ibid.*, p. 112.

37 Pryce-Jones, David, *Unity Mitford* (Weidenfeld & Nicolson,
1976), p. 73.

38 NM to DM, in *Love from Nancy*, p. 92.

39 OSU/1701, JM to SR, May 1934: 'I'm so glad you enjoyed your
voyage (to Gib) in spite of your thinking it wouldn't be much
fun . . .'

40 Mitford, Jessica, *A Fine Old Conflict* (Michael Joseph, 1977),
p. 25.

41 OSU/1701, JM to SR, various dates.

42 OSU/1642, JM to Idden (Ann Farrer Horne), 14 August 1980.

Chapter 8: Unity and the Führer, 1934–5

1 Mosley, Charlotte, *The Letters of Evelyn Waugh and Nancy Mitford*
(Sceptre, 1996), p. 366.

2 David Redesdale wrote in his copy of this book, against this disclaimer, 'A beastly lie!'

3 Mitford, Nancy, *Wigs on the Green* (Thornton and Butterworth,
1935), p. 16.

4 *Ibid.*, p. 193.

5 *Daily Sketch*, 9 February 1935, but most daily newspapers carried
this story.

6 OSU/1567, JM to DD, 14 May 1993.

7 DM to the author, January 2001.

8 Edmund Heines, a senior SA 'Brownshirts' officer.

9 UM to DM, 1 July 1934.

10 Pryce-Jones, David, *Unity Mitford* (Weidenfeld & Nicolson,
1976), p. 86.

11 The two children spent periods at their father's house,

Biddesden. Bryan and Diana remained on exceptionally good terms after their divorce. 'He was always in and out of Eaton Square,' Diana wrote to the author (16 January 2001), 'and I often went to Biddesden to see the little boys when they were not with me. I've got hundreds of letters from Bryan, we became great friends.'

12 Mitford, Diana, A *Life of Contrasts* (Hamish Hamilton, 1977), p. 118.

13 *Ibid.*

14 SR essay quoted in Guinness, Jonathan and Catherine, *The House of Mitford* (Hutchinson, 1985), p. 365.

15 Mitford, Jessica, *Hons and Rebels* (Victor Gollancz, 1960), p. 81.

16 Katz, Otto, *The Brown Book of Hitler Terror and the Burning of the Reichstag* (John Lane, 1933).

17 *Hons and Rebels*, p. 73.

18 Toynbee, Philip, *Friends Apart* (MacGibbon & Kee, 1954), p. 18.

19 JM to DM, 19 January 1935, in *House of Mitford*, p. 367.

20 JM to DR, *ibid.*, pp. 368–9.

21 JM to SR, *ibid.*, p. 369.

22 Michael Burn, telephone interview with the author, July 2000.

23 Diana Mosley's biographer, Jan Dalley, doubts that Hitler did not know of Unity's relationship with Mosley. She believes that Hitler would have had an intelligence dossier on Mosley and Diana, and might have been using Unity and, subsequently, Diana to obtain casual information during their regular fireside chats in the years leading up to the war. On the other hand it is obvious that from this time (the fourth recorded meeting of Unity and Hitler) her family connections were known.

24 22 June 1935.

25 *House of Mitford*, pp. 377–8.

26 *Unity Mitford*, chapter 7.

27 Acton, Harold *Nancy Mitford* (Hamish Hamilton, 1975), p. 78.

28 *Unity Mitford*, p. 127.

29 *Ibid.*, p. 84. However, it should be remembered that Paulette Helleu was never very friendly with either Unity or Diana, and

she never got over her jealousy of the latter's close friendship with her father.

30 Joe Allen, of J.A. Allen and Co. Ltd, publishers, in a private letter to the author, June 2000, and in conversation.

31 *Hons and Rebels*, p. 80.

32 DM to the author, January 2001.

Chapter 9: Secret Marriage, 1935–7

1   Pryce-Jones, David, *Unity Mitford* (Weidenfeld & Nicolson, 1976), pp. 144 and 149.

2   *Ibid.*

3   UM to SR, in Guinness, Jonathan and Catherine *The House of Mitford* (Hutchinson, 1984), p. 378.

4   NM to DM, 18 June 1935, in Mosley, Charlotte, *Love from Nancy* (Hodder & Stoughton, 1993), p. 100.

5   NM to UM, 21 June 1935, in *ibid.*, p. 101.

6   NM to DM, 7 November 1934, in *ibid.*, p. 94.

7   Bernard Shaw, Fabian Lecture: 'In Praise of Guy Fawkes', 1933.

8   Skidelsky, Robert, *Oswald Mosley* (Macmillan, 1975), p. 331.

9   Speech at Ealing, 11 November 1934.

10 OSU/1709, NM to JM, 26 May 1937: Nancy decided not to post this letter, she explained, 'because of my weak mind & not wanting to be tortured when the G[erman]s have conquered us'.

11 Lees-Milne, James, *Prophesying Peace* (John Murray, 1997), p. 444.

12 Mosley, Nicholas, *Beyond the Pale* (Secker & Warburg, 1983), p. 390.

13 Tavener vs Mosley, 1937.

14 DM to the author, November 2000.

15 Dalley, Jan, *Diana Mosley* (Faber and Faber, 2000), p. 196.

16 The villa was at Posillipo, and belonged to Lord Rennell, Peter Rodd's father.

17 Sir Oswald Mosley to DM, in *Beyond the Pale*, p. 366.

18 DM to the author, January 2001.

19 *Beyond the Pale*, p. 364.

20 *Ibid.*, p. 366

21 *Ibid.*

22 Mosley, Diana, *Loved Ones: Sir Oswald Mosley* (Sidgwick & Jackson, 1983), p. 167.

23 Mitford, Jessica, *Hons and Rebels* (Victor Gollancz, 1960), p. 87.

24 CHP, 1935/36, JM to NM, undated.

25 OSU/1566, JM to DD, 11 June 1990.

26 *Hons and Rebels*, pp. 87–8.

27 *Tea at Chartwell, c.* 1928. The picture depicts a scene in the dining room, around which are gathered Thérèse Sickert, Diana Mitford, Edward Marsh, Winston S. Churchill, Professor Lindemann, Randolph Churchill, Diana Churchill, Clementine Churchill and Richard Sickert. It can be viewed at Chartwell, in the studio.

28 *Unity Mitford*, p. 164.

29 Mosley, Diana, *A Life of Contrasts* (Hamish Hamilton, 1977), p. 142.

30 Julius Schaub, Hitler's adjutant and personal assistant.

31 She made visits in January, April, September, and in October for her wedding.

32 *Loved Ones*, p. 172

33 *Diana Mosley*, p. 213.

34 *A Life of Contrasts*, p. 142.

35 FO371/184721.

36 *A Life of Contrasts*, p. 143.

37 *House of Mitford*, p. 384.

38 *Beyond the Pale*, p. 390.

39 *Loved Ones*, p. 168.

40 For most of the details on Derek Jackson I am indebted to *Loved Ones* and the *Dictionary of National Biography*, 1981–5, p. 207.

41 Railway station roughly halfway between Oxford and Cambridge.

42 He won a first-class degree in the natural sciences tripos, part I, in 1926, and a second, in part II, a year later. Leading from this, his work enabled more accurate measurement of hyperfine structures and isotope shifts.

43 The result of Jackson's work, on the hyperfine structure of caesium, was published by the Royal Society in *Proceedings*, 1928.

44 OSU/1709, JM to NM, 13 October 1971.

45 *Prophesying Peace*, p. 444.

46 *Loved Ones*, p. 78.

Chapter 10: Elopement, 1937

1   OSU/1031, ER to JM, 27 June 1940.

2   Unless otherwise cited, I have used Jessica Mitford's *Hons and Rebels* (Victor Gollancz, 1960), chapter 14, for information on her elopement.

3   OSU/155.

4   Toynbee, Philip, *Friends Apart* (MacGibbon and Kee, 1954), p. 92.

5   CHP, JM papers, 1 February 1937.

6   *Ibid.*, 9 February 1937.

7   *Hons and Rebels*, pp. 116–17.

8   CHP, February 1937, and OSU, Esmond Romilly letters.

9   OSU/1697, SR to JM, 23 February 1937.

10 CHP and OSU, NR to SR, 23 February 1937.

11 Duchess of Devonshire, *My Early Childhood* (privately published, 1995), p. 15

12 *News Chronicle*, 13 February 1937.

13 CHP and OSU, JM to SR, 5 March 1937

14 OSU/1674, UM to JM, 3 April 1937.

15 CHP, cable in JM papers, 1 March 1937.

16 *Daily Express*, 1 March 1937.

17 OSU/1697, SR to JM, 3 March 1937.

18 OSU/1674, UM to JM, 3 April 1937.

19 *Ibid.*, Joan Farrer Rodzianko to JM, 4 April 1937.

20 *Ibid.*, Ann Farrer Horne to JM, *c.* 4 April 1937, and 23 April 1937.

21 DD, interview with the author, Chatsworth, May 2000; also Lees-Milne, James, *Ancient as the Hills* (John Murray, 1997), pp. 173–4.

22 OSU, JM to DD, 26 October 1976: 'When you said that my running away . . . was the worst thing in your life I was v. astonished . . . As I remember us in those days we weren't all that adoring . . . I was probably v. jealous of you for being much prettier, and it was far more Boud and me [who were close] . . . Then you also admitted in 1974 when we went over all this that if I had told you about running away you'd have told Muv and Farve, so do admit my instinct . . . was right.'

23 Arthur Pack is a previous subject of the author. See *Cast No Shadow* (Pantheon Books, 1992).

24 OSU/1709, Nancy Mitford file, JM to NM, undated, *c.* 29 May 1937.

25 *Ibid.* Also NM to JM, 14 March 1937.

26 Ingram, Kevin, *Rebel* (Weidenfeld & Nicolson, 1985), p. 151.

27 Now 45 pence, but probably worth the equivalent of £15 in today's terms.

28 OSU, UM to JM, 11 April 1937.

29 Romilly, Esmond, *Boadilla* (Hamish Hamilton, 1937), p. 196.

30 *Rebel,* p. 158.

31 OSU/1674, UM to DM, 16 May 1937.

32 OSU/1709, JM to NM, *c.* early June 1937.

33 OSU/1559, DD to JM, 7 July 1937.

Chapter 11: Family at Odds, 1937–8

1 OSU/1559, DM to JM, 21 May 1937.

2 Gilbert, Martin, *Prophet of Truth* (Heinemann, 1976), p. 911.

3 OSU/1700, SR to JM, 12 June 1937.

4 OSU/1700, SR to JM, 27 March 1960.

5 OSU/1559, combined: DD to JM, 13 June 1937 and 20 June 1937.

6 Guinness, Jonathan and Catherine, *The House of Mitford* (Hutchinson, 1984), p. 410.

7 CHP, SR to JM, 17 June 1937.

8 *Ibid.*

9   *Ibid.*, JM to NM, *c.* early June 1937.

10   OSU/1697, SR to JM, 12 July 1937.

11   OSU/1559, DD to JM, 20 June 1937.

12   *Ibid.*, DD to JM, 30 June 1937

13   OSU/1697, SR to JM, 3 July 1937.

14   OSU/1674, UM to JM, 10 August 1937.

15   *House of Mitford*, p. 415.

16   *Ibid.*, p. 386.

17   Speer, Albert, *Inside the Third Reich* (Sphere Books, 1960), p. 77.

18   FO371/211(97), 27 September 1937.

19   DM, interview with the author, 15 January 2000.

20   Riefenstahl, Leni, *The Sieve of Time* (Quartet Books, 1992), pp. 228–9.

21   Hanfstaengl, Ernst, *Hitler, The Missing* Years (Eyre & Spottiswoode, 1957), p. 224.

22   Ibid., p. 285.

23   *House of Mitford*, p. 387.

24   DM to the author, January 2001. 'Putzi had in fact become rather disloyal. He never stopped telling foreign press chiefs how terrible things were "at the top". E.g. how much Goering and Goebbels disliked each other, and how much both disliked Streicher. He [Putzi] was an inveterate gossip and just the sort of man one doesn't want set loose on hostile foreign journalists. Putzi should have been dropped years before but Hitler kept him on for old times' sake . . . he was a bit of a joke.'

25   *Hitler, the Missing Years*, p. 286.

26   *Ibid.*, p. 289.

27   Mosley, Diana, *A Life of Contrasts* (Hamish Hamilton, 1977), pp. 140ff.

28   Mosley, Nicholas, *Beyond the Pale* (Secker & Warburg, 1983), p. 400.

29   *Ibid.*, p. 399.

30   DM to the author, February 2001.

31   The Acton drawings are now owned by Desmond Guinness and kept at Leixslip Castle in Ireland.

32 Toynbee, Philip, *Friends Apart* (MacGibbon & Kee, 1954), p. 106.

33 *Ibid.*, p. 107.

34 In his diary he says she asked this of a car-park attendant. See Mitford, Jessica, *Faces of Philip* (Heinemann, 1984), p. 32

35 *Ibid.*, p. 112.

36 Ingram, Kevin, *Rebel* (Weidenfeld & Nicolson, 1985), p. 168.

37 OSU, MS by Bryan Guinness, 'Dichtung und Warheit among the Mitfords', *c.* 1959.

38 OSU/1678, JM to NM, 30 November 1968.

39 Later Dame Christian Howard.

40 OSU/1738, JM to Emma Tennant (and others), 3 September 1993.

41 PRO, birth certificate.

42 CHP, JM to DD, 31 May 1937.

43 Mitford, Jessica, *Hons and Rebels* (Victor Gollancz, 1960), p. 148.

44 DM, interview with the author, Paris, 2000.

45 *Hons and Rebels*, p. 149.

46 *Friends Apart*, pp. 115–16

47 DD, interview with the author, Chatsworth, 4 February 2000.

48 Widow of the late Clement Mitford (David's elder brother).

49 OSU/1559, DD to JM, 7 July 1937.

Chapter 12: Slide towards Conflict, 1938

1 Speech by Hitler at Nuremberg, 12 September 1938.

2 A study of statistics available in the Public Record Office shows that prior to 1938 the number of political and criminal prisoners in German concentration camps was approximately 25,000. This was similar to the number of convicted prisoners in modern Germany in 1977. The number confined in 1938 was a marked decrease from that of 1933–4. But even the figure of 25,000 was minute in comparison to the millions confined in Soviet slave-labour camps under Stalin, according to a letter in the *New Statesman* (22 April 1977). This only came to public knowledge two decades later.

3 See Bibliography.

4   Mitford, Jessica, *Hons and Rebels* (Victor Gollancz, 1960), pp. 145–6.

5   Interview notes, Paris, 2000.

6   DM to the author, 16 January 2001

7   Newspaper articles of the day named him as Edward Warburton.

8   Private letter to the author; Mr Allen is an old friend of the author's.

9   *Evening Standard*, 12 April 1937.

10 *The Times*, 2 June 1937, p. 14; *Daily Mirror*, 2 June 1937, pp. 1–2.

11 Guinness, Jonathan and Catherine, *The House of Mitford* (Hutchinson, 1984), p. 412.

12 Quoted in full in David Pryce-Jones, *Unity Mitford* (Weidenfeld & Nicolson, 1976), p. 187. FO/371/21581.

13 DM to the author, January 2001.

14 *House of Mitford*, p. 421.

15 *Ibid.*, p. 417.

16 *Ibid.*, p. 416.

17 *Unity Mitford*, p. 196.

18 *House of Mitford*, p. 417.

19 Cowles, Virginia, *Looking for Trouble* (Hamish Hamilton, 1941), p. 154.

20 *Ibid.*

21 Butler, Lucy (ed.), *Letters Home* (John Murray, 1991), p. 291.

22 Unity did spend Christmas in England. On 15 December a gossip column reported her sitting with her mother, nibbling at a plate of sausages on her lap (Sydney had clearly given up insisting that Unity stuck to Mosaic dietary law), at an Anglo-German Fellowship Christmas party in Bloomsbury.

23 *House of Mitford*, p. 371.

24 Typescript at OSU; partially published in *Forum* (undated).

25 Attallah, Naim, *More of a Certain Age* (Quartet Books, 1993), pp. 50–1.

26 *House of Mitford*, p. 385.

27 Mosley, Diana, *A Life of Contrasts* (Hamish Hamilton, 1977), p. 146.

28 *House of Mitford*, p. 383.

29 Mosley, Nicholas, *Beyond the Pale* (Secker & Warburg, 1983), p. 410.

30 Ravensdale, Irene, *In Many Rhythms* (Weidenfeld & Nicolson, 1953), p. 146.

31 *Ibid.*

32 Hastings, Selina, *Nancy Mitford* (Hamish Hamilton, 1985), p. 115.

33 Nancy also told friends that the 'wicked nanny' had suffered from syphilis and that it may have been passed to her, causing her inability to carry a child. This seems extremely unlikely.

34 OSU, Dr William K. Wallerstein, 5 December 1980.

35 *Hons and Rebels*, p. 152.

36 Toynbee, Philip, *Friends Apart* (MacGibbon & Kee, 1954), p. 122.

37 OSU/1711, Seldon Rodman to JM (undated).

38 *Friends Apart*, p. 154. It seems likely that it was at this point, when things looked very black for the couple, that Decca had her abortion.

39 *Ibid.*, p. 152.

Chapter 13: No Laughing Matter, 1939

1 *NY Daily Mirror*, 'Only Human', 21 April 1937.

2 *Ibid.*

3 *Ibid.*, 20 April 1937.

4 Mitford, Jessica, *Hons and Rebels* (Victor Gollancz, 1960), pp. 209 and 219–20.

5 *Daily Mirror*, 18 March 1937, p. 17.

6 Guinness, Jonathan and Catherine, *The House of Mitford* (Hutchinson, 1984), p. 423.

7 *Ibid.*

8 Pryce-Jones, David, *Unity Mitford* (Weidenfeld & Nicolson, 1976), p. 218.

9 *House of Mitford*, p. 424. Refers to Adolf Wagner, Gauleiter

of Munich. Schwabing is a student and artist district in Munich.

10 *Unity Mitford*, p. 149. Interview with Lady Gainer, widow of the British consul to Munich in 1936. Of the Jews taken to the island on the Danube, Unity told her, 'That's the way to treat them. I wish we could do that in England to our Jews.'

11 DM, interview with the author, Paris, January 2000.

12 *The Times*, 29 May 1940, p. 9.

13 Mosley, Diana, *A Life of Contrasts* (Hamish Hamilton, 1977), p. 160.

14 Trevor-Roper, Hugh (ed.), *Hitler's Table Talk* (Weidenfeld & Nicolson, 1953), p. 631. This conversation took place on the evening of 16 August 1942.

15 DM to the author, 11 November 2000.

16 DM to the author regarding the Hitler photograph, 6 February 2001: 'I still have the receipt (dated June 1940) but I never asked them about it after the war because I assumed the Home Office had probably stolen it. All our bank accounts were examined, and our safe at home forced open. Many things disappeared and our solicitor got apologies, but no more, from the Home Office people . . . One thing they stole was our marriage certificate . . . I had great trouble getting a copy from the ruins of Berlin.'

17 *House of Mitford*. p. 426.

18 *Ibid.*, p. 427.

19 CHP, JM to SR, 23 August 1939.

20 DM to the author, January 2001.

21 OSU/1651, PM to JM, 30 September 1937.

22 NM to SR, 25 May 1939, in Mosley, Charlotte, *Love from Nancy* (Hodder & Stoughton, 1993), p. 113.

23 *Ibid.*

24 *Ibid.*

25 OSU/1651, PM to JM, 19 February 1978.

26 *Love from Nancy*, p. 120.

27 *Unity Mitford*, p. 230.

28 *House of Mitford*, p. 428.

29 *Unity Mitford*, p. 235.

30 *Radio Times*, 11 April 1981, letter from Mr H.W. Koch of York, quoted in *House of Mitford*, p. 432.

31 It was the younger of the two Koch brothers who wrote the letter to the *Radio Times*.

32 *House of Mitford*, p. 434.

33 *Unity Mitford*, p. 236.

34 And, of course, Eva Braun would eventually die with Hitler in a suicide pact.

35 *Unity Mitford*, p. 231.

36 NM to Violet Hammersley, 15 September 1939, in *Love from Nancy*, p. 116.

37 OSU/1697, SR to JM, 29 October 1939.

38 NM to Violet Hammersley, 30 October 1939 in *Love from Nancy*, p. 123.

39 *Ibid.* Also OSU/1651, PM to JM, 30 September 1939.

40 Mitford, Jessica, *Hons and Rebels* (Victor Gollancz, 1960), pp. 196–202.

41 OSU/1679, Blor to JM, 10 December 1939.

42 OSU/1697, SR to JM, 8 December 1939.

Chapter 14: Irreconcilable Differences, 1940–41

1 DD, interview with the author, Chatsworth, 4 May 2000.

2 Mosley, Diana, A *Life of Contrasts* (Hamish Hamilton, 1977), p. 165.

3 Interview at Chatsworth, June 2000.

4 Not Unity's diaries. Janos kept these safely and later sent them to Lady Redesdale.

5 Guinness, Jonathan and Catherine, *The House of Mitford* (Hutchinson, 1984), p. 436.

6 OSU/1697, SR to JM, 28 January 1940: 'I see that doctors today have given up on pills and potions and taken to great mysterious engines, electrical and otherwise. This clinic is full of them and is more like the inside of a battleship than a hospital. She has had all

sorts of electrical tests and X-rays. We are certainly living in a mechanical age.'

7 NM to Violet Hammersley, 7 January 1940, in Mosley, Charlotte, *Love from Nancy* (Hodder & Stoughton, 1993), p. 126.

8 *House of Mitford*, p. 438.

9 A *Life of Contrasts*, p. 167.

10 NM to Violet Hammersley, 10 February 1940, in *Love from Nancy*, p. 130.

11 *House of Mitford*, pp. 439–40.

12 This quote appeared in English papers as 'Unity was always a headstrong girl'. See OSU/1673, TM to JM, 18 January 1940.

13 CHP, JM, to SR, 26 February 1940.

14 OSU/1697, SR to JM, 1 April 1940.

15 *The Times*, 9 March 1940, p. 4.

16 Unless otherwise stated, the information on Decca and Esmond's experiences in the USA is taken from Mitford, Jessica, *Hons and Rebels* (Victor Gollancz, 1960). For the Miami period, see pp. 210–14.

17 OSU/1628, Kay Graham file, 13 April 1978.

18 OSU/1032, Nellie Romilly to JM, 8 July 1940.

19 *Hons and Rebels*, p. 222.

20 Durr, Virginia Foster, *Outside the Magic Circle* (University of Alabama Press, 1990), p. 138.

21 OSU/1029, JM to ER, June 1940.

22 CHP, JM to DD, 17 November 1986.

23 OSU/1697, JM to SR, 22 July 1940.

24 OSU, Jessica Mitford Papers.

25 *Ibid.*

26 *Ibid.*

27 OSU/1020, JM to ER, 8 September 1940.

28 OSU/1031, ER to JM, 11 September 1940.

29 OSU/1029, Max Beaverbrook to Nellie Romilly, 19 November 1940.

30 Mosley, Nicholas, *Beyond the Pale* (Secker & Warburg, 1983), p. 443.

31 Winston Churchill thought this likely. See notes taken at a War Cabinet meeting 28 May 1940, in which Churchill discussed his decision against possible negotiations with Hitler: '"we should become a slave state, though a British Government which would be Hitler's puppet would undoubtedly be set up under Mosley or some such person" . . . no one expressed a flicker of dissent'. See Hugh Dalton, *The Fateful Years* (Frederick Muller, 1957), p. 336.

32 Dalley, Jan, *Diana Mosley* (Faber & Faber, 2000), p. 267.

33 Quoted in TV documentary *Churchill vs. Hitler: The Duel*, Channel 4, 8 May 2000.

34 DM to the author, January 2001.

35 Major Vidkun Quisling, leader of the Norwegian Fascists, proclaimed a puppet government on the day Norway was invaded by the Germans.

36 DM to the author, January 2001.

37 BBC2 programme, 2000, *The Age of Nazism – Tourists of the Revolution*.

38 Skidelsky, Robert, *Mosley* (Macmillan, 1981), p. 447.

39 *Ibid.*

40 Hubert Gladwyn Jebb (later 1st Baron Gladwyn) at the Ministry of Economic Warfare, 1940–42.

41 20 June 1940, in *Love from Nancy*, p. 132.

42 *House of Mitford*, p. 492.

43 *Ibid.*, p. 493.

44 *Ibid.* Jonathan Guinness points out that the statement regarding the profits of the radio station was incorrect. Half the profits were contracted to the German radio company, which was also involved in the venture.

45 DM to the author, January 2001.

46 *A Life of Contrasts*, p. 213.

47 *Ibid.*, p. 189.

48 OSU/1697, SR to JM, October 1940.

49 *Love from Nancy*, p. 139.

50 JM to VH, 1 October 1940, in *ibid.*, p. 140.

51 26 December 1940, in *ibid.*, p. 144.

52 *Ibid.*

53 OSU/1707, NM to JM, 4 July 1940.

54 OSU/1697, SR to JM 26 September 1940.

55 OSU/1700, referred to in JM, to SR, 2 April 1960.

56 3 March 1941, in *Love from Nancy*, p. 147.

57 André Roy was his *nomme de guerre*. His real name was Roy André Desplats-Pilter.

58 Mrs Rattenbury was a murderess.

59 OSU/1559, DD to JM, 6 May 1940.

60 *Ibid.*, DD to JM, 7 October 1940. Joseph Kennedy departed from London on 23 October 1940 at the height of the Blitz saying that he had the greatest respect for Londoners.

61 Lees-Milne, James, *Prophesying Peace* (John Murray, 1997), p. 345.

62 Collier, Peter and Horowitz, David, *The Kennedys* (Secker & Warburg), p. 94,

63 OSU/1679, 'Nannie' to JM, 15 September. Philip Toynbee, Esmond's old friend, was also at Sandhurst at the same time.

64 OSU/1697, SR to JM, 7 October 1940.

65 NM to VH 3 March 1941, in *Love from Nancy*, p. 147

66 *House of Mitford*, p. 581.

Chapter 15: Gains and Losses, 1941–3

1 In *Hons and Rebels* Decca says a nine-bed ward, but in her letters to Esmond she describes it, and draws a diagram of a five-bedded ward.

2 OSU/1648, JM to Anne Horne, 18 October 1984.

3 A Spanish grandee who left her home and family to join the Republicans fighting Franco. See *In Place of Splendour – the Biography of a Spanish Woman* (Michael Joseph, 1940).

4 OSU/1698, SR to JM, 15 April 1941.

5 *Ibid.*, 18 April 1941.

6 Madeau Stewart, interview with the author, Burford, spring 2000.

7 OSU, DD to JM, 1959 (undated).

8 DM to the author, January 2001.

9   Ingram, Kevin, *Rebel* (Weidenfeld & Nicolson, 1985), p. 217.

10 OSU/1030, Virginia Durr to ER, 1 August 1941.

11 OSU/1029, 3 September 1941.

12 *Ibid.*, ER, 6 September 1941.

13 OSU/1030, ER to JM, 11 November 1941.

14 OSU/1031, JM to ER, 1 December 1941.

15 *Ibid.*, Chief of Air Staff to JM (extract), 2 December 1941.

16 Durr, Virginia Foster, *Outside the Magic Circle* (University of Alabama Press, 1990), p. 141.

17 OSU/1029, Wing Commander Ronald Clark, O/C, 58 Squadron Linton on Ouse, York, 4 December 1941.

18 Churchill, Winston S., *The Second World War*, vol. III, *The Grand Alliance* (Cassell, 1950), pp. 539–40.

19 Moran, Lord, *Churchill – The Struggle for Survival* (Constable, 1966), p. 13. Also, Joyce McKee to author 29 January 2002. The church was The Foundry Methodist Church on 16th Street, Washington, DC.

20 Robert Treuhaft, interview with the author, San Francisco, October 1999.

21 OSU/1794, JM notes. Also OSU/1707, Nellie Romilly to SR, 19 March 1942.

22 Pearson, John, *Citadel of the Heart* (Macmillan, 1991), p. 306.

23 OSU, Romilly file, Nellie Romilly to SR, February 1942.

24 OSU/1032, Virginia Durr to SR, *c.* February 1942.

25 Lees-Milne, James, *Prophesying Peace* (John Murray, 1997), p. 349.

26 *Outside the Magic Circle*, p. 141.

27 OSU/1032, Virginia Durr to SR, *c.* February 1942. When Lady Redesdale replied to this she diplomatically repeated several phrases used by Mrs Durr, to let her know, without saying so, that her letter had been safely received.

28 Rosemary, Mrs Richard Bailey, interview with the author, Westwell, March 2000.

29 CHP, JM to SR, 22 February 1942.

30 NM to DM, 22 November 1941, in Mosley, Charlotte, *Love from Nancy* (Hodder & Stoughton, 1993), p. 151.

31 NM to DM, 24 August 1942, in *ibid.*, p. 155.

32 The shop still exists in Curzon Street. Today, a 'blue plaque' commemorates Nancy's association with the building.

33 Lees-Milne, James, *Ancestral Voices* (John Murray, 1975), p. 27.

34 *Ibid.*, p. 26.

35 *Ibid.*, p. 247. Anthony and Christopher, playmates of the Mitford children, were killed early in the war. Timothy's conversion to Roman Catholicism in 1943 while in a PoW camp is said to have distressed the Baileys 'more than the death in action of their two other sons'.

36 *Ibid.*, p. 201. The 'autobiography' became the basis of the novel *The Pursuit of Love*.

37 *Ibid.*, p. 343.

38 *Ibid.*, p. 351.

39 *Ibid.*, p. 249.

40 *Prophesying Peace*, p. 312.

41 Hastings, Selina, *Nancy Mitford* (Hamish Hamilton, 1985), p. 144

42 Mitford, Nancy, *The Pursuit of Love* (Hamish Hamilton, 1945), p. 189.

43 Hastings, *Nancy Mitford*, p. 149.

44 *Love from Nancy*, p. 162.

Chapter 16: Women at War, 1943–4

1 Churchill, Winston S., *The Second World War*, vol. III, *The Grand Alliance* (Cassell, 1950), p. 627

2 *Ibid.*, p. 750

3 Mosley, Diana, *A Life of Contrasts* (Hamish Hamilton, 1977), p. 192.

4 *Ibid.*

5 DM, interview with the author, June 2000.

6 *Ibid.*

7 Mosley, Nicholas, *Beyond the Pale* (Secker & Warburg, 1983), p. 483.

8   OSU/1698, JM to SR, 11 April 1943.

9   Mitford, Jessica, *A Fine Old Conflict* (Michael Joseph, 1977), p. 37.

10 OSU 1742, RT to Aranka, 28 December 1942.

11 *Ibid.*, 8 January 1943.

12 *A Fine Old Conflict*, p. 41.

13 *Ibid.*, p. 46.

14 Called 'Mrs Tibbs' in *A Fine Old Conflict*.

15 *A Fine Old Conflict*, p. 46.

16 OSU/1698, JM to SR, 16 March 1943.

17 *Ibid.*, 11 April 1943.

18 Even as an adult Dinky is unmistakably Mitford. I was easily able to identify her from among a jumbo jet-load of passengers when I first met her, merely because I was familiar with photographs of her Mitford aunts at the same age. However, she told me that when she was about nineteen she was walking in New York one day when she noticed a man walking towards her and staring as though transfixed. He passed by, then turned and came back to her. 'I say,' he said in an English voice, 'are you in any way related to Esmond Romilly?' She replied that Esmond was her father. 'Thank God,' he said. 'I thought I was seeing a ghost.'

19 OSU/1698, JM to SR, 11 April 1943.

20 *Ibid.*, 30 May, 1943.

21 *Ibid.*, BT to Aranka, 27 June 1943.

22 Doris Brin Walker, 'Dobbie', interview with the author, San Francisco, 23 October 1999.

23 OSU/1698, JM to SR, 28 June 1943.

24 *Ibid.*, 21 July 1943.

25 *Ibid.*, 22 November 1943.

26 OSU, misc., JM to Winston Churchill, 24 November 1943.

27 *A Fine Old Conflict*, p. 58.

28 When David found this question on forms he always answered, 'Honourable'.

29 Soames, Mary (ed.), *Speaking for Themselves* (Doubleday, 1998), p. 486.

30 *A Life of Contrasts*, p. 198.

31 *Speaking for Themselves*, p. 488.

32 Possibly the development of 'Window', bundles of thin strips of aluminium foil ejected from high-flying aircraft, designed to confuse enemy radar.

33 *A Life of Contrasts*, pp. 199–200.

34 Guinness, Jonathan and Catherine, *The House of Mitford* (Hutchinson, 1984), p. 508

35 OSU/1698, SR to JM, 1 January 1943.

36 *Ibid.*, JM to SR, 27 March 1944.

37 Sally Norton.

38 Kick kept in constant touch with Billy while in Washington. A friend of the author, Quentin Keynes, who worked at the British embassy in Washington, knew her well and used to send their letters through the diplomatic bag.

39 Collier, Peter and Horowitz, David, *The Kennedys* (Secker & Warburg, 1984), p. 129.

Chapter 17: The French Lady Writer, 1944–7

1 James Lees-Milne recorded in his diary that the Duke of Wellington was furious when he heard that Debo had called her son 'Morny', which appeared to be a diminutive of the Wellesley title Lord Mornington. 'How would you like it,' he complained to the Duke of Devonshire at a party, 'if I christened my grandson Harty of Burlington?' Nancy broke in, 'But Debo christened him after her favourite jockey. She's never heard of the Duke of Wellington.' See Lees-Milne, James, *Prophesying Peace* (John Murray, 1997), p. 345.

2 OSU/1698, JM to SR, 15 June 1944.

3 *Ibid.*, 27 March 1944.

4 *Ibid.*, DR to JM, 21 May 1944.

5 *Ibid.*, SR to JM, 16 May 1944.

6 Lord Hartington was killed on 10 September 1944.

7 Patsy White. See Collier, Peter, and Horowitz, David, *The Kennedys* (Secker & Warburg, 1984), p. 144.

8   *Ibid.*

9   *Ibid.*

10 Smith, Amanda, *A Hostage to Fortune* (Viking, 2001), p. 601.

11 NM to SR, 24 September 1944, in Mosley, Charlotte, *Love from Nancy* (Hodder & Stoughton, 1993), p. 167.

12 OSU/1698, SR to JM, 25 July 1944.

13 OSU/1709, NM to JM, 26 May 1944.

14 *Prophesying Peace*, p. 294.

15 Mitford, Nancy, *The Pursuit of Love* (Hamish Hamilton, 1945), p. 193.

16 *Prophesying Peace*, p. 344.

17 *Ibid.*, pp. 348–9.

18 *Ibid.*, p. 355.

19 *Ibid.*, p. 380.

20 *Ibid.*, p. 394.

21 Once part of British India, Burma became a separate state in 1937. Its government continued to function from India after occupation of the country by the Japanese.

22 The information on Major Freeman-Mitford's death is taken from (a) the official Statement of the Company Commander, Devonshire Regiment (OSU 1701) and (b) Commonwealth War Graves Commission records. His grave is at Taukyan War Cemetery, plot 17 F20. See also OSU/1698, SR to JM, 19 June 1945.

23 *Prophesying Peace*, p. 425.

24 Lees-Milne, James, *Deep Romantic Chasm* (John Murray, 2000), p. 101.

25 OSU/1698, SR to JM, 22 April 1945.

26 *Prophesying Peace*, p. 425.

27 *Ibid.*, p. 426.

28 *Ibid.*, p. 460.

29 RT, interview with the author, Oakland, California, October 1999.

30 OSU/1698, JM to NM.

31 OSU/1707, 13 April 1945.

32 OSU/1698, 22 April 1945.

33 NM to EW, 17 January 1945, in *Love from Nancy*, p. 175.

34 Author and publisher, editor of the *London Magazine*, and godson of Mrs Violet Hammersley.

35 NM to SR, 17 September 1945, in *Love from Nancy*, pp. 184–5.

36 NM to Randolph Churchill, 30 September 1945, in *ibid.*, p. 187.

37 John Betjeman to NM, 19 December 1945, in Lycett-Green, Candida (ed.), *John Betjeman Letters* (Methuen, 1990), p. 378.

38 NM to Gaston Palewski, 20 January 1946, in *Love from Nancy*, p. 195.

39 Guinness, Jonathan and Catherine, *The House of Mitford* (Hutchinson, 1984), p. 444.

40 11 February 1947.

41 OSU/1698, SR to JM, 24 March 1945.

42 *Ibid.*, Hasties (Mitford family solicitors) to JM, 15 June 1945.

43 Cockburn, Claud, 'Island Fling', *Punch*, 30 March 1960.

44 *Ibid.*

45 OSU/1698, JM to SR, 21 May 1946.

46 *Ibid.*, SR to JM, 4 February 1946.

47 956 Clayton Street, San Francisco.

48 Extract from RT's address at the memorial for JM held in London.

49 RT, interview with the author, Oakland, California, October 1999.

50 Pele de Lappe, interview with the author, Petaluma, California, October 1999.

51 OSU/1698, JM to SR, *c.* December 1947.

52 CHP, Constancia 'Dinky' Romilly to SR, 27 January 1948.

53 OSU/1709, JM to NM, 16 November 1971.

54 RT, interview with the author, Oakland, California, October 1999.

55 OSU/1709, JM to NM, 13 October 1971.

56 Constancia 'Dinky' Romilly, interview with the author, California, October 1999.

57 OSU/sundry. Transcript of an interview with Jessica Mitford by a TV crew.

58 OSU/1709, JM to NM, 13 October 1971.
59 NM to DM, 19 February 1947, in *Love from Nancy*, pp. 223–4
60 DM to the author, 16 January 2001.

Chapter 18: Truth and Consequences, 1948–55

1 Collier, Peter and Horowitz, David, *The Kennedys* (Secker & Warburg, 1984), pp. 169–71.
2 Guinness, Jonathan and Catherine, *The House of Mitford* (Hutchinson, 1984), p. 443.
3 Pryce-Jones, David, *Unity Mitford* (Weidenfeld & Nicolson, 1976), p. 260.
4 Interview with the author, October 1999.
5 OSU/1698, 26 June 1948.
6 YUL, SR to JLM, 18 June 1948.
7 Lycett-Green, Candida (ed.), *John Betjeman Letters 1926–1951* (Methuen, 1990), pp. 369–70.
8 DM to the author, January 2001.
9 *John Betjeman Letters.* p. 473.
10 Skidelsky, Robert, *Oswald Mosley* (Macmillan, 1975), p. 481.
11 *Ibid.*
12 *Ibid.*, p. 505.
13 Mosley, Diana, *A Life of Contrasts* (Hamish Hamilton, 1977), p. 218.
14 Mosley, Sir Oswald, *My Life* (Nelson, 1970), p. 424.
15 This began a long link between the family and OSU. Alexander Mosley would spend several years at OSU, and by coincidence the papers of Jessica were purchased by the Rare Books and MSS Department, making the college one of the main sources for Mitford researchers.
16 Victor Christian, 9th Duke of Devonshire (d. 1938) represented West Derbyshire from the age of twenty-three in 1891. Edward William Spencer, the 10th Duke (1895–1950) was MP for West Derbyshire from 1923–38.
17 Duchess of Devonshire, *The Estate* (Macmillan 1990), p. xxiii.

18　Increased to seven years in 1968.

19　After an old friend of Debo.

20　Murphy, Sophia, *The Mitford Family Album* (Sidgwick & Jackson, 1985), p. 123.

21　JM to Gaston Palewski, 23 September 1946, in Mosley, Charlotte, *Love from Nancy* (Hodder & Stoughton, 1993).

22　NM to DM, 17 May 1947, in *ibid.*, p. 229.

23　Margot de Gramont.

24　NM to Gaston Palewski, 26 July 1948, in *Love from Nancy*, p. 266.

35　*Ibid.*, 3 June 1949, p. 282.

Chapter 19: Return to the Old Country, 1955–8

1　CHP, JM to SR, *c.* February 1954.

2　*Ibid.*, SR to JM, 28 February 1954.

3　Extract from programme of testimonial dinner given for the Treuhafts in 1985.

4　Mitford, Jessica, *A Fine Old Conflict* (Michael Joseph, 1977), pp. 163–64.

5　*Ibid.*, p. 164.

6　Many years later they fought to obtain a copy of their FBI file through the Freedom of Information Act. Decca said that reading it she could see her old life flashing before her eyes as though she were drowning.

7　*A Fine Old Conflict*, p. 174.

8　OSU, Constancia 'Dinky' Romilly to RT, 21 March 1993.

9　OSU/1629, JM to Kay Graham, 13 March 1979.

10　OSU/1699, SR to JM, 26 February 1955.

11　OSU, RT file, Constancia 'Dinky' Romilly to RT, 21 March 1993.

12　RT, interview with the author, Oakland, October 1999.

13　CHP, JM to SR, 6 August 1955.

14　Mosley, Diana, *A Life of Contrasts* (Hamish Hamilton, 1977), p. 256.

15　OSU/1699, DR to SR, 7 June 1954.

16 RT, interview with the author, Oakland, October 1999.

17 OSU/1698, SR to JM, 26 March 1956.

18 Julia Budworth to the author, 29 May 2000.

19 *A Fine Old Conflict*, p. 183.

20 Pele de Lappe papers, JM to Pele de Lappe, 20 September 1955.

21 Since then the National Trust has changed the arrangements for acceptance of a property, and will only take houses where there is an endowment to ensure adequate upkeep. Also, many National Trust properties are now let at commercial rents to suitable tenants who run the properties partly as family homes. Even so, the difference between an unoccupied National Trust property and an ancestral seat still occupied by the family is marked, e.g. Hardwick vs Woburn.

22 *A Fine Old Conflict*, p. 194.

23 *Ibid.*

24 NM to Raymond Mortimer, 8 September 1955, in Mosley, Charlotte, *Love from Nancy* (Hodder & Stoughton, 1993), p. 407.

25 NM to Evelyn Waugh, 4 August 1955, in *ibid.*, p. 404.

26 *A Fine Old Conflict*, p. 197.

27 19 November 1955, in *Love from Nancy*, p. 410.

28 Decca believed Pam was a lesbian. It is true that Pam shared her home with another woman for a number of years but all the surviving written evidence points to this being a platonic rather than a sexual relationship.

29 OSU, RT file, JM to RT, 12 November 1955.

30 Constancia 'Dinky' Romilly, interview with the author, October 1999.

31 George Gutekunst, interview with the author, Sonoma, October 1999.

32 *A Fine Old Conflict*, p. 203.

33 Reprinted in *The Lively Arts*, date unknown. See transcript of interview in OSU/155.

34 Marge (Frantz), Pele (de Lappe) and Betty (Bacon).

35 OSU/1698, 4 January 1957; about $50,000.

36 NM to SR, 6 September 1952, in *Love from Nancy*, p. 358.

37   *Sunday Times*, 7 March 1954.

38   *Manchester Guardian*, 12 March 1954. See *Love from Nancy*, pp. 381–2.

39   *Ibid.*, p. 369.

40   Hastings, Selina, *Nancy Mitford* (Hamish Hamilton, 1985), p. 225.

41   Mitford, Nancy, *Noblesse Oblige* (Hamish Hamilton, 1956).

42   NM to Hugh Thomas, 15 March 1956, in *Love from Nancy*, p. 412.

43   Sophia Cavendish, b. 18 March 1957.

44   *A Life of Contrasts*, p. 257.

45   OSU/1699, SR to JM, 19 March 1958.

46   OSU/1707, NM to JM, 3 April 1958.

Chapter 20: A Cold Wind to the Heart, 1958–66

1   DM to the author, January 1999: 'my two Guinness sons went to Oxford, Jonathan to Trinity and Desmond to Christ Church – I tell you this in case you think that like us my sons never went to University'.

2   Mosley, Oswald, *My Life* (Nelson, 1970), p. 430.

3   Mosley, Diana, *A Life of Contrasts* (Hamish Hamilton, 1977), p. 240.

4   *My Life*, p. 428.

5   Guinness, Jonathan and Catherine, *The House of Mitford* (Hutchinson, 1984), p. 534.

6   Lord Longford, interview with the author, House of Lords, May 2000.

7   NM to JM, 15 November 1968, in Mosley, Charlotte, *Love from Nancy* (Hodder & Stoughton, 1993), p. 556.

8   NM to Gaston Palewski, 12 June 1958, in *ibid.*, p. 439.

9   OSU/1699, JM to SR, 30 June 1958.

10 RT recalls that the island was valued at $54,000 (about £11,000 then) so he and Decca were able to buy out the other shares for $27,000.

11 Decca had saved every penny she had ever received from the Canadian government widow's pension – even at her most hard-up she had never used it. It was Dinky's college fund.

12 OSU, RT file, JM to RT, 16 April 1959.

13 *Ibid.*, various letters.

14 Mitford, Jessica, *Hons and Rebels* (Victor Gollancz, 1960), p. 228.

15 OSU/RT file, RT to JM, 26 April 1959.

16 RT, interview with the author, Oakland, California, October 1999.

17 *Ibid.*

18 OSU/1746, JM to RT, 15 May 1959.

19 But published in the USA as *Daughters and Rebels*. There was an unexpected boost to sales in the Deep South where it was shelved in bookshops with civil-war materials.

20 OSU, JM to Marge Frantz, 5 June 1959.

21 CHP, JM to DD, 17 August 1959.

22 OSU, JM to RT, 29 July 1959.

23 OSU/1699, 14 October 1959.

24 OSU/1700, SR to JM, 21 April 1960.

25 Rosemary Bailey, Julia Budworth.

26 OSU/100, SR to JM, 10 April 1960.

27 *Ibid.*, 12 August 1959.

28 OSU/1707, NM to JM, 11 March 1960.

29 NM to Heywood Hill (2 letters), 9 and 16 March 1960, in *Love from Nancy*, pp. 446–7.

30 24 May 1960, in *ibid.*, p. 450.

31 RT, interview with the author, Oakland, California, October 1999.

32 *New York Post*, 5 June 1960.

33 19 November 1960.

34 CHP, JM to DD, 11 July 1962.

35 Mitford, Nancy, *The Water Beetle* (Hamish Hamilton, 1962), pp. 6–9.

36 Madeau Stewart was the granddaughter of Tello, Sydney's old governess and confidante. Tello had several children by Tap

Bowles and therefore Madeau was Sydney's half-niece. 'We never spoke of family matters, or the family connection,' Madeau told me, 'although our families were always in touch.' The Stewarts used to rent Sydney's cottage at High Wycombe, for instance, but Madeau was forty before she discovered there was some family connection. Madeau Stewart, interview with the author, Burford, Oxon, 1999.

37 *A Life of Contrasts*, p. 255.

38 NM to Mark Ogilvie-Grant, 14 May 1963, in *Love from Nancy*, p. 488

39 21 May 1963, in *ibid.*, p. 489.

40 OSU/1560, DD to JM, 31 May 1963.

41 OSU/1680, JM to Peter Nevile, 20 November 1991.

42 OSU, Constancia 'Dinky' Romilly to JM and RT, 25 September 1963. Also interview with the author, Oakland, California, 1999.

43 Mitford, Jessica, *The American Way of Death* (Simon & Schuster, 1963), p. 29.

44 OSU/1678, JM to Charlotte Mosley, 4 May 1996.

45 CHP, file, 1963. Cross-reference to JM letter, dated 30 January 1996. See also OSU, JM to RT, 23 June 1964: 'Said he had read my book and for that reason chose the $900 one [casket]. Otherwise would have felt he must get the most expensive, last gesture he could make to his brother etc.' When Bobby Kennedy was murdered Arthur Schlesinger was responsible for making the arrangements when the body arrived at Bethesda. He too recalled Decca's book and chose one of the least expensive caskets, but later agonized about whether he was being 'cheap' or just sensible: 'I remember thinking about how difficult it must be for everybody making that sort of decision.' See his *Robert Kennedy and His Times* (Houghton Mifflin, 1978).

46 The matter did not end with post-publication publicity. Decca began a campaign for inexpensive funerals and with the help of a friend a funeral co-operative was established, which is still active.

47 Mitford, Jessica *Poison Penmanship* (Farrar, Strauss and Giroux, 1979) p. 4.

Chapter 21: Views and Reviews, 1966–80

1 Her husband is Terry Webber.

2 OSU/709, NM to JM, 18 November 1965.

3 OSU/1776, RT file, RT to JM, 31 May 1965.

4 Pele de Lappe papers, JM to Pele, 11 August 1964, and interview with the author, California, October 1999.

5 Letter from Brigid Keenan to the author.

6 NM to DD, 29 March 1969, in Mosley, Charlotte, *Love from Nancy* (Hodder & Stoughton, 1993), p. 562.

7 OSU, JM to DD, 17 July 1969.

8 CHP, JM to DD, 13 May 1969.

9 Pele de Lappe, interview with the author, October 1999; JM to Pele, 26 May 1969.

10 RT, interview with the author, Oakland, California, 1999.

11 NM to DD, 24 October 1969, in *Love from Nancy*, p. 570.

12 OSU/1710, NM to JM, 23 May 1972.

13 CHP, JM to DD, 14 June 1973.

14 OSU, JM to RT, 14 June 1973.

15 OSU/1637, JM to William MacBrian, 30 September 1986.

16 A rare form of cancer, often called Hodgkin's lymphoma because it affects the lymph glands and the body's immune system. Treatment for this condition has now greatly improved and no sufferer would have to tolerate the pain that Nancy did.

17 OSU, JM to DD, 16 April 1994.

18 JM to James Lees-Milne, 24 May 1973.

19 JM to Gaston Palewski, 8 June 1973, in *Love from Nancy*, p. 606.

20 OSU/1712, Joan 'Rudbin' Rodzianko to JM, 5 July 1973.

21 OSU/1710, DD to JM, 8 July 1973.

22 Lees-Milne, James, *Ancient as the Hills* (John Murray, 1997), p. 57.

23 CHP, enclosure with JM to DD, *c.* June 1973.

24 *Ibid.*, JM to DD, 19 September 1974.

25 Pryce-Jones, David, *Unity Mitford* (Weidenfeld & Nicolson, 1976), p. 1.

26 OSU/1561, JM to DD, 25 January 1974.

27 OSU/1361, DD to JM, 11 February 1974.

28 OSU/1642, JM to Idden (Ann Farrer Horne), 23 February 1980.

29 OSU/1651, PJ to JM, 22 September 1976.

30 CHP, 26 October 1976.

31 OSU misc., Clementine, Lady Beit to JM, *c.* November 1976.

32 OSU/1738, JM to Emma Tennant, 24 July 1985.

33 Dalley, Jan, *Diana Mosley* (Faber and Faber, 2000), p. 284.

34 Lees-Milne, James, *Through Wood and Dale* (John Murray, 1998), p. 160.

35 Mosley, Diana, *A Life of Contrasts* (Hamish Hamilton, 1977), p. 264.

36 YUL, DD to JLM, 29 July 1988.

37 Mosley, Diana, *The Duchess of Windsor* (Sidgwick & Jackson, 1980).

38 OSU/1713, Joan 'Rudbin' Rodzianko to JM, 22 September 1980.

39 Lees-Milne, James, *Deep Romantic Chasm* (John Murray, 2000), p. 86.

40 *Sunday Times Magazine*, 'A Life in the Day', DM in interview, November 1983.

41 Guinness, Jonathan and Catherine, *The House of Mitford* (Hutchinson, 1984), p. 553. It is probably fair to say that Myra Hindley, sentenced to life imprisonment more than thirty years ago for her part in the torture and murder of child victims, is the most hated woman in Britain. Lord Longford has campaigned for years for her release on the grounds that she has repented and is a reformed character. Each time this is suggested British newspapers are besieged with angry letters. The Home Secretary has recently stated that for Myra Hindley life means the whole of her life.

Chapter 22: Relatively Calm Waters, 1980–2000

1 Marge Frantz, interview with the author, Santa Cruz, October 1999.

2 In 1977.

3 Decca's record choices included 'The Red Flag' and 'I'm Sex Appeal Sarah', a song she used to sing in Boudledidge to entertain visitors to Asthall.

4 *Sunday Times Magazine*, Julian Jebb, 'The Mitford Sisters', 25 May 1980.

5 Though it was a Raeburn, not an Aga.

6 OSU/1709, NM to JM, 15 November 1968.

7 'The Mitford Sisters'.

8 *The Mitford Girls* (1981) written by Ned Sherrin and Caryl Brahms.

9 OSU/1633, JM to Jonathan Guinness, 10 October 1983.

10 Guinness, Catherine, 'Words with my Aunt, Jessica Mitford', from an unidentified magazine, in JM's scrapbook at her home in Oakland.

11 Interview in JM's scrapbooks, at the Treuhaft home in Oakland.

12 *San Francisco Chronicle*, 21 September 1986.

13 OSU/1637, DD to JM, 2 December 1986.

14 One cannot help wondering if this DVT was caused by the long flight.

15 YUL, DM to JLM, 9 February 1988.

16 OSU/1783, JM to Dobbie Walker, 20 November 1989.

17 *Desert Island Discs*, presented by Sue Lawley, 26 November 1989.

18 *Daily Telegraph*, 27 November 1989, p. 36.

19 Her choice of records was entirely classical, pieces by Mozart, Beethoven and Puccini, a Chopin mazurka and two pieces of Wagner, the '*Liebestod*' from *Tristan and Isolde* and a duet from *The Valkyrie*.

20 OSU/1651, JM to Contancia 'Dinky' Romilly, 12 April 1994.

21 Interview, Oakland, California, October 1999.

22 OSU, Constancia 'Dinky' Romilly to Maya Angelou, 10 December 1994.

23 Dinky was, and still is, a highly qualified casualty nurse in A & E. Interestingly Decca identified Dinky as possessing many of Pam's 'Womanly' qualities even as a small child; see her letters to Sydney in 1941–3.

24 RT's address at the memorial service held for JM in London.

25 DM to the author, 25 February 2001.

26 During one visit to Chatsworth for research the author conducted a mini-census, asking people at nearby tables in the restaurant what had most impressed them. Almost universally they commented on the 'warm and well-cared-for atmosphere – like a family home'.

27 The author's late husband, Geoffrey A.H. Watts, chaired and served on the boards of over sixty companies. He said several colleagues told him that appointing Debo to the board of Tarmac Ltd was the best thing the company had ever done.

28 YUL, SR to JLM, 30 March 1958.

ACKNOWLEDGEMENTS
AND CREDITS

During the research for this book I was given a considerable amount of help and assistance by the family, primarily Debo (the Duchess of Devonshire), Diana (the Hon. Lady Mosley), Robert Treuhaft and Constancia 'Dinky' Romilly. I should like to express my immense gratitude to them, and also to the following who have helped in various ways:

Joe Allen, Rosemary Bailey, 'Rab' Bailey, Norman Bell, K.V. Blight (House of Lords Archivist), Julia Budworth, Michael Burn, Ruth Caruth (Beinecke Library, Yale University), Lady Elizabeth Cavendish, Richard Cohen, Betty Colchester Wemyss, Ellen R. Cordes (Beinecke Library, Yale University), Gill Day, Pele de Lappe, Katie Edwards (Decca's secretary), Penny Finchmullen, Marge Frantz, Elva Griffith (Ohio State University), the Hon. Desmond Guinness, Jonathan Guinness (Lord Moyne), George Gutekunst, Janie Hampton, Bevis Hillier, Quentin Keynes, Karen J. Leonard, Lady Elizabeth Longford, Lord Longford, Graeme R. Lovell (advice on inheritance taxes), Mrs J. MacKinnon, Priscilla McWilliams, Helen Marchant (secretary to the Duke and Duchess of Devonshire), Doreen Morris, Charlotte Mosley, the Hon. June Ogilvy, Bernadette Rivett,

Doug Scherer (Ohio State University), Geoffrey D. Smith (Ohio State University), Madeau Stewart, Peter Y. Sussman, Rosemary Taylor, Janet Topp-Fargion (British Library Sound Archive), Sally Toynbee, Michael Waite, Doris 'Dobbie' Walker.

Copyright Acknowledgements

The author wishes to thank the following for their generosity in granting permission for copyright material to be printed in this book, as follows:

Unpublished Material
The Duchess of Devonshire, for quotations from letters by Sydney (Lady Redesdale), Mrs Pamela Jackson, Unity Mitford, and her own unpublished writings, also the unpublished writings of Nancy Mitford and to quote the passage from *Wigs on the Green.*

Diana, Lady Mosley for unpublished and published quotations by herself and Sir Oswald Mosley, and other members of her immediate family.

Robert Treuhaft for quotations by Jessica (Decca) Mitford, himself and Constancia 'Dinky' Romilly.

The Rare Books and MSS Department of Ohio State University, which owns the physical property of Jessica Mitford's papers.

The Beinecke Library at Yale University, which owns the physical property of the James Lees-Milne papers.

Published Material
For quotations from various books (see bibliography for full details of publication):

Desmond Elliott and the Estate of Sir John Betjeman to quote from letters and poetry of Sir John Betjeman.

David Higham Associates for permission to quote from the works of James Lees-Milne.

Hodder & Stoughton for permission to quote from *Love from Nancy*.

Sally Toynbee for permission to quote from *Friends Apart*.

The *Lady* to quote from articles by Nancy Mitford.

Cassell Plc for quotations from *Beloved Infidel*.

Peters, Fraser & Dunlop Group for quotations from the published works of Nancy Mitford: *Love in a Cold Climate*, *The Pursuit of Love*, *The Water Beetle* and *Wigs on the Green*. And from the works of Nicholas Mosley: *Rules of the Game* and *Beyond the Pale*.

The *Sunday Times* for permission to quote from the Julian Jebb article 'The Mitford Sisters'.

The Trustees of the Jessica Mitford Estate for permission to quote from *Hons and Rebels* and *A Fine Old Conflict*.

NB The author has assumed 'fair usage' for quotations of less than 200 words from any publication. Strenuous attempts have been made to contact all copyright holders. In the few cases where it has not been possible to trace assigns and heirs, the author apologizes, and requests that copyright holders make contact through the publishers. Any such notification will be fully acknowledged in future editions of this book.

I should like to sincerely thank those involved in the various production processes of this book. At Little, Brown (London), Richard Beswick, Viv Redman and Hazel Orme. At W.W. Norton (NY), Starling Lawrence, who was responsible for the book's conception. And my literary agent Robert Ducas, who is a never-failing source of support.

Finally, my thanks to David Baldwin, Vanda Hamarneh, Fatie Darwish and Shadi Kabalan ('Song of a Tiger'), who, each in their own way, were of assistance when the page proofs of this book went astray between London and Damascus.

Picture Credits

Devonshire collection, Chatsworth, by kind permission of the Duchess of Devonshire: 1, 2, 3, 4, 5, 6, 7, 8, 9, 10, 11, 14, 15, 16, 18, 19, 20, 21, 22, 26, 27, 28, 29, 30, 31, 33, 34, 36, 38, 39, 40, 41, 43, 44, 45, 46, 47, 49, 50, 52, 54, 57, 61 (by kind permission of Desmond Guinness)

OSU: 12, 13, 17, 25, (by kind permission of Robert Treuhaft)

Diana Mosley: 23, 32, 42, 55, 56, 58, 59, 60

Hulton Getty: 24

Lawrence N. Hole: 37

Associated Press: 35

Popperfoto: 48

Bibliothèque Nationale: 51

Robert Treuhaft: 53, 62, 63

SELECT BIBLIOGRAPHY

All books published in London unless otherwise stated.

Acton, Harold, *Memoir of Nancy Mitford* (Hamish Hamilton, 1975).

Amory, Mark, *Letters of Evelyn Waugh* (Weidenfeld & Nicolson, 1980).

Attallah, Naim, *More of a Certain Age* (Quartet Books, 1993).

Barrow, Andrew, *Gossip* (Hamish Hamilton, 1978).

Boothby, Robert, *I Fight to Live* (Heinemann, 1947).
  Recollections of a Rebel (Hutchinson, 1978).

Bowles, Thomas Gibson, *The Log of the Nereid* (Simpkin, Marshall & Co., 1889).

Bullock, Alan, *Hitler – A Study in Tyranny* (Oldhams Press, 1952).

Butler, Lucy (ed.) *Letters Home: The Letters of Robert Byron* (John Murray, 1991).

Carpenter, Humphrey, *The Brideshead Generation* (Faber and Faber, 1989).

Carrington, Dora, *Letters and Diaries* (Cape, 1970).

Churchill, Winston, *The Second World War*, 5 vols (Cassell, 1948–54).

Collier, Peter and Horowitz, David, *The Kennedys* (Secker & Warburg, 1984).

Cowles, Virginia, *Looking for Trouble* (Hamish Hamilton, 1941).

Dalley, Jan, *Diana Mosley* (Faber and Faber, 2000).

Dalton, Hugh, *The Fateful Years* (Frederick Muller, 1957).

Davie, Mark, *Diaries of Evelyn Waugh* (Weidenfeld & Nicolson, 1976).

Devonshire, Duchess of, *The House* (Macmillan, 1982).
　The Estate (Macmillan, 1990).

Durr, Virginia Foster, *Outside the Magic Circle* (University of Alabama Press, 1990).

Graham, Sheilah, *Beloved Infidel* (Cassell, 1933).

Guinness, Bryan, *Singing out of Tune* (Putnam, 1933).
　Dairy Not Kept (Compton Press, 1981).

Guinness, Jonathan and Catherine, *The House of Mitford* (Hutchinson, 1984).

Halle, Kay, *The Young Unpretender* (Heinemann, 1971).

Hanfstaengl, Ernst ('Putzi'), *Hitler, the Missing Years* (Eyre & Spottiswoode, 1957).

Hastings, Selina, *Nancy Mitford* (Hamish Hamilton, 1985).

Hillier, Bevis, *Young Betjeman* (John Murray, 1988).

Holroyd, Michael, *Lytton Strachey* (Chatto & Windus, 1994).

Ingram, Kevin, *Rebel – The Life of Esmond Romilly* (Weidenfeld & Nicolson, 1985).

Lees-Milne, James, *Another Self* (Hamish Hamilton, 1970).
　Ancestral Voices (John Murray, 1975).
　Caves of Ice (John Murray, 1983).
　A Mingled Measure (John Murray, 1994).
　Ancient as the Hills (John Murray, 1997).
　Through Wood and Dale (John Murray, 1998).
　Deep Romantic Chasm (John Murray, 2000).

Leslie, Anita, *Cousin Randolph* (Hutchinson, 1985).
　The Gilt and the Gingerbread (Hutchinson, 1981).

Lewis, Jeremy, *Cyril Connolly* (Cape, 1997).

Lockhart, Sir Robert Bruce, *Diaries* (Macmillan, 1973).

Lycett-Green, Candida (ed.), *John Betjeman – Letters* (Methuen, 1990).

Mitford, Jessica, *Hons and Rebels* (Victor Gollancz, 1960).
　The American Way of Death (Simon & Schuster, 1963).
　A Fine Old Conflict (Michael Joseph, 1977).

Poison Penmanship (Farrar, Straus and Giroux, New York, 1979).

Kind and Unusual Punishment (Knopf, New York, 1973).

Faces of Philip (Heinemann, 1984).

Mitford, Nancy, *Wigs on the Green* (Butterworth, 1935).

The Pursuit of Love (Hamish Hamilton, 1947).

Love in a Cold Climate (Hamish Hamilton, 1949).

The Blessing (Hamish Hamilton, 1951).

Noblesse Oblige (Hamish Hamilton, 1956).

Don't Tell Alfred (Hamish Hamilton, 1960).

The Water Beetle (Hamish Hamilton, 1962).

Mosley, Charlotte, *Love from Nancy – The Letters of Nancy Mitford* (Hodder & Stoughton, 1993).

Letters of Nancy Mitford and Evelyn Waugh (Sceptre, 1996).

A Talent to Annoy (Beaufort Books, New York, 1986).

Mosley, Diana, *A Life of Contrasts* (Hamish Hamilton, 1977).

Loved Ones (Sidgwick & Jackson, 1985).

The Duchess of Windsor (Sidgwick & Jackson, 1980).

Mosley, Nicholas, *The Rules of the Game* (Secker & Warburg, 1982).

Beyond the Pale (Secker & Warburg, 1983).

Mosley, Sir Oswald, *My Life* (Nelson, 1970).

Murphy, Sophia, *The Mitford Family Album* (Sidgwick & Jackson, 1985).

Nicholson, Harold, *Diaries and Letters*, 3 vols (Collins, 1970).

Powell, Violet, *Five out of Six* (Heinemann, 1960).

Pryce-Jones, David, *Unity Mitford* (Weidenfeld & Nicolson, 1976).

Quennell, Peter, *The Marble Foot* (Collins, 1976).

Ravensdale, Irene, *In Many Rhythms* (Weidenfeld & Nicolson, 1953).

Redesdale, Lord, *Memories*, 2 vols (Hutchinson, 1915).

Romilly, Esmond, *Boadilla* (Macdonald, 1938).

Skidelsky, Robert, *Oswald Mosley* (Macmillan, 1975).

Soames, Mary, *Clementine Churchill* (Cassell, 1979).

Soames, Mary (ed.), *Speaking for Themselves: The Letters of Winston and Clementine Churchill* (Doubleday, 1998).

Speer, Albert, *Inside the Third Reich* (Sphere Books, 1975).

Sykes, Christopher, *Evelyn Waugh* (Collins, 1975).

Trevor-Roper, H.R., *Hitler's Table Talk* (Weidenfeld & Nicolson, 1953).

Toynbee, Philip, *Friends Apart* (MacGibbon and Kee, 1954).

Zeigler, Philip, *Diana Cooper* (Hamish Hamilton, 1981).

INDEX